Lecture Notes in Computer Sci

Edited by G. Goos, J. Hartmanis and J. van L

Advisory Board: W. Brauer   D. Gries   J. Stoer

Springer
Berlin
Heidelberg
New York
Barcelona
Budapest
Hong Kong
London
Milan
Paris
Santa Clara
Singapore
Tokyo

Gheorghe Păun Arto Salomaa (Eds.)

New Trends
in Formal Languages

Control, Cooperation,
and Combinatorics

 Springer

Series Editors

Gerhard Goos, Karlsruhe University, Germany

Juris Hartmanis, Cornell University, NY, USA

Jan van Leeuwen, Utrecht University, The Netherlands

Volume Editors

Gheorghe Păun
University of Bucharest, Institute of Mathematics
Str. Academiei 14, R-70109 Bucharest, Romania
E-mail: paun@roimar.imar.ro

Arto Salomaa
University of Turku, Department of Mathematics
FIN-20014 Turku, Finland
E-mail: asalomaa@sara.utu.fi

Cataloging-in-Publication data applied for

Die Deutsche Bibliothek - CIP-Einheitsaufnahme

New trends in formal languages : control, cooperation, and
combinatorics / Gheorge Păun ; Arto Salomaa (ed.). - Berlin ;
Heidelberg ; New York ; Barcelona ; Budapest ; Hong Kong ;
London ; Milan ; Paris ; Santa Clara ; Singapore ; Tokyo : Springer,
1997
    ISBN 3-540-62844-4 kart.

CR Subject Classification (1991): F.4.2, F.4.3, I.2.7

ISSN 0302-9743
ISBN 3-540-62844-4 Springer-Verlag Berlin Heidelberg New York

© Springer-Verlag Berlin Heidelberg 1997
Printed in Germany

Typesetting: Camera-ready by author
SPIN 10549399   06/3142 – 5 4 3 2 1 0   Printed on acid-free paper

Preface

The present volume has emerged from a twofold intention: (1) to collect and to present to the reader results in two important and active areas of formal language theory, regulated rewriting and grammar systems (both these areas have as one of their main goals to increase the generative power of grammars by adding certain features dealing with the control of the derivation process, the cooperation of parts, the distribution of tasks among parts, and other related ideas), and (2) to mark the 50th Birthday of *Jürgen Dassow*, an author who has made a significant contribution to the above mentioned areas (and who has been quite active in organizing meetings in formal language theory, as well as in theoretical computer science in general).

Most of the contributions are indeed devoted to regulated rewriting and grammar systems, but, because several of Jürgen's friends and collaborators are not working in these areas, we decided to enlarge the scope of the volume. Thus, the last two chapters were added.

The first chapter (*Regulated rewriting*) deals both with topics which can be considered classical in formal language theory (the LBA problem reformulated in terms of programmed grammars, the index of grammars and languages, the descriptional complexity in the form of the number of nonterminals used by a grammar) and with recent (controlling the work of a grammar/automaton by means of elements of a group, or by attributes associated to strings or to symbols), or emergent topics (fuzzy grammars, array grammars, restarting automata).

The next two chapters (*Cooperating distributed grammar systems* and *Parallel communicating grammar systems*) are devoted to the two main classes of grammar systems, the sequential ones (the components work in turn, one at each moment, on the same common sentential form) and the parallel ones (the components work synchronously, each on its own sentential form, and communicate on request or by command).

The papers included in these chapters prove the power and the fruitfulness – both from a theoretical and a practical point of view – of the distributed architectures specific to grammar systems. There are papers investigating basic generative capacity questions, computational complexity, variants (in general suggested by computer science aspects modelled in terms of grammar systems). Special mention should be made of the two papers about colonies, a particular case of cooperating distributed grammar systems, corresponding to multi-agent systems with very simple subsystems/agents, and the papers discussing the possible use(fulness) of parallel communicating grammar systems, of grammar systems in general, in modelling constructions and phenomena occurring in natural languages.

The fourth chapter (*Splicing systems*) deals with an exciting and hot area in computer science, which promises important developments also in automata and language theory: DNA computing. The basic ingredient here is the splicing operation modelling the DNA recombination. The first two papers investigate (parallel) grammar systems based on components using the splicing operation. (Thus, these papers can also be considered as continuations of the previous chapter.) The third paper of this chapter extends the splicing operation to arrays, opening a rich area of investigation.

Chapter five (*Infinite words*) contains three papers whose object of study are the infinite sequences, whereas Chapter six (*Algebraic approaches to languages*) contains papers where the main point of view is not generative but algebraic. These areas constitute well-established branches of formal language theory, important counterparts of the "classical" branches dealing with finite strings in a purely grammatical manner.

Of course, the volume does not intend to provide an overview of formal language theory; the reader interested in such an overview can consult *Handbook of Formal Languages* (three volumes), published this spring by Springer-Verlag (G. Rozenberg, A. Salomaa, eds.).

The contributions have been refereed in the usual way. We are very much indebted to all the people involved in the production of this volume. Most importantly, we want to thank the authors for excellent and timely cooperation, and regret that some other prospective authors who wanted to contribute were unable to do so because of time and other constraints. After fifty, other multiples of ten follow... So, Happy Birthday Jürgen, and see you at many multiples of ten from now on !

January 1997   Gh. Păun and A. Salomaa

Table of Contents

Chapter 1. Regulated Rewriting

A Grammatical Approach to the LBA Problem

Henning BORDIHN

Fakultät für Informatik
Otto-von-Guericke-Universität Magdeburg
Postfach 4120, D-39016 Magdeburg, Germany
Email: bordihn@irb.cs.uni-magdeburg.de

Abstract. In this paper, the degree of non-regulation for programmed grammars is introduced, as the largest number of elements in success or in failure fields. We show that this measure can be restricted to two without loss of generative capacity. Moreover, we present interrelations between the lba problem on the one hand and the relationship between the families of languages described by λ-free programmed grammars with degree of non-regulation one and two on the other hand. Especially, in case of accepting programmed grammars with monotone core rules and leftmost derivations this relationship exactly characterizes the lba problem.

1. Introduction

In [1], [2], it is proved that programmed grammars with λ-free context-free productions and with appearance checking features describe the family of context-sensitive languages if they are seen as accepting devices.

The idea of accepting grammars [7] is the following: Starting from a "terminal" word, the system tries to derive a given goal word (the axiom) where, following [1], [2], [3], the yield relation is defined by textually the same words as in generating case. Possible restrictions to production sets are turned "around", e.g., coming to productions of the form $v \to a$ in the context-free case, where v is a (possibly empty) word and a is a symbol.

In this paper, we present an approach to the family of languages recognized by deterministic linear-bounded automaton by restricting the number of possible choices of productions for continuing a derivation of programmed grammars in a certain situation, i.e. after a certain production has been applied leading a certain sentential form. For, we introduce a new measure of descriptional complexity for programmed grammars, the degree of non-regulation, which reflects this number of possible choices.

We assume that the reader is familiar with basic notions and basic knowledge of formal language and automata theory. Concerning our notations, we mostly follow [4]: $\subseteq$ denotes inclusion, $\subset$ denotes strict inclusion, $|M|$ is the number of elements in the set M. The empty word is denoted by λ. We consider two languages L_1, L_2 to be equal iff $L_1 \setminus \{\lambda\} = L_2 \setminus \{\lambda\}$, and we simply write $L_1 = L_2$ in this case. We term two devices describing languages equivalent if the two described languages are equal. Moreover, let $Sub(w)$ denote the set of subwords of w. The length of a word x is denoted by $|x|$. If $x \in V^*$, where V is some alphabet, and if $W \subseteq V$, then $|x|_W$ denotes the number of occurrences of letters from W in x. If W is a singleton set $\{a\}$, we simply write $|x|_a$ instead of $|x|_{\{a\}}$.

The families of regular, context-free, λ-free context-free, context-sensitive, monotone, and type-0 Chomsky grammars are denoted by REG, CF, CF-λ, CS, MON, and RE, respectively. If X is one of these families, $\mathcal{L}^{gen}(X)$ $(\mathcal{L}^{acc}(X))$ denotes the family of languages generated (accepted) by some device from the family X. Whenever we use bracket notations like $\mathcal{L}^{gen}(\text{CF}[-\lambda]) = \mathcal{L}^{acc}(\text{CF}[-\lambda])$ we mean that the statement is true both in case of neglecting the bracket contents and in case of ignoring the brackets themselves. If several parts of a formula (which can uniquelly be associated to each other) are enclosed in brackets then we can leave out none, one, or more of those associated parts.

2. Programmed Grammars and the Degree of Non-Regulation

First, we formally define the notion of programmed grammars in a way appropriate for generating and accepting case [1], [2].

A *programmed grammar* is a construct $G = (V_N, V_T, P, S)$, where V_N and V_T are two disjoint alphabets, the set of nonterminal symbols and the set of terminal symbols, $S \in V_N$ is the axiom, and P is a finite set of productions of the form $(r : \alpha \rightarrow \beta, \sigma(r), \phi(r))$, where $r : \alpha \rightarrow \beta$ is a rewriting rule labelled by r and $\sigma(r)$ and $\phi(r)$ are two sets of labels of such core rules in P. By $Lab(P)$, we denote the set of all labels of the productions appearing in P.

A sequence of words over V_G^*, $y_0, y_1, \ldots, y_n$, is referred to as a derivation in G iff, for $1 \leq i \leq n$, there are productions $(r_i : \alpha_i \rightarrow \beta_i, \sigma(r_i), \phi(r_i)) \in P$ such that

$$y_{i-1} = z_{i-1}\alpha_i z'_{i-1}, \quad y_i = z_{i-1}\beta_i z'_{i-1}, \text{ and, if } 1 \leq i < n, r_{i+1} \in \sigma(r_i)$$

or

$$\alpha_i \notin Sub(y_{i-1}), \quad y_{i-1} = y_i, \text{ and, if } 1 \leq i < n, r_{i+1} \in \phi(r_i).$$

Note that, in the latter case, the derivation step is done in the appearance checking mode. The set $\sigma(r_i)$ is called the success field and the set $\phi(r_i)$ the failure field of r_i. We also write the derivation as

$$y_0 \Longrightarrow_{r_1} y_1 \Longrightarrow_{r_2} \cdots \Longrightarrow_{r_n} y_n$$

or simply as $y_0 \Longrightarrow y_1 \Longrightarrow \cdots \Longrightarrow y_n$.

The language generated by G is defined as

$$L^{gen}(G) = \{w \in V_T^* \mid \text{there is a derivation } S = y_0, y_1, \ldots, y_n = w\}$$

if G is a generating programmed grammar and

$$L^{acc}(G) = \{w \in V_T^* \mid \text{there is a derivation } w = y_0, y_1, \ldots, y_n = S\}$$

if G is an accepting one.

A derivation according to G is said to be *leftmost* if each rule is either applied in a way such that it replaces the leftmost occurrence of its left-hand side or it is applied in appearance checking mode.[1] By $L^{gen}(G\text{-left})$ ($L^{acc}(G\text{-left})$) we denote the language generated (accepted) by G in this leftmost manner.

Let $X \in \{\text{REG, CF, CF-}\lambda\text{, CS, MON, RE}\}$. The family of languages generated (accepted) by programmed grammars of the form $G = (V_N, V_T, P, S)$ containing only core rules of type X is denoted by $\mathcal{L}^{gen}(\text{P}, X, \text{ac})$ ($\mathcal{L}^{acc}(\text{P}, X, \text{ac})$). When no appearance checking features are involved, i.e. $\phi(r) = \emptyset$ for each rule in P, we are led to the families $\mathcal{L}^{gen}(\text{P}, X)$ ($\mathcal{L}^{acc}(\text{P}, X)$). In order to denote the corresponding families of languages obtained by leftmost derivations we add *left* to the first component of that notation, e.g., leading to $\mathcal{L}^{gen}(\text{P-left,CF,ac})$.

Let us recall some results for the generating case [4] and extend them to further cases.[2]

Lemma 2.1. *For* $X \in \{CF, CF\text{-}\lambda\}$, *we have*

(i) $\mathcal{L}^{gen}(\text{P},X) \subseteq \mathcal{L}^{gen}(\text{P-left},X)$, *and*

(ii) $\mathcal{L}^{gen}(\text{P},X,\text{ac}) \subseteq \mathcal{L}^{gen}(\text{P-left},X,\text{ac})$.

For $X \in \{CS, MON, RE\}$,

(iii) $\mathcal{L}^{gen}(\text{P},X) = \mathcal{L}^{gen}(\text{P-left},X) = \mathcal{L}^{gen}(\text{P},X,\text{ac}) = \mathcal{L}^{gen}(X)$ *and*

(iv) $\mathcal{L}^{gen}(\text{P},X,\text{ac}) \subseteq \mathcal{L}^{gen}(\text{P-left},X,\text{ac})$.

Proof. For (i), (ii), and (iii), see [4]. In order to show (iv), we slightly modify the idea of the proof given for the context-free case (ii).

We consider the programmed grammar $G = (V_N, V_T, P, S)$ with productions of type CS, MON, or RE, and with each rule $(r : \alpha \to \beta, \sigma(r), \phi(r)) \in P$, we associate the productions

$$
\begin{aligned}
&(r : \alpha \to \alpha, \{r', r''\}, \phi(r)), \\
&(r' : A \to A', \{r', r''\}, \emptyset) && \text{if } \alpha = uA\gamma \text{ with } u \in V_T^*, A \in V_N, \gamma \in (V_N \cup V_T)^*, \\
&(r'' : \alpha \to \beta, \{r'''\}, \emptyset), \\
&(r''' : A' \to A, \{r'''\}, \sigma(r)).
\end{aligned}
$$

The remaining part of the construction is analogous to that one given for the context-free case in [4]. □

Now, we turn to the accepting case.

Lemma 2.2.

(i) *For* $X \in \{CF\text{-}\lambda, CS, MON\}$, $\mathcal{L}^{acc}(\text{P},X[,\text{ac}]) \subseteq \mathcal{L}^{acc}(\text{P-left},X[,\text{ac}])$,

(ii) $\mathcal{L}^{acc}(\text{P},RE[,\text{ac}]) = \mathcal{L}^{acc}(\text{P-left},RE[,\text{ac}]) = \mathcal{L}^{gen}(RE)$, *and*

(iii) $\mathcal{L}^{acc}(\text{P},CF) \subseteq \mathcal{L}^{acc}(\text{P-left},CF)$ *hold.*

---

[1]Note that this definition corresponds to the definition of leftmost derivations of type 3 in [4].

[2]For recent results about leftmost derivations in the special case of unconditional transfer cf. [5].

4

Proof. (i) The case with appearance checking can be proved similarly to the proof for generating grammars. We just have to rename the teminal symbols first in order to avoid terminals on the right-hand sides of rules. More precisely, for a given accepting programmed grammar $G = (V_N, V_T, P, S)$, we construct an equivalent accepting programmed grammar with leftmost derivations $G' = (V_N', V_T', P', S')$ as follows. Set $V_N' = V_N \cup \{A' \mid A \in V_N\} \cup \{\bar{a} \mid a \in V_T\}$ and $V_T' = V_T$. Now, let $\hat{\ } : (V_N \cup V_T)^* \longrightarrow (V_N')^*$ be the morphism defined by $\hat{A} = A$ for $A \in V_N$ and $\hat{a} = \bar{a}$ for $a \in V_T$. Furthermore, let P' contain the following productions:

$$((0, a) : a \to \bar{a}, \{(0, b) \mid b \in V_T\}, \{r, r', r^{\mathrm{ac}} \mid r \in \mathrm{Lab}(P)\}), \quad \text{for all } a \in V_T$$

and with each $(r : \alpha \to \beta, \sigma(r), \phi(r)) \in P$, we associate the productions

$$(r' : \hat{x} \to x', \{r, r'\}, \emptyset), \quad \text{if } \alpha = x\gamma, \ x \in V_N \cup V_T, \ \gamma \in (V_N \cup V_T)^*$$
$$(r : \hat{\alpha} \to \hat{\beta}, \{r''\}, \emptyset),$$
$$(r'' : x' \to \hat{x}, \{p''\}, \{p, p', p^{\mathrm{ac}} \mid p \in \sigma(r)\}),$$
$$(r^{\mathrm{ac}} : \hat{\alpha} \to \hat{\beta}, \emptyset, \{p, p', p^{\mathrm{ac}} \mid p \in \phi(r)\}),$$

Clearly, $L^{acc}(G') = L^{acc}(G)$. Note, that we have only productions of type X if every (given) rule $\alpha \to \beta$ is of type X.

If appearance checking features are not involved then we omit the productions r^{ac} and have productions

$$((0, a) : a \to \bar{a}, \{(0, b) \mid b \in V_T\} \cup \{r, r'\} \mid r \in \mathrm{Lab}(P)\}, \emptyset), \quad \text{for all } a \in V_T$$

and, for each $(r : \alpha \to \beta, \sigma(r), \phi(r)) \in P$,

$$(r' : \hat{x} \to x', \{r, r'\}, \emptyset), \quad \text{if } \alpha = x\gamma, \ x \in V_N \cup V_T, \ \gamma \in (V_N \cup V_T)^*$$
$$(r : \hat{\alpha} \to \hat{\beta}, \{r''\}, \emptyset),$$
$$(r'' : x' \to \hat{x}, \{p''\} \cup \{p, p' \mid p \in \sigma(r)\}, \emptyset).$$

Obviously, any derivation of G can be simulated by G', further possible derivations are either blocking or simulating derivations of the given grammar, as well. Hence, we find $L^{acc}(G') = L^{acc}(G)$ and the failure fields are empty for all rules in P'.

(ii) is a direct conclusion of Lemma 2.1 together with

$$\mathcal{L}^{gen}(\mathrm{P}, X, \mathrm{ac}) = \mathcal{L}^{gen}(\mathrm{RE}) \quad \text{and}$$
$$\mathcal{L}^{gen}(\mathrm{P}[\text{-left}], X[, \mathrm{ac}]) = \mathcal{L}^{acc}(\mathrm{P}[\text{-left}], X[, \mathrm{ac}])$$

for $X \in \{\mathrm{CF}, \mathrm{RE}\}$, cf. [4] and [1], [3], respectively. Let us remark that the idea of the proof for (i) cannot be used if λ-rules, i.e. rules of the form $\lambda \to \beta$ are allowed. $\square$

Let $G = (V_N, V_T, P, S)$ be a programmed grammar (with appearance checking) with productions of type X, $X \in \{\mathrm{REG}, \mathrm{CF}, \mathrm{CF}\text{--}\lambda, \mathrm{CS}, \mathrm{MON}, \mathrm{RE}\}$ in generating or in accepting mode. The *degree of non-regulation* $Rg(G)$ of G is defined in the following way: For any production $(r : \alpha \to \beta, \sigma(r), \phi(r))$ in P, we set

$$Rg(r) = \max\{|\sigma(r)|, |\phi(r)|\}$$

and

$$Rg(G) = \max\{Rg(r) \mid r \in \mathrm{Lab}(P)\}.$$

For a language $L \in \mathcal{L}^{gen}(\text{P[-left]},X,[\text{ac}])$, we define the degree of non-regulation as

$$Rg(L) \;=\; \min\{Rg(G) \mid L^{gen}(G) = L\}\,.$$

The degree of non-regulation of a language $L \in \mathcal{L}^{acc}(\text{P[-left]},X,[\text{ac}])$ is defined analogously. Furthermore, we set

$$
\begin{aligned}
\mathcal{L}^{gen}_n(\text{P[-left]},X[,\text{ac}])) &= \{L \in \mathcal{L}^{gen}(\text{P[-left]},X[,\text{ac}])) \mid Rg(L) \le n\}\,, \\
\mathcal{L}^{acc}_n(\text{P[-left]},X[,\text{ac}])) &= \{L \in \mathcal{L}^{acc}(\text{P[-left]},X[,\text{ac}])) \mid Rg(L) \le n\}\,.
\end{aligned}
$$

The inclusions

$$
\begin{aligned}
\mathcal{L}^{gen}_n(\text{P[-left]},X[,\text{ac}]) &\subseteq \mathcal{L}^{gen}_{n+1}(\text{P[-left]},X[,\text{ac}]) \subseteq \mathcal{L}^{gen}(\text{P[-left]},X[,\text{ac}]) \quad \text{and} \\
\mathcal{L}^{acc}_n(\text{P[-left]},X[,\text{ac}]) &\subseteq \mathcal{L}^{acc}_{n+1}(\text{P[-left]},X[,\text{ac}]) \subseteq \mathcal{L}^{acc}_n(\text{P[-left]},X[,\text{ac}])
\end{aligned}
$$

trivially hold for $n \ge 1$. Obviously, the degree of non-regulation of a programmed grammar is a measure for the maximum number of possibilities to continue a derivation of the form $z \Longrightarrow^* z' \Longrightarrow^*_p w$ according to G, for some sentential forms z, z', w and a label $p \in \text{Lab}(P)$.

Lemma 2.3. *Let* $X \in \{\text{REG, CF, CF--}\lambda, \text{CS, MON, RE}\}$.

(i) $\mathcal{L}^{gen}_2(\text{P},X[,\text{ac}]) = \mathcal{L}^{gen}(\text{P},X[,\text{ac}])$,

(ii) $\mathcal{L}^{acc}_2(\text{P},X[,\text{ac}]) = \mathcal{L}^{acc}(\text{P},X[,\text{ac}])$.

Proof. First, we consider a generating programmed grammar $G = (V_N, V_T, P, S)$. With each production

$$(r : \alpha \to \beta, \{s_1, s_2, \ldots, s_l\}, \{t_1, t_2, \ldots, t_k\}) \in P, \quad n > 2,$$

we associate the following groups of productions:

$$
\begin{aligned}
&(r : \alpha \to \alpha, \{r'_1, r_2\}, \{t_1, r_2\}), \\
&(r'_1 : \alpha \to \beta, \{s_1\}, \emptyset),
\end{aligned}
$$

if $l \ne k$, for $1 \le i \le \min\{l, k\}$,

$$
\begin{aligned}
&(r_i : \alpha \to \alpha, \{r'_i, r_{i+1}\}, \{t_i, r_{i+1}\}), \\
&(r'_i : \alpha \to \beta, \{s_i\}, \emptyset),
\end{aligned}
$$

and, if $l < k$, for $l < j < k$,

$$
\begin{aligned}
&(r_j : \alpha \to \alpha, \emptyset, \{t_j, r_{j+1}\}), \quad \text{and} \\
&(r_k : \alpha \to \alpha, \emptyset, \{t_k\}),
\end{aligned}
$$

if $k < l$, for $k < j < l$,

$$
\begin{aligned}
&(r_j : \alpha \to \alpha, \{r'_j, r_{j+1}\}, \emptyset), \quad \text{and} \\
&(r'_j : \alpha \to \beta, \{s_j\}, \emptyset) \\
&(r_l : \alpha \to \beta, \{s_l\}, \emptyset).
\end{aligned}
$$

6

In case of $l = k$, simply set $\sigma(r_k) = \{s_k\}$ and $\phi(r_k) = \{t_k\}$. If $\phi(r) = \emptyset$ we let the failure fields be empty in all these productions. Then we construct the programmed grammar $G' = (V_N, V_T, P', S)$ by replacing each rule $r \in P$ with $Rg(r) > 2$ by the corresponding group of productions as listed above in order to obtain P'. Clearly, G' is of the same type as G and $L^{gen}(G') = L^{gen}(G)$ holds.

In accepting case, replace any occurrence of $\alpha \to \alpha$ by $\alpha \to \beta$ and any occurrence of $\alpha \to \beta$ by $\beta \to \beta$ in the above groups of productions associated to rule r in order to obtain only accepting rules of the same type. Then we have $L^{acc}(G') = L^{acc}(G)$. □

Let us mention that a similar construction is possible for the special case of programmed grammars with unconditional transfer [4]. Moreover, the construction given in the proof of Lemma 2.3 is also working for the case of leftmost derivations, i.e., $L^{gen}(G'\text{-left}) = L^{gen}(G\text{-left})$ ($L^{acc}(G'\text{-left}) = L^{acc}(G\text{-left})$, respectively).

Corollary 2.4. *For $X \in \{REG, CF, CF\text{-}\lambda, CS, MON, RE\}$, we have*

(i) $\mathcal{L}_2^{gen}(\text{P-left},X[,\text{ac}]) = \mathcal{L}^{gen}(\text{P-left},X[,\text{ac}])$,

(ii) $\mathcal{L}_2^{acc}(\text{P-left},X[,\text{ac}]) = \mathcal{L}^{acc}(\text{P-left},X[,\text{ac}])$.

It is an open problem if the inclusions $\mathcal{L}_1^{acc}(\text{P-left},X[,\text{ac}]) \subseteq \mathcal{L}_2^{acc}(\text{P-left},X[,\text{ac}])$ are proper.

3. On Context-Sensitive and Deterministic Context-Sensitive Languages

In [1], [2], [3] it is proved that the familiy of accepting programmed grammars with λ-free context-free rules (with appearance checking) describes exactly the family $\mathcal{L}^{gen}(CS)$, i.e., the family of languages which are recognizable by linear-bounded automaton. If we take into consideration the results of the previous section, we can give some further characterizations of this language family.

Corollary 3.1. *For $X \in \{CF\text{-}\lambda, CS, MON\}$, we have*

$$\mathcal{L}^{acc}(\text{P},X,\text{ac}) = \mathcal{L}^{acc}(\text{P-left},X,\text{ac}) = \mathcal{L}_2^{acc}(\text{P},X,\text{ac}) = \mathcal{L}_2^{acc}(\text{P-left},X,\text{ac}) = \mathcal{L}^{gen}(CS).$$

Proof. $\mathcal{L}^{gen}(CS) \subseteq \mathcal{L}^{acc}(\text{P},CF\text{-}\lambda,\text{ac})$ is proved, e.g., in [2]. $\mathcal{L}^{acc}(\text{P},CF\text{-}\lambda,\text{ac}) \subseteq \mathcal{L}^{acc}(\text{P},X,\text{ac})$, for $X \in \{CF\text{-}\lambda, CS, MON\}$, holds by definition. The inclusions $\mathcal{L}_2^{acc}(\text{P}[\text{-left}],X,\text{ac}) \subseteq \mathcal{L}^{gen}(CS)$ can be shown by appropriate lba constructions. Thus, together with Lemma 2.2, Lemma 2.3, and Corollary 2.4, our statement is proved. □

Since the restriction of the degree of non-regulation of programmed grammars to one means the elimination of some nondeterministic aspect, it is natural to investigate the interrelations between the families $\mathcal{L}(DCS)$ and, e.g., $\mathcal{L}_1^{acc}(\text{P}[\text{-left}],CF\text{-}\lambda,\text{ac})$, where $\mathcal{L}(DCS)$ denotes the family of languages recognizable by deterministic linear-bounded automata which we call deterministic context-sensitive languages.

A *linear-bounded automaton* is a nondeterministic Turing machine in which the number of cells that can be used during a computation on an input word w is $O(|w|)$. A linear-bounded automaton is said to be *deterministic* iff the underlying Turing machine is deterministic. Concerning the notion of a Turing machine

$\mathcal{M} = (Q, \Sigma, \Gamma, \delta, q_0, B, F)$ (where Q is the set of states, Γ is the alphabet of tape symbols, $B \in \Gamma$ is the blank symbol, $\Sigma \subseteq \Gamma \setminus \{B\}$ is the alphabet of input symbols, δ is the transition function, $q_0 \in Q$ is the initial state, and $F \subseteq Q$ is the set of final states) and the notion of the accepted language we follow [6].

Lemma 3.2. *For $X \in \{CF\text{-}\lambda, CS, MON\}$, we have $\mathcal{L}_1^{acc}(\text{P-left},X,\text{ac}) \subseteq \mathcal{L}(\text{DCS})$.*

Idea of the proof. Let $G = (V_N, V_T, P, S)$ be an accepting progammed grammar with productions of type X (working in leftmost mode) and let $k = |P_T|$, where $P_T = \{\alpha \rightarrow \beta \in P \mid \alpha \in T^+\}$. Let $\{p_{i_1}, \ldots, p_{i_k}\}$ be the set of labels of the rules in P_T. Construct a deterministic linear-bounded automaton $\mathcal{M} = (Q, V_T, V_N \cup V_T \cup \{\#, \$, B\}, \delta, q_0, B, F)$, where the states are tuples with the first k components memorizing labels $r_{i_1}, \ldots, r_{i_k}$ from $\text{Lab}(P)$ initialized by $r_{i_j} = p_{i_j}$, $1 \le j \le k$, such that $\mathcal{M}$ performs the following steps.

Step 1. Copy $k - 1$ times the input word $w \in V_T^*$ such that we obtain the string

$$\underbrace{\#w\#w\#w \cdots w\#w\#}_{k-\text{times } w}.$$

Step 2. Perform stepwise simulations of leftmost derivation steps according to G in the following way. For $j = 1$ to k:

2.1 Search for the leftmost occurrence of the left-hand side α_{i_j} of rule r_{i_j} in the j-th subword between markers $\#$ on the tape from the left to the right (in the j-th occurrence of w, in the beginning).

2.2 If such substring is found, replace it by the right-hand side β_{i_j} of rule r_{i_j}, if $|\beta_{i_j}| = |\alpha_{i_j}|$, and replace it by $\beta_{i_j}\$^m$ if $|\alpha_{i_j}| - |\beta_{i_j}| = m$; change the j-th component of the current state to $\sigma(r_{i_j})$ if $|\sigma(r_{i_j})| = 1$ and do not accept if $|\sigma(r_{i_j})| = 0$. If $\#$ is reached and no subword α_{i_j} has been found in the current subword, then change the j-th component of the state to $\phi(r_{i_j})$ if possible and do not accept otherwise.

2.3 If $j < k$, move the read-write head over the first cell of the $(j+1)$-st subword and proceed with 2.1 for the next j. If $j = k$ then remove all occurrences of $\$$ and shift the remaining parts such that we obtain a "compact" word over $V_N \cup V_T \cup \{\#\}$. Then move the read-write head over the first cell of the first subword.

Step 3. Check whether a subword $\#S\#$ occurs in the current contents of the tape. If yes accept, otherwise repeat step 2 according to the currently memorized rules in the state.

Clearly, indeed $\mathcal{M}$ is deterministic and linear-bounded and accepts exactly the words in $L^{acc}(G\text{-left})$. □

Together with Lemma 2.3 we obtain the following statement.

Corollary 3.3. *For $X \in \{CF\text{-}\lambda, CS, MON\}$, we have*

$$\mathcal{L}_1^{acc}(\text{P-left},X,\text{ac}) \subseteq \mathcal{L}(\text{DCS}) \subseteq \mathcal{L}^{gen}(\text{CS}) = \mathcal{L}_2^{acc}(\text{P-left},X,\text{ac}).$$

If we take Lemma 2.1 into consideration, together with the fact that $\mathcal{L}_2^{gen}(\text{P[-left]},Y) = \mathcal{L}_2^{acc}(\text{P[-left]},Y)$, for $Y \in \{\text{CS, MON}\}$, we also find analogous characterizations without appearance checking features both in generating and in accepting mode.

Corollary 3.4. *For* $Y \in \{\text{CS, MON}\}$,

(i) $\mathcal{L}_1^{gen}(\text{P-left},Y) \subseteq \mathcal{L}(\text{DCS}) \subseteq \mathcal{L}^{gen}(\text{CS}) = \mathcal{L}_2^{gen}(\text{P[-left]},Y)$,

(ii) $\mathcal{L}_1^{acc}(\text{P-left},Y) \subseteq \mathcal{L}(\text{DCS}) \subseteq \mathcal{L}^{gen}(\text{CS}) = \mathcal{L}_2^{acc}(\text{[P-left]},Y)$

Proof. The statement is proved with the remark that the idea of the proof of Lemma 3.2 obviously applies also for languages in $\mathcal{L}_1^{gen}(\text{P-left},Y)$. □

Lemma 3.5. $\mathcal{L}(\text{DCS}) \subseteq \mathcal{L}_1^{acc}(\text{P[-left]},\text{MON},\text{ac})$

Proof. Given a deterministic linear-bounded automaton $\mathcal{M} = (Q,\Sigma,\Gamma,\delta,q_0,B,F)$, where $\Sigma = \{a_1,\ldots,a_k\}$. Construct an accepting programmed grammar $G = (V_N,\Sigma,P,S)$ with $V_N = \Gamma \cup \{\overline{x} \mid x \in \Gamma\} \cup Z \times \Gamma \cup Z \times \{\overline{x} \mid x \in \Gamma\} \cup \{S\}$ (the unions being disjoint) and where P contains the following productions.

$$([0,i]: a_i \to (q_0,\overline{a}_i), \{[q_0,\overline{a}_i]\}, \emptyset), \qquad 1 \le i \le k,$$
$$([q,\hat{x}_{i_j}]: (q,\hat{x}_{i_j})x_{i_{j+1}} \to \hat{x}'_{i_j}(q',x_{i_{j+1}}), \{[q',x_{i_{j+1}}]\}, \emptyset) \quad \text{if } \delta(q,x_{i_j}) = (q',x'_{i_j},R),$$
$$([q,\hat{x}_{i_j}]: \hat{x}_{i_{j-1}}(q,x_{i_j}) \to (q',\hat{x}_{i_{j-1}})x'_{i_j}, \{[q',\hat{x}_{i_{j-1}}]\}, \emptyset) \quad \text{if } \delta(q,x_{i_j}) = (q',x'_{i_j},L),$$
$$([q,\overline{x}_{i_j}]: B(q,\overline{x}_{i_j}) \to (q',\overline{B})x'_{i_j}, \{[q',\overline{B}]\}, \emptyset) \qquad \text{if } \delta(q,x_{i_j}) = (q',x'_{i_j},L),$$

where $\hat{x} \in \{x,\overline{x}\}$ for any $x \in \Gamma$.

Moreover, for $\Gamma = \{x_1,\ldots,x_\nu\}$, add the productions

$$([f,\hat{x}]: (f,\hat{x}) \to \hat{x}, \{1\}, \emptyset), \qquad \text{for all } x \in V_N,$$
$$(i: \overline{x}_i \to \overline{x}_i, \{< i,1 >\}, \{i+1\}) \qquad 1 \le i < \nu - 1,$$
$$(\nu - 1: \overline{x}_{\nu-1} \to \overline{x}_{\nu-1}, \{< \nu - 1,1 >\}, \{< \nu,1 >\})$$
$$(< i,j >: \overline{x}_i x_j \to \overline{x}_j, \{< j,1 >\}, \{< i,j+1 >\}), \qquad 1 \le i \le \nu, 1 \le j < \nu$$
$$(< i,\nu >: \overline{x}_i x_\nu \to \overline{x}_\nu, \{< \nu,1 >\}, \{< i,S >\}), \qquad 1 \le i \le \nu$$
$$(< i,S >: \overline{x}_i \to S, \emptyset, \emptyset), \qquad 1 \le i \le \nu.$$

Given a word $w \in \Sigma^*$, the only applicable rules are those with label $[0,i]$. If the "correct" i has been guessed then the leftmost symbol is overlined and it carries the initial state as an additional component. Now, the transitions of $\mathcal{M}$ can be simulated, where the barred symbol keeps on the leftmost position of the sentential form, until a sentential form is arrived which contains a symbol from $Q \times \Gamma \cup Q \times \{\overline{x} \mid x \in \Gamma\}$. Then the productions of the second group allow to derive S, but only if indeed the leftmost symbol has been overlined in the first step and w can be recognized by $\mathcal{M}$. If a symbol different from the leftmost symbol of w has been barred in the first step then it is impossible to derive the axiom since letters to the left of the barred one cannot be replaced. In conclusion, G accepts exactly the words recognized by $\mathcal{M}$. Note that this is true also in case of leftmost derivations. □

In conclusion, we have $\mathcal{L}_1^{acc}(\text{P-left},\text{MON},\text{ac}) = \mathcal{L}(\text{DCS})$ and the question whether or not the degree of non-regulation of accepting programmed grammars with monotone productions and with leftmost derivations can be reduced to one without loss of descriptional capacity is equivalent to the lba problem.

Corollary 3.6. $\mathcal{L}_1^{acc}(\text{P-left},\text{MON},\text{ac}) = \mathcal{L}(\text{DCS}) \subseteq \mathcal{L}^{gen}(\text{CS}) = \mathcal{L}_2^{acc}(\text{P-left},\text{MON},\text{ac})$.

4. Concluding Remarks

In this paper, we gave a grammatical characterization of the lba problem. Thus, a problem stemming from complexity theory can be expressed in terms of descriptional complexity of grammars. Unfortunately, for the precise characterization of the lba problem we needed monotone productions. It is an open problem whether the inclusion $\mathcal{L}_1^{acc}$(P-left,CF-λ,ac) $\subseteq \mathcal{L}$(DCS) is proper or $\mathcal{L}_1^{acc}$(P-left,CF-λ,ac) $= \mathcal{L}$(DCS) holds. In general, it is interesting to do further investigations of the language families with degree of non-regulation equal to one.

Moreover, it is remarkable that, in the proof of Lemma 3.5 we need appearance checking features only for the last part, where, after arriving at a final state, the sentential form is rewritten to the axiom by productions with context-free core rules. It is left open whether or not one can give up appearance checking at all for proving Lemma 3.5.

Acknowledgement. We are grateful to our colleague Bernd Reichel for some helpful comments on parts of the manuscript.

References

1. H. Bordihn and H. Fernau. Accepting grammars and systems. Technical Report 9/94, Universität Karlsruhe, Fakultät für Informatik, 1994.

2. H. Bordihn and H. Fernau. Accepting grammars with regulation. *International Journal of Computer Mathematics*, 53:1–18, 1994.

3. H. Bordihn and H. Fernau. Accepting grammars and systems via context condition grammars. *Journal of Automata, Languages and Combinatorics*, 1(2):97–112, 1996.

4. J. Dassow and Gh. Păun. *Regulated Rewriting in Formal Language Theory*, volume 18 of *EATCS Monographs in Theoretical Computer Science.* Berlin: Springer, 1989.

5. H. Fernau. Membership for 1-limited ET0L languages is not decidable. *J. Inf. Process. Cybern. EIK (formerly Elektron. Inf.verarb. Kybern.)*, 30(4):191–211, 1994.

6. J. E. Hopcroft and J. D. Ullman. *Introduction to Automata Theory, Languages, and Computation.* Reading (MA): Addison-Wesley, 1979.

7. A. K. Salomaa. *Formal Languages.* Academic Press, 1973.

Conditional Context-Free Languages of Finite Index

Henning FERNAU[1], Markus HOLZER

Wilhelm-Schickard-Institut für Informatik
Universität Tübingen
Sand 13, D-72076 Tübingen, Germany
Email: {fernau,holzer}@informatik.uni-tuebingen.de

Abstract. We consider conditional context-free grammars that generate languages of finite index. Thereby, we solve an open problem stated in Dassow and Păun's monograph on regulated rewriting. Moreover, we show that conditional context-free languages with context-free conditions of finite index are more powerful than conditional context-free languages with regular conditions of finite index. Furthermore, we study the complexity of membership and non-emptiness for conditional and programmed languages respectively grammars (of finite index) with regular, linear, and context-free core rules and conditions.

1. Introduction

Regulated rewriting is one of the main and classic topics of formal language theory [8], [36], since there, basically context-free rewriting mechanisms are enriched by different kinds of regulations, hence generally enhancing the generative power of such devices compared to the context-free languages. Such, it is possible to describe more natural phenomena using context-independent derivation rules [8].

In this paper, we are interested in the relation between formal languages which are built up by rewriting mechanisms—we restrict ourselves to context-free core rules—that generate languages of finite index. Loosely speaking, the index of a grammar is the maximal number of nonterminals simultaneously appearing in a sentential form during a terminating derivation (considering the most economical derivation for each string). Interestingly, such a notion has been introduced by several authors in the sixties on various motivations. Therefore, we start giving sort of historical overview over the topic.

Originally, the finite index restriction was investigated by Brainerd [5] motivated by combinatorial properties of context-free languages. He introduced this notion in order to generalize the statement:

> "If L is an infinite language generated by a context-free grammar, then L contains a sequence, $\{w_n\}$, of strings such that the sequence of lengths $\{|w_n|\}$ is a (nontrivial) arithmetic progression,"

(which is a corollary of the existence of pumping lemmata for context-free languages) to a class of languages that meets, but perhaps does not contain, the context-free languages. Brainerd showed that an analogous statement is valid in case of matrix grammars of finite index.

A similar notion (called bounded grammars here; a grammar is bounded if the total number of nonterminal symbols in any string derivable from the start symbol does not exceed an upper bound) has been introduced by Altman and Banerji [1], [3] motivated by an information theoretic reasoning.

"... languages have been studied for their efficiency for communication purposes, though in these studies the media of communication are referred to as channels [37] rather than languages. These studies use the concept of channel capacity, which is a direct measure of the total number of valid sentences of a given length that a language has."

In [3] it is studied how to compute the channel capacity for a restricted form of unambiguous bounded context-free languages. The capacity of bounded context-free languages (also called ultralinear languages) has been examined by Ginsburg and Spanier in [13]. It is shown that the family of ultralinear languages coincides with the language class characterized by finite-turn push-down automata.

Ginsburg and Spanier introduced derivation-bounded languages [14]. There, all words which have a successful derivation (in a given grammar G) consisting of sentential forms each of which does not contain more than k nonterminals are collected into the set $L_k(G)$. Even if G is a type-0 grammar, $L_k(G)$ is context-free.

Salomaa and Gruska investigated the index of a context-free grammar and language in [15], [35]. Later on, several authors have investigated finite index restrictions also to other rewriting mechanisms, as to, e.g., programmed, ordered, and random context with context-free core rules. In a sequence of papers of Rozenberg and Vermeir [28], [29], [30], [31], it is shown that the corresponding language families coincide. In fact, there are about fifteen different language description mechanisms which characterize the same language class when endowed with the finite index restriction. In these cases, also the slightly different notion of derivation-bounded grammars leads to the same language class.

Further relevant works are [4], [9], [10], [20], [21], [22], [24], [25], [26], [27], [32], [33], [38], [39]. More recently, the finite index restriction was studied in connection with grammar systems [6], [11], [12].

Most of the known results for these types of grammars (in general and in the finite index case) are contained in the first three chapters of the monograph of Dassow and Păun [8]. Results on conditional grammars can be found in [7], [23], [43], too.

In the present paper, we will contribute to the theory of conditional grammars in two ways: (a) we will study conditional grammars of finite index, hence solving a problem marked as open in the monograph [8], and (b) we will look at these models from a complexity theoretical viewpoint. The results of (a) are also contained in [12].

2. Definitions

We assume the reader to be familiar with the basic notions of formal language theory, as contained in Dassow and Păun [8] or Salomaa [36]. In addition, we use $\subseteq$ to denote inclusion, while $\subset$ denotes strict inclusion. The set of positive integers is denoted by $\mathbf{N}$, while $\mathbf{N}_0$ denotes the set of non-negative integers. The empty word is denoted by λ. We consider to languages L_1 and L_2 to be equal iff $L_1 \setminus \{\lambda\} = L_2 \setminus \{\lambda\}$.

The families of regular, linear, context-free, context-sensitive, and recursively enumerable languages are denoted by $\mathcal{L}(REG)$, $\mathcal{L}(LIN)$, $\mathcal{L}(CF)$, $\mathcal{L}(CS)$, and $\mathcal{L}(RE)$, respectively.

For the convenience of the reader, we repeat some definitions from the theory of regulated rewriting. A *programmed grammar (P grammar)* is a septuple $G = (V_N, V_T, P, S, \Lambda, \sigma, \phi)$, where V_N, V_T, and $S \in V_N$ are the set of nonterminals, the set of terminals, and the start symbol, respectively. In the following we use V_G to denote the set $V_N \cup V_T$. P is the finite set of rules $\alpha \to \beta$, and Λ is a finite set of labels (for the rules in P), such that Λ can be also interpreted as a function which outputs a rule when being given a label; σ and ϕ are functions from Λ into the set of subsets of Λ. For (x, r_1), (y, r_2) in $V_G^* \times \Lambda$ and $\Lambda(r_1) = (\alpha \to \beta)$, we write $(x, r_1) \Longrightarrow (y, r_2)$ iff either

1. $x = x_1 \alpha x_2$, $y = x_1 \beta x_2$ and $r_2 \in \sigma(r_1)$, or

2. $x = y$ and rule $\alpha \to \beta$ is not applicable to x, and $r_2 \in \phi(r_1)$.

In the latter case, the derivation step is done in *appearance checking mode*. The set $\sigma(r_1)$ is called success field and the set $\phi(r_1)$ failure field of r_1. As usual, the reflexive transitive closure of $\Longrightarrow$ is denoted by $\Longrightarrow^*$.[2] The language generated by G is defined as $L(G) = \{ w \in V_T^* \mid (S, r_1) \Longrightarrow^* (w, r_2) \text{ for some } r_1, r_2 \in \Lambda \}$. The family of languages generated by programmed grammars containing only context-free core rules is denoted by $\mathcal{L}(P, CF, ac)$. When no appearance checking features are involved, i.e., $\phi(r) = \emptyset$ for each label $r \in \Lambda$, we are led to the family $\mathcal{L}(P, CF)$.

A *conditional grammar (K grammar)* is a system $G = (V_N, V_T, P, S)$ where V_N, V_T, S are defined as above, and P is a finite set of rules $(\alpha \to \beta, Q)$, where Q is a regular language over V_G. The rule $(\alpha \to \beta, Q)$ is applicable to $x = x_1 \alpha x_2$ yielding $y = x_1 \beta x_2$ iff $x \in Q$. Then, we write $x \Longrightarrow y$ and define $\Longrightarrow^*$ as the reflexive transitive closure of $\Longrightarrow$ and $L(G) = \{ w \in V_T^* \mid S \Longrightarrow^* w \}$. The family of languages generated by conditional grammars containing only context-free rules $\alpha \to \beta$ is denoted by $\mathcal{L}(K, CF)$.

Up to now, we have only defined language families defined via grammars possibly containing λ-rules. If we want to exclude λ-rules, we add $-\lambda$ in our notations, e.g., the family of languages generated by conditional grammars containing only context-free λ-free rules is denoted by $\mathcal{L}(K, CF - \lambda)$.

We use bracket notations like $\mathcal{L}(P, CF[-\lambda]) \subset \mathcal{L}(P, CF[-\lambda], ac)$ in order to say that the equation holds both in case of forbidding λ-rules and in the case of admitting λ-rules (neglecting the bracket contents).

The length of a word $w \in V_G^*$, written as $|w|$ is the number of letters in w. For a subset V of V_G, we denote the number of occurrences of letter of V in $x \in V_G^*$ by $|w|_V$. If $V = \{a\}$, then we simply write $|w|_a$.

Let G be an arbitrary grammar type (from those discussed above). For a derivation $D : S = w_1 \Longrightarrow w_2 \Longrightarrow \cdots \Longrightarrow w_n = w \in V_T^*$ according to G, we set $ind(D, G) = \max\{ |w_i|_{V_N} \mid 1 \leq i \leq n \}$, and, for $w \in V_T^*$, we define $ind(w, G) = \min\{ ind(D, G) \mid D \text{ is a derivation for } w \text{ in } G \}$. The *index of grammar* G is defined as $ind(G) = \sup\{ ind(w, G) \mid w \in L(G) \}$. For a language L in the family $\mathcal{L}(X)$ of languages generated by grammars of type X we define $ind_X(L) = \inf\{ ind(G) \mid L(G) = L \text{ and } G \text{ is of type } X \}$. For a family $\mathcal{L}(X)$, we set $\mathcal{L}_k(X) = \{ L \mid L \in \mathcal{L}(X) \text{ and } ind_X(L) \leq k \}$ for $k \in \mathbf{N}$, and $\mathcal{L}_{fin}(X) = \bigcup_{k \geq 1} \mathcal{L}_k(X)$.

For our complexity considerations we need the following notations: we denote the class of languages accepted by deterministic (nondeterministic, respectively)

---

[2] If there is no confusion, we write $D : S \Longrightarrow_{r_1} w_2 \Longrightarrow_{r_2} \cdots \Longrightarrow_{r_{n-1}} w_n = w \in V_G^*$ instead of $D : (S, r_1) = (w_1, r_1) \Longrightarrow (w_2, r_2) \Longrightarrow \cdots \Longrightarrow (w_n, r_n) = (w, r_n) \in V_G^* \times \Lambda$ for a derivation of a programmed grammar.

$O(s(n))$ space bounded Turing machines by $DSPACE(s(n))$ ($NSPACE(s(n))$, respectively). In addition, we use $PSPACE$ as a short-hand notation for the class $\bigcup_k NSPACE(n^k)$. Moreover, the class of languages accepted by nondeterministic pushdown machines equipped with an auxiliary worktape of space $O(s(n))$ is called $NAuxPDASPACE(s(n))$. If in addition the running time is restricted to $O(t(n))$, the corresponding class is $NAuxPDATIMESPACE(t(n), s(n))$. Observe that $NAuxPDATIMESPACE(n^{O(1)}, \log n)$ equals $LOG(CF)$, that is the class of languages deterministic logspace many-one reducible to context-free languages [41]. Furthermore, the class of languages accepted by deterministic (nondeterministic, respectively) polynomially time bounded Turing machines is denoted by P (NP, respectively).

To describe our algorithms, we make use of nondeterministic space bounded oracle Turing machines, where the oracle tape is written deterministically. This oracle mechanism is known as RST-relativization in literature [34]. If L is a set, we denote the class of languages accepted by nondeterministic $O(s(n))$ space bounded RST oracle Turing machines with L oracle by $NSPACE^{\langle L \rangle}(s(n))$. If A is a class of sets, then $NSPACE^{\langle A \rangle}(s(n))$ is $\bigcup_{L \in A} NSPACE^{\langle L \rangle}(s(n))$.

Further, all completeness results are meant with respect to deterministic logspace many-one reducibilities. In case grammars are part of the input, the straight-forward coding of these grammars is assumed; the languages being part of the specification of conditional rules are given by standard grammars. Basic notions of complexity theory are contained in [2].

3. Conditional Languages

In this section, we give a positive answer to an open question listed in [8], Open problem 3.1.2, namely we show that the conditional and programmed context-free language coincide under the finite index restriction.

Without the finite index restriction we have the chain

$$\mathcal{L}(P, CF[-\lambda]) \subset \mathcal{L}(P, CF[-\lambda], ac) \subseteq \mathcal{L}(K, CF[-\lambda]),$$

where the latter inclusion is strict if and only if λ-rules are forbidden. Further, observe that conditional context-free grammars characterize the recursively enumerable languages in presence and the context-sensitive languages in absence of λ-rules.

Let us turn back to languages of finite index. We first show a normal form result for conditional grammars that generate languages of finite index.

Theorem 1. *For every conditional context-free grammar $G = (V_N, V_T, P, S)$ whose generated language is of index $k \in \mathbf{N}$, there exists an equivalent grammar $G' = (V_N', V_T, P', S')$ of same type whose generated language is also of index k and which satisfies the following two properties:*

1. *There exists a special start rule, which is the only rule where the start symbol S' appears.*

2. *If $D : S' = v_0 \Longrightarrow v_1 \Longrightarrow v_2 \Longrightarrow \cdots \Longrightarrow v_m = w$ is a derivation in G', then, for every v_i, $0 \le i \le m$, we have $|v_i|_{V_N'} \le k$, and moreover, for every nonterminal A, we have $|v_i|_A \le 1$.*

Proof. We construct a grammar $G' = (V'_N, V_T, P', S')$ of index k which is equivalent to $G = (V_N, V_T, P, S)$ and satisfies the two requirements.

Let $V'_N = V_N \times \{1, \ldots, k\} \cup \{S'\}$ and define the morphism h from $V_{G'} \setminus \{S'\}$ to V_G as follows: set $h(a) = a$ if $A \in V_T$, and $h((A, i)) = A$ otherwise. The start rule is $(S' \to (S, 1), \{S'\})$. Thus, the first property is ensured. Then, for every rule $(A \to w, Q)$ of the original grammar G, we construct for every i, $1 \le i \le k$, and for every $v \in h^{-1}(w)$ a rule of the form $((A, i) \to v, h^{-1}(Q) \cap R \cap T)$, where R and T are the regular sets

$$R = \bigcap_{A \in V'_N} (V_{G'} \setminus \{A\})^* \cdot (\{\lambda\} \cup \{A\}) \cdot (V_{G'} \setminus \{A\})^*, \quad \text{and} \quad T = \bigcup_{0 \le i \le k} (V_T^* V_N')^i \cdot V_T^*.$$

Note that the second property is controlled by the regular sets R and T, since R is the set of words such that every nonterminal occurs at most once, and language T ensures the additional property that only words that contain at most k nonterminals are derivable. $\quad\square$

Now, we are ready to prove that $\mathcal{L}_k(P, CF[-\lambda])$ and $\mathcal{L}_k(K, CF[-\lambda])$ coincide.

Theorem 2. *For every* $k \in \mathbf{N}$, $\mathcal{L}_k(P, CF[-\lambda]) = \mathcal{L}_k(K, CF[-\lambda])$.

Proof. It suffices to prove the inclusion $\mathcal{L}_k(K, CF[-\lambda]) \subseteq \mathcal{L}_k(P, CF[-\lambda])$, since it is known from [28], Lemma 3, that $\mathcal{L}_k(P, CF[-\lambda])$ coincides with the family of random context context-free languages of index k, which is a trivial subset of $\mathcal{L}_k(K, CF[-\lambda])$ (see, [8], page 121).

Let $G = (V_N, V_T, P, S)$ be a conditional context-free grammar of the normal form described above that generates a language of finite index k. Assume that every rule of P has a unique label r, $1 \le r \le m = |P|$, and that the start rule is labeled by 1.

In this way, we can refer to the regular language Q_r of the rth rule. Furthermore, we assume that Q_r is represented by some deterministic finite automaton $M_r = (K_r, V_G, \delta_r, q_{0,r}, F_r)$, where K_r is the finite set of states, V_G the input alphabet, $\delta_r : K_r \times V_G \to K_r$ the transition function, $q_{0,r} \in K_r$ the start state, and $F_r \subseteq K_r$ the set of final states.

Define $D = K_1^{K_1} \times \cdots \times K_m^{K_m}$. Note that D is finite. The elements d of D are tuples of state maps, such that the rth projection $d[r]$ is a map from K_r to itself. For each $v \in V_G^*$, one associates a map tuple $d_v \in D$ defined by: for every $1 \le r \le m$ and for every $p \in K_r$, $d_v[r](p) = \delta_r^*(p, v)$, where δ_r^* is the extension of the transition function δ_r to domain $K_r \times V_G^*$. For $d_v, d_w \in D$ let $d_v \circ d_w$ denote the component-wise extended composition of functions, i.e., for two functions f, g let $f \circ g(x)$ mean $g(f(x))$. Having this, one readily verifies that $d_v \circ d_w$ equals d_{vw}.

Now, we briefly describe the construction of an equivalent programmed grammar $G = (V'_N, V_T, P', S', \Lambda, \sigma, \phi)$ of index k. Set $V'_N = V_N$ and let

$$\Lambda \subseteq \{p_0\} \cup \{1, \ldots, m\} \times \left(\bigcup_{1 \le i \le k} (D \times V_N)^i \right) \times D.$$

The start rule is $S' \to S$ has the unique label p_0 and we set $\sigma(p_0) = \{(1, d_\lambda, S, d_\lambda)\}$. Observe that $d_\lambda[r]$ is the identity on K_r.

We say that a label $(r, d_{u_1}, A_1, d_{u_2}, A_2, \ldots, d_{u_j}, A_j, d_{u_{j+1}})$ is valid if and only if $1 \le r \le m$, $1 \le j \le k$, and all A_i's, $1 \le i \le j$, are distinct, and it is r-valid if and only if it is valid and satisfies

$$(d_{u_1} \circ d_{A_1} \circ d_{u_2} \circ d_{A_2} \circ \cdots \circ d_{u_j} \circ d_{A_j} \circ d_{u_{j+1}})[r](q_{0,r}) \in F_r,$$

i.e., the word $u_1 A_1 u_2 A_2 \ldots u_j A_j u_{j+1}$ belongs to Q_r.

For each rule r of the form $(A \to w, Q)$, we construct a bunch of labels with the corresponding σ and ϕ fields. Let

$$(r, d_{u_1}, A_1, d_{u_2}, A_2, \ldots, d_{u_i}, A_i, d_{u_{i+1}}, \ldots, d_{u_j}, A_j, d_{u_{j+1}})$$

be an r-valid label with $A_i = A$. We define

$$\Lambda\big((r, d_{u_1}, A_1, d_{u_2}, A_2, \ldots, d_{u_j}, A_j, d_{u_{j+1}})\big) = A \to w.$$

We have to distinguish two cases:

1. If $|w|_{V_N} > 0$, i.e., $w = w_1 B_1 w_2 B_2 \ldots w_s B_s w_{s+1}$, for some $s \geq 1$, $B_1, \ldots, B_s \in V_N$, and $w_1 \ldots w_{s+1} \in V_T^*$, then $\sigma\big((r, d_{u_1}, A_1, d_{u_2}, A_2, \ldots, d_{u_j}, A_j, d_{u_{j+1}})\big)$ consists of all r'-valid labels

$$(r', d_{u_1}, A_1, \ldots, d_{u_{i-1}}, A_{i-1}, d_{u_i} \circ d_{w_1}, B_1, d_{w_2}, \ldots$$
$$\ldots, d_{w_s}, B_s, d_{w_{s+1}} \circ d_{u_{i+1}}, A_{i+1}, \ldots, A_j, d_{u_{j+1}}).$$

Of course, we can assume $i + s \leq k$.

2. If $w \in V_T^*$, let $\sigma\big((r, d_{u_1}, A_1, d_{u_2}, A_2, \ldots, d_{u_j}, A_j, d_{u_{j+1}})\big)$ consist of all r'-valid labels

$$(r', d_{u_1}, A_1, \ldots, d_{u_{i-1}}, A_{i-1}, d_{u_i} \circ d_w \circ d_{u_{i+1}}, A_{i+1}, \ldots, A_j, d_{u_{j+1}}).$$

This completes our construction. It is seen that the index of the language is preserved, and that the constructed programmed grammar G' is equivalent to the originally given one. More precisely, by induction we have

$$S' \Longrightarrow_{p_0} S \Longrightarrow^* u \Longrightarrow_\alpha v,$$

where $\alpha = (r, d_{u_1}, A_1, d_{u_2}, \ldots, d_{u_j}, A_k, d_{u_{j+1}})$, in G' if and only if $S \Longrightarrow^* u \Longrightarrow v$ in G such that $u = w_1 A_1 w_2 \ldots w_j A_j w_{j+1}$, with $w_i \in V_T^*$ and $d_{u_i} = d_{w_i}$ for $1 \leq i \leq j + 1$. Furthermore, $u \in Q_r$. □

With our previous theorem, and the fact that erasing rules do not enlarge the family of programmed context-free languages of finite index [8], Lemma 3.1.2, we immediately obtain:

Corollary 1. *The language families $\mathcal{L}_{fin}(K, CF - \lambda)$ and $\mathcal{L}_{fin}(K, CF)$ coincide with the language family $\mathcal{L}_{fin}(P, CF)$. They strictly embrace the linear languages.*

4. Beyond the Finite Index Barrier

As mentioned in the introduction, about fifteen different language description mechanism coincide under the finite index restriction. Thus, the question arises whether one can think about "natural" rewriting mechanisms (based on context-free core rules), which generate languages of finite index which are not programmed context-free finite index languages.

Since in the non-finite index case, conditional context-free languages are a superset of programmed, random context, and ordered context-free languages, one way to break the programmed context-free finite index barrier might be to use conditional grammars with enlarged condition sets.

Conditional grammars with different Chomsky type-i languages for core rules and condition sets were already investigated in [23]. In all cases, characterizations of context-sensitive and recursively enumerable languages were obtained; the only exceptions are given below:

$$\mathcal{L}(REG) = \mathcal{L}(K, REG) \subset \mathcal{L}(CF) \subset \mathcal{L}(K_{CF}, REG) \subset \mathcal{L}(CS).$$

Here K_X denotes a conditional grammar with condition sets from $\mathcal{L}(X)$. Thus, e.g., $\mathcal{L}(K_{CF}, REG)$ denotes the family of languages generated by conditional grammars with context-free condition sets and regular core rules. Observe that by definition, $\mathcal{L}(K_X, REG)$ obviously contains only languages of finite index for any X.

We show that in the finite index case we can go beyond $\mathcal{L}_{fin}(P, CF)$ if one uses, e.g., conditional grammars with context-free core rules and context-free condition sets.

Theorem 3. $\mathcal{L}_{fin}(K, CF) \subset \mathcal{L}_{fin}(K_{CF}, CF[-\lambda])$.

Proof. The inclusion is obvious; it remains to proof the strictness. Since every one-letter language in $\mathcal{L}_{fin}(K, CF)$ is regular by [8] (Corollary, page 159), it is sufficient to prove that a conditional grammar with context-free core rules and context-free condition sets can generate a non-context-free one-letter language.

The conditional grammar $G = (\{S, A, B\}, \{a\}, P, S)$ with the rules

1: $(S \rightarrow AB, a^*S)$,

1a: $(S \rightarrow a, a^*S)$,

2: $(B \rightarrow aB, \{a^n A a^m B \mid n, m \geq 0 \text{ and } n > m\})$,

3: $(A \rightarrow a, \{a^n A a^m B \mid n, m \geq 0 \text{ and } n = m\})$, and

4: $(B \rightarrow S, a^*B)$

generates the language $\{a^{2^n} \mid n \geq 0\}$. This is seen as follows: Note that the rules $1, 3, 4, 1, 2, 3, 4, \ldots, 1, 2, 3, 4, 1a$ must be applied in this order and rule 2 can be repeated several times. Therefore, a successful derivation in G has the structure

$$
\begin{aligned}
S &\Longrightarrow_1 \quad AB \Longrightarrow_3 aB \Longrightarrow_4 aS \\
&\Longrightarrow_1 \quad aAB \Longrightarrow_2 aAaB \Longrightarrow_3 aaaB \Longrightarrow_4 aaaS \\
&\Longrightarrow_1 \quad aaaAB \Longrightarrow_2 \cdots \Longrightarrow_2 aaaAaaaB \Longrightarrow_3 aaaaaaaB \Longrightarrow_4 aaaaaaaS \\
&\quad \cdots \\
&\Longrightarrow_1 \quad a^{2^n-1}AB \Longrightarrow_2 \cdots \Longrightarrow_2 a^{2^n-1}Aa^{2^n-1}B \Longrightarrow_3 a^{2^n}a^{2^n-1}B \Longrightarrow_4 a^{2^n}a^{2^n-1}S \\
&\Longrightarrow_{1a} \quad a^{2^n}a^{2^n} = a^{2^{n+1}}.
\end{aligned}
$$

By induction, one proves that $L(G)$ equals the desired language. Obviously, language $L(G)$ has finite index 2. This proves our claim. $\qquad\square$

The previous proof shows a little bit more than only the separation of $\mathcal{L}_{fin}(K, CF)$ and $\mathcal{L}_{fin}(K_{CF}, CF[-\lambda])$. Since the condition sets of G are even linear languages, we obtain on the one hand:

Corollary 2. *If $\mathcal{L}(X)$ is a language family that contains the linear languages, then $\mathcal{L}_{fin}(K, CF) \subset \mathcal{L}_{fin}(K_X, CF[-\lambda])$.*

On the other hand, the language of the previous proof even separates the classes $\mathcal{L}(K_{CF}, REG)$ and $\mathcal{L}_{fin}(K_{CF}, CF[-\lambda])$, since every one-letter language in $\mathcal{L}(K_{CF}, REG)$ is regular by [23], page 184, Lemma 2.

Corollary 3. $\mathcal{L}(CF) \subset \mathcal{L}(K_{CF}, REG) \subset \mathcal{L}_{fin}(K_{CF}, CF[-\lambda])$.

Finally, we find it quite surprising that conditional languages of finite index with context-free condition sets and context-free core rules (even admitting λ-rules) belong to $\mathcal{L}(CS)$. Here, the presence of λ-rules is not crucial, because by the finite index restriction in every sentential form there are at most a constant number of nonterminals that can derive the word λ. Therefore, by a direct simulation of a (K_{CF}, CF) grammar of finite index k using a Turing machine, only a linear number (in the length of the input word) of additional cells on the work-tape may be used. Thus, we have:

Theorem 4. $\mathcal{L}_{fin}(K_{CF}, CF[-\lambda]) \subseteq \mathcal{L}(CS)$.

Unfortunately, we have to leave as open the question whether the inclusion of the last theorem is proper or not. Without the finite index restriction it is known from [23] that $\mathcal{L}(CS) = \mathcal{L}(K_{CF}, CF - \lambda)$ and $\mathcal{L}(RE) = \mathcal{L}(K_{CF}, CF)$. Employing a non-constant number of nonterminals during the simulation of a Turing machine (with a linear space bound) seems to be inherent in both cases. A natural idea for separating $\mathcal{L}_{fin}(K_{CF}, CF[-\lambda]) \subseteq \mathcal{L}(CS)$ might be to look at closure or decidability properties.

In the next section, we are going to investigate non-emptiness and word problems for conditional grammars. In the following, if we speak of a conditional grammar with say regular core rules and linear conditions, we also refer to these grammars as (K_{LIN}, REG)-grammars, and we assume that the condition sets are given by some grammar of the required type. The following lemma starts these investigations, underlining the difference between regular and non-regular context-conditions, since for programmed grammars of finite index with context-free core rules (and hence for (K_{REG}, CF)-grammars of finite index by Theorem 2, non-emptiness is known to be decidable, Theorem 3.2.4, [8].

Lemma 1. *For (K_{LIN}, REG)-grammars, the non-emptiness problem is undecidable.*

Proof. The Post correspondence problem (PCP), that is given two morphisms $g, h : V^* \to \{a, b\}^*$, is there a word $v \in V^+$ such that $g(v) = h(v)$, is well-known to be undecidable, if V contains at least nine letters.

Consider the conditional grammar $G = (\{S, T\}, \{a, b, \$\}, P, S)$ with rules

1: $(S \to aS, \{a, b, \$\}^*\{S\})$, $(S \to bS, \{a, b, \$\}^*\{S\})$, and $(S \to \$S, \{a, b, \$\}^*\{S\})$,

2: $(S \to T, \{ w\$w^R S \mid w \in \{a, b\}^* \})$, and

3: $(T \to \lambda, \{ g(v)\$h(v^R)T \mid v \in V^+ \})$,

where w^R denotes the reversal or mirror image of w. Clearly, the condition sets used for the latter two rules are linear. Obviously, $L(G) \neq \emptyset$ if and only if the PCP given by the morphisms g and h has a solution. □

5. Complexity Considerations

Up to now, the complexity of conditional languages respectively grammars (of finite index) was not studied in literature. We close this gap, studying fixed (FM), general or variable membership (GM), and non-emptiness (NE) for conditional grammars with regular, linear, and context-free core rules and conditions.

Grammars with regular or linear core rules are trivially of index 1. If we are interested in problems that deal with grammars of finite index having context-free core rules, we have two possibilities to vary each of the above-mentioned problems, because even for context-free grammars it is undecidable whether a given grammar is of finite index or not [8], Theorem 3.2.6. Hence, we can define the following fixed membership problems:

FM with fixed index (FMFI): Let $k \in \mathbf{N}$ and the grammar G, with context-free core rules, be fixed. For given word w, is $w \in L(G)$ and $ind(w, G) \leq k$?

FM with general index (FMGI): Let the grammar G, with context-free core rules, be fixed. For given 1^k and word w, is $w \in L(G)$ and $ind(w, G) \leq k$?

The corresponding general membership problems are denoted by GMFI and GMGI, and the non-emptiness problems by NEFI and NEGI. Obviously, FMFI reduces to GMFI which reduces to NEFI; FMGI reduces to GMGI which reduces to NEGI; finally FMFI reduces to FMGI, GMFI reduces to GMGI, and NEFI reduces to NEGI.

First let us summarize a few results that relates the classes of the Chomsky hierarchy with conditional language families [23]:

1. $\mathcal{L}(REG) = \mathcal{L}(K_{REG}, REG)$,

2. $\mathcal{L}(LIN) = \mathcal{L}(K_{REG}, LIN) \subseteq \mathcal{L}(K_{LIN}, REG)$

3. $\mathcal{L}(CF) \subseteq \mathcal{L}(K_{CF}, REG)$,

4. $\mathcal{L}(CS) = \mathcal{L}(K_X, CF - \lambda)$ for $X \in \{REG, LIN, CF\}$, and

5. $\mathcal{L}(RE) = \mathcal{L}(K_X, CF)$ for $X \in \{REG, LIN, CF\}$.

The inclusions in 2 and 3 are easily seen to be strict, e.g., $\{a^n b^n c^n \mid n \geq 0\} \in \mathcal{L}(K_{LIN}, REG)$ by a construction similar to Theorem 3.

Since the complexity of the classes on the left-hand sides of the equations are well-known ($LOG(REG) = DSPACE(\log n)$, $LOG(LIN) = NSPACE(\log n)$ [40], and $LOG(CS) = PSPACE$), we obtain either a few lower bound, completeness, or undecidability results. The two latter ones are stated below:

Theorem 5. *Fixed membership, general membership, and non-emptiness for (K_X, CF)-grammars, with $X \in \{REG, LIN, CF\}$, is undecidable. Even for λ-free context-free core rules, non-emptiness remains undecidable.*

Theorem 6. *Let $X \in \{REG, LIN, CF\}$. Fixed membership for $(K_X, CF - \lambda)$-grammars is PSPACE-complete.*

Theorem 7. *The fixed membership problem for* (K_{REG}, REG)*-grammars is* $DSPACE(\log n)$*-complete.*

In order to obtain upper bounds, let us show how to parse conditional languages nondeterministically in a top-down manner. So let $G = (V_N, V_T, P, S)$ be a conditional grammar and assume $w = a_1 \ldots a_n$ to be the input of length n. For simplicity of the description of the algorithm we assume that the productions of G are of the form $(A \to BC, Q)$ or $(A \to a, Q)$. It is easily seen that the algorithm generalizes to arbitrary context-free rules.

Define the triples $(A, i, j) \in V_N \times \{0, \ldots, n\} \times \{0, \ldots, n\}$. To each triple (A, i, j), with $0 \leq i < j \leq n$, we associate the word $a_1 a_2 \ldots a_i A a_{j+1} \ldots a_n$. This meaning generalizes to lists $(A_1, i_1, j_1), (A_2, i_2, j_2), \ldots, (A_k, i_k, j_k)$ in an obvious way; additionally we require $0 \leq i_1 < j_1 \leq i_2 < j_2 \leq \cdots \leq i_k < j_k \leq n$.

Start the algorithm with the list $(S, 0, n)$. (1) Guess a rule $r = (A \to \alpha, Q)$ whose left-hand side appears in the list. We assume (A, i, k) to be this triple. (2) Check whether the word associated to the list belongs to Q. If this is not the case then halt and reject. Otherwise, we continue the simulation of the derivation by replacing (A, i, k) in the list by $(B, i, j)(C, j, k)$ for some guessed j with $i < j < k$ if $r = (A \to BC, Q)$; erase (A, i, k) if $r = (A \to a, Q)$, $a = a_{i+1}$ and $i + 1 = k$. (4) If we have reached an empty sequence of triples, then we halt and accept, otherwise we continue the algorithm starting with (1). In passing, the algorithm can test the index restriction.

The interested reader may verify the correctness of the described algorithm. We implement the algorithm on an oracle Turing machine where the oracle tape is written deterministically [34], in order to simulate step (2). The oracle sets T we use are of the form

$$\langle r, w \rangle \in T \iff w \in Q \text{ if } r = (A \to \alpha, Q),$$

and the space of the machine (as usual the oracle tape is not taken into consideration) is bounded by the maximal number of triples ever written on the work tape times the space needed to encode *one* triple (A, i, j), which is $O(\log n)$.

Hence, if fixed membership with fixed index is checked for a conditional grammar with context-free core rules and linear conditions, we obtain $NSPACE(\log n)$ as an upper bound, because the space of the oracle Turing machine is logarithmically bounded, the oracle set T described above is contained in $NSPACE(\log n)$, and

$$NSPACE^{\langle NSPACE(\log n) \rangle}(\log n) \subseteq NSPACE(\log n) \quad [17], [42].$$

Analogously, we estimate the complexity of fixed membership with fixed index of conditional grammars with context-free core rules and context-free conditions with $NAuxPDATIMESPACE(n^{O(1)}, \log n)$. Combined with the lower bounds stated earlier, we obtain the following theorem:

Theorem 8.

1. *Let* $X, Y \in \{REG, LIN\}$*. Fixed membership for* (K_X, Y)*-grammars, except for* (K_{REG}, REG)*-grammars, and fixed membership with fixed index for* (K_X, CF)*-grammars, is* $NSPACE(\log n)$*-complete.*

2. *Fixed membership for* (K_{CF}, Y)*-grammars, with* $Y \in \{REG, LIN\}$*, and fixed membership with fixed index for* (K_{CF}, CF)*-grammars is* $LOG(CF)$*-complete.*

For the remaining three fixed membership problems we find the following upper bounds because the index is part of the input:

Theorem 9.

1. *The fixed membership with general index for (K_X, CF)-grammars, with $X \in \{REG, LIN\}$, is contained in $NSPACE(n \cdot \log n)$.*

2. *The fixed membership with general index for (K_{CF}, CF)-grammars is contained in $NAuxPDASPACE(n \cdot \log n)$.*

Let us turn our attention to general membership.

Theorem 10.

1. *Let $X, Y \in \{REG, LIN\}$. The general membership for (K_X, Y)-grammars is $NSPACE(\log n)$-complete.*

2. *The general membership for (K_{CF}, Y)-grammars, with $Y \in \{REG, LIN\}$, and general membership with fixed index for (K_{CF}, CF)-grammars, is P-complete.*

3. *The general membership with general index for (K_X, CF)-grammars, with $X \in \{REG, LIN, CF\}$, is $PSPACE$-complete.*

4. *The general membership for $(K_X, CF - \lambda)$-grammars, with $X \in \{REG, LIN, CF\}$, is $PSPACE$-complete.*

Proof. First consider general membership. Since general membership for regular (context-free, respectively) grammars is $NSPACE(\log n)$-complete (P-complete [18], respectively), we obtain $NSPACE(\log n)$ (P, respectively) as a lower bound for general membership for conditional grammars with regular core rules and regular (context-free, respectively) conditions.

The upper bounds follow with the algorithm to check membership. Observe that the space bound for the oracle Turing machine is $O(\log n)$ and the oracle sets to be used are from $NSPACE(\log n)$ in case of linear conditions and from P if context-free conditions are used. This is because the oracles have to check general membership for the condition sets. Note that $NSPACE^{(P)}(\log n) \subseteq P$. This leads us to the desired completeness results for general membership with fixed index.

In case of general membership (with general index), the space bounds for the oracle Turing machine get worse and remain $O(n \cdot \log n)$. In combination with an oracle from P to check general membership for a context-free conditions, we obtain $PSPACE$ as an upper bound, because $NSPACE^{(P)}(n \cdot \log n) \subseteq PSPACE$. The lower bound $PSPACE$, and hence the completeness results stated in 3 and 4 follow with the enclosed construction:

The intersection non-emptiness problem for deterministic finite automata, that is: given deterministic finite automata $M_1, \ldots, M_n$, i.e., a suitable coding $\langle M_1, \ldots, M_n \rangle$, is $\bigcap_{1 \leq i \leq n} L(M_i) \neq \emptyset$? This problem is $PSPACE$-complete [19].

Let $\langle M_1, \ldots, M_n \rangle$ be an instance of the non-emptiness intersection problem for deterministic finite automata. For technical reasons only, we assume that for the deterministic automata $M_i = (K_i, \Sigma, \delta_i, q_{0,i}, F_i)$, $1 \leq i \leq n$, with set of states K_i, input alphabet Σ, transition function $\delta_i : K_i \times \Sigma \to K_i$, start state $q_{0,i}$, and final set of states $F_i \subseteq K_i$ the following is satisfied: (1) $\Sigma = \{a, b\}$, (2) $K_i \cap K_j = \emptyset$ if $i \neq j$, and $\lambda \notin L(M_i)$ for each $1 \leq i \leq n$.

We construct a conditional grammar $G = (V_N, \{a\}, P, S)$ with context-free core rules and regular conditions. Set

$$V_N = \{S, A, B, C, D\} \cup \bigcup_{1 \leq i \leq n} K_i \cup \bigcup_{1 \leq i \leq n} \bar{K}_i,$$

where $\bar{K}_i = \{\bar{q} \mid q \in K_i\}$ and all unions being disjoint. The rules are as follows:

1. $(S \rightarrow q_{0,1} q_{0,2} \ldots q_{0,n} A, \{S\})$ and $(S \rightarrow q_{0,1} q_{0,2} \ldots q_{0,n} B, \{S\})$.

2. For each $(X, x) \in \{(A, a), (B, b)\}$ define

    (a) for every $q \in K_1$, $(q \rightarrow p, K_1 K_2 \ldots K_n \{X\})$ if $\delta_1(q, x) = p$,

    (b) for $q \in K_i$ with $2 \leq i \leq n$, define $(q \rightarrow \bar{p}, \bar{K}_1 \bar{K}_2 \ldots \bar{K}_{i-1} K_i \ldots K_n \{X\})$ if $\delta_i(q, x) = p$, and

    (c) $(X \rightarrow C, \bar{K}_1 \bar{K}_2 \ldots \bar{K}_n \{X\})$, and $(X \rightarrow D, \bar{K}_1 \bar{K}_2 \ldots \bar{K}_n \{X\})$.

3. Case nonterminal C:

    (a) For every $q \in K_1$ define $(\bar{q} \rightarrow q, \bar{K}_1 \bar{K}_2 \ldots \bar{K}_n \{C\})$,

    (b) for every $q \in K_i$, with $2 \leq i \leq n$, define $(\bar{q} \rightarrow q, K_1 \ldots K_{i-1} \bar{K}_i \ldots \bar{K}_n \{C\})$, and

    (c) $(C \rightarrow A, K_1 K_2 \ldots K_n \{C\})$, and $(C \rightarrow B, K_1 K_2 \ldots K_n \{C\})$.

4. Case nonterminal D:

    (a) For every $q \in K_i$, with $1 \leq i \leq n$, define $(\bar{q} \rightarrow a, a^{i-1} \bar{K}_i \ldots \bar{K}_n \{D\})$ if $q \in F_i$, and

    (b) $(D \rightarrow a, a^n \{D\})$.

Finally, it is easy to verify that $\bigcap_{1 \leq i \leq n} L(M_i) \neq \emptyset$ if and only if $\langle 1^{n+1}, a^{n+1}, G \rangle$ is an instance of general membership with general index if and only if $\langle a^{n+1}, G \rangle$ is an instance of general membership. Obviously, the latter instances are logspace computable if $\langle M_1, \ldots, M_n \rangle$ is given. This completes our construction. $\square$

In the remainder of this section we deal with non-emptiness problems. In Theorem 5 we have already seen, that some non-emptiness problems are undecidable. But these were only a few of them. By Lemma 1 we additional obtain:

Corollary 4. *Let $X \in \{LIN, CF\}$. Non-emptiness for (K_X, Y)-grammars, with $Y \in \{REG, LIN\}$, and non-emptiness with fixed and general index for (K_X, CF)-grammars, is undecidable.*

The remaining non-emptiness problems are shown to be *PSPACE*-complete.

Theorem 11. *The following problems are PSPACE-complete: non-emptiness for (K_{REG}, Y)-grammars, with $Y \in \{REG, LIN\}$, and non-emptiness for both fixed and general index for (K_{REG}, CF)-grammars.*

Proof. For the lower bound on non-emptiness, we again use the non-emptiness intersection problem for deterministic finite automata. For given $\langle M_1, \ldots, M_n \rangle$ we construct an instance of non-emptiness as follows: define the grammar $G = (\{S, T_1, \ldots, T_{n+1}\}, \{a, b\}, P, S)$ with rules

1. $(S \to aS, \{a, b\}^*S)$, $(S \to bS, \{a, b\}^*S)$, $(S \to T_1, \{a, b\}^*S)$,

2. $(T_i \to T_{i+1}, L(M_i) \cdot T_i)$, for $1 \le i \le n$, and $(T_{n+1} \to \lambda, \{a, b\}^*T_n)$.

It is easy to see that this construction is logspace computable and that $\bigcap_{1 \le i \le n} L(M_i) \ne \emptyset$ if and only if $L(G) \ne \emptyset$. Hence, $PSPACE$ is the desired lower bound.

Let G be a conditional grammar with context-free core rules and regular conditions. The easiest way to check non-emptiness with general index would be to guess a terminating derivation of finite index and to simulate it step by step, writing down the whole sentential form, say $u_1 A_1 u_2 \ldots u_k A_k u_{k+1}$, obtained so far. Unfortunately, this idea does not result in a $PSPACE$ algorithm in general. But we can do better, if we write down $d_{u_1} A_1 d_{u_2} \ldots d_{u_k} A_k d_{k+1}$, where the d_{u_i}'s are defined as in the proof of Theorem 2. Simple calculations show that this approach results in a polynomial space algorithm. □

6. Conclusions

We investigated conditional context-free grammars that generate languages of finite index. We proved a normal form theorem for these grammars, and showed that they coincide with programmed context-free languages of finite index, even when considering language families of finite index k, regardless whether erasing rules are allowed or not. In this way we solved an open problem stated in [8].

Furthermore, we classified various variants of fixed and general membership and non-emptiness for conditional languages (of finite index) according to their undecidability and complexity. Thereby, we closed a gap in the literature.

Let us remark that these results trivially carry over to programmed grammars of finite index, delivering easy upper bounds on the complexities. Regarding the lower bounds, we simply refer to the construction given in the proof of Theorem 10, where the regular condition sets are only used to prescribe the sequence of rule applications. Let us point to the surprising fact that non-emptiness with fixed index for programmed grammars with context-free core rules is $NSPACE(\log n)$-complete, while it is well-known to be P-complete for context-free grammars (without the finite index restriction).

So, we obtain the table given in Figure 1. If we write only the complexity class $\mathcal{C}$, we refer to a complete problem. If we write $\in \mathcal{C}$, we know only an upper bound. Finally, let us remark that it is known that fixed membership for $(P, CF - \lambda, ac)$ is NP-hard by a result of van Leeuwen [44].

We want to stimulate the readers to pursue complexity studies for problems given via regulated rewriting. Even if problems turn out to be undecidable, a further classification according to the criteria delivered by recursion theory would be of interest.

23

grammars	Problem		
	fixed membership	general membership	non-emptiness
(P, REG, ac)	$DSPACE(\log n)$		
(P, LIN, ac)			
(P, CF, ac) and FI			$NSPACE(\log n)$
(P, CF, ac) and GI	$\in NSPACE(n \cdot \log n)$		$PSPACE$
$(P, CF - \lambda, ac)$	$\in PSPACE$		
(P, CF, ac)			undecidable

Figure 1. Undecidability and complexity results for programmed languages

It is known that, e.g., programmed finite index languages have nice properties from the formal language theoretical point of view. Let's turn back to the original motivation of Brainerd [5] for introducing the notion of finite index. As already said in the introduction, he proved that the length set of each infinite context-free matrix language of finite index contains an infinite arithmetic progression. It is natural to ask whether this is a property special to languages of finite index in the regulated rewriting case with context-free core rules. There is a negative answer to this question in two senses:

1. The family $\mathcal{L}(P, CF)$ (without the finite index restriction) has the property that every infinite language in $\mathcal{L}(P, CF)$ contains an infinite arithmetic progression, because the class $\mathcal{L}(P, CF)$ is closed under homomorphisms, and every one-letter-language in $\mathcal{L}(P, CF)$ is semilinear, as proved in the paper of Hauschildt and Jantzen [16].

2. In Section 4, we have found a language class of finite index, namely $\mathcal{L}_{fin}(K_{CF}, CF[-\lambda])$, which contains the language $\{ a^{2^n} \mid n \geq 0 \}$ that does not have an infinite arithmetic progression.

References

1. E. Altman and R. Banerji. Some problems of finite representability. *Inf. Contr.*, 8:251–263, 1965.

2. J. Balcázar, J. Díaz, and J. Gabarró. *Structural Complexity Theory I*. Springer, 1988.

3. R. B. Banerji. Phrase structure languages, finite machines, and channel capacity. *Inf. Contr.*, 6:153–162, 1963.

4. J. Beauquier. Deux familles de langages incomparables. *Inf. Contr.*, 43:101–122, 1979.

5. B. Brainerd. An analog of a theorem about context-free languages. *Inf. Contr.*, 11:561–567, 1968.

6. E. Csuhaj-Varjú, J. Dassow, J. Kelemen, and Gh. Păun. *Grammar Systems: A Grammatical Approach to Distribution and Cooperation*. London: Gordon and Breach, 1994.

7. J. Dassow and H. Hornig. Conditional grammars with subregular conditions. In *2nd International Colloquium on Words, Languages, and Combinatorics*, pages 71–86. Kyoto Sangyo Unversity (Japan), World Scientific, August 1990.

8. J. Dassow and Gh. Păun. *Regulated Rewriting in Formal Language Theory*, volume 18 of *EATCS Monographs in Theoretical Computer Science*. Berlin: Springer, 1989.

9. G. Dong. On the index of positive programmed formal languages. *IPL*, 54:105–110, 1995.

10. D. Ferment. Principality results about some matrix language families. In J. Paredaens, editor, *11th ICALP'84*, volume 172 of *LNCS*, pages 151–161, 1984.

11. H. Fernau, R. Freund, and M. Holzer. External versus internal hybridization for cooperating distributed grammar systems. Technical Report TR 185–2/FR–1/96, Technische Universität Wien (Austria), 1996.

12. H. Fernau and M. Holzer. Regulated finite index language families collapse. Technical Report WSI–96–16, Universität Tübingen (Germany), Wilhelm-Schickard-Institut für Informatik, 1996.

13. S. Ginsburg and E. H. Spanier. Finite-turn pushdown automata. *SIAM Journal of Control*, 4(3):429–453, 1966.

14. S. Ginsburg and E. H. Spanier. Derivation-bounded languages. *JCSS*, 2:228–250, 1968.

15. J. Gruska. A few remarks on the index of context-free grammars and languages. *Inf. Contr.*, 19:216–223, 1971.

16. D. Hauschildt and M. Jantzen. Petri net algorithms in the theory of matrix grammars. *Acta Informatica*, 31:719–728, 1994.

17. N. Immerman. Nondeterministic space is closed under complementation. *SIAM Journal Comput.*, 17(5):935–938, 1988.

18. N. D. Jones and W. T. Laaser. Complete problems for deterministic polynomial time. *TCS*, 3:105–117, 1977.

19. D. Kozen. Lower bounds for natural proof systems. In *Proceedings of the 18th Annual Symposium on Foundations of Computer Science*, pages 254–266, 1977.

20. M. Latteux and A. Terlutte. The Parikh-boundedness of ET0L languages of finite index. In G. Rozenberg and A. K. Salomaa, editors, *The Book of L*, pages 327–338. Berlin: Springer, 1985.

21. Gh. Păun. On the index of grammars and languages. *Inf. Contr.*, 35:259–266, 1977.

22. Gh. Păun. On the family of finite index matrix languages. *JCSS*, 18(3):267–280, 1979.

23. Gh. Păun. On the generative capacity of conditional grammars. *Inf. Contr.*, 43:178–186, 1979.

24. Gh. Păun. Some consequences of a result of Ehrenfeucht and Rozenberg. *RAIRO Informatique théorique et Applications/Theoretical Informatics and Applications*, 14(1):119–122, 1980.

25. Gh. Păun. Length-increasing grammars of finite index. *Rev. Roumaine Math. Pures Appl.*, XXVIII(5):391–403, 1983.

26. Gh. Păun. Some context-free-like properties of finite index matrix languages. *Bull. Math. de la Soc. Sci. Math. de Roumanie*, 27(1):83–87, 1983.

27. V. Rajlich. Absolutely parallel grammars and two-way deterministic finite state transducers. *JCSS*, 6:324–342, 1972.

28. G. Rozenberg. More on ET0L systems versus random context grammars. *IPL*, 5(4):102–106, 1976.

29. G. Rozenberg and D. Vermeir. On ET0L systems of finite index. *Inf. Contr.*, 38:103–133, 1978.

30. G. Rozenberg and D. Vermeir. On the effect of the finite index restriction on several families of grammars. *Inf. Contr.*, 39:284–302, 1978.

31. G. Rozenberg and D. Vermeir. On the effect of the finite index restriction on several families of grammars; Part 2: context dependent systems and grammars. *Foundations of Control Engineering*, 3(3):126–142, 1978.

32. G. Rozenberg and D. Vermeir. Extending the notion of finite index. In H. A. Maurer, editor, *Colloquium on Automata, Languages and Programming (6)*, volume 71 of *LNCS*, pages 479–488. Berlin: Springer, July 1979.

33. B. Rozoy. The Dyck language D_1' is not generated by any matrix grammar of finite index. *Inf. Comp.*, 74:64–89, 1987.

34. W. L. Ruzzo, J. Simon, and M. Tompa. Space-bounded hierarchies and probabilistic computations. *JCSS*, 28:216–230, 1984.

35. A. K. Salomaa. On the index of a context-free grammar and language. *Inf. Contr.*, 14:474–477, 1969.

36. A. K. Salomaa. *Formal Languages*. Academic Press, 1973.

37. C. E. Shannon. A mathematical theory of communication. *The Bell System Technical Journal*, 27:379–423, 1948.

38. E. D. Stotskii. Formal grammars and limitations for derivations. *Problemy peredacii informacii* (in Russ.), VII(1):87–101, 1971.

39. E. D. Stotskii. On some strict hierarchies of languages. *Naucno-tehniceskaya informaciya, Seriya 2* (in Russ), (4):40–45, 1972.

40. I. H. Sudborough. A note on tape-bounded complexity classes and linear context-free languages. *JACM*, 22(4):499–500, October 1975.

41. I. H. Sudborough. On the tape complexity of deterministic context-free languages. *JACM*, 25:405–414, 1978.

42. R. Szelepcsényi. The method of forcing for nondeterministic automata. *EATCS Bull.*, 33:96–100, October 1987.

43. F. J. Urbanek. A note on conditional grammars. *Rev. Roumaine Math. Pures Appl.*, 28:341–342, 1983.

44. J. van Leeuwen. The membership problem for ET0L-languages is polynomially complete. *IPL*, 3(5):138–143, May 1975.

On the Number of Nonterminals in Matrix Grammars with Leftmost Derivations

Alexander MEDUNA

Computer Center of the Technical University of Brno
Udolni 19, Brno 60200, The Czech Republic

Abstract. The paper investigates the descriptional complexity of matrix grammars that always rewrites the leftmost possible occurrence of a non-terminal. Measuring this complexity by the number of nonterminals, this investigation proves that four-nonterminal matrix grammars working in this way characterize the family of recursively enumerable languages.

1. Introduction

A matrix grammar, G, is based upon sequences, referred to as matrices, that consist of context-free productions (see page 25 in [1]). According to its matrices, G makes derivation steps. More precisely, G makes a derivation step according to a matrix, m, so it applies m's productions one by one until all of them are used. This step is leftmost if G applies each of these productions to the leftmost possible occurrence of a nonterminal in the given sentential form.

The present paper reduces the number of nonterminals in matrix grammars making leftmost derivations. More precisely, it demonstrates that four-nonterminal matrix grammars with leftmost derivations characterize the family of recursively ennumerable languages. Analogously four-nonterminal matrix grammars with rightmost derivations define this family as well.

2. Definitions

This paper assumes that the reader is familiar with the language theory (see Chapter 0 in [1]).

For an alphabet V, V^* denotes the free monoid generated by V under the operation of concatenation; λ denotes the unit of V^*. Set $V^+ = V^* - \{\lambda\}$. For a word $w \in V^*$, $|w|$ denotes the length of w, $alph(w)$ is the set of symbols occurring in w, and $mi(w)$ is the mirror image of w. Set

$$suf(w) = \{x \mid x \text{ is a suffix of } w\}.$$

For a symbol $a \in V$ a word $w \in V^*$, $|w|_a$ denotes the number of occurrences of a in w. The definitions of $alph(w)$ and $mi(w)$ are extended in the natural way to languages.

A *matrix grammar* is a quadruple $G = (V, T, M, S)$, where V is an alphabet, $T \subseteq V$, $S \in V - T$, and M is a finite set of *matrices* of the form $(A_1 \to x_1, \ldots, A_n \to x_n)$, where n is a natural number, and for all $i = 1, 2, \ldots, n$, $A_i \in V - T, x_i \in V^*$.

Let $G = (V, T, M, S)$ be a matrix grammar. G uses a matrix $(A_1 \to x_1, \ldots, A_n \to x_n)$ in M by sequentially rewriting A_i with x_i in the order $i = 1, 2, \ldots, n$. Formally, if there exist $n + 1$ words $w_0, w_1, \ldots, w_n$ such that for $i = 1, 2, \ldots, n$, $w_{i-1} = u_i A_i v_i$

and $w_i = u_i x_i v_i$, for some $u_i, v_i \in V^*$, then we write $w_0 \Longrightarrow w_n \ [m]$. When the specification of m is unimportant we write $w_0 \Longrightarrow w_n$.

If $v_0 \Longrightarrow v_1 \Longrightarrow \ldots \Longrightarrow v_n$ such that $v_{i-1} \Longrightarrow v_i \ [m_i]$, $1 \leq i \leq n$, then we write $v_0 \Longrightarrow^* v_n \ [m_1 \ldots m_n]$. If $n = 0$, then $v_0 = v_n$ and $m_1 \ldots m_n = \lambda$. When the specification of $m_1 \ldots m_n$ is unimportant, we write $v_0 \Longrightarrow^n v_n$ or simply $v_0 \Longrightarrow^* v_n$ (for $n \geq 1$ we write $v_0 \Longrightarrow^+ v_n$). If $S \Longrightarrow^* w$ in G with $w \in T^*$, then $S \Longrightarrow^* w$ is a *successful derivation* in G. The language of G, $L(G)$, is the set of words successfully derived in G; formally,

$$L(G) = \{ w \in T^* \mid S \Longrightarrow^* w \}.$$

Let $G = (V, T, M, S)$ be a matrix grammar and $m = (A_1 \to x_1, \ldots, A_n \to x_n)$ be a matrix in M. In terms of this paper, G uses this matrix in a leftmost manner if for all $i = 1, 2, \ldots, n$, G substitutes x_i for the lefmost occurrence of A_i in the current sentential form ([1] classifies this manner as type-3 leftmost derivations). More formally, if there exist $n + 1$ words $w_0, w_1, \ldots, w_n$ such that for $i = 1, 2, \ldots, n$ we have $w_{i-1} = u_i A_i v_i, w_i = u_i x_i v_i, A_i \notin alph(u_i)$, for some $u_i, v_i \in V^*$, then we write $w_0 \Longrightarrow_{left} w_n \ [m]$. As for the usual derivation relation, also for the leftmost derivation relation we omit the specification of m when m is unimportant, and we write $u \Longrightarrow^*_{left} w \ [m_1 \ldots m_n]$ for denoting a sequence of leftmost derivation steps according to matrices $m_1, \ldots, m_n$, $n \geq 0$; when the specification of $m_1, \ldots, m_n$ is unimportant, we write simply $u \Longrightarrow^n_{left} w$ or $u \Longrightarrow^*_{left} w$.

If $S \Longrightarrow^*_{left} w$ in G and $w \in T^*$, then $S \Longrightarrow^*_{left} w$ is a *successful leftmost derivation* in G. $L_{left}(G)$ denotes the language consisting of words that G generates by these derivations; formally,

$$L_{left}(G) = \{ w \in T^* \mid S \Longrightarrow^*_{left} w \}.$$

We also recall the notion of a queue grammar (see [3]).

A *queue gramar* is a sextuple $Q = (V, T, W, F, R, g)$, where V, T, W, F are alphabets, $T \subseteq V, F \subseteq W, V \cap W = \emptyset$, $R \in (V - T)(W - F)$, $g \subseteq (V \times (W - F)) \times (V^* \times W)$ is a finite relation of Q such that for all $a \in V$ there is an element $(a, b, x, c) \in g$. V is referred to as the alphabet of Q, T is the terminal alphabet, W is the state alphabet, F is the final state alphabet, R is the axiom, g is the finite transition relation of Q.

If there are $a \in V, r, z \in V^*, b, c \in W$ such that $(a, b, z, c) \in g, u = arb, v = rzc$, then $u \Longrightarrow v \ [(a, b, z, c)]$, or, simply, $u \Longrightarrow v$. The language of Q, $L(Q)$, is defined as

$$L(Q) = \{ w \in T^* \mid R \Longrightarrow^* wf, \text{ for some } f \in F \},$$

where $\Longrightarrow^*$ is the reflexive and transitive closure of $\Longrightarrow$.

Recall that for any recursively enumerable language L, there exists a queue grammar Q such that $L = L(Q)$ (see Theorem 2.1 in [2]).

The following **observation** will be useful later: any successful derivation in Q, $R \Longrightarrow^* zd$, with $z \in T^*$ and $d \in F$, can be expressed as

$$
\begin{aligned}
R &\Longrightarrow^i a_1 u_1 b_1 \\
&\Longrightarrow u_1 x_1 y_1 c_1 \quad [(a_1, b_1, x_1 y_1, c_1)] \\
&\Longrightarrow^j y_1 z_1 d,
\end{aligned}
$$

where $i, j \geq 0, z = y_1 z_1, x_1, u_1 \in V^*, y_1, z_1 \in T^*, b_1, c_1 \in W$, and $d \in F$ ($i = 0$ implies $a_1 u_1 b_1 = u_1 x_1 y_1 c_1$, and $j = 0$ implies $u_1 x_1 y_1 c_1 = y_1 z_1 d$).

We denote by RE the family of recursively enumerable languages and by $MAT_{left}(i)$ the family of languages $L_{left}(G)$ generated by matrix grammars $G = (V, T, M, S)$ with $card(V - T) \leq i$.

3. Results

Theorem. $RE = MAT_{left}(4)$.

Proof. Obviously, $MAT_{left4}(4) \subseteq RE$. We prove the converse inclusion.

Let L be a recursively enumerable language. Take a queue grammar $Q = (V, T, W, F, R, g)$ such that $L(Q) = L$. We construct the four-nonterminal matrix grammar

$$G = (T \cup \{0, 1, 2, 3\}, T, M, S)$$

as follows.

Set

$$n = 2^{card(V \cup W)}.$$

Consider a morphism β from $V \cup W$ to $\{0, 1\}$. Extend β to $(V \cup W)^*$ in the standard manner. The set M of matrices is defined as follows.

1. If $a \in V - T$, $v \in W - F$, $ab = R$, then we introduce the matrix

$$(3 \rightarrow 0b_1 \ldots b_n 2a_1 \ldots a_n 23),$$

where $b_i, a_i \in \{0, 1\}$ for $1 \leq i \leq n$, $b_1 \ldots b_n = \beta(b)$, and $a_1 \ldots a_n = \beta(a)$.

2. If $(a, b, x, c) \in g$, then add

$$(0 \rightarrow 0, b_1 \rightarrow \lambda, \ldots, b_n \rightarrow \lambda, 2 \rightarrow \lambda, a_1 \rightarrow \lambda, \ldots, a_n \rightarrow \lambda,$$
$$2 \rightarrow \beta(c)22, 3 \rightarrow \beta(x)3)$$

to M, where $a_i, b_i \in \{0, 1\}$, for $1 \leq i \leq n$, $a_1 \ldots a_n = \beta(a)$, $b_1 \ldots b_n = \beta(b)$.

3. If $(a, b, xy, c) \in g$ with $x \in V^*$ and $y \in T^*$, then add

$$(0 \rightarrow 1, b_1 \rightarrow \lambda, \ldots, b_n \rightarrow \lambda, 2 \rightarrow \lambda, a_1 \rightarrow \lambda, \ldots, a_n \rightarrow \lambda,$$
$$2 \rightarrow \beta(c)22, 3 \rightarrow \beta(x)y3)$$

to M, where $a_i, b_i \in \{0, 1\}$, for $1 \leq i \leq n$, $a_1 \ldots a_n = \beta(a)$, $b_1 \ldots b_n = \beta(a)$.

4. If $(a, b, y, c) \in g$ with $y \in T^*$ and $c \notin F$, then add

$$(1 \rightarrow 1, b_1 \rightarrow \lambda, \ldots, b_n \rightarrow \lambda, 2 \rightarrow \lambda, a_1 \rightarrow \lambda, \ldots, a_n \rightarrow \lambda, 2 \rightarrow \beta(c)22, 3 \rightarrow y3)$$

to M, where $a_i, b_i \in \{0, 1\}$, for $1 \leq i \leq n$, $a_1 \ldots a_n = \beta(a)$, $b_1 \ldots b_n = \beta(b)$.

5. If $(a, b, y, c) \in g$ with $c \in F$ and $y \in T^*$, then add

$$(1 \rightarrow \lambda, b_1 \rightarrow \lambda, \ldots, b_n \rightarrow \lambda, 2 \rightarrow \lambda, a_1 \rightarrow \lambda, \ldots, a_n \rightarrow \lambda, 2 \rightarrow \lambda, 3 \rightarrow y)$$

to M, where $a_i, b_i, c_i \in \{0, 1\}$ for $1 \leq i \leq n$, $a_1 \ldots a_n = \beta(a)$, $b_1 \ldots b_n = \beta(b)$.

6. Add also

$$(2 \rightarrow 2, 2 \rightarrow \lambda, d \rightarrow d2, 3 \rightarrow 3)$$

to M, for $d = 0, 1$.

Notice that G has four nonterminals, 0, 1, 2, 3. The rest of this proof establishes several claims to demonstrate $L(Q) = L_{left}(G)$.

Claim 1. Let $3 \Longrightarrow^*_{left} z$ in G with $z \in T^*$. Then, in greater detail, $3 \Longrightarrow^*_{left} z$ can be expressed as

$$
\begin{aligned}
2 &\Longrightarrow_{left} & x & \quad [p] \\
&\Longrightarrow^*_{left} & u & \\
&\Longrightarrow^*_{left} & z & \quad [q],
\end{aligned}
$$

with $x, u \in (T \cup \{0, 1, 2, 3\})^*$, p is the matrix in group 1, p is a matrix in group 5, and during $x \Longrightarrow^*_{left} u$, G never uses a matrix in groups 1 or 5.

Proof of Claim 1. Consider a successful derivation $3 \Longrightarrow^*_{left} z$ in G. Observe that G surely uses the matrix in the first group, so express $3 \Longrightarrow^*_{left} z$ as $3 \Longrightarrow_{left} x \Longrightarrow^*_{left} z$, where the first step uses a matrix p introduced in the step 1 of the construction, that it p equals $(3 \rightarrow db_1 \ldots b_n 2a_1 \ldots a_n 23)$, where $d \in \{0, 1\}$, $b_i, a_i \in \{0, 1\}$, for $1 \le i \le n$, $b_1 \ldots b_n = \beta(b)$, $a_1 \ldots a_n = \beta(a)$, $ab = R$.

Notice that for every y such that $x \Longrightarrow^*_{left} \Longrightarrow^+_{left} z$, $|y|_3 = 1$.

As $z \in T^*$, G surely applies a matrix in group 5 in the last step of $3 \Longrightarrow^*_{left} z$, and before this application G never uses any matrix in group 5. Express

$$
\begin{aligned}
3 &\Longrightarrow_{left} & x & \quad [p] \\
&\Longrightarrow^*_{left} & z &
\end{aligned}
$$

as

$$
\begin{aligned}
3 &\Longrightarrow_{left} & x & \quad [p] \\
&\Longrightarrow^*_{left} & u & \\
&\Longrightarrow_{left} & z & \quad [q]
\end{aligned}
$$

where q is a matrix in group 5 and during $3 \Longrightarrow^*_{left} u$, G never uses a matrix in group 5. Assume that during $3 \Longrightarrow^*_{left} u$, G applies $(3 \rightarrow db_1 \ldots b_n 2a_1 \ldots a_n 23)$ t times, where $t \ge 1$. Then, $|u|_2 = 2t$ and $|u|_3 = 1$. G can remove 2's only by using matrices in group 5. However, during $3 \Longrightarrow^*_{left} u$, G never uses a matrix in group 5. Therefore, $3 \Longrightarrow^*_{left} z$ can be expressed as in Claim 1. □

Claim 2. Let $3 \Longrightarrow^+_{left} x \Longrightarrow^+_{left} z$ in G, where $x \in (\{0, 1, 2, 3\} \cup T)^*$ and $z \in T^*$. Then

$$x \in (\{0, 1\} \cup T)^* (\{2\} (\{0, 1\} \cup T)^*)^2 (\{0, 1\} \cup T)^* \{3\}.$$

Proof of Claim 2. Consider Claim 1. Then, examine M's matrices to see that Claim 2, whose rigorous proof is left to the reader, holds. □

Let

$$
\begin{aligned}
3 &\Longrightarrow^+_{left} & x & \\
&\Longrightarrow_{left} & y & \quad [p] \\
&\Longrightarrow^*_{left} & z &
\end{aligned}
$$

be a successful leftmost derivation in G, where p is a matrix in one of groups 2 – 5. The following claim demonstrate that at this point, $x = db_1 \ldots b_n 2x'$, where $d \in \{0, 1\}$, $b_i \in \{0, 1\}$, for $1 \le i \le n$, $x' \in (\{0, 1\} \cup T)^* \{2\} (\{0, 1\} \cup T)^* \{3\}$.

Claim 3. Let $3 \Longrightarrow_{left}^i x \Longrightarrow_{left}^+ z$ in G, where $i \geq 1, x \in (\{0,1,2,3\} \cup T)^*$, and $z \in T^*$. Then,

$$x \in \{0,1\}\{0,1\}^n\{2\}\{0,1\}^*\{2\}(\{0,1\} \cup T)^*\{3\}.$$

Proof of Claim 3. This proof is made by induction on i, where $i \geq 1$.

Basis: Let $3 \Longrightarrow_{left}^i x \Longrightarrow_{left}^+ z$ in G, where $i = 1, x \in (\{0,1,2,3\} \cup T)^*$, and $z \in T^*$. By Claim 1, G makes $3 \Longrightarrow_{left} x$ by the matrix p in group 1, that is p equals $(3 \rightarrow db_1 \ldots b_n 2a_1 \ldots a_n 23)$.

Express $3 \Longrightarrow_{left}^i x \Longrightarrow_{left}^+ z$ as $3 \Longrightarrow_{left} 0b_1 \ldots b_n 2a_1 \ldots a_n 23 \Longrightarrow_{left}^+ z$. Observe that $db_1 \ldots b_n 2a_1 \ldots a_n 23$ has the required form.

Induction step: Assume that the claim holds for all $i = 1, 2, \ldots, j$, where j is a natural number. Let $3 \Longrightarrow_{left}^{j+1} x \Longrightarrow_{left}^+ z$ in G, $x \in (\{0,1,2\} \cup T)^*$, and $z \in T^*$. Express this derivation as

$$
\begin{aligned}
3 &\Longrightarrow_{left}^j y \\
&\Longrightarrow_{left} x \quad [p] \\
&\Longrightarrow_{left}^+ z.
\end{aligned}
$$

By the induction hypothesis, $y \in \{0,1\}\{0,1\}^n\{2\}\{0,1\}^*\{2\}(\{0,1\}\cup T)^*\{3\}$. By Claim 1, p is a matrix in one of groups 2, 3, 4, or 6. Examine these matrices to see that G makes $y \Longrightarrow_{left} x$ $[p]$ so that $x \in \{0,1\}\{0,1\}^{n+k}\{2\}\{0,1\}^*\{2\}(\{0,1\} \cup T)^*\{3\}$.

By contradiction, this proof next demonstrates that $k = 0$. Assume that $k \geq 1$.

A. Suppose that $x \Longrightarrow_{left}^+ z$ is a one-step derivation. By Claim 1, G makes this step by using a matrix in group 5, so $z \notin T^*$, which contradicts $z \in T^*$.

B. Assume that $x \Longrightarrow_{left}^+ z$ consists of two or more steps. Observe that for every u such that $x \Longrightarrow_{left}^+ u \Longrightarrow_{left}^+ z$

$$u \in \{0,1\}\{0,1\}^{n+k+j}\{2\}\{0,1\}^*\{2\}(\{0,1\} \cup T)^*\{3\},$$

for some $j \geq 0$. Consequently, $z \notin T^*$, which contradicts $z \in T^*$.

Thus, $k = 0$ and Claim 3 holds. $\square$

To continue the derivation after applying a matrix in one of groups 2, 3, 4, G has to shift the second appearance of 2 right in the current sentential form. G makes this shift by using matrices in group 6 to generate a sentential form having precisely n occurrences of d, where $d \in \{0,1\}$, between the first appearance of 2 and the second appearance of 2. Indeed, the sentential form has to contain exactly n appearances of d between the first appearance of 2 and the second appearance of 2; otherwise, the successfulness of the derivation is contradicted by these two arguments:

A. If there exist fewer than n occurrences of d between the first appearance of 2 and the second appearance of 2, no matrix in groups 1 – 4 can be used, so the derivation ends. Because the last sentential form contains nonterminals, the derivation is not successful, a contradiction.

B. Assume that there exist more than n occurrences of d between the first appearance of 2 and the second appearance of 2. Then, after the next application of a rule in groups 1 – 5 at least $n + 2$ occurrences of d, where $d \in \{0,1\}$, appear before the first appearance of 2. Now, return to Claims 1 – 3, which imply these three observations:

B.1. The matrix in group 1 is always used in the first step of a successful derivation.

B.2. If $3 \Longrightarrow_{left}^+ x \Longrightarrow_{left}^+ z$ in G is a successful derivation, then $x \in \{0,1\}^{n+1}\{2\}\{0,1\}^*\{2\}(\{0,1\} \cup T)^*\{3\}$.

B.3. A matrix in group 5 is always used only in the last derivation step of a successful derivation; furthermore, observe that this matrix erases precisely $n + 1$ nonterminals preceding the first appearance of 2.

By B.1 through B.3, if a sentential form, x, contains more than n occurrences of d between the first appearance of 2 and the second appearance of 2, then x derives no sentence in G.

Thus, by A and B, the sentential form has to contain precisely n appearances of d between the first appearance of 2 and the second appearance of 2. The next claim verifies these observations rigorously.

Claim 4. Let

$$3 \underset{left}{\overset{i}{\Longrightarrow}} u$$
$$\underset{left}{\Longrightarrow} x \quad [p]$$
$$\underset{left}{\overset{+}{\Longrightarrow}} z$$

in G, where $i \geq 1, u, x \in (\{0, 1, 2, 3\} \cup T)^*$, p is a matrix in one of groups 1 – 5, and $z \in T^*$. Then,

$$x \in \{0, 1\}\{0, 1\}^n\{2\}\{0, 1\}^n\{2\}(\{0, 1\} \cup T)^*\{3\}.$$

Proof of Claim 4. This proof is made by induction on i, where $i \geq 0$.

Basis: Let $i = 0$; that is

$$3 \underset{left}{\Longrightarrow} x \quad [p]$$
$$\underset{left}{\overset{+}{\Longrightarrow}} z$$

in G, where $x \in (\{0, 1, 2, 3\} \cup T)^*$, p is a matrix in one of groups 1 – 5, and $z \in T^*$. Claim 1 implies that $3 \Longrightarrow_{left} x$ uses the matrix $(3 \rightarrow 1b_1 \ldots b_n 2a_1 \ldots a_n 23)$. As $1b_1 \ldots b_n 2a_1 \ldots a_n 23$ has the required form, the basis holds.

Induction step: Assume that the claim holds for all $i = 1, 2, \ldots, j$, where j is a natural number. Let

$$3 \underset{left}{\overset{i+}{\Longrightarrow}} u$$
$$\underset{left}{\Longrightarrow} x \quad [p]$$
$$\underset{left}{\overset{+}{\Longrightarrow}} z$$

in G, where $i \geq 1, u, x \in (\{0, 1, 2, 3\} \cup T)^*$, p is a matrix in one of groups 1 – 4, and $z \in T^*$. By the previous claim,

$$x \in \{0, 1\}\{0, 1\}^n\{2\}\{0, 1\}^m\{2\}(\{0, 1\} \cup T)^*\{3\}.$$

Assume $m < n$. This assumption leads to a contradiction because p is inapplicable at this point. Therefore, $m = n + k$, for some $k \geq 0$, so

$$x \in \{0, 1\}\{0, 1\}^n\{2\}\{0, 1\}^{n+k}\{2\}(\{0, 1\} \cup T)^*\{3\}.$$

By contradiction, this proof next demonstrates that $k = 0$. Assume that $k \geq 1$.

A. Suppose that $x \underset{left}{\overset{+}{\Longrightarrow}} z$ is a one-step derivation. By Claim 4, G makes this step by using a matrix in group 5, so $z \notin T^*$, which contradicts $z \in T^*$.

B. Suppose that $x \underset{left}{\overset{+}{\Longrightarrow}} z$ consists of two or more steps. Observe that

$$x \in \{0, 1\}\{0, 1\}^{n+k}\{2\}\{0, 1\}^n\{2\}(\{0, 1\} \cup T)^*\{3\}.$$

Consequently, $3 \underset{left}{\overset{+}{\Longrightarrow}} x \underset{left}{\overset{+}{\Longrightarrow}} z$ in G with $z \in T^*$ and

$$x \notin \{0, 1\}\{0, 1\}^n\{2\}\{0, 1\}^n\{2\}(\{0, 1\} \cup T)^*\{3\},$$

which contradicts Claim 3.

Thus, $k = 0$ and Claim 4 holds. □

Claim 5. Let $3 \Longrightarrow_{left}^{i} x \Longrightarrow_{left}^{+} z$ in G, where $i \geq 1$, $x \in (\{0,1,2,3\} \cup T)^*$, and $z \in T^*$. Then,

$$x \in \{0,1\}\{0,1\}^n\{2\}\{0,1\}^n\{2\}\{0,1\}^*T^*\{3\}.$$

Proof of Claim 5. Consider Claim 4 and examine M's matrices to see that this claim holds. □

Claim 6. In G, every successful derivation $3 \Longrightarrow_{left}^{+} v$ with $v \in T^*$, has the form

$$
\begin{aligned}
3 \ &\Longrightarrow_{left}^{+} \ 0a_1 \ldots a_n 2b_1 \ldots b_n 2\beta(c_1 \ldots c_n z)3 \\
&\Longrightarrow_{left} \ 1b_1 \ldots b_n 2c_1 \ldots c_n 2\beta(zx)y3 &[p] \\
&\Longrightarrow_{left}^{*} \ 1d_1 \ldots d_n 2e_1 \ldots e_n 2yu3 \\
&\Longrightarrow_{left} \ yu &[q]
\end{aligned}
$$

where $a_i, b_i, c_i, d_i, e_i \in \{0,1\}$, for all $i = 1, \ldots, n$, $z, x \in V^*$, $y, u \in T^*$, so $v = yu$, p is a matrix in group 3 and q is a matrix in group 5.

Proof of Claim 6. Claim 5 and the construction of M imply Claim 6, whose rigorous proof is left to the reader. □

Claim 7. Any successful derivation in G has the following form

$$
\begin{aligned}
3 \ &\Longrightarrow_{left}^{+} \ 0b_1 \ldots b_n 2a_1 \ldots a_n 23 &[p_1] \\
&\Longrightarrow_{left}^{i} \ u \\
&\Longrightarrow_{left} \ v \\
&\Longrightarrow_{left}^{k} \ w \\
&\Longrightarrow_{left} \ w_4 y_4 &[p_5]
\end{aligned}
$$

where $i, k \geq 0$ and the following properties A through E hold:

A. p_1 is of the form $(3 \rightarrow 0b_1 \ldots b_n 22a_1 \ldots a_n 3)$ (see step 1 of the construction of M).

B. In $v \Longrightarrow_{left}^{k} w$, consider any leftmost step that is not made by a matrix in group 6. This step has the following form

$$0b_{11} \ldots b_{1n} 2a_{11} \ldots a_{1n} 2\beta(u_1)3 \Longrightarrow_{left} 0c_{11} \ldots c_{1n} 22\beta(u_1 x_1)3 \quad [p_2]$$

where p_2 is of the form

$$
\begin{aligned}
(0 \rightarrow 0, b_{11} &\rightarrow \lambda, \ldots, b_{1n} \rightarrow \lambda, 2 \rightarrow \lambda, a_{11} \rightarrow \lambda, \ldots, a_{1n} \rightarrow \lambda, \\
2 &\rightarrow c_{11} \ldots c_{1n} 22, 3 \rightarrow \beta(x_1)3),
\end{aligned}
$$

so $0b_1 \ldots b_n 2a_1 \ldots a_n 23 \Longrightarrow_{left}^{i} u$ can be expressed as

$$0b_1 \ldots b_n 2a_1 \ldots a_n 23$$

. . . .

$$0b_{11} \ldots b_{1n} 2a_{11} \ldots a_{1n} 2\beta(u_1)3 \Longrightarrow_{left} 0c_{11} \ldots c_{1n} 22\beta(u_1 x_1)3 \quad [p_2]$$

. . . .

$$0b_{21} \ldots b_{2n} 2a_{21} \ldots a_{2n} 2\beta(u_2)3,$$

where $u = 0b_{21} \ldots b_{2n}2a_{21} \ldots a_{2n}2\beta(u_2)3$.

C. Consider $u \Longrightarrow_{left} v$. This step has the following form

$$0b_{21} \ldots b_{2n}2a_{21} \ldots a_{2n}2\beta(u_2)3 \Longrightarrow_{left} 1c_{21} \ldots c_{2n}22\beta(u_2x_2)y_23 \quad [p_3],$$

where

$$u = 0b_{21} \ldots b_{2n}2a_{21} \ldots a_{2n}2\beta(u_2)3,$$
$$v = 1c_{21} \ldots c_{2n}22\beta(u_2x_2)y_23,$$

and p_3 is of the form

$$(0 \to 1, b_{21} \to \lambda, \ldots, b_{2n} \to \lambda, 2 \to \lambda, a_{21} \to \lambda, \ldots, a_{2n} \to \lambda,$$
$$2 \to c_{21} \ldots c_{2n}22, 3 \to \beta(x_2)y_23).$$

D. In $v \Longrightarrow_{left}^{k} w$, consider any derivation step that is not made by a matrix in group 6. This step has the following form

$$1b_{31} \ldots b_{3n}2a_{31} \ldots a_{3n}2\beta(u_3)v_33 \Longrightarrow_{left} 1c_{31} \ldots c_{3n}22\beta(u_3)v_3y_33 \quad [p_4],$$

where p_4 is of the form

$$(1 \to 1, b_{31} \to \lambda, \ldots, b_{3n} \to \lambda, 2 \to \lambda, a_{31} \to \lambda, \ldots, a_{3n} \to \lambda,$$
$$2 \to c_{31} \ldots c_{3n}22, 3 \to y_33).$$

As a result, $v \Longrightarrow_{left}^{k} w$ can be expressed as

$$1c_{21} \ldots c_{2n}\beta(u_2x_2)y_23$$

$$\cdots\cdots\cdots$$

$$1b_{31} \ldots b_{3n}2a_{31} \ldots a_{3n}2\beta(u_3)3 \Longrightarrow_{left} 1c_{31} \ldots c_{3n}22\beta(u_3)v_3y_33 \quad [p_4]$$

$$\cdots\cdots\cdots$$

$$1b_{41} \ldots b_{4n}2a_{41} \ldots a_{4n}2w_43,$$

where

$$v = 1c_{21} \ldots c_{2n}22\beta(u_2x_2)y_23,$$
$$w = 1b_{41} \ldots b_{4n}2a_{41} \ldots a_{4n}2w_43.$$

E. p_5 is of the form

$$(1 \to \lambda, b_{41} \to \lambda, \ldots, b_{4n} \to \lambda, 2 \to \lambda, a_{41} \to \lambda, \ldots, a_{4n} \to \lambda,$$
$$2 \to \lambda, 3 \to y_4),$$

and w can be expressed as

$$w = 1b_{41} \ldots b_{4n}2a_{41} \ldots a_{4n}2w_4y_43.$$

Proof of Claim 7. A: The first step of any successful derivation is made according to $(3 \to 0b_1 \ldots b_n2a_1 \ldots a_n23)$, which thus produces $0b_1 \ldots b_n2a_1 \ldots a_n23$, with $b_i, a_i \in \{0,1\}$, for $1 \le i \le n$, $b_1 \ldots b_n = \beta(b)$, $a_1 \ldots a_n = \beta(a)$, $ab = R$.

Therefore, the first derivation has the form $3 \Rightarrow_{left} 0b_1 \ldots b_n 2a_1 \ldots a_n 23 \ [p_1]$, with $d \in \{0,1\}$. After this step, only matrices of the form p_2 or p_3, whose use is described next, can be used because the left-hand side of the first production in these matrices starts with 0.

B: Consider p_2, which is of the form

$$(0 \rightarrow 0, b_{11} \rightarrow \lambda, \ldots, b_{1n} \rightarrow \lambda, 2 \rightarrow \lambda, a_{11} \rightarrow \lambda, \ldots, a_{1n} \rightarrow \lambda,$$
$$2 \rightarrow c_{11} \ldots c_{1n} 22, 3 \rightarrow \beta(x_1)3).$$

By using p_2, the $2n+2$ leftmost symbols of the sentential form, $0b_{11} \ldots b_{1n} 2a_{11} \ldots a_{1n}$, are replaced with $0c_{11} \ldots c_{1n} 2$, and in addition 3 is replaced with $\beta(x_1)3$. Therefore, this step is of the form

$$0b_{11} \ldots b_{1n} 2a_{11} \ldots a_{1n} 2\beta(u_1)3 \Rightarrow_{left} 0c_{11} \ldots c_{1n} 22\beta(u_1 x_1)3 \quad [p_2]$$

To continue this derivation, the second appearance of 2 is shifted right by productions in group 4. By this shift, G produces a sentential form that has between the first appearance of 2 and the second appearance of 2 exactly n appearances of d, where $d \in \{0,1\}$; the concatenation of these n occurrences of d equals the n-symbol prefix of $\beta(u_1 x_1)$. Then, G can again use a matrix of the form p_i with $i \in \{2,3\}$.

C: Consider p_3, which is of the form

$$(0 \rightarrow 1, b_{21} \rightarrow \lambda, \ldots, b_{2n} \rightarrow \lambda, 2 \rightarrow \lambda, a_{21} \rightarrow \lambda, \ldots, a_{2n} \rightarrow \lambda,$$
$$2 \rightarrow c_{21} \ldots c_{2n} 22, 3 \rightarrow \beta(x_2)y_2 3).$$

By using p_3, G replaces the $2n + 2$ leftmost symbols of $0b_{21} \ldots b_{2n} 2a_{21} \ldots a_{2n} 2\beta(u_2)3$ with $1c_{21} \ldots c_{2n}$; in addition, it replaces 3 with $\beta(x_2)y_2 3$. Thus, this step has the following form

$$0b_{21} \ldots b_{2n} 2a_{21} \ldots a_{2n} 2\beta(u_2)3 \Rightarrow_{left} 1c_{21} \ldots c_{2n} 22\beta(u_2 x_2)y_2 3 \quad [p_3]$$

To continue, the second appearance of 2 is shifted by analogy with the case when p_2 is used (see B). Then, G uses a matrix of the form p_i, where $i \in \{4,5\}$, because the sentential form starts with 1.

D: Consider p_4, which has the form

$$(1 \rightarrow 1, b_{31} \rightarrow \lambda, \ldots, b_{3n} \rightarrow \lambda, 2 \rightarrow \lambda, a_{31} \rightarrow \lambda, \ldots, a_{3n} \rightarrow \lambda,$$
$$2 \rightarrow c_{31} \ldots c_{3n} 22, 3 \rightarrow y_3 3).$$

By using p_4, the $2n+2$ leftmost symbols of $1b_{31} \ldots b_{3n} 2a_{31} \ldots a_{3n} 2\beta(u_3)v_3 3$ are replaced with $1c_{31} \ldots c_{3n} 2$, and 3 is replaced with $y_3 3$. As a result, this step has the following form

$$1b_{31} \ldots b_{3n} 2a_{31} \ldots a_{3n} \beta(u_3)v_3 3 \Rightarrow_{left} 1c_{31} \ldots c_{3n} 22\beta(u_3)v_3 y_3 3 \quad [p_4]$$

To continue, the second 2 is shifted in the same way as described in the case when p_2 is used. Then, a matrix of the form p_i, where $i \in \{4,5\}$, because the sentential form starts with 1.

E: Consider p_5, which has the form

$$(1 \rightarrow \lambda, b_{41} \rightarrow \lambda, \ldots, b_{4n} \rightarrow \lambda, 2 \rightarrow \lambda, a_{41} \rightarrow \lambda, \ldots, a_{4n} \rightarrow \lambda,$$
$$2 \rightarrow \lambda, 3 \rightarrow y_4).$$

This matrix is used in the last derivation step, $w \Longrightarrow_{left} w_4 y_4 \ [p_5]$. Any successful derivation has thus the required form, so Claim 7 holds. □

Claim 8. For every successful derivation in Q, $R \Longrightarrow^* zd$, with $z \in T^*$ and $d \in F$, there exists a successful derivation in G of the form $3 \Longrightarrow^*_{left} z$.

Proof of Claim 8. Let $z \in L(Q)$. Recall that Q satisfies the *observation* at the end of the previous section. As a result, Q derives z as

$$
\begin{aligned}
R \Longrightarrow^i \ & a_1 u_1 b_1 \\
\Longrightarrow \ & u_1 x_1 y_1 c_1 \qquad [(a_1, b_1, x_1 y_1, c_1)] \\
\Longrightarrow^j \ & y_1 z_1 c_3 \in F,
\end{aligned}
$$

where $i, j \geq 1, z = y_1 z_1, x_1, u_1 \in V^*, y_1, z_1 \in T^*, b_1, c_1 \in W$, and $c_3 \in F$. In more detail, $R \Longrightarrow^* z c_3$ can be expressed as

$$
\begin{aligned}
R \Longrightarrow^* \ & a_0 u_0 b_0 \\
\Longrightarrow \ & u_0 x_0 c_0 \qquad [(a_0, b_0, x_0, c_0)] \\
\Longrightarrow^* \ & a_1 u_1 b_1 \\
\Longrightarrow \ & u_1 x_1 y_1 c_1 \qquad [(a_1, b_1, x_1 y_1, c_1)] \\
\Longrightarrow^* \ & a_2 u_2 y_1 v b_2 \\
\Longrightarrow \ & u_2 y_1 v y_2 c_2 \qquad [(a_2, b_2, y_2, c_2)] \\
\Longrightarrow \ & a_3 y_1 v y_2 w b_3 \\
\Longrightarrow \ & y_1 v y_2 w y_3 c_3 \qquad [(a_3, b_3, y_3, c_3)],
\end{aligned}
$$

where $x_0, x_1, u_0, u_1, u_2 \in V^*, v, w, y_1, y_2, y_3 \in T^*, c, c_1, c_2 \in W, c_3 \in F, z = y_1 z_1 = y_1 v y_2 w y_3 c_3, a_2 u_2 \in suf(u_1 x_1), a_3 \in suf(u_2)$ (note that $z_1 = v y_2 w y_3$). Next, this proof describes how G simulates the four direct derivations

$$
\begin{aligned}
a_0 u_0 b_0 &\Longrightarrow u_0 x_0 c_0 & [(a_0, b_0, x_0, c_0)] \\
a_1 u_1 b_1 &\Longrightarrow u_1 x_1 y_1 c_1 & [(a_1, b_1, x_1 y_1, c_1)] \\
a_2 u_2 y_1 v b_2 &\Longrightarrow u_2 y_1 v y_2 c_2 & [(a_2, b_2, y_2, c_2)] \\
a_3 y_1 v y_2 w b_3 &\Longrightarrow y_1 v y_2 w y_3 c_3 & [(a_3, b_3, y_3, c_3)]
\end{aligned}
$$

1. Consider

$$
a_0 u_0 b_0 \Longrightarrow u_0 x_0 c_0 \qquad [(a_0, b_0, x_0, c_0)]
$$

G simulates this step as

$$
0 b_{01} \ldots b_{0n} 2 a_{01} \ldots a_{0n} 2 \beta(u)3 \Longrightarrow_{left} 0 c_{01} \ldots c_{0n} 22 \beta(u_0 x_0)3
$$

according to

$$
\begin{aligned}
&(0 \to 0, b_{01} \to \lambda, \ldots, b_{0n} \to \lambda, 2 \to \lambda, a_{01} \to \lambda, \ldots, a_{0n} \to \lambda, \\
&\ 2 \to c_{01} \ldots c_{0n} 22, 3 \to \beta(x_1)3),
\end{aligned}
$$

where $a_{0i}, b_{0i}, c_{0i} \in \{0,1\}$, for $1 \leq i \leq n$, $a_{01} \ldots a_{0n} = \beta(a_0), b_{01} \ldots b_{0n} = \beta(b_0), c_{01} \ldots c_{0n} = \beta(c_0)$.

2. Consider

$$
a_1 u_1 b_1 \Longrightarrow u_1 x_1 y_1 c_1 \qquad [(a_1, b_1, x_1 y_1, c_1)]
$$

in Q. G simulates this step as

$$
0 b_{11} \ldots b_{1n} 2 a_{11} \ldots a_{1n} 2 \beta(u_1)3 \Longrightarrow_{left} 1 c_{11} \ldots c_{1n} 22 \beta(u_1 x_1) y_1 3
$$

according to

$$(0 \to 1, b_{11} \to \lambda, \ldots, b_{1n} \to \lambda, 2 \to \lambda, a_{11} \to \lambda, \ldots, a_{1n} \to \lambda,$$
$$2 \to c_{11} \ldots c_{1n} 22, 3 \to \beta(x_1) y_1 3),$$

where $a_{1i}, b_{1i}, c_{1i} \in \{0,1\}$, for $1 \le i \le n$, $a_{11} \ldots a_{1n} = \beta(a_1), b_{11} \ldots b_{1n} = \beta(b_1)$, $c_{11} \ldots c_{1n} = \beta(c_1)$.

3. The derivation step

$$a_2 u_2 y_1 v b_2 \Longrightarrow u_2 y_1 v y_2 c_2 \qquad [(a_2, b_2, y_2, c_2)]$$

in Q is simulated in G as

$$1 b_{21} \ldots b_{2n} 2 a_{21} \ldots a_{2n} 2\beta(u_2) y_1 v 3 \Longrightarrow_{left} 1 c_{21} \ldots c_{2n} 22\beta(u_2) y_1 v y_2 3$$

according to

$$(1 \to 1, b_{21} \to \lambda, \ldots, b_{2n} \to \lambda, 2 \to \lambda, a_{21} \to \lambda, \ldots, a_{2n} \to \lambda,$$
$$2 \to c_{21} \ldots c_{2n} 22, 3 \to y_2 3),$$

where $a_{2i}, b_{2i}, c_{2i} \in \{0,1\}$, for $1 \le i \le n$, $a_{21} \ldots a_{2n} = \beta(a_2), b_{21} \ldots b_{2n} = \beta(b_2)$, $c_{21} \ldots c_{2n} = \beta(c_2)$.

4. Consider

$$a_3 y_1 v y_2 w b_3 \Longrightarrow y_1 v y_2 w y_3 c_3 \qquad [(a_3, b_3, y_3, c_3)]$$

G simulates this step as

$$1 b_{31} \ldots b_{3n} 2 a_{31} \ldots a_{3n} 2 y_1 v y_2 w 3 \Longrightarrow_{left} y_1 v y_2 w y_3 3$$

according to

$$(1 \to \lambda, b_{31} \to \lambda, \ldots, b_{3n} \to \lambda, 2 \to \lambda, a_{31} \to \lambda, \ldots, a_{3n} \to \lambda,$$
$$2 \to \lambda, 3 \to y_3 3),$$

where $a_{3i}, b_{3i}, c_{3i} \in \{0,1\}$, for $1 \le i \le n$, $a_{31} \ldots a_{3n} = \beta(a_3), b_{31} \ldots b_{3n} = \beta(b_3)$, $c_{31} \ldots c_{3n} = \beta(c_3)$.

Thus, $3 \Longrightarrow_{left}^* z$ in G. Consequently, Claim 8 holds. $\square$

By Claim 8, $L(Q) \subseteq L_{left}(G)$.

Claim 9. For any successful leftmost derivation in G, $3 \Longrightarrow_{left}^* z$, with $z \in T^*$, there exists a successful derivation in Q of the form $R \Longrightarrow^* zd$ with $d \in F$.

Proof of Claim 9. This claim can be proved by analogy with the proof of Claim 8. A detailed version of this proof is left to the reader. $\square$

By Claim 9, $L_{left}(G) \subseteq L(Q)$. Thus, $L(Q) = L_{left}(G)$, which completes the proof of the Theorem. $\square$

4. Final Remarks

Symmetrically to the leftmost derivation, we can define a rightmost derivation in a matrix grammar: each rule replaces the rightmost occurrence of its left-hand nonterminal in the current sentential form. The construction in the previous section can be carried out also for the rightmost derivation: for $L \in RE$ consider the language $mi(L)$, which is also in RE, construct a four-nonterminal matrix grammar G as in the the the previous section such that $L_{left}(G) = mi(L)$, then "reverse" the matrices of G by replacing $(A_1 \rightarrow x_1, \ldots, A_n \rightarrow x_n)$ by $(A_1 \rightarrow mi(x_1), \ldots, A_n \rightarrow mi(x_n))$. We obtain a grammar G' which generates in the rightmost mode the language L. Thus, each recursively enumerable language can be generated by a matrix grammar with four nonterminals.

These characterizations of RE are closely related to the characterization of RE by six-nonterminal matrix grammars with appearance checking (see [3]). Can any of these characterizations be established for fewer nonterminals ?

References

1. J. Dassow, Gh. Păun, *Regulated Rewriting in Formal Language Theory*, Springer-Verlag, Berlin, Heidelberg, 1989.

2. H. C. K. Kleijn, G. Rozenberg, On the generative power of regular pattern grammars, *Acta Informatica*, 20 (1983), 391 – 411.

3. Gh. Păun, Six nonterminals are enough for generating each R.E. language by a matrix grammar, *Intern. J. Computer Math.*, 15 (1993), 23 – 37.

The Accepting Power of Finite Automata over Groups

Victor MITRANA[1]

Faculty of Mathematics, University of Bucharest
Str. Academiei 14, 70109, Bucharest, ROMANIA

Ralf STIEBE

Faculty of Computer Science, University of Magdeburg
P.O.Box 4120, D-39016, Magdeburg, GERMANY

Abstract. Some results from [2], [5], [6] are generalized for finite automata over arbitrary groups. The accepting power is smaller when abelian groups are considered, in comparison with the non-abelian groups. We prove that this is due to the commutativity. Each language accepted by a finite automaton over an abelian group is actually a unordered vector language. Finally, deterministic finite automata over groups are investigated.

1. Introduction

One of the oldest and most investigated machine in the automata theory is the finite automaton. Many fundamental properties have been established and many problems are still open.

Unfortunately, the finite automata without any external control have a very limited accepting power. Different directions of research have been considered for overcoming this limitation. The most known extension added to a finite automata is the pushdown memory. In this way, a considerable increasing of the accepting capacity has been achieved. The pushdown automata are able to recognize all context-free languages.

Another simple and natural extension, related somehow to the pushdown memory, was considered in a series of papers [2], [5], [6], [7], namely to associate to each configuration an element of a given group, but no information regarding the associated element is allowed. This value is stored in a counter. An input string is accepted if and only if the automaton reaches a designated final state with its counter containing the neutral element of the group.

Thus, new characterizations of unordered vector languages [6] or context-free languages [2] have been reported. These results are, in a certain sense, unexpected since in such an automaton the same choice is available regardless the content of its counter. More precisely, the next action is determined just by the input symbol currently scanned and the state of the machine.

In this paper, we shall consider only acceptors with a one-way input tape read from left to right and a counter able to store elements from a given group. The aforementioned papers deal with finite automata over very well defined groups e.g. the additive group of integers, the multiplicative group of non-null rational numbers

---

[1]Work supported by the Alexander von Humboldt Foundation and the Academy of Finland, Project 11281

or the free group. The aim of this paper is to provide some general results regardless the associated group.

We shall prove that the addition of an abelian group to a finite automaton is less powerful than the addition of the multiplicative group of rational numbers. An interchange lemma points out the main reason of the power decrease of finite automata over abelian groups. Characterizations of the context-free and recursively enumerable languages classes are set up in the case of non-abelian groups.

As far as the deterministic variants of finite automata over groups are concerned we shall show their considerable lack of accepting power.

2. Preliminaries

We assume the reader familiar with the basic concepts in automata and formal language theory and in the group theory. For further details, we refer to [4] and [8], respectively.

For an alphabet Σ, we denote by Σ^* the free monoid generated by Σ under the operation of concatenation; the empty string is denoted by λ and the semigroup $\Sigma^* - \{\lambda\}$ is denoted by Σ^+. The length of $x \in \Sigma^*$ is denoted by $|x|$.

Let $\mathbf{K} = (M, \circ, e)$ be a group under the operation denoted by $\circ$ with the neutral element denoted by e. An extended finite automaton (EFA shortly) over the group $\mathbf{K}$ is a construct

$$A = (Z, \Sigma, \mathbf{K}, q_0, F, \delta)$$

where Z, Σ, q_0, F have the same meaning as for a usual finite automaton [4], namely the set of states, the input alphabet, the initial state and the set of final states, respectively, and

$$\delta : Z \times \Sigma \cup \{\lambda\} \longrightarrow \mathcal{P}_f(Z \times M)$$

This sort of automaton can be viewed as a finite automaton having a counter in which any element of M can be stored. The relation $(q, m) \in \delta(s, a)$, $q, s \in Z$, $a \in \Sigma \cup \{\lambda\}$, $m \in M$ means that the automaton A changes its current state s into q, by reading the symbol a on the input tape, and writes in the register $x \circ m$, where x is the old content of the register. The initial value registered is e.

We shall use the notation

$$(q, aw, m) \models_A (s, w, m \circ r) \text{ iff } (s, r) \in \delta(q, a)$$

for all $s, q \in Z$ $a \in \Sigma \cup \{\lambda\}$, $m, r \in M$. The reflexive and transitive closure of the relation $\models_A$ is denoted by $\models_A^*$. Sometimes, the subscript identifying the automaton will be omitted when it is self-understood.

The word $x \in \Sigma^*$ is accepted by the automaton A if and only if there is a final state q such that $(q_0, x, e) \models^* (q, \lambda, e)$. In other words, a string is accepted if the automaton completely reads it and reaches a final state when the content of the register is the neutral element of M.

The language accepted by an extended finite automaton over a group A as above is

$$L(A) = \{x \in \Sigma^* | (q_0, x, e) \models_A^* (q, \lambda, e), \text{ for some } q \in F\}$$

For two groups $\mathbf{K}_1 = (M_1, \circ_1, e_1)$ and $\mathbf{K}_2 = (M_2, \circ_2, e_2)$, we define the triple $\mathbf{K}_1 \times \mathbf{K}_2 = (M_1 \times M_2, \circ, (e_1, e_2))$ with $(m_1, m_2) \circ (n_1, n_2) = (m_1 \circ_1 n_1, m_2 \circ_2 n_2)$. It is well-known that $\mathbf{K}_1 \times \mathbf{K}_2$ is also a group.

We are going to provide some results that will be useful in what follows. The notation $\mathcal{L}(REG)$ identifies the class of regular languages.

Theorem 1. *For any group* $\mathbf{K}$, $\mathcal{L}(EFA(\mathbf{K})) = \mathcal{L}(REG)$ *iff all finitely generated subgroups of* $\mathbf{K}$ *are finite.*

Proof. Let $\mathbf{K}$ be a group such that any finitely generated subgroup of $\mathbf{K}$ is finite. Let $A = (Z, \Sigma, \mathbf{K}, z_0, F, \delta)$ be an EFA over $\mathbf{K} = (M, \circ, e)$. We denote by X the finite subset of M

$$X = \{m \in M \mid (z', m) \in \delta(z, a) \text{ for some } z, z' \in Z, a \in \Sigma \cup \{\lambda\}\}.$$

Let $\mathbf{H} = (\langle X \rangle, \circ, e)$ be the subgroup generated by X.

We construct the finite automaton with λ-moves $B = (Z \times \langle X \rangle, \Sigma, (z_0, e), F \times \{e\}, \varphi)$ with $\varphi((z, m), a) = \{(z', m \circ n) \mid (z', n) \in \delta(z, a), \text{ for all } z \in Z, m \in M, a \in \Sigma \cup \{\lambda\}$. One can easily prove that $(z_0, w, e) \models_A^* (z, \lambda, m)$ iff $((z_0, e), w) \models_B^* ((z, m), \lambda)$, which implies $L(A) = L(B)$.

It remains to prove that for any infinite group $\mathbf{K}$, finitely generated, exists an EFA over $\mathbf{K}$ accepting a non-regular language. Let $\mathbf{K} = (\langle X \rangle, \circ, e)$ be such a group with the finite set of generators X. Consider the (deterministic) EFA $A = (\{z\}, Y, \mathbf{K}, z, \{z\}, \delta)$, with $Y = X \cup \{x^{-1} \mid x \in X\}$ and $\delta(z, a) = (z, a)$, for all $a \in Y$. The following facts about $L(A)$ are obvious:

1. For any $m \in \langle X \rangle$, exist a word $v \in Y^*$ such that $(z, v, e) \models_A^* (z, \lambda, m)$.

2. For any $v \in Y^*$, exists a word $w \in Y^*$ such that $vw \in L(A)$.

3. For any $k \geq 0$, the set

$$X_k = \{m \in \langle X \rangle \mid \exists v \in Y^*, |v| \leq k : (z, v, e) \models_A^* (z, \lambda, m)\}$$

is finite.

As a consequence of these facts and of the infiniteness of $\langle X \rangle$, we obtain: For all $k \geq 0$, there is a word v_k such that $v_k v \notin L(A)$, for all $v \in Y^*$, $|v| \leq k$.

But, one can easily prove that for any regular language $L \subseteq Y^*$, exists $k \geq 0$ such that for all $vw \in L$, there is $w' \in Y^*$, $|w'| \leq k$, with $vw' \in L$. Hence, $L(A)$ cannot be regular. □

A finitely generated abelian group is finite if all its elements are of finite order. Hence, for an abelian group $\mathbf{K}$, $\mathcal{L}(EFA(\mathbf{K})) = \mathcal{L}(REG)$ iff all elements of $\mathbf{K}$ have finite order. This is not necessarily true for non-abelian groups. We can, however, prove a pumping lemma which is very similar to the pumping lemma for regular languages.

Lemma 1. *Let* $\mathbf{K}$ *be some group without elements of infinite order. For any language* $L \in \mathcal{L}(EFA(\mathbf{K}))$, *there is a constant* $n \geq 1$ *such that, for all* $x \in L$, $|x| \geq n$, *there exist a decomposition* $x = uvw$ *and a natural number* $q \geq 1$ *with* $|uv| \leq n$, $|v| \geq 1$, $uv^{iq+1}w \in L$, *for all* $i \geq 0$.

Moreover, if $\mathbf{K}$ *has the finite exponent* p *then* q *can uniformly be chosen as* $q = p$.

Proof. Let $A = (Z, \Sigma, \mathbf{K}, z_0, F, \delta)$ be an EFA over $\mathbf{K}$. We choose $n = |Z| + 1$. Now consider a word $x \in \Sigma^*$ with $|x| \geq n$. Similar to the proof of the pumping lemma for regular languages, it can be shown that there is a decomposition $x = uvw$, $|uv| \leq n$, $|v| \geq 1$, such that

$$(z_0, uvw, e) \models_A^* (z, vw, m_1) \models_A^* (z, w, m_1 \circ m_2) \models_A^* (f, \lambda, e), z \in Z, f \in F.$$

Now choose q such that $m_2^q = e$. Obviously, any word $uv^{iq+1}w$ is accepted by A. $\square$

As a consequence of the above pumping lemma, we obtain:

Theorem 2. *For any group* **K**, $\mathcal{L}(EFA(\mathbf{K}))$ *contains the language* $L = \{a^n b^n \mid n \geq 1\}$ *iff at least one element of* **K** *has an infinite order.*

Proof. Let $\mathbf{K} = (M, \circ, e)$. If M contains an element m of infinite order then the finitely generated subgroup $(\langle m \rangle, \circ, e)$ is isomorphic to $(\mathbf{Z}, +, 0)$, hence L is in $\mathcal{L}(EFA(\mathbf{K}))$.

If all elements of M have finite order, a simple application of the above pumping lemma yields $L \notin \mathcal{L}(EFA(\mathbf{K}))$. $\square$

For a group **K**, let $\mathcal{F}(\mathbf{K})$ denote the family of all finitely generated subgroups of **K**.

Theorem 3. *For any group* **K**,

$$\mathcal{L}(EFA(\mathbf{K})) = \bigcup_{\mathbf{H} \in \mathcal{F}(\mathbf{K})} \mathcal{L}(EFA(\mathbf{H}))$$

Proof. Let $\mathbf{K} = (M, \circ, e)$ be a group. The inclusion

$$\mathcal{L}(EFA(\mathbf{K})) \supseteq \bigcup_{\mathbf{H} \in \mathcal{F}(\mathbf{K})} \mathcal{L}(EFA(\mathbf{H}))$$

holds, since $\mathcal{L}(EFA(\mathbf{K})) \supseteq \mathcal{L}(EFA(\mathbf{H}))$, for any subgroup **H** of **K**.

On the other hand, let $A = (Z, \Sigma, \mathbf{K}, z_0, F, \delta)$ be an EFA over **K**. The group $\mathbf{H} = (\langle X \rangle, \circ, e)$, where $X = \{m \in M | (q, m) \in \delta(z, a)$ for some $q, z \in Z, a \in \Sigma \cup \{\lambda\}\}$ is a finitely generated subgroup of **K**. Obviously, during any computation in the counter of A appear only elements of $\langle X \rangle$. Therefore, the automaton A can be viewed as an automaton over **H**. More precisely, $A' = (Z, \Sigma, \mathbf{H}, z_0, F, \delta)$ accepts the same language as A does. This proves the second inclusion and thus the theorem. $\square$

3. EFA over Abelian Groups

Valence grammars and EFA have initially been introduced for the groups $\mathbf{Z}_k = (\mathbf{Z}^k, +, 0)$, $k \geq 1$ and $\mathbf{Q} = (Q - \{0\}, \cdot, 1)$. In what follows we shall show that the accepting capacity of EFA does not increase if we consider arbitrary abelian groups instead of **Q**. Thus, every language accepted by an EFA over an abelian group is a (unordered) vector language [1]. The deeper reason of this fact is the following fundamental result in the group theory.

Theorem 4. *A finitely generated abelian group is the direct product of a finite number of cyclic groups.*

As a consequence, a finitely generated abelian group is either finite or isomorphic to a group $\mathbf{Z}_k \times \mathbf{H}$, where k is a positive integer and **H** is a finite abelian group.

Theorem 5. *For a group* $\mathbf{K}$ *and a finite group* $\mathbf{H}$,

$$\mathcal{L}(EFA(\mathbf{K} \times \mathbf{H})) = \mathcal{L}(EFA(\mathbf{K}))$$

Proof. Let $\mathbf{K}$ and $\mathbf{H}$ be given by $\mathbf{K} = (M_1, \circ_1, e_1)$ and $\mathbf{H} = (M_2, \circ_2, e_2)$, and let $A = (Z, \Sigma, \mathbf{K} \times \mathbf{H}, z_0, F, \delta)$ be an EFA over $\mathbf{K} \times \mathbf{H}$. We construct the EFA over $\mathbf{K}$, $A' = (Z', \Sigma, \mathbf{K}, z_0', F', \delta')$ with $Z' = Z \times M_2$, $z_0' = (z_0, e_2)$, $F' = F \times \{e_2\}$ and

$$\delta'((z, n_2), a) = \{((z', n_2 \circ_2 m_2), m_1) \mid (z', (m_1, m_2)) \in \delta(z, a)\},$$
$$z, z' \in Z, a \in \Sigma \cup \{\lambda\}, m_1 \in M_1, m_2, n_2 \in M_2.$$

By induction on the number of steps, one can show that $((z_0, e_2), w, e_1) \models_{A'}^* ((z, m_2), w', m_1)$ iff $(z_0, w, (e_1, e_2)) \models_A^* (z, w', (m_1, m_2))$, hence $L(A) = L(A')$. $\square$

We are now ready to prove the main result of this section.

Theorem 6. *For an abelian group* $\mathbf{K}$, *one of the following relations hold:*

$$\begin{aligned}
\mathcal{L}(EFA(\mathbf{K})) &= \mathcal{L}(REG), \\
\mathcal{L}(EFA(\mathbf{K})) &= \mathcal{L}(EFA(\mathbf{Z}_k)), \text{ for some } k, \\
\mathcal{L}(EFA(\mathbf{K})) &= \mathcal{L}(EFA(\mathbf{Q})).
\end{aligned}$$

Proof. As it was shown in Theorem 3, $\mathcal{L}(EFA(\mathbf{K})) = \bigcup_{\mathbf{H} \in \mathcal{F}(\mathbf{K})} \mathcal{L}(EFA(\mathbf{H}))$. Every $\mathbf{H} \in \mathcal{F}(\mathbf{K})$ is either finite or isomorphic to a group $\mathbf{Z}_k \times \mathbf{H}'$ where $k \geq 1$ and $\mathbf{H}'$ is a finite group. Hence for all $\mathbf{H} \in \mathcal{F}(\mathbf{K})$, either $\mathcal{L}(EFA(\mathbf{H})) = \mathcal{L}(REG)$, or $\mathcal{L}(EFA(\mathbf{H})) = \mathcal{L}(EFA(\mathbf{Z}_k \times \mathbf{H}')) = \mathcal{L}(EFA(\mathbf{Z}_k))$, for some $k \geq 1$.

If all finitely generated subgroups of $\mathbf{K}$ are finite, then $\mathcal{L}(EFA(\mathbf{K})) = \mathcal{L}(REG)$ holds, due to Theorem 1.

Otherwise, let $N(\mathbf{K})$ be the set of all k such that $\mathcal{L}(EFA(\mathbf{H})) = \mathcal{L}(EFA(\mathbf{Z}_k))$, for some $\mathbf{H} \in \mathcal{F}(\mathbf{K})$. If $N(\mathbf{K})$ is finite then $\mathcal{L}(EFA(\mathbf{K})) = \mathcal{L}(EFA(\mathbf{Z}_k))$, where $k = \max(N(\mathbf{K}))$. If $N(\mathbf{K})$ is infinite then $\mathcal{L}(EFA(\mathbf{K})) = \mathcal{L}(EFA(\mathbf{Q}))$. $\square$

It is known that languages as $L_1 = \{a^n b^n \mid n \geq 1\}^*$ or $L_2 = \{wcw^R \mid w \in \{a, b\}^+\}$ are not in $\mathcal{L}(EFA(\mathbf{Q}))$. Therefore, $L_1, L_2 \notin \mathcal{L}(EFA(\mathbf{K}))$, for any abelian group $\mathbf{K}$. In [2] it was conjectured that the commutativity of the multiplication of rational numbers is responsible for this fact. We shall formally prove this conjecture by help of the following "interchange lemma".

Lemma 2. *Let* $\mathbf{K} = (M, \circ, e)$ *be some abelian group, and let* L *be a language in* $\mathcal{L}(EFA(\mathbf{K}))$. *There is a constant* k *such that, for any* $x \in L$, $|x| \geq k$, *and any decomposition* $x = v_1 w_1 v_2 w_2 \ldots v_k w_k v_{k+1}$, $|w_i| \geq 1$, *exist two integers* $1 \leq r < s \leq k$ *such that the word* $x' = v_1 w_1' v_2 w_2' \ldots v_k w_k' v_{k+1}$ *with* $w_r' = w_s$, $w_s' = w_r$, $w_i' = w_i$, *for* $i \notin \{r, s\}$, *is in* L.

Proof. Let $A = (Z, \Sigma, \mathbf{K}, z_0, F, \delta)$ be an EFA over $\mathbf{K} = (M, \circ, e)$. We choose $k = |Z|^2 + 1$. For a word $x \in L(A)$, $|x| \geq k$, let be given a decomposition $x = v_1 w_1 v_2 w_2 \ldots v_k w_k v_{k+1}$, $|w_i| \geq 1$. There are the states $y_i, z_i \in Z$, $1 \leq i \leq k$, $q \in F$, with

$$\begin{aligned}
(z_{i-1}, v_i, e) &\models^* (y_i, \lambda, m_i), 1 \leq i \leq k, \\
(y_i, w_i, e) &\models^* (z_i, \lambda, n_i), 1 \leq i \leq k, \\
(z_k, v_{k+1}, e) &\models^* (q, \lambda, m_{k+1}),
\end{aligned}$$

and $m_1 \circ n_1 \circ m_2 \circ n_2 \circ \ldots \circ m_k \circ n_k \circ m_{k+1} = e$.

By the pigeon-hole principle, there are two numbers $1 \leq r < s \leq k$ with $(y_r, z_r) = (y_s, z_s)$.

Now consider $x' = v_1 w_1' v_2 w_2' \ldots v_k w_k' v_{k+1}$ with $w_r' = w_s$, $w_s' = w_r$, $w_i' = w_i$, for $i \notin \{r, s\}$. For the words v_i, $1 \leq i \leq k+1$, and w_i', $1 \leq i \leq k+1$ the relations

$$(z_{i-1}, v_i, e) \models^* (y_i, \lambda, m_i), 1 \leq i \leq k,$$
$$(y_i, w_i', e) \models^* (z_i, \lambda, n_i'), 1 \leq i \leq k,$$
$$(z_k, v_{k+1}, e) \models^* (q, \lambda, m_{k+1}),$$

hold, with $n_r' = n_s$, $n_s' = n_r$, $n_i' = n_i$, for $i \notin \{r, s\}$. By the commutativity of $\mathbf{K}$ it follows

$$m_1 \circ n_1' \circ m_2 \circ n_2' \circ \ldots \circ m_k \circ n_k' \circ m_{k+1}$$
$$= m_1 \circ n_1 \circ m_2 \circ n_2 \circ \ldots \circ m_k \circ n_k \circ m_{k+1}$$
$$= e,$$

implying that x' is accepted by A. $\qquad\square$

Theorem 7. *For any abelian group* $\mathbf{K}$, *the languages* $L_1 = \{a^n b^n \mid n \geq 1\}^*$ *and* $L_2 = \{wcw^R \mid w \in \{a, b\}^+\}$ *are not in* $\mathcal{L}(EFA(\mathbf{K}))$.

Proof. Assume that $L_1 \in \mathcal{L}(EFA(\mathbf{K}))$, for some $\mathbf{K}$, and let k be the constant from the interchange lemma. Now consider the word $x = aba^2b^2 \ldots a^k b^k$ and the decomposition $v_i = a^i, w_i = b^i$, $1 \leq i \leq k$, $v_{k+1} = \lambda$. There are $1 \leq r < s \leq k$ such that $x' = aw_1' a^2 w_2' \ldots a^k w_k'$ with $w_r' = b^s$, $w_s' = b^r$, $w_i' = b^i$, for $i \notin \{r, s\}$, is in L_1, contradiction.

A similar reasoning for the relation $L_2 \notin \mathcal{L}(EFA(\mathbf{K}))$ is left to the reader. $\qquad\square$

4. EFA over Non-Abelian Groups

In this section, we restrict our investigation to the free groups, since for any (non-abelian) group $\mathbf{K}$ there is a homomorphism from a free group to $\mathbf{K}$ [8].

In this way, we get a characterization of the context-free languages class in terms of languages accepted by extended finite automata over the free group with just two generators [2]. The free group with n generators is denoted by $\mathbf{F}_n$.

Recall from [2]

Theorem 8. *The family of context-free languages equals* $\mathcal{L}(EFA(\mathbf{F}_2))$.

Lemma 3. *Let* $\mathbf{K}_1$ *and* $\mathbf{K}_2$ *be two groups. For two languages* $L_i \in \mathcal{L}(EFA(\mathbf{K}_i))$, $i = 1, 2$, *the languages* $L_1 \cap L_2$ *and* $L_1 L_2$ *are in* $\mathcal{L}(EFA(\mathbf{K}_1 \times \mathbf{K}_2))$.

Proof. Let $A_i = (Z_i, \Sigma_i, \mathbf{K}_i, z_i^0, F_i, \delta_i)$, $i = 1, 2$, be two EFA over $\mathbf{K}_i$, respectively. We assume that $Z_1 \cap Z_2$ is empty.

We have $L(B) = L_1 \cap L_2$ and $L(C) = L_1 L_2$, where $B = (Z_1 \times Z_2, \Sigma_1 \cap \Sigma_2, \mathbf{K}_1 \times \mathbf{K}_2, (z_1^0, z_2^0), F_1 \times F_2, \delta)$ with

$$\delta((z_1, z_2), a) = \{((z_1', z_2'), (m_1, m_2)) \mid (z_1', m_1) \in \delta_1(z_1, a), (z_2', m_2) \in \delta_2(z_2, a)\},$$
$$z_1 \in Z_1, z_2 \in Z_2, a \in \Sigma_1 \cap \Sigma_2,$$
$$\delta((z_1, z_2), \lambda) = \{((z_1', z_2), (m_1, e_2)) \mid (z_1', m_1) \in \delta_1(z_1, \lambda)\}$$
$$\cup \{((z_1, z_2'), (e_1, m_2)) \mid (z_2', m_2) \in \delta_2(z_2, \lambda)\}, \quad z_1 \in Z_1, z_2 \in Z_2.$$

and $C = (Z_1 \cup Z_2, \Sigma_1 \cup \Sigma_2, \mathbf{K}_1 \times \mathbf{K}_2, z_1^0, F_2, \delta)$ with

$$\delta(z, a) = \{(z', (m, e_2)) \mid (z', m) \in \delta_1(z, a)\}, \quad z \in Z_1, a \in \Sigma_1,$$

$$\delta(z, \lambda) = \begin{cases} \{(z', (m, e_2)) \mid (z', m) \in \delta_1(z, \lambda)\}, & z \in Z_1 \setminus F_1, \\ \{(z', (m, e_2)) \mid (z', m) \in \delta_1(z, \lambda)\} \cup \{(z_2^0, (e_1, e_2))\}, & z \in F, \end{cases}$$

$$\delta(z, a) = \{(z', (e_1, m)) \mid (z', m) \in \delta_2(z, a)\}, \quad z \in Z_2, a \in \Sigma_2 \cup \{\lambda\}.$$

which concludes the proof. □

It is well-known that every recursively enumerable language can be expressed as the homomorphical image of the intersection of two linear languages. It is obvious that each family $\mathcal{L}(EFA(\mathbf{K}))$ is closed under homomorphims. In conclusion, due to the previous lemma as well as to Theorem 8, we have just proved:

Theorem 9. $\mathcal{L}(EFA(\mathbf{F}_2 \times \mathbf{F}_2))$ *equals the family of recursively enumerable languages.*

5. Deterministic EFA

In the case of EFA, the determinism significantly decreases the accepting capacity. Denote by $\mathcal{L}(DEFA(\mathbf{K}))$ the family of languages recognized by deterministic EFA over the group $\mathbf{K}$.

Lemma 4. *For any group $\mathbf{K}$, the languages $L_1 = \{a^n \mid n \geq 1\} \cup \{a^n b^n \mid n \geq 1\}$, $L_2 = \{a^m b^n \mid m \geq n\}$ and $L_3 = \{a, b\}^* \setminus \{a^n b^n \mid n \geq 1\}$ are not in $\mathcal{L}(DEFA(\mathbf{K}))$.*

Proof. Let $\mathbf{K} = (M, \circ, e)$, and let $A = (Z, \{a, b\}, \mathbf{K}, z_0, F, \delta)$ be a DEFA over $\mathbf{K}$ such that $L_1 = L(A)$. Since $a^n \in L(A)$, for all $n \geq 1$, there are the integers $1 \leq r < s \leq |F| + 1$ such that $(z_0, a^r, e) \models_A^* (q, \lambda, e)$ and $(z_0, a^s, e) \models_A^* (q, \lambda, e)$, for some $q \in Z$. Since $a^n b^n \in L(A)$, for all $n \geq 1$, we have also $(z_0, a^r b^r, e) \models_A^* (q, b^r, e) \models_A^* (q', \lambda, e)$, for some $q' \in F$. Hence, $(z_0, a^s b^r, e) \models_A^* (q, b^r, e) \models_A^* (q', \lambda, e)$, implying $a^s b^r \in L(A)$, contradiction. In conclusion, $L_1 \neq L(A)$.

By similar arguments it can be shown that $L_2, L_3 \notin \mathcal{L}(DEFA(\mathbf{K}))$. □

On the other hand, $\mathcal{L}(DEFA(\mathbf{K}))$ generally contains languages with undecidable membership problem.

Theorem 10. *There is a finitely generated group $\mathbf{K}$ such that the following question is undecidable. Given a DEFA A over $\mathbf{K}$ and a word w over the input alphabet of A, is $w \in L(A)$?*

Proof. For a finitely generated group $\mathbf{K} = (M, \circ, e)$ with the set of generators X, the word problem is the following question. Is a given term $x_1 \circ x_2 \circ \ldots x_n$, $x_i \in X \cup X^{-1}$, $1 \leq i \leq n$, $X^{-1} = \{x^{-1} \mid x \in X\}$ equal to the neutral element e? It is a well-known result from group theory that there is a finitely generated group $\mathbf{K}$ with undecidable word problem.

Let $\mathbf{K} = (M, \circ, e)$ with the finite set of generators X be such a group. We construct the DEFA $A = (\{z\}, X \cup X^{-1}, \mathbf{K}, z, \{z\}, \delta)$ with the transition function $\delta(z, x) = (z, x)$, for all $x \in X \cup X^{-1}$. Obviously, A accepts a word $x_1 x_2 \ldots x_n$ iff $x_1 \circ x_2 \circ \ldots \circ x_n = e$. The undecidability of the membership problem for A follows directly from the undecidability of the word problem for $\mathbf{K}$. □

Theorem 11. *For every group $\mathbf{K}$ having at least one element of infinite order, we have $\mathcal{L}(DEFA(\mathbf{K})) \subset \mathcal{L}(EFA(\mathbf{K}))$, strict inclusion.*

Proof. Let $\mathbf{K}$ be an arbitrary given group and $A = (Z, \Sigma, \mathbf{K}, z_0, F, \delta)$ be a deterministic EFA over $\mathbf{K}$.

If there is an element of M of infinite order, then the language $\{a^n | n \geq 1\} \cup \{a^n b^n | n \geq 1\} \in \mathcal{L}(EFA(\mathbf{K}))$, since $\mathcal{L}(EFA(\mathbf{K}))$ is closed under union. In conclusion, $\mathcal{L}(DEFA(\mathbf{K})) \subset \mathcal{L}(FEA(\mathbf{K}))$. $\qquad\qquad\square$

6. Deterministic EFA over Abelian Groups

The next result is a consequence of Theorem 11.

Theorem 12. *For every abelian group* $\mathbf{K}$*, we have either* $\mathcal{L}(DEFA(\mathbf{K})) = \mathcal{L}(REG)$ *or* $\mathcal{L}(DEFA(\mathbf{K})) \subset \mathcal{L}(EFA(\mathbf{K}))$*, strict inclusion.*

Obviously, the statement of Theorem 6 is also valid for the deterministic EFA over abelian groups.

As we have seen, neither $\mathcal{L}(EFA(\mathbf{Q}))$ [6] nor $\mathcal{L}(DEFA(\mathbf{Q}))$ are closed under complement. In the end of this section we will show that the complement of a language from $\mathcal{L}(DEFA(\mathbf{Q}))$ is in $\mathcal{L}(EFA(\mathbf{Q}))$. In order to handle the difficulties owing to the existence of λ-steps, we introduce some notations.

Let $A = (S, \Sigma, \mathbf{Z}_k, s_0, F, \delta)$ be a DEFA over $(\mathbf{Z}_k)$, for some $k \geq 1$. For all $s \in S$, we define the sets

$$N_s = \{r \in \mathbf{Z}^k \mid (s, \lambda, 0) \models^* (q, \lambda, r), \text{ for some } q \in F\}$$

Lemma 5. *Let* A *be a DEFA as above. For all* $s \in S$*, there is an EFA* $A_s = (Y_s, \Sigma, \mathbf{Z}_k, s, \{q_s\}, \delta_s)$ *such that* $\delta_s(s, a) = \emptyset$*, for all* $a \in \Sigma$*, and* $(s, \lambda, 0) \models^* (q_s, \lambda, r)$ *iff* $r \in \mathbf{Z}^k \setminus N_s$*.*

Proof. In what follows let e_i, $1 \leq i \leq k$, denote the i-th unit vector of $\mathbf{Z}^k$. For any $s \in S$, we construct the EFA $A_1(s) = (S \cup \{q\}, T, \mathbf{Z}_k, s, \{q\}, \delta_1)$ with $q \notin S$, $T = \{a_1, \ldots, a_k\} \cup \{b_1, \ldots, b_k\}$, and the transition relation δ_1 defined as

$$
\begin{aligned}
\delta_1(p, a) &= \emptyset, \text{ for } p \in S, a \in T, \\
\delta_1(p, \lambda) &= \delta(p, \lambda), \text{ for } p \in S \setminus F, \\
\delta_1(p, \lambda) &= \delta(p, \lambda) \cup \{(q, 0)\}, \text{ for } p \in F, \\
\delta_1(q, a_i) &= \{(q, -e_i), \text{ for } 1 \leq i \leq k, \\
\delta_1(q, b_i) &= \{(q, e_i), \text{ for } 1 \leq i \leq k, \\
\delta_1(q, \lambda) &= \emptyset.
\end{aligned}
$$

Obviously, the language accepted by $A_1(s)$ is

$$L_s = \{w \in T^* \mid (|w|_{a_1} - |w|_{b_1}, \ldots, |w|_{a_k} - |w|_{b_k}) \in N_s\}.$$

Let $\Psi : T^* \to \mathbf{N}^{2k}$ be the Parikh mapping with $\Psi(w) = (|w|_{a_1}, |w|_{b_1}, \ldots, |w|_{a_k}, |w|_{b_k})$, for all $w \in T^*$. The Parikh set $\Psi(L_s)$ is semilinear, and its complement $\overline{\Psi(L_s)}$ is semilinear, too. Therefore, there is a finite automaton $A_2(s) = (Y_s, T, s, \{q_s\}, \delta_s')$ such that the Parikh set of $L(A_2(s))$ is $\overline{\Psi(L_s)}$. From $A_2(s)$ we can construct A_s as follows: $A_s = (Y_s, \Sigma, \mathbf{Z}_k, s, \{q_s\}, \delta_s)$ with

$$
\begin{aligned}
\delta_s(p, a) &= \emptyset, \text{ for } p \in Y_s, a \in \Sigma, \\
\delta_s(p, \lambda) &= \{(p', e_i) \mid p' \in \delta_s'(p, a_i), 1 \leq i \leq k\} \\
&\quad \cup \{(p', -e_i) \mid p' \in \delta_s'(p, b_i), 1 \leq i \leq k\}, \text{ for } p \in Y_s.
\end{aligned}
$$

Obviously, $(s, \lambda, 0) \models^*_{A_s} (q_s, \lambda, r)$ iff $L(A_2(s))$ contains a word w with $r = (|w|_{a_1} - |w|_{b_1}, \ldots, |w|_{a_k} - |w|_{b_k})$, i.e. iff L_s contains no word v with $r = (|v|_{a_1} - |v|_{b_1}, \ldots, |v|_{a_k} - |v|_{b_k})$, hence iff $r \notin N_z$. $\square$

Theorem 13. *For all $L \in \mathcal{L}(DEFA(\mathbf{Q}))$, the complement of L is contained in $\mathcal{L}(EFA(\mathbf{Q}))$.*

Proof. Let $A = (S, \Sigma, \mathbf{Z}_k, s_0, F, \delta)$ be a DEFA over $\mathbf{Z}_k$. The set of states can be partitioned into the set R consisting of all states $s \in S$, such that A can perform only λ-steps if s is reached, and its complement $S \setminus R$.

The complement of $L(A)$ consists of two sets; first, the set of all words $w = w_1 w_2 \in \Sigma^+$ with $w_2 \neq \lambda$ and $(s_0, w, 0) \models^*_A (p, w_2, r)$ for some $r \in \mathbf{Z}^k$ and some $p \in R$; second, the set of all words $ww_1 a \in \Sigma^+$ with $a \in \Sigma$ and $(s_0, w, 0) \models^*_A (p, a, r') \models_A (s, \lambda, r)$ for some $p, s \in S$, and $r + t \neq 0$, for all $t \in N_s$. The last condition is equivalent to $r + t = 0$, for some $t \in \mathbf{Z}^k \setminus N_s$.

Now let for all $s \in S$, $A_s = (Y_s, \Sigma, \mathbf{Z}_k, s, \{q_s\}, \delta_s)$ be the DEFA constructed in the last lemma. Without loss of generality we may assume that Y_s and $Y_{s'}$ are disjoint for $s \neq s'$ and that Y_s and S are disjoint for all $s \in S$. Now we construct $B = (S', \Sigma, \mathbf{Z}_k, s_0, F', \delta')$ with the set of states $S' = S \cup \bigcup_{s \in S} Y_s \cup \{f\}$, the set of final states $F' = \{q_s \mid s \in S\} \cup \{f\}$, and the following transition mapping

$$\delta'(s, \lambda) = \begin{cases} \delta(s, \lambda) \text{ if } s \in S - \{s_0\} \\ \delta(s, \lambda) \cup \{(f, 0)\} \text{ if } s = s_0 \\ \delta_x(s, \lambda) \text{ if } s \in Y_x, \text{ for some } x \in S \end{cases}$$

$$\delta'(s, a) = \begin{cases} \delta(s, a) \cup \{(y_{s'}, r)|(s', r) \in \delta(s, a)\} \text{ if } s \in S - R \\ \delta(s, a) \cup \{(y_{s'}, r)|(s', r) \in \delta(s, a)\} \cup \{(f, 0)\} \text{ if } s \in R \end{cases}$$

$$\delta'(f, a) = \{(f, 0)\},$$

$$\delta'(f, \lambda) = \{(f, m \cdot e_i)\}, m \in \{-1, 0, 1\}, 1 \leq i \leq k.$$

for all $a \in \Sigma$.

It is easy to see that B accepts all words not in $L(A)$. On the other hand, no word from $L(A)$ is accepted by B. $\square$

An important consequence of the last theorem is the decidability of the inclusion problem (and of the equivalence problem, too) for DEFA over $\mathbf{Q}$, which is an interesting contrast to the undecidability of the universe problem for nondeterministic one-turn counter automata, a proper subclass of EFA over $(\mathbf{Z}, +, 0)$.

Theorem 14. *Let A and B be DEFA over $\mathbf{Q}$. It is decidable whether or not $L(A) \subseteq L(B)$.*

Proof. Given B, one can construct a (nondeterministic) EFA $\overline{B}$ over $\mathbf{Q}$ with $L(\overline{B}) = \overline{L(B)}$. Clearly, $L(A) \subseteq L(B)$ iff $L(\overline{B}) \cap L(A)$ is empty. Now an EFA C over $\mathbf{Q}$ can be constructed such that $L(C) = L(\overline{B}) \cap L(A)$. Hence, the inclusion problem for DEFA over $\mathbf{Q}$ is reduced to the emptiness problem for EFA over the same group, which is decidable [1]. $\square$

References

1. J. Dassow, Gh. Păun, *Regulated Rewriting in Formal Language Theory*, Akademie-Verlag, Berlin, 1989.

2. J. Dassow, V. Mitrana, Finite automata over free generated groups, submitted, 1996.

3. S. Ginsburg, S. A. Greibach, Abstract families of languages. *Memoirs Amer. Math. Soc.* 87(1969), 1–32.

4. S. Ginsburg, *Algebraic and automata-theoretic properties of formal languages*, North-Holl., Amsterdam, Oxford, 1975.

5. S. A. Greibach, Remarks on blind and partially blind one-way multicounter machines. *Th. Comp. Sci.* 7(1978), 311–324.

6. O. H. Ibarra, S. K. Sahni, C. E. Kim, Finite automata with multiplication. *Th. Comp. Sci.*, 2(1976), 271–294.

7. Gh. Păun, A new generative device: valence grammars, *Rev. Roum. Math. Pures et Appl.*, 25, 6(1980), 911–924.

8. J. J. Rotman, *An Introduction to the Theory of Groups*, Springer-Verlag, 1995.

Controlled Fuzzy Parallel Rewriting

Peter R. J. ASVELD

Department of Computer Science
Twente University of Technology
P.O. Box 217, 7500 AE Enschede, The Netherlands
E-mail: infprja@cs.utwente.nl

Abstract. We study a Lindenmayer-like parallel rewriting system to model the growth of filaments (arrays of cells) in which developmental errors may occur. In essence this model is the fuzzy analogue of the derivation-controlled iteration grammar. Under minor assumptions on the family of control languages and on the family of fuzzy languages in the underlying iteration grammar, we show that (i) regular control does not provide additional generating power to the model, (ii) the number of fuzzy substitutions in the underlying iteration grammar can be reduced to two, and (iii) the resulting family of fuzzy languages possesses strong closure properties, viz. it is a full hyper-AFFL, i.e., a hyper-algebraically closed full Abstract Family of Fuzzy Languages.

1. Introduction

The original motivation to introduce Lindenmayer systems, or L-systems for short, consisted of modeling the development of filamentous organisms [15], [16]. The state space of each individual cell of such an organism is a finite set, symbolically represented as an alphabet V, and rewrite rules over V provide for the development of single cells. More precisely, a rule $\alpha \to w$ with $\alpha \in V$ and $w \in V^*$, allows for a state change ($w \in V$, $w \neq \alpha$), a cell death ($w = \lambda$, λ is the empty word), or the splitting of a cell in more than a single off-spring ($\mid w \mid > 1$, where $\mid w \mid$ is the length of the string w). Starting from an initial filament, i.e. a string over V, and applying the rules for individual cells in parallel yields the global state of the filament after a discrete time step. Iterating this rewriting process shows the development of this filament as function of the discrete time parameter. From a mathematical point of view the set of rules is just a finite substitution over V that is applied iteratively to the initial string.

Subsequent contributions to the extension of this model resulted in the distinction between nonterminal and terminal symbols as in Chomsky phrase-structure grammars, in several sets of rules (several finite substitutions, also called *tables*) instead of just a single one, and numerous ways of restricting or regulating the parallel rewriting process. We refer the reader to [13], [21] for surveys of the early days of L-system theory; [13] is more elementary and devoted to biological applications, whereas [21] concentrates on mathematical properties. More recent developments and related approaches can be found in [7], [22], of which [7] treats derivation-controlled rewriting in general, whereas [22] shows a rich variety of results closely related to or inspired by L-systems.

The extension of the basic model with different sets of rules (a finite number of finite substitutions instead of a single one) stems from the observation that a filamentous organism might develop in a different way under different external conditions

[20]. A typical example is the difference between day and night; in that case we have two sets of rules, or tables, viz. a day table τ_d and a night table τ_n, each table being a finite substitution over the alphabet V. Closely related to this extension are the so-called derivation-controlled tabled L-systems in which the order of application is prescribed by a control language over the table names [10], [18], [1]. E.g. in order to obtain the right sequence of day, followed by night, followed by day, etc., a regular control language of the form $(\tau_d\tau_n)^\star\tau_d$ can be used, provided each sequence should start and end with the day table τ_d. Similarly, but on a larger time scale, the order of the four seasons can be described by a regular control language of the form $(\tau_{\text{spring}}\tau_{\text{summer}}\tau_{\text{autumn}}\tau_{\text{winter}})^\star\tau_{\text{spring}}$.

In this paper we introduce a further extension of this model which enables us to describe developmental errors. Such an error occurs when, instead of applying the correct rule $\alpha \to w$ from the table τ, the symbol α is replaced by a string w' with $w' \neq w$ and $\alpha \to w'$ is *not* a rule in τ. In such a situation the "quality" of this incorrect off-spring w' should be strictly less than the corresponding correct one and, consequently, the "quality" of the entire filament should also decrease by this developmental error. In addition we want that making two developmental errors is worse than a single error and, in general, that each additional developmental error should strictly decrease the "quality" of the filament under consideration.

But how do we measure the "quality" of a string or filament x derived by a controlled tabled L-system G? In traditional formal language theory there only are two possibilities, viz. (i) x belongs to the language $L(G)$ generated by G: its "quality" equals 100%, or (ii) x does not belong to $L(G)$: the "quality" of x is 0%. Clearly, there is no room for expressing statements like "x is slightly imperfect due to a minor developmental error" or "x has been severely damaged by a long sequence of considerable errors during its development". This lack of expressibility is, of course, due to restrictions in set theory: the membership function or characteristic function $\mu_{L(G)}$ of a set, or a language $L(G)$ in our case, has two possible values only: $\mu_{L(G)}(x) = 1$ if $x \in L(G)$, and $\mu_{L(G)}(x) = 0$ if $x \notin L(G)$. Thus, if $L(G) \subseteq \Sigma^\star$, then $\mu_{L(G)}$ is a mapping of type $\mu_{L(G)} : \Sigma^\star \to \{0,1\}$.

Fortunately, using fuzzy sets and fuzzy languages we are able to express "qualities" different from 0% and 100%, since $\mu_{L(G)}$ is now a mapping of type $\mu_{L(G)} : \Sigma^\star \to \mathcal{L}$ where $\mathcal{L}$ is a complete lattice, eventually provided with additional operations and properties. As a typical example, the reader may consider the case in which $\mathcal{L}$ equals the real interval [0,1] with min and max as lattice operations. Fuzzy languages have been introduced in [17], which is restricted to fuzzy analogues of Chomsky grammars and languages. In [19] fuzzy Lindenmayer systems and their languages have been studied, however, without any motivation in terms of developmental errors. This motivation is the obvious parallel Lindenmayer variant based on the idea of grammatical error studied in [3], [4], [5].

So in fuzzy L-system theory the "quality" of a string is a value in $\mathcal{L}$ which might be anything in between 0 (the smallest element of $\mathcal{L}$) and 1 (the greatest element of $\mathcal{L}$) depending on the actual structure of $\mathcal{L}$. And making a developmental error in the derivation of x means that the "quality" of x will not increase compared to the previous string. But whether it will strictly decrease depends on the structure and the operations of $\mathcal{L}$ as well as their relation with the definition of derivation step; cf. Section 4 for details.

In dealing with developmental errors there is another problem. Usually, an L-system has in each of its tables a finite number of rewrite rules. Making a developmental mistake, i.e., replacing α by w' instead of by the correct string w can be modeled by adding the rule $\alpha \to w'$ to the table τ to which $\alpha \to w$ belongs, and requiring $\mu_{\tau(\alpha)}(w') < 1$, where $\tau(\alpha)$ is the set of all strings ω such that $\alpha \to \omega$ belongs to τ. This construction works for a finite number of possible developmental errors only. But, in general, there is an infinite number of ways to make mistakes, and filamentous development does not form an exception to this observation. So we should add an infinite number of rules $\alpha \to w'$ to τ or, equivalently, an infinite number of strings to the fuzzy set $\tau(\alpha)$. So each set $\{\omega \in \tau(\alpha) \mid 0 < \mu_{\tau(\alpha)}(\omega) < 1\}$ is allowed to be infinite. But then the language $\{\omega \in \tau(\alpha) \mid \mu_{\tau(\alpha)}(\omega) = 1\}$ might be infinite as well, or, equivalently, each $\tau(\alpha)$ may be a fuzzy subset of $V^\star$, i.e., a fuzzy languages over V. However, we could not let be the sets $\tau(\alpha)$ arbitrary fuzzy languages over V: they should be restricted in some uniform way, otherwise we end up with languages $L(G)$ that are not even recursively enumerable; cf. [8]. A well-known way to restrict these fuzzy languages is the following: we require that each fuzzy language $\tau(\alpha)$ belongs to a given family K of fuzzy languages. The family K is a parameter in our approach: usually, we demand that K meets some minor conditions, but sometimes we simply take a concrete value for K, e.g., we take K equal to the family FIN_f of finite fuzzy languages.

This results in the notion of fuzzy K-iteration grammar which plays the main part in the present paper. Formally, such a grammar $G = (V, \Sigma, U, S)$ consists of an alphabet V, a terminal alphabet Σ ($\Sigma \subseteq V$), an initial symbol S ($S \in V - \Sigma$), and a finite set U of fuzzy K-substitutions over V. Thus for each τ in U, and for each α in V, $\tau(\alpha)$ is a fuzzy language over V that belongs to the family K. The controlled variant of this grammar concept is the so-called Γ-controlled fuzzy K-iteration grammar, or fuzzy (Γ, K)-iteration grammar where Γ is a family of (non-fuzzy) languages. A grammar $(G; M) = (V, \Sigma, U, S, M)$ of this type consists of a fuzzy K-iteration grammar (V, Σ, U, S) and a language M over U (considered as an alphabet) with $M \in \Gamma$. Each derivation D according to $(G; M)$ satisfies the condition that the sequence of fuzzy K-substitutions used in D constitutes a string in the control language M.

The remaining part of this paper is organized as follows. In Section 2 we introduce the basic notions with respect to fuzzy languages and operations on fuzzy languages. Section 3 is devoted to families of fuzzy languages. The formal definitions of fuzzy K-iteration grammar and of Γ-controlled fuzzy K-iteration grammar are provided in Section 4, where we also give a few examples of these grammars together with the fuzzy languages that they generate. Section 5 consists of some elementary but useful properties of fuzzy K-iteration and fuzzy (Γ, K)-iteration grammars. The main results, viz. Theorem 6.1 and its corollaries, which deal with the generating power of fuzzy (Γ, K)-iteration grammars, are in Section 6. Closure properties of the corresponding families of fuzzy languages are the subject of Section 7. Under minor conditions on the families Γ and K, the families $H_f(K)$ and $H_f(\Gamma, K)$ of fuzzy languages, generated by fuzzy K-iteration grammars and (Γ, K)-iteration grammars, respectively, possess strong closure properties very similar to the ones of the corresponding non-fuzzy language families; cf. [1]. Finally, Section 8 contains some concluding remarks.

2. Fuzzy Languages and Operations on Fuzzy Languages

We assume that the reader is familiar with basic formal language theory to the extend of the first few chapters of standard texts like [12], [14], [23]. L-systems and Abstract Families of Languages are treated much more thoroughly in [13], [21] and [9], respectively. Finally, we need some rudiments of lattice theory which can be found in most books on algebra; all what we use of lattice theory is also summarized in [2].

In order to define several types of fuzziness we need a few lattice-ordered structures. Instead of stacking adjectives, we collect some collections of properties under simple names as "type-bb lattice" for some short bit strings bb. The following definitions and examples are quoted from [5]. The definition of the principal notion of type 00-lattice is a slight modification of a structure originally introduced in [11].

Definition 2.1. An algebraic structure $\mathcal{L}$ or $(\mathcal{L}, \wedge, \vee, 0, 1, \star)$ is a *type-00 lattice* if it satisfies the following conditions.

- $(\mathcal{L}, \wedge, \vee, 0, 1)$ is a completely distributive complete lattice. Therefore for all a_i, a, b_i and b in $\mathcal{L}$, $a \wedge \bigvee_i b_i = \bigvee_i (a \wedge b_i)$ and $(\bigvee a_i) \wedge b = \bigvee_i (a_i \wedge b)$ hold. And 0 and 1 are the smallest and the greatest element of $\mathcal{L}$, respectively; so $0 = \bigwedge \mathcal{L}$ and $1 = \bigvee \mathcal{L}$.

- $(\mathcal{L}, \star)$ is a commutative semigroup.

- The following identities hold for all a_i's, b_i's, a and b in $\mathcal{L}$:

$$a \star \bigvee_i b_i = \bigvee_i (a \star b_i) \,,$$

$$(\bigvee_i a_i) \star b = \bigvee_i (a_i \star b) \,,$$

$$0 \wedge a = 0 \star a = a \star 0 = 0 \,,$$

$$1 \wedge a = 1 \star a = a \star 1 = a \,.$$

A *type-01 lattice* is a type-00 lattice in which the operation $\star$ coincides with the operation $\wedge$; so it is a completely distributive complete lattice actually. A *type-10 lattice* is a type-00 lattice in which $(\mathcal{L}, \wedge, \vee, 0, 1)$ is a totally ordered set or chain, i.e., for all a and b in $\mathcal{L}$, we have $a \wedge b = a$ or $a \wedge b = b$. In a type-10 lattice the operations $\vee$ and $\wedge$ are usually denoted by max and min, respectively. Finally, when $\mathcal{L}$ is both a type-01 lattice and a type-10 lattice, $\mathcal{L}$ is called a *type-11 lattice*.

Example 2.2. As usual we denote the closed interval of all real numbers in between 0 and 1 by $[0, 1]$.
(1) The structure $([0, 1] \times [0, 1], \wedge, \vee, (0, 0), (1, 1), \star)$ in which the operations are defined by $(x_1, y_1) \wedge (x_2, y_2) = (\min\{x_1, x_2\}, \min\{y_1, y_2\})$, $(x_1, y_1) \vee (x_2, y_2) = (\max\{x_1, x_2\}, \max\{y_1, y_2\})$ and $(x_1, y_1) \star (x_2, y_2) = (x_1 x_2, y_1 y_2)$ for all x_1, x_2, y_1 and y_2 in $[0, 1]$ is a type-00 lattice.
(2) Consequently, $([0, 1] \times [0, 1], \wedge, \vee, (0, 0), (1, 1), \star)$ where the operations $\wedge$ and $\vee$ are defined as in (1) and $(x_1, y_1) \star (x_2, y_2) = (\min\{x_1, x_2\}, \min\{y_1, y_2\})$ for all x_1, x_2, y_1 and y_2 in $[0, 1]$, is a type-01 lattice.
(3) The structure $([0, 1], \min, \max, 0, 1, \star)$ with $x_1 \star x_2 = x_1 x_2$ for all x_1 and x_2 in $[0, 1]$ is a type-10 lattice.
(4) Taking $\star$ equal to min in (3) yields a type-11 lattice.

The following useful fact is very easy to prove.

Lemma 2.3. *For each type-00 lattice $\mathcal{L}$, $a \star b \leq a \wedge b$ holds for all elements a and b in $\mathcal{L}$.*

Proof.
By the distributivity of $\star$ over $\vee$, $a \star (1 \vee b) = a \star 1 \vee a \star b$ holds. As $1 \vee b = 1$ and $a \star 1 = a$, we have $a = a \vee a \star b$, and therefore $a \star b \leq a$. Analogously, we obtain $a \star b \leq b$, and hence $a \star b \leq a \wedge b$. $\qquad\qquad\qquad\qquad\qquad\qquad\qquad\qquad\quad\square$

Of course, Lemma 2.3 implies that in a type-00 lattice the inequalities $a \star b \leq a$ and $a \star b \leq b$ also hold for all a and b.

Now we are ready to define fuzzy languages relative to the lattice-ordered structures of Definition 2.1.

Definition 2.4. Let $\mathcal{L}$ be a type-00 lattice and let Σ be an alphabet. A $\mathcal{L}$-*fuzzy language* over Σ is a $\mathcal{L}$-fuzzy subset of Σ^*, i.e., it is a triple (Σ, μ_{L_0}, L_0) where μ_{L_0} is a function $\mu_{L_0} : \Sigma^* \to \mathcal{L}$, the *degree of membership function*, and L_0 is the support of μ_{L_0}; i.e., $L_0 = \{w \in \Sigma^* \mid \mu_{L_0}(w) > 0\}$. Very often we will write L_0 rather than (Σ, μ_{L_0}, L_0).

Henceforth, when $\mathcal{L}$ is clear from the context, we use "fuzzy language" instead of "$\mathcal{L}$-fuzzy language". Usually we write $\mu(x; L_0)$ instead of $\mu_{L_0}(x)$ in order to reduce the number of subscript levels.

For each fuzzy language L_0 over Σ, the *crisp language* $c(L_0)$ induced by L_0 —also known as the *crisp part* of L_0— is the subset of Σ^* defined by $c(L_0) = \{w \in \Sigma^* \mid \mu(w; L_0) = 1\}$. Each ordinary (non-fuzzy) language L_0 coincides with its crisp part $c(L_0)$. Therefore an ordinary language will also be called a *crisp* language.

In dealing with fuzzy languages (Σ, μ_{L_0}, L_0) the degree of membership function μ_{L_0} is actually the principal concept, whereas the languages L_0, $c(L_0)$ and many other crisp languages like

$$L_{\geq a} = \{w \in \Sigma^* \mid \mu(w; L_0) \geq a\},$$

$$L_{>a} = \{w \in \Sigma^* \mid \mu(w; L_0) > a\},$$

$$L_{\leq a} = \{w \in \Sigma^* \mid \mu(w; L_0) \leq a\},$$

$$L_{<a} = \{w \in \Sigma^* \mid \mu(w; L_0) < a\},$$

$$L_{a \leq; \leq b} = \{w \in \Sigma^* \mid a \leq \mu(w; L_0) \leq b\},$$

where a and b are elements in $\mathcal{L}$, are derived notions.

Example 2.5. (1) Let $\mathcal{L}$ be the type-00 lattice of Example 2.2.(1). Consider the $\mathcal{L}$-fuzzy language L_0 over $\Sigma = \{a, b\}$ defined by

$$\mu(a^m b^n; L_0) = \left(\frac{m}{\max\{1, m, n\}}, \frac{n}{\max\{1, m, n\}} \right) \text{ if } m, n \geq 0.$$

In defining the degree of membership function is such a concrete case, we always tacitly assume that $\mu(x; L_0) = (0, 0)$ in all other, unmentioned cases for x in Σ^*. Consequently, we have, e.g., $\mu(b^3 a^2; L_0) = \mu(a^2 b a^5; L_0) = \mu(a b^3 a^2 b^4; L_0) = (0, 0)$, etc.

Then the crisp part of L_0 equals $c(L_0) = \{a^m b^m \mid m \geq 1\}$; for each x in $c(L_0)$, we have $\mu(x; L_0) = (1, 1)$. Note that for each $m \geq 1$, $\mu(a^m; L_0) = (1, 0)$ and $\mu(b^m; L_0) = (0, 1)$, whereas for the empty word λ, we have $\mu(\lambda; L_0) = (0, 0)$.

(2) Now we take for $\mathcal{L}$ the type-10 lattice of Example 2.2.(3). Let L be the fuzzy language over $\{a, b\}$ defined by

$$\mu(w; L) = 0 \qquad \text{if } |w| \neq 2^k \text{ for some } k \geq 0, \text{ and}$$
$$\mu(w; L) = 2^{-\#_b(w)} \qquad \text{if } |w| = 2^k \text{ for some } k \geq 0.$$

As usual, $\#_\sigma(w)$ denotes the number of times that the symbol σ occurs in the word w. Then $c(L) = \{a^{2^k} \mid k \geq 0\}$.

Throughout this paper we will restrict ourselves to the computable or even to the rational elements in $[0, 1]$. For an account on the impact of computability constraints in fuzzy formal languages we refer the reader to [8].

Starting from simple fuzzy languages we can define more complicated ones by means of operations on fuzzy languages. First, we consider the operations union, intersection and concatenation for fuzzy languages; they have been defined originally in [17] for the type-11 lattice $[0, 1]$; cf. Example 2.2(4). In [4] we remarked that a generalization to the type-10 lattice of Example 2.2(3) is possible. However, it is straightforward to define these operations for arbitrary type-00 lattices; cf. [5] from which we cite the following definitions.

Let $(\Sigma_1, \mu_{L_1}, L_1)$ and $(\Sigma_2, \mu_{L_2}, L_2)$ be fuzzy languages, then the *union* of the fuzzy languages L_1 and L_2, denoted by $(\Sigma_1 \cup \Sigma_2, \mu_{L_1 \cup L_2}, L_1 \cup L_2)$ or abbreviated by $L_1 \cup L_2$, is defined by

$$\mu(x; L_1 \cup L_2) = \mu(x; L_1) \vee \mu(x; L_2) \,,$$

for all x in $(\Sigma_1 \cup \Sigma_2)^\star$. And for the *intersection* of fuzzy languages L_1 and L_2, denoted by $(\Sigma_1 \cap \Sigma_2, \mu_{L_1 \cap L_2}, L_1 \cap L_2)$ or $L_1 \cap L_2$ for short, the equality

$$\mu(x; L_1 \cap L_2) = \mu(x; L_1) \wedge \mu(x; L_2) \,,$$

holds for all x in $(\Sigma_1 \cap \Sigma_2)^\star$. Finally, for the *concatenation* of fuzzy languages L_1 and L_2, denoted by $(\Sigma_1 \cup \Sigma_2, \mu_{L_1 L_2}, L_1 L_2)$ or abbreviated to $L_1 L_2$, we have

$$\mu(x; L_1 L_2) = \bigvee \{\mu(y; L_1) \star \mu(z; L_2) \mid x = yz\}$$

for all x in $(\Sigma_1 \cup \Sigma_2)^\star$.

Example 2.6. Let $\mathcal{P}(X)$ denote the power set of the set X. Then $\mathcal{P}(\Sigma^\star)$ is the collection of all crisp languages over the alphabet Σ. Let $\mathcal{P}_f(\Sigma^\star)$ be the class of all fuzzy languages over Σ. Clearly, we have $\mathcal{P}(\Sigma^\star) = \{c(L) \mid L \in \mathcal{P}_f(\Sigma^\star)\}$. And $(\mathcal{P}_f(\Sigma^\star), \cap, \cup, \emptyset, \Sigma^\star, \cdot)$ —where $\cap$, $\cup$ and $\cdot$ denote the operations union, intersection and concatenation for fuzzy languages, respectively— is *not* an example of a type-00 lattice, since $(\mathcal{P}_f, \cdot)$ is not a commutative semigroup. In case Σ contains a single letter only, $(\mathcal{P}_f, \cdot)$ is a commutative semigroup and $(\mathcal{P}_f(\Sigma^\star), \cap, \cup, \emptyset, \Sigma^\star, \cdot)$ is a type-00 lattice. The same remarks apply to the structure $(\mathcal{P}(\Sigma^\star), \cap, \cup, \emptyset, \Sigma^\star, \cdot)$ of crisp languages.

Once we have defined the operations of union and concatenation it is straightforward to define the operations of *Kleene* $+$ and *Kleene* $\star$ for a fuzzy language L; viz. by

$$L^+ = L \cup LL \cup LLL \cup \ldots = \bigcup \{L^i \mid i \geq 1\} \,, \qquad \text{and}$$
$$L^\star = \{\lambda\} \cup L \cup LL \cup LLL \cup \ldots = \bigcup \{L^i \mid i \geq 0\} \,,$$

respectively, where $L^0 = \{\lambda\}$, and $L^{n+1} = L^n L$ with $n \geq 0$. In defining $L^\star$ we demand that $\mu(\lambda; L^\star) = 1$. Consequently, $L^\star = L^+ \cup \{\lambda\}$ where the latter set in this union is a crisp set.

Apart from these simple operations we need some other well-known ones, like homomorphisms and substitutions. They can be extended to fuzzy languages as well by means of the concept of fuzzy function; cf. [5] for the original definitions.

A *fuzzy relation* R between crisp sets X and Y is a fuzzy subset of $X \times Y$. If $R \subseteq X \times Y$ and $S \subseteq Y \times Z$ are fuzzy relations, then their composition $R \circ S$ is defined by

$$\mu((x,z); R \circ S) = \bigvee \{\mu((x,y); R) \star \mu((y,z); S) \mid y \in Y\}. \tag{1}$$

A *fuzzy function* $f : X \to Y$ in its turn, is a fuzzy relation $f \subseteq X \times Y$, satisfying the condition that for all x in X: if $\mu((x,y); f) > 0$ and $\mu((x,z); f) > 0$ hold, then $y = z$ and hence $\mu((x,y); f) = \mu((x,z); f)$. For fuzzy functions (1) holds as well, but we write the composition of two functions $f : X \to Y$ and $g : Y \to Z$ as $g \circ f : X \to Z$ rather than as $f \circ g$.

As mentioned before, $\mathcal{P}(X)$ denotes the power set of the set X. In the sequel we need functions $f : V^* \to \mathcal{P}(V^*)$ that will be extended to $f : \mathcal{P}(V^*) \to \mathcal{P}(V^*)$ by $f(L) = \bigcup \{f(x) \mid x \in L\}$ and for each subset L of V^*,

$$\mu(y; f(L)) = \bigvee \{\mu(x; L) \star \mu((x,y); f) \mid x \in V^*\}. \tag{2}$$

Consequently, by (1) and (2) iterating a single fuzzy function f, yielding functions like $f \circ f$, $f \circ f \circ f$, and so on, are now defined. Clearly, each of these functions $f^{(n)}$ is of type $f^{(n)} : \mathcal{P}(V^*) \to \mathcal{P}(V^*)$. Of course, we can iterated a finite set of such functions $\{f_1, \ldots, f_n\}$ in the very same way.

3. Families of Fuzzy Languages

This section is devoted to some families of simple fuzzy languages, their crisp counterparts, and a few operators that transform families of fuzzy languages into other families. The next few definitions are simple generalizations based on well-known concepts for families of crisp languages; cf. [5].

Throughout this paper Σ_ω denotes a countably infinite set of symbols. All families of languages that we will consider in the sequel only use symbols from this set. Henceforth, $\mathcal{L}$ is a type-00 lattice, and "fuzzy" means "$\mathcal{L}$-fuzzy" actually.

Definition 3.1. A *family of fuzzy languages* K is a set of fuzzy languages (Σ_L, μ_L, L) such that each Σ_L is a finite subset of Σ_ω. As usual, we assume that for each fuzzy language (Σ_L, μ_L, L) in the family K, the alphabet Σ_L is minimal with respect to μ_L, i.e., a symbol α belongs to Σ_L if and only if there exists a word w in which α occurs and for which $\mu_L(w) > 0$ or, equivalently, for which $w \in L$ holds.

A family K of fuzzy languages is called *nontrivial* if K contains a language (Σ_L, μ_L, L) with $L \cap \Sigma_L^+ \neq \emptyset$, i.e., (Σ_L, μ_L, L) satisfies $\mu(x; L) > 0$ for some $x \in \Sigma_L^+$.

For each family K of fuzzy languages, the *crisp part* of K, denoted by $c(K)$, is defined by $c(K) = \{c(L) \mid L \in K\}$.

We already remarked that we write L rather than (Σ_L, μ_L, L) for members of a family of fuzzy languages. And we also assume that each family of fuzzy languages, that we will use in this paper, is closed under isomorphism ("renaming of symbols"), i.e., for each family K we assume that for each fuzzy language L in K over some alphabet Σ_L and for each bijective non-fuzzy mapping $i : \Sigma_L \to \Sigma'_L$ —extended to words and to languages in the usual way— we have that the language $i(L)$ also belongs to K. Consequently, we have the equality $\mu(x; L) = \mu(i(x); i(L))$ for all x in Σ_L^*.

We will encounter a few simple, nontrivial families of fuzzy languages in the sequel: they are the family FIN_f of finite fuzzy languages

$$\mathrm{FIN}_f = \{(\Sigma_L, \mu_L, L) \mid \Sigma_L \subset \Sigma_\omega, \ L \text{ is finite}\} \ ,$$

the family ONE_f of singleton fuzzy languages

$$\mathrm{ONE}_f = \{(\Sigma_L, \mu_L, L) \mid \Sigma_L \subset \Sigma_\omega, \ L \text{ is a singleton}\} \ ,$$

the family ALPHA_f of fuzzy alphabets

$$\mathrm{ALPHA}_f = \{(\Sigma_L, \mu_L, L) \mid \Sigma_L \subset \Sigma_\omega, \ L = \Sigma_L\} \ ,$$

and the family SYMBOL_f of singleton fuzzy alphabets

$$\mathrm{SYMBOL}_f = \{(\Sigma_L, \mu_L, L) \mid \Sigma_L \subset \Sigma_\omega, \ L = \Sigma_L \ , \ L \text{ is a singleton }\} \ .$$

The crisp counterparts of these language families are denoted by FIN, ONE, ALPHA, and SYMBOL, respectively. Clearly, the equality $c(\mathrm{FIN}_f) = \mathrm{FIN}$ holds, as well as similar statements for the other families of languages.

Another important role will be played by the family REG_f of regular fuzzy languages, which is defined in a way very similar to its crisp counterpart REG.

Definition 3.2. Let Σ be an alphabet. The *regular fuzzy languages* over Σ are defined as follows:
(1) The fuzzy subsets $\oslash$, $\{\lambda\}$, and $\{\sigma\}$ (for each σ in Σ) of Σ^*, are regular fuzzy languages over Σ.
(2) If R_1 and R_2 are regular fuzzy languages over Σ, then so are $R_1 \cup R_2$, $R_1 R_2$, and R_1^*.
(3) A fuzzy subset R of Σ^* is regular fuzzy language over Σ if and only if R can be obtained from the basic elements in (1) by a finite number of applications of the operations in (2).

The family of regular fuzzy languages us denoted by REG_f.

In the remainder of this paper we frequently need the concept of fuzzy substitution. It is defined in a way very similar to the notion of substitution for crisp languages; cf. [5], [6].

Definition 3.3. Let K be a family of fuzzy languages and let V be an alphabet. A mapping $\tau : V \to K$ is called a *fuzzy K-substitution τ on V*; it is extended to words over V by $\tau(\lambda) = \{\lambda\}$ with $\mu(\lambda; \tau(\lambda)) = 1$, and $\tau(\alpha_1 \ldots \alpha_n) = \tau(\alpha_1) \ldots \tau(\alpha_n)$ where $\alpha_i \in V$ $(1 \le i \le n)$, and to languages L over V by $\tau(L) = \bigcup\{\tau(w) \mid w \in L\}$. If for each $\alpha \in V$, $\tau(\alpha) \subseteq V^*$, then $\tau : V \to K$ is called a *fuzzy K-substitution over V*. If K equals FIN_f or REG_f, τ is called a *fuzzy finite* or a *fuzzy regular substitution*, respectively.

Given families K and K' of fuzzy languages, let $\mathrm{Sûb}(K, K') = \{\tau(L) \mid L \in K;$ τ is a fuzzy K'-substitution$\}$. A family K is *closed* under fuzzy K'-substitution if $\mathrm{Sûb}(K, K') \subseteq K$, and K is *closed under fuzzy substitution*, if K is closed under fuzzy K-substitution.

When we take K and K' equal to families of crisp languages we obtain the well-known definition of (ordinary, non-fuzzy) substitution. Therefore a ONE-substitution is just a homomorphism and an isomorphism ("renaming of symbols") is a one-to-one SYMBOL-substitution. And a fuzzy ONE_f-substitution may be called a fuzzy homomorphism.

Definition 3.4. A *fuzzy prequasoid* K is a nontrivial family of fuzzy languages that is closed under fuzzy finite substitution (i.e., $\mathrm{Sûb}(K, \mathrm{FIN}_f) \subseteq K$) and under intersection with regular fuzzy languages. A *fuzzy quasoid* is a fuzzy prequasoid that contains an infinite fuzzy language.

It is a straightforward exercise to show that each fuzzy [pre]quasoid includes the smallest fuzzy [pre]quasoid REG_f [FIN_f, respectively], whereas FIN_f is the only fuzzy prequasoid that is not a fuzzy quasoid; cf. [6].

Let $\Pi_f(K)$ denote the smallest fuzzy prequasoid that includes the family K of fuzzy languages. Similarly, let $\Phi_f(K)$ [$\Delta_f(K)$, $\Theta_f(K)$, respectively] be the smallest family of fuzzy languages that includes K and is closed under fuzzy finite substitutions [intersection with regular fuzzy languages, fuzzy homomorphisms, respectively]. Then, obviously, for each family K of fuzzy languages, we have $\Pi_f(K) = \{\Phi_f, \Delta_f, \Theta_f\}^*(K)$ or even $\Pi_f(K) = \{\Phi_f, \Delta_f\}^*(K)$. But instead of this infinite set of strings over $\{\Phi_f, \Delta_f, \Theta_f\}$ a single string suffices; viz.

Proposition 3.5. [6] *For each family K of fuzzy languages*, $\Pi_f(K) = \Theta_f \Delta_f \Phi_f(K)$.

Definition 3.6. A *full Abstract Family of Fuzzy Languages* or *full AFFL* is a nontrivial family of fuzzy languages closed under union, concatenation, Kleene $\star$, (possibly erasing) fuzzy homomorphism, inverse fuzzy homomorphism, and intersection with fuzzy regular languages. A *full substitution-closed AFFL* is a full AFFL closed under fuzzy substitution.

In many situations the following characterization of full AFFL happens to be more useful than the original definition.

Proposition 3.7. [6] *A family K of fuzzy languages is a full AFFL if and only if K is a fuzzy prequasoid closed under fuzzy regular substitution (i.e., $\mathrm{Sûb}(K, \mathrm{REG}_f) \subseteq K$), and under substitution in the regular fuzzy languages (i.e., $\mathrm{Sûb}(\mathrm{REG}_f, K) \subseteq K$).*

Closely related to regular fuzzy languages is a kind of fuzzy finite automaton. The next definition and equivalence result is useful, and should not come as a surprise. A proof of this characterization can be found in [6].

Definition 3.8. A *nondeterministic fuzzy finite automaton* or *NFFA* is a 5-tuple $M = (Q, \Sigma, \delta, q_0, F)$ where Q is a finite fuzzy set of states, Σ is an alphabet, q_0 is an element of Q with $\mu(q_0; Q) > 0$, F is a crisp subset of the crisp set $\{q \mid \mu(q; Q) > 0\}$, and δ is a fuzzy function of type $\delta : Q \times (\Sigma \cup \{\lambda\}) \to \mathcal{P}_f(Q)$. Note that M may have λ-moves.

The fuzzy function δ is extended to $\delta' : Q \times \Sigma^* \to \mathcal{P}_f(Q)$ by $\delta'(q, \lambda) = \delta(q, \lambda)$ and $\delta'(q, \sigma\omega) = \bigcup \{\delta'(q', \omega) \mid q' \in \delta(q, \sigma)\}$ for all q in Q.

The language $L(M)$ accepted by an NFFA M is defined by $\mu(x; L(M)) = \bigvee \{\mu(q; \delta'(q_0, x))) \mid q \in F\}$.

Proposition 3.9. *A fuzzy language L is regular if and only if L is accepted by a nondeterministic fuzzy finite automaton.*

4. Controlled Fuzzy Iteration Grammars

The notion of fuzzy K-iteration grammar is a straightforward modification of the definition of (ordinary) K-iteration grammar: we just replace the ordinary K-substitutions by fuzzy K-substitutions; cf. [1].

Definition 4.1. Let K be a family of fuzzy languages. A *fuzzy K-iteration grammar* G is a four-tuple $G = (V, \Sigma, U, S)$ where
- V is an alphabet (the *alphabet* of G);
- Σ is an alphabet with $\Sigma \subseteq V$ (the *terminal alphabet* of G);
- S is a symbol in V (the *initial symbol* of G);
- U is a finite set of fuzzy K-substitutions over V.

The fuzzy language $L(G)$ generated by G is defined by

$$L(G) = U^*(S) \cap \Sigma^* = \bigcup \{\tau_p(\ldots(\tau_1(S))\ldots) \mid p \geq 0; \ \tau_i \in U, \ 1 \leq i \leq p\}.$$

The family of fuzzy languages generated by fuzzy K-iteration grammars is denoted by $H_f(K)$. For each $m \geq 1$, $H_{f,m}(K)$ is the family of fuzzy languages generated by fuzzy K-iteration grammars that contain at most m fuzzy K-substitutions in U.

Definition 4.2. Let Γ be a family of crisp languages and let K be a family of fuzzy languages. A Γ-*controlled fuzzy K-iteration grammar* or *fuzzy (Γ, K)-iteration grammar* is a pair (G, M) that consists of a fuzzy K-iteration grammar $G = (V, \Sigma, U, S)$ and a *control language* M, i.e., M is a crisp language over the alphabet U. The fuzzy language $L(G, M)$ generated by (G, M) is defined by

$$L(G, M) = M(S) \cap \Sigma^* = \bigcup \{\tau_p(\ldots(\tau_1(S))\ldots) \mid p \geq 0; \ \tau_i \in U, \ \tau_1 \ldots \tau_p \in M\}.$$

The family of fuzzy languages generated by fuzzy (Γ, K)-iteration grammars is denoted by $H_f(\Gamma, K)$. And $H_{f,m}(\Gamma, K)$ is the family of fuzzy languages generated by fuzzy (Γ, K)-iteration grammars that contain at most m fuzzy K-substitutions in U ($m \geq 1$).

Note that in Definitions 4.1 and 4.2 $L(G)$ and $L(G, M)$, respectively, are defined in terms of union, intersection, concatenation and iterated function application for fuzzy sets; cf. Section 2 for the precise definitions of these fundamental concepts.

Clearly, we have that $H_f(K) = \bigcup\{H_{f,m}(K) \mid m \geq 1\}$ and $H_f(\Gamma, K) = \bigcup\{H_{f,m}(\Gamma, K) \mid m \geq 1\}$ for each family K of fuzzy languages and each family Γ of crisp languages.

Example 4.3. Let $\mathcal{L}$ be the type-10 lattice of Example 2.2.(3).
(1) Consider the fuzzy FIN_f-iteration grammar $G = (V, \Sigma, U, S)$ defined by $\Sigma = \{a, b\}$, $V = \Sigma \cup \{S\}$, and $U = \{\tau_1, \tau_2\}$ where τ_1 is an ordinary or crisp FIN-substitution with $\tau_1(S) = \{SS\}$ and $\tau_1(\alpha) = \{\alpha\}$ ($\alpha \in \Sigma$), whereas τ_2 is a FIN_f-substitution with $\tau_2(S) = \{a, b\}$, $\tau_2(\alpha) = \{\alpha\}$, $\mu(b; \tau_2(S)) = 0.5$ and $\mu(a; \tau_2(S)) = \mu(\alpha; \tau_2(\alpha)) = 1$ ($\alpha \in \Sigma$).

Then $L(G)$ consists of all strings w with length 2^n for some $n \geq 0$ and $\mu(w; L(G)) = 2^{-\#_b(w)}$; $\#_\sigma(x)$ denotes the number of times that the symbol σ occurs in the word x. Clearly, $c(L(G)) = \{a^{2^n} \mid n \geq 0\}$ which is the set of strings that are obtained without making any "developmental error"; cf. the discussion in Section 1. A developmental error occurs when S changes into a b rather than into an a; the quality of the string reduces to 50% of its previous value by each such erroneous replacement.

(2) Define the REG-controlled fuzzy FIN_f-iteration grammar or (REG, FIN_f)-iteration grammar (G, M) where G is as in (1) and $M = \{\tau_1^{2k+1}\tau_2 \mid k \geq 0\}$. Now $L(G, M)$ equals the set of all strings w with length 2^n for some odd $n \geq 1$ and still we have $\mu(w; L(G, M)) = 2^{-\#_b(w)}$. Remark that $c(L(G, M)) = \{a^{2^n} \mid n \geq 0, \ n \text{ is odd } \}$.

(3) We modify (G, M) of (2) to a REG-controlled fuzzy REG_f-iteration grammar or (REG, REG_f)-iteration grammar (G_1, M) by redefining $\tau_2(S)$ to a REG_f-substitution with $\tau_2(S) = \{a\} \cup \{b^k \mid k \geq 1\}$, $\tau_2(\alpha) = \{\alpha\}$ for each α in Σ, $\mu(b^k; \tau_2(S)) = 2^{-k}$ for each $k \geq 1$ and $\mu(a; \tau_2(S)) = \mu(\alpha; \tau_2(\alpha)) = 1$ $(\alpha \in \Sigma)$. Then for all strings x over $\{a, b\}$, we have $\mu(x; L(G_1, M)) \geq \mu(x; L(G, M))$, $L(G, M)$ is a proper subset of $L(G_1, M)$, but $c(L(G_1, M)) = c(L(G, M))$.

Since in Example 4.3 K equals FIN_f in both (1) and (2), G may be called a fuzzy ETOL-system and (G, M) a regularly controlled fuzzy ETOL-system.

Example 4.4. By taking concrete values for the parameter K we obtain fuzzy analogues for some families of (ordinary or crisp) Lindenmayer languages; viz.

$$H_f(ONE_f) = EDTOL_f, \qquad H_{f,1}(ONE_f) = EDOL_f,$$
$$H_f(FIN_f) = ETOL_f, \qquad H_{f,1}(FIN_f) = EOL_f.$$

Readers unfamiliar with L-systems are referred to [21] for the meaning of these abbreviations.

5. Elementary Properties

In this section we establish some basic properties of Γ-controlled fuzzy K-iteration grammars and their languages that already hold under very mild restrictions on the parameters Γ and K. These results turn out to be very useful in proving more complicated and more interesting propositions to which the following two sections are devoted.

First we show that regular control does not extend the generating power of fuzzy K-iteration grammars; cf. Theorem 2.1 in [1].

Theorem 5.1. *For each family K of fuzzy languages, $H_f(REG, K) = H_f(K)$ provided $K \supseteq ONE$.*

Proof. Since $U^\star$ is regular for each alphabet U, the inclusion $H_f(REG, K) \supseteq H_f(K)$ is obvious.

Conversely, let $(G, M) = (V, \Sigma, U, S, M)$ be an arbitrary fuzzy (REG, K)-iteration grammar where M is accepted by a complete deterministic finite automaton (Q, U, δ, q_0, Q_F) with finite set of states Q, input alphabet U, transition function $\delta : Q \times U \to Q$, initial state q_0, and set of final states Q_F.

We define a new initial symbol S_0, a set of new nonterminal symbols $N_\Sigma = \{A_a \mid a \in \Sigma\}$, and a new alphabet $V_0 = Q \cup V \cup \{S_0, F\} \cup N_\Sigma$. Define an isomorphism $\psi : V \to (V - \Sigma) \cup N_\Sigma$ by $\psi(a) = A_a$ $(a \in \Sigma)$ and $\psi(A) = A$ $(A \in V - \Sigma)$. The isomorphism ψ is extended to words and to languages in the usual way. Remember that we assumed that each family of (fuzzy) languages is closed under isomorphism.

Define the fuzzy K-iteration grammar $G_0 = (V_0, \Sigma, U_0, S_0)$ with $U_0 = \{\tau' \mid \tau \in U\} \cup \{\tau_0\}$. So for each fuzzy K-substitution τ in U there is corresponding fuzzy K-substitution τ' in U_0, defined by

$$\tau'(S_0) = \{q_0 S\}, \qquad \mu(q_0 S; \tau'(S_0)) = 1,$$

$\tau'(\alpha) = \psi(\tau(\alpha)),$ for each α in $V - \Sigma$,

$\tau(A_a) = \psi(\tau(a)),$ for each A_a in N_Σ $(a$ in $\Sigma)$,

$\tau'(q) = \{q'\}, \qquad \mu(q'; \tau'(q)) = 1,$ iff $\delta(q, \tau) = q'$ $(q$ in $Q)$,

$\tau'(\alpha) = \{F\}, \qquad \mu(F; \tau'(\alpha)) = 1,$ for each α in $\Sigma \cup \{F\}$.

The additional fuzzy K-substitution τ_0 is defined as follows.

$\tau_0(q) = \{\lambda\}, \qquad \mu(\lambda; \tau_0(q)) = 1,$ for each q in Q_F,

$\tau_0(q) = \{F\}, \qquad \mu(F; \tau_0(q)) = 1,$ for each q in $Q - Q_F$,

$\tau_0(A_a) = \{a\}, \qquad \mu(a; \tau_0(A_a)) = 1,$ for each A_a in N_Σ $(a$ in $\Sigma)$,

$\tau_0(\alpha) = \{F\}, \qquad \mu(F; \tau_0(\alpha)) = 1,$ for each α in $V \cup \{S_0, F\}$.

This construction implies that for each string x in Σ^*, we have $\mu(x; L(G_0)) = \mu(x; L(G, M))$, and hence $H_f(\text{REG}, K) \subseteq H_f(K)$. $\square$

There exists a sort of reverse of Theorem 5.1 in the sense that all "productive" sequences of substitutions in a fuzzy K-iteration grammar G —i.e., those sequences that yield at least one terminal string x with $\mu(x; L(G)) > 0$— form a regular language over U; cf. Definition 5.2, Theorem 5.3 and [24].

Definition 5.2. Let $G = (V, \Sigma, U, S)$ be a fuzzy K-iteration grammar. Then the *Szilard language* of G —denoted by $Sz(G)$— is

$$Sz(G) = \{\omega \in U^* \mid \exists x \in \Sigma^* : \mu(x; \omega(S)) > 0\}.$$

The following theorem is the straightforward fuzzy counterpart of one of the main results in [24].

Theorem 5.3. *If G is a fuzzy K-iteration grammar, then its Szilard language $Sz(G)$ is a regular language.*

Proof. Let $G = (V, \Sigma, U, S)$ be a fuzzy K-iteration grammar. For each word x, we denote the set of all symbols that occur in x by $\Diamond(x)$; formally, $\Diamond(x) = \bigcap \{\Sigma \mid \Sigma \subseteq \Sigma_\omega, \ x \in \Sigma^*\}$.

Consider the right-linear grammar $G_0 = (V_0, U, P_0, S_0)$ where $V_0 - U = \{X \mid X \subseteq V\}$, $S_0 = \{S\}$, and P_0 is defined by

$$P_0 = \{X \to \tau Y \mid \exists x, y \in V^* : \ \Diamond(x) = X, \ \Diamond(y) = Y, \ \mu(y; \tau(x)) > 0\} \cup$$

$$\cup \{X \to \lambda \mid X \subseteq \Sigma\}.$$

Clearly, $L(G_0)$ is regular, and it is a routine matter to verify that $S_0 \Rightarrow^*_{G_0} \omega$ with $\omega \in U^*$ if and only if $\exists x \in \Sigma^* : \mu(x; \omega(S)) > 0$. $\square$

Next we show that the number of fuzzy K-substitutions in a Γ-controlled K-iteration grammar can be reduced to two in case the parameters Γ and K satisfy some very simple conditions as in the corresponding crisp case; cf. [1].

Theorem 5.4. *Let Γ be a family of crisp languages closed under λ-free homomorphism, and let K be a family of fuzzy languages with $K \supseteq \text{SYMBOL}$. Then $H_{f,2}(\Gamma, K) = H_{f,m}(\Gamma, K) = H_f(\Gamma, K)$ for each $m \geq 2$.*

Proof. Of course, $H_{f,2}(\Gamma, K) \subseteq H_{f,m}(\Gamma, K) \subseteq H_f(\Gamma, K)$ holds for each $m \geq 2$. So it remains to prove that $H_f(\Gamma, K) \subseteq H_{f,2}(\Gamma, K)$.

Let $(G, M) = (V, \Sigma, U, S, M)$ be a fuzzy (Γ, K)-iteration grammar with m $(m \geq 3)$ fuzzy K-substitutions in U —say, $U = \{\tau_1, \ldots, \tau_m\}$— and let for each i $(1 \leq i \leq m)$ ψ_i be the isomorphism defined by $\psi_i(\alpha) = \alpha_i$ (α in V; each α_i is a new, unique symbol).

Construct the fuzzy (Γ, K)-iteration grammar $(G_0, M_0) = (V_0, \Sigma, U_0, S, M_0)$ with

- $V_0 = V \cup \{F\} \cup \{\psi_i(\alpha) \mid \alpha \in V, 1 \leq i \leq m\}$,
- $U_0 = \{\sigma_1, \sigma_2\}$ where the fuzzy K-substitutions σ_1 and σ_2 are defined respectively by

$$
\begin{array}{lll}
\sigma_1(\alpha) = \{\alpha_1\}, & \mu(\alpha_1; \sigma_1(\alpha)) = 1, & \alpha \text{ in } V, \\
\sigma_1(\alpha_i) = \{\alpha_{i+1}\}, & \mu(\alpha_{i+1}; \sigma_1(\alpha_i)) = 1, & \alpha \text{ in } V \text{ and } 1 \leq i < m, \\
\sigma_1(\beta) = \{F\}, & \mu(F; \sigma_1(\beta)) = 1, & \beta \text{ in } \{F\} \cup \{\psi_m(\alpha) \mid \alpha \in V\}, \\
\sigma_2(\alpha_i) = \tau_i(\alpha), & & \alpha \text{ in } V \text{ and } 1 \leq i \leq m, \\
\sigma_2(\beta) = \{F\}, & \mu(F; \sigma_2(\beta)) = 1, & \beta \text{ in } V \cup \{F\}.
\end{array}
$$

- $M_0 = h(M)$ where the homomorphism $h : U^\star \to U_0^\star$ is defined by $h(\tau_i) = \sigma_1^i \sigma_2$ $(1 \leq i \leq m)$.

An application of τ_i of (G, M) is simulated by i times applying σ_1 (by which each α is changed into α_i) and a single application of σ_2 which carries out the actual simulation of τ_i and removes all subscripts from the symbols.

It is left to the reader to show that $\mu(x; L(G_0, M_0)) = \mu(x; L(G, M))$ for each x over Σ. Hence $H_f(\Gamma, K) \subseteq H_{f,2}(\Gamma, K)$. $\qquad\square$

Obviously, we can combine Theorems 5.1 and 5.4 to establish a similar result for the uncontrolled case. However, we can achieve this under weaker assumptions on K by slightly modifying the proof of Theorem 5.4.

Corollary 5.5. *If K is a family of fuzzy languages with $K \supseteq$ SYMBOL, then $H_{f,2}(K) = H_{f,m}(K) = H_f(K)$ for each $m \geq 2$.*

Proof. Take M and M_0 in the proof of Theorem 5.4 equal to $M = U^\star$ and $M_0 = U_0^\star = \{\sigma_1, \sigma_2\}^\star$, respectively. Then for each x in $\Sigma^\star$, $\mu(x; L(G_0)) = \mu(x; L(G))$ holds and, consequently, $H_f(K) \subseteq H_{f,m}(K) \subseteq H_{f,2}(K)$. The converse inclusions are trivial. $\qquad\square$

We conclude this section with a few useful inclusion properties for which we need some additional terminology.

Definition 5.6. A family Γ of crisp languages is closed under *left marking* [*right marking*] if for each language L in Γ with $L \subseteq \Sigma^\star$ for some Σ, and for each symbol c not in Σ, the language $\{c\}L$ [$L\{c\}$, respectively] belongs to Γ. And Γ is closed under *full marking* if Γ is closed under both left and right marking. Frequently, we write cL and Lc rather than $\{c\}L$ and $L\{c\}$, respectively.

Proposition 5.7. *(1) Let Γ be a family of crisp languages closed under right marking, and let K be a family of fuzzy languages with $K \supseteq$ ONE. Then the inclusions $\Gamma \subseteq H_f(\Gamma, K)$ and $K \subseteq H_f(\Gamma, K)$ hold.*
(2) Let Γ be a family of crisp languages closed under (i) left or right marking, (ii) union or concatenation, and (iii) Kleene star. If K is a family of fuzzy languages with $K \supseteq$ SYMBOL, then $H_f(K) \subseteq H_f(\Gamma, K)$.

Proof. (1) Consider an arbitrary crisp language L_0 over U_0 in the family Γ. Define the fuzzy (Γ, K)-iteration grammar $(G, M) = (V, U_0, U, S, M)$ with $U = U_0 \cup \{\sigma\}$, $M = L_0\sigma$, and U consists of fuzzy K-substitutions defined by

$$\tau(S) = \{\tau S\}, \qquad \tau \in U_0,$$
$$\tau(\alpha) = \{\alpha\}, \qquad \alpha \in U_0, \tau \in U_0,$$
$$\sigma(S) = \{\lambda\},$$
$$\sigma(\alpha) = \{\alpha\}, \qquad \alpha \in U_0.$$

All degrees of membership are equal to 1 (or to 0 in all other, unmentioned cases). So (G, M) is actually a crisp (Γ, K)-iteration grammar with $L(G, M) = L_0$. Consequently, we have $\Gamma \subseteq H_f(\Gamma, K)$.

Similarly, let L_0 be a fuzzy language over Σ and let M_0 be an arbitrary nonempty crisp language over U_0. We define the fuzzy (Γ, K)-iteration grammar $(G, M) = (V, \Sigma, U, S, M)$ where $V = \Sigma \cup \{S\}$, $U = U_0 \cup \{\sigma\}$ $(\sigma \notin U_0)$, $M = M_0 \sigma$, and the fuzzy K-substitutions are defined by

$$\tau(\alpha) = \{\alpha\}, \qquad \mu(\alpha; \tau(\alpha)) = 1, \qquad \alpha \in V, \tau \in U,$$
$$\sigma(S) = L_0, \qquad \mu(x; \sigma(S)) = \mu(x; L_0), \qquad \text{for all } x \text{ over } \Sigma,$$
$$\sigma(\alpha) = \{\alpha\}, \qquad \mu(\alpha; \sigma(\alpha)) = 1, \qquad \alpha \in \Sigma.$$

Then $\mu(x; L(G, M)) = \mu(x; L_0)$ for all x over Σ, and thus $K \subseteq H_f(\Gamma, K)$.

(2) Let $G = (V, \Sigma, U, S)$ be an arbitrary fuzzy K-iteration grammar with $U = \{\tau_1, \ldots, \tau_n\}$ and let M_0 be a nonempty crisp language over U_0 from Γ such that $U \cap U_0 = \varnothing$. If the family Γ is closed under union [concatenation], then the crisp language $M = (M_0\tau_1 \cup M_0\tau_2 \cup \ldots \cup M_0\tau_n)^*$ [or $M = ((M_0\tau_1)^*(M_0\tau_2)^* \ldots (M_0\tau_n)^*)^*$, respectively] is also in Γ.

Finally, we define the fuzzy (Γ, K)-iteration grammar (G_1, M) by $(G_1, M) = (V, \Sigma, U_1, S, M)$ with $U_1 = U \cup U_0$ and for each τ in U_0 and for each α in V, $\tau(\alpha) = \{\alpha\}$ with $\mu(\alpha; \tau(\alpha)) = 1$. Then $\mu(x; L(G_1, M)) = \mu(x; L(G))$ for each x over Σ and, consequently, $H_f(K) \subseteq H_f(\Gamma, K)$. $\qquad \square$

6. The Main Results

In Section 1 we argued that in order to model developmental errors we should allow a countable rather than a finite number of productions in each table (or substitution). This resulted in the notion of Γ-controlled fuzzy K-iteration grammar and the corresponding language family $H_f(\Gamma, K)$.

In this section we address the question to which extend we can enlarge the family K of fuzzy languages and still remain within the family $H_f(\Gamma, K)$. The answer (Theorem 6.1 and Corollaries 6.2, 6.3 and 6.4)) is rather surprising and implies that both families $H_f(\Gamma, K)$ and $H_f(K)$ possess very strong closure properties; this latter subject will be discussed in Section 7.

For families Γ_1 and Γ_2 of crisp languages, $\text{Sûb}(\Gamma_1, \Gamma_2)$ denotes the family of crisp languages that results from substituting Γ_2-languages into Γ_1-languages, i.e., $\text{Sûb}(\Gamma_1, \Gamma_2) = \{\tau(L) \mid L \in \Gamma_1, \tau \text{ is a } \Gamma_2\text{-substitution}\}$. A family Γ is closed under substitution if $\text{Sûb}(\Gamma, \Gamma) \subseteq \Gamma$. Of course, these concepts are well-known special instances of Definition 3.3.

Theorem 6.1. Let Γ_1 and Γ_2 be families of crisp languages and let Γ_2 be closed under full marking, union or concatenation, and Kleene $\star$. If K is a family of fuzzy languages with $K \supseteq \text{ALPHA}$, then $H_f(\Gamma_1, H_f(\Gamma_2, K)) \subseteq H_f(\text{Sûb}(\Gamma_1, \Gamma_2), K)$.

Proof. Consider an arbitrary Γ_1-controlled fuzzy $H_f(\Gamma_2, K)$-iteration grammar $(G, M) = (V, \Sigma, U, S, M)$, where each τ in U is a fuzzy $H_f(\Gamma_2, K)$-substitution over V. For each such fuzzy $H_f(\Gamma_2, K)$-substitution τ in U and each symbol α in V, we assume that $\mu(x; \tau(\alpha)) = \mu(x; L(G_{\tau\alpha}, M_{\tau\alpha}))$ holds for each x over V. Here $(G_{\tau\alpha}, M_{\tau\alpha}) = (V_{\tau\alpha}, V, U_{\tau\alpha}, S_{\tau\alpha}, M_{\tau\alpha})$ ($\tau \in U$ and $\alpha \in V$) are fuzzy (Γ_2, K)-iteration grammars that have mutually disjoint nonterminal alphabets $V_{\tau\alpha} - V$ as well as mutually disjoint sets of fuzzy K-substitution names $U_{\tau\alpha}$.

We also assume that the fuzzy (Γ_2, K)-iteration grammars $(G_{\tau\alpha}, M_{\tau\alpha})$ meet the following conditions: (i) for each a in V and each σ in $U_{\tau\alpha}$: $\sigma(a) = \{a\}$ with $\mu(a; \sigma(a)) = 1$, and (ii) if an intermediate string ω in a derivation due to $(G_{\tau\alpha}, M_{\tau\alpha})$ contains a symbol of V, then for each σ in $U_{\tau\alpha}$: $\sigma(\omega) = \{\omega\}$, while for all u over $U_{\tau\alpha}$ and each w over $V_{\tau\alpha}$, we have $\mu(\omega; \sigma u(w)) = \mu(\omega; u(w))$. Otherwise, we introduce for each a in V a new nonterminal symbol A_a and we replace each occurrence of a in $(G_{\tau\alpha}, M_{\tau\alpha})$ by A_a. Each fuzzy substitution is extended with $\sigma(\beta) = \{\beta\}$, $\mu(\beta; \sigma(\beta)) = 1$ with $\beta \in V \cup \{F_0\}$, where F_0 is a new rejection symbol. Finally, we add a new fuzzy substitution φ defined by

$$\begin{aligned}
\varphi(A_a) &= \{a\}, & \mu(a; \varphi(A_a)) &= 1, & &\text{for each } a \text{ in } V, \\
\varphi(a) &= \{a\}, & \mu(a; \varphi(a)) &= 1, & &\text{for each } a \text{ in } V \cup \{F_0\}, \\
\varphi(\beta) &= \{F_0\}, & \mu(F_0; \varphi(\beta)) &= 1, & &\text{for each } \beta \text{ in } V_{\tau\alpha} - V,
\end{aligned}$$

and we replace the control language $M_{\tau\alpha}$ by $M_{\tau\alpha}\varphi$.

In order to show that the fuzzy language $L(G, M)$ belongs to the family $H_f(\text{Sûb}(\Gamma_1, \Gamma_2), K)$, we construct a fuzzy $(\text{Sûb}(\Gamma_1, \Gamma_2), K)$-iteration grammar $(G_0, M_0) = (V_0, \Sigma, U_0, S, M_0)$ such that $\mu(x; L(G_0, M_0)) = \mu(x; L(G, M))$ holds for each x in Σ^*. The definition of (G_0, M_0) is as follows.

- $V_0 = \bigcup_{\tau,\alpha}(V_{\tau\alpha} \cup \{S'_{\tau\alpha}\}) \cup \{F\}$ where F is a rejection symbol and each $S'_{\tau\alpha}$ is a new nonterminal symbol associated with $S_{\tau\alpha}$. Remark that $S \in V$, and since $V \subseteq V_{\tau\alpha} \subseteq V_0$, we have $S \in V_0$.
- $U_0 = \{\sigma_0\} \cup \{\sigma_\tau \mid \tau \in U\} \cup \{\sigma'_{\tau\alpha k} \mid \sigma_{\tau\alpha k} \in U_{\tau\alpha}\}$.
- The fuzzy K-substitutions in U_0 are defined in the following way:

(a) For the initial fuzzy K-substitution σ_0 we have with degree of membership equal to 1 in all the following instances:

$$\begin{aligned}
\sigma_0(\alpha) &= \{S'_{\tau\alpha} \mid \tau \in U\}, & \alpha &\in V, \\
\sigma_0(\alpha) &= \{F\}, & \alpha &\notin V.
\end{aligned}$$

(b) For each τ in U the fuzzy K-substitution σ_τ is defined by

$$\begin{aligned}
\sigma_\tau(S'_{\tau\alpha}) &= \{S'_{\tau\alpha}, S_{\tau\alpha}\}, & \alpha &\in V, \\
\sigma_\tau(\alpha) &= \{\alpha\}, & \alpha &\in V, \\
\sigma_\tau(\alpha) &= \{F\}, & \alpha &\notin V \cup \{S'_{\tau\alpha}\},
\end{aligned}$$

where all degrees of membership are again equal to 1.

(c) For each fuzzy K-substitution $\sigma_{\tau\alpha k}$ from $U_{\tau\alpha}$ we define a corresponding fuzzy K-substitution $\sigma'_{\tau\alpha k}$ by

$$\begin{aligned}
\sigma'_{\tau\alpha k}(\beta) &= \sigma_{\tau\alpha k}(\beta), & & & \beta &\in V_{\tau\alpha}, \\
\sigma'_{\tau\alpha k}(S'_{\tau\beta}) &= \{S'_{\tau\beta}\}, & \mu(S'_{\tau\beta}; \sigma'_{\tau\alpha k}(S'_{\tau\beta})) &= 1, & \beta &\in V, \\
\sigma'_{\tau\alpha k}(\beta) &= \{F\}, & \mu(F; \sigma_{\tau\alpha k}(\beta)) &= 1, & &\text{otherwise.}
\end{aligned}$$

• The control language M_0 is defined by $M_0 = \gamma(M)$ where γ is the Γ_2-substitution defined by

$$\gamma(\tau) = M_\tau, \qquad \tau \in U,$$

where the languages M_τ with $\tau \in U$ satisfy —assuming $V = \{\alpha_1, \ldots, \alpha_n\}$—

$$M_\tau = \sigma_0(\sigma_\tau M_{\tau\alpha_1} \cup \ldots \cup \sigma_\tau M_{\tau\alpha_n})^*, \qquad \text{if } \Gamma_2 \text{ is closed under union, and}$$
$$M_\tau = \sigma_0(\sigma_\tau M_{\tau\alpha_1} \ldots \sigma_\tau M_{\tau\alpha_n})^*, \qquad \text{if } \Gamma_2 \text{ is closed under concatenation.}$$

Clearly, each language M_τ ($\tau \in U$) belongs to the family Γ_2.

Each step in any derivation according to the Γ_1-controlled fuzzy (Γ_2, K)-iteration grammar (G, M) is simulated by a finite number of derivational steps of the fuzzy $(\text{Sûb}(\Gamma_1, \Gamma_2), K)$-iteration grammar (G_0, M_0) in the following way.

For each intermediate string in a derivation of (G, M) there is an identical string over V in the simulation by (G_0, M_0). However, going from such a string to the next one over V —i.e., the actual simulation of the application of a fuzzy (Γ_2, K)-substitution τ from U in a (G, M)-derivation— takes a finite number of steps controlled by the language M_τ. So the simulation of a single step according to τ by M_τ proceeds as follows. First, all symbols α from V are converted into $S'_{\tau\alpha}$ by a single application of σ_0. Next an application of σ_τ checks whether all first indices of these primed initial symbols are indeed equal to τ, otherwise at least one occurrence of the rejection symbol F is introduced. Simultaneously, some of the occurrences of the primed initial symbols $S'_{\tau\alpha}$ may be changed into their unprimed counterparts $S_{\tau\alpha}$. And symbols from $\bigcup_{\rho,\beta} V_{\rho\beta} - V$ are rewritten into the rejection symbol F. Obviously, the unprimed symbols $S_{\tau\alpha}$ start an actual derivation according to $(G_{\tau\alpha}, M_{\tau\alpha})$, i.e., according to the fuzzy K-substitutions $\sigma'_{\tau\alpha k}$ due to the control language $M_{\tau\alpha}$. Clearly, the definitions of M_τ and of σ_τ allow different occurrences of $S_{\tau\alpha}$ be rewritten under different control words from $M_{\tau\alpha}$. Finally, after the simulation of a τ-step only occurrences of symbols from V will survive the simulation of a subsequent τ'-step and contribute to the derivation of a possible terminal substring in the end.

By a long, straightforward correctness proof —which we leave to the interested reader— one can establish that for each string x over Σ, we have $\mu(x; L(G_0, M_0)) = \mu(x; L(G, M))$, and, consequently, we have established the inclusion $H_f(\Gamma_1, H_f(\Gamma_2, K)) \subseteq H_f(\text{Sûb}(\Gamma_1, \Gamma_2), K)$. □

Corollary 6.2. *(1) Let Γ be a family of crisp languages closed under full marking and under substitution that satisfies $\Gamma \supseteq \text{REG}$. If K is a family of fuzzy languages with $K \supseteq \text{ALPHA} \cup \text{ONE}$, then $H_f(\Gamma, H_f(\Gamma, K)) = H_f(\Gamma, K)$.*
(2) Let Γ be a family of crisp languages that is closed under full marking, union, concatenation, and Kleene $\star$. If K is a family of fuzzy languages with $K \supseteq \text{ALPHA} \cup \text{ONE}$, then $H_f(H_f(\Gamma, K)) = H_f(\Gamma, K)$.

Proof. (1) follows from Theorem 6.1 in which we take $\Gamma_1 = \Gamma_2 = \Gamma$, Proposition 5.7.(1), and the fact that a family of crisp languages is closed under union, concatenation, and Kleene $\star$ if and only if it is closed under substitution into the regular languages (Proposition 3.3.1 in [9]).

(2) is implied by (i) Theorem 6.1 (where we take Γ_1 and Γ_2 equal to REG and Γ, respectively), (ii) Theorem 5.1, (iii) Proposition 3.3.1 in [9] (as in the proof of

6.2.(1)), and finally (iv) the inclusion $H_f(\Gamma, K) \subseteq H_f(H_f(\Gamma, K))$ due to Proposition 5.7(1). □

Corollary 6.3. *If K is a family of fuzzy languages with $K \supseteq$ ALPHA $\cup$ ONE, then $H_f(H_f(K)) = H_f(K)$.*

Proof. If we take Γ equal to REG, then the result follows from Theorem 5.1 and Corollary 6.2.(2) immediately. □

Corollary 6.4. $\text{ETOL}_f = H_f(\text{ETOL}_f) = H_f(H_f(\text{FIN}_f)) = H_f(\text{FIN}_f)$.

Proof. Example 4.4 and Corollary 6.3 with K equal to FIN_f. □

This latter corollary shows that, in order to stay within the framework of ETOL_f-languages (i.e., $H_f(\text{FIN}_f)$-languages; cf. Example 4.4.), we have to restrict the infinite fuzzy sets $\tau(\alpha)$ consisting of developmental rules together with developmental errors to ETOL_f-languages as $H_f(\text{ETOL}_f) \subseteq \text{ETOL}_f$; cf. the discussion in Section 1. Of course, a similar remark applies in the more general case (Corollary 6.3) but the extension from finite sets to countably infinite fuzzy sets is a more striking phenomenon.

7. Closure Properties

We already remarked that Theorem 6.1 and its corollaries imply that the families $H_f(\Gamma, K)$ and $H_f(K)$ of fuzzy languages possess very strong closure properties under minor assumptions and the families Γ and K. In this section we first consider some simple closure properties (Lemmas 7.1 and 7.2) before we consider the more important ones (Theorem 7.5) due to our results from Section 6.

Lemma 7.1. *Let K be a family of fuzzy languages with $K \supseteq \text{FIN}_f$, and let Γ be a family of crisp languages closed under right marking. Then the families of fuzzy languages $H_f(K)$ and $H_f(\Gamma, K)$ are closed under fuzzy finite substitution.*

Proof. Let $G = (V, \Sigma, U, S)$ be a fuzzy K-iteration grammar and let $\sigma : \Sigma \to \Delta^*$ be a fuzzy finite substitution. Without loss of generality we assume that the alphabets Σ and Δ are disjoint.

Consider the fuzzy K-iteration grammar $G_0 = (V_0, \Delta, U_0, S)$ where $V_0 = V \cup \Delta \cup \{F\}$, $U_0 = \{\tau' \mid \tau \in U\} \cup \{\sigma'\}$ with

$$\begin{array}{lll} \sigma'(\alpha) = \sigma(\alpha), & & \alpha \in \Sigma, \\ \sigma'(\alpha) = \{F\}, & \mu(F; \sigma'(\alpha)) = 1, & \alpha \notin \Sigma, \end{array}$$

and for each τ in U we define

$$\begin{array}{lll} \tau'(\alpha) = \tau(\alpha), & & \alpha \in V, \\ \tau'(\alpha) = \{F\}, & \mu(F; \tau'(\alpha)) = 1, & \alpha \in \Delta \cup \{F\}. \end{array}$$

Then for each string x over Δ, we have $\mu(x; \sigma(L(G))) = \mu(x; L(G_0))$.

In the Γ-controlled case we depart from (G, M) and we construct (G_0, M_0) with G_0 as above and $M_0 = \varphi(M)\{\sigma'\}$ where φ is the isomorphism that maps each τ on τ'. □

Lemma 7.2. *Let K be a fuzzy prequasoid, and let Γ be a family of crisp languages closed under full marking. Then the familes of fuzzy languages $H_f(K)$ and $H_f(\Gamma, K)$ are closed under intersection with regular fuzzy languages.*

Proof. Let $G = (V, \Sigma, U, S)$ be a fuzzy K-iteration grammar, and let R be a regular fuzzy language accepted by a nondeterministic fuzzy finite automaton $(Q, \Sigma, \delta, q_0, F)$; cf. Proposition 3.9.

Consider the fuzzy K-iteration grammar $G_0 = (V_0, \Sigma, U_0, S_0)$ where $V_0 = \Sigma \cup \{S_0, F\} \cup \{[q, \alpha, q'] \mid q, q' \in Q, \ \alpha \in V\}$, $U_0 = \{\sigma_0, \sigma_1\} \cup \{\tau' \mid \tau \in U\}$, with

$$\sigma_0(S_0) = \{[q_0, S, q] \mid q \in F\}, \qquad q \in F,$$
$$\sigma_0(\alpha) = \{\alpha\}, \qquad \alpha \in V_0 - \{S_0\},$$
$$\sigma_1(\alpha) = \{\alpha\}, \qquad \alpha \in \Delta \cup \{S_0, F\};$$

the degrees of membership are equal to 1 for all these instances. But for

$$\sigma_1([q, \alpha, q']) = \{\alpha \mid q' \in \delta(q, \alpha)\} \cup \{F\}, \qquad \alpha \in V, \ q, q' \in Q,$$

we have $\mu(\alpha; \sigma_1([q, \alpha, q'])) = \mu(q'; \delta(q, \alpha))$ and $\mu(F; \sigma_1([q, \alpha, q'])) = 1$.

For each τ in U, we define the fuzzy substitution τ' over V_0 by

$$\tau'([q, \alpha, q']) = \{[q, \alpha_1, q_1][q_1, \alpha_2, q_2] \ldots [q_{n-1}, \alpha_n, q'] \mid q_1, \ldots, q_{n-1} \in Q;$$
$$\alpha_1 \alpha_2 \ldots \alpha_n \in \tau(\alpha), \ n \geq 1\} \cup E((\tau, \alpha, q, q'), \qquad \alpha \in V, \ q, q' \in Q,$$

with $E((\tau, \alpha, q, q') = \textbf{if } \lambda \in \tau(\alpha)$ and $q = q'$ **then** $\{\lambda\}$ **else** $\{F\}$. For the degrees of membership we have

$$\mu([q, \alpha_1, q_1] \ldots [q_{n-1}, \alpha_n, q']; \tau'([q, \alpha, q'])) = \mu(\alpha_1 \ldots \alpha_n; \tau(\alpha)), \quad n \geq 1,$$
$$\mu(\lambda; \tau'([q, \alpha, q'])) = \textbf{if } \lambda \in \tau(\alpha) \text{ and } q = q' \textbf{ then } \mu(\lambda; \tau(\alpha)) \textbf{ else } 0,$$
$$\mu(F; \tau'([q, \alpha, q'])) = 1.$$

Since K is a fuzzy prequasoid, it easy to show that each τ' is a fuzzy K-substitution over V_0. The proof that for each string x over Σ, $\mu(x; L(G_0)) = \mu(x; L(G) \cap R)$ holds is also left to the reader.

When G is provided with a crisp control language M from the family Γ, we construct (G_0, M_0) with $M_0 = \{\sigma_0\}\varphi(M)\{\sigma_1\}$, where φ is as in the proof of Lemma 7.1. $\qquad\square$

We now turn to more complicated closure properties for fuzzy languages.

Definition 7.3. A family K of fuzzy languages is closed under *iterated fuzzy substitution* if for each fuzzy language L in K over some alphabet V ($L \subseteq V^*$), and each finite set U of fuzzy K-substitutions over V, the language $U^*(L)$ defined by

$$U^*(L) = \bigcup \{\tau_p(\ldots(\tau_1(L))\ldots) \mid p \geq 0; \ \tau_i \in U, \ 1 \leq i \leq p\}$$

belongs to K.

A *hyper-algebraically closed full Abstract Family of Fuzzy Languages*, or *full hyper-AFFL* for short, is a full AFFL closed under nested iterated fuzzy substitution.

For a fuzzy prequasoid closure under iterated fuzzy substitution implies closure under many of the operations related to the notion of full AFFL; using Proposition 3.7, Definitions 7.3 and 3.6 it is straightforward to establish the following characterization.

Proposition 7.4. *A family K of fuzzy languages is a full hyper-AFFL if and only if K is a fuzzy prequasoid and $H_f(K) = K$.*

Each full hyper-AFFL is a full super-AFFL (i.e., a full AFFL closed under iterated nested fuzzy substitution; a substitution τ is *nested* if $\alpha \in \tau(\alpha)$ holds for each symbol α.), and each full super AFFL is in its turn a full substitution-closed AFFL [5], but none of the converse implications holds.

Now we are ready for the main results of this section.

Theorem 7.5. *If K is a fuzzy prequasoid and if Γ is a family of crisp languages closed under full marking, union, concatenation, and Kleene $\star$, then the family of fuzzy languages $H_f(\Gamma, K)$ is a full hyper-AFFL.*

Proof. By Lemmas 7.1 and 7.2 we obtain the fact that $H_f(\Gamma, K)$ is a fuzzy prequasoid. Then by Proposition 7.4 and Corollary 6.2.(2) the result follows. □

Theorem 7.6. *(1) If K is a fuzzy prequasoid, then $H_f(K)$ is a full hyper-AFFL.*
(2) For each arbitrary family K of fuzzy languages, $H_f \Pi_f(K)$ is the smallest full hyper-AFFL that includes K.
(3) For each arbitrary family K of fuzzy languages, $H_f \Theta_f \Delta_f \Phi_f(K)$ is the smallest full hyper-AFFL that includes K.

Proof. (1) The statement follows immediately from Lemmas 7.1 and 7.2 together with Corollary 6.3.
(2) Let $\hat{\mathcal{H}}_f(K)$ be the smallest full hyper-AFFL that includes K. By the inclusion $K \subseteq \hat{\mathcal{H}}_f(K)$ and the monotonicity of both H_f and Π_f, we have $H_f \Pi_f(K) \subseteq H_f \Pi_f \hat{\mathcal{H}}_f(K)$. According to Proposition 7.4 this yields $H_f \Pi_f(K) \subseteq \hat{\mathcal{H}}_f(K)$. Now Theorem 7.6.(1) implies that $H_f \Pi_f(K)$ is a full hyper-AFFL that includes K. Hence we obtain that $\hat{\mathcal{H}}_f(K) = H_f \Pi_f(K)$.
(3) By Theorem 7.6.(2) and Proposition 3.5. □

By Proposition 7.4 we have that a family of fuzzy languages K is a full hyper-AFFL if and only if $\Pi_f(K) = K$ and $H_f(K) = K$. Consequently, the smallest full hyper-AFFL $\hat{\mathcal{H}}_f(K)$, that includes a family K of fuzzy languages, equals $\hat{\mathcal{H}}_f(K) = \bigcup \{w(K) \mid w \in \{\Pi_f, H_f\}^\star\}$ or, written equivalently, $\hat{\mathcal{H}}_f(K) = \{\Pi_f, H_f\}^\star(K)$. According Theorem 7.6.(2) this infinite set of strings over the alphabet $\{\Pi_f, H_f\}$ can be reduced to the single string $H_f \Pi_f$. Of course, a similar remark applies to Theorem 7.6.(3).

From the fact that FIN_f is the smallest fuzzy prequasoid, Theorem 7.6.(1), Corollary 6.4, Example 4.4, and the monotonicity of the operator H_f we obtain

Corollary 7.7. ETOL_f *is the smallest full hyper-AFFL.*

8. Concluding Remarks

In the previous sections we extended the concept of Γ-controlled K-iteration grammar from [1] to its fuzzy analogue in order to model the phenomenon of "developmental error". Many of the results that we have established are straightforward generalizations of similar statements for the crisp case from [1], [24] once the language-theoretic operations —like homomorphism, substitution and concatenation— are extended in the right way for fuzzy languages; cf. Section 2. On the other hand non-fuzzy versions of Theorem 6.1 and Corollary 6.2.(1) are proper generalizations of the main result in [1] which is more or less equivalent to the crisp counterpart of Corollary 6.2.(2).

Obviously, all our results apply to fuzzy ETOL languages as well; they are obtained by taking the parameter family K of fuzzy languages equal to the family FIN$_f$ of finite fuzzy languages. The precise formulation of these statements for Γ-controlled ETOL$_f$-languages are left to the interested reader.

In the definition of fuzzy K-iteration grammar each element in U is an arbitrary fuzzy K-substitution over V. Restricting each τ in U to a nested fuzzy K-substitution —i.e., $\mu(\alpha; \tau(\alpha)) = 1$ for each $\alpha \in V$— results in the concept of fuzzy context-free K-grammar; cf. [3], [4]. A further restriction to not-self-embedding nested fuzzy K-substitutions yields the notion of fuzzy regular K-grammar; cf. [5]. Both types of grammars have properties rather similar than those presented in this paper. Particularly with respect to closure properties there are many similarities and the question arises whether a uniform approach as the one in [2] for crisp languages is also possible for families of fuzzy languages. On the other hand there are some differences between fuzzy regular or context-free K-grammars and fuzzy K-iteration grammars. E.g., for fuzzy regular and fuzzy context-free K-grammars we can reduce the number of substitutions to 1 rather than to 2 (cf. Theorem 5.4), which implies that providing these grammars with a control language is probably not very challenging.

Next we return to a few matters discussed in Section 1. First, we want to reconsider the effect of developmental errors on the quality of the filament. In Section 1 we argued that each developmental error should properly change this quality, and therefore the underlying lattice-ordered structure $\mathcal{L}$ should possess an infinite number of elements. Clearly, the real closed interval $[0, 1]$ —even restricted to its computable or rational elements; cf. [8]— satisfies this condition, which is one reason for its popularity. But other instances of $\mathcal{L}$ may be useful too. E.g. in case we want to count symbols, i.e. to count cell states in filaments, the elements of $\mathcal{L}$ may be Parikh-vectors with $0 = [0, 0, \ldots, 0]$, and $1 = [\infty, \infty, \ldots, \infty]$ as smallest and largest element in $\mathcal{L}$. Note that $\mathcal{L}$ has countably infinite elements too in this example.

Two examples of biologically motivated control languages have been mentioned in Section 1: the sequence of days and nights, and the sequence of seasons. Both sets of sequences are regular languages. So the obvious question is: are there any non-regular events in biology/nature? Other sets of sequences —like the proper order of the days in a week, of the months in a year— are unsuitable candidates: apart from being regular sets, they are also human artifacts rather than natural or biological events.

References

1. Asveld, P.R.J.: Controlled iteration grammars and full hyper-AFL's, *Inform. Contr.* **34** (1977) 248–269.

2. Asveld, P.R.J.: An algebraic approach to incomparable families of formal languages, pp. 455–475 in [22].

3. Asveld, P.R.J.: Towards robustness in parsing — Fuzzifying context-free language recognition, pp. 443–453 in: J. Dassow, G. Rozenberg & A. Salomaa (eds.): *Developments in Language Theory II – At the Crossroads of Mathematics, Computer Science and Biology* (1996), World Scientific, Singapore.

4. Asveld, P.R.J.: A fuzzy approach to erroneous inputs in context-free language recognition, pp. 14–25 in: *Proc. 4th Internat. Workshop on Parsing Technologies* (1995), Prague/Karlovy Vary, Czech Republic.

5. Asveld, P.R.J.: The non-self-embedding property for generalized fuzzy context-free grammars, Memorandum Informatica 96-08 (1996), Dept. of Comp. Sci., Twente University of Technology, Enschede, the Netherlands. Presented at *8th Internat. Conf. on Automata and Formal Languages* (1996), Salgótarján, Hungary.

6. Asveld, P.R.J.: A note on Full Abstract Families of Fuzzy Languages (Full AFFL). In preparation.

7. Dassow, J. & Păun, G.: *Regulated Rewriting in Formal Language Theory* (1989), Springer-Verlag, Berlin, etc.

8. Gerla, G.: Fuzzy grammars and recursively enumerable fuzzy languages, *Inform. Sci.* **60** (1992) 137–143.

9. Ginsburg, S.: *Algebraic and Automata-Theoretic Properties of Formal Languages* (1975), North-Holland, Amsterdam.

10. Ginsburg, S. & Rozenberg, G.: TOL schemes and control sets, *Inform. Contr.* **27** (1975) 109–125.

11. Goguen, J.A.: L-fuzzy sets, *J. Math. Analysis Appl.* **18** (1967) 145–174.

12. Harrison, M.A.: *Introduction to Formal Language Theory* (1978), Addison-Wesley, Reading, Mass.

13. Herman, G.T. & Rozenberg, G.: *Developmental Systems and Languages* (1975), North-Holland, Amsterdam.

14. Hopcroft, J.E. & Ullman, J.D.: *Introduction to Automata Theory, Languages, and Computation* (1979), Addison-Wesley, Reading, Mass.

15. Lindenmayer, A.: Mathematical models for cellular interactions in development, Parts I and II, *J. Theor. Biology* **18** (1968) 280–315.

16. Lindenmayer, A.: Developmental systems without cellular interaction, their languages and grammars, *J. Theor. Biology* **30** (1971) 455–484.

17. Lee, E.T. & Zadeh, L.A.: Note on fuzzy languages, *Inform. Sci.* **1** (1969) 421–434.

18. Nielsen, M.: EOL systems with control devices, *Acta Inform.* **4** (1975) 373–386.

19. Prasad, N., Mahajan, M. & Krithivasan, K.: Fuzzy L-systems, *Internat. J. Comput. Math.* **36** (1990) 139–161.

20. Rozenberg, G.: Extensions of tabled OL-systems and languages, *Internat. J. Comp. Inform. Sci.* **2** (1973) 311–336.

21. Rozenberg, G. & Salomaa, A.: *The Mathematical Theory of L Systems* (1980), Academic Press, New York.

22. Rozenberg, G. & Salomaa, A. (eds.): *Lindenmayer Systems — Impacts on Theoretical Computer Science, Computer Graphics, and Developmental Biology* (1992), Springer-Verlag, Berlin, etc.

23. Salomaa, A.: *Formal Languages* (1973), Academic Press, New York.

24. Wood, D.: A note on Lindenmayer systems, Szilard languages, spectra, and equivalence, *Internat. J. Comp. Inform. Sci.* **4** (1975) 53–62.

On Controlling Rewriting by Properties of Strings and Symbols

Paolo BOTTONI

Università "La Sapienza" di Roma, Dip. Scienze dell'Informazione
via Salaria 113, 00198 Roma, Italy

Giancarlo MAURI

Università degli Studi di Milano, Dip. Scienze dell'Informazione
via Comelico 39, 20100 Milano, Italy

Piero MUSSIO

Università degli Studi di Brescia
Dipartimento di Elettronica per l'Automazione
via Branze 38, 25123 Brescia, Italy

Abstract. In this paper we explore forms of organization of rewriting systems which allow the systematic modelling of systems for human-computer interaction and the control of their dynamics. To this end we exploit tools from formal languages, adopting forms of parallel rewriting from L-systems tradition. Based on this formalisation, a notion of controlled rewriting is proposed where information about how to rewrite strings is embedded into the strings themselves or in properties of symbols. The main contribution of the paper is the introduction of a variety of families of L-systems with new control mechanisms in their rewriting relations. Hierarchies in the families are discussed and some relations among them presented. We also start the exploration of the closure properties of these language families. Finally, we discuss some relations among the proposed families of L-systems and families of grammar systems.

0. Introduction

The theory of grammar systems has been mainly originated by attempts to formalise within the theory of formal languages control mechanisms developed in the distributed/decentralised artificial intelligence and multi-agent systems fields (for a foundation, see [6]; for a survey of applications, see [18]).

Different types of grammar systems have been proposed, in particular cooperating distributed (CD) grammars were aimed at modelling the behaviour of a blackboard system, by having several grammars taking turns to rewrite a single string [5]. Forms of parallelism in the development of the activity of agents, in particular having agents which operate independently and report to a master, motivated Parallel Communicating Grammar Systems (PCGS) [29]. Different models of communication were also studied, based on communication upon request or upon command [10]. Research in artificial life led to the development of systems based on parallel rewriting, in particular combining the evolution of individual agents with their action on a common environment [9].

Starting from the basic models, several variants were considered to model specific forms of cooperation and of synchronisation among the action of the independent grammars in the system. For instance, partial or linear orders can be defined on the set of grammars forming a CD system [6], [24]; forms of synchronisation in the choice of rules can be imposed on CD systems in the form of teams [20], or on PCGS [27].

In this paper we explore forms of organisation of rewriting systems which allow the systematic modelling of systems for human-computer interaction and the control of their dynamics. To this end we exploit tools from formal languages, adopting forms of parallel rewriting from the L-system tradition. In particular, we will account for the simultaneous evolution of several strings, without necessarily having a notion of master string; we will adopt forms of parallel rewriting from the theory of L-systems and, again in the L-system tradition, we will drop the distinction between terminal and non terminal alphabets and will consider the possibility of having several strings as initial axioms [14]. Furthermore, we enrich symbols with properties, in the line of the use of attributed grammars as specification tools [17], [25]. In this way we gain in expressivity, as well as in generative power, with respect to traditional L-systems.

The evolution of an interactive system is modelled by considering the state of the different components of the system, as it evolves under commands issued by a user. We do not enter into details of implementation, but we propose to consider the components as individual agents in a population whose behaviour is controlled by mechanisms of constraints and synchronisation on their dynamics. These constraints can be at different levels: hierarchical, mutual, physical. From an abstract point of view, these constraints are modelled by mechanisms of stratification, grouping, fragmentation. A special case of stratification is defined by observation morphisms which produce the representation to a user of the state of a population of agents.

Based on this formalisation, a notion of controlled rewriting is proposed, different from those studied in classical formal language theory and based on some specific organisation and refinements of the sets of rules [11]. In the proposed approach, instead, information about how to rewrite strings is embedded into the strings themselves or in properties of symbols.

The main contribution of the paper is the introduction of a variety of families of L-systems with new control mechanisms in their rewriting relations. Hierarchies in the families are discussed and some relations among them presented. We also start the exploration of the closure properties of these languages. Finally, we discuss some relations among the proposed families of L-systems and families of grammar systems.

Paper organization. First, we present a scenario from a realistic case in the development of interactive systems for scientific purposes. Then we formalise the notions introduced in the scenario in terms of systems of L-systems. In Section 3 we give details on the mechanisms of regulation in rewriting and in Section 4 we compare them with notions from grammar systems theory. Finally, the conclusions draw some lines for further research.

1. Scenario

In this Section we illustrate by an example how mechanisms which control the interleaving and synchronisation of several rewriting systems model the definition and use of a human-computer interactive environment.

Some preliminary definitions are needed. An *image* is a 2-D string. A *tile* is a 2-D substring of an image. Hence, an image is seen as the composition of one or more tiles of different size. A *tile language* is a set of images built from the juxtaposition of tiles.

Tile languages have been formally introduced and studied as an extension of formal language theory to the two-dimensional case. In particular, the problem of recognising picture languages by finite state mechanisms has been studied [12], [15]. Here, we are only interested in the use of tile languages as a tool for layout definition, rather than in studying their properties in the usual terms of formal language theory.

The scenario: a scientist prepares his/her electronic document for programming the simulation of a galaxy evolution, studying the galaxy behaviour and documenting both the programming and the simulation activity.

To this end s/he uses a system of L-systems, presented in Appendix 1: one, the Screen Tile Language (STL), to define the organisation of the interface; the others to describe the set of data which must be displayed by the interface at any instant. Hence, the string describing the interactive system is organised into two *strata*: the first describing the organisation of the interface layout; the second describing the different sets of data. In turn, each stratum is organised into *fragments*. Each fragment in the first stratum is a tile defining a different part of the interface; each fragment in the second stratum defines a different set of data.

In practice, the scientist first specifies the layout of the electronic document as a sentence in STL, defined by the L-system reported in Appendix 1A. S/he decides to work with two windows, each one showing a different plausible evolution of the galaxy under study. Then s/he starts the processes of naming the two windows and simulating the galaxy evolution (L-system of Appendix 1B). To this end, s/he initialises each fragment in the second stratum with the appropriate axiom, thus also determining the rules used in the subsequent rewriting process. The decision of which L-system to use in each fragment is non-deterministic and depends on scientist interaction.

This process is exemplified in Appendix 2, showing the derivation up to the third step of galaxy evolution. A function *mat* materialises the description as an image on the screen [2]. Figure A1 schematises the images which appear on the screen after each derivation step.

The use of systems of L-systems also opens the possibility of describing how the interface can be adapted to user needs during the simulation, without losing the results already obtained. Suppose that during the simulation the scientist realises that the document clarity can be improved by adding a new window which represents the galaxy by a different convention and grouping the two windows so that when scrolling one of the two, the other is similarly scrolled. In this way corresponding pixels in the two images represent the same element of the galaxy. In this case, s/he suspends the simulation, goes back to the use of the tile language, adapts the electronic document and restarts his/her work without losing the previously obtained results. The same applies if the user has only modified the size or some other property of a window. This is possible because when several strata are used, rules for each stratum evolution are applied in an interleaved way. The stratified organisation is left untouched. New fragments have been generated at the first stratum to accommodate the new window and its title. A new fragment has been generated at the second stratum, which defines the content of the new window. Due to lack of space, the Appendix does not report the rules to manage these situations, discussed in [4].

The L-Systems of Appendix 1 are not deterministic both at syntactic and semantic level, as shown for example by the splitting rules. The syntax specifies that a tile can be split in two horizontal or vertical subtiles. The semantics indicate that the type of a tile is associated with a specific subset of types and not only one. Again, this form of non-determinism is resolved in interactive systems by an interaction with the user.

The description of the whole interactive environment as a system of L-systems drives its implementation as a Cooperative Visual Environment, [1].

2. Systems of L-Systems

In the next Section we explore several augmentations on the classical structure of 0L-systems. In particular, we consider families of rewriting systems that model the evolution of populations of agents under the influence of the environment. Each agent is modelled through a symbol from a finite alphabet.

This marks a difference with the classical approach of grammar systems, where each individual agent is modelled by associating it with a grammar. In grammar systems, the agents operate on a common support (case of CD), or provide information to a master (case of PCGS). We give a first extension to the classical theory of formal languages and L-system, by augmenting symbols with attributes. Moreover, we consider four basic extensions. First, we use attributes to assign properties to symbols and to condition their evolution on the values of these attributes. This models the independent evolution of agents. It is observed that this allows the generation of a richer family of languages than in classical 0L systems [14]. Second, we consider the possibility of coordinating the evolution of several strings on different alphabets in which symbols are subject to different sets of rules. This models the possibility of considering the evolution of a system under different levels of detail and allows the introduction of a notion of observation. Third, we consider the evolution of a single string where a fragment structure is imposed on the string and different sets of rules are used in different fragments. This models the effect of the environment on the independent evolution of individual agents. Finally, the evolution of a string is studied when constraints are imposed on the simultaneous application of rules to different symbols. This models forms of cooperation or competition in the evolution of populations of agents.

We assume that the reader is familiar with the theory of formal languages and we just give some basic definitions.

A 0L-system is a construct $0L = \langle T, Ax, P, \Longrightarrow \rangle$, where T is a finite alphabet of symbols, Ax is a finite collection of strings on T, i.e. $Ax \subseteq T^*$, P is a finite collection of rules of the form $x \rightarrow \omega$, with $x \in T$ and $\omega \in T^*$. The constraint holds that $\forall x \in T, \exists (x \rightarrow \omega) \in P$ for some ω. The rewriting relation $\Longrightarrow \subset T^* \times T^*$ holds between two strings x and z such that z can be obtained from x by simultaneously substituting all symbols in x as allowed by the given rules, i.e. $x \Longrightarrow z$ iff $x = a_1, \ldots, a_n, z = \beta_1, \ldots, \beta_n$ and $a_i \rightarrow \beta_i \in P$ for each a_i. The language generated by a 0L system is the set $L = \{x \mid \exists y \in Ax, y \Longrightarrow^* x\}$.

In the above formulation the axioms belong to the generated language, in the following we will adopt the same conventions as above to define the generated languages for any type of system.

OL-systems with attributes are defined following the tradition of associating semantics with syntax, introduced by Knuth [21]. An *attributed* 0L-system is a construct
$a0L = \langle T, Ax, P, At, D, \Phi, \Longrightarrow \rangle$, where T and P are as above, $At = \{\alpha_1, \ldots, \alpha_k\}$ is
a finite set of attributes, $D = \{D_1, \ldots, D_k\}$ is a finite set of domains, one for each
element of At, Φ a set of functions of the form $f : D_{i_1} \times \ldots \times D_{i_s} \to D_{i_k}$. With each
symbol $x \in T$ a finite set of attributes $At(x) \subset At$ is associated. We will indicate the
attribute α of the symbol x with $x.\alpha$. Ax is a set of strings on T with an initial assign-
ment of properties to attributes of symbols in the string. With each rule $x \to \omega \in P$,
a finite set of functions $r_p \subset \Phi$ is associated (called *semantic rule*) which computes
the values of the attributes of the elements in ω based on the values of the attributes
of x. The rewriting relation is augmented with the prescription that the application
of a rule is always followed by the evaluation of the associated semantic rule. The
language defined by an attributed 0L-system is the set of strings on the alphabet T
derived from an axiom (i.e. in the definition of the language the value of attributes is
not accounted for). In the following we omit the 0 from the definition of L-systems.
In any case the treatment will be restricted to the 0L case.

3. Control Mechanisms for Rewriting

In this Section we describe control mechanisms that generalise those introduced
in the Appendices.

3.1. Conditioning

The use of attributes can affect the definition of the generated language, if the
rewriting relation is extended so that the application of a rule is guarded by the
satisfaction of a condition. This allows context to be taken into account on a context-
free structure of rules. As an example, most of the rules presented in Appendix 1 are
conditioned.

An attributed L-system *with conditions* is a construct $caL = \langle T, Ax, P, At, D,$
$\Phi, \Gamma, \Longrightarrow \rangle$ where T, Ax, At, P, D, and Φ, are as in the definition of aL systems.
Γ is a set of predicates, comprising the constant predicates *true* and *false*. $\forall p \in$
$P, \exists \gamma \in \Gamma, \gamma : D_{i_1} \times \ldots \times D_{i_s} \to \{true, false\}$. γ is called the *condition* of the
rule. The relation $\Longrightarrow$ specifies that rules in P are applied in parallel and that a
rule is applied only if the associated condition is satisfied. Formally, $\Longrightarrow \subset T^* \times T^*$
holds between two strings x and z ($x \Longrightarrow z$) iff $x = a_1, \ldots, a_n$, $z = \beta_1, \ldots, \beta_n$,
and, for each a_i: 1) $\exists (a_i \to \beta_i) \in P$, 2) the condition associated with this rule is
$\gamma : D_{i_1} \times \ldots \times D_{i_s} \to \{true, false\}$, 3) the set of attributes of a_i includes the subset
$\{\alpha_{i_1}, \ldots, \alpha_{i_s}\}$, and 4) $\gamma(a_i.\alpha_{i_1}, \ldots a_i.\alpha_{i_s}) = true$. The semantic rule is then evaluated
to assign values to each symbol in each β_i. In the following we will adopt a notation for
conditional attributed rules which synthesises their syntactic, semantic and condition
components. In particular, a rule

$$a \to x_1 \ldots x_m \gamma(a.\alpha_{c_1}, \ldots, a.\alpha_{c_k})$$
$$x_1.\alpha_{1_1} = f(a.\alpha_{s_{11}}, \ldots, a.\alpha_{s_{1r}}); \ldots; x_m.\alpha_{k_m} = f(a.\alpha_{s_{m1}}, \ldots, a.\alpha_{s_{mr}})$$

is written

$$(\mathbf{a}, a.\alpha_{h_1}, \ldots, a.\alpha_{h_k}) \to (\mathbf{x_1}, \alpha_{1_1}, \ldots, \alpha_{1_s}) \ldots (\mathbf{x_m}, \alpha_{m_1}, \ldots \alpha_{m_s}),$$

where $\{\alpha_{h_1}, \ldots, \alpha_{h_k}\} = \{\alpha_{c_1}, \ldots, \alpha_{c_k}\} \cup \bigcup_{i=1}^{m} \bigcup_{j=1}^{r} \{\alpha_{s_{ij}}\}$.

The rules in the Appendix are instead written in the first form.

Claim 3.1.1. The L-system $caL = \langle\{a,b,c\}, Ax, P, \{gen\}, \mathbf{N}, \Phi, \Gamma, \Longrightarrow\rangle$, with $Ax = \{(\mathbf{a},0)(\mathbf{b},0)(\mathbf{c},0)\}$ and $P = \{(a,0) \to (\mathbf{a},1)(\mathbf{a},0), (\mathbf{b},0) \to (\mathbf{b},1)(\mathbf{b},0), (\mathbf{c},0) \to (\mathbf{c},1)(\mathbf{c},0), (\mathbf{a},1) \to (\mathbf{a},1), (\mathbf{b},1) \to (\mathbf{b},1), (\mathbf{c},1) \to (\mathbf{c},1)\}$ generates the language $\{a^n b^n c^n \mid n \geq 1\}$.

Here, the synchronisation of string evolution is achieved by having in the string, at each step, only one instance, for each type of symbol, which is able to reproduce.

This models systems where individual agents have a limited capacity of reproduction. Different capacities can generate languages $\{a^{nk} b^{nk} c^{nk} \mid n \geq 1\}$, with k any number. In this model agents never disappear. More sophisticated behaviours can be obtained with agents with limited resources, modelled by letting symbols disappear when properties reach a certain value.

3.2. Stratification

In a string-stratified rewriting system several strings evolve together with mutual constraints on their evolution. This concept is the counterpart in terms of strings of the notion of stratified grammar systems, where sets of rules are ordered and the derivation of a single string occurs starting with the application of rules in the first set and ends with the application of rules in the last set, respecting the ordering of the sets [8]. Here, each generation step involves the evolution of all the strata, in a prescribed way. As an example, process generating rules in Appendix 1A are used to start a new process in a different stratum.

A *string-stratified* (from here on simply stratified) L-system is a construct $sL = \langle(T_1, Ax_1, HP_1, VP_1, \Longrightarrow_1, \Downarrow_1), \ldots, (T_n, Ax_n, HP_n, VP_n, \Longrightarrow_n, \Downarrow_n)\rangle$, where, for $i = 1, \ldots, n, T_i$ is an alphabet, Ax_i is a set of axioms, HP_i is a collection of intra-stratum (horizontal) rules, VP_i is a collection of inter-stratum (vertical) rules, from symbols in the alphabet T_i into strings in the alphabets T_{i-1} or T_{i+1}, $\Longrightarrow_i$ and $\Downarrow_i$ are the horizontal and vertical direct generation relation for the i-th stratum respectively. Conditions, if any, can regard symbols in the same stratum or in adjacent strata (the lower and the upper one).

The case in which no attributes (and a fortiori no conditions) are considered and only two strata are present reduces to the case of 0L-systems with coding [29].

Each stratum is equipped with a direct generation relation for the intra-stratum rules. For each stratum a metarule specifies when to apply the inter-stratum rules. Intra-stratum rules are applied in parallel and each stratum is rewritten when no generation can be performed in any other stratum. Two basic definitions can be adopted for the generated language: either consider the language formed by the vector of the strings, or consider the language of the strings at some designated level. Languages formed by specific configuration of strings can be defined. Moreover, languages of strings of one level can be defined using strings of other levels as control words.

A stratification mechanism allows the formalisation of observation as a mapping from a stratum to the lower one. An *observational stratified* L-system osL is a stratified system with the limitation that no condition is admissible from a lower stratum to an upper one.

In an osL-system the relation $\Downarrow_1$ is such that the string at the first level is not modified (except possibly for the modification of attributes) by the application of inter-strata rules. This reflects an assumption of non-destructive observation.

For the other levels, instead, observation is destructive, so that each symbol in the stratum above is deleted when a vertical rule is applied. (Indeed, strings in strata different from the first are valid only until a new observation is performed, while the first stratum provides the dynamics of the observed phenomenon). For reasons of homogeneity, the existence of vertical rules $x \downarrow x$ for each x is assumed for the string at the lowest level in the observation hierarchy.

As an example, consider the following conditional attributed observational stratified system on the one-letter alphabet $T = \{a\}$ and using the single attribute gen with domain the set of natural numbers.

I   intra-stratum rules: $\{(\mathbf{a}, 0) \to (\mathbf{a}, 0)(\mathbf{a}, 3), (\mathbf{a}, n) \to (\mathbf{a}, n + 2); \text{ with } n \neq 0\}$,
     inter-strata rules: $\{(\mathbf{a}, n) \downarrow (\mathbf{a}, n)\}$,

II   intra-stratum rules: $\{(\mathbf{a}, 0) \to (\mathbf{a}, 0); (\mathbf{a}, n) \to (\mathbf{a}, n - 1)\}$, with $n \neq 0$,
     inter-strata rules: $\{(\mathbf{a}, 0) \downarrow a\}$,

III intra-stratum rules: $\{a \to a\}$.

The rewriting relation prescribes that rules from the first to the second stratum be applied after each step; rules from the second to the third stratum are applied when no more rules (different from identity) are applicable at the second stratum. This generates the language $\{a^{n^2} \mid n \geq 1\}$, which is an ED T0L language. The control mechanism here introduced is similar to the t-mode of derivation in the formalism of grammar systems, in which a grammar continues to apply rules as long as it can do so [6]. The difference lies in the fact that we are dealing with parallel rewriting and we consider to have identity rules always available.

3.3. Fragmentation

An n-fragmented string on an alphabet T is a string $\alpha_1 \# \ldots \# \alpha_n \#$, where $\alpha_i \in T^*$ for $i = 1, \ldots, n$ and $\#$ is a separator symbol not in T. As an example, process generating rules in Appendix 1A create fragments in the lower stratum which are initialised with different axioms.

3.3.1. Fixed number of fragments

An n-fragmented L-system is a construct $fL_n = \langle T \cup \{\#\}, Ax, P, \mu, \Longrightarrow \rangle$, where T is a set of symbols, $T \cap \{\#\} = \emptyset$, $Ax = Ax_1 \# \ldots Ax_n \#$ and each Ax_i is a finite set of strings from T^*, $P = \{P_1, P_2, \ldots, P_m\}$ is a collection of sets of rules, with $P_i \subset T \times T^*$, and $\mu : \{1, \ldots, n\} \to P$ is a function associating a set of rules from P with each fragment. Symbols in the same fragment are rewritten only by rules in the same set (in the original formulation by Mayoh [22], μ is implicitly assumed as $\mu : \mathbf{N} \times \{1, \ldots, \mathbf{n}\} \to \mathbf{P}$, letting the association vary at each step of derivation). n is called the *degree of frgmentation* of fL_n.

The direct generation relation is defined as follows: $x \Longrightarrow y$ iff $x = \alpha_1 \# \alpha_2 \# \ldots \# \alpha_n \#, y = \beta_1 \# \beta_2 \# \ldots \# \beta_n \#$ and for $i = 1, \ldots, n, \alpha_i \Longrightarrow_{\mu(i)} \beta_i$. As usual, the language generated by a rewriting system with fragments is the set of strings obtained by hiding the symbols $\#$. This can be formulated in the context of observational stratified systems, by considering the interstrata rules $x \downarrow x, \forall x \in T$ and $\# \downarrow \lambda$. As an example, consider the system $fL = \langle \{a, \#\}, \{a\#a\#\}, \{\{a \to aa\}, \{a \to a\}\}, \mu, \Longrightarrow \rangle$, where μ is defined by the pairs $(1, P_1), (2, P_2)$. This generates the language $\{a^{1+2^n} \mid n \geq 1\}$, which is not a 0L language.

3.3.2. Migration

Let us consider the case in which symbols are allowed to migrate from one fragment to another. Migration is modelled as the disappearing of one symbol in a fragment and its reappearing in another. We assume that only one symbol per fragment can migrate at a time, namely the one adjoining to a separator symbol. To restrict migration to such a symbol, we must enrich the 0L scheme with special rules for migration.

A fragmented L-system *with migration* is a construct $mfL = \langle T \cup \{\#\}, Ax, P, \mu, M, \Longrightarrow \rangle$, where T, P, Ax and μ are the same as for fL-systems, and M is a set of migration rules. Let $T_M \subset T$ be the set of symbols which are allowed to migrate, $M \subset T_M\{\#\} \times \{\#\}T_M$. Each rule in M has the form $x\# \rightarrow \#x$, for any $x \in T_M$. In the following we consider $T_M = T$.

The rewriting relation $\Longrightarrow$ is defined as follows. Let $\Longrightarrow_P$ denote the rewriting relation of fragmented L systems as discussed above, with application of rules only from P. Let $\Longrightarrow_M$ be defined as follows: $x \Longrightarrow_M y$ if $x = \alpha_1 x_1 \# \alpha_2 x_2 \# \ldots \# \alpha_n \#$, $y = \alpha_1 \# \beta_2 \# \ldots \# \beta_n \#$, and $\beta_i = x_{i-1}\alpha_i$ if $(x_i\# \rightarrow \#x_i)$, $(x_{i-1}\# \rightarrow \#x_{i-1}) \in M$, and $\alpha_i \in T^*, x_i \in T$, for $i = 1, \ldots, n$. Here we consider the deterministic case in which a migration rule is forced to occur for all fragments. Then $x \Longrightarrow y$ iff a string z exists such that $x \Longrightarrow_P z$ and $z \Longrightarrow_M y$. In other words, a rewriting step is composed of an evolution step and a migration step. The language generated by an L-system with migration is therefore the set of strings generated after a migration step.

Two variants can be considered as regards migration from the last fragment. In the mode described above, called *blocking* and denoted by b, no migration is possible from the last fragment. Otherwise, in the *leaping* mode, denoted by l, migration from the last fragment results into the deletion of the migrating symbol. In the following we consider only the l-mode.

Let $L(fL)$ be a language generated by a fragmented L-system fL. It can be expressed as $L(fL) = \bigcup_{i=1}^{\infty} L_i$, where each L_i is the set of strings which can be generated in i steps from an initial string. The language $L' = L(mfL)$ generated by the system mfL, obtained by adding migration to fL, is defined as follows: $L(mfL) = \bigcup_{i=1}^{\infty} L_i'$, where $L_i' = \{\sigma \mid \exists \zeta = \alpha_1 \alpha_2 \ldots \alpha_n \in L_i$ and $\sigma = \beta_1 \beta_2 \ldots \beta_n$, with each $\beta_j = x_0 h(x_1) \ldots h^{i-1}(x_{i-1}) Pref(i, \alpha_j)\}$ and $h^k(x)$ indicates one of the possible strings generated in k steps starting with a symbol x. Each x_k indicates the symbol which is migrated to a fragment k steps before. In particular $x_0 = last(\alpha_{i-1})$ and $x_k = last(\alpha_{i-1}^{n-k})$ where α_{i-1}^{n-k} indicates the state of fragment α_{i-1} at the derivation step $n-k$.

Claim 3.3.2.1. The 3-fragmented L-system with migration on a one-letter alphabet $mfL = \langle \{a, \#\}, \{a\#a\#a\#\}, \{\{a \rightarrow aa\}, \{a \rightarrow aaa\}\} \{(1, P_1), (2, P_2), (3, P_1)\}, \{a\# \rightarrow \#a\}, \Longrightarrow \rangle$ generates the language $\{a^{3^n} a^{2^n+1} \mid n \geq 1\}$. This language is obtainable by a 3-fragmented one-letter 0L-system (without migration) only if one of the fragments has only the trivial rule $a \rightarrow a$. It is not obtainable from a one-letter 0L-system.

Consider now the case in which μ is defined by the pairs $(1, P_2), (2, P_2), (3, P_1)$. The resulting language is $\{a^{g(n)} a^{3^n} a^{h(n)} \mid n \geq 1\}$, where $g(n)$ is defined recursively as follows: $g(0) = 1, g(n) = (3 \times g(n-1)) - 1$, and $h(n)$ is $h(0) = 1, h(n) = 1 + 2 \times h(n-1)$.

This is not obtainable by any 0L-system without migration. Actually, for one-letter alphabets, the case with migration reduces to the case without migration if and only if the first and last fragment are rewritten by the same set of rules. Indeed, for all other fragments the incoming symbol compensates the outgoing symbol, while the first is not compensated by anyone and the last fragment only receives contributions from the fragment before.

3.3.3. Dynamic generation of fragments

Let us now consider the case in which fragments can be generated dynamically, through rules of the type $\# \rightarrow \#\#$. These rules, called *fragmentation rules*, are typically conditioned, but this is not relevant to the present discussion. We assume that for each new fragment the association with a set of rules is the same as for the originating fragment. Hence an L-system *with fragment generation* is a construct $gfL = \langle T \cup \{\#\}, Ax, P, \mu, F, \Longrightarrow \rangle$, where T, P, Ax and μ are the same as for fL systems, and F is a set of fragmentation rules, including the identity rule for fragments.

Two variants can be considered for defining the starting string in the new fragment, based on the characteristics of the fragment to the left of the instance to which the fragmentation rule was applied. This fragment is called the *originating* fragment. First, in the *setting* mode, indicated by s, the fragmentation control mechanism is defined so that, when applying a fragmentation rule, a new fragment is generated with an axiom from the set of axioms for the originating fragment. This is expressed by the following rewriting relation: if $\# \rightarrow \#\#$ is applied to the i-th occurrence of $\#$, then if $x = \alpha_1 \# \ldots \alpha_i \# \alpha_{i+1} \# \ldots \alpha_n \#$, $x' = \alpha_1 \# \ldots \alpha_i \# \xi_i \# \alpha_{i+1} \# \ldots \# \alpha_n \#$ where $\xi_i \in Ax_i$. This simulates a class-based mechanism in object-oriented programming language, where new instances are generated from the mould of the class. Second, in the *doubling* mode, indicated by d, the fragmentation control mechanism is defined so that when applying a fragmentation rule, a new fragment is generated equal to the originating fragment. This is expressed by the following rewriting relation: if $\# \rightarrow \#\#$ is applied to the i-th occurrence of $\#$, then if $x = \alpha_1 \# \ldots \alpha_i \# \alpha_{i+1} \# \ldots \alpha_n \#$, $x' = \alpha_1 \# \ldots \alpha_i \# \alpha_i \# \alpha_{i+1} \# \ldots \# \alpha_n \#$. This simulates the cloning mechanism in object-based programming languages. Two variants are define for what happens to the originating fragment. In the *fragment-non-returning* mode, indicated by n, the originating fragment remains unchanged after application of a fragmentation rule. This variant has implicitly been adopted in the discussion above. In the *fragment-returning* mode, indicated by r, the originating fragment (i.e. the i-th fragment) is deleted after the application of a fragmentation rule and substituted by a string $\xi \in Ax_i$.

In any case, the set of rules for the new fragment is the same as the one for the originating fragment.

We adopt the notation $(X, Y)\mathbf{gfL}$ to indicate the family of fragmented L-systems with generation using the $X \in \{r, n\}$ mode for the originating fragment, and the $Y \in \{s, d\}$ mode for the created fragment.

The rewriting relation $\Longrightarrow$ is as follows. Let $\Longrightarrow_P$ denote the rewriting relation of fragmented L systems with application of rules only from P. Let $\Longrightarrow_F$ be one of the variants of the rewriting relation defined above. Then $x \Longrightarrow y$ iff a string z exists such that $x \Longrightarrow_P z$ and $z \Longrightarrow_F y$. In other words, a rewriting step is composed of an evolution step and a fragment generation step.

The family of L-systems with migration and fragment generation is denoted by $\mathbf{mgfL}$. In this family, the rewriting relation is defined by the sequence $\Longrightarrow_P, \Longrightarrow_F, \Longrightarrow_M$.

3.3.4. Hierarchies of languages

Let $\mathbf{fL_k}$ be the set of k-fragmented L-systems and $\mathcal{L}(\mathbf{fL_k})$ the family of languages generated by L-systems in $\mathbf{fL_k}$. Then the following holds:

Theorem 3.3.4.1. *The families of languages generated by L-systems in* $\mathbf{fL_1}$, $\mathbf{fL_2}$, ..., $\mathbf{fL_n}$, ... *form an infinite hierarchy.*

Proof (of inclusion). For each n, a system L in $\mathbf{fL_n}$ can be simulated by a system L' in $\mathbf{fL_{n+1}}$ in the following way: L' has exactly the same sets of rules $P_1, \ldots, P_m$ as L, together with a set P_0, which has rules $x \to \lambda, \forall x \in T$. The function μ_{n+1} is an extension of μ_n to $n+1$, with $\mu_{n+1}(n+1) = P_0$. For each $ax \in Ax$, where Ax is the set of axioms of L, $ax = \alpha_1 \# \ldots \alpha_n \#$, the set Ax' of axioms of L' contains an axiom $ax' = \alpha_1 \# \ldots \alpha_n \# \#$ (i.e. the fragment $n+1$ contains the null string).

(of strictness) For each n the one-letter language $\{a^{2^k} a^{3^k} \ldots a^{(n+2)^k} \mid k \geq 1\}$ is in $\mathcal{L}(\mathbf{fL_{n+1}})$, but not in $\mathcal{L}(\mathbf{fL_n})$. □

Theorem 3.3.4.2. $\mathcal{L}(\mathbf{fL}) \subset \mathcal{L}(\mathbf{gfL})$.

Proof: A fL is a gfL in which the fragment generation rule is never used. □

Fragmented L-systems with only one fragment reduce to ordinary 0-L systems.

3.3.5. Properties of closure

Let $\mathbf{fL} = \bigcup_{i=1}^{\infty} \mathbf{fL_k}$. We now consider the properties of closure of the classes of fragmented L-systems above defined with respect to the usual operations.

Theorem 3.3.5.1. *For any number k of fragments, the following table collects the results about the closure of the classes* $\mathbf{fL}$, $\mathbf{gfL}$, $\mathbf{mfL}$, $\mathbf{mgfL}$ *and* $\mathbf{fL_k}$ *w.r.t. union and concatenation. Y means that the family in the row is closed under the operation in the column, N that it is not closed, Y(cond.) that it is closed only if conditional rules are used.*

Family	Union	Concat.	Kleene's $*$
fL	Y (cond.)	Y	N
gfL	Y (cond.)	Y	N
mfL	Y (cond.)	N	N
mgfL	Y (cond.)	N	N
fL$_k$	Y (cond.)	N	N

Proof.

<u>Union.</u> Without loss of generality, we will consider languages and systems over one same alphabet T. Let $L(A)$ and $L(B)$ be two languages generated by the fragmented L-systems $A = \langle T \cup \{\#\}, Ax_a, P_a, \mu_a, \Longrightarrow \rangle$ and $B = \langle T \cup \{\#\}, Ax_b, P_b, \mu_b, \Longrightarrow \rangle$, respectively. Then, the language $L = L(A) \cup L(B)$ is generated by the conditional attributed fragmented system: $C = \langle T \cup \{\#\}, Ax'_a \cup Ax'_b, \mathcal{P}(P'_a \cup P'_b), \{origin\}, \{\{0,1\}\}, \Gamma, \mu_c, \Longrightarrow \rangle$, where $origin$ is a new attribute, with domain $\{0,1\}$, Ax'_x is obtained from Ax_x by assigning to symbols in the axioms in Ax_a (resp. Ax_b) the value 0 (resp. 1) for the attribute $origin$, and P'_x is obtained by associating with each rule in P_x a condition in Γ on the value of the attribute $origin$ so that rules in P_a (resp., P_b) can be applied iff $origin$ has value 0 (resp., 1). The function μ_c is defined by associating with each fragment i the primed version union of the sets of rules defined for the fragment i in A and B.

Here we resort to conditioned rules, where rules depend on the value of an attribute. It is obvious that every string in $L(A)$ or in $L(B)$ can be generated by C, and no other strings can be generated.

The proof for other classes is analogous.

Concatenation. Let $L(A)$ and $L(B)$ be two languages generated by the fragmented L-systems $A = \langle T \cup \{\#\}, Ax_a, P_a, \mu_a, \Longrightarrow \rangle$ and $B = \langle T \cup \{\#\}, Ax_b, P_b, \mu_b, \Longrightarrow \rangle$, respectively, and let k_a be the degree of fragmentation of A and k_b the degree of fragmentation of B. $L = L(A) \cup L(B)$ is generated by the $k_a + k_b$-fragmented system: $C = \langle T \cup \{\#\}, Ax_a \cdot Ax_b, P_a \cup P_b, \mu_c, \Longrightarrow \rangle$, where $\mu_c = \mu_a(i)$ for $i \leq k_a$, $\mu_c = \mu_b(i - k_a)$ for $k_a < i \leq k_b$.

The same proof holds for **gfL**. However, concatenation is not closed on $\mathbf{fL_k}$, since it increases the number of fragments. Moreover, it is not closed even on systems with migration, in either variant, since migration would now be allowed for a symbol in the k_a-th fragment, which would become subject to rules from a set in P_b. Hence, for any two languages $L(A), L(B) \in X, X \in \{\mathbf{mfL}, \mathbf{mgfL}\}$, we can only state the weaker result that there exists a language $L(C) \in X$, such that $L(C) \supset L(A) \cdot L(B)$ and such that if a string is in $L(C) \setminus (L(A) \cdot L(B))$, then a symbol migrated from the k_a-th fragment during its derivation.

Kleene. Fragmented languages are not closed under Kleene since, they would require an infinite set of axioms. However, it can be proved that $(r,s)gfL$-systems can generate the Kleene's $*$ of 0L languages. □

If we consider stratified systems, so as to allow observation, we have the following result:

Theorem 3.3.5.2. *The facts described in the table hold.*

Operation	Union	Concat.
ssfL	Y	Y
ssgfL	Y	Y
ssmfL	Y	N
ssmgfL	Y	N
ssfL$_\mathbf{k}$	Y	N

Proof. The proof procedes in a way analogous to that of Theorem 3.3.5.1. In this case, union does not require conditioning. It is in fact possible to use disjoint isomorphic copies T' and T'' of the alphabet, and hence of the sets of rules, for the two original systems. Inverse morphisms from T' and T'' to T are then applied in the observation phase. □.

3.4. Grouping

Groups allow the definition of synchronisation constraints on the action of different agents, so that if a certain agent performs a given action (application of a rule), then the associated agents will perform related actions. In particular this allows the modelling of forms of multicast communication where several agents receive simultaneously the same message and each agent reacts according to its abilities [1]. As an example, the notion of group has been used in the L-system of Appendix 1B, where the belonging of all symbols to one same group forces the process to consistently evolve either in the horizontal or in the vertical direction.

An L-system *with groups* is a construct $gL = \langle T, Ax, P, At, D, \Phi, \rho, \nu, \Longrightarrow \rangle$ with T, Ax, At, D, Φ as for aL-systems, ρ a symmetrical predicate $\rho : (T \times \prod_{i=1}^{k} D_i)^2 \to \{true, false\}$, assessing whether two symbols belong to a same group, ν a mapping

$\nu : P \setminus I \rightarrow \wp(P)$, where I is the set of identity rules, with the property that if $p_i \in \nu(p_j)$, $p_i \notin I$, then $p_j \in \nu(p_i)$. If ν is extended to I, the property holds also in I.

In particular, ρ defines for each symbol the group it belongs to, ν defines for each rule the associated set of rules.

The direct generation relation is as follows: $w \Longrightarrow z$ iff $w = a_1 a_2 \ldots a_n$, $z = \beta_1 \beta_2 \ldots \beta_n$, $a_i \rightarrow \beta_i \in P$ for each $i = 1, \ldots, n$, and if $\rho(a_i, a_j) = true$, and a rule $a_j \rightarrow \beta_j$ has been applied, a rule $a_i \rightarrow \beta_i$ has also been applied, where $a_i \rightarrow \beta_i \in \nu(a_j \rightarrow \beta_j)$.

Claim 3.4.1 The language $Z = \{xx \mid x \in T^*\}$ on an alphabet T, is generated by an L-system with groups.

Proof. Consider, without loss of generality, $T = \{a, b\}$. Let us assume that we start with a string respecting the pattern, say $abab$, and that we have the set of rules $P = \{a \rightarrow ab, a \rightarrow ba, a \rightarrow aa, a \rightarrow bb, b \rightarrow bb, b \rightarrow ab, b \rightarrow ba, b \rightarrow aa, a \rightarrow a, b \rightarrow b, a \rightarrow b, b \rightarrow a\}$. Let $\nu : P \rightarrow \wp(P)$ be the injection in the powerset of the identity function on P. Let us attach to a symbol in a string derived from the axiom a property formed by a pair (id, ln), where id is the identifier of the symbol, i.e. its derivation path from the axiom, and ln denotes the symbol with which it must be coupled to form a group.

Thus, the axiom is rewritten $(\mathbf{a}, 1, 3)(\mathbf{b}, 2, 4)(\mathbf{a}, 3, 1), (\mathbf{b}, 4, 2)$. With each rule an action on this property is defined, namely, for a generic rule $(\mathbf{x}, id, ln) \rightarrow (\mathbf{y}, id \cdot 1, ln \cdot 1)(\mathbf{z}, id \cdot 2, ln \cdot 2)$ or $(\mathbf{x}, id, ln) \rightarrow (\mathbf{y}, id \cdot 1, ln \cdot 1)$. Two symbols $(\mathbf{x}, id, ln)$ and $(\mathbf{y}, id, ln)$ belong to the same group iff $x.id = y.ln$ and $y.ln = x.id$. □

As an example, consider the following steps in derivation: $(\mathbf{a}, 1, 3)$ $(\mathbf{b}, 2, 4)$ $(\mathbf{a}, 3, 1)$, $(\mathbf{b}, 4, 2) \Longrightarrow (\mathbf{a}, 1 \cdot 1, 3 \cdot 1)(\mathbf{b}, 1 \cdot 2, 3 \cdot 2)(\mathbf{b}, 2 \cdot 1, 4 \cdot 1)(\mathbf{b}, 2 \cdot 2, 4 \cdot 2)(\mathbf{a}, 3 \cdot 1, 1 \cdot 1)(\mathbf{b}, 3 \cdot 2, 1 \cdot 2)(\mathbf{b}, 4 \cdot 1, 1 \cdot 1)(\mathbf{b}, 4 \cdot 2, 1 \cdot 2) \Longrightarrow (\mathbf{b}, 1 \cdot 1 \cdot 1, 3 \cdot 1 \cdot 1)(\mathbf{a}, 1 \cdot 1 \cdot 2, 3 \cdot 1 \cdot 2)(\mathbf{b}, 1 \cdot 2 \cdot 1, 3 \cdot 2 \cdot 1)(\mathbf{a}, 2 \cdot 1 \cdot 1, 4 \cdot 1 \cdot 1)(\mathbf{b}, 2 \cdot 1 \cdot 2, 4 \cdot 1 \cdot 2)(\mathbf{b}, 2 \cdot 2 \cdot 1, 4 \cdot 2 \cdot 1)(\mathbf{b}, 3 \cdot 1 \cdot 1, 1 \cdot 1 \cdot 1)(\mathbf{a}, 3 \cdot 1 \cdot 2, 1 \cdot 1 \cdot 2)(\mathbf{b}, 3 \cdot 2 \cdot 1, 1 \cdot 2 \cdot 1)(\mathbf{a}, 4 \cdot 1 \cdot 1, 2 \cdot 1 \cdot 1)(\mathbf{b}, 4 \cdot 1 \cdot 2, 2 \cdot 1 \cdot 2)(\mathbf{b}, 4 \cdot 2 \cdot 1, 2 \cdot 2 \cdot 1)$. Each string in L can be generated from a string in the finite set of axioms $\{aa, bb\}$.

3.4.1. Fixed number of groups

We distinguish the case where the number of groups remains fixed from the case where it increases with the time.

Consider the following gL, built on the alphabet $T = \{a, b, c\}$, with set of rules $P = \{a \rightarrow aa, b \rightarrow bb, c \rightarrow cc, a \rightarrow a, b \rightarrow b, c \rightarrow c\}$. Each rule is labelled with its position in the set and the mapping ν is defined by $\{I \rightarrow \{I, II, III\}, II \rightarrow \{I, II, III\}, III \rightarrow \{I, II, III\}, IV \rightarrow \{IV, V, VI\}, V \rightarrow \{IV, V, VI\}, VI \rightarrow \{IV, V, VI\}\}$. To each symbol in a string derived from the axiom a property grp is attached, where grp indicates the group to which a symbol belongs. With each rule an action on this property is defined, namely, for a generic rule $(\mathbf{x}, -) \rightarrow (\mathbf{x}, 1)(x, 2)$ or $(\mathbf{x}, GrP) \rightarrow (\mathbf{x}, Grp)$. Two symbols $(\mathbf{x}, Grp1)$ and $(\mathbf{y}, Grp2)$ belong to the same group iff $Grp1 = Grp2$. Starting from the axiom $(\mathbf{a}, 1)(\mathbf{a}, 2)(\mathbf{b}, 1)(\mathbf{b}, 2)(\mathbf{c}, 1)(\mathbf{c}, 2)$, this gL generates the language $\{a^n b^n c^n \mid n \geq 2\}$.

Let $i\mathbf{gL}$ be the set of L-systems with i groups. The following holds:

Theorem 3.4.1.1. $\mathcal{L}(i\mathbf{gL})$ *is incomparable with* $\mathcal{L}((i+1)\mathbf{gL})$ *for each* i.

Proof. Consider a language in $\mathcal{L}(i\mathbf{gL})$ generated starting from an axiom of i symbols. It is not possible to have $i+1$ groups on such an axiom, so that the axiom is not in $\mathcal{L}((i+1)\mathbf{gL})$. On the other hand, consider a language $L \in \mathcal{L}((i+1)\mathbf{gL})$ with an axiom $\zeta \in L$, such that $|\zeta| = i+1$. Let us suppose that there exists a language

$H \in \mathcal{L}(\mathbf{igL})$ such that $\zeta \in H$. Hence, there are at least two symbols, say ζ_k and ζ_l, which belong to a same group. Any string directly generated from ζ is such that if ζ_k is rewritten according to a rule r, ζ_l will be rewritten according to a rule $\nu(r)$. Hence, indicated with $c(r)$, the consequent of rule r, we have $\zeta = \zeta_1 \ldots \zeta_l \ldots \zeta_k \ldots \zeta_{|\zeta|} \Longrightarrow \sigma = \sigma_1 \ldots c(r) \ldots c(s) \ldots \sigma_{|\zeta|}$ with $s \in \nu(r)$. In general, any string in H derived from ζ will present some relation between the l-th and the k-th substrings. On the other hand, there is no such relation forced on strings in L, so that there is a string in L, directly generated from ζ, of the form $\omega = \omega_1 \ldots c(r) \ldots c(s) \ldots \omega_{|\zeta|}$, with $s \notin \nu(r)$. $\square$

3.4.2. Dynamic number of groups

Consider the same gL as in Section 3.4.1 above, this time starting from the axiom $(a, 1)(b, 1)(c, 1)$. This gL generates the language $\{a^n b^n c^n \mid n \geq 1\}$. Here we have at most two groups, but we are not in the situation where this language can be obtained with exactly two groups (since the axiom accommodates only one group).

Hence, we can define the set $\mathcal{L}(\mathbf{digL})$ of languages from L-systems with dynamically generated groups up to a number i. By generalising the example, one can infer the following:

Theorem 3.4.2.1. $\mathcal{L}(\mathbf{digL})$ *properly contains* $\mathcal{L}(\mathbf{igL})$ *for each* i.

Theorem 3.4.2.2. $\mathcal{L}(\mathbf{d(i+1)gL})$ *properly contains* $\mathcal{L}(\mathbf{digL})$ *for each* i.

The set $\mathcal{L}(\mathbf{dgL}) = \bigcup_{i \in N} \mathcal{L}(\mathbf{digL})$ of languages generated by L-systems with dynamically generated groups is a superior for $\mathcal{L}(\mathbf{NgL}) = \bigcup_{i \in N} \mathcal{L}(\mathbf{igL})$ the set of languages generated by systems with a fixed finite number of groups. In particular, the following theorem states that unrestricted dynamical generation of fragments provides more generative power than the use of any finite number of fragments.

Theorem 3.4.2.3. *The language* $Z = \{xx \mid x \in \{a, b\}^*\}$ *is not generated by any L-system with a limited number of groups.*

Proof. Let us consider a $digL$-system K with $T = \{a, b\}$, and rule set P, able to generate all the words in $X = Z \cap \{\omega \mid |\omega| \leq 2 \times (i + 1)\}$, and no word in $Z^c \cap \{\omega \mid |\omega| \leq 2 \times (i + 1)\}$. Let $Y = L(K) \cap \{\omega \mid |\omega| > 2 \times (i + n + 2)\}$, where n is the maximum length for any of the consequents in P. Then, there are strings in Y which K is not able to generate. Indeed, for any string $\sigma \in Y$ there are at least a string $\omega \in Z$, and $\zeta \in (Z \setminus X) \cup (Z \setminus Y)$ and a derivation $\omega \Longrightarrow \zeta \Longrightarrow^* \sigma$. By the argument in the demonstration of Claim 3.4.1, the sequence of groups in the first half of the string, must be replicated in the second half. Hence, for each such string $\zeta \in Y$ there are at least two instances of the same symbol x, say ζ_k, and ζ_l, with $l \leq |\zeta|/2$, which belong to a same group. Hence, let $d(\zeta_i)$ indicate a string derived from a generic symbol ζ_i. Any string derived from will comply with the pattern $d(\zeta_1) \ldots d(\zeta_{k-1}) d(\zeta_k) \ldots d(\zeta_{l-1}) d(\zeta_l) \ldots d(\zeta_{|\zeta|/2}) \ldots d(\zeta_{|\zeta|})$.

In general, any string in Y will present some replication of substrings in its first half. Hence, for instance no string whose first half is of the form $abbaaabbbb \ldots a^k b^{k+1}$ can be generated, and $Z \setminus L(K) \neq \emptyset$. $\square$

3.4.3. Properties of closure

Theorem 3.4.3.1. *The facts in the table hold.*

Family	Union	Concat.
dgL	Y (cond.)	Y (cond.)
NgL	Y (cond.)	Y (cond.)

Proof. As for Theorem 3.3.4.1, we resort to conditioned rules, where rules depend on the value of an attribute. For union and concatenation one introduces a new attribute *origin*; takes the axioms of the two systems and sets *origin* to 0 or 1, according to the system from which is taken. Then one adds to the rules a condition on *origin*. If it is 0 the rules will be chosen from those of the first system, if it is 1 from those of the second.

<u>Concatenation</u>. Again, one uses *origin*.   □.

4. Relation with Control Mechanisms in Grammar Systems

4.1. Fragments and PCLS

The behaviour of fragmented L-systems can be related to the action of Parallel Communicating Lindenmayer Systems with Communication by Command. This family of L-systems combines the notion of Parallel Communicating L-systems, introduced in [26] with the notion of communication by command, introduced for grammar systems in [10].

In particular, we define a PCLS as a construct $\Gamma = \langle T, L_1 \ldots, L_n \rangle$, with $L_i = \langle T, P_i, Ax_i, \pi_i, X_i \rangle$, for $i = 1, \ldots, n$, where π_i is the pattern of strings for which communication occurs and X_i is a set of components to which messages have to be sent. Several variants can be defined as to whether the messages sent by a component i are the whole current string (*without splitting* indicated with w) or substrings from it (splitting, indicated with x), or as to what happens of the string of a component after sending a message (*returning*, r, or not, n).

Theorem 4.1.1. $\mathcal{L}((n,d)fL) \subset \mathcal{L}((w,r)PCLS)$.

Proof. Given a system $Z = \langle T \cup \{\#\}, Ax, P, \mu, \Longrightarrow \rangle \in (n,d)fL_k$, let $Q \in (w,r)PCLS$ a system built as follows. $Q = \langle T, L_0, L_1, \ldots, L_n \rangle$ with $L_i = \langle T, p_i, Ax_i, T^*, \{L_0\} \rangle$, $p_i = \mu(i)$, and Ax_i is the set of axioms for the i-th fragment of Z, and $L_0 = \langle T, P_0, Ax_0, \emptyset, \emptyset \rangle$, P_0 contains only rules $x \to \lambda$ for each $x \in T$ and $Ax_0 = \{\#_1\#_2 \ldots \#_{n-1}\#_n\}$. Since for each component of Q the communication pattern is T^*, every string is valid for performing a communication step. The rule for receiving messages is: concatenate a string α_i coming from component i before the i-th occurrence of $\#$. The language $L(L_0) - \{\lambda\}$ is equal to $L(Z)$.   □

If we apply the simulation in the proof of Theorem 4.1.1 to the case of L-systems with fragment generation, we find that for each string $\alpha_1\alpha_2 \ldots \alpha_n$ produced by the PCLS simulating a system without fragment generation, we can generate strings of type $K_1(\alpha_1) \ldots K_i(\alpha_i) \ldots K_n(\alpha_n)$. K_i indicates that a string is repeated as many times as the rule for fragment generation has been applied to the i-th separator symbol. On the other hand, in fragmented L-systems with generation, no relation exists after generation between a fragment and its originator, so that no pattern of dependency can be defined. Hence, L-systems with fragment generation cannot be simulated by PCLS with the above rule. For the returning mode of fragmentation, i.e. for $(r,d)fL_k$, no simulation is possible by PCLS, since any simulation should mix the returning and the non returning mode for the same component of the PCLS.

4.2. Migration and Immigration

The concept of fragmented L-systems with migration subsumes the recently proposed notion of L-systems with immigration [30]. In this latter notion an axiom can be non-deterministically added to a string at each step and the resulting language derives from the concatenation of the contributions of the axioms through the steps. The case when axioms are strings of length one can be simulated by considering a string with two fragments, where the first fragment has rules of type $\lambda \rightarrow x$, for each $x \in T$ and the second fragment has all the rules of the original L-system. The case of generic axioms can be simulated by introducing migration rules with antecedents of arbitrary length and conditioning application of a rule to the antecedent belonging to a finite set of patterns (exactly the set of axioms). Called B the set of axioms, the language generated by an L-system G with immigration is described in [30] as $L(G) = \{b_0\bar{h}(b_1; \ldots; b_n) \mid n \geq 0, b_i \in B\}$, where $\bar{h}(\omega_1; \omega_2; \ldots; \omega_n) = h(\omega_1)h^2(\omega_2)\ldots h^n(\omega_n)$ and h indicates the same morphism as in the definition of L' above. Since L-systems with immigration, indicated with **imL**, can be simulated by **mfL**s, we have that $\mathcal{L}(\mathbf{imL}) \subset \mathcal{L}(\mathbf{mfL})$. The additional constraint for **imL** that the morphism is unique for the whole string, causes the inclusion to be strict.

On the other hand, **imL**s can be simulated by fragmented L-systems with fragment generation as stated by the following:

Theorem 4.2.1. $\mathcal{L}(\mathbf{imL}) \subset \mathcal{L}((\mathbf{r, d})\mathbf{gfL})$.

Proof. An L-system with immigration can be simulated by a **(r,d)gfL** system starting with a single fragment and applying at each step exactly a fragmentation rule to the first fragment. □.

4.3. Groups, CD grammars and Teams

We study here the relation between groups and cooperating distributed grammar systems [6] where rules from a same set are used up to a certain restriction. In general, the mechanism of generation of CD grammar systems can be simulated with groups by distinguishing terminals and non terminals and defining the mapping ν so as to constrain the simultaneous application of rules to rules from a same component. Note that the simulation regards the synchronisation aspect, since CD systems operate on distinct alphabets of terminals and non terminals. The following theorem states the exact relation between sentential forms in derivations in a CD system and the language produced by the L-system with groups which simulates it. We first introduce a normal form lemma for CD systems.

Lemma 4.3.1. *For any CD system Γ there exists a CD-system Δ such that all its components have disjoint rules and $L_*(\Gamma) = L_*(\Delta)$.*

Proof. An equivalent CD is constructed according to the following procedure: For any subset of rules in a component that is a subset of at least another component remove the subset from all components it appears in and build a new component with this set. Repeat the procedure considering the newly added components, until no intersections among components are found. The procedure terminates since at most there will be as many components as rules. Since in the *-mode rules can be chosen from any component at each rewriting step, the set of sentential forms produced by the two CD systems in *-mode are the same. □

Theorem 4.3.1. *for any CD system* Γ, *there is a gL system* G *with two groups, such that* $A(G) = L_*(\Gamma)$, *i.e. the adult language of* G *is the language produced by* Γ *in the *-mode. Moreover,* $L(G) = Sen_*(\Gamma)$, *where* $Sen_*(\Gamma)$ *is the set of sentential forms produced in the *-mode of derivation.*

Proof. Given the CD system $\Gamma = \langle T, G_1, \ldots, G_n, S \rangle$, G is built in the following way: $G = \langle \bigcup_i T_i \cup \bigcup_i N_i, \{(S,0)\}, P_0 \cup \bigcup_i P_i \cup P_{n+1}, \Phi, \{term\}, \{\{0,1\}\}, \rho, \nu, \Longrightarrow \rangle$ with $P_0 = \{x \to x \mid x \in \bigcup_i T_i\}, P_{n+1} = \{X \to X \mid X \in \bigcup_i N_i\}, \Phi$ a set of semantic actions associating the value 0 with each non terminal and 1 with each terminal, ρ stating that two symbols belong in the same group if they have the same value of *term*, and ν defined by the rule $\nu(p) = P_i \cup P_0 \cup P_{n+1}, \forall p \in P_i$, for $i \leq n$ (remember that identity rules can be freely applied within a group, unless ν states otherwise). Let $S \stackrel{*}{\Longrightarrow}_* \omega \in T^*$ be a derivation in Γ. Such a derivation can be replicated in G by having only one symbol from a N_i rewritten at each step by a non-identity rule, while all other symbols are rewritten by identity rules. Hence any string of terminals produced by Γ is also generated by G, and is no longer modified in G. On the other hand, let $(S,0) \Longrightarrow^* \zeta \Longrightarrow \xi \Longrightarrow^* \omega \in (\bigcup_i T_i)^*$ be a derivation in G. If in the generation from ζ to ξ only one symbol is rewritten by a rule different from identity, this same step can be performed in Γ. Suppose this step rewrites k symbols by non identity rules. For the definition of ν, all the applied rules must belong to the same component. Hence the string ξ is a sentential form obtainable from ζ in k steps in which rules from a same component are applied. (Remember that in the *-mode there is no restriction on the number of times that rules from a component can be used). Any string of terminals in $L(G)$ is therefore also produced by Γ in the *-mode of derivation. □

We here briefly sketch an apparent symmetry between L-systems with groups and teams, which will be the subject of further studies. In teams, rules are applied in parallel by subsets of the set of sets of rules. Subsets are formed on the fly by taking any combination of sets of rules [20], or are predefined in a fixed number [28]. At each step each member of a team applies a rule. Teams can operate until all sets in the team have available a rule [28], or until all sets may be used simultaneously [13]. In general, several occurrences of symbols are rewritten simultaneously, each by a different member of a team. On the other hand, it is not required that all the occurrences of non terminals be rewritten at each step.

In groups, rules are applied in parallel to all the occurrences of symbols, subject to restrictions of synchronisation. A symbol is rewritten only if all the elements in the group have a rule to apply. Symbols for which the group cannot behave as a whole are rewritten by the identity rule.

4.4. Groups and fragments

A relation can be established between groups and fragments in a restricted case, if rules in the L-system with groups are also conditioned. In particular, it holds that:

Theorem 4.4.1. *Given a* fL_k-*system* F, *there is a ckgL-system* G, *such that* $L(F) = L(G)$.

Proof. Given a fL_k-system, the corresponding *ckgL*-system is defined by associating an attribute *fragm* with each symbol, to simulate membership in a fragment. Two symbols belong to the same group if they have the same value for *fragm*. The set P is composed of the union of the sets P_i in the fragmented system and $\nu(p) = P_i$, $\forall p \in P_i$. Each rule is associated with a condition, so that a rule from the set P_k is applicable to a symbol $(x, fragm)$ if and only if $k = \nu(fragm)$. □

The inverse simulation is not possible, since fragments restrict the possibility of synchronisation to adjacent symbols, while groups allow synchronisation among symbols at arbitrary distance.

5. Conclusions

Four abstract mechanisms to control the evolution of interactive systems - conditioning, stratification, fragmentation and grouping - have been abstracted from experimental studies on interactive systems [1] and placed in the framework of formal language theory. In particular, in a simulation of the immune system antigens, antibodies and immunocomplexes were modelled as agents subject to conditions depending on the tissue they are in, [3]. Mechanisms of fragmentation restricted communication among agents, and grouping modelled the coordinated evolution of agents. Agents were able to migrate from a tissue to another under certain conditions.

As shown in the example in Appendix 2, these abstract mechanisms allow the formal description of interactive systems and of their dynamics, characterised by: conditioning of system dynamics to user choices, synchronisation of responses of different parts of the system to a user action, coordination of the evolution of computational processes with their representation, management of different processes evolving in parallel, with forms both of synchronisation and of independence.

The defined forms of control are common to many situations in which the evolution and the viability of a system depend on the coordination of independent agents evolving in parallel and subject to environmental constraints [23]. In general, as discussed in [19], the ability of an agent to sense its environment defines the kind of environmental actions it can be subject to.

A different form of modelling the relation between agents and environments comes from the formalism of eco-grammar systems where there is a mutual dependency in the evolution of two different strings [9]. This mechanism can be seen as a special form of the stratification mechanism discussed in this paper.

Further research will both explore the potential of the control mechanism proposed in this paper in satisfying requirements for coordination in different fields and extend the characterisation of the families here introduced.

References

1. N. Bianchi, P. Bottoni, P. Mussio, M. Protti, "Cooperative Visual Environments for the Design of Effective Visual Systems", *JVLC*, vol. 4, n. 4, pp. 357-381, 1993

2. P. Bottoni, M. F. Costabile, S. Levialdi, P. Mussio, "Formalizing visual languages", *Proc. IEEE Symp. on Vis. Lang. '95.* IEEE CS Press, 1995, pp. 334-341.

3. P. Bottoni, M. Mariotto, P. Mussio, "LiSEB: a Language for Modeling Living Systems with APL2", *APL Quote Quad*, vol. 25, n. 1, 1994, pp. 7-16

4. P. Bottoni, G. Mauri, P. Mussio, "On controlling rewriting in Cooperative Systems", *Technical report* in preparation.

5. E. Csuhaj-Varju, J. Dassow, "On cooperating distributed grammar systems", *J. Inform. Process. Cybern., EIK*, vol. 26, pp. 49-63, 1990

6. E. Csuhaj-Varju, J. Dassow, J. Kelemen, G. Păun, *Grammar Systems: A Grammatical Approach to Distribution and Cooperation*, Gordon & Breach, 1994

7. E. Csuhaj-Varju, J. Dassow, J. Kelemen, G. Păun, "Stratified Grammar Systems", *Computers and Artificial Intelligence*, vol. 13, n. 5, pp. 409-422, 1994

8. E. Csuhaj-Varju, J. Dassow, G. Păun, "Stratified Grammar Systems", *Computers and Artificial Intelligence*, vol. 13, n. 5, pp. 409-422, 1994

9. E. Csuhaj-Varju, J. Kelemen, A. Kelemenova, G. Păun, "Eco-grammar systems: A grammatical framework for studying life-like interaction", *Artificial Life*, vol. 3, nr. 1, 1997.

10. E. Csuhaj-Varju, J. Kelemen, G. Păun, "Grammar Systems with WAVE-Like Communication", *Computers and Artificial Intelligence*, vol. 15, n. 5, pp. 419-436, 1996.

11. J. Dassow, G. Păun, *Regulated Rewriting in Formal Language Theory*, Springer, 1989

12. D. Giammarresi, A. Restivo, "Recognizable picture languages", *International Journal of Pattern Recognition and Artificial Intelligence*, vol. 6, pp. 31-46, 1992.

13. R. Freund, G. Păun, "A Variant of Team Cooperation in Grammar Systems", *J. Universal Computer Science*, vol. 1, n. 2, pp. 105-130, 1995

14. G. T. Herman, G. Rozenberg, *Developmental Systems and Languages*, North-Holland, 1975

15. K. Inoue, I. Takanami, "A survey of two-dimensional automata theory", *Information Science*, vol. 55, pp. 99-121, 1991.

16. L. Kari-Sântean, "Parallel Communicating Grammar Systems:", in G. Rozenberg, A. Salomaa eds., *Current Trends in Theoretical Computer Science. Essays and Tutorials*, World Scientific, pp. 603-615, 1993.

17. U. Kastens, "Attribute Grammars as a Specification Method", *Attribute Grammars, Applications and Systems, LNCS 545*, 1991, Springer, pp. 16-47.

18. J. Kelemen ed. , "Distributed AI, Decentralized AI and Multiagent Systems", Special Issue of *Computers and Artificial Intelligence*, vol. 12, n. 1, 1993

19. J. Kelemen, "Artificial life: Describing life-like behaviors in computational frameworks", in G. Păun ed. , *Artificial life: grammatical models*, Black Sea press, pp. 1-21, 1995

20. L. Kari, A. Mateescu, G. Paun, A. Salomaa, "Teams in cooperating grammar systems", *J. Exp. and Theoret. Artif. Intel.*, vol. 7, pp. 347-359, 1995

21. D. Knuth, "Semantics of context-free languages", *J. Math Syst. Theory*, vol. 2, pp. 127-145, 1968

22. B. Mayoh, "Templates, fragments and skins", in G. Rozenberg, A. Salomaa eds., *Lindenmayer Systems*, Springer, 1992, pp. 497-514

23. T. W. Malone, K. Crowston, "The Interdisciplinary Study of Coordination", *ACM Computing Surveys*, vol. 26, n. 1, pp. 87-121, 1994

24. V. Mitrana, G. Păun, G. Rozenberg, "Structuring grammar systems by priorities and hierarchies", *Acta Cybernetica*, vol. 11, n. 3, pp. 189-204, 1994

25. J. Paakki, "Attribute Grammar Paradigms, A High-Level Methodology in Language Implementation", *ACM Computing Surveys*, vol. 27, n. 2, pp. 196-255, 1995

26. G. Păun, "Parallel communicating Lindenmayer systems", in G. Rozenberg, A. Salomaa, *Lindenmayer Systems*, Springer, 1992, pp. 405-417

27. G. Păun, "On the synchronization in parallel communicating grammar systems", *Acta Informatica*, vol. 30, pp. 351-367, 1993

28. G. Păun, G. Rozenberg, "Prescribed teams of grammars", *Acta Informatica*, vol. 31, pp. 525-537, 1994

29. G. Păun, L. Sântean, "Parallel communicating grammar systems: the regular case, *Annals of Bucharest Univ., Mathematics-Informatics Series*, vol. 38, pp. 55-63, 1989

30. G. Rozenberg, "Theory of L-systems: From the point of view of formal language theory", in G. Rozenberg, A. Salomaa eds. , *L Systems*, Springer, 1974, pp. 1-24

31. A. Salomaa, "L codes and L systems with immigration", in G. Rozenberg, A. Salomaa eds. , *Current Trends in Theoretical Computer Science. Essays and Tutorials*, pp. 595-602, World Scientific, 1993

32. L. Santean, "Parallel Communicating Grammar Systems", in G. Rozenberg, A. Salomaa eds. , *Current Trends in Theoretical Computer Science. Essays and Tutorials*, pp. 603-615, World Scientific, 1993

Appendix 1. The system of L-systems for definition of electronic documents for galaxy simulation

A. LAYOUT DEFINITION

ALPHABET

The alphabet is $T_l = \{s, t, h, v\}$ where s stands for screen, t for tile, h for horizontal, v for vertical. The value of the attribute a for a symbol s is denoted by $s.a$.

A screen or a tile is described by a vector of attributes organized as follows: $a = \langle u, v \rangle$ where $u = \langle tp, state \rangle$ and $v = \langle links \rangle$; $state$ is a vector $state = \langle id, ds, ht, wt, pos \rangle$ and $links$ is a vector $links = \langle son\_of, father\_of \rangle$. On the whole, $a = \langle\langle tp, \langle id, ds, ht, wt, pos \rangle\rangle, \langle son\_of, father\_of \rangle\rangle$. tp is the type and takes value in the powerset of tile types $Tp = ul, ur, ll, lr, title, comm, display \cup \{ax_1, \ldots, ax_n\}$ where ul stands for *upper_left*, ur for *upper_right*, ll for *low_left*, lr for *low_right* and each ax_i is a domain-dependent type (e.g. *text*, *Nh*, *Nv*). We will not distinguish between an element of Tp and the corresponding singleton in the powerset.

id is an identifier (an integer) which characterises the symbol at hand, ds is a string of integers memorising the derivation of the tile from the screen. The value of the attribute ds for the symbol s is *1*.

pos identifies the position of the upper left corner of the tile in the image; ht identifies the height and wt the width of the tile.

son_of and $father\_of$ are used to maintain a link through the strata

AXIOM

The axiom is a screen symbol s with attributes $tp=ul$, $id=0$, $ds=1$, $ht=H$, $wt=W$; $pos=(0,0)$; $father\_of=void$.

RULES

In the semantic part we only show those attributes which are computed by the rules. When a symbol is created in the generation process, attributes which are not specified in the semantic part of the creating rule are set to void. When a symbol is rewritten, attributes which are not specified in the semantic part of the rewriting rule are copied. Symbols h, v have an empty set of attributes. We indicate by the symbol $=$ assignments of values to attributes specified by the rule, by the symbol $\leftarrow$ assignments which require user interaction. The symbol $\in$ indicates that the rule constrains the value to be in a certain set, from which the user can choose.

Splitting rules

For the sake of simplicity we impose rigid constraints on the computation of the attributes wt and ht.

1) $s \rightarrow t_1 \cdot v \cdot t_2$ $t_1.tp=ul$; $t_1.id=1$; $t_1.tds=1.1$; $t_1.ht=s.ht$; $t_1.wt \leftarrow w_c(s.wt)$;
   $t_1.pos=(0,0)$; $t_2.tp=ur$; $t_2.id=2$; $t_2.ds=1.2$;
   $t_2.ht=s.ht$; $t_2.wt \leftarrow s.wt\text{-}w_c(s.wt)$; $t_2.pos=w_c(s.wt)+1$.

2) $s \rightarrow t_1 \cdot h \cdot t_2$ $t_1.tp=title$; $t_1.id=1$; $t_1.ds=1.1$; $t_1.ht \leftarrow h_c(s.ht)$; $t_1.wt=s.wt$;
   $t_1.\ pos=(0,0)$; $t_2.tp=ll$; $t_2.id=2$; $t_2.ds=1.2$;
   $t_2.ht \leftarrow s.ht\text{-}h_c(s.ht)$; $t_2.wt = s.wt$; $t_2.pos=(0,h \div 2)$.

where $h_c(s.ht)=\{1, \ldots, s.ht\text{-}1$ and $w_c(s.wt)=\{1, \ldots, s.wt\text{-}1\}$. The following rules are guarded by a condition.

3) $t \rightarrow t_1 \cdot v \cdot t_2$ $\gamma \equiv t.tp \in \{ul, ur, ll, lr\}$

$\qquad t_1.tp \in r_1(t.tp); \; t_1.id=(t.id \times 2)+1; \; t_1.ds=t.ds \cdot 1; \; t_1.ht=t.ht;$

$\qquad t_1.wt \leftarrow w_c(t.wt); \; t_1.pos=t.pos; \; t_2.tp \in r_2(t.tp); \; t_2.id=(t.id \times 2)+2;$

$\qquad t_2.ds=t.ds \cdot 2; \; t_2.ht=t.ht; \; t_2.wt \leftarrow t.wt - w_c(t.wt);$

$\qquad t_2.pos=t.pos+w_c(t.wt+1);$

4) $t \rightarrow t_1 \cdot h \cdot t_2$ $\gamma \equiv t.tp \in \{ul, ur, ll, lr\}$

$\qquad t_1.tp \in r_3(t.tp); \; t_1.id=(t.id \times 2)+1; \; t_1.ds=t.ds \cdot 1;$

$\qquad t_1.ht \leftarrow h_c(t.ht); \; t_1.wt=t.wt;$

$\qquad t_1.pos=t.pos; \; t_2.tp \in r_4(t.tp); \; t_2.id=(t.id \times 2)+2; \; t_2.ds=t.ds \cdot 2;$

$\qquad t_2.ht \leftarrow t.ht - h_c(t.ht); \; t_2.wt=t.wt; \; t_2.pos=t.pos+(0,h_c(t.ht+1));$

where r_1, r_2 and r_3, r_4 indicate a set of possible values determined by the following rules. The non-determinism in their definition is resolved by the interaction of the user.

r_1: $\quad ul \mapsto \{ul, \; title\}; \; ur \mapsto \{ul, \; title\}; \; ll \mapsto \{ll, \; title\}; \; lr \mapsto \{ll, \; title\}$

r_2: $\quad ul \mapsto \{ur, \; title\}; \; ur \mapsto \{ur, \; title\}; \; ll \mapsto \{lr, \; title\}; \; lr \mapsto \{lr, \; title\}$

r_3: $\quad ul \mapsto \{ul, \; title\}; \; ur \mapsto \{ur, \; title\}; \; ll \mapsto \{ll, \; title, \; display\};$

$\qquad lr \mapsto \{lr, \; title, \; display\}$

r_4: $\quad ul \mapsto \{ul, \; display, \; comm, \; \{display, comm\}\};$

$\qquad ur \mapsto \{ur, \; display, \; comm, \; \{display, comm\}\};$

$\qquad ll \mapsto \{ll, \; display, \; comm, \; \{display, \; comm\}\};$

$\qquad lr \mapsto \{lr, \; display, \; comm, \; \{display, \; comm\}\}$

Process generating rules

Tiles t of type *display* may generate at a lower stratum the axioms of different processes.

5) $\quad t_1 \downarrow t_2 \qquad \gamma \equiv (t.tp=display \land t_1.father\_of=void)$

$\qquad ax \# \quad ax.id=(t1.id,0); \; ax.son\_of=t_1.id;$

$\qquad ax.pos=(t.pos[1]+t.ht \div 2, \; t.pos[2]+t.wt \div 2 \; t_2.father\_of=ax.id$

6) $\quad t_1 \downarrow t_2 \qquad \gamma \equiv (t.tp=title \land t_1.father\_of=void)$

$\qquad Tx \# \quad Tx.id=(t1.id,0); \; Tx.son\_of=t_1.id;$

$\qquad Tx.pos=(t.pos[1]+t.ht \div 2, \; t.pos[2]+t.wt \div 2 \; t_2.father\_of=Tx.id$

Process generating rules can be applied after each rewriting step using only splitting rules.

B. SIMULATION OF GALAXY EVOLUTION

ALPHABET

The alphabet is $T=\{Nh, Nv, A\}$ where Nh stands for nucleus generating in horizontal, Nv for nucleus generating in vertical A for arm. A galaxy is composed of a nucleus and two arms developing at opposite sides of the nucleus. The galaxy expands by spawning new elements of the arms from the nucleus and each element of the arm moves in a way that combines expansion towards the exit as the result of the push from new formed elements and a tendency to rotate around the nucleus due to gravitational effects. The galaxy has also a translational movement. For the sake of simplicity the galaxy is described as having a one pixel nucleus, while arms have one pixel width and translation is assumed to be always in the horizontal sense. All movements are here discretised and assumed to occur at a speed of one pixel per rewriting step. Let us consider the display tile in which the simulation of the galaxy dynamics is represented. The process is halted when an element of the galaxy touches the border of the tile, i. e. the representation would exceed the window limits. The elements of the alphabet T_g have a common set of attributes: $A_g=\{x, y, xmax, ymax, xmin, ymin, age, arm, grp\}$. The tile L-system STL of appendix 1 is used to generate an interface, using a materialisation function which represents a tile t of size $(t.wt,t.ht)$ and in position $t.pos$ as a rectangle of width $t.wt$, height $t.ht$ and with the upper left corner in position $(x=t.pos[1]$, $y=t.pos[2])$ of the screen. The process generating rules are here defined as follows:

7) $t_1 \downarrow t_2$ $\quad \gamma \equiv (t.tp=display \wedge t_1.father\_of=void)$
$\quad\quad Nh \# Nh.id=(t_1.id,0); Nh.son\_of=t_1.id; Nh.xmax=t_1.pos[1]+t.wt;$
$\quad\quad Nh.ymax=t_1.pos[2]+t.ht, Nh.pos=t_1.pos+(t_1.wt \div 2,t_1.ht \div 2);$
$\quad\quad Nh.xmin=t_1.pos[1]+1; Nh.ymin=t_1.pos[2]+1; Nh.grp=1;$
$\quad\quad t_2.father\_of=Nh.id$

8) $t_1 \downarrow t_2$ $\quad \gamma \equiv (t.tp=display \wedge t_1.father\_of=void)$
$\quad\quad Nv \# Nv.id=(t_1.id,0); Nv.son\_of=t_1.id; Nv.xmax=t_1.pos[1]+t.wt;$
$\quad\quad Nv.ymax=t_1.pos[2]+t.ht, Nv.pos=t_1.pos+(t_1.wt \div 2,t_1.ht \div 2;$
$\quad\quad Nv.xmin=t_1.pos[1]+1; Nv.ymin=t_1.pos[2]+1; Nv.grp = 1;$
$\quad\quad t_2.father\_of = Nh.id.$

The evolution of the galaxy in the horizontal direction is described by two rules which combine expansion and translation. In these two rules the values of the attributes $\{grp,xmax,ymax,xmin,ymin,son\_of\}$ of the antecedent are are transmitted to each generated symbol in the consequent.

9) $Nh_1 \rightarrow A_1 \cdot Nh_2 \cdot A_2$
$\quad\quad Nh_2.pos=Nh_1.pos+(1,0), A_1.pos=Nh_1.pos, A_2.pos=Nh_1.$
$\quad\quad pos+(2,0) A_1.arm=-1, A_2.arm=1, A_1.age=1, A_2.age=1$

10) $A_1 \rightarrow A_2$ $\quad \gamma \equiv (A_1.pos[1] <A_1.xmax-1) \wedge (A_1.ymin+1 <A_1.pos[2] \leq A_1.$
$\quad\quad ymax-1) A_2.age=A_1.age+1,$
$\quad\quad A_2.pos[1]=A_1.pos[1]+1+A_1.arm \times \cos(45° \times \lfloor \log A_1.age \rfloor),$
$\quad\quad A_2.pos[2]=A_1.pos[2]+A_1.arm \times \sin(45° \times \lfloor \log A_1.age \rfloor)+1.$

An analogous pair of rules is defined to simulate upward movement and expansion, not reported here due to lack of space.

C. Text Generation

The process generating rules in the experiment are assumed to be coordinated so that for each tile of type *display*, the tile above it is of type *title*. Such tile can create a text axiom, from which the string of the title is derived. Such a derivation can be modelled with specific sets of rules for text generation. We do not report them due to lack of space.

Appendix 2. Example: Interactive generation of an interface and a simulation process

The system of L-Systems of Appendix 1 is used to generate a simple interface and to run the simple experiment described in the scenario. Table 1 displays the derivation process with the following conventions. A rewriting step is denoted by an arrow $\Longrightarrow$ over which a vector of numbers is written. The numbers denote the rules from Appendix 1 which are simultaneously applied in the step. In the first two steps, some values used in the computation of the semantic part are interactively determined by the scientist interaction. In this case, the vector of values input by the scientist is written after the arrow and the arrow and the vector are enclosed between braces.

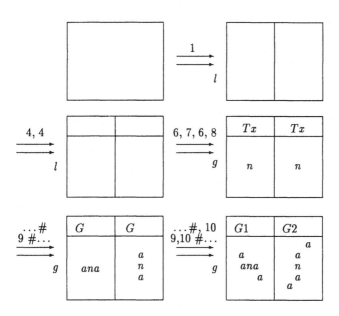

Figure A1

Each symbol in the derivation is materialised by a function *mat* which associates with each symbol t a rectangular shape, with each string in a tile of type *title* the string itself, and which represents a symbol $x \in \{Nh, Nv\}$ as a letter "n" in position x. *pos* and a symbol A as a letter "a" in position A. *pos*.

$\langle$ **s**, *ul*, 0, 1, H, W, (0,0), *void* $\rangle$

$$\{\xrightarrow{(1)}_l, (W/2)\}$$

$\langle$ **t**, *ul*, 1, 1.1 ,H, W/2, (0,0), *void* $\rangle$ **v** $\langle$ **t**, *ur*, 2, 1.2, H, W/2, (W/2+1,0), *void* $\rangle$

$$\{\xrightarrow{(4,4)}_l, (tp=title, ht=h_1), (tp=display, ht=H-h_1), (tp=title, ht=h_1),$$
$$(tp=display, ht=H-h_1)\}$$

$\langle$ **t**, *title*, 3, 1.1.1 , h_1, W/2, (0,0), *void* $\rangle$ **h**
$\langle$ **t**, *display*, 4, 1.1.2 , H-h_1, W/2, (0,h_1+1), *void* $\rangle$ **v**
$\langle$ **t**, *title*, 5, 1.2.1, h_1, W/2, (W/2+1,0), *void* $\rangle$ **h**
$\langle$ **t**, *display*, 6, 1.2.2 , H-h_1, W/2, (W/2+1,h_1+1), *void* $\rangle$

$$\{\xdownarrow{6,7,6,8}_l, ((ax=Tx, rules=rtx), (ax=Nh, rules=rgal), (ax=Tx, rules=rtx),$$
$$(ax=Nv, rules=rgal)\}$$

⟨t, ..., *3.0* ⟩ h ⟨t, ..., *4.0* ⟩ v ⟨t, ..., *5.0* ⟩ h ⟨t, ..., *6.0* ⟩

⟨**Tx**, *3.0*, $W/2, h_1$, *1, 1, (1,h_1), 1, 3* ⟩ #
⟨**Nh**, *4.0*, $W/2$, H, *1*, h_1+1, $(W/4, ((H-h_1)/2+h_1))$, *1, 4* ⟩#
⟨**Tx**, *5.0*, W, h_1, $W/2+1$, *1*, $(W/2+1, h_1)$, *1, 5* ⟩ #
⟨**Nv**, *6.0*, W, H, $W/2+1$, h_1+1, $(W/2+W/4, ((H-h_1)/2+h_1)), 1, 6$ ⟩

$$\overset{9}{\Longrightarrow}_g$$

...# ⟨**A**, ..., $(W/4, (H-h_1)/2+h_1)$, *1* ⟩
⟨**Nh**, ..., $(W/4+1, (H-h_1)/2+h_1)$ ⟩ ⟨**A**, ..., $(W/4+2, (H-h_1)/2+h_1)$, *1* ⟩# ...#

$$\overset{10,9,10}{\Longrightarrow}_g$$

...# ⟨**A**, ..., $(W/4, (H-h_1)/2+h_1-1)$, *2* ⟩ ⟨**A**, ..., $(W/4+1, (H-h_1)/2+h_1)$, *1* ⟩
⟨**Nh**, ..., $(W/4+2, (H-h_1)/2+h_1)$ ...⟩
⟨**A**, ..., $(W/4+3, (H-h_1)/2+h_1)$, *1* ⟩ ⟨**A**, ..., $(W/4+4, (H-h_1)/2+h_1+1)$, *2* ⟩# ...

Accepting Array Grammars
with Control Mechanisms

Henning FERNAU

Wilhelm-Schickard-Institut für Informatik
Universität Tübingen
Sand13, D-72076 Tübingen, Germany

Rudolf FREUND

Institut für Computersprachen
Technische Universität Wien
Resselgasse3, A-1040 Wien, Austria

Abstract. We consider (n-dimensional) array grammars in the accepting mode with various control mechanisms and compare these families of array grammars with the corresponding families obtained by array grammars in the generating mode.

1. Introduction

Accepting grammars together with various control mechanisms were introduced in [1] for the string case. Recent ideas concerning these grammars were exposed in [2]. The main results of the paper concern the relations between the families of array languages obtained by accepting array grammars in this way and array languages described by the corresponding types of generating array grammars.

Compared with the string case, we find many similarities, e.g., accepting programmed array grammars without appearance checking are just as powerful as their generating counterparts, and accepting ordered grammars can describe every recursively enumerable array language. On the other hand, the family of accepting regular programmed two-dimensional array languages with unconditional transfer is incomparable with the corresponding family of generating regular programmed array languages, while the respective string language classes coincide. Moreover, such incomparability results have not been observed in the string case except for pure grammars [3].

2. Definitions and Examples

In the main part of this section, we will introduce the definitions and notations for arrays and sequential array grammars [5], [11], [14], [17], [19] and give some explanatory examples, but first we recall some basic notions from the theory of formal languages (for more details, the reader is referred to [18]).

Definition 2.1. For an alphabet V, by V^* we denote the free monoid generated by V under the operation of concatenation; the *empty string* is denoted by λ, and $V^* \setminus \{\lambda\}$ is denoted by V^+. Any subset of V^+ is called a *λ-free (string) language*.

A *(string) grammar* is a quadruple $G = (V_N, V_T, P, S)$, where V_N and V_T are finite sets of *non-terminal* and *terminal symbols,* respectively, with $V_N \cap V_T = \emptyset$, P is a finite set of *productions* $\alpha \to \beta$ with $\alpha \in V^+$ and $\beta \in V^*$, where $V = V_N \cup V_T$, and $S \in V_N$

is the *start symbol*. For $x, y \in V^*$ we say that y *is directly derivable from x in G*, denoted by $x \vdash_G y$, if and only if for some $\alpha \to \beta$ in P and $u, v \in V^*$ we get $x = u\alpha v$ and $y = u\beta v$. Denoting the reflexive and transitive closure of the derivation relation $\vdash_G$ by $\vdash_G^*$, the *(string) language generated by G* is $L(G) = \{w \in V_T^* \mid S \vdash_G^* w\}$.

The families of λ-free (string) languages generated by arbitrary, monotonic, context-free, respectively regular grammars are denoted by $L(enum)$, $L(mon)$, $L(cf)$, respectively $L(reg)$. The following relations are known as the CHOMSKY-hierarchy [18]: $L(reg) \subset L(cf) \subset L(mon) \subset L(enum)$.

Definition 2.2. Let Z denote the set of integers, let N denote the set of positive integers, $N = \{1, 2, ...\}$, and let $n \in N$. Then an *n-dimensional array $\mathcal{A}$* over an alphabet V is a function $\mathcal{A} : Z^n \to V \cup \{\#\}$, where $shape(\mathcal{A}) = \{v \in Z^n \mid \mathcal{A}(v) \neq \#\}$ is finite and $\# \notin V$ is called the *background* or *blank symbol*. We usually shall write $\mathcal{A} = \{(v, \mathcal{A}(v)) \mid v \in shape(\mathcal{A})\}$.

The set of all n-dimensional arrays over V shall be denoted by V^{*n}. The *empty array* in V^{*n} with empty shape shall be denoted by Λ_n. Moreover, we define $V^{+n} = V^{*n} \setminus \{\Lambda_n\}$. Any subset of V^{+n} is called a Λ-free n-dimensional array language.

Definition 2.3. Let $v \in Z^n$. Then the *translation* $\tau_v : Z^n \to Z^n$ is defined by $\tau_v(w) = w + v$ for all $w \in Z^n$, and for any array $\mathcal{A} \in V^{*n}$ we define $\tau_v(\mathcal{A})$, the corresponding n-dimensional array translated by v, by

$$(\tau_v(\mathcal{A}))(w) = \mathcal{A}(w - v) \text{ for all } w \in Z^n.$$

The vector $(0, \dots, 0) \in Z^n$ is denoted by Ω_n, while $(1, \dots, 1)$ is denoted by E_n.

Usually [5], [17], [19], [20], arrays are regarded as equivalence classes of arrays with respect to linear translations, i.e. only the relative positions of the symbols $\neq \#$ in the plane are taken into account: The equivalence class $[\mathcal{A}]$ of an array $\mathcal{A} \in V^{*n}$ is defined by $[\mathcal{A}] = \{\mathcal{B} \in V^{*n} \mid \mathcal{B} = \tau_v(\mathcal{A}) \text{ for some } v \in Z^n\}$.

The set of all equivalence classes of n-dimensional arrays over V with respect to linear translations shall be denoted by $[V^{*n}]$ etc. Most of the results elaborated in this paper immediately carry over from the families of array languages we consider to the corresponding families of array languages with respect to linear translations, therefore, in general we shall not consider these families of array languages with respect to linear translations explicitly in the following any more.

In order to be able to define the notion of connectedness of n-dimensional arrays, we need the following definitions:

Definition 2.4. An (undirected) *graph* g is an ordered pair (K, E), where K is a finite set of nodes and E is a set of undirected edges $\{x, y\}$ with $x, y \in K$. A sequence of different nodes $x_0, x_1, \dots, x_m$, $m \in N$, is called a *path of length m* in g with the starting-point x_0 and the ending-point x_m, if for all i with $1 \leq i \leq m$ an edge $\{x_{i-1}, x_i\}$ in E exists. A graph g is said to be *connected*, if for any two nodes $x, y \in K$, $x \neq y$, a path in g with starting point x and ending point y exists. Observe that a graph $(\{x\}, \emptyset)$ with only one node and an empty set of edges is connected, too.

Let W be a non-empty finite subset of Z^n. For any $k \in N \cup \{0\}$, a graph $g_k(W) = (W, E_k)$ can be assigned to W such that E_k for $v, w \in W$ contains the edge $\{v, w\}$ if and only if $0 < \|v - w\| \leq k$, where the norm $\|u\|$ of a vector $u \in Z^n$, $u = (u(1), \dots, u(n))$, is defined by $\|u\| = \max\{|u(i)| \mid 1 \leq i \leq n\}$. Then, W is said to be *k-connected* if $g_k(W)$ is a connected graph. Observe that W is 0-connected if and only if $card(W) = 1$, where $card(W)$ denotes the number of elements in the set W.

Now let V be a finite alphabet and $\mathcal{A}$ an n-dimensional array over V, $\mathcal{A} \neq \Lambda_n$. Then $\mathcal{A}$ is said to be *k-connected* if $g_k(shape(\mathcal{A}))$ is a connected graph. Obviously, if $\mathcal{A}$ is k-connected then $\mathcal{A}$ is m-connected for all $m > k$, too. The *norm of* $\mathcal{A}$ is the smallest number $k \in N \cup \{0\}$ such that $\mathcal{A}$ is k-connected, and is denoted by $\|\mathcal{A}\|$. Observe that $\|\mathcal{A}\| = 0$ if and only if $card(shape(\mathcal{A})) = 1$.

Example 2.1. The n-dimensional array $\mathcal{E}(n,k) = \{(\Omega_n, a), (kE_n, a)\} \in \{a\}^{*n}$ is m-connected only for every $m \geq k$, and therefore $\|\mathcal{E}(n,k)\| = k$.

Definition 2.5. An *n-dimensional generating array production* p over V is a triple $(W, \mathcal{A}_1, \mathcal{A}_2)$, where $W \subseteq Z^n$ is a finite set and $\mathcal{A}_1$ and $\mathcal{A}_2$ are mappings from W to $V \cup \{\#\}$; p is called Λ-*free* if $shape(\mathcal{A}_2) \neq \emptyset$, where we define $shape(\mathcal{A}_i) = \{v \in W \mid \mathcal{A}_i(v) \neq \#\}$, $1 \leq i \leq 2$. The norm of the n-dimensional array production $(W, \mathcal{A}_1, \mathcal{A}_2)$ is defined by $\|(W, \mathcal{A}_1, \mathcal{A}_2)\| = \max\{\|v\| \mid v \in W\}$. We say that the array $\mathcal{C}_2 \in V^{*n}$ is *directly derivable* from the array $\mathcal{C}_1 \in V^{*n}$ by the n-dimensional array production $(W, \mathcal{A}_1, \mathcal{A}_2)$ if and only if there exists a vector $v \in Z^n$ such that $\mathcal{C}_1(w) = \mathcal{C}_2(w)$ for all $w \in Z^n \setminus \tau_v(W)$ as well as $\mathcal{C}_1(w) = \mathcal{A}_1(\tau_{-v}(w))$ and $\mathcal{C}_2(w) = \mathcal{A}_2(\tau_{-v}(w))$ for all $w \in \tau_v(W)$, i.e. the subarray of $\mathcal{C}_1$ corresponding to $\mathcal{A}_1$ is replaced by $\mathcal{A}_2$, thus yielding $\mathcal{C}_2$; we also write $\mathcal{C}_1 \vdash_p \mathcal{C}_2$.

As can already be seen from the definitions of an n-dimensional array production, the conditions for an application to an n-dimensional array $\mathcal{B}$ and the result of an application to $\mathcal{B}$, an n-dimensional array production $(W, \mathcal{A}_1, \mathcal{A}_2)$ is a representative for the infinite set of equivalent n-dimensional array productions of the form $(\tau_v(W), \tau_v(\mathcal{A}_1), \tau_v(\mathcal{A}_2))$ with $v \in Z^n$. Hence, without loss of generality, in the sequel we shall assume $\Omega_n \in W$ as well as $\mathcal{A}_1(\Omega_n) \neq \#$. Moreover, we often will omit the set W, because it is uniquely reconstructible from the description of the two mappings $\mathcal{A}_1$ and $\mathcal{A}_2$ by $\mathcal{A}_i = \{(v, \mathcal{A}_i(v)) \mid v \in W\}$, $1 \leq i \leq 2$. Thus in the sequel we will represent the n-dimensional array production $(W, \mathcal{A}_1, \mathcal{A}_2)$ also by writing $\mathcal{A}_1 \rightarrow \mathcal{A}_2$, i.e. $\{(v, \mathcal{A}_1(v)) \mid v \in W\} \rightarrow \{(v, \mathcal{A}_2(v)) \mid v \in W\}$.

Definition 2.6. An *n-dimensional (generating) array grammar* is a quintuple

$$G = (n, V_N, V_T, \#, P, \{(v_0, S)\}),$$

where V_N is the alphabet of *non-terminal symbols*, V_T is the alphabet of *terminal symbols*, $V_N \cap V_T = \emptyset$, $\# \notin V_N \cup V_T$; P is a finite non-empty set of n-dimensional array productions over $V_N \cup V_T$ and $\{(v_0, S)\}$ is the *start array (axiom)*, v_0 is the start vector, and S is the *start symbol*. G is called Λ-*free* if every production in P is Λ-free.

We say that the array $\mathcal{B}_2 \in V^{*n}$ is *directly derivable* from the array $\mathcal{B}_1 \in V^{*n}$ in G, denoted $\mathcal{B}_1 \vdash_G \mathcal{B}_2$, if and only if there exists an n-dimensional array production $p = (W, \mathcal{A}_1, \mathcal{A}_2)$ in P such that $\mathcal{B}_1 \vdash_p \mathcal{B}_2$. Let $\vdash_G^*$ be the reflexive transitive closure of $\vdash_G$. Then the *(n-dimensional) array language* generated by G, $L_{gen}(G)$, is defined by $L_{gen}(G) = \{\mathcal{A} \mid \mathcal{A} \in V_T^{*n}, \{(v_0, S)\} \vdash_G^* \mathcal{A}\}$. The norm of the n-dimensional array grammar G is defined by $\|G\| = \max\{\|p\| \mid p \in P\}$.

An n-dimensional generating array production $p = (W, \mathcal{A}_1, \mathcal{A}_2)$ in P is called

- *monotonic*, if $shape(\mathcal{A}_1) \subseteq shape(\mathcal{A}_2)$;

- *strictly monotonic*, if $shape(\mathcal{A}_2) = W$ and $\|p\| = 1$;

- *#-context-free*, if $card(shape(\mathcal{A}_1)) = 1$;

- *context-free*, if p is monotonic, $card(shape(\mathcal{A}_1)) = 1$, and $\mathcal{A}_1(\Omega_n) \in V_N$; the condition $\mathcal{A}_1(\Omega_n) \in V_N$ allows the representation of a context-free array production as $(A, \{(v, \mathcal{A}_2(v)) \mid v \in W\})$ or $A \to \{(v, \mathcal{A}_2(v)) \mid v \in W\}$ instead of $(W, \{(\Omega_n, A)\} \cup \{(v, \#) \mid v \in W \setminus \{\Omega_n\}\}, \{(v, \mathcal{A}_2(v)) \mid v \in W\})$; if $card(W) = 1$, we only write $A \to \mathcal{A}_2(\Omega_n)$;

- *strictly context-free*, if p is strictly monotonic as well as context-free;

- *regular*, if either

    1. $W = \{\Omega_n, v\}$ for some $v \in U_n$, where $U_n = \{(i_1, \ldots, i_n) \mid \sum_{k=1}^{n} |i_k| = 1\}$, and $\mathcal{A}_1 = \{(\Omega_n, B), (v, \#)\}$, $\mathcal{A}_2 = \{(\Omega_n, a), (v, C)\}$, with $B, C \in V_N$ and $a \in V_T$ (we also write $Bv\# \to avC$), *or*

    2. $W = \{\Omega_n\}$, $\mathcal{A}_1 = \{(\Omega_n, B)\}$, $\mathcal{A}_2 = \{(\Omega_n, a)\}$, with $B \in V_N$ and $a \in V_T$ (we also write $B \to a$).

G is called an n-dimensional array grammar of type (gen, X), $X \in \{enum, \# - cf, mon, smon, cf, scf, reg\}$, if every array production in P is of the corresponding type, i.e. a generating arbitrary $(gen, enum)$, #-context-free $(gen, \# - cf)$, monotonic (gen, mon), strictly monotonic $(gen, smon)$, context-free (gen, cf), strictly context-free (gen, scf), respectively regular (gen, reg) n-dimensional (generating) array production; the corresponding families of Λ-free n-dimensional array languages are denoted by $L(n, (gen, X))$. If for two types (gen, X), (gen, Y) with $X, Y \in \{enum, \# - cf, mon, smon, cf, scf, reg\}$ every array production of type (gen, X) is also an array production of type (gen, Y), we write $(gen, X) \subseteq (gen, Y)$ or even $X \subseteq Y$.

Remark 2.1. Let $G = (n, V_N, V_T, \#, P, \{(v_0, S)\})$ be an n-dimensional (generating) array grammar. If G is regular, strictly context-free, respectively strictly monotonic, then according to the previous definition of regular, strictly context-free, and strictly monotonic n-dimensional generating array productions we immediately see that every array in $L_{gen}(G)$ must be 1-connected. If G is context-free or monotonic, then $\|A\| \leq \|G\|$ for all $A \in L_{gen}(G)$. In the case of arbitrary n-dimensional array grammars, additional restrictive conditions on the n-dimensional array productions in P are required in order to guarantee every n-dimensional array in $L_{gen}(G)$ to be $\|G\|$-connected or even to be 1-connected as it is often required in the literature [5], [17], [19], [20]. In the following, we also consider the case of monotonic n-dimensional generating array grammars with norm 1 and denote the corresponding family of array languages generated by such array grammars by $L(n, (gen, mon_1))$.

Like in the string case, some of the families of array languages defined above form a strict hierarchy (compare with the results stated in [11], [12], [14].

Proposition 2.1. (CHOMSKY-*Hierarchy of array languages*) *For all* $n \in N$, $L(n, (gen, reg)) \subset L(n, (gen, scf)) \subset L(n, (gen, mon)) \subset L(n, (gen, enum))$.

Obviously, the inclusions

$$L(n, (gen, scf)) \subset L(n, (gen, smon)) \text{ and } L(n, (gen, cf)) \subset L(n, (gen, mon))$$

are true, too, whereas the families $L(n,(gen,cf))$ and $L(n,(gen,smon))$ are incomparable. Furthermore, we have the inclusions

$$L(n,(gen,cf)) \subset L(n,(gen,\# - cf)) \subset L(n,(gen,enum)),$$

whereas $L(n,(gen,\# - cf))$ and $L(n,(gen,mon))$ are incomparable.

An interesting feature of n-dimensional (generating) array grammars is the fact that even regular and context-free array productions make use of some special context, namely the context of blank symbols $\#$. This $\#$-sensing ability (which is reduced to a minimum in the case of strictly context-free respectively strictly monotonic array grammars in contrast to context-free respectively monotonic array grammars) induces a relatively high generating power even of only regular two-dimensional-dimenensional array grammars and yields some rather astonishing results, e.g. the set of all solid squares can be generated by a regular two-dimensional array grammar [20].

As many results for n-dimensional arrays for a special n can be taken over immediately for higher dimensions, we introduce the following notion:

Definition 2.7. Let $n, m \in N$ with $n \leq m$. For $n < m$, the natural embedding $i_{n,m} : Z^n \to Z^m$ is defined by $i_{n,m}(v) = (v, \Omega_{m-n})$ for all $v \in Z^n$; for $n = m$ we define $i_{n,n} : Z^n \to Z^n$ by $i_{n,n}(v) = v$ for all $v \in Z^n$. To an n-dimensional array $\mathcal{A} \in V^{+n}$ with $\mathcal{A} = \{(v, \mathcal{A}(v)) \mid v \in shape(\mathcal{A})\}$ we assign the m-dimensional array $i_{n,m}(\mathcal{A}) = \{(i_{n,m}(v), \mathcal{A}(v)) \mid v \in shape(\mathcal{A})\}$.

3. Accepting Array Grammars: Definitions and Examples

First we introduce the concept of accepting array productions and grammars:

Definition 3.1. An n-*dimensional accepting array production* p over V is a triple $(W, \mathcal{A}_2, \mathcal{A}_1)$, where $W \subseteq Z^n$ is a finite set and $\mathcal{A}_1$ and $\mathcal{A}_2$ are mappings from W to $V \cup \{\#\}$; p is called Λ-*free* if $shape(\mathcal{A}_2) \neq \emptyset$. We say that the array $\mathcal{C}_1 \in V^{*n}$ is *directly derivable (reducible)* from the array $\mathcal{C}_2 \in V^{*n}$ by the n-dimensional accepting array production $(W, \mathcal{A}_2, \mathcal{A}_1)$ if and only if there exists a vector $v \in Z^n$ such that $\mathcal{C}_1(w) = \mathcal{C}_2(w)$ for all $w \in Z^n \setminus \tau_v(W)$ as well as $\mathcal{C}_2(w) = \mathcal{A}_2(\tau_{-v}(w))$ and $\mathcal{C}_1(w) = \mathcal{A}_1(\tau_{-v}(w))$ for all $w \in \tau_v(W)$, i.e. the subarray of $\mathcal{C}_2$ corresponding to $\mathcal{A}_2$ is replaced by $\mathcal{A}_1$, thus yielding $\mathcal{C}_1$; we also write $\mathcal{C}_2 \vdash_p \mathcal{C}_1$. For short, if $(W, \mathcal{A}_1, \mathcal{A}_2)$ is a generating array production, then $(W, \mathcal{A}_2, \mathcal{A}_1)$ is the corresponding (dual) accepting array production; for the accepting array production $(W, \mathcal{A}_2, \mathcal{A}_1)$ the dual generating array production is $(W, \mathcal{A}_1, \mathcal{A}_2)$.

An n-*dimensional accepting array grammar* is a construct

$$G = (n, V_N, V_T, \#, P, \{(v_0, S)\}),$$

where V_N is the alphabet of *non-terminal symbols*, V_T is the alphabet of *terminal symbols*, $V_N \cap V_T = \emptyset$, $\# \notin V_N \cup V_T$; P is a finite non-empty set of n-dimensional accepting array productions over $V_N \cup V_T$, and $\{(v_0, S)\}$ is the *final array (goal)*. G is called Λ-*free* if every production in P is Λ-free.

We say that the array $\mathcal{B}_1 \in V^{*n}$ is *directly derivable* from the array $\mathcal{B}_2 \in V^{*n}$ in G, denoted $\mathcal{B}_2 \vdash_G \mathcal{B}_1$, if and only if there exists an n-dimensional accepting array production $p = (W, \mathcal{A}_2, \mathcal{A}_1)$ in P such that $\mathcal{B}_2 \vdash_p \mathcal{B}_1$. Let $\vdash_G^*$ be the reflexive transitive closure of $\vdash_G$. Then the *(n-dimensional) array language accepted by G, $L_{acc}(G)$*, is defined by $L_{acc}(G) = \{A \mid A \in V_T^{*n}, A \vdash_G^* \{(v_0, S)\}\}$.

For any $X \in \{enum, \# - cf, mon, smon, cf, scf, reg\}$ the accepting array production (W, A_2, A_1) is said to be of type (acc, X), if the dual generating array production (W, A_1, A_2) is of type (gen, X). G is called to be of type (acc, X), if every accepting array production in P is of the corresponding type. The corresponding families of Λ-free n-dimensional array languages are denoted by $L(n, (acc, X))$.

For any n-dimensional (generating respectively accepting) array grammar $G = (n, V_N, V_T, \#, P, \{(v_0, S)\})$, the corresponding dual n-dimensional (accepting respectively generating) array grammar $G^d = (n, V_N, V_T, \#, P^d, \{(v_0, S)\})$ is defined by

$$P^d = \{(W, A_2, A_1) \mid (W, A_1, A_2) \in P\}.$$

The following result is obvious from our definitions:

Lemma 3.1. *If G is a generating (accepting, respectively) array grammar and G^d is its dual accepting (generating, respectively) array grammar, then $L_{gen}(G) = L_{acc}(G^d)$ (and $L_{acc}(G) = L_{gen}(G^d)$, respectively). Hence, for every $n \in N$ and for every $X \in \{enum, \# - cf, mon, smon, cf, scf, reg\}$ we obtain*

$$L(n, (acc, X)) = L(n, (gen, X)).$$

Therefore, as in the string case we can also use the notation $L(n, X)$ for both $L(n, (acc, X))$ and $L(n, (gen, X))$. We shall also omit the subscripts *gen* and *acc*, respectively, in $L_{gen}(G)$ and $L_{acc}(G)$, respectively, if the derivation mode is clear from the context.

4. Control Mechanisms on Array Grammars

In the following, we give the necessary definitions of ordered and programmed (graph controlled) array grammars and languages in the generating as well as in the accepting case. For detailed informations concerning these control mechanisms as well as many other interesting results about regulated rewriting in the theory of string languages, the reader is referred to [6].

Definition 4.1. An *ordered (string) grammar* is a construct

$$G_O = (V_N, V_T, (P, <), S),$$

where V_N and V_T are disjoint alphabets of non-terminal respectively terminal symbols, $S \in V_N$ is the start symbol, P is a finite set of (string) productions over $V_N \cup V_T$, and $<$ is a partial order relation on the productions in P. For $v, w \in (V_N \cup V_T)^*$ we define $v \vdash_{G_O} w$ if and only if there exists a production $p \in P$ such that w is the result of the application of p to v, whereas no other production $q \in P$ with $q > p$ is applicable to v. With $\vdash_{G_O}^*$ denoting the reflexive and transitive closure of the derivation relation $\vdash_{G_O}$ the string language generated by G_O is $L_{gen}(G_O) = \{w \in V_T^* \mid S \vdash_{G_O}^* w\}$.

A *programmed (string) grammar (or graph controlled (string) grammar) with appearance checking* is a construct $G_P = (V_N, V_T, (R, L_i, L_f), S)$; V_N and V_T are disjoint alphabets of non-terminal and terminal symbols, respectively; $S \in V_N$ is the start symbol; R is a finite set of rules r of the form $(l(r) : p(l(r)), \sigma(l(r)), \varphi(l(r)))$, where $l(r) \in Lab(G_P)$, $Lab(G_P)$ being a set of labels associated (in a one-to-one manner) to the rules r in R, $p(l(r))$ is a string production over $V_N \cup V_T$, $\sigma(l(r)) \subseteq Lab(G_P)$ is the *success field* of the rule r, and $\varphi(l(r))$ is the *failure field* of the rule r; $L_i \subseteq Lab(G_P)$ is the set of initial labels, and $L_f \subseteq Lab(G_P)$ is the set of final labels. For $r = (l(r) : p(l(r)), \sigma(l(r)), \varphi(l(r)))$ and $v, w \in (V_N \cup V_T)^*$ we define $(v, l(r)) \vdash_{G_P} (w, k)$ if and only if

- **either** $p(l(r))$ is applicable to v, the result of the application of the production $p(l(r))$ to v is w, and $k \in \sigma(l(r))$,

- **or** $p(l(r))$ is not applicable to v, $w = v$, and $k \in \varphi(l(r))$.

The (string) language generated by G_P is

$$L(G_P) = \{ w \in V_T^* \mid (S, l_0) \vdash_{G_P} (w_1, l_1) \vdash_{G_P} \ldots (w_k, l_k), \ k \geq 1,$$
$$w_j \in (V_N \cup V_T)^* \text{ and } l_j \in Lab(G_P) \text{ for } 0 \leq j \leq k,$$
$$w_k = w, \ l_0 \in L_i, \ l_k \in L_f \}.$$

If the failure fields $\varphi(l(r))$ are empty for all $r \in R$, then G_P is called a *programmed grammar without appearance checking*. If $\varphi(l(r)) = \sigma(l(r))$ for all $r \in R$, then G_P is called a *programmed grammar with unconditional transfer*.

An ordered (string) grammar, or a programmed (string) grammar, respectively, is said to be of type *enum, mon, cf, cf* $- \lambda$, or *reg*, respectively, if every production appearing in this grammar is of the corresponding type, i.e. an arbitrary, monotonic, context-free, λ-free context-free, respectively regular production. For the types $X \in \{enum, mon, cf, cf - \lambda, reg\}$, by

$$L(gen, X), \ O(gen, X), \ P_{ac}(gen, X), \ P_{ut}(gen, X), \ P(gen, X),$$

we denote the λ-free (string) languages generated by grammars of type X and ordered grammars, programmed grammars with appearance checking, programmed grammars with unconditional transfer, and programmed grammars without appearance checking, respectively, of type X.

In the following we list some of the most important results known [6], [8], [9], [15] for the control mechanisms defined above (for the sake of conciseness, we use $U(X)$ instead of $U(gen, X)$):

- $L(X) = Y(X)$ for $X \in \{reg, mon, enum\}$ and $Y \in \{O, P_{ac}, P_{ut}, P\}$;

- $L(cf - \lambda) \subset P(cf - \lambda) \subset P_{ac}(cf - \lambda) \subset L(mon)$;

- $L(cf - \lambda) \subset P_{ut}(cf - \lambda) \subseteq P_{ac}(cf - \lambda) \subset L(mon)$;

- $P(cf - \lambda) \subseteq P(cf) \subset P_{ac}(cf) = L(enum)$;

- $O(cf - \lambda) \subset P_{ut}(cf - \lambda) \subset P_{ut}(cf) \subseteq P_{ac}(cf) = L(enum)$;

- $L(cf - \lambda) = L(cf) \subset O(cf - \lambda) \subseteq O(cf) \subset P_{ut}(cf) \subseteq L(enum)$.

The definitions of ordered grammars and graph controlled grammars can immediately be taken over for accepting (string) grammars as well as for generating and accepting array grammars by taking accepting string productions or generating and accepting array productions, respectively, instead of generating string productions in the definitions given above, e.g. an *ordered array grammar* is a construct $G = (n, V_N, V_T, \#, (P, <), \{(v_0, S)\})$, where V_N, V_T, P, and $\{(v_0, S)\}$ are defined as for an array grammar and $<$ is a partial order relation on the array productions in P etc.

An ordered array grammar (generating or accepting, respectively) or a graph controlled array grammar (generating or accepting, respectively) is said to be of type X if every array production appearing in this grammar is of the corresponding type X, too.

Definition 4.2. For every $X \in \{enum, \# - cf, mon, smon, cf, scf, reg\}$ and every $\delta \in \{gen, acc\}$, by $L(n, (\delta, X), O)$, $L(n, (\delta, X), P)$, $L(n, (\delta, X), P_{ut})$, $L(n, (\delta, X), P_{ac})$ we denote the Λ-free array languages described by ordered array grammars, programmed array grammars without appearance checking, programmed array grammars with unconditional transfer, and programmed array grammars with appearance checking, respectively, of type (δ, X).

In the following we give some examples elucidating the control mechanisms defined above.

Example 4.1. According to [20], the set R_H of hollow rectangles of thickness one over the one-letter alphabet $\{a\}$ (with the left lower corner lying in the origin) cannot be generated by a context-free array grammar. Yet the following regular ordered array grammar G can generate R_H, i.e. $R_H \in L(2, (gen, reg), O)$.

$$G = (2, \{S, A, B, C, D, E, F, Q\}, \{a\}, \#, (P, <), \{((0,1), S)\}),$$

$$P = \left\{ \begin{matrix} \# \\ S \end{matrix} \rightarrow \begin{matrix} A \\ a \end{matrix}, \begin{matrix} \# \\ A \end{matrix} \rightarrow \begin{matrix} A \\ a \end{matrix}, A\# \rightarrow aB, B\# \rightarrow aB, B\# \rightarrow aC, \begin{matrix} C \\ \# \end{matrix} \rightarrow \begin{matrix} a \\ D \end{matrix}, \right.$$

$$\left. \begin{matrix} D \\ \# \end{matrix} \rightarrow \begin{matrix} a \\ D \end{matrix}, \begin{matrix} D \\ \# \end{matrix} \rightarrow \begin{matrix} a \\ E \end{matrix}, \#E \rightarrow Ea, \#E \rightarrow Fa, \begin{matrix} \# \\ F \end{matrix} \rightarrow \begin{matrix} Q \\ a \end{matrix}, F \rightarrow a \right\}.$$

The order relation $<$ only consists of $F \rightarrow a < \begin{matrix} \# \\ F \end{matrix} \rightarrow \begin{matrix} Q \\ a \end{matrix}$, which guarantees that $F \rightarrow a$ is only applied when no blank symbol appears above the non-terminal symbol F, or otherwise the (forced) application of $\begin{matrix} \# \\ F \end{matrix} \rightarrow \begin{matrix} Q \\ a \end{matrix}$ introduces the trap symbol Q.

The derivation of a rectangle of side lengths n and m, $n, m \geq 3$, proceeds as follows: The left vertical line of the hollow rectangle is generated by first using the rule $\begin{matrix} \# \\ S \end{matrix} \rightarrow \begin{matrix} A \\ a \end{matrix}$ and then using $n-3$ times the rule $\begin{matrix} \# \\ A \end{matrix} \rightarrow \begin{matrix} A \\ a \end{matrix}$. After applying the rule $A\# \rightarrow aB$, the upper horizontal line of the rectangle is generated by using $m-3$ times the rule $B\# \rightarrow aB$. The generation of the right vertical line of the rectangle starts with applications of the array productions $B\# \rightarrow aC$ and $\begin{matrix} C \\ \# \end{matrix} \rightarrow \begin{matrix} a \\ D \end{matrix}$, whereafter we can proceed with repeated applications of $\begin{matrix} D \\ \# \end{matrix} \rightarrow \begin{matrix} a \\ D \end{matrix}$. By applying $\begin{matrix} D \\ \# \end{matrix} \rightarrow \begin{matrix} a \\ E \end{matrix}$ the generation of the lower horizontal line is started, which proceeds by repeatedly applying $\#E \rightarrow Ea$. After the application of $\#E \rightarrow Fa$ the final array production $F \rightarrow a$ can only be applied, if with the non-terminal F we have arrived exactly below the starting point of our derivation; otherwise the trap symbol Q is introduced by the application of $\dfrac{\#}{F} \to \dfrac{Q}{a}$, which is forced by the order relation $<$. Hence, we conclude

$$L(G) = \{\{((0,j),a),((i,n-1),a),((m-1,j+1),a),((i+1,0),a) \mid \\ 0 \le j \le n-2,\ 0 \le i \le m-2\} \mid n \ge 3,\ m \ge 3\} = R_H.$$

For the generation of the set S_H of hollow squares with the left lower corner positioned in the origin (see [14]) regular array productions are not sufficient, i.e. S_H can only be generated by a context-free graph controlled array grammar with appearance checking:

Example 4.2. We consider the context-free graph controlled array grammar $G = (2,\{S,U,R,D,L,Q\},\{a\},(R,\{0\},\{0\}),\{((0,0),S)\})$ (with appearance checking), where P contains the labelled rules listed in Figure 1.

$$\left(0:\ \dfrac{\#}{S}\ \# \ \to\ \dfrac{U}{a}\ R\ ,\{1\},\emptyset\right);\qquad \left(1:\ \dfrac{\#}{U}\ \to\ \dfrac{U}{a}\ ,\{2\},\emptyset\right);$$

$$(2:\ R\# \to aR,\{1,3\},\emptyset);\qquad \left(3:\ \dfrac{\#\ \#}{U}\ \to\ \dfrac{a\ D}{a}\ ,\{4\},\emptyset\right);$$

$$(4:\ R\# \to aL,\{5\},\emptyset);\qquad (5:\ D\# \to aD,\{6,7\},\emptyset);$$

$$\left(6:\ \dfrac{\#}{L}\ \to\ \dfrac{L}{a}\ ,\{5\},\emptyset\right);\qquad \left(7:\ \dfrac{\#}{L}\ \to\ \dfrac{Q}{L}\ ,\emptyset,\{8\}\right);$$

$$(8:\ L \to a,\{9\},\emptyset);\qquad (9:\ D \to a,\{0\},\emptyset).$$

Figure 1. The rule set belonging to Example 4.2

After using the initial rule 0, the generation of the hollow square of side length $n \ge 3$ proceeds as follows: By repeatedly using rules 1 and 2 in a loop, the left vertical line and the lower horizontal line grow in a synchronized manner. After the application of the sequence 3 and 4, the upper horizontal line and the right vertical line are grown in a synchronized manner by using the array productions 5 and 6 in a loop. Only if L has arrived just below D, the array production 7 can be skipped in the appearance checking mode without introducing the trap symbol Q, whereafter the derivation is finished by using the sequence of array productions 8 and 9. Hence, we conclude

$$L(G) = \{\{((0,i),a),((i,n-1),a),((n-1,i+1),a),((i+1,0),a) \mid \\ 0 \le i \le n-2\} \mid n \ge 3\} = S_H,$$

and therefore $S_H \in L(2,(gen,scf),P_{ac})$.

By replacing empty success or failure fields, respectively, in the rules above by the corresponding non-empty failure and success fields, respectively, we immediately obtain a graph controlled array grammar with unconditional transfer generating the same array language, i.e. $S_H \in L(2,(gen,scf),P_{ut})$, too.

The previous two examples reveal an important difference between the applicability of a context-free string production to an underlying string and the applicability of a context-free array production to an underlying array: Whereas a context-free string production $A \to w$ is applicable to the underlying string if and only if the non-terminal symbol A appears in this string, the applicability of a context-free array production $(W, \mathcal{A}_1, \mathcal{A}_2)$ with $\mathcal{A}_1 (\Omega_n) = A$ to an underlying array not only depends on the occurrence of the non-terminal symbol A in the underlying array, but also on the "availability" of blank symbols in the neighbourhood of A on the relative positions $v \in W \setminus \{\Omega_n\}$. This #-sensing ability is the basis of the some results proved in [14], i.e. in contrast to the string case, even #-context-free ordered array grammars can generate any recursively enumerable Λ-free array language.

The following results directly follow from the definitions:

Lemma 4.1. *For all $n \in N$, for all derivation modes $\delta \in \{gen, acc\}$, and for all types $X, Y \in \{enum, \# - cf, mon, smon, cf, scf, reg\}$ with $X \subseteq Y$, as well as for all control types $U \in \{P, P_{ut}, P_{ac}, O\}$ we have $L(n, (\delta, X), U) \subseteq L(n, (\delta, Y), U)$.*

Lemma 4.2. *For all $n \in N$, for all derivation modes $\delta \in \{gen, acc\}$, and for all types $X \in \{enum, \# - cf, mon, smon, cf, scf, reg\}$ we have*

$$L(n, (\delta, X)) \subseteq L(n, (\delta, X), P) \subseteq L(n, (\delta, X), P_{ac}),$$
$$L(n, (\delta, X)) \subseteq L(n, (\delta, X), P_{ut}) \subseteq L(n, (\delta, X), P_{ac})$$

as well as $L(n, (\delta, X)) \subseteq L(n, (\delta, X), O)$.

Lemma 4.3. *For every $n \in N$ and for every $X \in \{enum, \# - cf, mon, smon, cf, scf, reg\}$, we have $L(n, (gen, X), O) \subseteq L(n, (gen, X), P_{ut})$.*

Proof. Let $G = (n, V_N, V_T, \#, (R, <), \{(v_0, S)\})$ be an ordered generating array grammar of type X, and let Lab be the set of unique labels for the rules in R. We construct an equivalent graph controlled generating array grammar with unconditional transfer of type X, $G' = (n, V_N \cup \{F\}, V_T, \#, (R', Lab, Lab), \{(v_0, S)\})$, in the following way: For each labelled rule $r : (W, \mathcal{A}_1, \mathcal{A}_2)$ from R, $r \in Lab$, with $F(r) = \{(r, i) \mid 1 \le i \le k(r)\}$ denoting the set of labels of the rules $p_{r,i}$ greater than r with respect to the order relation $<$, in R' we take

$$((r, i) : p_{r,i}^{\ominus}, \{(r, i+1)\}, \{(r, i+1)\}), \quad \text{for } 1 \le i \le k(r) \text{ and}$$
$$((r, k(r) + 1) : (W, \mathcal{A}_1, \mathcal{A}_2), Lab, Lab),$$

where we identify the labels $(r, 1)$ and r.

For any generating array production p in R, $p = (W, \mathcal{A}_1, \mathcal{A}_2)$, the corresponding failure production $p^{\ominus}$ is defined by $p^{\ominus} = (W, \mathcal{A}_1, F_W)$, where $F_W = \{(v, F) \mid v \in W\}$. Such a failure production $p^{\ominus}$ therefore introduces the trap symbol F whenever it cannot be skipped in the sequence controlling the application of an array production from R.

In the regular case, for the rules of the form $r : A \to a$ and of the form $r : Av\# \to avB$, respectively, we need a slight modification of the construction given above: If the set $F(r)$ contains a label identifying a production of the form $A \to b$ we simply can forget about the rule r. Otherwise, we only have to check the applicability of the rules greater than r of the form $Au\# \to CuD$, and therefore we can exclude all labels belonging to productions being not of this form $Au\# \to CuD$ from $F(r)$ and then proceed as above with this reduced set of labels of productions greater than r. The corresponding failure production $p^{\ominus}$ for $p = Cu\# \to cuD$ is defined by $p^{\ominus} = Cu\# \to cuF$. $\qquad\square$

Lemma 4.4. *For every $n \in N$ and for every $X \in \{enum, \# - cf, mon, smon, cf, scf, reg\}$, we have $L(n, (acc, X), O) \subseteq L_{acc}(n, (acc, X), P_{ut})$.*

Proof. Let $G = (n, V_N, V_T, \#, (R, <), \{(v_0, S)\})$ be an ordered accepting array grammar of type X, and let Lab be the set of unique labels for the rules in R. We construct an equivalent graph controlled accepting array grammar with unconditional transfer of type X, $G' = (n, V_N \cup \{F\}, V_T, \#, (R', Lab, Lab), \{(v_0, S)\})$, in the following way: For each labelled rule $r : (W, \mathcal{A}_1, \mathcal{A}_2)$ from R with $F(r) = \{(r, i) \mid 1 \leq i \leq k(r)\}$ denoting the set of labels of the rules $p_{r,i}$ greater than r with respect to the order relation $<$, in R' we again take

$$((r, i) : p_{r,i}^{\ominus}, \{(r, i+1)\}, \{(r, i+1)\}) \quad \text{for } 1 \leq i \leq k(r) \text{ and}$$
$$((r, k(r) + 1) : (W, \mathcal{A}_1, \mathcal{A}_2), Lab, Lab),$$

where we identify the labels $(r, 1)$ and r.

For any accepting array production in R, $p = (W, \mathcal{A}_1, \mathcal{A}_2)$, the corresponding failure production $p^{\ominus}$ now is defined by $p^{\ominus} = (W, \mathcal{A}_1, \mathcal{A}_2^F)$, where $\mathcal{A}_2^F = \{(\Omega_n, F)\} \cup \{(v, \mathcal{A}_2(v)) \mid v \in (W \setminus \{\Omega_n\})\}$, i.e. at the position Ω_n, which is always occupied by a non-blank symbol, the trap symbol F is introduced instead of the original symbol $\mathcal{A}_2(\Omega_n)$ in case the production $p^{\ominus}$ has to be applied. $\square$

Observe that in the accepting case, the proof also works for the regular array grammars.

As in the string case (see [1], [2]), it is easy to see that generating and accepting programmed array grammars without appearance checking describe the same family of languages. Hence, we find:

Lemma 4.5. *For every $n \in N$ and for every $X \in \{enum, \# - cf, mon, smon, cf, scf, reg\}$, we have $L(n, (gen, X), P) = L(n, (acc, X), P)$.*

Proof. The results directly follow from the duality of generating and accepting array productions, respectively, and the corresponding derivation mechanisms:

Let $G = (n, V_N, V_T, \#, (R, L_i, L_f), \{(v_0, S)\})$ be a graph controlled generating array grammar of type X without appearance checking. Then we can construct a graph controlled accepting array grammar of type X without appearance checking $G^d = (n, V_N \cup \{F\}, V_T, \#, (R^d, L_i^d, L_f^d), \{(v_0, S)\})$, where F is a new non-terminal symbol $\notin V_N \cup V_T \cup \{\#\}$. We take a new accepting (regular) array production $a \to F$ and assign a new label f to it, i.e. R^d contains $(f : a \to F, \emptyset, \emptyset)$. Moreover, we define $L_f^d = \{f\}$ and $L_i^d = \{s \mid r \in \sigma(s) \text{ for some } r \in L_f\}$. For $(r : (W, \mathcal{A}_1, \mathcal{A}_2), \sigma(r), \emptyset)$ in R we take $(r : (W, \mathcal{A}_2, \mathcal{A}_1), \sigma^{-1}(r), \emptyset)$ into R^d; the set $\sigma^{-1}(r)$ is defined by $\sigma^{-1}(r) = \{s \mid r \in \sigma(s)\}$ for $r \notin L_i$ and $\sigma^{-1}(r) = \{s \mid r \in \sigma(s)\} \cup \{f\}$ for $r \in L_i$. Hence, to every (generating) derivation in G,

$$(\{(v_0, S)\}, r_0) \vdash_G \dots (\mathcal{B}_{m-1}, r_{m-1}) \vdash_G (\mathcal{B}_m, r_m)$$

of a terminal array $\mathcal{B}_m \in V_T^{+n}$ with $r_0 \in L_i$ and $r_m \in L_f$ there corresponds the (accepting) derivation in G^d

$$(\mathcal{B}_m, r_{m-1}) \vdash_{G^d} (\mathcal{B}_{m-1}, r_{m-2}) \vdash_{G^d} \dots (\mathcal{B}_1, r_0) \vdash_{G^d} (\{(v_0, S)\}, f).$$

A similar construction allows us to build up a graph controlled generating array grammar of type X without appearance checking for a given graph controlled accepting array grammar of type X without appearance checking. □

In the string case, the analogue of the following result (with the same idea of a purely structural proof) has been shown in [3].

Lemma 4.6. *For every $n \in N$ and for every $X \in \{enum, \# - cf, mon, cf\}$,*
$$L(n, (gen, X), P_{ac}) \subseteq L(n, (acc, X), P_{ac}).$$

Proof. Let $G = (n, V_N, V_T, \#, (R, L_i, L_f), \{(v_0, S)\})$ be a graph controlled generating array grammar of type X. Then we can construct a graph controlled accepting array grammar of type X

$$
\begin{aligned}
G^d &= \left(n, V_N \cup \{F\}, V_T, \#, \left(R^d, L_i^d, L_f^d\right), \{(v_0, S)\}\right), \\
R^d &= R' \cup R'', L_i^d = \{s', s'' \mid r \in \sigma(s) \text{ for some } r \in L_f\}, L_f^d = \{f', f''\},
\end{aligned}
$$

where for $(r : (W, \mathcal{A}_1, \mathcal{A}_2), \sigma(r), \varphi(r))$ in R we take

$$
\begin{aligned}
\left(r' : (W, \mathcal{A}_2, \mathcal{A}_1), (\sigma^{-1}(r))' \cup (\varphi^{-1}(r))'', \emptyset\right) &\quad \text{into } R' \text{ and} \\
\left(r'' : (W, \mathcal{A}_1, \mathcal{A}_1), \emptyset, (\sigma^{-1}(r))' \cup (\varphi^{-1}(r))''\right) &\quad \text{into } R'';
\end{aligned}
$$

moreover, we take $(f' : F \to F, \emptyset, \emptyset)$ into R' and $(f'' : F \to F, \emptyset, \emptyset)$ into R''; the sets $\sigma^{-1}(r), \varphi^{-1}(r)$ are defined by

$$
\begin{aligned}
\sigma^{-1}(r) &= \{s \mid r \in \sigma(s)\} \text{ and } \varphi^{-1}(r) = \{s \mid r \in \varphi(s)\} \text{ for } r \notin L_i \text{ and} \\
\sigma^{-1}(r) &= \{s \mid r \in \sigma(s)\} \cup \{f\} \text{ and } \varphi^{-1}(r) = \{s \mid r \in \varphi(s)\} \cup \{f\} \text{ for } r \in L_i.
\end{aligned}
$$

For any set of labels L we define

$$L' = \{s' \mid s \in L\}, \qquad L'' = \{s'' \mid s \in L\}.$$

With the accepting array productions assigned to primed labels we simulate the dual generating array production in the reverse direction, whereas when choosing a rule with a doubly primed label we can only proceed (without changing the current array) if the corresponding generating array production could not be applied. □

Observe that the proof method used in the proof of the preceding lemma does not work for the types $smon$, scf, and reg, because the productions $(W, \mathcal{A}_1, \mathcal{A}_1)$ we use are not of the desired type.

In the regular case, the families of array languages $L(n, (gen, reg), O)$ and $L(n, (acc, reg), P_{ac})$ as well as $L(n, (gen, reg), P_{ac})$ and $L(n, (acc, reg), O)$ are even incomparable for each $n \geq 2$, which we shall prove next.

Lemma 4.7. *For each $n \geq 2$,*

$$i_{2,n}(R_H) \in L(n, (gen, reg), O) \setminus (L(n, (acc, reg), P_{ac}) \cup L(n, scf)).$$

Proof. According to Example 4.1, $i_{2,n}(R_H) \in L(n, (gen, reg), O)$, because by replacing every vector v occurring in the two-dimensional ordered array grammar there by the corresponding n-dimensional vector $i_{2,n}(v)$ we immediately obtain an n-dimensional ordered array grammar generating $i_{2,n}(R_H)$.

On the other hand, no n-dimensional accepting graph controlled array grammar with appearance checking can exist that describes $i_{2,n}(R_H)$:

After the first derivation step the underlying array contains exactly one non-terminal symbol. The rectangle is cut at some position, yet with accepting array productions we cannot check the closure of the line to both directions from this starting position, hence if we proceed in one direction from the starting point, even the control mechanism of programming cannot guarantee that we close the line at the end of the analysing procedure. A usual pumping argument shows that the last of the four lines of the rectangle need not be analysed in total, which would allow the acceptance of arrays not in R_H; the details of this pumping argument are left to the reader.

As we proceed along a single line when analysing a rectangle, even by using strictly context-free accepting array productions we can follow the argumentation in the preceding lines and conclude $R_H \notin L(2,(acc, scf))$. □

On the other hand, the arguments used in the previous proof do not carry over to ordered array grammars with regular accepting array productions as well as array productions of the form

$$\{((0,0),A),(v,\#)\} \to \{((0,0),B),(v,\#)\}$$

for some $v \in Z^2$ with $\|v\| = 1$, i.e. the construction in the following example using only one rule of this special form already allows us to generate R_H :

Example 4.3. The set R_H of hollow rectangles of thickness one over the one-letter alphabet $\{a\}$ (with the left lower corner lying in the origin) can be described by the following context-free ordered accepting array grammar G :

$$G = (2,\{S,A,B,C,D,E,F,Q\},\{a\},\#,(P,<),\{((0,1),S)\}),$$

$$P = \left\{ \begin{matrix} A \\ a \end{matrix} \to \begin{matrix} \# \\ S \end{matrix}, \begin{matrix} A \\ a \end{matrix} \to \begin{matrix} \# \\ A \end{matrix}, aB \to A\#, aB \to B\#, \right.$$

$$aC \to B\#, \begin{matrix} a \\ D \end{matrix} \to \begin{matrix} C \\ \# \end{matrix}, \begin{matrix} a \\ D \end{matrix} \to \begin{matrix} D \\ \# \end{matrix}, \begin{matrix} a \\ E \end{matrix} \to \begin{matrix} D \\ \# \end{matrix},$$

$$\left. Ea \to \#E, Fa \to \#E, \begin{matrix} \# \\ F \end{matrix} \to \begin{matrix} \# \\ Q \end{matrix}, a \to F \right\}.$$

The order relation $<$ only consists of $Fa \to \#E < \begin{matrix} \# \\ F \end{matrix} \to \begin{matrix} \# \\ Q \end{matrix}$. The rule $a \to F$ initiates the parsing process; this rule can only be applied once at the first step of the derivation, otherwise the goal $\{((1,0),S)\}$ cannot be derived.

In the second derivation step we have to apply the rule $Fa \to \#E$, which is supervised by the rule $\begin{matrix} \# \\ F \end{matrix} \to \begin{matrix} \# \\ Q \end{matrix}$ introducing the trap symbol Q, which guarantees that above the starting position indicated by the generation of the symbol F we will find a symbol a at the end of the derivation.

The remaining rules accomplish the analysis of the array just in the opposite direction as the generation of the same array was described by the corresponding dual rules in the ordered regular array grammar in Example 4.1. In sum, we obtain $L(G) = R_H$, i.e. we conclude $R_H \in L(2, (acc, cf), O)$.

In fact, taking into account the duality of these two array grammars, the only difference between the ordered accepting array grammar in this example and the ordered generating array grammar is that here we have to use the (context-free but non-regular) blank-sensing trap rule $\begin{matrix} \# \\ F \end{matrix} \rightarrow \begin{matrix} \# \\ Q \end{matrix}$ instead of the (regular generating) trap rule $\begin{matrix} \# \\ F \end{matrix} \rightarrow \begin{matrix} Q \\ a \end{matrix}$, which not even is monotonic accepting.

Observe that Lemma 4.6 is also valid for an extended regular case where we admit array productions of the form $\{(\Omega_n, A), (v, \#)\} \rightarrow \{(\Omega_n, B), (v, \#)\}$, since we then can simulate a generating rule $(r : (W, A_1, A_2), \sigma(r), \varphi(r))$ with $A_1 = \{(\Omega_n, B), (v, \#)\}$, $A_2 = \{(\Omega_m, a), (v, C)\}$, via r' and r'' as defined in the proof of Lemma 4.6, because now the array production (W, A_1, A_1) used in r'' is of this new form.

Also the programmed use of strictly context-free accepting array productions allows us to accept R_H :

Example 4.4. The set R_H of hollow rectangles of thickness one over the one-letter alphabet $\{a\}$ (with the left lower corner lying in the origin) can be accepted by the following strictly context-free graph controlled accepting array grammar G without appearance checking:

$$G = (2, \{S, A, B\}, \{a\}, \#, (R, \{1\}, \{10\}), \{((0,1), S)\})$$

with R containing the rules listed in Fig. 2.

$$
\begin{aligned}
&(1 : \ a \rightarrow S, \{2\}, \emptyset); && (2 : \ Sa \rightarrow \#S, \{3\}, \emptyset); \\
&(3 : \ a \rightarrow B, \{2, 4\}, \emptyset); && (4 : \ Sa \rightarrow \#S, \{5\}, \emptyset); \\
&\left(5 : \ \begin{matrix} a \\ S \end{matrix} \rightarrow \begin{matrix} S \\ \# \end{matrix}, \{6\}, \emptyset\right); && (6 : \ a \rightarrow A, \{5, 7\}, \emptyset); \\
&\left(7 : \ \begin{matrix} a \\ S \end{matrix} \rightarrow \begin{matrix} S \\ \# \end{matrix}, \{8\}, \emptyset\right); && (8 : \ BS \rightarrow S\#, \{8, 9\}, \emptyset); \\
&(9 : \ aS \rightarrow S\#, \{10\}, \emptyset); && \left(10 : \ \begin{matrix} S \\ A \end{matrix} \rightarrow \begin{matrix} \# \\ S \end{matrix}, \{10\}, \emptyset\right).
\end{aligned}
$$

Figure 2. The rule set belonging to Example 4.4

With each symbol a consumed by rule 2 on the lower horizontal line, a symbol B arises on the upper horizontal line, which symbol afterwards is consumed by rule 8. In the same way, a symbol A arises on the left vertical line with each application of the rules 5 and 6, which then is consumed by an application of rule 10. In this way we can control the corresponding lengths of the horizontal and the vertical lines, respectively. In sum, we obtain $L(G) = R_H$, i.e. we conclude $R_H \in L(2, (acc, scf), P)$.

Example 4.5. The set L_F^1 of lines of thickness one over the one-letter alphabet $\{a\}$ with the starting point lying in the origin and ending with a free end can be defined by being generated by the following context-free array grammar G :

$$
\begin{aligned}
G &= (2, \{S\}, \{a\}, \#, P, \{((0,0), S)\}), \\
P &= \{\{((0,0), S), (v, \#)\} \rightarrow \{((0,0), a), (v, S)\} \mid v \in U_4\} \cup \\
&\quad \{\{((0,0), S)\} \cup \{(v, \#) \mid v \in U_4 \setminus \{u\}\} \rightarrow \\
&\quad \{((0,0), a)\} \cup \{(v, \#) \mid v \in U_4 \setminus \{u\}\} \mid u \in U_4\}, \quad \text{where} \\
U_4 &= \{(0,1), (0,-1), (1,0), (-1,0)\}.
\end{aligned}
$$

On the other hand, the array language generated by this context-free array grammar G can also be accepted by an ordered regular array grammar G' the construction of which is rather obvious but tedious and therefore left to the reader.

Lemma 4.8. *For each $n \geq 2$,*

$$
i_{2,n}\left(L_F^1\right) \in (L(n, (acc, reg), O) \cap L(n, cf)) \setminus L(n, (gen, reg), P_{ac}).
$$

Proof. From the preceding example we immediately infer

$$
i_{2,n}\left(L_F^1\right) \in (L(n, (acc, reg), O) \cap L(n, cf)).
$$

A pumping argument shows that $i_{2,n}\left(L_F^1\right) \notin L(n, (gen, reg), P_{ac})$. The details are left to the reader. □

We even conjecture that

$$
i_{2,n}\left(L_F^1\right) \in L(n, (gen, smon)) \setminus L(n, (gen, scf), P_{ac}).
$$

Moreover, we conjecture that the array language $i_{2,n}(L_F)$, where L_F is the array language from $L(n, (gen, cf))$ defined in the following example, even is not in $L(n, (gen, smon), P_{ac})$. So far proofs of these conjectures remain as open problems.

Example 4.6. The array language L_F containing arrays representing an arbitrary number of lines starting in the origin and ending with free ends is generated by the following context-free array grammar:

$$
\begin{aligned}
G &= (2, \{S\}, \{a\}, \#, P, \{((0,0), S)\}), \\
P &= \{\{((0,0), S), (v, \#)\} \rightarrow \{((0,0), a), (v, S)\} \mid v \in U_4\} \cup \\
&\quad \{\{((0,0), S)\} \cup \{(v, \#) \mid v \in U_4 \setminus \{u\}\} \rightarrow \\
&\quad \{((0,0), a)\} \cup \{(v, \#) \mid v \in U_4 \setminus \{u\}\} \mid u \in U_4\} \cup \\
&\quad \{\{((0,0), S), (v, \#)\} \rightarrow \{((0,0), S), (v, S)\} \mid v \in U_4\}.
\end{aligned}
$$

Most of the examples elaborated above cannot be taken over to the one-dimensional case. As a consequence, in the one-dimensional case, some more families of array languages collapse into one class:

Theorem 4.1. *For every $U \in \{O, P, P_{ut}, P_{ac}\}$, we have*

$$
L(1, reg) = L(1, (acc, reg), U) = L(1, (gen, reg), U) \subset L(1, scf)
$$

110

Proof. Obviously, $L(1, reg) \subseteq L(1, scf)$. The strictness of this inclusion follows from the fact that one-dimensional arrays generated by a regular array grammar can grow only to the left or to the right from the start position, whereas strictly context-free array grammars can grow the array to the left as well as to the right; hence, e.g. $\{\{((-i), a) \mid 1 \le i \le k\} \cup \{((j), a) \mid 0 \le j \le m\} \mid k \ge 0, m \ge 0\} \in L(1, scf) \setminus L(1, reg)$. Therefore, it only remains to prove that we have $L(1, reg) \supseteq L(1, (\delta, reg), P_{ac})$ for $\delta \in \{gen, acc\}$.

Yet these inclusions can be proved by the standard techniques known from the string case, i.e. all we need for the control mechanism can be stored in the single nonterminal of the intermediate sentential forms together with the information to which side from the start position the array is grown. The technical details are obvious and therefore left to the reader. □

When considering equivalence classes of arrays, we even obtain (see [12]).

Corollary 4.1. *For every* $U \in \{O, P, P_{ut}, P_{ac}\}$, *we have*

$$[L(1, reg)] = [L(1, (acc, reg), U)] = [L(1, (gen, reg), U)] = [L(1, scf)].$$

Proof. The inclusion $[L(1, scf)] \subseteq [L(1, reg)]$ was proved in [12]. The remaining statements then follow from Theorem 4.1. □

For families of strictly context-free one-dimensional array languages we obtain the following inclusions implied by the results in [13], [14] and some results previously proved in this paper.

Theorem 4.2. *For every* $U \in \{O, P, P_{ut}, P_{ac}\}$ *we have*

$$L(1, scf) \subset L(1, (gen, scf), U) \subset L(1, smon) = L(1, mon_1) \subset L(1, mon),$$
$$L(1, scf) \subset L(1, (acc, scf), U) \subseteq L(1, smon), \text{ and moreover,}$$
$$L(1, scf) \subset L(1, (gen, scf), P) \subset L(1, (gen, scf), P_{ac}) \subset L(1, mon_1),$$
$$L(1, scf) \subset L(1, (acc, scf), O) \subseteq L(1, (acc, scf), P_{ut})$$
$$\subseteq L(1, (acc, scf), P_{ac}) \subset L(1, mon_1).$$

Proof. The strictness of the relation $L(n, (gen, scf), U) \subset L(n, mon)$ was proved in [13], where the array representation of the context-free string language

$$L = \{xcx^R dycy^R \mid x, y \in \{a, b\}^+\}$$

(x^R is the mirror image of x) was shown to be in $L(1, mon) \setminus L(1, (gen, scf), U)$; from the proof given there it is clear that even for any $n \in N$ we have

$$i_{1,n}(L) \in L(n, mon) \setminus L(n, (gen, scf), U),$$

which concludes the proof. □

In the string case, the analogue of the following result has been shown in [1].

Theorem 4.3. *For every* $n \in N$, *we have* $L(n, mon) \subseteq L(n, (acc, cf), O)$.

Proof. Combining the KURODA-like normal form result for generating monotonic array grammars [14] with Lemma 3.1, we can assume that an arbitrary monotonic array language is given by a monotonic accepting array grammar

$$G = (n, V_N, V_T, \#, P, \{(v_0, S)\})$$

which only contains accepting array productions of one of the following forms:

1. $a \to X$, where $X \in V_N$, $a \in V_T$;

2. $Y \to X$, where $X \in V_N$, $Y \in V_N$;

3. $\{(\Omega_n, B), (v, C)\} \to \{(\Omega_n, A), (v, \#)\}$, where $A, B, C \in V_N$;

4. $\{(\Omega_n, B), (v, \#)\} \to \{(\Omega_n, A), (v, \#)\}$, where $A, B \in V_N$;

5. $\{(\Omega_n, B), (v, C)\} \to \{(\Omega_n, A), (v, D)\}$, where $A, B, C, D \in V_N$.

As the first four kinds of rules are already accepting context-free, we only have to show how the inherent non-context-free array productions of the form $\{(\Omega_n, B), (v, C)\} \to \{(\Omega_n, A), (v, D)\}$, where $A, B, C, D \in V_N$, can be simulated by using only context-free array productions together with the control mechanism of an order relation:

For each labelled array production $r : \{(\Omega_n, B), (v, C)\} \to \{(\Omega_n, A), (v, D)\}$, $r \in Lab$, we introduce the following accepting array productions:

1. $B \to [B, r, 0]$ less than (supervised by) $[X, s, i] \to F$ for all $X \in V_N$, $s \in Lab$, $i \in \{0, 1, 2\}$;

2. $C \to [C, r, 1]$ supervised by $[X, s, i] \to F$

   for all $X \in V_N$, $s \in Lab$, $i \in \{0, 1, 2\}$ such that $(X, s, i) \neq (B, r, 0)$;

3. $[B, r, 0] \to [A, r, 2]$ supervised by:

   $[B, r, 0] v Y \to F v \#$ for all $Y \in V_N \cup V_T \cup \{\#\}$,

   $[B, r, 0] v [X, s, i] \to F v \#$ for all $X \in V_N$, $s \in Lab$, $i \in \{0, 1, 2\}$ such that $(X, s, i) \neq (C, r, 1)$,

   $[X, s, i] \to F$ for all $X \in V_N$, $s \in Lab$, $i \in \{0, 1, 2\}$ such that $(X, s, i) \notin \{(B, r, 0), (C, r, 1)\}$;

4. $[C, r, 1] \to D$ supervised by:

   $[C, r, 1] (-v) Y \to F (-v) \#$ for all $Y \in V_N \cup V_T \cup \{\#\}$,

   $[C, r, 1] (-v) [X, s, i] \to F (-v) \#$ for all $X \in V_N$, $s \in Lab$, $i \in \{0, 1, 2\}$ such that $(X, s, i) \neq (A, r, 2)$,

   $[X, s, i] \to F$ for all $X \in V_N$, $s \in Lab$, $i \in \{0, 1, 2\}$ such that $(X, s, i) \notin \{(A, r, 2), (C, r, 1)\}$;

5. $[A, r, 2] \to A$ supervised by $[X, s, i] \to F$

   for all $X \in V_N$, $s \in Lab$, $i \in \{0, 1, 2\}$ such that $(X, s, i) \neq (A, r, 2)$.

Hence, each derivation step in G using an accepting array production of the form $\{(\Omega_n, B), (v, C)\} \rightarrow \{(\Omega_n, A), (v, D)\}$ is simulated by a sequence of five context-free accepting array productions in the ordered accepting array grammar constructed above: By the array productions $B \rightarrow [B, r, 0]$ and $C \rightarrow [C, r, 1]$, respectively, two positions in the underlying sentential form are marked. By the supervising array productions in 3 it is guaranteed that we can only proceed without generating the trap symbol F if in the first two simulation steps a subarray of the desired form, i.e. $\{(w, [B, r, 0]), (w + v, [C, r, 1])\}$, has been marked. No more than two symbols can be marked at the same time without finally enforcing the generation of the trap symbol F. By the array productions $[B, r, 0] \rightarrow [A, r, 2]$, $[C, r, 1] \rightarrow D$, and $[A, r, 2] \rightarrow A$ in 3, 4, and 5 we can finish the simulation of the array production labelled by r, thus yielding the subarray $\{(w, A), (w + v, D)\}$. The supervising array productions guarantee the correct sequence of applying these simulating accepting array productions. □

Remark 4.1. As we shall show later in this paper, we even have

$$L(n, mon) = L(n, (acc, cf), O).$$

By also allowing accepting array productions of the form $\# \rightarrow A$, $A \in V_N$, in the normal form given above, we immediately obtain a normal form for arbitrary accepting array productions and grammars, respectively, as well as according to the definition of the type $\#$-context-free, we readily obtain

$$L(n, enum) = L(n, (acc, \# - cf), O).$$

In [14] it was already proved that (for $n = 2$, yet the result holds true for every $n \geq 1$) we have $L(n, enum) = L(n, (gen, \# - cf), O)$.

Hence, according to the thesis of Turing and Church, for the arbitrary case we can already state (also using Lemmas 4.2, 4.3, and 4.4 as well as results from [14]):

$$L(n, enum) = L(n, (\delta, \# - cf), U)$$

for all $\delta \in \{gen, acc\}$ and $U \in \{O, P_{ut}, P_{ac}\}$.

In the monotonic accepting case, so far we have shown (see Lemma 4.2, Lemma 4.4, and Theorem 4.3) that

$$L(n, mon) \subseteq L(n, (acc, cf), O) \subseteq L(n, (acc, cf), P_{ut}) \subseteq L(n, (acc, cf), P_{ac}).$$

In order to show that all these inclusions are equalities, it only remains to show the following lemma:

Lemma 4.9. *For every* $n \in N$, $L(n, (acc, mon), P_{ac}) \subseteq L(n, mon)$.

Proof. Let $G = (n, V_N, V_T, \#, (R, L_i, L_f), \{(v_0, S)\})$ be a graph controlled accepting monotonic array grammar, and let Lab be the set of unique labels of the rules in R as well as $U_G = \{v \in Z^n \mid 0 < \|v\| \leq \|G\|\}$. Then we can construct an equivalent monotonic generating array grammar $G' = (n, V'_N, V_T, \#, P, \{(v_0, S)\})$ with

$$
\begin{aligned}
V'_N \;=\; & \{[x, Y, s, u, U] \mid x \in V_T, Y \in V_N \cup V_T \cup \{\#\}, u \in U_G, \emptyset \subseteq U \subseteq U_G, \\
& s \in \{A, I, F\} \cup \{(p, d) \mid p \in Lab, d \in \{Y, N, C, D, R\}\}\} \cup \{S\}
\end{aligned}
$$

and P containing the following array productions:

1. $S \rightarrow [a, a, A, \Omega_n, \emptyset]$ for all $a \in V_T$.

   Such an array production starts the non-deterministic generation of an arbitrary array, which is continued by the array productions in 2.

2. $\{(\Omega_n, [a, a, A, u, U]), (v, \#)\} \rightarrow$

   $\{(\Omega_n, [a, a, A, u, U \cup \{v\}]), (v, [b, b, I, -v, \emptyset])\}$

   for all $a, b \in V_T$, $u \in U_G \cup \{\Omega_n\}$, $v \in U_G$, $\emptyset \subseteq U \subseteq U_G$.

   The quintuples of the form $[x, Y, s, u, U]$ contain the following information:

   (a) x is the symbol that finally has to appear in the terminal array generated by G'.

   (b) Y is the current symbol at this position during the simulation of G by G'.

   (c) The state s describes the current phase of the simulation at the underlying position.

   (d) The vector u points to the relative position from which the underlying position has been reached first by an array production in 2 (except for the starting position v_0, which therefore contains Ω_n as fourth component). In this way, a connectivity tree (with the root in v_0) is codified.

   (e) The set U contains the relative positions of the children (successors) of the underlying position in this connectivity tree. Hence the fourth and the fifth component allow us to go forth and back in the connectivity tree.

3. $\{(\Omega_n, [a, a, A, u, U]), (v, [b, b, I, w, W])\} \rightarrow$

   $\{(\Omega_n, [a, a, I, u, U]), (v, [b, b, A, w, W])\}$

   for all $a, b \in V_T$, $u, w \in U_G \cup \{\Omega_n\}$, $v \in U_G$, $\emptyset \subseteq U, W \subseteq U_G$.

   In the first phase, when generating an arbitrary array by using the array productions in 1,2, and 3, exactly one position in the current sentential form carries the active state A, whereas all the other non-blank positions carry the non-active state I. The array productions in 3 allow us to move the active state from one non-blank position to another one.

4. $[a, a, A, \Omega_n, U] \rightarrow [a, a, (p, \delta), \Omega_n, U]$

   for all $a \in V_T$, $\emptyset \subseteq U \subseteq U_G$, $p \in L_i$, $\delta \in \{Y, N\}$.

   The simulation of G is started by introducing an initial active state (p, δ), which can be moved around by the array productions in 5.

5. $\{(\Omega_n, [a, X, (p, \delta), u, U]), (v, [b, Y, I, w, W])\} \rightarrow$

   $\{(\Omega_n, [a, X, I, u, U]), (v, [b, Y, (p, \delta), w, W])\}$

   for all $a, b \in V_T$, $X, Y \in V_N \cup V_T \cup \{\#\}$, $u, w \in U_G \cup \{\Omega_n\}$, $v \in U_G$, $\emptyset \subseteq U, W \subseteq U_G$, $p \in Lab$, $\delta \in \{Y, N\}$.

6. $\{(\Omega_n, [a_{\Omega_n}, X_{\Omega_n}, (p, Y), w_{\Omega_n}, W_{\Omega_n}])\} \cup$

   $\{(v, [a_v, X_v, I, w_v, W_v]) \mid v \in V\} \rightarrow$

$$\{(\Omega_n, [a_{\Omega_n}, Y_{\Omega_n}, (q, \delta), w_{\Omega_n}, W_{\Omega_n}])\} \cup$$

$$\{(v, [a_v, Y_v, I, w_v, W_v]) \mid v \in V\}$$

for all $a_v \in V_T$, $X_v, Y_v \in V_N \cup V_T \cup \{\#\}$, $w_v \in U_G \cup \{\Omega_n\}$, $\emptyset \subseteq W_v \subseteq U_G$,

for $v \in V \cup \{\Omega_n\}$, $p \in Lab$, $q \in \sigma(p)$, $\delta \in \{Y, N\}$,

and the rule labelled with p is

$$\{(v, X_v) \mid v \in V \cup \{\Omega_n\}\} \rightarrow \{(v, Y_v) \mid v \in V \cup \{\Omega_n\}\}, \Omega_n \notin V.$$

If the application of the array production p has to be simulated, the active state (p, Y) is moved to a suitable position from which the simulation is possible.

7. $[a, X, (p, N), \Omega_n, U] \rightarrow [a, X, (p, C), \Omega_n, U]$

   for all $a \in V_T$, $X \in V_N \cup V_T \cup \{\#\}$, $\emptyset \subseteq U \subseteq U_G$, $p \in Lab$.

   The check for the non-applicability of an array production p (which non-deterministically has been guessed by introducing the active state (p, N)) is started at the position v_0 by the suitable array production in 7. From there, the state (p, C) is propagated forward to all non-blank positions along the connectivity tree by the array productions in 8.

8. $\{(\Omega_n, [a_{\Omega_n}, X_{\Omega_n}, (p, C), w_{\Omega_n}, W_{\Omega_n}])\} \cup$

   $\{(v, [a_v, X_v, I, w_v, W_v]) \mid v \in W_{\Omega_n}\} \rightarrow$

   $\{(\Omega_n, [a_{\Omega_n}, X_{\Omega_n}, (p, C), w_{\Omega_n}, W_{\Omega_n}])\} \cup$

   $\{(v, [a_v, X_v, (p, C), w_v, W_v]) \mid v \in W_{\Omega_n}\}$

   for all $a_v \in V_T$, $X_v \in V_N \cup V_T \cup \{\#\}$, $w_v \in U_G \cup \{\Omega_n\}$, $\emptyset \subseteq W_v \subseteq U_G$,

   for $v \in W_{\Omega_n} \cup \{\Omega_n\}$, $p \in Lab$.

9. $\{(\Omega_n, [a_{\Omega_n}, X_{\Omega_n}, (p, C), w_{\Omega_n}, W_{\Omega_n}])\} \cup$

   $\{(v, [a_v, X_v, \delta_v, w_v, W_v]) \mid v \in V_1\} \cup \{(v, \#) \mid v \in V_2\} \rightarrow$

   $\{(\Omega_n, [a_{\Omega_n}, X_{\Omega_n}, (p, D), w_{\Omega_n}, W_{\Omega_n}])\} \cup$

   $\{(v, [a_v, X_v, \delta_v, w_v, W_v]) \mid v \in V_1\} \cup \{(v, \#) \mid v \in V_2\}$,

   where V_1 and V_2 are disjoint finite subsets of Z^n, $V_1 \cup V_2 \subseteq U_G$,

   for all $a_v \in V_T$, $X_v \in V_N \cup V_T \cup \{\#\}$, $w_v \in U_G \cup \{\Omega_n\}$, $\emptyset \subseteq W_v \subseteq U_G$,

   for $v \in V_1 \cup \{\Omega_n\}$, $p \in Lab$, $\delta_v \in \{(p, C), (p, D)\}$,

   and the rule labelled with p is of the form

   $\{(v, Z_v) \mid v \in V_1 \cup V_2 \cup \{\Omega_n\}\} \rightarrow \{(v, Y_v) \mid v \in V_1 \cup V_2 \cup \{\Omega_n\}\}$,

   $Z_v, Y_v \in V_N \cup V_T \cup \{\#\}$ for $v \in V_1 \cup V_2 \cup \{\Omega_n\}$,

   but not of the form

   $\{(v, X_v) \mid v \in V_1 \cup \{\Omega_n\}\} \cup \{(v, \#) \mid v \in V_2\} \rightarrow$

   $\{(v, Y_v) \mid v \in V_1 \cup V_2 \cup \{\Omega_n\}\}$.

   At each position, from the state (p, C) the state (p, D) is generated if the array production p cannot be applied here.

10. $[a, X, (p, D), u, \emptyset] \to [a, X, (p, R), u, \emptyset]$

    for all $a \in V_T$, $X \in V_N \cup V_T \cup \{\#\}$, $u \in U_G \cup \{\Omega_n\}$.

    From the leaves of the connectivity tree (indicated by the empty set as the fifth component), the information of the non-applicability of p is propagated back to the root at position v_0 by the array productions 10 and 11.

11. $\{(\Omega_n, [a_{\Omega_n}, X_{\Omega_n}, (p, D), w_{\Omega_n}, W_{\Omega_n}])\} \cup$
    $\{(v, [a_v, X_v, (p, R), w_v, W_v]) \mid v \in W_{\Omega_n}\} \to$
    $\{(\Omega_n, [a_{\Omega_n}, X_{\Omega_n}, (p, R), w_{\Omega_n}, W_{\Omega_n}])\} \cup$
    $\{(v, [a_v, X_v, I, w_v, W_v]) \mid v \in W_{\Omega_n}\}$

    for all $a_v \in V_T$, $X_v \in V_N \cup V_T \cup \{\#\}$, $w_v \in U_G \cup \{\Omega_n\}$, $\emptyset \subseteq W_v \subseteq U_G$,
    for $v \in W_{\Omega_n} \cup \{\Omega_n\}$, $p \in Lab$, $W_{\Omega_n} \neq \emptyset$.

12. $[a, X, (p, R), \Omega_n, U] \to [a, X, (q, \delta), \Omega_n, U]$

    for all $a \in V_T$, $X \in V_N \cup V_T \cup \{\#\}$, $\emptyset \subseteq U \subseteq U_G$,
    $p \in Lab$, $q \in \varphi(p)$, $\delta \in \{Y, N\}$.

    At the root, i.e. at position v_0 marked with the fourth component being Ω_n, the successful check for the non-applicability of p allows us to guess the next active state (q, δ), where q has to be from the failure field $\varphi(p)$.

13. $\{(\Omega_n, [a_{\Omega_n}, S, (p, \delta), \Omega_n, W_{\Omega_n}])\} \cup \{(v, [a_v, \#, I, w_v, W_v]) \mid v \in W_{\Omega_n}\} \to$
    $\{(\Omega_n, a_{\Omega_n})\} \cup \{(v, [a_v, \#, F, w_v, W_v]) \mid v \in W_{\Omega_n}\}$

    for all $a_v \in V_T$, $w_v \in U_G$, $\emptyset \subseteq W_v \subseteq U_G$, for $v \in W_{\Omega_n} \cup \{\Omega_n\}$,
    $p \in L_f$, $\delta \in \{Y, N\}$.

14. $\{(\Omega_n, [a_{\Omega_n}, \#, F, w_{\Omega_n}, W_{\Omega_n}])\} \cup \{(v, [a_v, \#, I, w_v, W_v]) \mid v \in W_{\Omega_n}\} \to$
    $\{(\Omega_n, a_{\Omega_n})\} \cup \{(v, [a_v, \#, F, w_v, W_v]) \mid v \in W_{\Omega_n}\}$

    for all $a_v \in V_T$, $w_v \in U_G$, $\emptyset \subseteq W_v \subseteq U_G$, for $v \in W_{\Omega_n} \cup \{\Omega_n\}$.

    When we reach a final state, indicated by the active state (p, δ) with $p \in L_f$, we can initiate the generation of the terminal array by applying an array production 13, provided that at position v_0 the third component is S, by introducing the active symbol F and then continue with the array productions in 14, provided that at every other position the third component is $\#$. This terminating phase, indicated by the state F, successfully ends at the leaves of the connectivity tree (which have the empty set as fifth component) if and only if we first have successfully guessed the initial array generated by the array productions 1,2, and 3, and then have successfully simulated an accepting derivation of the array in G by G' finally obtaining the array $\{(v_0, S)\}$ encoded in the third components. $\square$

Hence, for the monotonic case we have proved that for every $n \in N$ and every $U \in \{O, P_{ut}, P_{ac}\}$:

$$L(n, mon) = L(n, (acc, cf), U) = L(n, (acc, mon), U) = L(n, (gen, mon), U).$$

Finally, let us mention that the proof of Lemma 4.7 given above is considerably more involved than its analogue in the string case, where a simulation of non-erasing grammars by linear bounded automata is quite obvious.

Strictly monotonic array grammars cannot check for the context of blank symbols as monotonic or even context-free array grammars can do by using array productions like

$$\{(\Omega_n, A), (v, \#)\} \rightarrow \{(\Omega_n, B), (v, \#)\},$$

which were inevitably used in the previous proofs. Surprisingly enough, appearance checking can overcome this difficulty when we restrict ourselves to array grammars with norm 1, which is shown in the following lemma:

Lemma 4.10. *For every $n \in N$, if G is an n-dimensional monotonic generating or accepting array grammar with $\|G\| = 1$, then we can construct an n-dimensional ordered strictly monotonic generating or accepting, respectively, array grammar G' with $\|G'\| = 1$ such that $L(G') = L(G)$.*

Proof. Let $G = (n, V_N, V_T, \#, P, \{(v_0, S)\})$ be a generating or accepting monotonic array grammar in normal form (see Theorem 4.3). Then we construct an equivalent ordered monotonic generating or accepting array grammar $G' = (n, V'_N, V_T, \#, (P, <), \{(v_0, S)\})$, with $L(G') = L(G)$ by eliminating the rules r of the form $\{(\Omega_n, A), (v, \#)\} \rightarrow \{(\Omega_n, B), (v, \#)\}$. We replace such a rule by the following set of rules:

1. $A \rightarrow A_r$ supervised by

   $X_q \rightarrow F$ for all $X \in V_N$ and all q that are labels of a rule of the form above;

2. $A_r \rightarrow B$ supervised by

   $\{(\Omega_n, A_r), (v, X)\} \rightarrow \{(\Omega_n, F), (v, F)\}$ for all $X \in V_N \cup V_T$ (which inevitably destroys the normal form). Observe that the newly introduced array productions are of the desired type. □

Summarizing some of the most important results elaborated in this paper, we can state the following theorem (for the string case, analogous results concerning the accepting mode of derivation were stated in Theorem 3.3 and Corollaries 3.5 and 4.8 in [1]):

Theorem 4.4. *For every $n \in N$ and every $U \in \{O, P_{ut}, P_{ac}\}$, we have*

$$L(n, enum) = L(n, (gen, \# - cf), U) = L(n, (acc, \# - cf), U);$$
$$L(n, mon) = L(n, (gen, mon), U) = L(n, (acc, mon), U);$$
$$L(n, mon) = L(n, (acc, cf), U) \supseteq L(n, (gen, cf), U).$$

5. Final Remarks

Several problems for accepting array grammars with various control mechanisms have remained open in this paper, but some problems for generating array grammars with various control mechanisms are still open, too.

In [10], we discussed how to interpret generating array grammars in an analysing manner for character recognition purposes. This is done in the following way:

1. productions are read from left to right, i.e. we use the generating rules as they are given, indeed,

2. a production is applicable if the result of the derivation step still matches the given pattern.

Point (2) allows to prune subcases which can never lead to a complete match with the given pattern, hence reducing the non-deterministic choices inherent in Chomsky-like grammars. In this way, we can accelerate the derivation considerably. Observe that there is a crucial difference between this interpretation of an analysing grammar and the accepting grammars discussed in this paper. It is not obvious how to use the matching interpretation described above when applying the accepting grammars in the sense introduced in this paper. This remains as an interesting theoretical problem with possibly significant impact on practical algorithms for syntactical pattern recognition.

Acknowledgements. The work of the first author was supported by Deutsche Forschungsgemeinschaft grant DFG La 618/3-1.

References

1. H. Bordihn and H. Fernau, Accepting regulated grammars, *IJCM* **53** (1994), pp. 1-18.

2. H. Bordihn and H. Fernau, Accepting grammars and systems, *JALC* **1** (2) (1996). A short version appeared in: J. Dassow, G. Rozenberg, and A. Salomaa (eds.), *Developments in Language Theory II* (World Scientific Publ., Singapore, 1996), pp. 199–208.

3. H. Bordihn and H. Fernau, Accepting pure grammars, *5th Theorietag der GI 'Automaten und Formale Sprachen', Rauischholzhausen 1995* (Technischer Bericht 9503 of the Universität Gießen, Arbeitsgruppe Informatik, 1995), pp. 4–16.

4. E. Csuhaj-Varjù, J. Dassow, J. Kelemen, and Gh. Păun, *Grammar Systems* (Gordon and Breach, London, 1994).

5. C. R. Cook and P. S.-P. Wang, A Chomsky hierarchy of isotonic array grammars and languages, *Computer Graphics and Image Processing* **8** (1978), pp. 144-152.

6. J. Dassow and Gh. Păun, *Regulated Rewriting in Formal Language Theory* (Springer, Berlin, 1989).

7. J. Dassow, R. Freund, and Gh. Păun, Cooperating array grammar systems, *International Journal of Pattern Recognition and Artificial Intelligence* **9** (6) (1995), pp. 1029-1053.

8. H. Fernau, Membership for 1-limited ET0L languages is not decidable, *J. Inform. Process. Cybernet.* **EIK 30** (4) (1994), pp. 191-211.

9. H. Fernau, On unconditional transfer. In: W. Penczek, and A. Szałłas (eds.), *Proceedings MFCS'96, LNCS 1113* (Springer, Berlin, 1996), pp. 348–359.

10. H. Fernau and R. Freund, Bounded parallelism in array grammars used for character recognition. In: P. Perner, P. Wang, and A. Rosenfeld (eds.), *Proceedings SSPR'96, LNCS 1121* (Springer, Berlin, 1996), pp. 40–49.

11. R. Freund, Aspects of n-dimensional Lindenmayer systems. In: G. Rozenberg, and A. Salomaa (eds.), *Developments in Language Theory* (World Scientific Publ., Singapore, 1994), pp. 250–261.

12. R. Freund, One-dimensional #-sensing context-free array grammars, Technical report, Universität Magdeburg, 1994.

13. R. Freund and Gh. Păun, One-dimensional matrix array grammars, *J. Inform. Process. Cybernet.* **EIK 29** (6) (1993), pp. 1-18.

14. R. Freund, Control mechanisms on #-context-free array grammars. In: Gh. Păun (ed.), *Mathematical Aspects of Natural and Formal Languages* (World Scientific Publ., Singapore, 1994), pp. 97-137.

15. D. Hauschildt and M. Jantzen, Petri net algorithms in the theory of matrix grammars, *Acta Informatica* **31** (1994), pp. 719–728.

16. H. Maurer, G. Rozenberg, and E. Welzl, Using string languages to describe picture languages, *Information and Control* **54** (1982), pp. 155-185.

17. A. Rosenfeld, *Picture Languages* (Academic Press, Reading, MA, 1979).

18. A. Salomaa, *Formal Languages* (Academic Press, Reading, MA, 1973).

19. P. S.-P. Wang, Some New Results on Isotonic Array Grammars, *Information Processing Letters* **10** (1980), pp. 129-131.

20. Y. Yamamoto, K. Morita, and K. Sugata, Context-sensitivity of two-dimensional regular array grammars. In: P. S.-P. Wang (ed.), *Array Grammars, Patterns and Recognizers*, WSP Series in Computer Science, Vol. 18 (World Scientific Publ., Singapore, 1989), pp. 17-41.

On Restarting Automata with Rewriting[1]

Petr JANČAR

University of Ostrava, Department of Computer Science
Bráfova 7, 701 03 OSTRAVA, Czech Republic
E-mail: jancar@osu.cz

František MRÁZ, Martin PLÁTEK

Charles University, Department of Computer Science
Malostranské nám. 25, 118 00 PRAHA 1, Czech Republic
E-mail: mraz@ksvi.mff.cuni.cz, platek@ksi.mff.cuni.cz

Jörg VOGEL

Friedrich Schiller University, Computer Science Institute
07740 Jena, Germany
E-mail: vogel@informatik.uni-jena.de

Abstract. Motivated by natural language analysis we introduce restarting automata with rewriting. They are acceptors on the one hand, and (special) regulated rewriting systems on the other hand. The computation of a restarting automaton proceeds in cycles: in each cycle, a bounded substring of the input word is rewritten by a shorter string, and the computation restarts on the arising shorter word.

We show a taxonomy of (sub)variants of these automata taking into account (non)determinism and two other natural properties.

Theoretical significance of the restarting automata is also demonstrated by relating it to context-free languages (CFL), by which a characterization of deterministic CFL is obtained.

1. Introduction

Our motivation for introducing the restarting automata is to model so called elementary syntactic analysis of natural languages. The elementary syntactic analysis consists in stepwise simplification of an extended sentence until a simple sentence is got or an error is found. Let us show it on the sentence

'Martin, Peter and Jane work very slowly.'

We work with the wordforms in the examples; instead of wordforms, the elementary analysis uses their lexical characterizations (categories). This sentence can be simplified for example in this way:

'Martin, Peter and Jane work slowly.'

'Martin, Peter and Jane work.'

*'Martin **and** Peter work.'* or *'Peter and Jane work.'* or *'Martin and Jane work.'*

*'Martin **works**.'* or some other variant of the corresponding simple sentence.

---

[1]Supported by the Grant Agency of the Czech Republic, Grant-No. 201/96/0195

120

Notice, that every simplification is realized by deleting and possible rewriting (marked by the bold face) of words.

The restarting automaton with rewriting (RW-automaton), introduced in [7], can be roughly described as follows. It has a finite control unit, a head with a lookahead window attached to a linear (doubly linked) list with sentinels, and it works in certain cycles. In a cycle, it moves the head from left to right along the word on the list (any item contains exactly one symbol); according to its instructions, it can at some point replace the scanned string by a shorter string and "restart" – i.e. reset the control unit to the initial state and place the head on the left end of the list (which now contains the shortened word). The computation halts in an accepting or a rejecting state.

Using cycles we define *yield relation* for a RW-automaton M. From a string α contained in the list by the start of a cycle M yields a string β remaining in the list after finishing the cycle (denoted by $\alpha \Rightarrow_M \beta$). Together with the yield relation, a RW-automaton can also be considered as a (regulated) rewriting system.

Formerly, in [4], we have introduced restarting automata without rewriting – R-automata – by which the replacing string is a proper subsequence of the replaced string. They are considered as a transparent model for grammar checker (of natural and formal languages as well). Having found an error in a sentence, the grammar checker should specify it – often by exhibiting the parts (words or more exactly their lexical characterizations) which do not match each other. The method can be based on stepwise leaving out some parts not affecting the (non)correctness of the sentence. E.g. applying it to the sentence

'The little boys I mentioned runs very quickly'

we get after some steps the "error core"

'boys runs'.

There are other paradigms modelling the elementary syntax in the generative way, e.g. *pure (generalized) grammars with strictly length-increasing rules* (c.f. [8]). These grammars work on strings of terminals and do not introduce any nonterminals. This type of grammars realize, similarly as Marcus grammars ([6][2]), a (generalized) rewriting system with an yield relation $\Rightarrow_G$ ($\alpha \Rightarrow_G \beta$ means that α can be rewritten to β in one step according to a grammar G), which should capture the stepwise development from simple sentences. The yield relation has the so called *correctness preserving property*, which means that if α is a correct string according to some grammar G and $\alpha \Rightarrow_G \beta$, then β is a correct string again.

The yield relation corresponding to a RW-automaton has a dual property comparing to the yield relation corresponding to a pure (generalized) grammar with strictly length-increasing rules. RW-automaton yields strings in the strictly length-decreasing way, and has the *error preserving property*: if α contains error (is not in the language recognized by the RW-automaton M) and $\alpha \Rightarrow_M \beta$, then β contains an error. This duality will allow to consider RW-automata as another type of generalization of pure grammars with strictly length-increasing rules. The RW-automata allow to add regulation of the yielding by their control units.

---

[2]A comprehensive presentation of these grammars can be found in the forthcoming monograph Gh. Păun, *Contextual Grammars. From Natural Languages to Formal Languages and Back*.

Section 2 contains definitions of *RW*-automata and *R*-automata. There are also described some basic properties of these automata and their computations. As usual, we define nondeterministic and deterministic versions of the automata. In second subsection we show that *RW*-automata are stronger than pure grammars. In the third subsection we consider a natural property of monotonicity (during any computation, "the places of restarting do not increase their distances from the right end") and show that the monotonicity is a decidable property. In Section 3 we show that monotonic *RW*-automata recognize a subset of the class of context-free languages (*CFL*) and deterministic monotonic *RW*-automata recognize only deterministic *CFL* (*DCFL*). Moreover any deterministic context-free language can be recognized by a deterministic monotonic *R*-automaton. From this results we get two characterizations of *DCFL*. The paper continues in Section 4 with separation theorems for rewriting and non-rewriting classes of automata and some related results. In conclusions (Section 5) beside discussion of future directions of our study, also another type of automata with similar features as *RW*-automata – contraction automata – is mentioned.

2. Definitions and Basic Properties

We present the definitions informally; the formal technical details could be added in a standard way of the automata theory. In the first subsection we introduce restarting automata with rewriting, in the second subsection we relate *RW*-automata to pure grammars and in the last subsection we introduce the monotonicity property for *RW*-automata and a normal form of this automata – (strong) cyclic form.

2.1. Restarting Automata with Rewriting

A *restarting automaton with rewriting*, or a *RW-automaton*, M (with bounded lookahead) is a device with a finite state control unit and one head moving on a finite linear (doubly linked) list of items (cells). The first item always contains a special symbol ¢, the last one another special symbol $, and each other item contains a symbol from a finite alphabet (not containing ¢, $). The head has a lookahead "window" of length k (for some $k \geq 0$) – besides the current item, M also scans the next k right neighbour items (or simply the end of the word when the distance to $ is less than k). In the *initial configuration*, the control unit is in a fixed, initial, state and the head is attached to the item with the left sentinel ¢ (scanning also the first k symbols of the input word).

The *computation* of M is controlled by a finite set of *instructions* of the following two types:

(1) $(q, au) \rightarrow_M (q', MVR)$

(2) $(q, au) \rightarrow_M RESTART(v)$

The left-hand side of an instruction determines when it is applicable – q means the current state (of the control unit), a the symbol being scanned by the head, and u means the contents of the lookahead window (u being a string of length k or less if it ends with $). The right-hand side describes the activity to be performed. In case (1), M changes the current state to q' and moves the head to the right neighbour item. In case (2), au is replaced with v, where v must be shorter than au, and M restarts – i.e. it enters the initial state and places the head on the first item of the list (containing ¢).

We say that M is a *restarting automaton (R-automaton)* if in each instruction of the form $(q, au) \rightarrow_M REST\,ART(v)$ the word v is a proper subsequence of the word au.

We will suppose that the control unit states of M are divided into two groups: the *regulating states* (nonhalting states – an instruction is always applicable when the unit is in such a state) and the *halting states* (a computation finishes by entering such a state); the *halting states* are further divided into the *accepting states* and the *rejecting states*.

In general, a *RW*-automaton is *nondeterministic*, i.e. there can be two or more instructions with the same left-hand side (q, au). If it is not the case, the automaton is *deterministic* (*det-RW*-automaton).

An input *word w is accepted by M* if there is a computation which starts in the initial configuration with w (bounded by sentinels ¢,$) on the list and finishes in an *accepting configuration* where the control unit is in one of the accepting states. $L(M)$ denotes the language consisting of all words accepted by M; we say that M *recognizes the language $L(M)$*.

It is natural to divide any computation of a *RW*-automaton into *cycles*: in one cycle, the head moves right along the input list (with a bounded lookahead) until a halting state is entered or something in a bounded space is rewritten – in that case the computation is resumed in the initial configuration on the shortened word (thus a new cycle starts). It immediately implies that any computation of any *RW*-automaton is finite (finishing in a halting state).

The notation $u \longrightarrow_M v$ means that there exists a cycle of M starting in the initial configuration with the word u and finishing in the initial configuration with the word v; the relation $\longrightarrow_M^*$ is the reflexive and transitive closure of $\longrightarrow_M$. We say that u *yields v by M* if $u \longrightarrow_M v$.

The next three claims express the basic properties of the yield relations corresponding to *RW*-automata.

Claim 2.1. (The error preserving property (for all RW-automata)) *Let M be a RW-automaton, and $u \longrightarrow_M^* v$ for some words u, v. If $u \notin L(M)$, then $v \notin L(M)$.*

Proof. Let $u \longrightarrow_M^* v$ such that $v \in L(M)$. Since $v \in L(M)$ there is some y such that $v \longrightarrow_M^* y$, where y can be accepted by M in one cycle. Because of $u \longrightarrow_M^* v$, the relation $u \longrightarrow_M^* y$ holds. Hence u is accepted by M. $\square$

Claim 2.2. (The correctness preserving property (for det-RW-automata)) *Let M be a deterministic RW-automaton and $u \longrightarrow_M^* v$ for some words u, v. If $u \in L(M)$, then $v \in L(M)$.*

Proof. Let M be a deterministic *RW*-automaton, $u \in L(M)$ and $u \longrightarrow_M^* v$ for some word v. Because of determinism of M there exists exactly one accepting computation for u by M. The computation represented by sequence of cycles $u \longrightarrow_M^* v$ is a prefix of this computation. Thus the rest of this computation (starting in the initial configuration with v on the list) is an accepting computation for v and $v \in L(M)$. $\square$

As a consequence of the previous two claims 2.1 and 2.2 we get:

Claim 2.3. *Let M be a deterministic R-automaton and $u \longrightarrow_M^* v$ for some words u, v. Then $v \in L(M)$ if and only if $u \in L(M)$.*

2.2. Pure Grammars

Next we will show that RW-automata can be considered as regulated acceptors (analysers) for pure grammars with strictly length-increasing rules.

A *pure grammar* is a triple $G = (V, P, S)$ where V is a finite set of symbols, S is a finite subset of V^*, and P is finite set of productions of the form $v \to_G w$, $v, w \in V^*$.

For $x, y \in V^*$, the yield relation $x \Rightarrow_G y$ is defined by $x = z_1 v z_2$, $y = z_1 w z_2$, $v \to_G w \in P$, where $v, w, z_1, z_2 \in V^*$.

$\Rightarrow_G^*$ is the reflexive and transitive closure of $\Rightarrow_G$. The language generated by G is defined as $L(G) = \{y \mid x \Rightarrow_G^* y \text{ for some } x \in S\}$.

We can easily see that $\Rightarrow_G^*$ has the correctness preserving property, i.e. if $x \in L(G)$ and $x \Rightarrow_G^* y$ then $y \in L(G)$.

We say that a grammar G has strictly length-increasing rules if $|v| < |w|$ for each $v \to_G w \in P$.

We can easily see that for any pure grammar G with strictly length-increasing rules there is a RW-automaton M with one regulating state (the starting state), one rejecting and one accepting state only, such that $L(G) = L(M)$, and the relation $\Rightarrow_G$ is the opposite relation to $\Rightarrow_M$.

The opposite implication is not true. Let us show that the RW-automata with one regulating state are more powerful than pure grammars.

Let us take the following language $L_a = \{a^n b^n \mid n \geq 0\} \cup \{a^n \mid n \geq 0\}$.

Claim 2.4. *The language L_a cannot be generated by any pure grammar G with strictly length-increasing rules.*

Proof. Let us suppose that some pure grammar $G = (V, P, S)$ with strictly length-increasing rules generates L_a.

Let us consider a sufficiently long word $w = a^m$, where m is greater than the size of any string from S. We can see that there is $v = a^n$ such that $v \Rightarrow_G w$, and therefore P contains a rule of the form $a^p \to_G a^{p+q}$, where $p \geq 0$ and $q > 0$.

Let us consider word $z = a^m b^m$. We can see that $z \in L_a$ and $z \Rightarrow_G z'$, where $z' = a^{m+q} b^m$. Since $m + q > m > 0$ the word z' is not in L_a, that is a contradiction to the correctness preserving property of $\Rightarrow_G$. $\qquad\square$

Claim 2.5. *There is a RW-automaton M with one regulating state recognizing the language L_a.*

Proof. Let us describe the automaton M: M has lookahead of the length 3, one regulating state (the initial state q_0), the accepting state q_a and the rejecting state q_r. The automaton in one cycle accepts the empty word, deletes a from the words containing only a's, deletes ab from the word ab and deletes ab from the words with the prefix $a^+ bb$. The working alphabet of M is $\{a, b\}$ and M has the following instructions:

$$
\begin{aligned}
&(q_0, \mathrm{\mathcal{c}}\$) \to_M (q_a, MVR), &&(q_0, \mathrm{\mathcal{c}}aab) \to_M (q_0, MVR),\\
&(q_0, \mathrm{\mathcal{c}}a\$) \to_M REST ART(\mathrm{\mathcal{c}}\$), &&(q_0, aaaa) \to_M (q_0, MVR),\\
&(q_0, \mathrm{\mathcal{c}}ab\$) \to_M REST ART(\mathrm{\mathcal{c}}\$), &&(q_0, aaab) \to_M (q_0, MVR),\\
&(q_0, \mathrm{\mathcal{c}}aa\$) \to_M REST ART(\mathrm{\mathcal{c}}a\$), &&(q_0, aabb) \to_M REST ART(ab),\\
&(q_0, \mathrm{\mathcal{c}}aaa) \to_M (q_0, MVR), &&(q_0, aaa\$) \to_M REST ART(aa\$)
\end{aligned}
$$

$(q_0, u) \to_M (q_r, MVR)$ for any u of the length four not covered in the previous cases.

We can see that M recognizes L_a and that M is actually a deterministic R-automaton. □

2.3. Monotonicity and Cyclic Forms of RW-Automata

In this subsection the monotonicity property of RW-automata is defined, its decidability is shown and so called cyclic forms of restarting automata with rewriting are introduced.

The property of monotonicity (for a computation of a RW-automaton): All items which appeared in the lookahead window (and were not deleted) during one cycle will appear in the lookahead in the next cycle as well – if it does not finish in a halting state (i.e., during a computation, "the places of changes in the list do not increase their distances from the right endmarker $").

By a *monotonic RW-automaton* we mean a RW-automaton where the property of monotonicity holds for all computations.

Theorem 2.6. *There is an algorithm which for any RW-automaton M decides whether M is monotonic or not.*

Proof. We sketch the idea briefly. Consider a given (nondeterministic) RW-automaton M; let its lookahead be of length k. Recall that all computations of a monotonic automaton have to be monotonic. The idea is to construct a (nondeterministic) finite automaton which accepts a nonempty language if and only if there is a nonmonotonic computation of M.

Suppose there is a nonmonotonic computation of M. Then there is a word w on which M can perform two cycles where in the second cycle it does not scan all (remaining) items scanned in the first cycle.

Now consider the construction of the mentioned finite automaton A; we can suppose that it has lookahead of length k. A supposes reading the described w. It moves right simulating two consecutive cycles of M simultaneously. At a certain moment, A decides nondeterministically that it has entered the area of rewriting in the second cycle – it guesses the appropriate contents of the lookahead window which would be encountered in the second cycle. Then it moves right coming to the place of the (guessed) rewriting in the first cycle and verifies that the previously guessed lookahead was guessed correctly; if so, A accepts. □

Considering a deterministic RW-automaton M, it is sometimes convenient to suppose it in the *strong cyclic form*; it means that the words of length less than k, k being the length of lookahead, are immediately (hence in the first cycle) accepted or rejected, and that M performs at least two cycles (at least one restarting) for any longer word.

For a nondeterministic RW-automaton M, we can suppose the *weak cyclic form* – any word from $L(M)$ longer than k (the length of lookahead) can be accepted only by performing two cycles at least. The cyclic forms are justified by the following claim.

Claim 2.7. *For any RW-automaton (R-automaton) M, with lookahead k, there exists an RW-automaton (R-automaton) M', with some lookahead n, $n \geq k$, such that M' is in the weak cyclic form and $L(M) = L(M')$. Moreover, if M is deterministic then M' is deterministic and in the strong cyclic form, if M is monotonic deterministic then M' is monotonic deterministic and in strong cyclic form.*

Proof. To prove this claim we can proceed in the same way as for R-automata (see [5]).

First notice that we can easily force an RW-automaton M to visit all items of the input list before accepting or rejecting – instead of an "original" accepting (rejecting) state, it would enter a special state which causes moving to the right end and then accepting (rejecting).

Now suppose that (the modified) M accepts a long word w in the first cycle (without restarting). If w is sufficiently long then it surely can be written $w = v_1 a u v_2 a u v_3$ where M enters both occurrences of a in the same state q during the corresponding computation (as above, by a we mean a symbol and by u a string of length k). Then it is clear that the word $v_1 a u v_3$ ($a u v_2$ has been deleted) is also accepted. In addition, we can suppose that the length of $a u v_2 a u v_3$ is less than a fixed (sufficiently large) n.

We sketch a desired M' with lookahead n. Any word w shorter than n is immediately accepted or rejected by M' according to whether $w \in L(M)$ or not. On a longer w, M' simulates M with the following exception: when \$ appears in the lookahead window, M' checks whether M could move to the right end and accept; if so, M' deletes the relevant $a u v_2$ (cf. the above notation) and restarts (recall that n has been chosen so that such $a u v_2$ surely exists). Obviously, $L(M) = L(M')$ holds.

In case M is deterministic, M' can work as above; in addition it can safely delete the relevant $a u v_2$ also when M would reject (due to determinism, the resulting word is also rejected by M).

It should be clear that monotonicity of M implies monotonicity of M' in the deterministic case.

Further it should be clear that we get by this construction from a R-automaton M a R-automaton M'. $\square$

Remark 2.1. For the nondeterministic monotonic RW-automata the construction does not ensure monotonicity of the resulted automaton.

For brevity, we use the following obvious notation. RW denotes the class of all (nondeterministic) restarting automata (with rewriting and some lookahead). R denotes the class of all (nondeterministic) restarting automata without rewriting. Prefix *det-* denotes the deterministic version, similarly *mon-* the monotonic version. For any class $\mathcal{A}$ of automata, $\mathcal{L}(\mathcal{A})$ denotes the class of languages recognizable by automata from $\mathcal{A}$, and $\mathcal{A}$-language is a language from $\mathcal{L}(\mathcal{A})$. E.g. the class of languages recognizable by deterministic monotonic R-automata is denoted by $\mathcal{L}(det\text{-}mon\text{-}R)$.

Throughout the article we will use the following notations for the inclusion relations: $A \subseteq B$ means that A is a subset of B and $A \subset B$ means that A is a proper subset of B ($A \subseteq B$ and $A \neq B$). $\emptyset$ denotes the empty set.

3. Characterization of $DCFL$

In this section, we show a (twofold) characterization of $DCFL$, namely $DCFL = \mathcal{L}(det\text{-}mon\text{-}R) = \mathcal{L}(det\text{-}mon\text{-}RW)$. In addition, we also get $\mathcal{L}(mon\text{-}RW) \subset CFL$.

Lemma 3.1. $DCFL \subseteq \mathcal{L}(det\text{-}mon\text{-}R)$.

Proof. We use the characterization of deterministic context-free languages by means of $LR(0)$–grammars and $LR(0)$–analysers (cf. e.g. [2]); generally $LR(1)$–

grammars (lookahead 1) are needed, but it is not necessary when each word is finished by the special sentinel $.

Let L' be a deterministic context-free language. Then there is an $LR(0)$–grammar G generating $L = L'\$$ (the concatenation $L' \cdot \{\$\}$ supposing $\$$ being not in the alphabet of L'), and there is a corresponding $LR(0)$–analyser P.

For any word $w \in L$ there is only one derivation tree T_w; it corresponds to the analysis of w by the analyser P. In fact, P simulates constructing T_w in the left-to-right and bottom-up fashion. Due to the standard pumping lemma for context-free languages, there are constants p, q s.t. for any w with length greater than p there are a (complete) subtree T_1 of T_w and a (complete) subtree T_2 of T_1 with the same root labelling; in addition, T_2 has fewer leaves than T_1 and T_1 has q leaves at most. (Cf. Fig. 1; A is a nonterminal of G). Replacing T_1 with T_2, we get the derivation tree for a shorter word w' (w could be written $w = u_1 v_1 u_2 v_2 u_3$ in such a way that $w' = u_1 u_2 u_3$).

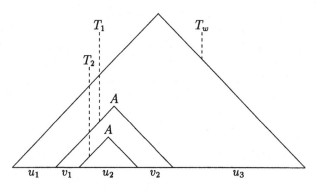

Figure 1.

Now we outline a *det-mon-R*-automaton M with lookahead of length $k > q$ which recognizes L'.

M stores the contents of the lookahead in a buffer in the control unit. Simulating the $LR(0)$–analyser P, it constructs (in a bounded space in the control unit) all maximal subtrees of the derivation tree which have all their leaves in the buffer. If one of the subtrees is like the T_1 above, M performs the relevant deleting (of at most two continuous segments) in the input list and restarts. If it is not the case then M forgets the leftmost of these subtrees with all its $n \geq 1$ leaves, and reads n new symbols to the right end of the buffer (shifting the contents left). Then M continues constructing the maximal subtrees with all leaves in the (updated) buffer (simulating P).

In general, the input word w is either shorter than p, such words can be checked using finite memory, or it is longer. If it is longer and belongs to L then M must meet the leftmost above described T_1 (with the subtree T_2); it performs the relevant deleting and restarts on a new, shorter, word. If the (long) input word w does not belong to L, M either meets $\$$ without restarting and stops in a rejecting state or performs some deleting and restarts. It suffices to show that the resulting shorter word (in both cases) is in L if and only if w is in L.

It can be verified using the following properties of the $LR(0)$–analyser.

a) For each word $w \in L$ there is exactly one derivation of w in G which corresponds to the analysis of w by P.

b) Let u be the prefix of the input word $w = uv$ which has been already read by the $LR(0)$–analyser P. If P did not reject the word until now, then there exists a suffix word v' s.t. uv' is in L, and the computation of P on the prefix u is independent w.r.t. the suffix.

Let u be the prefix of the input word, the last symbol of which corresponds to the last symbol in the lookahead window just before M performs a RESTART-operation; let $\bar{u}$ be the rest of u after performing the RESTART-operation. There exists a suffix v' such that uv' is in L. uv' has a derivation tree in which there is a complete subtree T_1 (with a subtree T_2; as above) corresponding to the place of cutting. Then in the computation of M on $\bar{u}$ the tree T_2 will appear in the buffer above the same terminal leaves as in the computation on u (it follows from the presence of T_2 in the derivation tree of $\bar{u}v'$ and from the independence of computation on the suffix).

Let $w = uv$ is in L, then obviously $\bar{u}v$ is in L. Conversely if uv is not in L then $\bar{u}v$ is not in L (otherwise, in the corresponding derivation tree of $\bar{u}v$, the subtree T_2 appears over the corresponding terminal leaves of $\bar{u}$ and replacing the tree T_2 by T_1 yields a derivation tree for uv – a contradiction).

The monotonicity of M should be clear from the above description.   □

Lemma 3.1 (together with Claim 2.7) is a means for short proving that some languages are not in $DCFL$. We illustrate it by the next two examples.

Example 3.2. Consider the language $L_1 = \{ww^R \mid w \in \{a, b\}^*\}$. If it were in $DCFL$, it would be recognized by a deterministic R-automaton M with the length of lookahead k (for some k); M can be supposed in the strong cyclic form. Let us now take a word $a^n b^m b^m a^n$ $(n, m > k)$, on which M performs two cycles at least. In the first cycle, M can only shorten the segment of $b's$. But due to determinism, it would behave in the same way on the word $a^n b^m b^m a^n a^n b^m b^m a^n$, which is a contradiction to the correctness preserving property (Claim 2.2).

Example 3.3. The language $L_2 = \{a^m b^n c^p \mid m, n, p \geq 0 : (m = n \text{ or } n = p)\}$ is not in $DCFL$. This can be shown in a similar way as in the previous example. But using the error preserving property for RW-automata we will show stronger result – the language L_2 cannot be recognized by any RW-automaton.

The next claim shows that RW-automata do not recognize all context-free languages and will be used in the proof of the next lemma.

Claim 3.4. *The language* $L_2 = \{a^m b^n c^p \mid m, n, p \geq 0 : (m = n \text{ or } n = p)\}$ *is not a RW-language.*

Proof. Let us suppose that L_2 is recognized by some RW-automaton M_2 in the weak cyclic form with the size of lookahead k. Let us consider an accepting computation on a word $a^r b^r$, where $r > 2(k + 1)$. In the first cycle of the accepting computation, M_2 can only shorten both segments of a's and b's in such way that after the first cycle the resulting word will be $a^{r-m} b^{r-m}$ for some $0 < m < k$ (i.e. the restart with rewriting occurs in the middle of the word; M_2 cannot rewrite a suffix of the word in order to get a word of the form $a^r b^m c^m$ for some $m \geq 0$). But M_2 can behave in the same way also on the word $a^r b^{r+m} c^r \notin L_2$ from which it can get after the first cycle $a^{r-m}b^r c^r \in L_2$. This is a contradiction to the error preserving property of RW-automata (Claim 2.1). $\square$

Lemma 3.5.

a) $\mathcal{L}(mon\text{-}RW) \subset CFL$,

b) $\mathcal{L}(det\text{-}mon\text{-}RW \subseteq \mathcal{L}(DCFL)$.

Proof. At first we show that $\mathcal{L}(mon\text{-}RW)$ is a subclass of CFL. Let L be a language recognized by $mon\text{-}RW$-automaton M, with lookahead of length k. We show how to construct a pushdown automaton P which simulates M. The construction is similar to the construction of a deterministic pushdown automaton which should simulate a given $det\text{-}mon\text{-}R$-automaton (see [4]). The difference is following: Instead of one step simulation of a single MVR-step, P will simulate in one step all possible "nondeterministic" MVR-steps performed on the simulated scanned item simultaneously, and the simulation of a restart without rewriting is replaced by a simulation of a restart with rewriting.

P is able to store in its control unit in a component CSt the set of possible current states of M (i.e. any subset of the set of states of M) and in a component B a word of length at most $1 + 2k$. P starts by storing $\{q_0\}$, where q_0 is the initial state of M, in CSt and pushing $\math{\c{c}}$ (the left endmarker of M) into the first cell of the buffer B and the first k symbols of the input word of M into the next k cells of the buffer B (cells $2, 3, \ldots, k + 1$).

During the simulation, the following conditions will hold invariantly:
- CSt contains the set of all states of M, in which can be M visiting the simulated (currently scanned) item, with the current left-hand side, and the current lookahead,
- the first cell of B contains the current symbol of M (scanned by the head) and the rest of B contains m right neighbour symbols of the current one (lookahead of length m) where m varies between k and $2k$,
- the pushdown contains the left-hand side (w.r.t. the head) of the list, the leftmost symbol ($\math{\c{c}}$) being at the bottom. In fact, any pushdown symbol will be composed
- it will contain the relevant symbol of the input list and the set of states of M in which this symbol (this item) could be entered (from the left) by the situation, which corresponds to the last simulated visit.

The mentioned invariant will be maintained by the following simulation of instructions of M; the left-hand side (q, au) of the instruction to be simulated is determined by the information stored in the control unit. The activity to be performed depends on the right-hand sides of applicable instructions of M. P can either

1. nondeterministically simulate one of RESTART instructions of M, or

2. simulate all possible MVR instructions in one step.

(1) $RESTART(v)$ is simulated by deleting and rewriting in the buffer B (some of the first $k + 1$ symbols are deleted and the rest is pushed to the left and possibly rewritten). Then $k + 1$ (composed) symbols are successively taken from the pushdown and the relevant symbols are added from the left to B (shifting the rest to the right). The state parts of k (composed) symbols are forgotten, the state part of the $(k+1)$-th symbol (the leftmost in the buffer) is stored in CSt. Thus not only the $RESTART(v)$

- operation is simulated but also the beginning part of the next cycle, the part which was prepared in the previous cycle.

(2) P puts the contents of the first cell of B and CSt as a composed symbol on the top of the pushdown, stores the set $\{q' \mid (q, au) \to_M (q', MVR), q \in CSt\}$ of simulated new states which can be entered after MVR-step from some state in the original CSt with the lookahead au, and shifts the contents of B one symbol to the left; if the $(k+1)$-th cell of B is then empty, then P reads the next input symbol into it.

It should be clear that due to monotonicity of M the second half of B (cells $k+2, k+3, \ldots, 2k$) is empty at the time of simulating a $RESTART(v)$–operation. Hence the described construction is correct which proves $\mathcal{L}(mon\text{-}RW) \subseteq CFL$. To finish the proof of the first part of the proposition can show a context-free language which cannot be recognized by any RW-automaton. But this was already done in Claim 3.4.

Obviously the above construction applied to a $det\text{-}mon\text{-}R$-automaton yields a deterministic push-down automaton – this proves part b) of the statement.   □

Theorem 3.6. $\mathcal{L}(det\text{-}mon\text{-}RW) = DCFL = \mathcal{L}(det\text{-}mon\text{-}R)$.

Proof. The statement is a consequence of Lemma 3.1, Lemma 3.5 and the trivial inclusion $\mathcal{L}(det\text{-}mon\text{-}R) \subseteq \mathcal{L}(det\text{-}mon\ RW)$.   □

It can be worth noting that the closure of deterministic RW-languages under complement is immediately clear when considering deterministic RW-automata ($det\text{-}R$-, $det\text{-}RW$-, $det\text{-}mon\text{-}R$- and $det\text{-}mon\text{-}RW$-automata). Since all computations of deterministic RW-automata are finite it suffices to exchange the accepting and the rejecting states to get a deterministic automaton of the same type ($det\text{-}R$-, $det\text{-}RW$-, $det\text{-}mon\text{-}R$- or $det\text{-}mon\text{-}RW$-automaton) recognizing the complementary language.

Claim 3.7. *The classes of languages $\mathcal{L}(det\text{-}mon\text{-}R)$, $\mathcal{L}(det\text{-}mon\text{-}RW)$, $\mathcal{L}(det\text{-}R)$ and $\mathcal{L}(det\text{-}RW)$ are closed under complement.*

4. Taxonomy of RW-languages

In this section we will study relations between different subclasses of $\mathcal{L}(RW)$. The resulting relations are depicted in Figure 2.

Next we will prove all the relations depicted in this figure. We will start by proving that a $det\text{-}R$-automaton can recognize a language which is not $mon\text{-}RW$-language.

Theorem 4.1. $\mathcal{L}(det\text{-}R) - \mathcal{L}(mon\text{-}RW) \neq \emptyset$

Proof. To prove the theorem, it is sufficient to give a $det\text{-}R$-automaton M which recognizes a non context-free language $L = L(M)$. L cannot be recognized by any $mon\text{-}RW$-automaton, because according Lemma 3.5 all languages recognized by $mon\text{-}R$-automata are context-free. We will use a $det\text{-}R$-automaton M which recognizes a non context-free language from [5].

The main idea is to start with a non context-free language $L' = \{a^{2^k} \mid k \geq 0\}$. The automaton M will work in phases. A phase starts with a word from L' on the list and consists of several cycles in which the length of the current word is reduced by factor 2 and simultaneously the parity of the length of the word on the start of the phase is checked. But restarting automaton can shorten the word by at most constant number of symbols in one cycle. Thus we must modify the language to enable to "mark"

130

already shortened part of the working list – instead of one symbol a we use a pair ab. Working on a word of the form $(ab)^n$ for some $n > 1$, M at first deletes the second a out of each subword $abab$, proceeding stepwise from the right to the left. Then M deletes one b out of each abb and proceeds also stepwise from the right to the left. The automaton recognizes the language $L(M)$ for which

$$L(M) \cap \{(ab)^n \mid n \geq 1\} = \{(ab)^{2^k} \mid k \geq 0\}$$

Thus the language $L(M)$ is not context-free and also is not a *mon-RW*-language (Lemma 3.5).

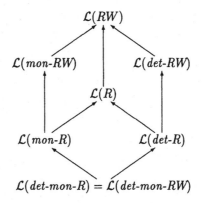

Figure 2. Taxonomy of RW-languages. Solid arrows show the proper inclusion relations, depicted classes not connected (by an oriented path) are incomparable.

The automaton M works as follows:

1. reading ¢*abab* or ¢*abba* it moves to the right;

2. reading *ababa* or *babab* it moves to the right;

3. reading *abab*\$ it deletes second a and restarts;

4. reading *ababb* it deletes the first a and restarts;

5. reading *abbab* or *bbabb* or *babba* it moves to the right;

6. reading *babb*\$ it deletes the second b and restarts;

7. reading *bbab*\$ or *bbaba* it deletes the first b and restarts;

8. reading ¢*abb*\$ it deletes the first b and restarts;

9. reading ¢*ab*\$ it accepts;

10. in all other cases the automaton halts in a nonaccepting state.

Clearly the automaton M is deterministic. To prove (1) let us consider a word of the form $(ab)^n$ for some $n \geq 1$. Then the following two conditions hold

$$(i) \quad (ab)^n \longrightarrow_M^* (ab)^{\frac{n}{2}} \qquad \text{when } n \text{ is even,}$$
$$\text{or } (ii) \quad (ab)^n \longrightarrow_M^* b(abb)^{\frac{n-1}{2}} \quad \text{when } n \text{ is odd.}$$

In the case (i) the automaton makes $\frac{n}{2}$ cycles (using points 1, 2–4), and gets the word $(abb)^{\frac{n}{2}}$, then after another $\frac{n}{2}$ cycles it gets the word $(ab)^{\frac{n}{2}}$ (using points 1, 5–8)

In the case (ii) the automaton makes $\frac{n-1}{2}$ cycles (using points 1, 2–4), and gets the word $b(abb)^{\frac{n-1}{2}}$, which will be rejected in the next cycle.

Thus let the input word be of the form $(ab)^n$, where $n = l2^k$ for some integer $k \geq 0$ and some odd integer $l \geq 1$.

- If n is a power of 2 (i.e. $l = 1$ and $k \geq 1$), then according (i) $(ab)^n \longrightarrow_M^* (ab)^{2^{k-1}} \longrightarrow_M^* (ab)^{2^{k-2}} \longrightarrow_M^* \cdots \longrightarrow_M^* ab$ and according point 9 the input word will be accepted.

- If n is not a power of 2 (i.e. $l > 1$), then according (i) $(ab)^n \longrightarrow_M^* (ab)^l$, $l > 1$ and odd. Further according (ii) $(ab)^l \longrightarrow_M^* b(abb)^{\frac{l-1}{2}}$ and this word will be rejected by 10. $\qquad \square$

This theorem implies some relations between several classes of languages from Figure 2. These relations are depicted in Figure 3. Solid arrow from A to B means that $A \subset B$, dotted arrow from A to B means that $B - A \neq \emptyset$ (and $A \subset B$ is still not excluded).

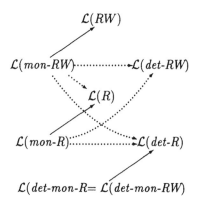

$$\mathcal{L}(RW)$$
$$\mathcal{L}(mon\text{-}RW) \cdots\cdots\cdots \mathcal{L}(det\text{-}RW)$$
$$\mathcal{L}(R)$$
$$\mathcal{L}(mon\text{-}R) \cdots\cdots\cdots \mathcal{L}(det\text{-}R)$$
$$\mathcal{L}(det\text{-}mon\text{-}R) = \mathcal{L}(det\text{-}mon\text{-}RW)$$

Figure 3. Relations which follow from the Theorem 4.1. Solid arrows depict proper inclusion relations, dotted arrows depict non-inclusion relations (in the following shown as incomparable by inclusion) – dotted arrow from A to B means $A \not\supseteq B$.

The next theorem shows a symmetric statement to the previous theorem.

Theorem 4.2. $\mathcal{L}(mon\text{-}R) - \mathcal{L}(det\text{-}RW) \neq \emptyset$

Proof. We will show that the language

$$L = \{a^i b^j \mid 0 \leq i \leq j \leq 2i\}$$

is a *mon-R*-language and is not a *det-RW*-language.

L is recognized by a (nondeterministic) *mon-R*-automaton M with lookahead 4 which:

- immediately accepts the empty word,

- immediately rejects any nonempty word starting by b,

- on a nonempty word starting by a, moves to the right to this a. If the lookahead contains b$ (bb$, abb$, resp.) then deletes ab (abb, aabb resp.) and restarts. Otherwise M moves through a's to the right until its head scans a followed immediately by a different symbol. If its lookahead is not bbbb or bbb$, the word is rejected, else M nondeterministically deletes ab or abb and restarts.

Obviously M recognizes L.

On the other hand the language L cannot be accepted by a deterministic *RW*-automaton (in the strong cyclic form). Working on the word $a^n b^n$ for sufficiently large n (greater than lookahead of the automaton) this deterministic automaton should shorten the word in a cycle by keeping the correctness preserving property. Thus $a^n b^n \longrightarrow_M a^r b^s$ for some $r < n$ and $s \geq r$, i.e the automaton must decrease the number of a's in the word, thus rewriting can occur only when the head is visiting some a in the word. Because of determinism and fixed size of lookahead the automaton must work in the same way on the word $a^n b^{2n}$. But the resulting word at the end of the first cycle is $a^r b^{s+n}$, where $s + n > 2r$, which is not in L. This is a contradiction to the correctness preserving property of *det-RW*-automata (Claim 2.2). □

This theorem implies new proper inclusion relations and non-inclusion relations. We compose them with the relations depicted in Figure 3. In the resulting Figure 4 we use the same notation as in Figure 3 except that the incomparability relations which follow from the already proved theorems are depicted by dotted arcs.

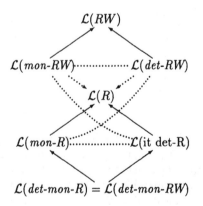

Figure 4. Relations which follow from Theorem 4.1 and Theorem 4.2. Dotted arcs (not the dotted arrows) denote already proved incomparability relations.

As a consequence of the next theorem and Theorem 4.2 we get the incomparability of classes $\mathcal{L}(det\text{-}RW)$ and $\mathcal{L}(R)$.

Theorem 4.3. $\mathcal{L}(det\text{-}RW) - \mathcal{L}(R) \neq \emptyset$

Proof. We will construct a deterministic RW-automaton M such, that $L(M)$ cannot be recognized by any R-automaton. The idea of the construction is similar to that one used in the proof of Theorem 4.1. We are going out of the language $\{a^{3^n} \mid n \geq 0\}$. The automaton M will work in phases. One phase consists of several cycles. During a phase the working word will be reduced by factor 3 and its length will be checked whether it is divisible by 3. A marking of the already reduced part of the word is done by a single symbol b in the list. Let us describe the automaton M: M has lookahead of the length 3, and three states only – the initial state q_0, the accepting state q_a and the rejecting state q_r. The working alphabet of M is $\{a, b\}$ and M has the following instructions:

1. $(q_0, \text{¢}a\$) \to_M (q_a, MVR)$,
2. $(q_0, \text{¢}ba\$) \to_M REST ART(\text{¢}a\$)$,
3. $(q_0, \text{¢}baa) \to_M REST ART(\text{¢}aa)$,
4. $(q_0, \text{¢}aaa) \to_M (q_0, MVR)$,
5. $(q_0, aaaa) \to_M (q_0, MVR)$,
6. $(q_0, aaab) \to_M REST ART(ba)$,
7. $(q_0, aaa\$) \to_M REST ART(ba\$)$,
8. $(q_0, u) \to_M (q_r, MVR)$ for any other u of the length four not covered in the previous cases.

Actually

$$L(M) \cap \{a^i \mid i \geq 1\} = \{a^{3^n} \mid n \geq 0\} \qquad (2)$$

i.e. an intersection of $L(M)$ and the regular language a^* is a non context-free language, thus $L(M)$ cannot be from CFL. We can show that:

$$a^{3i+j} \longrightarrow_M^* a^j ba^i \text{ for } i > 0 \text{ and } 2 \geq j \geq 0$$

The automaton M makes cycles (using instructions 4 – 7) until the symbol b appears in the lookahead window in the initial configuration of a cycle. If it is the first symbol after ¢ then this b is deleted (according 3 or 2). Otherwise the current word is rejected. From this the observation (2) directly follows.

$L(M)$ cannot be recognized by any R-automaton: Suppose that an R-automaton M_R in the weak cyclic form recognizes $L(M)$ and the length of its lookahead is k. Then for a sufficiently large m (e.g. greater than k) such automaton accepts the word a^{3^m} and $a^{3^m} \longrightarrow_{M_R} a^l$ in the first cycle of an accepting computation on the word a^{3^m}. But l cannot be a power of 3 ($3^{m-1} < 3^m - k - 1 \leq l < 3^m$). This fact contradicts the error preserving property (Claim 2.1). $\square$

Moreover the previous proof shows, that RW-automata are stronger than R-automata outside CFL.

As a consequence of the next theorem and Theorem 4.1 we get the incomparability of classes $\mathcal{L}(mon\text{-}RW)$ and $\mathcal{L}(R)$.

Theorem 4.4. $\mathcal{L}(mon\text{-}RW) - \mathcal{L}(R) \neq \emptyset$.

Proof. Obviously $\mathcal{L}(R)$ is a subclass of $\mathcal{L}(RW)$.

At first, we will show that the language

$$L_c = \{ww^R \mid w \in \{a, b\}^*\} \cup \{wcw^R \mid w \in \{a, b\}^*\}$$

can be recognized by a *mon-RW*-automaton M_c:

1. M_c immediately accepts the empty word and the word c.

2. Working on a word (of length greater than 1) containing one symbol c the automaton M_c can scan the word until this symbol and to check whether it is surrounded by the same symbols (a or b). If it is so, then M_c deletes the left and right neighbour of c and restarts, otherwise rejects.

3. Working on a word without c the automaton can "guess aa or bb in the center" of the word, replace it by c and restart.

4. M_c is nondeterministic, but when it makes a mistake – inserts c in a word already containing c or inserts c not in its center, then the test according the point 2 above will fail later.

M_c can be constructed in such a way that the following properties holds:

(i_1) $xaay \longrightarrow_{M_c} xcy$, for any words $x, y \in \{a, b\}^*$.

(i_2) $xbby \longrightarrow_{M_c} xcy$, for any words $x, y \in \{a, b\}^*$.

(i_3) $xacay \longrightarrow_{M_c} xcy$, for any words $x, y \in \{a, b\}^*$.

(i_4) $xbcby \longrightarrow_{M_c} xcy$, for any words $x, y \in \{a, b\}^*$.

(i_5) M_c accepts the one-symbol-word c immediately.

(i_6) M_c rejects in a cycle any word of the form cy or yc, where y is any nonempty word.

(i_7) Any cycle performed by M_c is one of the types $i_1, ..., i_6$.

Secondly, we will show that L_c cannot be recognized by any R-automaton by a contradiction. W.l.o.g. let us suppose that L_c is recognized by some R-automaton M in the weak cyclic form. Let us consider an accepting computation on a sufficiently long word $a^n b^m b^m a^n$, where m, n are greater than the size of lookahead of M. In the first cycle of the accepting computation, M can only shorten the segment of b's. We will get a word of the form $a^n b^{2m'} a^n$, for some $m' < m$, after the first cycle. But M can make the same first cycle in the computation on the word $a^n b^{2m} a^n a^n b^{2m'} a^n$, which is not in $L(M)$ and get the word $a^n b^{2m'} a^n a^n b^{2m'} a^n$ which is from $L(M)$. This is a contradiction to the error preserving property of RW-automata (cf. Claim 2.1; R-automata are a special type of RW-automata). $\square$

The language L_c used in the previous proof is a context-free language. Thus we have proved that RW-automata are stronger than R-automata even inside CFL.

The last two theorems imply the relations depicted in Figure 5.

Composing Figure 4 and Figure 5 we get the complete picture in Figure 2.

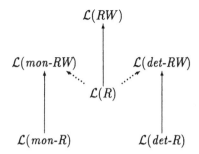

Figure 5. Relations which follow from Theorem 4.3 and Theorem 4.4.

5. Conclusions

In the previous sections we have shown typical results concerning RW-languages and R-languages. We have compared deterministic, nondeterministic, monotonic, nonmonotonic, rewriting and nonrewriting RW-languages. The nondeterministic RW-languages can be possibly studied in a similar way by (regulated) generative tools. On the other hand the results concerning the deterministic RW-languages can be hardly achieved by generative tools in a natural way.

Considering RW-automata as analysers we are interested in properties of the corresponding yield relations as well. There is exactly one difference between the presented taxonomy of languages and the corresponding taxonomy of yield relations. The class of yield relations corresponding to det-mon-RW-automata is greater than the class of yield relations corresponding to det-mon-R-automata. We have omitted the part about the taxonomy of yield relations here, because the nonequality results can be obtained by simple observations of finite yield relations (with finite number of pairs $u \Rightarrow v$).

In [4], we have introduced restarting automata as a further model of list automata (in particular forgetting automata (see [3])). Later, by reading the book by Dassow and Păun (see [1]) we have met contraction automata (introduced by von Solms in [9]). The contraction automata have (some) similar features as RW-automata. A contraction automaton works as a restricted linear bounded automaton. It simulates the operation deleting using a special symbol, and works in cycles. Any cycle starts on the right sentinel, and uses one reversal on the left sentinel. To any contraction automaton M, a complexity (n, k) is associated where, roughly speaking, n means the number of non-input symbols which can be used by M, and k is the maximal number of changes, which can be performed on the tape during a cycle. The contraction automata work also with some technical restrictions, which allow characterizations of matrix languages, certain class of random context languages and a type of ETOL languages.

Inspired by contraction automata we propose to study measures of regulation of (generalized) RW-automata in the future. Also we propose to compare (generalized) RW-automata with different types of regulated generative tools. Some such steps been already done for (generalized) R-automata.

We plan to take RW-automata as theoretical background for a program for (robust) syntactic analysis of Czech sentences. That can be a nice tool to learn the basic syntax of the Czech language.

References

1. J. Dassow, G. Păun: *Regulated Rewriting in Formal Language Theory*, EATCS Monographs on Theoretical Computer Science, Springer Verlag, 1989

2. J. Hopcroft, J. Ullman: *Introduction to Automata Theory, Languages, and Computation*; Addison-Wesley, 1979

3. P. Jančar, F. Mráz, M. Plátek: *A Taxonomy of Forgetting Automata*; in: *Proc. of MFCS 1993*; Gdańsk, Poland, LNCS 711, Springer Verlag, 1993, pp. 527–536

4. P. Jančar, F. Mráz, M. Plátek, J. Vogel: *Restarting Automata*; in: *Proc. of FCT'95*; Dresden, Germany, LNCS 965, Springer Verlag, 1995, pp. 283–292

5. P. Jančar, F. Mráz, M. Plátek, M. Procházka, J. Vogel: *Restarting Automata, Marcus Grammars and Context-Free Languages*; in: J. Dassow, G. Rozenberg, A. Salomaa (eds.): *Developments in Language Theory*; World Scientific Publ., 1995, pp. 102–111

6. S. Marcus: *Contextual grammars*; Revue Roum. Math. Pures Appl.,14, 10, 1969, pp.1525–1534

7. F. Mráz, M. Plátek, J. Vogel: *Restarting Automata with Rewriting*; in *Proc. of SOFSEM'96*; LNCS 1175, Springer Verlag 1996, to appear

8. M. Novotný: *S algebrou od jazyka ke gramatice a zpět*; Academia, Praha, 1988 (*in Czech*)

9. S. H. von Solms: *The Characterization by Automata of Certain Classes of Languages in the Context Sensitive Area*; Inform. Control 27, 1975, pp. 262–271

Chapter 2. Cooperating Distributed Grammar Systems

Deterministic Cooperating Distributed Grammar Systems[1]

Valeria MIHALACHE[2], Victor MITRANA

Faculty of Mathematics, University of Bucharest
Str. Academiei 14, 70109, Bucharest, ROMANIA

Abstract. Subclasses of grammar systems that can facilitate parser construction appear to be of interest. In this paper, some syntactical conditions considered for strict deterministic grammars are extended to cooperating distributed grammar systems, restricted to the terminal derivation mode. Two variants are considered according to the level to which the conditions address. The local variant, which introduces strict deterministic restrictions for each component of the system apart, results in local unambiguity of the derivations. The total variant, which extends the strict deterministic constraints at the level of the entire system, results in some cases in global unambiguity of the derivations.

1. Introduction

Cooperating distributed (CD, for short) grammar systems have been introduced in [3]. A similar generating device was considered in [11], while a particular variant of it appears in [1]. Most of the results known in this area until the middle of 1992 can be found in [4], while newer results are surveyed in [7].

However, there are still lots of classical topics in formal languages theory or in related areas which have not been studied so far in the grammar systems set-up. Constructing parsers is such a topic, which is not only of theoretical interest, but it will make grammar systems more appealing to researchers in applied computer science as well, since it will open the possibility of using grammar systems in domains where just Chomsky-like grammars are currently used (for instance, in natural language processing, or in compiler construction). This will clearly bring to the user all the advantages of having a model which can cope with such phenomena as cooperation and distribution of the work carried out by several processors.

Of interest to this aim are the results of [2] and [6]. Thus, [2] approaches CD grammar systems from the accepting point of view, comparing their accepting capacity to their own generating capacity, or to that of other classes of grammars in the regulated rewriting area. [6] considers pushdown automata systems, with the scope of

---

[1]Research supported by the Academy of Finland, Project 11281, and the Alexander von Humboldt Foundation
[2]Current address: Turku Centre for Computer Science (TUCS), Lemminkäisenkatu 14 A, 4th Floor, 20520, Turku, Finland

characterizing the languages generated by grammar systems in terms of recognizers; but their model turns out to be much more powerful from the point of view of the recognized languages class.

We believe that a more involved study of the derivations in a CD grammar system would be very useful to a possible parser constructor for the languages generated by grammar systems. This is the aim of the present paper: we address subclasses of CD grammar systems which can facilitate a parser construction, due to some unambiguity properties of the derivations in such systems.

More precisely, the present paper studies the effect on CD grammar systems of syntactical constraints similar to those considered for strict deterministic context-free grammars. It is known that the family of languages generated by strict deterministic context-free grammars is the same as the family of languages generated by $LR(0)$ grammars (see Theorem 11.5.5 in [8] and Theorem 10.12 in [9]), which are ones of the most useful class of grammars for parsing. Therefore, our intention was to see what happens if the conditions for strict deterministic grammars are extended to CD grammar systems. To our surprise, we obtained that the *unambiguity* of the derivations holds for some classes of grammar systems as well.

When introducing the restrictions for strict determinism in CD grammar systems, two variants should be taken into consideration, depending on the level, *local/global*, to which the restrictions address. In the local level case, the generative capacity of the systems remains the same, but the behaviour of each component is unambiguous. The generative power decreases when global level is considered, whereas for some more restrictive classes the derivation is totally unambiguous.

2. Definitions and Examples

We assume the reader accustomed to the basic facts in formal language theory [9]. For details concerning the grammar systems we refer to [4].

For an alphabet V, we denote by V^* the set of all words over V and by λ the empty word; moreover, $V^+ = V^* - \{\lambda\}$, while $|V|$ stands for the cardinality of V. For a string x, denote by $|x|$ the length of x and by $Pref_k(x)$ the prefix of length k of $x, |x| \geq k$.

If π is a partition of V, then we write $a \sim^\pi b$ iff there exists $M \in \pi$ such that $\{a, b\} \subseteq M$.

A *cooperating distributed grammar system* is a construct

$$\Gamma = (N, T, S, P_1, P_2, \ldots, P_n),$$

where N, T are disjoint alphabets, $S \in N$, and $P_i, 1 \leq i \leq n$, are finite sets of context-free rules over $N \cup T$.

The sets P_i are called the *components* of Γ. (If we want to point out *grammars* as components, then we can consider grammars without axioms, of the form $G_i = (N, T, P_i), 1 \leq i \leq n$.)

For a component P_i of a grammar system Γ as above, we denote $dom(P_i) = \{A \in N \mid A \to x \in P_i\}$, and $T_i = (N \cup T) - dom(P_i)$.

Let $\Gamma = (N, T, S, P_1, P_2, \ldots, P_n)$ be a CD grammar system as above and let π_i be a partition of $N \cup T$, for any $1 \leq i \leq n$. The partition π_i is a *local strict partition* if the following conditions hold:

a) $T \in \pi_i$,

b) $T_i - T \in \pi_i$,

c) for any $A, A' \in dom(P_i)$, if $A \sim^{\pi_i} A'$ and $A \longrightarrow xy, A' \longrightarrow xy' \in P_i$,
   $x, y, y' \in (N \cup T)^*$, then we have either

   (i) $y, y' \neq \lambda$ and $Pref_1(y) \sim^{\pi_i} Pref_1(y')$, or

   (ii) $y = y' = \lambda$ and $A = A'$.

We say that a component P_i is a *strict deterministic* component of Γ iff there exists a local strict partition π_i.

The system Γ is said to be *local strict deterministic* iff all its components are strict deterministic.

If Γ is a CD grammar system and π is a partition of $N \cup T$, then π is a *total strict partition* iff:

a) $T \in \pi$,

b) for any $A, A' \in N$, if $A \sim^{\pi} A'$ and $A \longrightarrow xy, A' \longrightarrow xy' \in \bigcup_{i=1}^{n} P_i$,
   $x, y, y' \in (N \cup T)^*$, then we have either

   (i) $y, y' \neq \lambda$ and $Pref_1(y) \sim^{\pi} Pref_1(y')$, or

   (ii) $y = y' = \lambda$ and $A = A'$.

The system Γ is said to be *total strict deterministic* iff there exists a total strict partition of $N \cup T$.

We will later on provide grammar systems which are total strict deterministic but not local strict deterministic, and vice versa.

Among the derivation modes in CD grammar systems, our concern here is restricted to the *terminal* (t) mode. Therefore, we next recall only the definition of this one.

On $(N \cup T)^*$ one can define the usual one step derivation with respect to P_i, denoted by $\Longrightarrow_{P_i}$. Formally, $x \Longrightarrow_{P_i} y$ iff $x = x_1 A \alpha$, $y = x_1 z \alpha$, $x_1 \in T_i^*$, $z, \alpha \in (N \cup T)^*$, and $A \longrightarrow z \in P_i$. The reflexive and transitive closure of the relation $\Longrightarrow_{P_i}$ is denoted by $\Longrightarrow_{P_i}^*$. Furthermore, we write $x \Longrightarrow_{P_i}^t y$ if $z \Longrightarrow_{P_i}^* y$ and there is no $z \in (N \cup T)^*$ such that $y \Longrightarrow_{P_i} z$.

Note that we work here with leftmost derivations: see again the condition $x_1 \in T^*$ in the previous definition of $x \Longrightarrow_{P_i} y$.

The language generated by the system Γ is

$$L(\Gamma) = \{w \mid w \in T^*, S \Longrightarrow_{P_{i_1}}^t w_1 \Longrightarrow_{P_{i_2}}^t \cdots \Longrightarrow_{P_{i_m}}^t w_m = w,$$
$$m \geq 1, 1 \leq i_j \leq n, 1 \leq j \leq m\}.$$

Example 1. Consider the system

$$\Gamma_1 = (\{S, A, C, X, Y\}, \{a, b, c\}, S, P_1, P_2, P_3),$$
$$P_1 = \{S \longrightarrow AC, X \longrightarrow A, Y \longrightarrow C\},$$
$$P_2 = \{A \longrightarrow aXb, C \longrightarrow cY\},$$
$$P_3 = \{A \longrightarrow ab, C \longrightarrow c\}.$$

One can observe that Γ_1 is local strict deterministic under the local partitions

$$\pi_1 = \{\{S\}, \{A, C\}, \{X, Y\}, \{a, b, c\}\},$$
$$\pi_2 = \pi_3 = \{\{S, X, Y\}, \{A, C\}, \{a, b, c\}\},$$

but it is not total strict deterministic.

The language generated by Γ_1 is $\{a^n b^n c^n \mid n \geq 1\}$.

Example 2. Consider now

$$\Gamma_2 = (\{S, A, B, C, D\}, \{a, b, c\}, S, P_1, P_2),$$
$$P_1 = \{S \longrightarrow aA, S \longrightarrow aB, A \longrightarrow aAa, A \longrightarrow bC\},$$
$$P_2 = \{B \longrightarrow aB, B \longrightarrow bD, C \longrightarrow bC, C \longrightarrow a, D \longrightarrow bDc, D \longrightarrow c\}.$$

The grammar system above is total strict deterministic under the partition

$$\pi = \{\{S\}, \{A, B\}, \{C, D\}, \{a, b, c\}\}$$

which is a total strict partition. However, its first component is not deterministic.

The generated language is

$$L(\Gamma_2) = \{a^n b^k a^n \mid n, k \geq 1\} \cup \{a^n b^k c^k \mid n, k \geq 1\}.$$

3. Properties of Derivations

Due to the explicit motivation for the introduction of local/total strict deterministic restrictions on CD grammar systems, we first study the derivations in such systems.

In the local case, we obtain that all the components of the system are unambiguous. This is not the situation anymore for total strict deterministic CD grammar systems. However, also in this case the deterministic constraints have a clear impact on the derivations: one can eliminate left-recursion from a total strict deterministic CD grammar system. Moreover, if the system is such that no production rule belongs to two different components, then the unambiguity of the derivations (properly defined) at the level of the system holds as well.

A few additional notations and definitions are necessary.

Let $\Gamma = (N, T, S, P_1, P_2, \ldots, P_n)$ be a CD grammar system whose rules are labelled. Let $Lab(P_i)$ be the set of labels of the rules in P_i. For a derivation $D : x \Longrightarrow_{P_i}^t y$ we denote by $C(D)$ the control word associated to the derivation D (that is, the word consisting of the labels of productions used in the derivation D, in the corresponding order). Therefore, $C(D)$ is a string in $(Lab(P_i))^*$ that represents the sequence of rules of P_i used in the derivation D.

A component P_i is *ambiguous* if there exist two derivations $D_1 : x \Longrightarrow_{P_i}^t y$ and $D_2 : x \Longrightarrow_{P_i}^t y$ with $C(D_1) \neq C(D_2)$, for some $x, y \in (N \cup T)^*$. Otherwise, the component is called unambiguous.

For a word $w \in L(\Gamma)$, we say that a derivation

$$S = x_0 \Longrightarrow_{P_{i_1}}^t x_1 \Longrightarrow_{P_{i_2}}^t x_2 \Longrightarrow_{P_{i_3}}^t \cdots \Longrightarrow_{P_{i_s}}^t x_s = w$$

is a *leftmost derivation* of w if for any j, $1 \leq j \leq s$, the derivation in the component P_{i_j} is such that at the first step the very leftmost nonterminal symbol in x_{j-1} is rewritten, and afterwards, the leftmost possible nonterminal in the resulted sentential form is rewritten by P_{i_j}. Formally, the following conditions hold:

i) $x_{j-1} = \alpha_{j-1} A_j \beta_{j-1}$, for $\alpha_{j-1} \in T^*$,

ii) the first production used in the derivation $x_{j-1} \Longrightarrow_{P_{i_j}}^t x_j$ is of the form $A_j \rightarrow \gamma_{j-1} \in P_{i_j}$, resulting in the string $z = \alpha_{j-1} \gamma_{j-1} \beta_{j-1}$,

iii) afterwards, the derivation $z \Longrightarrow_{P_{i_j}}^t x_j$ proceeds by rewriting at any step the leftmost possible nonterminal in the current sentential form.

In order to point out that a derivation is leftmost, we will use the notation tl (terminal leftmost) instead of t, when we specify the derivation mode.

A CD grammar system Γ is said to be *unambiguos* if for any $w \in L(\Gamma)$ and for any two leftmost derivations of w in Γ,

$$D_1 : \quad S = x_0 \Longrightarrow_{P_{i_1}}^{tl} x_1 \Longrightarrow_{P_{i_2}}^{tl} \cdots \Longrightarrow_{P_{i_s}}^{tl} x_s = w,$$

$$D_2 : \quad S = x_0' \Longrightarrow_{P_{j_1}}^{tl} x_1' \Longrightarrow_{P_{j_2}}^{tl} \cdots \Longrightarrow_{P_{j_l}}^{tl} x_l' = w,$$

the following hold:

$$(i) \quad s = l,$$
$$(ii) \quad P_{i_r} = P_{j_r}, \ 1 \leq r \leq s,$$
$$(iii) \quad x_r = x_r', \ 0 \leq r \leq s.$$

We shall shortly say that $D_1 = D_2$ holds.

Remark that the definition of leftmost derivation does not imply that for any $w \in L(\Gamma)$ a leftmost derivation of w exists.

We can now proceed in analysing the derivations in a CD grammar system. We first consider the case of local strict deterministic systems. The next theorem states the *local unambiguity* of such systems.

Theorem 1. *Any local strict grammar system has only unambiguous components.*

Proof. Let $\Gamma = (N, T, S, P_1, \ldots, P_n)$ be a CD grammar system, local strict deterministic under the partitions $\pi_i, 1 \leq i \leq n$. We have to prove that for any i, $1 \leq i \leq n$, and for any two derivations

$$D_1 : \alpha \Longrightarrow_{P_i}^t x, \quad D_2 : \alpha \Longrightarrow_{P_i}^t x,$$

the relation $C(D_1) = C(D_2)$ holds.

We need the following fact which we give without proof. The reader interested in details may consult [8] (Lemma 11.4.1), since the corresponding proof there can be easily adapted to our situation.

Fact: For any $A, A' \in N$ with $A \sim^\pi A'$ such that $A \Longrightarrow_{P_i}^k xy$ and $A' \Longrightarrow_{P_i}^k xy'$, one of the following situations holds:

i) $y, y' \neq \lambda$, and $Pref_1(y) \sim^\pi Pref_1(y')$,

ii) $y = y' = \lambda$, and $A = A'$.

Here $\Longrightarrow^k_{P_i}$ means a k-steps derivation in the component P_i. We shall prove now our theorem by induction on the length of α.

Suppose $|\alpha| = 1$, hence $\alpha = A$. Assume that each of the derivations D_i, $1 \leq i \leq 2$, uses q_i productions, respectively. Then $q_1 = q_2$ must hold. Indeed, if $q_1 < q_2$ or $q_2 < q_1$, by the above fact, a symbol in $dom(P_i)$ would result equivalent with respect to π_i to a symbol in T_i, which contradicts the definition of local strict determinism. Denote $q = q_1 = q_2$.

We continue the proof by induction on q. The assertion is trivially true for $q = 1$. Assume that the assertion is true for any derivations of length $q - 1$, and let

$$D_1 : A \Longrightarrow^{q-1}_{P_i} x_1 B x_2 \Longrightarrow_{P_i} x,$$
$$D_2 : A \Longrightarrow^{q-1}_{P_i} x_1' B' x_2' \Longrightarrow_{P_i} x.$$

Clearly, $x_1 = x_1'$ (since the derivation is leftmost) and $B \sim^\pi_i B'$.

Assume now that $x_1 B x_2 \Longrightarrow_{P_i} x$ by using a rule $B \to z$, while $x_1 B' x_2' \Longrightarrow_{P_i} x$ by using a rule $B' \to z'$. Since $x = x_1 z x_2 = x_1 z' x_2'$, it follows that z is a prefix of z', or z' is a prefix of z, or $z = z'$. Due to $B \sim^\pi_i B'$, none of the first two cases can hold. Therefore, $z = z'$, which implies $B = B'$, and $x_2 = x_2'$.

By the induction hypothesis, it then follows that the derivation

$$A \Longrightarrow^{q-1}_{P_i} x_1 B x_2$$

is unambiguous, hence $C(D_1) = C(D_2)$.

Suppose now the statement holds true for each word α with $|\alpha| < p$, and let

$$D_1 : \alpha \Longrightarrow^t_{P_i} x, \qquad D_2 : \alpha \Longrightarrow^t_{P_i} x,$$

with $|\alpha| = p$.

If $\alpha = A\alpha'$, with $A \in (N \cup T) - dom(P_i)$, then $C(D_1) = C(D_2)$ holds by the induction hypothesis.

If $A \in dom(P_i)$, then there are $y_1, y_2, z_1, z_2 \in (T_i)^*$ such that

$$A \Longrightarrow^t_{P_i} y_1, \qquad \alpha' \Longrightarrow^t_{P_i} z_1,$$
$$A \Longrightarrow^t_{P_i} y_2, \qquad \alpha' \Longrightarrow^t_{P_i} z_2,$$

and $x = y_1 z_1 = y_2 z_2$.

Assume that y_1 is a proper prefix of y_2 (the case of y_2 a proper prefix of y_1 can be treated similarly), and let us point out the lengths of the derivations resulting into y_1, y_2, that is, let $A \Longrightarrow^{q_1}_{P_i} y_1$, $A \Longrightarrow^{q_2}_{P_i} y_2$. We have neither $q_1 < q_2$, nor $q_2 < q_1$. Consequently, $q_1 = q_2$ and $y_1 = y_2$. Moreover, the derivation $A \Longrightarrow^t_{P_i} y_1$ is unambiguous. It then follows that $z_1 = z_2$. Since $|\alpha_1| < p$, by the induction hypothesis we infer that the derivation $\alpha' \Longrightarrow^t_{P_i} z_1$ is unambiguous, which concludes the proof. $\square$

For the case of total strict deterministic systems, some global (i.e. at the level of the system) properties of the derivations follow directly from the case of strict deterministic context-free grammars, see [8]. The two propositions that follow present them.

Proposition 1. *Let $\Gamma = (N, T, S, P_1, \ldots, P_n)$ be a reduced CD grammar system (i. e. all the productions and all the nonterminals of Γ are used during terminal derivations) without λ - productions, and let $P = \bigcup_{i=1}^{n} P_i$. If Γ is total strict deterministic under the partition π, then for any $A, B \in N$ such that $A \sim^\pi B$, no derivation $B \Longrightarrow_P^+ A\alpha$, $\alpha \in (N \cup T)^*$, is possible.*

We make the observation that the requirement for the system Γ to be reduced in the theorem above is not a restriction at all, due to the fact that for any CD grammar system there exists an equivalent (with respect to the generated language) reduced CD grammar system, [10]. Moreover, the proof of [10] only eliminates the non-necessary productions and nonterminals, and therefore does not affect the eventually total strict deterministic partition of the system.

Yet remark that for the case of local strict deterministic systems, a property similar to Proposition 1 holds locally, in each component grammar.

As a consequence, one can eliminate left recursion from a total strict deterministic CD grammar system.

Proposition 2. *For any total strict deterministic CD grammar system $\Gamma = (N, T, S, P_1, \ldots, P_n)$, there exists a total strict deterministic CD grammar system $\Gamma' = (N', T, S, P_1', \ldots, P_n')$, with $L(\Gamma') = L(\Gamma)$, such that no derivation $A \Longrightarrow_{\Gamma'}^+ A\alpha$, $\alpha \in (N' \cup T)^*$ is possible, for any $A \in N'$.*

It is worthwhile mentioning that in case of total strict deterministic systems, a property similar to Theorem 1, with respect to a global derivation in the system, does not hold. For instance, consider the grammar system in Example 2, to which we add a new component, P_3, defined as

$$P_3 = \{C \to bC, C \to a\}.$$

One can observe that for any word of the form $a^n b^k a^n$, $n, k \geq 1$, two distinct leftmost derivations can be pointed out: one in the components P_1 and P_2, and the other in the components P_1 and P_3.

Therefore, additional restrictions to the system should be considered in order to cope with such situations. Surprisingly enough, we find out that if the components of the system are mutually disjoint, than the unambiguity of the system follows as well.

Theorem 2. *Any total strict deterministic CD grammar system whose components are mutually disjoint is unambiguous.*

Proof. Let $\Gamma = (N, T, S, P_1, \ldots, P_n)$ be a total strict deterministic CD grammar system such that $P_i \cap P_j = \emptyset$ for any i, j, $1 \leq i, j \leq n$, $i \neq j$.

Denote $P = \bigcup_{i=1}^{n} P_i$, and let $G = (N, T, S, P)$ be the context-free grammar associated to Γ. Clearly $L(\Gamma) \subseteq L(G)$. Due to Γ being total strict deterministic, G is a strict deterministic context-free grammar ([8]). In particular, the fact that G is unambiguous follows, i.e. for no word in $L(G)$ two distinct leftmost derivations exist.

We prove that for any word $w \in L(\Gamma)$ such that there exist leftmost derivations

$$D_1: \ S = x_0 \Longrightarrow_{P_{i_1}}^{tl} x_1 \Longrightarrow_{P_{i_2}}^{tl} \ldots \Longrightarrow_{P_{i_s}}^{tl} x_s = w,$$

$$D_2: \ S = x'_0 \Longrightarrow^{tl}_{P_{j_1}} x'_1 \Longrightarrow^{tl}_{P_{j_2}} \dots \Longrightarrow^{tl}_{P_{j_l}} x'_l = w,$$

then $D_1 = D_2$ follows.

We first prove $i_1 = j_1$, by contradiction.

Assume $i_1 \neq j_1$. Let p_1, p'_1 be the productions used at the first derivation steps in P_{i_1}, P_{j_1}, respectively. Since $P_{i_1} \cap P_{j_1} = \emptyset$, then $p_1 \neq p'_1$ results. But this implies that in the grammar G there exists two distinct leftmost derivations of the word w, that is, there exists leftmost derivation

$$S \Longrightarrow^{p_1}_{G} \alpha \Longrightarrow^{*}_{G} w, \quad S \Longrightarrow^{p'_1}_{G} \beta \Longrightarrow^{*}_{G} w,$$

which contradicts the unambiguity of G.

Hence $i_1 = j_1$ holds. Denote $i = i_1$.

We now prove that any two leftmost derivations

$$\alpha \Longrightarrow^{tl}_{P_i} \beta \quad (1),$$

$$\alpha \Longrightarrow^{tl}_{P_i} \gamma \quad (2),$$

which are used in leftmost rewritings of w, actually coincide.

The assumption that the derivations above are used in leftmost rewritings of w implies that there exist leftmost derivations (in Γ)

$$S \Longrightarrow^{*}_{\Gamma} \alpha \Longrightarrow^{tl}_{P_i} \beta \Longrightarrow^{*}_{\Gamma} w,$$

$$S \Longrightarrow^{*}_{\Gamma} \alpha \Longrightarrow^{tl}_{P_i} \gamma \Longrightarrow^{*}_{\Gamma} w.$$

We point out the first productions applied in the rewriting of α, that is, $\alpha = \alpha_1 A \alpha_2$, with $\alpha_1 \in ((N \cup T) - dom(P_i))^*$, $\bar{p}_1$ is a production $\bar{p}_1 : A \to \delta_1 \in P_i$, $\bar{p}_2$ is a production $\bar{p}_2 : A \to \delta_2 \in P_i$, and in the derivations above we have

$$\alpha = \alpha_1 A \alpha_2 \Longrightarrow^{\bar{p}_1}_{P_i} \alpha_1 \delta_1 \alpha_2 \Longrightarrow^{tl}_{P_i} \beta \Longrightarrow^{*}_{P_i} w,$$

$$\alpha = \alpha_1 A \alpha_2 \Longrightarrow^{\bar{p}_2}_{P_i} \alpha_1 \delta_2 \alpha_2 \Longrightarrow^{tl}_{P_i} \gamma \Longrightarrow^{*}_{P_i} w.$$

Two situations might occur:

Case a): $\alpha_1 \in T^*$.

Then, in a similar manner as in the proof above for $i_1 = j_1$, one can deduce that if $\bar{p}_1 \neq \bar{p}_2$, then a contradiction results.

Case b): $\alpha_1 = y_1 B y_2$, for a $B \in N - dom(P_i)$, $y_1 \in T^*, y_2 \in (T \cup (N - dom(P_i)))^*$.

Then one can point out leftmost derivations in the associated grammar G of the form

$$S \Longrightarrow^{*}_{G} \alpha = \alpha_1 A \alpha_2 = y_1 B y_2 A \alpha_2 \Longrightarrow^{*}_{G} y_1 z_1 A \alpha_2 \Longrightarrow^{\bar{p}_1}_{G} y_1 z_1 \delta_1 \alpha_2 \Longrightarrow^{*}_{G} w,$$

$$S \Longrightarrow^{*}_{G} \alpha = \alpha_1 A \alpha_2 = y_1 B y_2 A \alpha_2 \Longrightarrow^{*}_{G} y_1 z_2 A \alpha_2 \Longrightarrow^{\bar{p}_2}_{G} G y_1 z_2 \delta_2 \alpha_2 \Longrightarrow^{*}_{G} w,$$

where $B y_2 \Longrightarrow^{*}_{G} z_1$ and $B y_2 \Longrightarrow^{*}_{G} z_2$ are leftmost terminal derivations in G. Since either z_1 is a prefix of z_2 or z_2 is a prefix of z_1, it follows that $z_1 = z_2$ holds. But this again leads to a contradiction if $\bar{p}_1 \neq \bar{p}_2$ is assumed.

In any of the two cases, $\bar{p}_1 = \bar{p}_2$ must hold. By inductively repeating this argument, we obtain that the derivations (1) and (2) above are actually the same.

But this assertion allows us to repeat the reasoning which lead to concluding $i_1 = j_1$, and we then obtain that in derivations D_1 and D_2 we have $s = l$, $i_k = j_k$ for any k, $1 \leq k \leq s$, and any two leftmost derivations in a component concide, and therefore the theorem follows. $\qquad\square$

4. The Generative Power

The subject matter of this section is the language generated by local/total strict deterministic CD grammar systems. We first prove that a total system is local as well, if some additional constraints are satisfied. Then we show that the problem of whether or not a system is local or total strict deterministic is decidable. Also the hierachy on the number of components is addressed, proving that it collapeses to systems with only 3 components for the local case. Finally, the generative capacity of the systems is compared to that of usual CD grammar systems, or to that of context-free grammars.

Theorem 3. *Let* $\Gamma = (N, T, S, P_1, \ldots, P_n)$, *be a CD grammar sysetm, strict deterministic under the partition* π, *satisfying the additional restriction that for any* $A, B \in N$, $A \sim^\pi B$, *such that* $A \in dom(P_i)$ *for an* $i, 1 \leq i \leq n$, *then* $B \in dom(P_i)$ *holds as well. Then* Γ *is local deterministic.*

Proof. Let Γ be a CD grammar system as in the hypotheses of the theorem and let π be the partition. One can observe that partition π can be written as

$$\pi = \{T\} \cup \{[A]_\pi \mid A \in N\}.$$

The requirement that for any $A, B \in N$, $A \sim^\pi B, A \in dom(P_i)$, for an $i, 1 \leq i \leq n$, implies $B \in dom(P_i)$ as well, means that for any $A \in N$, and for a ny $i, 1 \leq i \leq n$, either $[A]_\pi \subseteq dom(P_i)$, or $[A]_\pi \subseteq N - dom(P_i)$. Then for any $i, 1 \leq i \leq n$, one can consider the partition

$$\pi_i = \{T\} \cup \{N - dom(P_i)\} \cup \{[A]_\pi \mid A \in dom(P_i).\}$$

The fact that Γ is local deterministic under the partitions π_i, $1 \leq i \leq n$, follows. $\quad\square$

Theorem 4. *Let* $\Gamma = (N, T, S, P_1, P_2, \ldots, P_n)$ *be a CD grammar system and let* $k = |\cup_{i=1}^n P_i|$.
 1. *It is decidable in* $O(k^2 \cdot |N|)$ *whether or not* Γ *is total strict deterministic.*
 2. *It is decidable in* $O(\sum_{i=1}^n |dom(P_i)| \cdot |P_i|^2)$ *whether or not* Γ *is local strict deterministic.*

Proof. The assertions above can be proved by constructing algorithms which rely on the same idea. We shall briefly explain it in the hypothesis of the first point. See [8] for more details.

For two partitions of $N \cup T$ we say that π_1 is smaller or equal than π_2, if $[X]_{\pi_1} \subseteq [X]_{\pi_2}$, for any $X \in N \cup T$. The notation $[X]_\pi$ stands for the equivalence class of X with respect to the partition π.

One starts with the smallest possible partition $\pi = \{T\} \cup \{\{A\} | A \in N\}$. By examining the rules of $\cup_{i=1}^n P_i$ whose left-hand sides are in the same equivalence classes, with respect to the current partition, the following situations may occur:

1. A nonterminal and a terminal are to be put in the same equivalence class. But this is not possible, due to the definition of the total strict deterministic partition, therefore the grammar system is not total strict deterministic follows. This is a consequence of choosing the sequence of current partitions in increasing order.

2. Two nonterminals, say A and B, should be considered in the same equivalence class, and they are not equivalent with respect to the current partition. Then, the current partition becomes

$$\pi = (\pi \setminus \{[A]_\pi, [B]_\pi\}) \cup \{[A]_\pi \cup [B]_\pi\}$$

Now, the process goes on by examinating again the productions of Γ.

3. No change of the current partition had to be performed during the last examination of the productions of Γ. Then it follows that the grammar system is total strict deterministic, and the current partition is a total strict partition.

The correctness and the complexity of the algorithm are easy to be checked. □

We now turn our attention to the generative capacity of total/local strict deterministic CD grammar systems.

Theorem 5. *For any local strict deterministic CD grammar system of degree n, there exists an equivalent (with respect to the generated language) local strict deterministic CD grammar system of degree 3.*

Proof. The proof parallels the reduction of the number of components to 3 in the case of usual CD grammar systems (deriving in the terminal mode), see [1]. Let $\Gamma = (N, T, S, P_1, P_2, \ldots, P_n)$ be a system of degree n, which is local strict deterministic under the partitions π_i, $1 \le i \le n$. Consider

$$N' = \bigcup_{i=0}^{n} \{A^{(i)} \mid A \in N\},$$

and for any i, $0 \le i \le n$, define the morphisms $h_i : N \cup T \Longrightarrow N' \cup T$ by

$$h_i(X) = \begin{cases} X, & \text{for } X \in T \\ X^{(i)}, & \text{for } X \in N. \end{cases}$$

For the sake of simplicity, for a set M, we denote $h_i(M) = \{h_i(A) \mid A \in M\}$. Consider $\Gamma' = (N', T, P_1', P_2', P_3', S^{(0)})$, where

$$P_1' = \bigcup_{i=1}^{n} \{A^{(i)} \to h_i(\alpha) \mid A \to \alpha \in P_i\},$$

$$P_2' = \begin{cases} \{A^{(i)} \to A^{(i+1)} \mid A \in N, 0 \le i < n, i \text{ even number}\}, & \text{if } n \text{ is odd}, \\ \{A^{(i)} \to A^{(i+1)} \mid A \in N, 0 \le i < n, i \text{ even number}\} \cup \\ \cup \{A^{(n)} \to A^{(1)}\}, & \text{if } n \text{ is even} \end{cases}$$

$$P_3' = \begin{cases} \{A^{(i)} \to A^{(i+1)} \mid A \in N, 0 \le i < n, i \text{ odd number}\}, & \text{if } n \text{ is even}, \\ \{A^{(i)} \to A^{(i+1)} \mid A \in N, 0 \le i < n, i \text{ odd number}\} \cup \\ \cup \{A^{(n)} \to A^{(0)}\}, & \text{if } n \text{ is odd} \end{cases}$$

Then Γ' is local strict deterministic under the partitions

$$\pi'_1 \;=\; \{T\} \cup \bigcup_{i=1}^{n} \{h_i([A]_{\pi_i}) \mid A \in dom(P_i)\} \cup \{N' - dom(P'_1),$$

$$\pi'_2 = \pi'_3 \;=\; \{T\} \cup \{\, \{A^{(i)}\} \mid A \in N, 0 \le i \le n,\ i \text{ even number}\}$$
$$\cup \;\; \{\, \{A^{(i)}\} \mid A \in N, 0 \le i \le n,\ i \text{ odd number}\}.$$

On the other hand, $L(\Gamma') = L(\Gamma)$ can be proved in a similar manner as in [1]. □

Theorem 6. *For any CD grammar system there exists an equivalent local strict deterministic CD grammar system.*

Proof. Let $\Gamma = (N, T, S, P_1, P_2, \ldots, P_n)$ be a CD grammar system in which all rules are labelled by distinct labels. Without loss of generality, we may assume that no P_i contains erasing rules. If the rules of P_i are labelled by $r_{i,1}, r_{i,2}, \ldots, r_{i,k_i}$, then consider the set of new nonterminals

$$N' = (\bigcup_{i=1}^{n} \{[i, j, X] \mid 1 \le j \le k_i, X \in N \cup T\}) \cup \{X_i \mid 1 \le i \le n, X \in N\} \cup \{F\}$$

We construct the grammar system

$$\Gamma' = (N \cup N', T, S, P'_1, P'_2, \ldots, P'_n, P_{n+1}),$$

where

$$
\begin{aligned}
P'_i \;=\;& \{A \longrightarrow [i, j, X]y \mid r_{i,j} : A \longrightarrow Xy \in P_i\} \cup \{A_i \longrightarrow A \mid A \in N\} \\
\cup\;& \{[t, s, X] \longrightarrow F \mid 1 \le t \le n, t \ne i, 1 \le s \le k_t, X \in N \cup T\} \\
\cup\;& \{A_j \longrightarrow F \mid A \in N, 1 \le j \le n. j \ne i\},\ 1 \le i \le n, \\
P_{n+1} \;=\;& \{[i, j, a] \longrightarrow a \mid a \in T, 1 \le i \le n, 1 \le j \le k_i\} \\
\cup\;& \{[i, j, A] \longrightarrow A_i \mid A \in N, 1 \le i \le n, 1 \le j \le k_i\}
\end{aligned}
$$

For any $1 \le i \le n$, denote by Q_i the set of all A_i such that A is a nonterminal in which appears on the first position of a right-hand side of a rule in P_i. Consider the partitions

$$
\begin{aligned}
\pi_i \;=\;& \{dom(P_i) \cup Q_i \cup \{A_j \mid j \ne i, A \in N\}\} \\
\cup\;& \{N' \setminus (dom(P_i) \cup Q_i \cup \{A_j \mid j \ne i, A \in N\}), T\}, 1 \le i \le n, \\
\pi_{n+1} \;=\;& \{T, N \cup \{A_i \mid A \in N, 1 \le i \le n\}\} \\
\cup\;& \{\{[i, j, X]\} \mid 1 \le i \le n, 1 \le j \le k_i, X \in N \cup T\}.
\end{aligned}
$$

Obviously, the above partitions are local strict partitions. Since any derivation in a component P_i is simulated by an arbitrary number of derivations in the pair of components P'_i, P_{n+1}, it follows that $L(\Gamma) = L(\Gamma')$. □

As far as the generative power of total strict deterministic CD grammar systems is concerned, one can observe that this decreases as shown by the next theorem.

Theorem 7. *Every language generated by a total strict deterministic CD grammar system is prefix-free.*

Proof. It is known that every language accepted by an $LR(0)$ grammar is prefix-free. If $\Gamma = (N, T, S, P_1, P_2, \ldots, P_n)$ is a total strict deterministic CD grammar system, then $L(\Gamma) \subseteq L(G)$, where $G = (N, T, S, \cup_{i=1}^{n} P_i)$.

But $L(G)$ generates a language that can be generated by an $LR(0)$ grammar, hence prefix-free and the proof is complete. □

On the other hand, there are non-context-free languages that can be generated by total strict deterministic CD grammar systems. An example is provided by the CD grammar system with the components given by

$$\begin{aligned} P_1 &= \{S \rightarrow AC, X \rightarrow A, Y \rightarrow C\} \\ P_2 &= \{A \rightarrow aXb, C \rightarrow cY\} \\ P_3 &= \{A \rightarrow d, C \rightarrow d\} \end{aligned}$$

and the total strict partition

$$\pi = \{\{S\}, \{A\}, \{C\}, \{X\}, \{Y\}, \{a, b, c, d\}\}$$

The language generated by the above grammar system is $\{a^n db^n dc^n d \mid n \geq 1\}$. Therefore, we have proved:

Theorem 8. *The family of context-free languages and the family of languages generated by total strict deterministic CD grammar systems are incomparable.*

5. Final Remarks

It is worthwhile mentioning that the restrictions we have imposed on CD grammar systems have meaningful interpretations in terms of the *blackboard architecture* of problem solving, which CD grammar systems are a formal representation for, [5]. Briefly stated, the blackboard model consists of three basic parts [12]):

- the *knowledge* needed to solve a given problem, which is partitioned into separate and independent *knowledge sources*;

- the *global data base*, the blackboard, representing the current state of the problem solving process, and in which the knowledge sources can make changes;

- the *control* of the opportunistic responds of the knowledge sources to make changes in the blackboard.

In the formal modelization, the knowledge sources correspond to grammars and the blackboard to a sentential form. Rewriting a nonterminal can be interpreted as a developmental step of the information contained in the current state of the blackboard, a solution of the problem corresponds to a terminal word, and the control mechanism states the conditions under which a grammar can start or stop its work.

Therefore, it is natural to try to encapture in the CD grammar systems architecture other features of their Artificial Intelligence counterpart. To this aim, if one regards nonterminal symbols as corresponding to subproblems to be solved, then it is of interest to study in detail CD grammar systems in which a relation partitioning the subproblems, according to their state of the art with respect to the process of finding solutions, holds. But this is exactly what the strict determinism features considered here for CD grammar systems formally model. More precisely, the partitions of the symbol set of a system can be regarded as follows:

i) all the terminal symbols (at the level of the system, and also at the level of each component, when a local relation is considered) are related, since they all are (partial) solutions to some problems, the presence of a terminal symbol on the blackboard does not require any subsequent study of this symbol;

ii) nonterminal symbols (corresponding to subproblems to be solved) are considered related if, once one has started to build a solution of a subproblem, this is a beginning of a solution of a related subproblem as well.

References

1. A. Atanasiu, V. Mitrana, The Modular Grammars, *Internat. J. Comp. Math.* 30 (1989), 17–35

2. H. Fernau, M. Holzer, H. Bordihn, Accepting Multi-Agent Systems: The Case of Cooperating Grammar Systems, *Computers and Artificial Intelligence* 15 (1996), No. 2-3, 123-139

3. E. Csuhaj-Varju, J. Dassow, On Cooperating Distributed Grammar Systems, *J. Inform. Process. Cybern., EIK*, 26 (1990), 49 – 63.

4. E. Csuhaj-Varju, J. Dassow, J. Kelemen, Gh. Păun, *Grammar Systems*, Gordon and Breach, London, 1994.

5. E. Csuhaj-Varju, J. Kelemen, Cooperating Grammar Systems: A Syntactical Framework for the Blackboard Model of Problem Solving, *Proc. Artificial Intelligence and Information-Control Systems of Robots '89*, North-Holland Publ. Co. (I. Plander, ed.), 1989, 121 – 127.

6. J. Dassow, V. Mitrana, Cooperating Pushdown Automata Systems, *Submitted*, 1995.

7. J. Dassow, Gh. Păun, G. Rozenberg, Grammar Systems, in *The Handbook of Formal Languages* (G. Rozenberg, A. Salomaa, eds.), Springer-Verlag, 1997.

8. M. Harrison, *Introduction to Formal Language Theory*, Addison-Wesley Publ. Co., 1978

9. J. E. Hopcroft, J. D. Ullman, *Introduction to Automata Theory, Languages and Computation*, Addison-Wesley, Reading Mass., 1979.

10. V. Mihalache, Coverability Trees for Grammar Systems: A Strong Decidability Tool, *submitted*

11. R. Meersman, G. Rozenberg, Cooperating Grammar Systems, *Proc. MFCS '78 Symp., LNCS 64*, Springer-Verlag, 1978, 364 – 374.

12. P. H. Nii, Blackboard Systems, in *The Handbook of AI*, vol. 4 (A. Barr, P. R. Cohen, E. A. Feigenbaum, eds.), Addison-Wesley, 1989.

Grammar Systems with Counting Derivation and Dynamical Priorities

Tudor BĂLĂNESCU, Horia GEORGESCU, Marian GHEORGHE

Faculty of Mathematics, University of Bucharest
Str. Academiei 14, 70109 Bucharest, Romania

Abstract. The paper deals with a new type of restriction considered for the cooperation protocol of grammar systems. The effect of this strategy is investigated for all modes of derivation. Some connections are made with the usual concept of fairness [1], [6] and that introduced for grammar systems [5].

1. Introduction

The cooperating/distributed (CD for short) grammar systems were introduced first in [9] with motivations related to two level grammars. An intensive study of CD grammar systems has been started after relating them with artificial intelligence concepts [2], [4] such as the blackboard models in problem solving [10]. A CD grammar system is a construct consisting of several usual grammars, working together on the same sentential form to generate words. Informally, such systems and their work can be described as follows (see [3]): initially, the axiom is the common sentential form. At each moment, one grammar is active, that means it rewrites the common string, while the others are not active. The conditions under which a component can become active or it is disabled and leaves the sentential form to other component are specified by the cooperation protocol. The language of terminal strings generated in this way is the language generated by the system. As basic stop conditions usually considered, we mention: each component, when active, has to work exactly k, at least k, at most k, or the maximal number of steps (a step means the application of a rewriting rule). Many other stopping conditions were considered or added to the above mentioned ones (see [3]). Among these strategies a fairness restriction is considered in [5]. Under the *fairness* assumption, the strategy of cooperation requires that all components of the system have approximately the same contribution to the common work, concerning the time spent by each of them during the derivation process. In [5] two fairness strategy are considered. The first one, called *weak fairness*, requires that each component has to be activated almost the same number of times (the difference between the number of times for which any two components are activated is bounded). But this concept says nothing about the period of time in which a component is working. The second one, called *strong fairness*, requires more fair behavior from the system by imposing the number of applications of rules of components during the whole derivation, to be almost the same - the difference between the number of applications of any two arbitrary components is bounded.

In this paper we focus on the case when a rule from a component P is applied and there are some applicable rules in a component Q. We view this as a *neglect* of Q and we consider Q will recover later all or at least a part of these lost opportunities to use its rules. Moreover, if there are more "neglected" components at a given moment, then the most neglected is selected as active component, having the highest priority. This approach has some links with the fairness concepts introduced and studied in relation with the behavior of parallel processes [1], [6]. Our concept is different from the strategies used in [5] due to the fact that a component which had no opportunity to apply its rules does not disturb the derivation process.

Informally, we associate to each component P an integer variable v to hold the difference between the number of applications of the rules from P and the number of neglects of P. The higher this difference is, the lower is the priority. Initially, $v = 0$ for all components, giving equal priorities to all the components. If a rule from P is applied in a derivation, then the value of v is increased by one ($v := v + 1$), *decreasing* its priority. By contrast, the values of all neglected components are decreased by one, *increasing* their priorities. The other components does not change their current priorities. Hence the priority of a component may *be changed* during the derivation. In the strongest strategy, all neglected components are recovered and the derivation have to end with $v = 0$ for all components. Weaker strategies may be considered by allowing a fixed number of components to have a bounded number of unrecovered neglects or surplus of applications. This new strategy of cooperation is considered together with the well known modes of derivation, usually applied for CD grammar systems, and it is proven that the generative capacity of these mechanisms is generally increased. The strong fairness concept [1], [6] is also studied in connection with these CD grammar systems.

2. Basic Definitions, Notations and Preliminary Results

For an alphabet V, we denote by V^* the free monoid generated by V under the operation of concatenation; the empty string is denoted by λ, and we set $V^+ = V^* \setminus \{\lambda\}$.

The length of $x \in V^*$ is denoted by $|x|$. If $x \in V^*$ and $U \subseteq V$, then $|x|_U$ is the number of occurrences of symbols of U in x (the length of the string obtained by erasing from x all symbols in $V \setminus U$).

By REG, CF and $ETOL$ we denote the families of regular, context-free and ETOL languages, respectively (see [11], [12]).

A *CD grammar system of degree* $n, n \geq 1$, is a construct

$$\Gamma = (N, T, S, P_1, \ldots, P_n),$$

where N, T are disjoint alphabets, $S \in N$, and $P_1, \ldots, P_n$ are finite sets of rewriting rules over $N \cup T$.

The elements of N are *nonterminals*, those of T are *terminals*; $P_1, \ldots, P_n$ are called *components* of the system. Here we work with CD grammar systems having only regular rules, i.e. rules of the form $A \to aB$ or $A \to a$ with $A, B \in N$, $a \in T$, right-linear rules, i.e. rules of the form $A \to xB$ or $A \to x$ with $A, B \in N$, $x \in T \cup \{\lambda\}$ or context-free rules, i.e. rules of the form $A \to w$ with $A \in N$, $w \in (N \cup T)^*$ and denote them by REG, RL and CF, respectively.

The domain of the ith component denoted by $dom(P_i)$ is defined as

$$dom(P_i) = \{A \mid A \to x \in P_i\}.$$

For $(N \cup T)^*$ one can define the usual one step derivation with respect to P_i, denoted by $\Longrightarrow_{P_i}$. The derivations consisting of exactly k, at most k (but at least one), at least k such steps $\Longrightarrow_{P_i}$ are denoted by $\Longrightarrow_{\overline{P_i}}^{=k}$, $\Longrightarrow_{\overline{P_i}}^{\leq k}$, $\Longrightarrow_{\overline{P_i}}^{\geq k}$, respectively. Furthermore, we write $x \Longrightarrow_{P_i}^{t} y$ iff $x \Longrightarrow_{\overline{P_i}}^{\geq 1} y$ and there is no $z \in (N \cup T)^*$ such that $y \Longrightarrow_{P_i} z$. We note also by $x \Longrightarrow_{P_i}^{*} y$ an arbitrary derivation. Let

$$M = \{t, *\} \cup \bigcup_{k \geq 1}\{\leq k, = k, \geq k\}.$$

Let

$$D : S \Longrightarrow_{P_{i_1}}^{=m_1} w_1 \Longrightarrow_{P_{i_2}}^{=m_2} \cdots \Longrightarrow_{P_{i_t}}^{=m_t} w_k$$

be a derivation in the f-mode, $f \in M$, $1 \leq i_j \leq n$, with $i_j \neq i_{j+1}$ for all j (i.e. m_j gives the number of derivation steps performed by the component P_{i_j} in D). For any $1 \leq p \leq n$, we write

$$\psi_D(p) = \sum_{i_j=p} 1 \quad \text{and} \quad \varphi_D(p) = \sum_{i_j=p} m_j,$$

Conventionally, the empty sum delivers zero.

Let Γ be a CD grammar system with at least two components. Then we set

$$dw(D) = max\{|\psi_D(i) - \psi_D(j)| \mid 1 \leq i, j \leq n\}$$

and

$$ds(D) = max\{|\varphi_D(i) - \varphi_D(j)| \mid 1 \leq i, j \leq n\}.$$

Moreover, for $u \in \{w, s\}$, $x \in (N \cup T)^*$ and $f \in M$, we define

$$du(x, f) = min\{du(D) \mid D \text{ is a derivation in the } f - \text{mode for } x\}.$$

For a CD grammar system Γ of degree $n \geq 2$ and $f \in M$ it is denoted by $L_f(\Gamma)$ the language generated by Γ. Taking Γ and f as above and a natural number $q \geq 0$, in [5] it is defined the *weakly q-fair* language generated by Γ in the f-mode as

$$L_f(\Gamma, w - q) = \{x \mid x \in L_f(\Gamma) \text{ and } dw(x, f) \leq q\}$$

and the *strongly q-fair* language of Γ as

$$L_f(\Gamma, s - q) = \{x \mid x \in L_f(\Gamma) \text{ and } ds(x, f) \leq q\}.$$

For $X \in \{REG, RL, CF\}$, $f \in M$, $n \geq 1$, the family of languages generated by CD grammar systems with n components in $f - mode$ are denoted by $CDL_n(X, f)$. The union of the families $CDL_n(X, f)$, for all n, is denoted by $CDL_\infty(X, f)$.

For $X \in \{REG, RL, CF\}$, $f \in M$, and integers $n \geq 2$ and $q \geq 0$, $CDL_n(X, f, w - q)$ and $CDL_n(X, f, s-q)$ represent the families of weakly and strongly q-fair languages, respectively, generated by CD grammar systems with n components.

Definition 1. On $(N \cup T)^*$ we define the one step *counting derivation* with respect to P_i, denoted by $^c \Longrightarrow_{P_i}$. Let $v_1, ..., v_n$ and $u_1, ..., u_n$ be integer values associated to $P_1, ..., P_n$ before and after a derivation step, respectively. Formally, we write

$$(v, v_1, ..., v_n) \;^c \Longrightarrow_{P_i} (u, u_1, ..., u_n)$$

if $v = xAy, u = xwy, A \rightarrow w \in P_i$ and:

$u_i = v_i + 1$;

$u_j = v_j - 1$ if $i \neq j$ and $|v|_{dom(P_j)} \neq 0$ (i.e. P_j is a neglected component);

$u_k = v_k$ otherwise.

Moreover, if $v_i = min\{v_j \mid 1 \leq j \leq n$ and $|v|_{dom(P_j)} \neq 0\}$ then we have a *prior derivation*. It is denoted by $(v, v_1, ..., v_n) \; ^p \Longrightarrow_{P_i} (u, u_1, ..., u_n)$.

The derivation $^c \Longrightarrow_{P_i}^f$ with $f \in M$ has the usual meaning, each step being a *counting* derivation and the first one is a *prior* derivation.

Remark. When the symbol f used in the above notation is understood, it can be replaced by another symbol denoting how many times is applied the derivation.

Definition 2. Let Γ be a CD grammar system with n components, p and q natural numbers, $0 \leq p \leq n$. One can define the *language generated* by Γ in the *counting derivation mode* $f \in M$ with p components *relaxed* to the interval $[-q, q]$, as being the set:

$$L_f(\Gamma, p, q) = \{w \mid w \in T^*, (S, V_0) = (w_0, V_0) \; ^c \Longrightarrow_{P_{i_1}}^f (w_1, V_1) \; ^c \Longrightarrow_{P_{i_2}}^f \cdots$$
$$^c \Longrightarrow_{P_{i_m}}^f (w_m, V_m), w_m = w, \; m \geq 1, 1 \leq i_j \leq n, 1 \leq j \leq m\}.$$

where: $V_i = (v_{i,1}, \ldots, v_{i,n})$, is the vector with the associated values for the n components of Γ,

1) the first step in $(w_{j-1}, V_{j-1}) \; ^c \Longrightarrow_{P_{i_j}}^f (w_j, V_j)$ is a prior derivation,

2) $V_0 = (0, ..., 0)$,

3) there are p components $P_{j_1}, ..., P_{j_p}$ such that $-q \leq v_{m,j_r} \leq q$, for all $1 \leq r \leq p$, and $v_{m,i} = 0$ for $i \neq j_r$, $1 \leq r \leq p$.

Remark. This type of derivation introduces a kind of priorities among the components to be chosen after P_i was used. These priorities are computed at each step.

The corresponding classes of languages are denoted by $CDL_n(X, f, p, q)$, where n is the degree of the grammar system, $X \in \{REG, RL, CF\}$ indicates the type of the components (regular, right-linear or context-free) and $f \in M$.

Theorem 1. *For all modes of derivation $f \in M$ and any type of grammars X, we have $CDL_n(X, f, p, q) \subseteq CDL_{n'}(X, f, p', q')$, $n \leq n', p \leq p', q \leq q'$.*

Proof. Directly from the definitions. □

Remark. The meaning of $CDL_n(X, f, p, 0)$, $CDL_n(X, f, 0, q)$, $L_f(\Gamma, p, 0)$, $L_f(\Gamma, 0, q)$ does not depend on p or q. We frequently use $CDL_n(X, f, 0, 0)$ and $L_f(\Gamma, 0, 0)$ for expressing these cases.

Let us illustrate the introduced concepts by two examples. We shall give just the components of the systems, the other elements can easily be deduced under the assumption that S is the axiom.

Example 1. We consider the grammar system Γ with the components

$$P_1 = \{S \rightarrow aS, S \rightarrow aA, A \rightarrow aX\},$$
$$P_2 = \{A \rightarrow bA, A \rightarrow b, S \rightarrow bX\}$$

We have

$$L_{\geq k}(\Gamma, 0, 0) = \{a^p b^p \mid p \geq k\}$$
$$L_*(\Gamma, 0, 0) = \{a^p b^p \mid p \geq 1\}.$$

Indeed, any counting derivation producing a terminal string in Γ has the form

$$(S, 0, 0) \ ^c \Longrightarrow_{P_1}^f (a^k A, u_1, u_2) \ ^c \Longrightarrow_{P_2}^f (a^k b^m, v_1, v_2)$$

where $u_1 = k$, $u_2 = -k$, $v_1 = k - m$, $v_2 = -k + m$. From $a^k b^m \in L_f(\Gamma, 0, 0)$ we deduce $v_1 = v_2 = 0$, i.e. $k = m$.

Note that the rules $A \to aX$, $S \to bX$ are used only for counting.

Example 2. Let Γ be the grammar system having the following components

$$P_1 = \{S \to abB, S \to aAbB, A \to aAb, A \to ab, B \to F\},$$
$$P_2 = \{B \to cB, B \to c, S \to F, A \to F\}.$$

It follows that, for all $f \in \{= 1, \geq 1, *\} \cup \{\leq k \mid k \geq 1\}$ and $q \geq 1$,

$$L_f(\Gamma, 2, q) = \{a^n b^n c^m \mid n \geq 1, m \geq 1, |n - m| \leq q\}$$

holds (the two components are alternatively used) whereas for $q = 0$

$$L_f(\Gamma, 0, 0) = \{a^n b^n c^n \mid n \geq 1\}.$$

We mention that all the above mentioned languages are not context-free. Moreover, by taking $q = 0$ and $= k$ or $\geq k$ derivation mode, for all $k \geq 1$, we have

$$L_{=k}(\Gamma, 0, 0) = \{a^n b^n c^n \mid n = p \cdot k, p \geq 1\},$$
$$L_{\geq k}(\Gamma, 0, 0) = \{a^n b^n c^n \mid n \geq k\}.$$

Theorem 2. *Let Γ be a CD grammar system with the degree $n = 2$. Every counting derivation*

$$(S, 0, 0) \ ^c \Longrightarrow_{P_{i_1}}^f (\alpha_1, u_1, v_1) \ ^c \Longrightarrow_{P_{i_2}}^f \ldots (\alpha_k, u_k, v_k)$$

has the property $u_k + v_k \geq 0$, for $k \geq 0$ and $f \in M$. Moreover, if there is an i such that $u_i + v_i > 0$ then $u_{i+j} + v_{i+j} > 0$, for $j \geq 0$.

Proof. We prove by induction on the length of the derivation. For $k = 0$ the result is trivial. Suppose that $u_k + v_k \geq 0$ and $(\alpha_k, u_k, v_k) \ ^c \Longrightarrow_{P_{i_{k+1}}}^f (\alpha_{k+1}, u_{k+1}, v_{k+1})$. Let us consider $i_{k+1} = 1$ (the other case is similar). Then we have $u_{k+1} = u_k + j$, $v_{k+1} = v_k - r$, $0 \leq r \leq j$, where r counts how many times the component P_2 was neglected. Obviously, $u_{k+1} + v_{k+1} \geq 0$. □

Corollary 3. *Let Γ be a CD grammar system with the degree $n = 2$. Every counting derivation*

$$(S, 0, 0) \ ^c \Longrightarrow_{P_{i_1}}^f \ldots (\alpha_k, u_k, v_k) \ ^c \Longrightarrow_{P_{i_{k+1}}}^f \ldots (x, 0, 0)$$

has the property $u_k + v_k = 0$ for $k \geq 0$ and $f \in M$.

Corollary 4. $CDL_2(X,t,0,0) = \{\emptyset\}, X \in \{REG, RL, CF\}$.

Proof. Suppose there exists Γ such that $L_t(\Gamma,2,0) \neq \emptyset$. Then we have a counting derivation

$$(S,0,0) \;{}^c\!\Longrightarrow^t_{P_{i_1}} (\alpha_1, u_1, v_1) \;{}^c\!\Longrightarrow^t_{P_{i_2}} \ldots (x, u_k, v_k)$$

where $x \in T^*$, $k \geq 1$ and $u_k = v_k = 0$.

Assume $i_1 = 1$. In fact we have $k \geq 2$, otherwise $u_k \neq 0$. If after the derivation $(S,0,0) \;{}^c\!\Longrightarrow^t_{P_{i_1}} (\alpha_1, u_1, v_1)$, the first applied rule is of the form $B \to x \in P_2$, then there is no rule $B \to y \in P_1$. Hence after applying the rule $B \to x \in P_2$ we get

$$(\alpha_1, u_1, v_1)^c \Longrightarrow (\alpha', u', v'), u' = u_1, v' = v_1 + 1,$$

so, $u' + v' > 0$, a contradiction with Theorem 2. $\qquad\square$

Lemma 5. $CDL_1(X, f, 0, 0) = \{\emptyset\}, X \in \{REG, RL, CF\}, f \in M$.

Proof. For a counting derivation $(S,0) \;{}^c\!\Longrightarrow^f_{P_1} (x, v)$ having at least one step we have $v > 0$. $\qquad\square$

3. The Regular Case

Lemma 6. $\{a\} \notin CDL_n(REG, f, 0, 0)$ for all $n \geq 2, f \in M$.

Proof. Suppose we have a CD grammar system Γ such that $L_f(\Gamma, 0, 0) = \{a\}$. In this case there is a component P_i such that $S \to a \in P_i$. The only way to generate a is to use such a rule. But in a counting derivation $(S, 0, \ldots, 0) \;{}^c\!\Longrightarrow^f_{P_i} (a, v_1, \ldots, v_n)$ we have $v_i = 1$. This contradicts $a \in L_f(\Gamma, 0, 0)$. $\qquad\square$

Theorem 7. $CDL_2(REG, f, 0, 0) \subset REG, f \in \{= k \mid k \geq 1\}$.

Proof. Let $\Gamma = (N, T, S, P_1, P_2)$ be a CD grammar system with two components and a derivation

$$(x, u_1, u_2) \;{}^c\!\Longrightarrow^f_{P_i} (y, v_1, v_2).$$

From Corollary 3 we have $u_1 + u_2 = v_1 + v_2 = 0$, so it results that $dom(P_1) = dom(P_2)$. The rules of the two components are alternatively applied, k times each one. The following regular grammar is constructed:

$$G = (N', T, S, P),$$

where, for $k \geq 2$

$$
\begin{aligned}
N' &= \{S\} \cup \{A_{i,j,l} \mid A \in N, 1 \leq i \leq 2, 1 \leq j \leq k, 1 \leq l \leq 2\}, \\
P &= \{A_{i,j,l} \to aB_{i,j+1,l} \mid A \to aB \in P_i, 1 \leq i \leq 2, 1 \leq j < k, 1 \leq l \leq 2\} \\
&\cup \{A_{1,k,l} \to aB_{2,1,l} \mid A \to aB \in P_1, 1 \leq l \leq 2\} \\
&\cup \{A_{2,k,l} \to aB_{1,1,l} \mid A \to aB \in P_2, 1 \leq l \leq 2\} \\
&\cup \{A_{1,k,2} \to a \mid A \to a \in P_1\} \cup \{A_{2,k,1} \to a \mid A \to a \in P_2\} \\
&\cup \{S \to aA_{i,2,i} \mid S \to aA \in P_i, 1 \leq i \leq 2\}.
\end{aligned}
$$

Clearly, each derivation in Γ, in the above specified conditions, is simulated by a derivation in P, starting with $S \Longrightarrow aA_{i,2,i}$ and continuing by alternatively applying k times rules from P_1, P_2; at the end a rule $A_{1,k,2} \to a$ or $A_{2,k,1} \to a$ is used. The strict inclusion follows from Lemma 6. $\qquad\square$

Theorem 8. *REG and $CDL_n(REG, f, 0, 0)$ are incomparable for:*
a) $f \in \{*\} \cup \{\geq k \mid k \geq 1\}$ and $n \geq 2$;
b) $f \in \{\leq k \mid k \geq 1\} \cup \{= k \mid k \geq 1\} \cup \{t\}$ and $n \geq 3$.

Proof. From Lemma 6 we have a regular language which can not be generated with counting derivation.

Conversely, the point a may be proved using Example 1. To prove b we first show that $\{a^m b^m c^m \mid m \geq 1\} \in CDL_3(REG, t, 0, 0)$. Indeed, the system having the following components:

$$P_1 = \{S \to aS, S \to aA, B \to bX\},$$
$$P_2 = \{A \to bA, A \to bB, S \to aX\},$$
$$P_3 = \{B \to cB, B \to c, A \to cX\}$$

generates the considered language in the counting derivation mode t.

We see that such a derivation has only the form

$$(S, 0, 0) \overset{c}{\Longrightarrow}^t_{P_1} (a^k A, k, -k, 0) \overset{c}{\Longrightarrow}^t_{P_2} (a^k b^m B, k, m-k, -m)$$

and then

$$(a^k b^m B, k, m-k, -m) \overset{c}{\Longrightarrow}^t_{P_3} (a^k b^m c^r, k-r, m-k, r-m).$$

Note that the first step in $\overset{c}{\Longrightarrow}^t_{P_i}$ must be a *prior* derivation and after the last derivation all priorities have to be zero. Thus, we get $k = m = r$. Finally, Theorem 1 and Corollary 4 state that $n \neq 2$.

For the derivation modes $\leq k, = k$ we consider the system Γ with

$$P_1 = \{S \to aS, S \to aA, A \to aX\},$$
$$P_2 = \{A \to bA, A \to b\},$$
$$P_3 = P_2.$$

We have $L_{=k}(\Gamma, 0, 0) = \{a^{2pk} b^{2pk} \mid p \geq 1\}$. It is easy to see that every counting derivation producing terminal strings in the mode $= k$ has the form

$$(S, 0, 0, 0) \overset{c}{\Longrightarrow}^{=k}_{P_1} (a^k S, k, 0, 0) \overset{c}{\Longrightarrow}^{=k}_{P_1} \ldots$$
$$\ldots (a^{rk} A, rk, 0, 0) \overset{c}{\Longrightarrow}^{=k}_{P_2} (a^{rk} b^k A, (r-1)k, k, -k)$$
$$\overset{c}{\Longrightarrow}^{=k}_{P_3} (a^{rk} b^{2k} A, (r-2)k, 0, 0) \ldots \overset{c}{\Longrightarrow}^{=k}_{P_3} (a^{rk} b^{2pk}, (r-2p)k, 0, 0)$$

where $p \geq 1$. We must get $(r - 2p)k = 0$, hence the result is proved.

We also have

$$L_{\leq k}(\Gamma, 0, 0) = \{a^{2p} b^{2p} \mid p \geq 1\}.$$

Indeed, every counting derivation producing terminal strings in the mode $\leq k$ has the form

$$(S, 0, 0, 0) \overset{c}{\Longrightarrow}^{\leq k}_{P_1} (a_r A, r, 0, 0) \overset{c}{\Longrightarrow}^{\leq k}_{P_2}$$
$$(a^r b^{r_1} A, r - r_1, r_1, -r_1) \overset{c}{\Longrightarrow}^{\leq k}_{P_3} (a^r b^{r_1} b^{r'_1}, r - r_1 - r'_1, r_1 - r'_1, r'_1 - r_1)$$
$$\overset{c}{\Longrightarrow}^{\leq k}_{P_2} \ldots (a^r b^{q+m}, r - q - m, q - m, m - q).$$

We must get $r - q - m = q - m = m - q = 0$ and the result is proved. □

Theorem 9. a) $REG \subseteq CDL_n(REG, f, 2, 1)$, for all $n \geq 2, f \in \{*, = 1, \geq 1\} \cup \{\leq k \mid k \geq 1\}$,

b) $REG \subseteq CDL_n(REG, t, 2, 1)$, for $n \geq 3$; the inclusion is strict for:

c) $n \geq 2, f \in \{*, \geq 1\}$,

d) $n \geq 3, f \in \{t, = 1\} \cup \{\leq k \mid k \geq 1\}$.

Proof. Let $G = (N, T, S, P)$ be a regular grammar. We consider another set $N' = \{A' \mid A \in N\}$ containing copies of G nonterminals and a new *trap* nonterminal $X \notin N \cup N'$. Let $\Gamma = (N \cup N' \cup \{X\}, T, S, P_1, P_2)$ be a grammar system of degree 2 where

$$P_1 = \{A \to aB' \mid A \to aB \in P\} \cup \{A \to a \mid A \to a \in P\} \cup \{A' \to aX \mid A \in N\},$$
$$P_2 = \{A' \to aB \mid A \to aB \in P\} \cup \{A' \to a \mid A \to a \in P\} \cup \{A \to aX \mid A \in N\}.$$

We note that in the mentioned modes f every counting derivation in Γ starts with a rule from P_1 and uses alternatively rules from P_1 and P_2 due to the parasitic rules $A \to aX, A' \to aX$. It is easy to see that every derivation of G

$$S \Longrightarrow x_1 A_1 \Longrightarrow x_2 A_2 \ldots$$

can be simulated by the counting derivation in Γ

$$(S, 0, 0) \overset{c}{\Longrightarrow}{}^f_{P_1} (x_1 A'_1, 1, -1) \overset{c}{\Longrightarrow}{}^f_{P_2} (x_2, A_2, 0, 0) \ldots$$

Hence, $L(G) \subseteq L_f(\Gamma, 2, 1)$. Conversely, $L_f(\Gamma, 2, 1) \subseteq L(G)$ due to the fact that excepting the parasitic rules the productions from P_1 and P_2 are copies of those from P.

For $f = t$ the following grammar system is taken

$$\Gamma = (N, T, S_1, P_1, P_2, P_3),$$

where

$$P_1 = \{A_1 \to aB_2 \mid A \to aB \in P\} \cup \{A_1 \to a \mid A \to a \in P\} \cup \{A_3 \to aX \mid A \in N, a \in T\}$$
$$P_2 = \{A_2 \to aB_3 \mid A \to aB \in P\} \cup \{A_2 \to a \mid A \to a \in P\} \cup \{A_1 \to aX \mid A \in N, a \in T\}$$
$$P_3 = \{A_3 \to aB_1 \mid A \to aB \in P\} \cup \{A_3 \to a \mid A \to a \in P\} \cup \{A_2 \to aX \mid A \in N, a \in T\}$$

Clearly, $L_t(\Gamma, 2, 1) = L(G)$.

Applying Theorem 1 and Theorem 8 the proof is over. □

Theorem 10. a) $REG \subseteq CDL_n(RL, f, 0, 0)$, for $n \geq 2, f \in M \setminus \{t\}$ and for $n \geq 3, f = t$. The strict inclusion holds for

b) $n \geq 2, f \in \{*\} \cup \{\geq k \mid k \geq 1\}$,

c) $n \geq 3, f \in \{t\} \cup \{= k \mid k \geq 1\} \cup \{\leq k \mid k \geq 1\}$.

Proof. Let $G = (N, T, S, P)$ be a regular grammar. We construct the grammar system $\Gamma = (N, T, S, P_1, P_2)$ where $P_1 = P_2 = P \cup \{A \to A \mid A \in N\}$. It is easy to see that $L(G) \subseteq L_f(\Gamma, 0, 0)$. Indeed, every derivation $S \Longrightarrow^*_G x$ may be written as a derivation with right linear rules having an even numbers of steps (we may start with $S \to S$ whenever needed). Such a derivation may be simulated in Γ by alternatively applying rules from P_1 and P_2. For the cases $= k$, $\geq k$ the rules $A \to A$ may be used to obtain a derivation

$$(S, 0, 0) \stackrel{c}{\Longrightarrow}{}^f_{P_1} (\alpha_1, k, -k) \stackrel{c}{\Longrightarrow}{}^f_{P_2} \dots (x, 0, 0)$$

in an even number of steps. For the case $f = t$, the last part of the proof of Theorem 9 is considered and appropriately modified to prove the required inclusion.

The strict inclusions follow from Theorem 8 and using Theorem 1 the proof is over. $\square$

The following two results set out some relations among the *strong fair* languages and the languages generated by CD grammar systems with *counting/priority* mechanism in the case $f = t$.

Theorem 11. *For any right linear CD grammar system* $\Gamma = (N, T, S, P_1, \dots, P_n)$ *there exists a right linear CD grammar system* $\Gamma' = (N', T, S', P_0, P_1, \dots, P_n)$ *such that S' occurs only in the left hand side of the rules belonging to P_0 and $L_t(\Gamma, s - 0) = L_t(\Gamma', s - 0)$.*

Proof. If $\Gamma = (N, T, S, P_1, \dots, P_n)$ is an arbitrary CD grammar system, then the new elements defining Γ' are

$$N' = N \cup \{S'\}$$
$$P_0 = \{S' \to S', S' \to S\}.$$

If $S \Longrightarrow^* w$ in Γ and each component works p times, then in Γ' the following derivation occurs $S' \Longrightarrow^{p-1} S' \Longrightarrow S \Longrightarrow^* w$. $\square$

Theorem 12. $CDL_n(RL, t, s - 0) \subseteq CDL_{n+2}(RL, t, 0, 0)$.

Proof. Let us consider for an arbitrary language $L \in CDL_n(RL, t, s - 0)$ a right linear grammar system Γ with n components. From Theorem 11 we get an equivalent grammar system $\Gamma' = (N', T, S', P_0, P_1, \dots, P_n)$. The following grammar system is constructed, using the definition of Γ'

$$\Gamma'' = (N'', T, S', P'_0, P_1, \dots, P_n, P_{n+1})$$

where

$$
\begin{aligned}
N'' &= \{A_i \mid A \in N \setminus \{S'\}, 1 \leq i \leq n\} \cup \{F, X\}, \\
P'_0 &= \{S' \to S', X \to X\} \cup \{S' \to S_i \mid 1 \leq i \leq n\}, \\
P'_i &= \{A_i \to aB_j \mid A \to aB \in P_i, B \notin dom(P_i), 1 \leq j \leq n, j \neq i\} \\
&\quad \cup \{A_i \to aB_i \mid A \to aB \in P_i\} \\
&\quad \cup \{A_i \to aX \mid A \to a \in P_i\} \\
&\quad \cup \{S' \to F\}, 1 \leq i \leq n, \\
P_{n+1} &= \{S' \to F, X \to X, X \to \lambda\}.
\end{aligned}
$$

For any derivation in Γ', $S' \Longrightarrow^* w$, having for each component the same number of applications, p, the following derivation steps are constructed in Γ'':

$$(S', 0, \dots, 0) \stackrel{c}{\Longrightarrow}{}^t_{P_0} (S_i, p, -p, \dots, -p)$$

(due to the rules $S' \to F \in P_i, 1 \le i \le n+1$) and then

$$(S_i, p, -p, \ldots, -p) \overset{c}{\Longrightarrow}{}^t_{P_i} \ \ldots \ (wX, p, 0, \ldots, 0, -p)$$

(using the rules of $P_1, \ldots, P_n$, p times each); at the end the rules of P_{n+1} are used p times and so we get

$$(wX, p, 0, \ldots, 0, -p) \overset{c}{\Longrightarrow}{}^t_{P_{n+1}} \ (w, 0, \ldots, 0).$$

It follows that $w \in L_t(\Gamma'', 0, 0)$ and the proof is over. $\qquad \square$

4. The Context-Free Case

The main results concerning the generative capacity of the context-free grammar systems with the *counting/priority* support are stated by the next theorem.
Let

$$M_1 = \{= 1, \ge 1, *, t\} \cup \bigcup_{k \ge 1} \{\le k\}.$$

Theorem 13. i) *For all $n \ge 2$, and*
• $f \in M_1 \setminus \{t\}$,

$$CDL_n(CF, f) \subset CDL_n(CF, f, 0, 0).$$

• $q \ge 1$,

$$CDL_2(CF, t) \subset CDL_2(CF, t, 1, q).$$

ii) *For all $n \ge 3$*

$$CDL_n(CF, t) \subseteq CDL_n(CF, t, 0, 0).$$

iii) *For all $n \ge 2$ and $k \ge 2$*

$$CF \subset CDL_n(CF, = k, 0, 0) \cap CDL_n(CF, \ge k, 0, 0)$$

Proof. First we recall (see [3])

    a) $CF = CDL_\infty(CF, f), f \in M_1 \setminus \{t\}$,
    b) $CF = CDL_1(CF, t) = CDL_2(CF, t) \subset CDL_n(CF, t) = ETOL$,
    c) $CF \subset CDL_n(CF, = k) \cap CDL_n(CF, \ge k), n \ge 2, k \ge 2$.

i) For $f \in M_1 \setminus \{t\}$ and an arbitrary context-free grammar $G = (N, T, S, P)$, the following grammar system is constructed

$$\Gamma = (N', T, S', P_1, P_2\}$$

with

$$
\begin{aligned}
N &= N \cup \{S', X\}, S', X \\
P_1 &= P_2 = P \cup \{S' \to SX, X \to X, X \to \lambda\}.
\end{aligned}
$$

For a derivation $S \Longrightarrow^* u$ in G, the following derivation steps are obtained in Γ

$$(S', 0, 0) \overset{c}{\Longrightarrow}{}^f_{P_1} (SX, 1, -1) \ \ldots \ \overset{c}{\Longrightarrow}{}^f_P (uX, a, b) \overset{c}{\Longrightarrow}{}^f_{P'} (u, 0, 0)$$

where P, P' are any of P_1, P_2 and $a + b = 0$.

For $f = t$ and an arbitrary context free grammar, it can be constructed the grammar system with the components:

$$P_1 = P \cup \{S' \rightarrow SX, Y \rightarrow F\},$$
$$P_2 = P \cup \{X \rightarrow Y, Y \rightarrow Y, Y \rightarrow \lambda, S' \rightarrow F\},$$

where S', X, Y are new symbols, S' being the start symbol. A derivation in G for a word u has the following corresponding derivation steps in Γ:

$$(S', 0, 0) \stackrel{c}{\Longrightarrow}_{P_1} (SX, 1, -1) \stackrel{c}{\Longrightarrow}_{P_1}^s (uX, s+1, -s-1),$$
$$\stackrel{p}{\Longrightarrow}_{P_2} (uY, s+1, -s) \stackrel{c}{\Longrightarrow}_{P_2}^s (u, 1, 0).$$

For f mode, $f \in M_1 \setminus \{t\}$, the grammar system Γ considered in Example 2 gives, for counting derivation style, non-context free languages. In the t mode the grammar system can be modified such that it also generates a non-context free language. Combining these results with the relations $a), b)$, mentioned at the beginning of this proof, we get the announced inclusions.

ii) For showing $CDL_n(CF, t) \subseteq CDL_n(CF, t, 0, 0), n \geq 3$, let us consider a language $L \in CDL_n(CF, t)$. From the last inclusion stated by relation $b)$ it follows that L can be generated by some ETOL system $G = (V, T, S, T_1, T_2, \ldots, T_m)$ with the alphabet V, containing the set T of terminals, the start word S which can be considered without loss of generality as an element of $V \setminus T$ and the tables $T_1, T_2, \ldots, T_m$.

For an element $a \in V, 0 \leq i \leq m$ and $1 \leq k \leq 3$, we introduce the new elements $a_{i,k}$. For a word x over the alphabet V, the string $x_{i,k}$ is defined inductively in an obvious way.

The following CD grammar system is constructed:

$$\Gamma = (N, T, S, P_1, P_2, P_3)$$

with

$$
\begin{aligned}
N \;=\; & \{S, F, Z, E_1, E_2, R, R_1, R_2, V, V_1, V_2, V_3, W, X\} \\
& \cup \{a_{i,k} \mid a \in V, 0 \leq i \leq m, 1 \leq k \leq 3\} \\
& \cup \{Z_{i,k} \mid 0 \leq i \leq m, 1 \leq k \leq 3\} \\
& \cup \{X_{i,k} \mid 0 \leq i \leq m, 1 \leq k \leq 3\},
\end{aligned}
$$

$$P_1 \;=\; \bigcup_{i=1}^{5} P_{1,i},$$
$$P_{1,1} \;=\; \{a_{i,1} \rightarrow a_{i,2} \mid a \in V, 0 \leq i \leq m\} \cup \{Z_{i,1} \rightarrow Z_{i,2} \mid 0 \leq i \leq m\},$$
$$P_{1,2} \;=\; \{X_{i,1} \rightarrow X_{i,2} \mid 0 \leq i \leq m\},$$
$$P_{1,3} \;=\; \{E_1 \rightarrow E_1, E_1 \rightarrow E_2, E_1 \rightarrow R, E_1 \rightarrow R_2, E_1 \rightarrow Z, E_1 \rightarrow \lambda\},$$
$$P_{1,4} \;=\; \{R_1 \rightarrow F\},$$
$$P_{1,5} \;=\; \{V \rightarrow V_1, V_1 \rightarrow V_1, V_1 \rightarrow V_2, W \rightarrow F, V_3 \rightarrow F\},$$
$$P_2 \;=\; \bigcup_{i=1}^{5} P_{2,i},$$
$$P_{2,1} \;=\; \{a_{i,1} \rightarrow a_{i,3} \mid a \in V, 0 \leq i \leq m\} \cup \{Z_{i,1} \rightarrow Z_{i,3} \mid 0 \leq i \leq m\},$$

$$P_{2,2} = \{X_{i,2} \rightarrow X_{i,1} \mid 0 \le i \le m\},$$
$$P_{2,3} = \{E_2 \rightarrow E_2, E_2 \rightarrow R, E_2 \rightarrow R_1, E_2 \rightarrow Z, E_2 \rightarrow \lambda\},$$
$$P_{2,4} = \{R_2 \rightarrow F\},$$
$$P_{2,5} = \{V_2 \rightarrow V_3, V_3 \rightarrow V_3, V_3 \rightarrow W, V_1 \rightarrow F\},$$
$$P_3 = \bigcup_{i=1}^{8} P_{3,i},$$
$$P_{3,1} = \{S \rightarrow X_{0,1}, X_{0,1} \rightarrow X_{0,1}, X_{0,1} \rightarrow S_{0,1}Z_{0,1}\},$$
$$P_{3,2} = \{a_{i,2} \rightarrow a_{i+1,1} \mid a \in V, 0 \le i \le m-1\}$$
$$\qquad \cup\{Z_{i,2} \rightarrow Z_{i+1,1} \mid 0 \le i \le m-1\},$$
$$P_{3,3} = \{a_{i,3} \rightarrow w_{0,1} \mid a \rightarrow w \in T_i, 1 \le i \le m\},$$
$$P_{3,4} = \{Z_{i,3} \rightarrow Z_{0,1} \mid 1 \le i \le m\}$$
$$\qquad \cup\{Z_{i,3} \rightarrow X_{i,j} \mid 1 \le i \le m, j = 1, 2\}$$
$$\qquad \cup\{X_{i,j} \rightarrow Z_{i,3} \mid 1 \le i \le m, j = 1, 2\}$$
$$\qquad \cup\{X_{i,j} \rightarrow Z_{0,1} \mid 1 \le i \le m, j = 1, 2\},$$
$$P_{3,5} = \{a_{0,3} \rightarrow a \mid a \in T\} \cup \{a_{0,3} \rightarrow F \mid a \in V \setminus T\}$$
$$\qquad \cup\{Z_{0,3} \rightarrow Z, Z_{0,3} \rightarrow \lambda\},$$
$$P_{3,6} = \{Z \rightarrow E_1, Z \rightarrow E_2, Z \rightarrow R, R \rightarrow R, R \rightarrow \lambda\},$$
$$P_{3,7} = \{Z \rightarrow R_1, Z \rightarrow R_2, R_1 \rightarrow R_1, R_1 \rightarrow R_2, R_2 \rightarrow R_2,$$
$$\qquad R_2 \rightarrow R, R_1 \rightarrow \lambda, R_2 \rightarrow \lambda\},$$
$$P_{3,8} = \{R \rightarrow V, W \rightarrow W, W \rightarrow X, X \rightarrow X, X \rightarrow \lambda, V_1 \rightarrow F\}.$$

For a derivation

$$D : S \Longrightarrow x^{(1)} \Longrightarrow x^{(2)} \Longrightarrow \ldots \Longrightarrow x^{(n)} = x, x \in T^*,$$

in the ETOL system, with the observation that $x^{(j)}$ is obtained in the table T_{i_j}, we construct the following derivation steps in Γ:

a) The derivation starts by applying only some rules from P_3 component ($P_{3,1}$ subset); so we get

$$(S, 0, 0, 0) \overset{c}{\Longrightarrow}{}_{P_3}^{n} (X_{0,1}, -n+1, 0, n) \overset{c}{\Longrightarrow}_{P_3} (S_{0,1}Z_{0,1}, -n, 0, n+1).$$

After getting the last string, the component P_3 is left. Let us denote by k, the length of the string $S_{0,1}Z_{0,1}$. Clearly, we have $n \ge 1, k \ge 2$.

b) For simulating the first step in G, $S \Longrightarrow x^{(1)}$ (using the rules of the table T_{i_1}), it is necessary to apply in Γ, alternatively rules from P_1 ($P_{1,1}$ subset) and P_3 ($P_{3,2}$ subset) and then P_2 ($P_{2,1}$ subset) followed by P_3 ($P_{3,3}, P_{3,4}$ subsets). Applying first rules from $P_{1,1}$ and then from $P_{3,2}$, we get the derivation

$$(S_{0,1}Z_{0,1}, -n, 0, n+1) \overset{c}{\Longrightarrow}{}_{P_1}^{t} (S_{0,2}Z_{0,2}, -n+k, -k, n+1-(k-1))$$
$$\overset{c}{\Longrightarrow}{}_{P_3}^{t} (S_{1,1}Z_{1,1}, -n+1, -2k+1, n+1+1).$$

The number of rules used in each mentioned component is the same and it equals the length of the string.

c) Applying j times the rules of the components $P_{1,1}$ and $P_{3,2}$, alternatively, the following derivation can be defined

$$(S_{0,1}Z_{0,1}, -n, 0, n+1) \overset{c}{\Longrightarrow_{P_1}^t} \ \ldots \ (S_{j,1}Z_{j,1}, -n+j, (-2k+1)j, n+1+j).$$

After leaving P_3 component, and for applying again P_1 component instead of P_2 (both components could be applied to the string $S_{j,1}Z_{j,1}$), it is necessary to have $-n+j < (-2k+1)j$, i.e.:

$$n > 2kj.$$

Let us denote by l the first value of j for which the relation above is not true; so we have

$$2k(l-1) < n \le 2kl.$$

In this case (when $j = l$), the rules from P_2 ($P_{2,1}$ subset) and then those from P_3 can be applied. So the derivation becomes:

$$(S, 0, 0, 0) \overset{c}{\Longrightarrow_{P_3}^t} \ \ldots \ (S_{l,1}Z_{l,1}, u_1, u_2, u_3)$$

$$\overset{c}{\Longrightarrow_{P_2}^t} (S_{l,3}Z_{l,3}, v_1, v_2, v_3) \overset{c}{\Longrightarrow_{P_3}^t} (x_{0,1}^{(1)}Z_{0,1}, w_1, w_2, w_3).$$

After leaving $P_{2,1}$ only the rules of P_3 ($P_{3,3}$ or $P_{3,4}$ subsets) can be applied. Clearly, $l = i_1$ and then $x_{0,1}^{(1)}$ corresponds to $x^{(1)}$, the first string in the derivation D.

d) After getting $(x_{0,1}^{(s)}Z_{0,1}, n_1, n_2, n_3)$, for some $s < n$, for restarting the derivation in order to simulate the application of the table $T_{i_{s+1}}$, it is necessary to have

$$n_1 = n_2 - n,$$

where n satisfies $2k(l-1) < n \le 2kl$ for $l = i_{s+1}, k = |x_{0,1}^{(s)}Z_{0,1}|$. In order to obtain relation $n_1 = n_2 - n$ the string $(x_{0,1}^{(s)}Z_{0,1}, n_1, n_2, n_3)$ must be derived from $(x_{i_s,3}Z_{i_s,3}, m_1, m_2, m_3)$ by applying the rules of $P_{3,3}$ and $P_{3,4}$ in the following way:

• if we need to decrease m_1 instead of m_2 (m_2 instead of m_1) then are applied first the rules from $P_{3,4}$ for $j = 1$ ($j = 2$) and we get the string $(x_{i_s,3}Z_{0,1}, h_1, h_2, h_3)$;

• at the end are applied the rules belonging to $P_{3,3}$ (these rules change both h_1 and h_2 at each step of the derivation).

e) The process described until now, ends when the string $(x_{0,1}^{(n)}Z_{0,1}, p_1, p_2, p_3)$ is obtained ($x_{0,1}^{(n)}$ corresponds to $x^{(n)}$, the last string in D). For ending the derivation in Γ, the string above mentioned must be derived using rules of P_2 ($P_{2,1}$ subset) instead of P_1 ($P_{1,1}$ subset), so it is required to have $p_1 \ge p_2$. In order to get this relation the rules belonging to P_3 applied to the string deriving $(x_{0,1}^{(n)}Z_{0,1}, p_1, p_2, p_3)$ are managed in a similar way to those used for step d). The derivation can further be described as

$$(x_{0,1}^{(n)}Z_{0,1}, p_1, p_2, p_3) \overset{c}{\Longrightarrow_{P_2}^t} (x_{0,3}^{(n)}Z_{0,3}, s_1, s_2, s_3) \overset{c}{\Longrightarrow_{P_3}^t} (x^{(n)}U, u, v, p).$$

The rules used for the last part of the derivation are those from P_3 ($P_{3,5}$ subset). The string $x^{(n)}$ is just the string obtained in the derivation D and U is Z or λ.

f) If $u = v = p = 0$, U is λ and the derivation stops. Otherwise U is Z and from $(x^{(n)}Z, u, v, p)$ we get the string $(x^{(n)}, 0, 0, 0)$.

Indeed, if $u \ne 0$ or $v \ne 0$ then we first transform $(x^{(n)}Z, u, v, p)$ into $(x^{(n)}U, 0, 0, m)$, where U is R if $m \ne 0$ otherwise U is λ. For getting the string $(x^{(n)}U, 0, 0, m)$ the following cases are distinguished:

• for $u \leq 0, v \leq 0$, the string $(x^{(n)}Z, u, v, p)$ is derived using $Z \to E_1$ or $Z \to E_2$ belonging to $P_{3,6}$ and then the rules from $P_{1,3}$ and/or $P_{2,3}$;

• for $u \geq 0, v \geq 0$, the string $(x^{(n)}Z, u, v, p)$ is derived starting with $Z \to R_1$ or $Z \to R_2$ from $P_{3,7}$ and continues by using suitable rules belonging to $P_{3,7}$, getting $u = 0, v = 0$ due to the rules from P_1 ($P_{1,4}$ subset) or P_2 ($P_{2,4}$ subset);

• for $u > 0, v < 0$ or $u < 0, v > 0$, the string $(x^{(n)}Z, u, v, p)$ is derived starting with $Z \to E_1$ if $u < 0$ ($Z \to E_2$ if $v < 0$) continues by applying the rules belonging to $P_{1,3}$ ($P_{2,3}$), obtaining $(x^{(n)}R_2, u', v', p')$ (or obtaining $(x^{(n)}R_1, u', v', p')$) and ends by using rules of $P_{3,7}$. When the rules from $P_{3,7}$ are selected it is necessary to have $v' > p'(u' > p')$. This condition can be achieved by first using $Z \to E_2, E_2 \to E_2$ (arbitrary times) and then $E_2 \to Z$ (or $Z \to E_1, E_1 \to E_1$ (arbitrary times) and then $E_1 \to Z$)

If we get $(x^{(n)}R, 0, 0, m), m \neq 0$, then we distinguish two cases:

• For $m < 0$ we get $(x^{(n)}, 0, 0, 0)$ from $(x^{(n)}R, 0, 0, m)$ by iteratively applying $R \to R$ and then $R \to \lambda$.

• For $m > 0$ we first derive $(x^{(n)}R, 0, 0, m)$ with $R \to V$ from P_3 ($P_{3,8}$ subset) and so we get $m > 1$. The rules $V \to V_1, V_1 \to V_1$ ($2 \cdot m - 1$ times) and $V_1 \to V_2$ from P_1 are then used to get the string $(x^{(n)}V_2, 2 \cdot m + 1, -2 \cdot m, -m)$ (due to the rules $V_1 \to F$ belonging to both $P_{2,5}$ and $P_{3,8}$). This last obtained string is further derived by applying the rules $V_2 \to V_3, V_3 \to V_3$ ($2 \cdot m - 2$ times) and $V_3 \to W$ from P_2 and getting $(x^{(n)}W, 2, 0, -m)$ (due to the rule $V_3 \to F$ of $P_{1,5}$). At the end, this string is transformed by using the rules of $P_{3,8}$: $W \to W, W \to X, X \to X$ ($m - 3$ times) and then $X \to \lambda, m \geq 3$ or $W \to X, X \to \lambda, m = 2$.

iii) Let us consider a context free grammar $G = (N, T, S, P)$ and construct similar to Theorem 4 (see [5])

$$\Gamma = (N \cup \{X\}, T, S, P_1, P_2),$$

with

$$P_1 = P_2 = P \cup \{A \to wX : A \to w \in P\} \cup \{X \to X, X \to \lambda\}.$$

Clearly, $L_f(\Gamma) = L(G), f \in \{= k : k \geq 2\} \cup \{\geq k : k \geq 2\}$. Combining this construction with Example 2, the proof is over. $\square$

5. Strong Fairness and Grammar Systems with Priority

Usually, *fairness* is defined as a restriction on some infinite behavior according to *eventual occurrence* of some events. The term is used as a generic name for a multitude of concepts. In the contexts where an *event occurrence* can be either *enabled* or *disabled*, two kinds of requirements are stated by *weak fairness* and *strong fairness* concepts [1], [6]. According to *weak fairness*, an event will not be indefinitely postponed provided that it remains *continuously enabled* from some time instant until occurring. *Strong fairness* guarantees eventual occurrence under the condition of being *infinitely often enabled*, but not necessarily continuously.

In CD grammar systems we consider as *event occurrence* the intervention of some given component P in the derivation process, i.e. the $\Longrightarrow_P^f$ occurrence. Such an event occurrence is considered *enabled* at a given step of the derivation process if the given component contains some rules that can be applied in the current sentential form. From among the enabled components the component with the highest priority will be activated.

In this section we confine our attention to *strong fairness* of the CD grammar systems with dynamical priorities.

Definition 3. Let $D : (\alpha_0, 0, \ldots, 0) \overset{c}{\Longrightarrow}\!\!{}^f_{P_{i_0}} \ldots \overset{c}{\Longrightarrow}\!\!{}^f_{P_{i_{k-1}}} (\alpha_k, v_{k,1}, \ldots, v_{k,n}) \ldots$ be a counting derivation (possibly an infinite one), where $\alpha_0 = S$, $k \geq 0$. A component P is said to be *enabled* at the kth step of the derivation if $|\alpha_k|_{dom(P)} \geq 1$, i.e. there are some rule $A \to \beta \in P$ and $\alpha_k = \gamma A \delta$. A component P_{i_j}, $0 \leq j \leq k-1$, appearing in this derivation is said to be the *activated component* at the step j. By E_j, $0 \leq j \leq k$, we denote the set of all components enabled at the jth step. The pair (E_j, i_j), $0 \leq j \leq k-1$, is said to be a *selection* (from among n components) and consists of the nonempty set $E_j \subseteq \{1, \ldots, n\}$ of enabled components and the activated component $i_j \in E_j$. Of course, $v_{j,i_j} \leq v_{j_r}$ for all $r \in E_j$. We associate to the derivation D a *run*, i.e. the sequence of selections $(E_0, i_0) \ldots (E_j, i_j) \ldots$

Note. Instead of a component name P_i we simply use the index i.

Example 3. Let Γ be a CD grammar system with the following components:

$$P_1 = \{S \to A, A \to B, B \to C, C \to D, D \to E, E \to F\},$$
$$P_2 = \{F \to A, A \to S, C \to X, E \to X\},$$
$$P_3 = \{F \to a\}.$$

For the mode $= 2$, we have the following counting derivation:

$$(S, 0, 0, 0) \overset{c}{\Longrightarrow}_{P_1} (A, 1, 0, 0) \overset{c}{\Longrightarrow}_{P_1} (B, 2, -1, 0) \overset{c}{\Longrightarrow}_{P_1} (C, 3, -1, 0)$$
$$\overset{c}{\Longrightarrow}_{P_1} (D, 4, -2, 0) \overset{c}{\Longrightarrow}_{P_1} (E, 5, -2, 0) \overset{c}{\Longrightarrow}_{P_1} (F, 6, -3, 0)$$
$$\overset{c}{\Longrightarrow}_{P_2} (A, 6, -2, -1) \overset{c}{\Longrightarrow}_{P_2} (S, 5, -1, -1) \overset{c}{\Longrightarrow}_{P_1} \ldots,$$

that is

$$(S, 0, 0, 0) \overset{c}{\Longrightarrow}\!\!{}^{=2}_{P_1} (B, 2, -1, 0) \overset{c}{\Longrightarrow}\!\!{}^{=2}_{P_1} (D, 4, -2, 0)$$
$$\overset{c}{\Longrightarrow}\!\!{}^{=2}_{P_1} (F, 6, -3, 0) \overset{c}{\Longrightarrow}\!\!{}^{=2}_{P_2} (S, 5, -1, -1) \overset{c}{\Longrightarrow}\!\!{}^{=2}_{P_1} (B, 7, -2, -1) \ldots$$

Its associated run is:

$$[(\{1\}, 1)(\{1\}, 1)(\{1\}, 1)(\{2, 3\}, 2)] \ldots$$

The component P_3 is never activated, despite the fact that it is enabled infinitely often at the steps $3, 7, 11 \ldots$ of the $= 2$ derivation. Obviously, the intervention of the component P_3 which could terminate the derivation is systematically forbidden.

Definition 4. A derivation is called *strong fair* if its associated run satisfies the following condition:

$$\forall i (1 \leq i \leq n) \wedge \overset{\infty}{\exists} j \in N_0 (i \in E_j) \to \overset{\infty}{\exists} j \in N_0 (i = i_j)$$

Here, the quantifier $\overset{\infty}{\exists}$ stands for "there exists infinitely many" and N_0 denotes the set $0, 1, \ldots$ of natural numbers.

Remark. In a strong fair derivation every component which is enabled infinitely often, is also activated infinitely often. In particular, every finite derivation is strong fair.

Definition 5. A CD grammar system Γ is said to be *strong fair* in the derivation mode f if all the mode f counting derivation are strong fair.

Theorem 14. *For the degree $n \geq 3$ and for the derivation modes $t, *, \leq k, = k, \geq k$, where $k \geq 2$, there are CD grammar systems which are not strong fair.*

Proof. See Example 3 for $t, *, \leq k$. For $= k, \geq k$ this example can be slightly modified. $\square$

Theorem 15. *Let Γ be a CD grammar system with the degree $n = 3$. For the derivation mode $= 1$, at every step of a counting derivation we have at most two components with the priority value less than or equal to -1, at most one component with the priority value less than or equal to -2 and no component with the value less than or equal to -3.*

Proof. We proceed by induction on the length k of the counting derivation. For

$$(S, 0, 0, 0) \;{}^c\!\!\Longrightarrow_{P_{i_1}}^{=1} \;\ldots\; {}^c\!\!\Longrightarrow_{P_{i_k}}^{=1} (w_k, u_k, v_k, z_k) \;{}^c\!\!\Longrightarrow_{P_{i_{k+1}}}^{=1} (w_{k+1}, u_{k+1}, v_{k+1}, z_{k+1})$$

let us assume $i_{k+1} = 1$. We have $u_{k+1} = u_k + 1$ and for v_{k+1}, z_{k+1} the following cases:

   a) $v_{k+1} = v_k - 1$, $z_{k+1} = z_k - 1$, $u_k \leq v_k$, $u_k \leq z_k$;

b) $v_{k+1} = v_k$, $z_{k+1} = z_k - 1$, $u_k \leq z_k$;

c) $v_{k+1} = v_k$, $z_{k+1} = z_k$.

It is easy to see that assuming one component has the value less than or equal to -3 we contradicts the inductive hypothesis. The other cases are similar. $\square$

Theorem 16. *For the degree $n = 3$ and for the derivation mode $= 1$, the CD grammar systems are strong fair.*

Proof. Let us assume that there exists a CD grammar system with a derivation which is not strong fair. We deduce that in its associated run $(E_0, i_0) \ldots (E_j, i_j)$ there exists a component i and a step k of the derivation such that $\overset{\infty}{\exists} j \; (j \geq k) \wedge \forall m (m \geq k \rightarrow i \neq i_m)$. Let $j_0, \ldots j_l \ldots$ be the infinite sequence deduced from $\overset{\infty}{\exists} j \; (j \geq k)$. If $v_{k,i}$ is the associated priority of the component i at the step k, from $i \in E_{j_0}, \ldots i \in E_{j_l} \ldots$ and $i \neq i_{j_l}$ we deduce that $v_{i,j_0}, \ldots v_{i,j_l} \ldots$ is a strict decreasing infinite sequence. So, we obtain that there exists a component i having its priority less than or equal to -3, a contradiction with Theorem 15. $\square$

Theorem 17. *For the degree $n = 2$ and for all modes of derivation $f \in M$ the CD grammar systems are strong fair.*

Proof. Let assume that there exists a derivation D which is not strong fair. Hence, we have a component infinitely often enabled but never activated from some moment on. Let 2 be this component. We deduce that in the run of D there exists a j_0 such that for all $j \geq j_0$ we have $E_j = \{1, 2\}$, $i_j = 1$, $v_{j,1} \leq v_{j,2}$ and $v_{j+1,2} < v_{j,2}$. Let $m \geq j_0$ be a value such that $v_{m,2} < 0$. From Theorem 2 we have $v_{m,1} \geq -v_{m,2} > 0$, a contradiction with $v_{j,1} \leq v_{j,2}$. $\square$

6. Conclusions

In this paper we introduced and studied a new protocol mechanism for cooperation in CD grammar systems. The generative devices obtained have an increased generative power for all types of production rules. Connections between the dynamical priorities and strong fairness concepts (see [6], [1]) are also made.

Some open problems remain to be solved, especially related to context-free case and concerning the relations with other families of languages generated by different CD grammar systems.

We are further interested to study other kind of counting/priority conditions offering more opportunities for studying the behavior of some parallel computations (see [8], [7]). Also, all these restrictions can be studied as regulated rewritings for context-free grammar case.

References

1. K. R. Apt, E.-R. Olderog, *Verification of sequential and concurrent programs*, Springer-Verlag, 1991.

2. E. Csuhaj-Varju, J. Dassow, On cooperating distributed grammar systems. *J. Inform. Process. Cybern. (EIK)* 26 (1990) 49–63.

3. E. Csuhaj-Varju, J. Dassow, J. Kelemen, Gh. Păun, *Grammar Systems. A Grammatical Approach to Distribution and Cooperation.* Gordon & Breach, London, 1994.

4. J. Dassow, J. Kelemen, Cooperating distributed grammar systems: a link between formal languages and artificial intelligence. *Bulletin of EATCS* 45 (1991) 131–145.

5. J. Dassow, V. Mitrana, Fairness in Grammar Systems. *Acta Cybernetica, submitted.*

6. N. Francez, *Fairness*, Springer-Verlag, 1986.

7. H. Georgescu, *Concurrent Programming. Theory and Practice (in Romanian).* Editura Tehnică, 1996.

8. D. Hemmendinger, Specifying Ada Server Tasks with Executable Formal Grammars. *IEEE Transactions on Software Engineering*, 16 7, July 1990.

9. R. Meersman, G. Rozenberg, Cooperating grammar systems. In: *Proc. MFCS 78*, LNCS 64, Springer-Verlag, Berlin, 1978, 364–374.

10. P. H. Nii, Blackboard systems. In: *The Handbook of AI*, vol. 4 (Eds.: A. Barr, P. R. Cohen, E. A. Feigenbaum), Addison-Wesley, Reading, Mass., 1989.

11. G. Rozenberg, A. Salomaa, *The Mathematical Theory of L Systems.* Academic Press, New York, 1980.

12. A. Salomaa, *Formal Languages.* Academic Press, New York, 1973.

Characterization of RE Using CD Grammar Systems with Two Registers and RL Rules[1]

Sorina DUMITRESCU

Faculty of Mathematics, University of Bucharest
Str. Academiei 14, Bucharest, 70109 Romania

Abstract. We prove that each recursively enumerable language can be generated by a cooperating distributed grammar system with two $\mathbf{Q}_+$ registers and right-linear rules.

1. Introduction

The *cooperating distributed* (CD, for short) *grammar systems* were introduced in [1] as a model of the blackboard architecture in the artificial intelligence. Intuitively, a CD grammar system consists of *a set* of grammars, each grammar working, in turn, on the same sentential form. Different conditions for the start or the stop of the work of each grammar may be imposed. All the terminal strings obtained in this way form the generated language.

The CD grammar systems with two *registers* were defined in [3], starting from usual CD grammar systems, in which two *valences* are assigned to each production rule, a valence being an element of a given group. The valences of the rules contribute to the contents of the registers. When the derivation starts these contents are empty (i.e. equal to the neutral element of the group). When a rule is applied the content of each register changes according to the corresponding valence of the rule applied. The work of a grammar of the system may stop only if the first register is empty. After the stop of the application of one grammar, a transfer step must be performed. This means that the whole content of the second register is transferred into the first one. The system stops its work only if a terminal string is obtained and both registers are empty.

Results obtained so far concerning the CD grammar systems with registers can be found in [3], [4], [6], [7]. For a survey of the results in the area of CD grammar systems we refer the reader to [2].

We prove in this paper that the CD grammar systems with two registers and right-linear rules, in which the valences of the rules are elements of the multiplicative group of strictly positive rational numbers, can generate all the recursively enumerable languages.

2. Definitions and Notations

For an alphabet V, we denote by V^* the free monoid generated by V; λ is the empty string, $|x|$ is the length of $x \in V^*$, $|x|_U$ is the number of occurrences of symbols in $U \subseteq V$ in $x \in V^*$. We assume the reader familiar with the basic notions and results of formal language theory. For details we refer to [5].

---

[1]Research supported by the Academy of Finland, project 11281

168

Definition 1. A *cooperating distributed* (CD, for short) *grammar system* of degree $n, n \geq 1$, is a structure
$$\gamma = (N, T, P_1, \ldots, P_n, S),$$
where N and T are finite, disjoint alphabets (called the nonterminal and the terminal alphabet, respectively), $P_1, \ldots, P_n$ are sets of production rules (they are called the components of the grammar system) and $S \in N$ is the axiom.

Definition 2. Take a group $(H, \circ, e)$.

(i). A *cooperating distributed* (CD) *grammar system with two H registers*, of degree $n, n \geq 1$, is a structure of the form
$$\gamma = (N, T, P_1, \ldots, P_n, v_1, \ldots, v_n, u_1, \ldots, u_n, S),$$
where $(N, T, P_1, \ldots, P_n, S)$ is a CD grammar system and v_i and u_i are applications $v_i, u_i : P_i \longrightarrow H, 1 \leq i \leq n$.

(ii). Take $(x, \alpha, \beta), (y, \alpha', \beta') \in (N \cup T)^* \times H \times H$ and $r \in P_i$ for some $i, 1 \leq i \leq n$. Then we write
$$(x, \alpha, \beta) \Longrightarrow_r (y, \alpha', \beta')$$
iff $x = x_1 u x_2, y = x_1 w x_2, r : u \to w$ and $\alpha' = \alpha \circ v_i(r), \beta' = \beta \circ u_i(r)$.

(iii). For $(x, \alpha, \beta), (y, \alpha', \beta') \in (N \cup T)^* \times H \times H$ and $i \in \{1, \ldots, n\}$ we write
$$(x, \alpha, \beta) \Longrightarrow_{P_i}^* (y, \alpha', \beta')$$
iff $x = y, \alpha = \alpha', \beta = \beta'$ or there are $t \geq 0, r_1, \ldots, r_{t+1} \in P_i, \alpha_1, \ldots, \alpha_t, \beta_1, \ldots, \beta_t \in H$ and $x_1, \ldots, x_t \in (N \cup T)^*$ such that $(x, \alpha, \beta) \Longrightarrow_{r_1} (x_1, \alpha_1, \beta_1) \Longrightarrow_{r_2} \ldots \Longrightarrow_{r_t} (x_t, \alpha_t, \beta_t) \Longrightarrow_{r_{t+1}} (y, \alpha', \beta')$.

(iv). *The language generated* by γ is
$$\begin{aligned} L(\gamma) = \{ &z \in T^* \mid \text{there are } t \geq 0, x_1, \ldots, x_t \in (N \cup T)^*, i_1, \ldots, i_{t+1} \in \\ &\{1, \ldots, n\}, \text{ and } \beta_1, \ldots, \beta_t \in H \text{ such that } (S, e, e) \Longrightarrow_{P_{i_1}}^* \\ &(x_1, e, \beta_1) \models (x_1, \beta_1, e) \Longrightarrow_{P_{i_2}}^* (x_2, e, \beta_2) \models (x_2, \beta_2, e) \\ &\Longrightarrow_{P_{i_3}}^* \ldots \Longrightarrow_{P_{i_t}}^* (x_t, e, \beta_t) \models (x_t, \beta_t, e) \Longrightarrow_{P_{i_{t+1}}}^* (z, e, e) \}. \end{aligned}$$

(For any triple (x, α, β) which appears in a derivation as above – we shall call such a triple a configuration – we say that α is the content of the first register and β is the content of the second register. The step denoted by $\models$ represents the transfer of the whole content of the second register in the first register and may be performed only after the first register becomes empty (i.e. its content becomes equal to e). Note that the change of the component which is working at one moment may have place only if the first register is empty and before this change a transfer step must be performed. On the other hand, it is allowed that, after a transfer step, the applied component is not changed (it means that we may have $P_{i_j} = P_{i_{j+1}}$ for some $j, 1 \leq j \leq t$). Also mention that a terminal derivation starts and ends with both registers empty.)

We denote by $CD(X, 2\mathbf{Q}_+)$ the family of languages generated by CD grammar systems with two $\mathbf{Q}_+$ registers $((\mathbf{Q}_+, \cdot, 1)$ is the multiplicative group of strictly positive rational numbers) and rules of type X. In what follows we consider $X = RL$ (right-linear rules; we also allow λ-rules). The notations CF and RE are for the families of context-free and recursively enumerable languages, respectively.

3. Characterizing RE

In [4] it is proved (Theorem 14) that $CF \subseteq CD(RL, 2\mathbf{Q}_+)$. We shall prove here that the family $CD(RL, 2\mathbf{Q}_+)$ is closed under intersection. Using the well-known characterization of recursively enumerable languages as homomorphic images of the intersection of two context-free languages, we shall obtain that $RE \subseteq CD(RL, 2\mathbf{Q}_+)$. According to Turing-Church thesis the converse inclusion is also true. Hence the equality of the two families follows.

Lemma 1. *Let γ be a CD grammar system with two $\mathbf{Q}_+$ registers and right-linear rules. Then there is a CD grammar system with two $\mathbf{Q}_+$ registers, γ', such that $L(\gamma) = L(\gamma')$ and whose components have only rules of the form $A \to aB, A \to B, A \to a$ or $A \to \lambda$, for A and B nonterminals and a terminal symbol.*

Proof. Take $\gamma = (N, T, P_1, \ldots, P_n, v_1, \ldots, v_n, u_1, \ldots, u_n, S)$. Take $i, 1 \leq i \leq n$, and the rule $r \in P_i, r : A \to xB$, where $x \in T^*, |x| \geq 2$, and $B \in N \cup \{\lambda\}$. Assume that $x = a_1 a_2 \ldots a_p$, where $a_1, \ldots, a_p \in T$. Replace the rule r in P_i by the rules

$$r_1 : A \to a_1[r, 1], r_2 : [r, 1] \to a_2[r, 2], \ldots, r_p : [r, p-1] \to a_p B,$$

with the valences $v_i(r_1) = \ldots = v_i(r_{p-1}) = u_i(r_1) = \ldots = u_i(r_{p-1}) = 1, v_i(r_p) = v_i(r)$, $u_i(r_p) = u_i(r)$, where $[r, 1], [r, 2], \ldots, [r, p-1]$ are new nonterminals.

We continue in this way until we replace all the uncorresponding productions from P_i. Denote the obtained set by P_i'. Denote by γ' the grammar system obtained after we have modified in this way all the components $P_i, 1 \leq i \leq n$. Hence

$$\gamma' = (N', T, P_1', \ldots, P_n', v_1, \ldots, v_n, u_1, \ldots, u_n, S).$$

We will show that $L(\gamma) = L(\gamma')$. The inclusion $\subseteq$ is obvious. It remains to prove the other inclusion. Let D' be a derivation in γ'. We will show that for any configuration (zB, β, β') in D' obtained during the application of a component $P_i', 1 \leq i \leq n$, and not immediately after a transfer step, where $B \in N \cup \{\lambda\}$ (hence B is not a new nonterminal) there is a derivation $(S, 1, 1) \Longrightarrow^* (zB, \beta, \beta')$ in γ, where the last applied component is P_i. We shall prove this by induction on the length of the subderivation $(S, 1, 1) \Longrightarrow^* (zB, \beta, \beta')$ of D'. (By the length of a derivation we mean the number of the rewriting steps, hence we do not count the transfer steps.) For the configuration $(S, 1, 1)$ the statement is true. Suppose that the assertion is valid for any subderivation of D' which fulfils the conditions in the hypothesis and of length at most m, for some $m \geq 1$. Take the configuration (zB, β, β') in D' such that the corresponding subderivation has the length $m+1$ and $B \in N \cup \{\lambda\}$. If the last applied rule is a rule r in P_i' which is also in P_i, then we consider the previous configuration or, if this is obtained immediately after a transfer step, we take the configuration before it. Then this configuration has the form $(z'A, \alpha, \alpha'), A \in N$. In the first case we have $(z'A, \alpha, \alpha') \Longrightarrow_r (zB, \beta, \beta')$ in γ', hence $\beta = \alpha \cdot v_i(r), \beta' = \beta \cdot u_i(r)$. In the second case we have $(z'A, \alpha, \alpha') \models (z'A, \alpha', 1) \Longrightarrow_r (zB, \beta, \beta')$ in γ'. Hence, $\alpha = 1, \beta = \alpha' \cdot v_i(r)$ and $\beta' = u_i(r)$. In both cases $(z'A, \alpha, \alpha')$ satisfies the necessary conditions to apply the inductive hypothesis, hence there is a derivation $(S, 1, 1) \Longrightarrow^* (z'A, \alpha, \alpha')$ in γ

which, in the first case has the last applied component P_i. This derivation can be continued by using the rule r in the first situation and by using a transfer step and then the rule r in the second situation. In both situations we obtain a derivation in γ of the form $(S, 1, 1) \Longrightarrow^* (zB, \beta, \beta')$, in which the last applied component is P_i.

If the rule applied before obtaining (zB, β, β') is one of the new rules, then it follows that all the productions that replace the corresponding rule in P_i have been applied (in the corresponding order). Let $r_1, \ldots, r_p \in P_i'$ be these productions and r be the rule from P_i which was replaced by them. If the applications of the rules $r_1, \ldots, r_p$ are not separated by transfer steps, then these applications can be simulated in γ by using the production r and the proof is similar to the proof of the previous case. If the applications of the rules $r_1, \ldots, r_p$ are separated by transfer steps, then, supposing that $(z'A, \alpha, \alpha')$ is the configuration obtained before the use of r_1, we must have $A \in N$ and $\alpha = 1$. (Indeed, the rules $r_1, \ldots, r_{p-1}$ does not change the content of the first register and since before a transfer step the content of the first register has to be equal to 1, it follows that $\alpha = 1$.) If there is only one transfer step, then we have

$$(z'A, 1, \alpha') \Longrightarrow^*_{P_i'} (z'x_1A_1, 1, \alpha') \models (z'x_1A_1, \alpha', 1) \Longrightarrow^*_{P_i'} (zB, \alpha' \cdot v_i(r), u_i(r)),$$

with $A \in N', x_1 \in T^+$. Consequently, $\alpha' \cdot v_i(r) = \beta$ and $u_i(r) = \beta'$. When $(z'A, 1, \alpha')$ follows immediately after a transfer step, we must have $\alpha' = 1$, hence the next transfer step can be removed. Thus we are in the previous situation. When $(z'A, 1, \alpha')$ does not follow immediately after a transfer step, we can apply the inductive hypothesis, hence there is a derivation in γ of the form $(S, 1, 1) \Longrightarrow^* (z'A, 1, \alpha')$. This derivation can be continued as follows:

$$(z'A, 1, \alpha') \models (z'A, \alpha', 1) \Longrightarrow^*_{P_i} (zB, \alpha' \cdot v_i(r), u_i(r)) = (zB, \beta, \beta').$$

(After the transfer step the rule $r \in P_i$ have been applied.)

If the applications of the rules $r_1, \ldots, r_p$ are separated by several transfer steps, then $\alpha' = 1$ and the transfers can be eliminated. Thus we come back to one of the previous situations. The proof is complete. $\qquad \square$

Lemma 2. *The family* $CD(RL, 2\mathbf{Q}_+)$ *is closed under intersection.*

Proof. Take the CD grammar systems with two $\mathbf{Q}_+$ registers and right-linear rules γ_1 and γ_2,

$$\gamma_i = (N_i, T, P_1^{(i)}, \ldots, P_{n_i}^{(i)}, v_1^{(i)}, \ldots, v_{n_i}^{(i)}, u_1^{(i)}, \ldots, u_{n_i}^{(i)}, S_i),$$

$i = 1, 2$. According to the previous lemma we may assume that γ_1 and γ_2 have only rules of the form $A \to aB, A \to B, A \to a$ or $A \to \lambda$, where A and B are nonterminals and a is a terminal symbol. For each $\gamma_i, i = 1, 2$, construct the system γ_i' of same type, as follows. Mention first that if R is a subset of $\mathbf{Q}_+$, then we denote by $prim(R)$ the set of all prime numbers that appear in the decomposition in prime factors of the numerator or of the denominator of a number of R, written as irreducible rational fraction. Suppose that

$$prim(\{v_j^{(i)}(r), u_j^{(i)}(r) \mid r \in P_j^{(i)}, 1 \le j \le n_i\}) = \{p_1^{(i)}, \ldots, p_{t_i}^{(i)}\}, i \in \{1, 2\}.$$

Consider the sets of prime numbers $R_j^{(i)} = \{q_{j,1}^{(i)}, \ldots, q_{j,t_i}^{(i)}\}$, $1 \le j \le n_i$, such that $R_j^{(i)} \cap R_{j'}^{(i)} = \emptyset$, $R_j^{(i)} \cap \{p_1^{(i)}, \ldots, p_{t_i}^{(i)}\} = \emptyset$, $1 \le j, j' \le n_i, j \ne j'$.

Construct the functions $v_j'^{(i)} : P_j^{(i)} \longrightarrow \mathbf{Q}_+, 1 \leq j \leq n_i, i \in \{1,2\}$, such that for any $i \in \{1,2\}, 1 \leq j \leq n_i$, and $r \in P_j^{(i)}, v_j'^{(i)}(r)$ is obtained from $v_j^{(i)}(r)$ by replacing, in its writing using prime numbers, $p_k^{(i)}$ by $q_{j,k}^{(i)}$, for any $k, 1 \leq k \leq t_i$.

Consider for each $i \in \{1,2\}$ the CD grammar system with two $\mathbf{Q}_+$ registers γ_i', in which the set of terminal symbols is T, the set of nonterminal symbols is

$$N_i' = N_i \cup \{A', A'' \mid A \in N_i\} \cup \{(A,k),(A',k),(A'',k) \mid A \in N_i, 1 \leq k \leq 2t_i\}$$

and the components are denoted by $P_j'^{(i)}, P_{j,r}^{(i)}, 1 \leq j \leq n_i, r \in P_j^{(i)}$, and constructed as follows.

For $j \in \{1,\dots,n_i\}$ and $r \in P_j^{(i)}, r : A \to x$ (it follows that $x = aB$ or $x = B$ or $x = a$ or $x = \lambda$, for $A, B \in N_i, a \in T$) we have

$$
\begin{aligned}
P_{j,r}^{(i)} = & \; \{(r, v_j'^{(i)}(r), u_j^{(i)}(r))\} \cup \\
& \cup \bigcup_{k=1}^{2t_i} \{(A \to (A,k),1,1),((A,k) \to A,1,1),((A \to (A',k),1,1)), \\
& \qquad ((A',k) \to A,1,1)\} \cup \\
& \cup \bigcup_{k=1}^{t_i} \{((A,k) \to (A,k), q_{j,k}^{(i)}, \frac{1}{q_{j,k}^{(i)}}),((A,t_i+k) \to (A,t_i+k), \frac{1}{q_{j,k}^{(i)}}, q_{j,k}^{(i)}), \\
& \qquad ((A',k) \to (A',k), p_k^{(i)}, \frac{1}{p_k^{(i)}}),((A',t_i+k) \to (A',t_i+k), \frac{1}{p_k^{(i)}}, p_k^{(i)})\}.
\end{aligned}
$$

For $1 \leq j \leq n_i$ we have

$$
\begin{aligned}
P_j'^{(i)} = & \; \bigcup_{A \in N_i} \bigcup_{k=1}^{2t_i} \{(A \to (A'',k),1,1),((A'',k) \to A,1,1)\} \cup \\
& \cup \bigcup_{A \in N_i} \bigcup_{k=1}^{t_i} \{((A'',k) \to (A'',k), p_k^{(i)}, \frac{1}{q_{j,k}^{(i)}}), \\
& \qquad ((A'',t_i+k) \to (A'',t_i+k), \frac{1}{p_k^{(i)}}, q_{j,k}^{(i)})\}.
\end{aligned}
$$

The initial symbol of the system γ_i' is S_i, too.

Note that each component of the system $\gamma_i', i = 1, 2$, contains at most one rule which introduces a terminal symbol in the sentential form.

Assertion 1. $L(\gamma_i) = L(\gamma_i'), i = 1, 2$.

Proof of Assertion 1. During this proof we shall not use the index i. Hence γ will mean γ_i, γ' will mean γ_i' and the elements of the two systems γ and γ' will be denoted as the corresponding ones in the systems γ_i, γ_i', respectively, removing the index i.

($\subseteq$) Take a derivation D in γ,

$$
\begin{aligned}
D : \; & (xA, \beta, 1) \Longrightarrow_{r_1} (x_1 A_1, \beta_1, \beta_1') \Longrightarrow_{r_2} (x_2 A_2, \beta_2, \beta_2') \Longrightarrow_{r_3} \dots \\
& \Longrightarrow_{r_m} (x_m A_m, \beta_m, \beta_m'),
\end{aligned}
$$

where $r_1, \ldots, r_m \in P_j$, for some $j, 1 \leq j \leq n$, and $\beta_m = 1$. We have the following corresponding derivation in γ'

$$D' \; : \; (xA, \beta, 1) \Longrightarrow^*_{P'_j} (xA, 1, \delta) \models (xA, \delta, 1) \Longrightarrow^*_{P_{j,r_1}} (x_1A_1, 1, \delta_1) \models$$
$$(x_1A_1, \delta_1, 1) \Longrightarrow^*_{P_{j,r_2}} (x_2A_2, 1, \delta_2) \models \ldots \Longrightarrow^*_{P_{j,r_m}} (x_mA_m, 1, \delta_m),$$

where δ is obtained from β by replacing each occurrence of the factor p_k in the writing of β by $q_{j,k}, 1 \leq k \leq t$ and $\delta_1 = \delta \cdot v'_j(r_1) \cdot u_j(r)$, $\delta_2 = \delta_1 \cdot v'_j(r_2) \cdot u_j(r_2), \ldots, \delta_m = \delta_{m-1} \cdot v'_j(r_m) \cdot u_j(r_m)$. Hence $\delta_m = \delta \cdot v'_j(r_1) \cdot \ldots \cdot v'_j(r_m) \cdot u_j(r_1) \cdot \ldots \cdot u_j(r_m)$. Since $\beta \cdot v_j(r_1) \cdot \ldots \cdot v_j(r_m) = 1$, it follows that $\delta \cdot v'_j(r_1) \cdot \ldots \cdot v'_j(r_m) = 1$. Moreover, $u_j(r_1) \cdot \ldots \cdot u_j(r_m) = \beta'_m$. From here we obtain that $\delta_m = \beta'_m$. It is clear now that for any terminal derivation in γ there is a terminal derivation in γ' of the same word.

($\supseteq$) Let us consider a derivation in γ' of the form

$$D' \; : \; (xY, \delta, 1) \Longrightarrow^*_{P_{j_1,r_1}} (x_1Y_1, 1, \delta_1) \models (x_1Y_1, \delta_1, 1) \Longrightarrow^*_{P_{j_2,r_2}} (x_2Y_2, 1, \delta_2) \models$$
$$\models (x_2Y_2, \delta_2, 1) \Longrightarrow^*_{P_{j_3,r_3}} \ldots \Longrightarrow^*_{P_{j_m,r_m}} (x_mY_m, 1, \delta_m) \models (x_mY_m, \delta_m, 1)$$
$$\Longrightarrow^*_{P_{j_{m+1}}} (x_mY_{m+1}, 1, \delta_{m+1}),$$

where $m \geq 1$, $1 \leq j_1, j_1, \ldots, j_{m+1} \leq n$, $r_k \in P_{j_k}$, $x, x_k \in T^*$, $1 \leq k \leq m$, $Y \in N$, $Y_k \in N'$, $\delta, \delta_k \in \mathbf{Q}_+$, $1 \leq k \leq m+1$, δ does not contain any prime factor $p_k, 1 \leq k \leq t$. Note that if during the application of a component P_{j_k,r_k} the rule r_k is not used, then we obtain $\delta_k = \delta_{k-1}$ for $k \geq 2$ or $\delta_k = \delta$ for $k = 1$, hence the application of this component changes nothing and it can be removed. That is why we assume that at the application of the component P_{j_k,r_k} the rule r_k is used at least once, $1 \leq k \leq m$. Let us denote by s_k the number of applications of the rule r_k during the application of $P_{j_k,r_k}, 1 \leq k \leq m$ (hence $s_k \geq 1, 1 \leq k \leq m$). It follows that

$$\delta_1 = \delta \cdot (v'_{j_1}(r_1) \cdot u_{j_1}(r_1))^{s_1},$$
$$\delta_2 = \delta_1 \cdot (v'_{j_2}(r_2) \cdot u_{j_2}(r_2))^{s_2}, \qquad (1)$$
$$\ldots \ldots \ldots \ldots$$
$$\delta_m = \delta_{m-1} \cdot (v'_{j_m}(r_m) \cdot u_{j_m}(r_m))^{s_m},$$

and, further,

$$\delta_m = \delta \cdot (v'_{j_1}(r_1))^{s_1} \cdot \ldots \cdot (v'_{j_m}(r_m))^{s_m} \cdot (u_{j_1}(r_1))^{s_1} \cdot \ldots \cdot (u_{j_m}(r_m))^{s_m}. \qquad (2)$$

Since at the last step the component $P'_{j_{m+1}}$ can be applied, it follows that δ_m contains in its writing (as irreducible fraction) only prime factors from the set $\{p_1, \ldots, p_t\}$. On the other hand, δ does not contain any factor $p_k, 1 \leq k \leq t$, hence, using relation (2) it follows that

$$\delta \cdot (v'_{j_1}(r_1))^{s_1} \cdot \ldots \cdot (v'_{j_m}(r_m))^{s_m} = 1. \qquad (3)$$

There are two cases:

Case 1. We have $\delta \cdot (v'_{j_1}(r_1))^{s_1} \neq 1, \delta \cdot (v'_{j_1}(r_1))^{s_1} \cdot (v'_{j_2}(r_2))^{s_2} \neq 1, \ldots, \delta \cdot (v'_{j_1}(r_1))^{s_1} \cdot \ldots \cdot (v'_{j_{m-1}}(r_{m-1}))^{s_{m-1}} \neq 1$.

Since at the first step the component P_{j_1,r_1} can be applied, it follows that δ does not contain factors $q_{j,k}, 1 \leq j \leq n, j \neq j_1, 1 \leq k \leq t$. As after that the component

P_{j_2,r_2} can be applied, we obtain, by using the first of the relations (1) and the fact that the sets $R_j, R_{j'}$ are disjoint, $1 \leq j, j' \leq n, j \neq j'$, that $j_1 = j_2$ or $\delta \cdot (v'_{j_1}(r_1))^{s_1} = 1$. But the second situation is not possible, hence $j_1 = j_2$. By a similar reasoning, it follows that $j_1 = j_2 = \ldots = j_m$.

Note that δ_{m+1} is obtained from δ_m by replacing the occurrences of the factors p_k by $q_{j_{m+1},k}, 1 \leq k \leq t$. Denoting by β the number which is obtained by replacing in δ any factor $q_{j_1,k}$ by $p_k, 1 \leq k \leq t$, and by using the fact that $Y \in N$ and the relations (1), it follows that there is a derivation D in γ which consists of the application of the component P_{j_1} as follows

$$D \; : \; (xY, \beta, 1) \underbrace{\Longrightarrow_{r_1} \ldots \Longrightarrow_{r_1}}_{s_1 \; ori} (x_1 A_1, \beta_1, \beta'_1) \underbrace{\Longrightarrow_{r_2} \ldots \Longrightarrow_{r_2}}_{s_2 \; ori}$$

$$(x_2 A_2, \beta_2, \beta'_2) \Longrightarrow_{r_3} \ldots \Longrightarrow_{r_m} (x_m A_m, \beta_m, \beta'_m),$$

where $A_m = Y_{m+1}$ (by applying the component $P'_{j_{m+1}}$ in γ', in the second register only factors from the set $R_{j_{m+1}}$ are introduced, hence, when continuing the subderivation D', after a transfer step it is compulsory to apply a component $P_{j_{m+1},r}$, hence $Y_{m+1} \in N$ – from the form of the productions of the system γ'), $A_1, \ldots, A_m \in N, \beta_1 = \beta \cdot (v_{j_1}(r_1))^{s_1}, \beta_2 = \beta_1 \cdot (v_{j_1}(r_2))^{s_2}, \ldots, \beta_m = \beta_{m-1} \cdot (v_{j_1}(r_m))^{s_m}, \beta'_1 = (u_{j_1}(r_1))^{s_1}, \ldots, \beta'_m = \beta'_{m-1} \cdot (u_{j_1}(r_m))^{s_m}$. It follows that $\beta_m = \beta \cdot (v_{j_1}(r_1))^{s_1} \cdot \ldots \cdot (v_{j_1}(r_m))^{s_m}$ and $\beta'_m = (u_{j_1}(r_1))^{s_1} \cdot \ldots \cdot (u_{j_1}(r_m))^{s_m}$. From the relation (3) and from the way we defined β, it follows that $\beta_m = 1$ and β'_m is the number obtained from δ_{m+1} by replacing the occurrences of $q_{j_{m+1},k}$ by $p_k, 1 \leq k \leq t$.

Case 2. There is some $u, 1 \leq u < m$, such that

$$\delta \cdot (v'_{j_1}(r_1))^{s_1} \cdot \ldots \cdot (v'_{j_u}(r_u))^{s_u} = 1 \qquad (4)$$

Assume, without restricting the generality, that u is the smallest number for which the relation (4) is fulfilled. Then the subderivation D'' of D',

$$D'' \; : \; (xY, \delta, 1) \Longrightarrow^*_{P_{j_1,r_1}} (x_1 Y_1, 1, \delta_1) \models (x_1 Y_1, \delta_1, 1) \Longrightarrow^*_{P_{j_2,r_2}} \ldots$$
$$\Longrightarrow^*_{P_{j_u,r_u}} (x_u Y_u, 1, \delta_u)$$

fulfils the conditions in Case 1 (replacing m by u). By a similar reasoning to that in Case 1, it follows that $j_1 = j_2 = \ldots = j_u$ and there is a derivation D_1 in γ corresponding to the subderivation D'' it will correspond a derivation D_1 in γ using the component P_{j_1}

$$D_1 : (xY, \beta, 1) \underbrace{\Longrightarrow_{r_1} \ldots \Longrightarrow_{r_1}}_{s_1 \; times} (x_1 A_1, \beta_1, \beta'_1) \Longrightarrow_{r_2} \ldots \Longrightarrow_{r_u} (x_u Y_u, 1, \beta'_u)$$

(for the derivation D we have proved that $\beta_m = 1$ and $A_m = Y_m$, hence the corresponding relation for u is also valid here).

The subderivation which continues the subderivation D'' – after the transfer step has been performed – until D' is obtained, can satisfy or not the conditions in Case 1. If the second situation occurs, then we do the same as for D' (in Case 2) and so on, until we obtain that D' is a chain of subderivations – separated by transfer steps – all of them, excepting the last, being as D'' and the last as D', all satisfying the conditions in Case 1. Hence we can associate to D' a derivation in γ obtained by chaining the derivations as D_1 or D, with transfer steps in between, corresponding to the subderivations of D'. It is easy to see now that a terminal derivation of γ' is a chain of subderivations of the form D' separated by transfer steps and which, being replaced by subderivations similar to D or D_1 corresponding in γ, lead to a terminal derivation in γ.

Now the proof of the fact that $L(\gamma_i) = L(\gamma_i'), i = 1, 2$, is completed.

We shall construct now a CD grammar system with two $\mathbf{Q}_+$ registers, γ, as follows. The set of terminal symbols of γ is T, the set of nonterminal symbols is $N = N_1' \times N_2'$ and the axiom is (S_1, S_2). For each pair (P_1, P_2), P_i being a component of γ_i', we construct a component in γ with the following rules:

(i) $((A_1, A_2) \rightarrow x(B_1, B_2), \alpha_1 \cdot \alpha_2, \beta_1 \cdot \beta_2)$,

where $(A_i \rightarrow xB_i, \alpha_i, \beta_i) \in P_i, x \in T \cup \{\lambda\}, A_i, B_i \in N_i', \alpha_i, \beta_i \in \mathbf{Q}_+$,

$i = 1, 2$,

(ii) $((A_1, A_2) \rightarrow x, \alpha_1 \cdot \alpha_2, \beta_1 \cdot \beta_2)$,

where $(A_i \rightarrow x, \alpha_i, \beta_i) \in P_i, x \in T \cup \{\lambda\}, A_i \in N_i', \alpha_i, \beta_i \in \mathbf{Q}_+$,

$i = 1, 2$,

(iii) $((A_1, A_2) \rightarrow (B_1, B_2), \alpha_1 \cdot \alpha_2, \beta_1 \cdot \beta_2)$,

where $(A_i \rightarrow B_i, \alpha_i, \beta_i) \in P_i, A_{3-i} = B_{3-i}, \alpha_{3-i} = \beta_{3-i} = 1, A_i, B_i \in N_i'$,

$A_{3-i} \in N_{3-i}', \alpha_i, \beta_i \in \mathbf{Q}_+$, for some $i \in \{1, 2\}$.

Assertion 2. $L(\gamma) = L(\gamma_1') \cap L(\gamma_2')$.

Proof of Assertion 2. Let us examine first the way the rules in γ are constructed. Note that each rule of the form (i) or (ii) corresponds to a pair of rules – one from γ_1' and the other one from γ_2' – which have in common the terminal symbol in the right side of the rule and the presence or the absence of the nonterminal symbol in the right side. Each rule of the form (iii) is associated to a pair containing a rule of one of the systems γ_i' and a nonterminal of the other system. We may assume, without restricting the generality, that the valences of the rules in γ_1' have no common prime factor with the valences of the rules in γ_2' (we speak about prime factors appearring in the decomposition in prime factors of the numerator or of the denominator of a valence when it is written as an irreductible fraction).

($\subseteq$) Take $z \in L(\gamma)$. Then there is a terminal derivation γ,

$$D : ((S_1, S_2), 1, 1) \Longrightarrow_{P_1'}^* (z_1(A_1^{(1)}, A_2^{(1)}), 1, \delta_1) \models (z_1(A_1^{(1)}, A_2^{(1)}), \delta_1, 1) \Longrightarrow_{P_2'}^*$$

$$\Longrightarrow_{P_2'}^* (z_2(A_1^{(2)}, A_2^{(2)}), 1, \delta_2) \models (z_2(A_1^{(2)}, A_2^{(2)}), \delta_2, 1) \Longrightarrow_{P_3'}^* \cdots$$

$$\cdots \Longrightarrow_{P_m'}^* (z_m(A_1^{(m)}, A_2^{(m)}), 1, \delta_m) \models (z_m(A_1^{(m)}, A_2^{(m)}), \delta_m, 1) \Longrightarrow_{P_{m+1}'}^*$$

$$\Longrightarrow_{P_{m+1}'}^* (z, 1, 1).$$

Let us suppose that for each $i, 1 \le i \le m + 1, P_i'$ corresponds to the pair $(P_{1,i}, P_{2,i})$ of components of the two systems γ_1', γ_2', respectively. Note that to the first part of the subderivation D – until the first transfer step – it corresponds a pair of subderivations D_1 and D_2 in the systems γ_1, γ_2, respectively,

$$D_j : (S_j, 1, 1) \Longrightarrow^*_{P_{j,1}} (z_1 A_j^{(1)}, \alpha_j, \beta_j),$$

where $j = 1, 2$. From the form of the rules in γ, it follows that $\alpha_1 \cdot \alpha_2 = 1$ and $\beta_1 \cdot \beta_2 = \delta_1$. According to the supposition made above, the valences of the rules in γ_1' and the valences of the rules in γ_2' have no common prime factor, hence $\alpha_1 \cdot \alpha_2 = 1$ if and only if $\alpha_1 = 1$ and $\alpha_2 = 1$. It follows that each of the derivations D_j may be continued by a transfer step and then by applying the component $P_{j,2}$. By a similar reasoning we obtain the derivations D_1' and D_2' in γ_1', γ_2', respectively,

$$
\begin{aligned}
D_j' \ : \ &(S_j, 1, 1) \Longrightarrow^*_{P_{j,1}} (z_1 A_j^{(1)}, 1, \beta_j) \vDash (z_1 A_j^{(1)}, \beta_j, 1) \Longrightarrow^*_{P_{j,2}} \\
&\Longrightarrow^*_{P_{j,2}} (z_2 A_j^{(2)}, 1, \beta_j^{(2)}) \vDash (z_2 A_j^{(2)}, \beta_j^{(2)}, 1) \Longrightarrow^*_{P_{j,3}} \cdots \\
&\Longrightarrow^*_{P_{j,m}} (z_m A_j^{(m)}, 1, \beta_j^{(m)}) \vDash (z_m A_j^{(m)}, \beta_j^{(m)}, 1) \Longrightarrow^*_{P_{j,m+1}} (z, 1, 1),
\end{aligned}
$$

for $j = 1, 2$.

($\supseteq$) First we shall prove that, if D is a terminal derivation in γ_i' (for $i = 1$ or $i = 2$), then there is a terminal derivation D' in γ_i' of the same word such that at each application of a component $P_{j,r}^{(i)}$, $1 \leq j \leq n_i, r \in P_j^{(i)}$, the rule r is used at most once. Let us suppose that in D we have an application of the component $P_{j,r}^{(i)}$ in which the rule r is used s times, $s \geq 2$. This fact is possible only if r has the form $A \to aA, A \in N_i$ and $a \in T$. We may assume, without restricting the generality, that all the s applications of the rule r are consecutive. Hence the application of the component $P_{j,r}^{(i)}$ can be represented as follows

$$
\begin{aligned}
D_1'' \ : \ &(wX, \alpha, 1) \Longrightarrow^* (wA, \alpha_1, \beta_1) \Longrightarrow_r (waA, \alpha_2, \beta_2) \Longrightarrow_r \cdots \\
&\Longrightarrow_r (wa^s A, \alpha_s, \beta_s) \Longrightarrow^* (wa^s Y, 1, \beta),
\end{aligned}
$$

for $w \in T^*, X \in N_i', Y \in N_i' \cup \{\lambda\}$ and $\alpha_m = \alpha_{m-1} \cdot v_j^{(i)'}(r), \beta_m = \beta_{m-1} \cdot u_j^{(i)}(r), 2 \leq m \leq s$.

This subderivation may be replaced by the subderivation D_2'' which consists of s consecutive aplications of the component $P_{j,r}^{(i)}$, in each application the rule r being used only once:

$$
\begin{aligned}
D_2'' \ : \ &(wX, \alpha, 1) \Longrightarrow^* (wA, \alpha_1, \beta_1) \Longrightarrow_r (waA, \alpha_2, \beta_2) \Longrightarrow^* (waA, 1, \beta_2 \cdot \alpha_2) \\
&\vDash (waA, \beta_2 \cdot \alpha_2, 1) \Longrightarrow_r (wa^2 A, \beta_2 \cdot \alpha_3, u_j^{(i)}(r)) \Longrightarrow^* \\
&\Longrightarrow^* (za^2 A, 1, \beta_3 \cdot \alpha_3) \vDash (za^2 A, \beta_3 \cdot \alpha_3, 1) \Longrightarrow^*_{P_{j,r}^{(i)}} \cdots \\
&\cdots \vDash (za^{s-1} A, \beta_{s-1} \cdot \alpha_{s-1}, 1) \Longrightarrow_r (za^s A, \beta_{s-1} \cdot \alpha_s, u_j^{(i)}(r)) \Longrightarrow^* \\
&\Longrightarrow^* (za^s A, \alpha_s, \beta_s) \Longrightarrow^* (za^s Y, 1, \beta).
\end{aligned}
$$

We have also used above the fact that the rules of the component $P_{j,r}^{(i)}$, different from r have the role to transfer the content of the first register into the second one.

Take now a word $x \in L(\gamma_1') \cap L(\gamma_2')$. Then there is a derivation D_1 in γ_1' of x and a derivation D_2 in γ_2' of x. We shall construct a derivation D of x in γ by following step by step the derivations D_1, D_2, sometimes simultaneously, othertimes advancing only in one of them and waiting in the same position of the other. The derivation D begins, obviously, by the configuration $((S_1, S_2), 1, 1)$. Let us assume that at one moment we are in the derivation D at the configuration $(z(X_1, X_2), \delta_1 \cdot \delta_2, 1)$ obtained immediately after a transfer step, the corresponding configurations in D_1, D_2 being $(zX_1, \delta_1, 1)$ and $(zX_2, \delta_2, 1)$, respectively, obtained after a transfer step, too. Assume that in D_i the application of the component $P_i, i = 1, 2$ follows. We obtain several situations:

1) If the application of the two components leads to the occurrence of a terminal symbol both in D_1 and in D_2, then this symbol is the same. Let us denote it by b. (According to the facts proved above we may assume that in D_1 and in D_2, during the application of a component, at most one terminal symbol is introduced.) In this case in the derivation D will follow the application of the component corresponding to the pair (P_1, P_2) by using once a rule of the form $(A_1, A_2) \to b(B_1, B_2)$ or $(A_1, A_2) \to b$ and, if neccesary, rules of the other forms until the configuration $(zb(Y_1, Y_2), 1, \delta_1' \cdot \delta_2')$ is obtained, corresponding to the configurations $(zbY_i, 1, \delta_i')$ in $D_i, i = 1, 2$, situated before the transfer step. Then the transfer step follows in D (the same way as in D_1 and D_2) and $(zb(Y_1, Y_2), \delta_1' \cdot \delta_2', 1)$ is obtained (if the derivation is not finished yet).

2) If the application of the components P_1 and P_2 does not lead to the insertion of a terminal symbol, then in the derivation D it follows the application of the component corresponding to the pair (P_1, P_2), in a similar way as in case **1)** (the only difference is that in the obtained sentential form a new terminal symbol does not appear).

3) In the case when, for some $i_0 \in \{1, 2\}$, the application of P_{i_0} in D_{i_0} leads to the appearence of a new terminal symbol b, and the application of P_{3-i_0} in D_{3-i_0} does not introduce any symbol, we introduce in D_{i_0} a subderivation of the form

$$(zX_{i_0}, S_{i_0}, 1) \Longrightarrow^*_{P^{(i_0)}_{j,r}} (zX_{i_0}, 1, \delta_{i_0}) \models (zX_{i_0}, \delta_{i_0} 1)$$

before the application of P_{i_0}, for some $j \in \{1, \ldots, n\}$ and $r \in P_j^{(i_0)}$ suitably choosen such that the applications of $P^{(i_0)}_{j,r}$ to be possible. In this way P_{i_0} will be replaced by $P^{(i_0)}_{j,r}$ and we will be in situation **2)**.

The above considerations should be enough for describing the form of the derivation D.

Now the proof of Assertion 2 is over.

From Assertions 1 and 2 it follows that $L(\gamma) = L(\gamma_1) \cap L(\gamma_2)$. Hence the family $CD(RL, 2\mathbf{Q}_+)$ is closed under intersection. $\qquad \square$

Lemma 3. *The family $CD(RL, 2\mathbf{Q}_+)$ is closed under arbitrary homomorphisms.*

Proof. Take the CD grammar system with two $\mathbf{Q}_+$ registers and right-linear rules

$$\gamma = (N, T, P_1, \ldots, P_n, v_1, \ldots, v_n, u_1, \ldots, u_n, S),$$

and the homomorphism $h : T^* \longrightarrow V^*$. Construct the CD grammar system γ'

$$\gamma' = (N, T, P_1', \ldots, P_n', v_1', \ldots, v_n', u_1', \ldots, u_n', S),$$

where, for each $i, 1 \le i \le n$, we have

$$P_i' = \{(A \to h(x)B, \alpha, \beta) \mid (A \to xB, \alpha, \beta) \in P_i, A \in N, B \in N \cup \{\lambda\},$$
$$x \in T^*, \alpha, \beta \in \mathbf{Q_+}\}.$$

It is easy to see that $L(\gamma') = h(L(\gamma))$. $\qquad \square$

Theorem. $RE = CD(RL, 2\mathbf{Q_+})$.

Proof. Using the result proved in [4] (Theorem 14) that $CF \subseteq CD(RL, 2\mathbf{Q_+})$, Lemmas 2 and 3 and the characterization of recursively enumerable languages as homomorphic images of the intersection of two context-free languages, we obtain that $RE \subseteq CD(RL, 2\mathbf{Q_+})$. The other inclusion follows from the Turing-Church thesis. Hence the equality in the theorem is valid. $\qquad \square$

References

1. E. Csuhaj-Varju, J. Dassow, On cooperating distributed grammar systems, *J. Inform. Process. Cybern.*, EIK, 26 (1990), 49-63.

2. E. Csuhaj-Varju, J. Dassow, J. Kelemen, Gh. Păun, *Grammar Systems. A Grammatical Aproach to Distribution and Cooperation*, Gordon and Breach, London, 1994.

3. J. Dassow, Gh. Păun, Cooperating distributed grammar systems with registers, *Found. Control Engineering*, 15 (1990), 19-38.

4. J. Dassow, Gh. Păun, S. Vicolov, On the power of *CDGS* with regular components, *Foundations of Computing and Decision Sciences*, 18, 2 (1993), 83-108.

5. G. Rozenberg, A. Salomaa (eds.), *Handbook of Formal Languages*, Springer-Verlag, Berlin, 1997.

6. S. Vicolov, Cooperating distributed grammar systems with registers: the regular case, *Computers and AI*, 12, 1 (1993), 89-98.

7. S. Vicolov-Dumitrescu, Grammars, grammar systems and g.s.m. mappings with valences, in vol. *Mathematical Aspects of Natural and Formal Languages* (Gh. Păun, ed.), World Sci. Publ., Singapore, 1994, 473-491.

On Cooperating Distributed Uniformly Limited 0L Systems

Dietmar WÄTJEN

Institut für Theoretische Informatik
Technische Universität Braunschweig
Postfach 3329, D-38023 Braunschweig, Germany
Email: waetjen@iti.cs.tu-bs.de

Abstract. Cooperating distributed grammar systems [1] constitute a formal model of the blackboard model for problem solving. In this paper, we replace the grammars in such systems by uniformly k-limited 0L systems [9]. In this way we can define quite a lot of different language families. We compare these families with each other in respect to inclusion. The connections with other language families and closure properties are also investigated. For instance, it is shown that the new introduced families are incomparable with the families of T0L or uniformly k-limited T0L languages.

1. Introduction

Motivated by the blackboard model of artificial intelligence, Csuhaj-Varjú and Dassow [1] introduced the concept of cooperating distributed grammar systems. In their model, the distributed knowledge sources are represented by grammars, the actual state of the problem corresponds to a sentential form, and the application of some production of a grammar corresponds to an action at the blackboard. The distributed grammars have to cooperate to obtain a solution. The actions at the blackboard are controlled according to different modes. These modes determine how long a certain grammar is allowed to manipulate the sentential forms before giving back control to the system. Cooperating distributed grammar systems and some variants have been also considered in [2], [4] and [5]. A comprehensive text-book presentation is given in [3].

In [9], we have introduced the notion of uniformly k-limited T0L systems (see also [6], [12]). These systems represent a limitation of the parallel rewriting of T0L systems. In short, a *uniformly k-limited* T0L *system* (abbreviated as uklT0L *system*) $G = (\Sigma, H, \omega, k)$ is given by the *limitation* $k \in \mathbf{N}$ (where $\mathbf{N}$ is the set of natural numbers) and a T0L system (Σ, H, ω) with *alphabet* Σ, finite set of *tables* H (where a table is a finite substitution on Σ), and *axiom* $\omega \in \Sigma^*$. A derivation step of a uklT0L system differs from that of a T0L system in such a way that instead of the fully parallel rewriting of L systems, now at each step of the rewriting process, exactly $\min\{k, |w|\}$ symbols in the word w considered have to be rewritten (where $|w|$ is the length of w). A derivation step from w_1 to w_2 according to G is denoted by $w_1 \Longrightarrow_G w_2$. If no misunderstanding is possible we write $\Longrightarrow$ instead of $\Longrightarrow_G$. Let $\Longrightarrow^*$ be the reflexive transitive closure of the relation $\Longrightarrow$. Then $L(G) = \{w \in \Sigma^* \mid \omega \Longrightarrow^* w\}$ is the uklT0L *language generated by* G. If there is only one table, we talk of a ukl0L system and write $G = (\Sigma, h, \omega, k)$ where h is a finite substitution on Σ. By $\mathcal{L}(uklT0L)$ and $\mathcal{L}(ukl0L)$, we denote the corresponding families of all uklT0L or ukl0L languages, respectively.

If the derivation mechanism is changed in such a way that at each step of the rewriting process, for every $a \in \Sigma$ exactly $\min\{k, \#_a w\}$ occurrences of the symbol a in the word w considered have to be rewritten (where $\#_a w$ is the number of occurrences of the symbol a in w), then we get the definition of klT0L and kl0L systems as introduced in [8].

Every derivation step of a uklT0L system (or klT0L system) has to be carried out with the same limitation k. If we want to change the limitation during the derivation process then we can reach this aim by replacing the grammars of cooperating distributed grammar systems by ukl0L systems (or kl0L systems, respectively) with different limitations k.

In the case of kl0L systems, such cooperating distributed limited 0L systems (CDl0L systems) have been already investigated in [10]. Furthermore, in [11] there have been considered extended CDl0L systems. In this paper, we start the investigation of cooperated/distributed uniformly-limited 0L systems. The exact definition of such a system (CDul0L system) is given in Section 2. Quite a lot of different language families are defined. In Section 3 we compare CDul0L language families with each other in respect to inclusion. Relative to this aspect we get nice characterizations of the so-called CD$(k_1, \ldots, k_r)$ul0L language families where only some special cases remain open. In Section 4 we compare the CDul0L language families with other families. Especially, all propagating CDul0L languages are context-sensitive. Finally, in Section 5 we shall see that all CDul0L families are anti-AFL's.

In the sequel, we denote by $\mathbf{N}$ the set of all natural numbers (where $0 \notin \mathbf{N}$). Then $\mathbf{N}_0 = \mathbf{N} \cup \{0\}$.

2. CDul0L Systems, Definitions and Simple Results

A *cooperating distributed uniformly limited* 0L *system* (CDul0L *system* for short) is a construct

$$G = (\Sigma, (h_1, k_1), \ldots, (h_r, k_r), \omega)$$

for $r \in \mathbf{N}$ (the number of *components* of the system), *alphabet* Σ, a word $\omega \in \Sigma^*$ (the *axiom*), finite substitutions h_ρ (the *tables* of the system) and natural numbers $k_\rho \in \mathbf{N}$ (the *limitations*) where $\rho = 1, \ldots, r$. Obviously, $G_\rho = (\Sigma, h_\rho, \omega, k_\rho)$, $\rho = 1, \ldots, r$, can be considered as a uk_ρl0L system. Especially, a system G as above is also called a CD$(k_1, \ldots, k_r)$ul0L *system*. If $r = 1$, we also write CD$k_1$ul0L system. G is called *deterministic* if all h_ρ, $\rho = 1, \ldots, r$, are homomorphisms. G is called propagating if the empty word $\varepsilon \notin h_\rho(a)$ for all $\rho \in \{1, \ldots, r\}$ and $a \in \Sigma$. If $w \in h_\rho(a)$ for some $a \in \Sigma$, $w \in \Sigma^*$, then $a \to w$ is called a production of h_ρ. We also talk of the production $w \in h_\rho(a)$.

Let $v, w \in \Sigma^*$, $\rho = 1, \ldots, r$, and $s \in \mathbf{N}$. We write

$$v \Longrightarrow_\rho^s w$$

if there are words $w_1, \ldots, w_s = w \in \Sigma^*$ such that there exists a derivation

$$v \Longrightarrow_{G_\rho} w_1 \Longrightarrow_{G_\rho} w_2 \Longrightarrow_{G_\rho} \cdots \Longrightarrow_{G_\rho} w_{s-1} \Longrightarrow_{G_\rho} w_s = w$$

according to the uniformly k_ρ-limited 0L system G_ρ. s is called the *length* of the derivation $v \Longrightarrow_\rho^s w$. We write

$$u \Longrightarrow_\rho^{\leq s} w \quad (u \Longrightarrow_\rho^{\geq s} w, \text{ respectively})$$

if $u \Longrightarrow_\rho^{s'} w$ for some $s' \le s$ ($s' \ge s$, respectively). Finally, let

$$u \Longrightarrow_\rho^* w$$

if $u \Longrightarrow_\rho^s w$ for some $s \in \mathbf{N}_0$. Sometimes, the index ρ is replaced by G_ρ.

Let G be a CDul0L system as above and

$$m \in \{*, 1, 2, 3, \ldots, \le 1, \le 2, \le 3, \ldots, \ge 1, \ge 2, \ge 3, \ldots\}.$$

The *language generated according to the m-mode by G* is defined by

$$L_m(G) = \{w \in \Sigma^* | w = \omega \text{ or there exist } n \in \mathbf{N}_0, w_i \in \Sigma^* \text{ and } \rho_i \in \{1, \ldots, r\},$$
$$i = 1, \ldots, n, \text{ such that } \omega \Longrightarrow_{\rho_1}^m w_1 \Longrightarrow_{\rho_2}^m \ldots \Longrightarrow_{\rho_n}^m w_n = w\}.$$

By $\mathcal{L}_m(CDul0L)$ we denote the *family of all those languages generated according to the m-mode by CDul0L systems.* Omitting the index m we have $\mathcal{L}(CDul0L)$ as the *family of languages generated according to an arbitrary m-mode by CDul0L systems.* We call it also *family of CDul0L languages.* If $k_1, \ldots, k_r \in \mathbf{N}$ for some $r \in \mathbf{N}$, then by $\mathcal{L}_m(k_1, k_2, \ldots, k_r, ul0L)$ we denote the *family of those languages generated according to the m-mode by $CD(k_1, \ldots, k_r)ul0L$ systems.* Especially, if $k_1 = \ldots = k_r = k$, we write $\mathcal{L}_m(k^r, ul0L)$. For every $r \in \mathbf{N}$, we define

$$\mathcal{L}_m^r(CDul0L) = \bigcup_{\substack{k_i \in \mathbf{N} \\ i=1,\ldots,r}} \mathcal{L}_m(k_1, \ldots, k_r, ul0L),$$

and furthermore, if $k \in \mathbf{N}$, we set

$$\mathcal{L}_m^r(\le k)(CDul0L) = \bigcup_{\substack{k_i \in \mathbf{N}, k_i \le k \\ i=1,\ldots,r}} \mathcal{L}_m(k_1, \ldots, k_r, ul0L) \text{ for } r \in \mathbf{N},$$

$$\mathcal{L}_m(\le k)(CDul0L) = \bigcup_{r \in \mathbf{N}} \mathcal{L}_m^r(\le k)(CDul0L).$$

We see that k is a common bound for all limitations of the components of the systems generating these families. Let

$$\mathcal{L}_m^r(k)(CDul0L) = \bigcup_{\substack{k_i = k \\ i=1,\ldots,r}} \mathcal{L}_m(k_1, \ldots, k_r, ul0L) \text{ for } r \in \mathbf{N},$$

$$\mathcal{L}_m(k)(CDul0L) = \bigcup_{r \in \mathbf{N}} \mathcal{L}_m^r(k)(CDul0L).$$

We remark that in all these cases we can consider deterministic and/or propagating such systems which give rise to corresponding language families. For instance, by $\mathcal{L}(CDulPD0L)$ we denote the family of propagating and deterministic CDul0L languages. If we write $\mathcal{L}(CDul(P)(D)0L)$ we mean that the letters P and D may be present in the corresponding position or not. This leads to four language families.

Because of the definitions the following results are obvious.

Theorem 2.1. *Let G be a CDul0L system. For all $t \in \mathbf{N}$, we have*

$$L_*(G) = L_1(G) = L_{\ge 1}(G) = L_{\le t}(G).$$

Corollary 2.1. *Let $r \in \mathbf{N}$, $k_1, \ldots, k_r \in \mathbf{N}$, $t \in \mathbf{N}$. Then*

$$\mathcal{L}_*(k_1, \ldots, k_r, ul0L) = \mathcal{L}_1(k_1, \ldots, k_r, ul0L) =$$
$$\mathcal{L}_{\geq 1}(k_1, \ldots, k_r, ul0L) = \mathcal{L}_{\leq t}(k_1, \ldots, k_r, ul0L)$$

and

$$\mathcal{L}_*(CDul0L) = \mathcal{L}_1(CDul0L) = \mathcal{L}_{\geq 1}(CDul0L) = \mathcal{L}_{\leq t}(CDul0L).$$

Because of this Corollary, the m-mode is considered in the following only for $m \in \{1, 2, 3, \ldots, \geq 2, \geq 3, \ldots\}$.

As in the case of uniformly k-limited T0L systems (see [9], Theorem 2.1) the growth of the lengths of the words in a CDul0L language is bounded. More precisely, let $G = (\Sigma, (h_1, k_1), \ldots, (h_r, k_r), \omega)$ be a CD$(k_1, \ldots, k_r)$ul0L system and $L_m(G)$ its language generated according to the m-mode. Let $m = t$ or $m = (\geq t)$. Set

$$s = \max(\{s_\rho | s_\rho = tk_\rho(s'_\rho - 1), s'_\rho = \max\{|w| \, | w \in h_\rho(a), a \in \Sigma\}, \rho = 1, \ldots, r\}$$

$$\cup \{\bar{s}_\rho | \bar{s}_\rho = tk_\rho, \varepsilon \in h_\rho(a), a \in \Sigma, \rho = 1, \ldots, r\}).$$

Then for all words $w, w' \in L_m(G)$, there exist $q \in \mathbf{N}$ and words $w_0 = w, w_1, \ldots, w_q = w' \in L_m(G)$ such that $|\, |w_i| - |w_{i-1}| \,| \leq s$ for all i, $i = 1, \ldots, q$.

In case of the t- or $\geq t$-mode, $t \geq 2$, for some CD$(k_1, \ldots, k_r)$ul0L system G there may exist symbols of the alphabet which are used in elementary derivation steps (according to some uk_ρl0L system G_ρ) but which do not occur in any word of $L(G)$. We consider the following example.

Example 2.1. We define the deterministic CD4ul0L system

$$G = (\{a, b, c, d\}, (h, 4), a^2 c)$$

with $h(a) = b$, $h(b) = cd$, $h(c) = c^2$ and $h(d) = d^2$. According to the 2-mode,

$$a^2 c \text{ and } cdcdc^4$$

are the shortest words of $L_2(G)$. Other words belong to $c^+ d^+ c^+ d^+ c^+$, but obviously,

$$c^4 dcdc^4, \ c^2 dc^2 dc^4 \notin L_2(G).$$

Assume that this language is generated by a CD4ul0L system

$$G' = (\{a, c, d\}, (h', 4), \omega)$$

according to the 2-mode. Assume that $\varepsilon \in h'(c)$ or $u_1 x u_2 \in h'(c)$ for $x \in \{a, d\}$ and some $u_1, u_2 \in \{a, c, d\}^*$. We get the derivations

$$cdcdc^4 \Longrightarrow_{h'}^2 cdcd \text{ or } cdcdc^4 \Longrightarrow_{h'}^2 (u_1 x u_2) d(u_1 x u_2) dc^2 (u_1 x u_2)^2, \text{ respectively.}$$

c must be a prefix of u_1. It follows that both derivations lead to words not belonging to $L_2(G)$, a contradiction. We conclude that $h'(c) \subset c^+$. Analogously, $h'(d) \subset d^+$. Frequently, a similar conclusion shall be used in the sequel. It follows that $\omega = a^2 c$ and

$$D: \ a^2 c \Longrightarrow_{h'}^2 cdcdc^4.$$

First we note that $\varepsilon \in h'(a)$ is not possible since otherwise a production $u_1 x u_2 \in h'(c)$ with $x \neq c$ would be necesarry which is not possible as demonstrated above. Since there are words with arbitrary many occurrences of c, a production $c^i \in h'(c)$ for some $i > 1$ must exist. Therefore, if $a \in h'(a)$, the word $a^2 c$ would derive words with 2 occurrences of a and more than one occurrence of c, a contradiction. If $c \in h'(a)$, then from $a^2 c$ words of c^+ could be generated. If $cdc \in h'(a)$ is used in D, then we need $du \in h'(a)$ to generate, if at all, the word $cdcdc^4$, but then a word beginning with d would belong to $L_2(G)$. A production $cdcd \in h'(a)$ would again lead to words not belonging to $L_2(G)$. We conclude that $cd \in h'(a)$. Thus, the derivation D is of the form

$$a^2 c \Longrightarrow_{h'} cdcdc^i \Longrightarrow_{h'} cdcdc^4$$

for some $i \in \{1, 2, 3, 4\}$. If $i = 1$ or $i = 4$, then $\{c, c^4\} \subset h'(c)$. We conclude that $cdcdc^4 \Longrightarrow_{h'}^2 c^4 dcdc^4$. If $i = 2$ or $i = 3$, then $c^2 \in h'(c)$ and $c \in h'(c)$ or $d \in h'(d)$. It follows that $cdcdc^4 \Longrightarrow_{h'}^2 c^2 dc^2 dc^4$. In both cases we get a contradiction to the shape of the words in $L_2(G)$.

We see that the language $L_2(G)$ cannot be generated by a CD4ul0L system according to the 2-mode without an auxiliary symbol.

While in this example a symbol not occurring in a word of the language has been necessary, it is trivial that in case of the 1-mode every symbol occurring in a derivation belongs to a word of the language. The following lemma shows that for many languages we can assume that no auxiliary symbols occur.

Lemma 2.1. *Let $m = t$ or $m = (\geq t)$ where $t \in \mathbf{N}$. Let $L \in \mathcal{L}_m(k_1, \ldots, k_r, CDul0L)$ with $L \subset \Sigma^*$ where every symbol of Σ occurs in some word of L. If for every $a \in \Sigma$ there exists a word $w \in L$ with*

$$\#_a w \geq 1 \text{ and } |w| \geq k_\rho t \forall \rho \in \{1, \ldots, r\},$$

then L can be generated by a $CD(k_1, \ldots, k_r)ul0L$ system with alphabet Σ.

Proof. Assume the contrary. Then there must exist a $CD(k_1, \ldots, k_r)ul0L$ system $G = (\Sigma', (h_1, k_1), \ldots, (h_r, k_r), \omega)$ with $\Sigma \subset \Sigma'$ and $L_m(G) = L$ which fulfills the following property: there are symbols $x \in \Sigma' - \Sigma$ and $a \in \Sigma$ such that $u_1 x u_2 \in h_\rho(a)$ for some $\rho \in \{1, \ldots, r\}$ and $u_1, u_2 \in \Sigma'^*$. Let $w \in L$ with $\#_a w \geq 1$ and $|w| \geq k_\rho t$. We conclude that $w \Longrightarrow_\rho^t w'$ with $w' \in L$ and $\#_x w' \geq 1$, a contradiction. $\square$

We mention that in the non-uniformly limited case, cooperated/distributed limited 0L systems (CDl0L systems) and languages are defined from $kl0L$ systems analogously to the definition of CDul0L systems and languages from $ukl0L$ systems above (see [10]).

3. Comparison of Different Families of CDul0L Languages

The following lemma is obvious.

Lemma 3.1. *Let $m \in \{1, 2, 3, \ldots, \geq 2, \geq 3, \ldots\}$, $r, s \in \mathbf{N}$ with $r \leq s$, and furthermore, let $k_1, \ldots, k_r, k'_1, \ldots, k'_s \in \mathbf{N}$. If the multiset $\{k_1, \ldots, k_r\}$ is included in the multiset $\{k'_1, \ldots, k'_s\}$, then*

$$\mathcal{L}_m(k_1, \ldots, k_r, ul0L) \subset \mathcal{L}_m(k'_1, \ldots, k'_s, ul0L).$$

We shall see (Corollary 3.2) that this result can be strengthened in nearly all cases in such a way that the inclusion of the language families is strict if the multiset inclusion is strict. But the case of limitation 1 behaves a little bit individually. By the definitions, we get

Theorem 3.1. *For all* $r \in \mathbf{N}$, $\mathcal{L}_1(1^r, ul0L) = \mathcal{L}(uelT0L) = \mathcal{L}(uel0L)$.

Lemma 3.2. *For all* $m \in \{1, 2, 3, \ldots, \geq 2, \geq 3, \ldots\}$ *and all* $r, s, k_1, \ldots, k_s \in \mathbf{N}$,

$$\mathcal{L}_1(1^r, ul0L) \subset \mathcal{L}_m(k_1, \ldots, k_s, ul0L).$$

Proof. By Theorem 3.1, it suffices to consider an arbitrary ul1T0L system $G = (\Sigma, h, \omega, 1)$. We choose any $k \in \{k_1, \ldots, k_s\}$ and consider the CDk'ul0L system

$$G' = (\Sigma, (h', k'), \omega) \text{ with } h'(a) = \{w \mid w \in h(a)\} \cup \{a\} \forall a \in \Sigma.$$

According to any m-mode, G' generates $L(G)$. With Lemma 3.1 we get $\mathcal{L}_1(1^r, ul0L) \subset \mathcal{L}_m(k', ul0L) \subset \mathcal{L}_m(k_1, \ldots, k_s, ul0L)$. $\qquad\square$

In the next theorems we shall show that in nearly all other cases, if the modes do not coincide, the resulting language families are incomparable.

Theorem 3.2. *Let* $m' = t_1$ *or* $m' = (\geq t_1)$ *and* $m = t_2$ *or* $m = (\geq t_2)$, $t_1, t_2 \in \mathbf{N}$, *and let* $r, s \in \mathbf{N}$, $k_1, \ldots, k_r, k_1', \ldots, k_s' \in \mathbf{N}$. *If* $t_1 \neq t_2$, $k_\rho t_1 \neq 1$ *for at least one* $\rho \in \{1, \ldots, r\}$, *and if it is not true that* $k_\rho = 1$ *for all* $\rho \in \{1, \ldots, r\}$ *such that there exists* $\sigma \in \{1, \ldots, s\}$ *with* $k_\sigma' = 2$ *and* $k_\rho t_1 = t_1 = 2t_2 = k_\sigma' t_2$, *then*

$$\mathcal{L}_{m'}(k_1, \ldots, k_r, ul0L) \not\subset \mathcal{L}_m(k_1', \ldots, k_s', ul0L).$$

Proof. There are two cases. In case (1),

(a) there exists $\rho \in \{1, \ldots, r\}$ such that $1 \neq k_\rho \cdot t_1 \neq k_\sigma' \cdot t_2 \forall \sigma = 1, \ldots, s$, or
(b) there exist $\rho \in \{1, \ldots, r\}, \sigma \in \{1, \ldots, s\}$ such that $k_\rho \cdot t_1 = k_\sigma' \cdot t_2$ and $k_\sigma' < k_\rho$.

By the assumptions, in the opposite case (2),

$$\forall \rho \in \{1, \ldots, r\}, \text{ there exists } \sigma \in \{1, \ldots, s\} \text{ such that}$$
$$k_\rho \cdot t_1 = k_\sigma' \cdot t_2, \ k_\sigma' > k_\rho \text{ and } k_\sigma' \geq 3.$$

We consider case (1). We choose an index ρ with the properties above. Without restricting generality, we assume that $\rho = 1$. Set $p = k_1 t_1$ and $g = \max\{k_1', \ldots, k_s'\}$. We remember that by the assumptions $p > 1$. We define a CD$k_1$ul0L system (also being a uk_1l0L system)

$$G_1 = (\{a_1, \ldots, a_p\}, (h, k_1), a_1 \ldots a_p a_1^g \ldots a_p^g)$$

by $h(a_i) = \{a_i^2\}$ for all $i \in \{1, \ldots, p\}$. By L_1, we denote the language generated by G_1 according to the m'-mode. By Theorem 3.1, $L_1 \in \mathcal{L}_{m'}(k_1, \ldots, k_r, ul0L)$. L_1 contains the axiom $a_1 \ldots a_p a_1^g \ldots a_p^g$, and the words of second shortest length are of the form

$$a_1^{1+x_1} \ldots a_p^{1+x_p} a_1^{g+x_{p+1}} \ldots a_p^{g+x_{2p}} \text{ with } x_1 + \cdots + x_{2p} = k_1 t_1 \text{ for } x_i \in \mathbf{N}_0, i \in \{1, \ldots, p\}.$$

Especially, we have $w_1 = a_1^2 \ldots a_p^2 a_1^g \ldots a_p^g \in L_1$. Obviously, $L_1 \subset a_1^+ \ldots a_p^+ a_1^+ \ldots a_p^+$, and for every $n \in \mathbf{N}$ there exist $n_i, m_i \in \mathbf{N}$, $i \in \{1, \ldots, p\}$, $n_i, m_i > n$, with $a_1^{n_1} \ldots a_p^{n_p} a_1^{m_1} \ldots a_p^{m_p} \in L_1$.

Assume that L_1 is generated by a $CD(k_1', \ldots, k_s')$ul0L system

$$G_1' = (\Sigma, (h_1, k_1'), \ldots, (h_s, k_s'), \omega)$$

according to the m-mode. By Lemma 2.1 we can assume that $\Sigma = \{a_1, \ldots, a_p\}$. By the shape of the language L_1, it is clear that G_1' is propagating and $h_\sigma'(a_i) \subset a_i^+$ for all $\sigma \in \{1, \ldots, s\}$ and $i \in \{1, \ldots, p\}$. Thus $\omega = a_1 \ldots a_p a_1^g \ldots a_p^g$. Since there does not exist a production $\varepsilon \in h_\sigma'(a_i)$ for any i and σ, we conclude that no word of second shortest length can be generated from a longer word or from another word of second shortest length according to the 1-mode or according to an arbitrary m-mode. Especially, it follows that there exists $\sigma \in \{1, \ldots, s\}$ such that

$$D: \quad a_1 \ldots a_p a_1^g \ldots a_p^g \Longrightarrow_\sigma^m a_1^2 \ldots a_p^2 a_1^g \ldots a_p^g = w_1.$$

Thus $a_i^2 \in h_\sigma'(a_i)$ for all $i \in \{1, \ldots, p\}$. If $m = (\geq t_2)$, then only the subderivations

$$\omega \Longrightarrow_\sigma^{t_2} \omega \Longrightarrow_\sigma^* w_1 \quad \text{or} \quad \omega \Longrightarrow_\sigma^{t_2} w_1 \Longrightarrow_\sigma^* w_1$$

are possible. In the first case there must exist an $i' \in \{1, \ldots, p\}$ such that $a_{i'} \in h_\sigma'(a_{i'})$. It follows that

$$\omega \Longrightarrow_\sigma^{t_2} a_1^2 a_2 \ldots a_p a_1^g \ldots a_p^g.$$

Since $p > 1$ the derived word does not belong to L_1, a contradiction. Thus we can assume that

$$D: \quad a_1 \ldots a_p a_1^g \ldots a_p^g \Longrightarrow_\sigma^{t_2} a_1^2 \ldots a_p^2 a_1^g \ldots a_p^g = w_1.$$

We see that at least the first occurrences of the symbols $a_1, \ldots, a_p$ have to be substituted during this derivation process. Obviously, this is not possible for $k_\sigma' t_2 < k_1 t_1$. For $k_\sigma' t_2 > k_1 t_1$, there must exist an $i' \in \{1, \ldots, p\}$ with $a_{i'} \in h_\sigma'(a_{i'})$. It follows that

$$a_1 \ldots a_p a_1^g \ldots a_p^g \Longrightarrow_\sigma^{t_2} a_1^2 a_2 \ldots a_p a_1^g \ldots a_p^g$$

which is a contradiction as proved above. In the subcase (a), we are ready. In the subcase (b) let the derivation D be given by a table h_σ' with $k_\sigma' t_2 = k_1 t_1$ and $k_\sigma' < k_1$. Obviously, we get

$$a_1 \ldots a_p a_1^g \ldots a_p^g \Longrightarrow_\sigma^{t_2} a_1^{1+t_2} \ldots a_{k_\sigma'}^{1+t_2} a_{k_\sigma'+1} \ldots a_p a_1^g \ldots a_p^g.$$

This derivation again leads to a word not belonging to L_1, a contradiction.

Finally, we consider case (2). Since $k_1 < k_1'$ where $k_1' \geq 3$ we know that $t_1 > 1$. Let $g = \max\{k_1', \ldots, k_s'\}$ again. We regard the CDk_1ul0L system

$$G_2 = (\{a, x\}, (h, k_1), a^{k_1'-2} x^g a)$$

where $h(a) = \{a^2\}$ and $h(x) = \{x^2\}$. Let L_2 be the language generated by G_2 according to the m'-mode. Then

$$a^{k_1'-2+k_1 t_1-1} x^g a^2$$

is one of the words of second shortest length $g + k_1' + k_1 t_1 - 1$ of $L_2 \in \mathcal{L}_{m'}(k_1, \ldots, k_r, ul0L)$. Obviously, $L_2 \subset a^+ x^+ a^+$, and for every $n \in \mathbf{N}$ there exist n_1, n_2, n_3 such that $a^{n_1} x^{n_2} a^{n_3} \in L_2$.

Assume that L_2 is generated by a $\mathrm{CD}(k_1', \ldots, k_s')ul0L$ system

$$G_2' = (\{a, x\}, (h_1, k_1'), \ldots, (h_s, k_s'), \omega)$$

according to the m-mode. Obviously, G_2' is propagating, $\omega = a^{k_1' - 2} x^g a$, $h(a) \subset a^+$, $h(x) \subset x^+$, and analogously to case (1) we can assume that

$$D : \omega \Longrightarrow_\sigma^{t_2} a^{k_1' - 2 + k_1 t_1 - 1} x^g a^2$$

for some $\sigma \in \{1, \ldots, s\}$. Because of this derivation there must exist a production $a^2 \in h_\sigma'(a)$.

If $k_\sigma' t_2 < k_1 t_1 = k_1' t_2$, then $k_\sigma' < k_1'$. Then from ω, we may derive a word w with $g + k_1' - 1 < |w| < g + k_1' + k_1 t_1 - 1$ which does not belong to L_2, a contradiction.

If $k_\sigma' t_2 \geq k_1 t_1$, then $k_\sigma' \geq k_1'$. Since $\#_a \omega = k_1' - 1$, in the first step of the derivation D the symbol x has to be substituted at least once. It follows that $x \in h_\sigma'(x)$. Since $a^2 \in h_\sigma'(a)$, we conclude that $\omega \Longrightarrow_\sigma^{t_2} a^{k_1' - 2} x^g a^2$. Because of $t_1 > 1$, such a word does not belong to L_2. □

If $k_\rho t_1 = 1$ for all $\rho \in \{1, \ldots, r\}$, we have the situation of Lemma 3.2. If $k_\rho = 1$ for all $\rho \in \{1, \ldots, r\}$ such that there exists $\sigma \in \{1, \ldots, s\}$ with $k_\sigma' = 2$ and $k_\rho t_1 = t_1 = 2t_2 = k_\sigma' t_2$, then the exact status of the comparison is not known.

Corollary 3.1. *Let* $m \in \{t, \geq t \mid t \in \mathbf{N}\}$, $r, s \in \mathbf{N}$, $k_1, \ldots, k_s \in \mathbf{N}$, *such that* $k_\sigma \cdot t \neq 1$ *for ar least one* $\sigma \in \{1, \ldots, s\}$. *Then*

$$\mathcal{L}_1(1^r, ul0L) \subset \mathcal{L}_m(k_1, \ldots, k_s, ul0L).$$

Proof. Case (1) of the proof of Theorem 3.2 shows that $\mathcal{L}_m(k_1, \ldots, k_s, ul0L) \not\subset \mathcal{L}_1(1^r, ul0L)$. By Lemma 3.2, the result follows. □

In Theorem 3.2 we have assumed that $t_1 \neq t_2$. In the following theorems, we consider the case $t_1 = t_2$ with $m \neq m'$.

In Lemma 3.1, if $m = m'$ and the multiset inclusion is given, then we have $\mathcal{L}_m(k_1, \ldots, k_r, ul0L) \subset \mathcal{L}_m(k_1', \ldots, k_s', ul0L)$. If the multiset inclusion is not valid, non-inclusion results follow. More generally, we get the following theorem.

Theorem 3.3. *Let* $t \in \mathbf{N}$, $m = t$ *or* $m = (\geq t)$ *and* $m' = t$ *or* $m' = (\geq t)$. *Furthermore, let* $r, s \in \mathbf{N}$ *and* $k_1, \ldots, k_r, k_1', \ldots, k_s' \in \mathbf{N}$. *If there exists* $k \in \mathbf{N}$ *such that* $\#\{\rho | k_\rho = k, \rho = 1, \ldots, r\} > \#\{\sigma | k_\sigma' = k, \sigma = 1, \ldots, s\}$ *and* $kt \neq 1$, *then we have*

$$\mathcal{L}_m(k_1, \ldots, k_r, ul0L) \not\subset \mathcal{L}_{m'}(k_1', \ldots, k_s', ul0L).$$

Proof. Set

$$p = \#\{\rho | k_\rho = k, \rho = 1, \ldots, r\} \text{ and } q = \#\{\sigma | k_\sigma' = k, \sigma = 1, \ldots, s\}.$$

By the assumptions, $p > q$. Without restricting generality, let

$$k_1 = \ldots = k_p = k \text{ and } k_1' = \ldots = k_q' = k.$$

Since $\mathcal{L}_m(k_1,\ldots,k_p,ul0L) \subset \mathcal{L}_m(k_1,\ldots,k_r,ul0L)$ it suffices to prove

$$\mathcal{L}_m(k^p,ul0L) \not\subset \mathcal{L}_{m'}(k_1',\ldots,k_s',ul0L).$$

Let $g = \max\{k_1',\ldots,k_s'\}$. Consider the $CDk^p ul0L$ system

$$G = (\{a_1,\ldots,a_{kt}\},(h_1,k),\ldots,(h_p,k),a_1^g \ldots a_{kt}^g)$$

where $h_j(a_i) = \{a_i^{p+j}\}$ for all $i \in \{1,\ldots,kt\}$ and $j \in \{1,\ldots,p\}$. Obviously, $L = L_m(G) \subset a_1^+ \ldots a_{kt}^+$. The words

$$a_1^g \ldots a_{kt}^g \text{ and } w_j = a_1^{g+p+j-1} \ldots a_{kt}^{g+p+j-1}, \ j = 1,\ldots,p,$$

belong to L where w_1 is one of the words of second shortest length of L. For other words $w \in L$ there exists $i \in \{1,\ldots,kt\}$ with $\#_{a_i}w \geq g + 2p$.

Suppose that L is generated by a $CD(k_1',\ldots,k_s')ul0L$ system

$$G' = (\Sigma,(h_1',k),\ldots,(h_q',k),(h_{q+1}',k_{q+1}'),\ldots,(h_s',k_s'),\omega)$$

according to the m'-mode. By Lemma 2.1, $\Sigma = \{a_1,\ldots,a_{kt}\}$. Obviously, G' is propagating and $\omega = a_1^g \ldots a_{kt}^g$. Since G' is propagating, all words w_j, $j = 1,\ldots,p$, can only be directly generated, if at all, from ω or from some $w_{j'}$ with $j' < j$. A derivation $w_{j'} \Longrightarrow_\sigma^m w_j$ ($\sigma \in \{1,\ldots,s\}$) would imply $\omega \Longrightarrow_\sigma^m w$ with $g < \#_{a_i}w \leq g + p - 1$ for all $i \in \{1,\ldots,kt\}$, a contradiction. We conclude that $D : \omega \Longrightarrow_\sigma^m w_j$ where we can assume, analogously to the proof of Theorem 3.2, that

$$D : \omega \Longrightarrow_\sigma^t w_j.$$

Obviously, if $k_\sigma' < k$ such a derivation step is not possible. If $k_\sigma' > k$, there must exist an $i \in \{1,\ldots,kt\}$ such that $a_i^{x_i} \in h_\sigma'(a_i)$ with $x_i \leq p$ where at least two occurrences of a_i are substituted in the course of the derivation D. If $1 < x_i \leq p$, by substituting only one occurrence of a_i, we get $\omega \Longrightarrow_\sigma^t w$ with $g < \#_{a_i}w \leq g + p - 1$, but $w \notin L$. Else it is necessary that $\{a_i,a_i^{p+j}\} \subset h_\sigma'(a_i)$ where both the corresponding productions have to be used in D. If an application of $a_i \to a_i^{p+j}$ in D is replaced by an application of $a_i \to a_i$, then $\omega \Longrightarrow_\sigma^t a_1^{g+p+j-1} \ldots a_{i-1}^{g+p+j-1} a_i^g a_{i+1}^{g+p+j-1} \ldots a_{kt}^{g+p+j-1} \notin L$, a contradiction. We conclude that $k_\sigma' = k$.

Thus we know that for all $j \in \{1,\ldots,p\}$, $\omega \Longrightarrow_{\sigma'}^t w_j$ for some $\sigma' \in \{1,\ldots,q\}$. It follows that $a_i^{p+j} \in h_{\sigma'}'(a_i)$ for all $i \in \{1,\ldots,kt\}$. Assume that some w_j and $w_{j'}$, $j,j' \in \{1,\ldots,p\}$, $j \neq j'$, are generated by the same table $h_{\sigma'}$. Then $\{a_i^{p+j},a_i^{p+j'}\} \subset h_{\sigma'}'(a_i)$ for all $i \in \{1,\ldots,kt\}$. It follows that from ω, we may generate $a_1^{g+p+j'-1} a_2^{g+p+j-1} \ldots a_{kt}^{g+p+j-1}$ which does not belong to L, a contradiction. $\square$

By Theorem 3.3 and Lemma 3.1 we get the following corollary.

Corollary 3.2. Let $m \in \{1,2,3,\ldots,\geq 2,\geq 3,\ldots\}$, $r,s \in \mathbb{N}$ with $r \leq s$, and furthermore, let $k_1,\ldots,k_r,k_1',\ldots,k_s' \in \mathbb{N}$ where the multiset $\{k_1,\ldots,k_r\}$ is strictly included in the multiset $\{k_1',\ldots,k_s'\}$. If $m = 1$, assume that there exists a $\sigma \in \{1,\ldots,s\}$ with $k_\sigma' \neq 1$. Then

$$\mathcal{L}_m(k_1,\ldots,k_r,ul0L) \subset \mathcal{L}_m(k_1',\ldots,k_s',ul0L).$$

It remains the case that $t_1 = t_2$, $m \neq m'$ and that the multiset inclusion is given.

Theorem 3.4. *Let $t \in \mathbf{N}$, $t \geq 2$, and $r, s \in \mathbf{N}$, $k_1, \ldots, k_r \in \mathbf{N}$, $k'_1, \ldots, k'_s \in \mathbf{N}$ where the multiset $\{k_1, \ldots, k_r\}$ is included in the multiset $\{k'_1, \ldots, k'_s\}$. Then*

$$\mathcal{L}_t(k_1, \ldots, k_r, ul0L) \not\subset \mathcal{L}_{\geq t}(k'_1, \ldots, k'_s, ul0L).$$

If in addition, there exists $\rho \in \{1, \ldots, r\}$ such that $k'_\sigma \neq \frac{k_\rho(t+1)}{t}$ for all $\sigma \in \{1, \ldots, s\}$, then

$$\mathcal{L}_{\geq t}(k_1, \ldots, k_r, ul0L) \not\subset \mathcal{L}_t(k'_1, \ldots, k'_s, ul0L).$$

Proof. Especially, we choose $k = k_1$. Let $g = \max\{k'_1, \ldots, k'_s\}$. We define a CDkul0L system by $G_t = (\{a\}, (h, k), a^{(g+1)kt})$ with $h(a) = \{\varepsilon\}$. Obviously,

$$L_t(G_t) = \{a^{(g+1)kt}\} \cup \{a^{\nu kt} \mid \nu = 0, \ldots, g\} \text{ and}$$
$$L_{\geq t}(G_t) = \{a^{(g+1)kt}\} \cup \{a^{\nu k} \mid \nu = 0, \ldots, gt\}.$$

First, assume that $L_t(G_t)$ is generated by a $CD(k'_1, \ldots, k'_s)ul0L$ system $G'_t = (\Sigma, (h'_1, k'_1), \ldots, (h'_s, k'_s), \omega)$ according to the $(\geq t)$-mode. By Lemma 2.1 we can assume that $\Sigma = \{a\}$. We conclude that $\omega = a^{(g+1)kt}$ and $h'_\sigma(a) \subset \{\varepsilon, a\}$. For some $\sigma \in \{1, \ldots, s\}$, we have

$$D : a^{(g+1)kt} \Longrightarrow^t_\sigma a^{gkt}.$$

Obviously, $\varepsilon \in h'_\sigma(a)$. If $k'_\sigma < k$, then we get $a^{(g+1)kt} \Longrightarrow a^{(g+1)kt - k'_\sigma t}$ where $(g+1)kt - k'_\sigma t > gkt$, a contradiction. If $k'_\sigma > k$, then we also need $a \in h'_\sigma(a)$. We conclude that $\omega \Longrightarrow^t_\sigma a^{(g+1)kt-1} \notin L_t(G_t)$, a contradiction. This implies that the derivation D is only possible if $k'_\sigma = k$. It follows that the derivation

$$a^{(g+1)kt} \Longrightarrow^t_\sigma a^{gkt} \Longrightarrow_\sigma a^{gkt-k}$$

leads to a word of $L_{\geq t}(G'_t)$ not belonging to $L_t(G_t)$, a contradiction.

Next, assume that the additional condition of the theorem is valid. Without restricting generality, let $k = k_\rho$ and $k'_\sigma \neq \frac{k(t+1)}{t}$ for all $\sigma \in \{1, \ldots, s\}$. Suppose that $L_{\geq t}(G_t)$ is generated according to the t-mode by a $CD(k'_1, \ldots, k'_s)ul0L$ system G'_t as above. Again, we have $\omega = a^{(g+1)kt}$ and $h'_\sigma(a) \subset \{\varepsilon, a\}$. Consider

$$D' : a^{gkt} \Longrightarrow^t_\sigma a^{gkt-k},$$

a derivation from the word of second longest length to the word of third longest length. If $k'_\sigma < k$, we get a contradiction as demonstrated before. If $k'_\sigma \geq k$, then the derivation D' would be only possible if $h'_\sigma(a) = \{\varepsilon, a\}$. It follows that $a^{(g+1)kt} \Longrightarrow a^{(g+1)kt-1}$, a contradiction. This implies that

$$\omega \Longrightarrow^t_\sigma a^{gkt-k}.$$

As above, $a \notin h'_\sigma(a)$. We conclude that

$$k'_\sigma = kt + k$$

which contradicts the additional assumption. Thus, $L_{\geq t}(G_t)$ cannot be generated according to the t-mode. $\square$

Unfortunately, we have not succeeded in proving this theorem for all k'_σ. The equation $k'_\sigma = \frac{k_\rho(t+1)}{t}$ is only possible if t divides k_ρ. If for all $\rho \in \{1, \ldots, r\}$ there exists $\sigma \in \{1, \ldots, s\}$ such that this equation is fulfilled and if the multiset $\{k_1, \ldots, k_r\}$ is included in $\{k'_1, \ldots, k'_s\}$, then we do not know whether $\mathcal{L}_{\geq t}(k_1, \ldots, k_r, ul0L) \not\subset \mathcal{L}_t(k'_1, \ldots, k'_s, ul0L)$ or not. To prove the non-inclusion result also for this case, we tried different examples of propagating systems, but all these examples only worked under the restriction of Theorem 3.4.

Example 3.1. We give some examples for the case $m = 4$, $m' = (\geq 4)$ and vice versa. By Theorem 3.3

$$\mathcal{L}_4(4, 5, 8, ul0L) \not\subset \mathcal{L}_{\geq 4}(4, ul0L) \text{ and } \mathcal{L}_{\geq 4}(4, ul0L) \not\subset \mathcal{L}_4(5, 8, ul0L).$$

By Theorem 3.4, we know that

$$\mathcal{L}_4(4, ul0L) \not\subset \mathcal{L}_{\geq 4}(4, 5, 8, ul0L),$$

but it is open whether $\mathcal{L}_{\geq 4}(4, ul0L) \not\subset \mathcal{L}_4(4, 5, 8, ul0L)$ or not.

Theorem 3.2, Theorem 3.3 and Theorem 3.4 give a nearly full characterization of the families $\mathcal{L}_m(k_1, \ldots, k_r, ul0L)$ in respect to mutual inclusion, but some special cases remain open. For the different theorems, we have used different examples and we could not find a common example for all cases. In the non-uniform case, Theorem 3.1 of [10] gives a full characterization of the corresponding families $\mathcal{L}_m(k_1, \ldots, k_r, l0L)$. In contrast to the corresponding cases here, its proof has been carried out with the help of only one common example for all cases. Since the k-limitation of a $kl0L$ system is imposed seperately on each symbol of the alphabet Σ, the special structure of the example in [10] implies that all its generating systems have to be deterministic. Thus, the possible derivations remain better arranged than in the case considered here.

In [9] we have introduced, for all $r \in \mathbf{N}$, the family $\mathcal{L}_r(uklT0L)$ of languages which are generated by $uklT0L$ systems which possess r tables. Since $\mathcal{L}_1(k^r, ul0L) = \mathcal{L}_r(uklT0L)$, from Corollary 3.2 we derive

Corollary 3.3. *For all $k \in \mathbf{N}$, $k \geq 2$, and $r \in \mathbf{N}$, $\mathcal{L}_r(uklT0L) \subset \mathcal{L}_{r+1}(uklT0L)$.*

Corollary 3.3 equals Theorem 5.1 of [9].

Corollary 3.4. *Let $k, k' \in \mathbf{N}$, $k \neq k'$, $k \neq 1$, $k' \neq 1$. Then any of the eight families of $\mathcal{L}(uklPDT0L)$ is incomparable to any of the eight families of $\mathcal{L}(uk'lPDT0L)$.*

Proof. Consider $\mathcal{L}(ukl0L) = \mathcal{L}_1(k, ul0L)$ and, for all $s \in \mathbf{N}$, $schrL_1(k'^s, ul0L)$. Let $L \in \mathcal{L}_1(k, ul0L)$ with $L \notin \mathcal{L}_1(k'^s, ul0L)$ for all $s \in \mathbf{N}$ be the language of the proof of Theorem 3.3 which is independent of s because of $g = \max\{k'_1, \ldots, k'_s\} = k'$. It follows that $L \notin \mathcal{L}(uk'lT0L) = \bigcup_{s \in \mathbf{N}} \mathcal{L}_1(k'^s, ul0L)$. The system G of the proof of Theorem 3.3 is also deterministic and propagating. Thus we conclude that $L \in \mathcal{L}(uk\ lPD0L)$. Since $\mathcal{L}(uk\ lPD0L) \subset \mathcal{L}_1(k, ul0L) \subset \mathcal{L}(uklT0L)$, the result follows. $\square$

Corollary 3.4 equals Theorem 3.6 in [9]. The proof using Theorem 3.3 given here depends on another example than that of [9].

More generally than Corollary 3.3, we get

Theorem 3.5. *Let $t \in \mathbf{N}$, $m = t$ or $m = (\geq t)$. Furthermore, let $r \in \mathbf{N}$ and $k \in \mathbf{N}$. Then*

$$\mathcal{L}_m^r(\leq k)(CDul0L) \subset \mathcal{L}_m^r(\leq (k+1))(CDul0L)$$

$$\text{and } \mathcal{L}_m^r(\leq k)(CDul0L) \subset \mathcal{L}_m^r(CDul0L) \subset \mathcal{L}_m^{r+1}(CDul0L).$$

If also $kt \neq 1$, *then*

$$\mathcal{L}_m^r(\leq k)(CDul0L) \subset \mathcal{L}_m^{r+1}(\leq k)(CDul0L).$$

Proof. The simple inclusions are obvious by Lemma 3.1 and the definitions. To prove the last strict inclusion, for $k_1 = \ldots = k_{r+1} = k \in \mathbf{N}$ with $kt \neq 1$, we define a $CDk^{r+1}ul0L$ system G according to the proof of Theorem 3.3 where $g = k$. Clearly, $L = L(G) \in \mathcal{L}_m^{r+1}(\leq k)(CDul0L)$. By the construction of the proof of Theorem 3.3, $L \notin \mathcal{L}_m(k'_1, \ldots, k'_r, 10L)$ for all $k'_i \in \mathbf{N}$, $k'_i \leq k$, $i = 1, \ldots, r$. We conclude that $L \notin \mathcal{L}_m^r(\leq k)(CDul0L)$. Thus, the last inclusion is proved.

Similarly, we define a $CD(k+1)^r ul0L$ system G' according to the proof of Theorem 3.3 where $g = k$ again. It follows that $L_m(G') \in \mathcal{L}_m^r(\leq (k+1))(CDul0L)$, but $L_m(G') \notin \mathcal{L}_m^r(\leq k)(CDul0L)$ which proves $\mathcal{L}_m^r(\leq k)(CDul0L) \subset \mathcal{L}_m^r(\leq (k+1))(CDul0L)$ and thus also $\mathcal{L}_m^r(\leq k)(CDul0L) \subset \mathcal{L}_m^r(CDul0L)$.

The proof of $\mathcal{L}_m^r(CDul0L) \subset \mathcal{L}_m^{r+1}(CDul0L)$ cannot be directly carried over from Theorem 3.3 because there does not exist a common g which may be used for all $CD(k'_1, \ldots, k'_r)ul0L$ systems in the same way as in that theorem. Therefore, the construction must be changed a little bit. We define a $CD2^{r+1}ul0L$ system

$$G = (\{a_1, \ldots, a_{2t}\}, (h_1, 2), \ldots, (h_{r+1}, 2), a_1^2 \ldots a_{2t}^2)$$

with $h_\rho(a_i) = \{a_i^{r+1+\rho}\}$ for all $i \in \{1, \ldots, 2t\}$ and $\rho = 1, \ldots, r+1$. Obviously, $L = L_m(G) \subset a_1^+ \ldots a_{2t}^+$. The words

$$a_1^2 \ldots a_{2t}^2 \text{ and } w_\rho = a_1^{r+2+\rho} \ldots a_{2t}^{r+2+\rho}, \; \rho = 1, \ldots, r+1,$$

belong to L. For other words $w \in L$, there exists $i \in \{1, \ldots, 2t\}$ with $\#_{a_i} w \geq 2 + 2(r+1)$. Every word $w \in L$ fulfills $\#_{a_i} = 2$ or $\#_{a_i} \geq r+3$ for all $i \in \{1, \ldots, 2t\}$.

Suppose that, according to the m-mode, L is generated by an arbitrary $CD(k_1, \ldots, k_r)ul0L$ system

$$G' = (\Sigma, (h'_1, k_1), \ldots, (h'_r, k_r), \omega).$$

By Lemma 2.1, $\Sigma = \{a_1, \ldots, a_{2t}\}$. As in the case of the proof of Theorem 3.3, G' is propagating, $\omega = a_1^2 \ldots a_{2t}^2$ and the words w_ρ, $\rho = 1, \ldots, r+1$, can only be generated, if at all, from ω or from some $w_{\rho'}$ with $\rho' < \rho$. Since $1 < \#_{a_i} w_\rho - \#_{a_i} w_{\rho'} \leq r$ for all $i \in \{1, \ldots, 2t\}$, a derivation step $w_{\rho'} \Longrightarrow_\sigma^m w_\rho$ for some $\sigma \in \{1, \ldots, r\}$ would imply $a_i^{x_i} \in h'_\sigma(a_i)$ with $1 < x_i \leq r+1$ for all $i \in \{1, \ldots, 2t\}$. Since $|\omega| \geq 4 > 2$ according to G and using h_1 we may derive a word $w' = a_1^2 a_2^{2+z_2} \ldots a_{2t}^{z_{2t}+2t} \in L$ with $z_2 + \ldots z_{2t} = 2t(r+1)$. Using the table h'_σ above and substituting one occurrence of a_1, we have a derivation $w' \Longrightarrow_\sigma^t w''$ with $2 < \#_{a_1} w'' = 1 + x_1 \leq r+2$, a contradiction to the shape of the words of L. We conclude that for all $\rho \in \{1, \ldots, r+1\}$,

$$D : \omega \Longrightarrow_\sigma^t w_\rho$$

for some $\sigma \in \{1, \ldots, r\}$. Obviously, if $k'_\sigma < k$, such a derivation step is not possible. We consider the case $k'_\sigma \geq k$. By the considerations above we know that $a_i^{x_i} \in h'_\sigma(a_i)$ with $1 < x_i \leq r+1$ is not possible. This implies that the derivation D is only possible if $a_i^{r+1+\rho} \in h'_\sigma(a_i)$ for all $i \in \{1, \ldots, 2t\}$. It follows that the $r + 1$ derivations $\omega \Longrightarrow_\sigma^t w_\rho$ are carried out by at most r different tables h'_σ. Assume that w_ρ and $w_{\rho'}$, $\rho < \rho'$, are generated by the same table $h_{\sigma'}$. Then $\{a_i^{r+1+\rho}, a_i^{r+1+\rho'}\} \subset h'_{\sigma'}(a_i)$ for all $i \in \{1, \ldots, 2t\}$. In the last step of the derivation $\omega \Longrightarrow_{\sigma'}^t w_\rho$ using a non-trivial production $a_i \rightarrow a_i^{r+1+\rho}$ for some i, we replace this production by $a_i \rightarrow a_i^{r+1+\rho'}$ which leads to a derivation $\omega \Longrightarrow_{\sigma'}^t a_1^{r+2+\rho} \ldots a_{i-1}^{r+2+\rho} a_i^{r+2+\rho'} a_{i+1}^{r+2+\rho} \ldots a_{2t}^{r+2+\rho}$ generating a word not belonging to L, a contradiction. $\quad\square$

By Theorem 3.1 we know that $\mathcal{L}_1^r(\leq 1)(CDul0L) = \mathcal{L}(uel0L)$.

The different results show that there exist infinitely many language families which are incomparable to one another. But on the other side we have also recognized that there exist infinitely many infinite hierarchies of language families.

4. Comparison of CDul0L Language Families with Other Language Families

In case of the non-uniformly limited systems, we have shown in [10], Theorem 4.1, that $\mathcal{L}_m(k_1, \ldots, k_r, l0L)$, $\mathcal{L}(k_1 lT0L)$, $\mathcal{L}_m(CDl0L)$, $\mathcal{L}_m^r(CDl0L)$, $\mathcal{L}_m^r(\leq k')(CDl0L)$ (for all $k' \in \mathbf{N}$) and $\mathcal{L}(CDl0L)$ are incomparable with any family of $\mathcal{L}((P)(D)(T)0L)$ or with the families of finite, regular or context-free languages. We begin this section with the comparison of CDul0L language families with the families of T0L languages and with the families of CDl0L languages. The proof of the corresponding results is similar to that of the special case of the comparison of $\mathcal{L}(uklT0L)$ with $\mathcal{L}((P)(D)(T)0L)$ and $\mathcal{L}(kl(P)(D)(T)0L)$ in [9], Theorem 3.1 and Theorem 3.2, but some modifications are necessary.

Theorem 4.1. *For all $m \in \{1, 2, 3, \ldots, \geq 2, \geq 3, \ldots\}$, $r, s, k_1, \ldots, k_r \in \mathbf{N}$ with $k_1 \cdot \ldots \cdot k_r \neq 1$, and $k'_1, \ldots, k'_s \in \mathbf{N}$, any family*

$$\mathcal{L}_m(k_1, \ldots, k_r, ulpd0L), \mathcal{L}(k_1 ulpdT0L), \mathcal{L}_m(CDulpd0L),$$
$$\mathcal{L}_m^r(CDulpd0L), \mathcal{L}_m^r(\leq k')(CDulpd0L),$$

for all $k' \in \mathbf{N}$ and $\mathcal{L}(CDulpd0L)$ is incomparable with any family

$$\mathcal{L}((P)(D)(T)0L), \mathcal{L}_m(k'_1, \ldots, k'_s, lpd0L), \mathcal{L}(k'_1 lpdT0L),$$
$$\mathcal{L}_m(CDlpd0L), \mathcal{L}_m^s(CDlpd0L), \mathcal{L}_m^s(\leq k'')(CDlpd0L)$$

for all $k'' \in \mathbf{N}$ and $\mathcal{L}(CDlpd0L)$, but the families are not disjoint.

Proof. $\{a\}$ is a member of all language families considered. Furthermore, we have $L = \{a^{2^n} | n \in \mathbf{N}_0\} \in \mathcal{L}(PDT0L)$, but L is not a member of any of the CDul0L language families because of the remarks after Corollary 2.1 concerning the difference of the lengths of the words in a CDul0L language. By the definitions we know that

$$\mathcal{L}_m(k_1, ul0L) \subset \mathcal{L}_m(k_1, \ldots, k_r, ul0L) \subset \mathcal{L}_m^r(CDul0L) \subset \mathcal{L}_m(CDul0L) \subset \mathcal{L}(CDul0L),$$

$$\mathcal{L}_m(k_1, ul0L) \subset \mathcal{L}_m^r(\leq k_1)(CDul0L) \subset \mathcal{L}(CDul0L) \quad \text{and}$$

$$\mathcal{L}_1(k_1, ul0L) = \mathcal{L}(k_1 ul0L) \subset \mathcal{L}(k_1 ulT0L) \subset \mathcal{L}(CDul0L).$$

The corresponding inclusions are also valid in the propagating and/or deterministic case and also for non-uniformly limited systems. It remains to prove that there exists

$L' \in \mathcal{L}_m(k_1, ulPD0L)$ with $L' \notin \mathcal{L}(T0L) \cup \mathcal{L}(CDl0L)$ and that there exists $L'' \in \mathcal{L}_m(k_1, lPD0L)$ with $L'' \notin \mathcal{L}(CDul0L)$. We begin with the latter case. Denote $k = k_1$ and consider the CDklPD0L system

$$G_2 = (\{a, b\}, (h, k), a^k b^k) \text{ with } h(a) = a^2 \text{ and } h(b) = b^2.$$

Let $m = t$ or $m = (\geq t)$ for some $t \in \mathbf{N}$. Obviously, $\{a^{k+stk} b^{k+stk} \mid s \in \mathbf{N}_0\} subset L'' = L_m(G_2) \subset a^+ b^+$, and if $w \in L''$, then $\#_a w = \#_b w$. Let $m = t'$ or $m' = (\geq t')$ for some $t' \in \mathbf{N}$. Assume that according to the m'-mode, L'' is generated by a CD$(k_1, \ldots, k_r)$ul0L system

$$G_2'' = (\Sigma, (h_1, k_1), \ldots, (h_r, k_r), \omega).$$

By Lemma 2.1, $\Sigma = \{a, b\}$. Obviously, G_2'' must be propagating. There must exist a table h_ρ, $\rho \in \{1, \ldots, r\}$, with $a^i \in h_\rho(a)$ and $i > 1$. Choose an $s_0 \in \mathbf{N}$ with $k + s_0 tk > k_\rho \cdot t'$. Then a derivation $a^{k+s_0 tk} b^{k+s_0 tk} \Longrightarrow_\rho^{m'} w''$ with $\#_a w'' \neq k + s_0 tk = \#_b w''$ is possible. But this contradicts the shape of the language L''. Thus $L'' \notin \mathcal{L}(CDul0L)$.

Next, for $k \geq 2$ we consider the CD$k$ulPD0L system

$$G_1 = (\{a, b\}, (h, k), ab) \text{ with } h(a) = a^2, h(b) = b^2.$$

Assume that $k = 2^p + q$ for some q with $0 \leq q < k$. Depending on m, the shortest words of $L' = L_m(G_1)$ are among the words

$$ab, a^2 b^2, a^4 b^4, \ldots, a^{2^p} b^{2^p}.$$

Other words of L' which do not possess more than k occurrences of a, are of the form $a^k b^{2^{p+1}+\nu k}$ for appropriate $\nu \in \mathbf{N}$ depending on m. But obviously, there exist infinitely many different such words belonging to L'. Assume that L' is generated according to the m'-mode by a CD$(k_1', \ldots, k_s')$l0L system

$$G_1' = (\{a, b\}, (h_1', k_1'), \ldots, (h_s', k_s'), \omega).$$

It is clear that G_1' must be propagating. Suppose that there exists a $\sigma \in \{1, \ldots, s\}$ and an $i \in \mathbf{N}$, $i > 1$, such that $a \in h_\sigma'(a)$ and $b^i \in h_\sigma'(b)$. It follows that $ab \Longrightarrow_\sigma^{m'} ab^j$ for an appropriate $j \in \mathbf{N}$, $j > 1$. Since $k \neq 1$, $ab^j \notin L'$. Therefore, the infinitely many words of L' of the form $a^k b^{2^{p+1}+\nu k}$ can only be directly generated from words with less than k occurrences of a. But there are only finitely many such words, a contradiction. Thus $L' \notin \mathcal{L}(CDl0L)$.

If we assume that L' is generated by a T0L system, we get the same contradiction. $\square$

By $\mathcal{L}(FIN)$, $\mathcal{L}(REG)$, $\mathcal{L}(CF)$, $\mathcal{L}(CS)$, we denote the families of finite, regular, context-free, or context-sensitive languages, respectively. The following result shows that in case of propagating systems, all generated languages are context-sensitive.

Theorem 4.2. $\mathcal{L}(CDulP0L) \subset \mathcal{L}(CF)$.

Proof. We consider an arbitrary $t \in \mathbf{N}$ and an arbitrary CD$(k_1, \ldots, k_r)$ulP0L system

$$G = (\Sigma, (h_1, k_1), \ldots, (h_r, k_r), \omega).$$

We define a grammar H generating $L_t(G)$ which can be generalized to a grammar for $L_{\geq t}(G)$. The terminal alphabet of H is given by Σ. The nonterminal symbols are given, together with the productions, in the course of the following construction. Let X_0 be the start symbol. The production

$$X_0 \to \omega$$

is only necessary to derive the axiom of G. After an application of a production

$$X_0 \to LT_0^\rho \omega R_1 \text{ for } \rho \in \{1, \dots, r\}$$

begins the simulation of a derivation step $\omega \Longrightarrow_\rho^t \hat{w}$ according to a table h_ρ. If $LT_0^\rho w R_1$ with $w \in L_t(G)$ has already been derived, then

$$D : w \Longrightarrow_\rho^t w'$$

is simulated with the help of the following productions where the non-terminals T_i^ρ, $i = 0, \dots, k$, count the number of substitutions effected in a single derivation step of D while the non-terminals R_j, $j = 1, \dots, t$, count the number of these single derivation steps. First, a single derivation step of D is simulated with the help of the productions

$$T_i^\rho a \to a' T_i^\rho, \ T_i^\rho a \to v T_{i+1}^\rho \text{ for } a \in \Sigma, \ v \in h_\rho(a) \text{ and } i \in \{0, \dots, k_\rho - 1\},$$

where, for every $a \in \Sigma$, a' is a new nonterminal symbol. By these productions, the symbol T_i^ρ passes from left to right in the course of which the index i is incremented by 1 if an application of a production is simulated. If at the right side of the word considered, the symbol $T_{k_\rho}^\rho$ meets R_j, then in this simulation step exactly k_ρ symbols of the word considered have been substituted. By the productions

$$T_{k_\rho}^\rho R_j \to Z^\rho R_{j+1}, \ j \in \{1, \dots, t-1\},$$
$$a Z^\rho \to Z^\rho a, a' Z^\rho \to Z^\rho a \text{ for } a \in \Sigma \text{ and } L Z^\rho \to L T_0^\rho,$$

the $(j+1)$-st derivation step according to h_ρ is initiated. If instead of the situation above, at the right side of the word considered, a symbol T_i^ρ, $i \in \{0, \dots, k_\rho - 1\}$, meets a symbol R_j, then a single derivation step has only been successfully simulated if no symbol a' for $a \in \Sigma$ occurs in the word considered. Thus, by

$$T_i^\rho R_j \to \hat{Z}^\rho R_{j+1}, \ j \in \{1, \dots, t-1\}, \ i \in \{0, \dots, k_\rho - 1\},$$
$$a \hat{Z}^\rho \to \hat{Z}^\rho a \text{ for } a \in \Sigma \text{ and } L \hat{Z}^\rho \to L T_0^\rho,$$

only if there is no such a', a next single derivation step according to h_ρ is initiated. Otherwise, the derivation stops. After the last single derivation step, that is after the simulation of D, T_i^ρ, $i \in \{0, \dots, k_\rho\}$, meets the symbol R_t at the right side of the word considered. Then by a production

$$T_k^\rho R_t \to Z^{\rho'} R_0 \text{ for } \rho' \in \{1, \dots, r\}$$

or

$$T_i^\rho R_t \to \hat{Z}^{\rho'} R_0 \text{ for } \rho' \in \{1, \dots, r\}, \ i \in \{0, \dots, k_\rho - 1\},$$

we can start a further derivation $w' \Longrightarrow_{\rho'}^t w''$, or else by

$$T_k^\rho R_t \to S, \ aS \to Sa, \ a'S \to Sa \text{ for } a \in \Sigma \text{ and } LS \to \varepsilon$$

or

$$T_i^\rho R_t \to \hat{S}, \; a\hat{S} \to \hat{S}a \text{ for } i \in \{0, \dots, k_\rho - 1\}, \; a \in \Sigma \text{ and } L\hat{S} \to \varepsilon,$$

we derive the word $w' \in L_t(G)$. By the construction it is obvious that the grammar generates $L_t(G)$. Since G is propagating, the workspace theorem (see [7], Theorem III.10.1) shows that $L_t(G)$ is context-sensitive. If we want to generate $L_{\geq t}(G)$, then it is clear that we only have to add the productions

$$T_k^\rho R_t \to Z^\rho R_t \text{ and } T_i^\rho R_t \to \hat{Z}^\rho R_t, \; i \in \{0, \dots, k_\rho - 1\}.$$

The language $\{a^{2^n} \mid n \in \mathbf{N}_0\} \in \mathcal{L}(CF)$ cannot be a CDu0L language because of the considerations following Corollary 2.1. Thus the strict inclusion holds. $\square$

It is open if the result of Theorem 4.2 is also valid for arbitrary CDul0L languages.

The following theorem shows that the different CDul0L language families cannot be inserted into the hierarchy $\mathcal{L}(FIN) \subset \mathcal{L}(REG) \subset \mathcal{L}(CF)$ of Chomsky language families. The corresponding result for the families $\mathcal{L}(k'\mathrm{l}\mathrm{T}0\mathrm{L})$ has already been proved in [9], Theorem 3.9, and for the families of CDl0L languages in [10], Theorem 4.2.

Theorem 4.3. *For all*

$$\mathcal{L}_1 \in \{\mathcal{L}(FIN), \mathcal{L}(REG) - \mathcal{L}(FIN), \mathcal{L}(CF) - \mathcal{L}(REG), \mathcal{L}(CF) - \mathcal{L}(CF)\},$$
$$\mathcal{L}_2 \in \{\mathcal{L}_m(k_1, \dots, k_r, ul0L), \mathcal{L}_m^r(CDul0L), \mathcal{L}_m(CDul0L), \mathcal{L}_m^r(\leq k_1)(CDul0L),$$
$$\mathcal{L}(CDul0L), \mathcal{L}(k_1 ul\mathrm{T}0L) \mid m = t \text{ or } m = (\geq t), t \in \mathbf{N}, r \in \mathbf{N}, k_1, \dots, k_r \in \mathbf{N}\}$$

there exist languages $L_1 \in \mathcal{L}_1$ with $L_1 \in \mathcal{L}_2$ (with the exception of the case $\mathcal{L}_1 = \mathcal{L}(CF) - \mathcal{L}(CF)$ together with $\mathcal{L}_2 \in \{\mathcal{L}_m(k_1, \dots, k_r, ul0L), \mathcal{L}(k_1 ul\mathrm{T}0L) \mid k_1 \cdot \dots \cdot k_r = 1\}$) and $L_2 \in \mathcal{L}_1$ with $L_2 \notin \mathcal{L}_2$.

Proof. Let $m = t$ or $m = (\geq t)$ for $t \in \mathbf{N}$. We begin by proving the first half of the statement of the theorem. Because of the inclusions of the proof of Theorem 4.1, it suffices to demonstrate that for every $\mathcal{L}_1$ as above there exists $L_1 \in \mathcal{L}_m(k_1, ul0L)$ with $L_1 \in \mathcal{L}_1$. We set $k = k_1$.

Obviously, $\{b\} \in \mathcal{L}_m(k, ul0L) \cap \mathcal{L}(FIN)$. Furthermore, the CD$k$ul PD0L system $G_1 = (\{b\}, (h_1, k), b^k)$ with $h_1(b) = b^2$ generates

$$L_t(G_1) = b^k(b^{tk})^* \in \mathcal{L}_t(k, ul0L) \cap (\mathcal{L}(REG) - \mathcal{L}(FIN)) \text{ and}$$
$$L_{\geq t}(G_1) = b^k \cup b^{(t+1)k}(b^k)^* \in \mathcal{L}_{\geq t}(k, ul0L) \cap (\mathcal{L}(REG) - \mathcal{L}(FIN)).$$

The language $\{a^{k+n}ba^{k+n} \mid n \in \mathbf{N}_0\} \in \mathcal{L}(CF) - \mathcal{L}(REG)$ is generated, according to any m-mode, by the CD$k$ul PD0L system $G_2 = (\{a, b\}, (h_2, k), a^k ba^k)$ with $h_2(a) = a$ and $h_2(b) = aba$.

For $k \geq 2$, we consider the CD$k$ul PD0L system

$$G_3 = (\{a_1, \dots, a_k\}, (h_3, k), a_1 \dots a_k a_1)$$

with $h_3(a_1) = a_1^2 a_2, \; h_3(a_2) = a_2 a_3, \dots, h_3(a_k) = a_k a_1$. Obviously,

$$L_t(G_3) \cap a_1^+ a_2^+ \dots a_k^+ a_1^+ = \{a_1^{1+tn} \dots a_k^{1+tn} a_1^{1+tn} \mid n \in \mathbf{N}_0\} \text{ and}$$
$$L_{\geq t}(G_3) \cap a_1^+ a_2^+ \dots a_k^+ a_1^+ = \{a_1 \dots a_k a_1\} \cup \{a_1^{t+n} \dots a_k^{t+n} a_1^{t+n} \mid n \in \mathbf{N}\}.$$

By the Lemma of Bar-Hillel, these intersections are not context-free. Since $a_1^+ \dots a_k^+ a_1^+$ is regular, $L_t(G_3)$ and $L_{\geq t}(G_3)$ cannot be context-free, too. On the other side, by Theorem 4.2 we know that $L_t(G_3)$ and $L_{\geq t}(G_3)$ are context-sensitive.

For the second half of the proof it suffices to show that for every family $\mathcal{L}_1$ as above there exists a language of $\mathcal{L}_1$ which cannot be generated by any $CD(k_1, \ldots, k_r)$ul0L system. First we consider the finite language $L_1 = \{b, b^2\}$ and assume that it is generated by a system $G = (\Sigma, (h_1, k_1), \ldots, (h_r, k_r), \omega)$. (Note that for $t \neq 1$ we cannot assume that $\Sigma = \{b\}$.) If $\omega = b$ is the axiom of G then $b \Longrightarrow_\rho^m b^2$ for some ρ, $\rho = 1, \ldots, r$. This means that there exists $t' \in \mathbf{N}$, $t' \geq t$, such that b^2 is derived from b in t' derivation steps according to the underlying uk_ρl0L system. We continue the derivation with further t' steps according to h_ρ such that from the first b of b^2 the derivation is carried out exactly as before. From the second b we try to do the same but depending on k_ρ, it might be possible that some substitutions have to be postponed to later steps. But in any case it is obvious that in any intermediate word of this derivation $b^2 \Longrightarrow_\rho^m w$, there exists at least one symbol arising from the second b. It follows that $|w| \geq 3$, a contradiction. If $\omega = b^2$, then $b^2 \Longrightarrow_\rho^m b$ according to t' steps as before. Similarly as before, it follows that $b \Longrightarrow_\rho^m \varepsilon$, a contradiction.

For the next cases, consider $L_i = \{b, b^2\} \cup A_i$, $i = 2, 3$, where $A_2 = \{b^2\}^+ c^+$ and $A_3 = \{b^n c^n \mid n \in \mathbf{N}, n \geq 2\}$. Obviously, $L_2 \in \mathcal{L}(REG) - \mathcal{L}(FIN)$, $L_3 \in \mathcal{L}(CF) - \mathcal{L}(REG)$. Assume that L_i, $i = 2, 3$, is generated by a $CD(k_1, \ldots, k_r)$ul0L system. By Lemma 2.1 we can assume that $\Sigma = \{b, c\}$. It follows that G is propagating, $\omega = b$ and $h_\rho(b) \subset b^+$, $h_\rho(c) \subset c^+$ for all ρ, $\rho = 1, \ldots, r$. $h_\rho(b) \subset b^+$ implies that $\omega = b$ cannot derive $b^2 c^2 \in L_i$, $i = 2, 3$, a contradiction.

Finally, let $L_4 = \{a^{2^n} \mid n \in \mathbf{N}_0\} \in \mathcal{L}(CF) - \mathcal{L}(CF)$. In Theorem 4.2 we have shown that $L_4 \notin \mathcal{L}(CDul0L)$. □

5. Non-Closure Properties

Theorem 5.1. *All CDul0L language families $\mathcal{L}_2$ of the set of Theorem 4.3 are not closed with respect to (a) union, (b) intersection with regular sets, (c) ε-free iteration, (d) ε-free homomorphism, (e) inverse homomorphism, (f) concatenation.*

Proof. For a derivation according to the m-mode we assume that $m = t$ or $m = (\geq t)$ for some $t \in \mathbf{N}$.

(a) Obviously, $\{b\}$, $\{b^2\} \in \mathcal{L}_2$ for all such language families, but $\{b, b^2\} \notin \mathcal{L}(CDul0L)$ (see proof of Theorem 4.3.).

(b) For an arbitrary $k \in \mathbf{N}$, consider the CDkul0L system $G = (\{b\}, (h, k), b)$ with $h(b) = \{b, b^2\}$. According to any m-mode, $\{b, b^2\} \subset L_m(G)$. But $\{b, b^2\} \in \mathcal{L}(REG)$, and $L_m(G) \cap \{b, b^2\} = \{b, b^2\} \notin \mathcal{L}(CDul0L)$.

(c) We have $\{b^2 c^2\} \in \mathcal{L}_2$ for all $CDul0L$ language families $\mathcal{L}_2$. Let $L = \{b^2 c^2\}^+ \in \mathcal{L}(CDul0L)$. By Lemma 2.1 we can assume that L is generated by a $CD(k_1, \ldots, k_r)$ul0L system $G = (\{b, c\}, (h_1, k_1), \ldots, (h_r, k_r), \omega)$. Obviously, G is propagating. To derive words longer than the axiom $b^2 c^2$, it is necessary that there exists h_ρ, $\rho = 1, \ldots, r$, such that $\beta \in h_\rho(b)$ or $\gamma \in h_\rho(c)$ with $|\beta| \geq 2$ or $|\gamma| \geq 2$. Without loss of generality let $\beta \in h_\rho(b)$. Consider $(b^2 c^2)^{k_\rho t} \in L$. Then there is a derivation step $(b^2 c^2)^{k_\rho t} \Longrightarrow_\rho^t (\beta b c^2)^{k_\rho t}$. Since $|\beta| \geq 2$, $(\beta b c^2)^{k_\rho t} \in L$ implies that b^2 is a prefix of β. Now we consider the also possible derivation step $(b^2 c^2)^{k_\rho t} \Longrightarrow_\rho^t (b\beta c^2)^{k_\rho t}$. We recognize that b^3 is a prefix of the derived word, a contradiction.

(d) For an arbitrary $k \in \mathbf{N}$, consider the CD$k$ul0L system $(\{c, d\}, (h, k), c)$ with $h(c) = d$ and $h(d) = d$ which generates $\{c, d\}$. Let g be an ε-free homomorphism defined by $g(c) = b$, $g(d) = b^2$. Then $g(\{c, d\}) = \{b, b^2\} \notin \mathcal{L}(CDul0L)$.

(e) For any $k \in \mathbf{N}$, the language $\{c, b, b^2\}$ is generated by the CD$k$ul0L system $G = (\{b, c\}, (h, k), c)$ with $h(c) = \{b, b^2\}$ and $h(b) = \{b\}$. Define a homomorphism g by $g(b) = b$. It follows that $g^{-1}(\{c, b, b^2\}) = \{b, b^2\} \notin \mathcal{L}(CDul0L)$.

(f) Obviously, $\{b\}$ and $\{\varepsilon, b\}$ are languages of every CDul0L language family $\mathcal{L}_2$. But $\{b\}\{\varepsilon, b\} = \{b, b^2\} \notin \mathcal{L}(CDul0L)$. □

The theorem proves that all CDul0L language families are anti-AFL's. The case $\mathcal{L}(kulT0L)$ has been proved in [9], Theorem 4.1. The proof given here is shorter than that of [9]. As a simple positive closure result we get at once that all CDul0L language families are closed with respect to mirror image.

References

1. Csuhaj-Varjú, E. and J. Dassow, On Cooperating/Distributed Grammar Systems. *J. Inform. Process. Cybern. EIK* **26**(1990), 49–63.

2. Csuhaj-Varjú, E., J. Dassow and Gh. Păun, Dynamically controlled cooperating/distributed grammar systems. *Information Sciences* **69**(1993), 1–25.

3. Csuhaj-Varjú, E., J. Dassow, J. Kelemen and Gh. Păun, *Grammar Systems: A Grammatical Approach to Distribution and Cooperation.* Gordon and Breach Science Publishers, London, 1994.

4. Dassow, J., Cooperating/distributed grammar systems with hypothesis languages. *J. Expt. Theor. Artif. Intell.* **3**(1991), 11–16.

5. Dassow, J and Gh. Păun, On the succinctness of descriptions of context-free languages by cooperating distributed grammar systems. *Computers and Artificial Intelligence* **10**(1991), 513–527.

6. Dassow, J. and D. Wätjen, On the relations between the degree of synchronization and the degree of nondeterminism in k-limited and uniformly k-limited T0L systems. *Intern. J. Computer Math.* **35**(1990), 69–82.

7. Salomaa, A., *Formal Languages.* Academic Press, New York 1973.

8. Wätjen, D., k-limited 0L Systems and Languages. *J. Inform. Process. Cybern. EIK* **24**(1988), 267–285.

9. Wätjen, D., On k-uniformly-limited T0L Systems and Languages. *J. Inform. Process. Cybern. EIK* **26**(1990), 229–238.

10. Wätjen, D., On Cooperating distributed Limited 0L Systems. *J. Inform. Process. Cybern. EIK* **29**(1993), 129–142.

11. Wätjen, D., On Cooperating distributed Extended Limited 0L Systems. To appear in Intern. J. Computer Math. **61**.

12. Wätjen, D. and E. Unruh, On Extended k-uniformly-limited T0L Systems and Languages. *J. Inform. Process. Cybern. EIK* **26**(1990), 283–299.

Teams in Grammar Systems: Sub-Context-Free Cases

Maurice H. ter BEEK[1]

Department of Computer Science, Leiden University,
P.O. Box 9512, 2300 RA Leiden, The Netherlands
E-mail: mtbeek@wi.leidenuniv.nl

Abstract. The study of teams in grammar systems so far has evolved around teams being formed from a finite number of sets of *context-free* productions. Here, the generative power of teams in grammar systems consisting of regular, linear and metalinear sets of productions is investigated.

For these sub-context-free cases the forming of teams strictly increases the generative power of the underlying grammar systems in many cases.

1. Introduction

When an agent is unable to tackle a complex problem, due to limited capabilities, it seems natural to try to tackle the problem by more than one agent. This results in what they call in *Artificial Intelligence* (AI) a *multi-agent system.* An example of the idea of multi-agent systems in *Distributed AI* are is the so-called *blackboard model of problem solving.*

This model starts with a given problem specified on the blackboard. Several knowledge sources contribute, regulated by a certain strategy, to solving the problem by changing the current state of the blackboard. During the problem solving, the only way in which these knowledge sources can communicate with each other is by using the blackboard. Finally, in the case of successful cooperation, the solution appears on the blackboard.

The link between this blackboard model of problem solving and formal languages was established in [5]. The knowledge sources correspond to grammars, changing the current state of the blackboard corresponds to rewriting the sentential form, the strategy is regulated by so-called derivation modes and the solution is represented by a terminal word. In [3], *cooperating distributed grammar systems*, CD grammars systems for short, have been introduced as a formal realisation of this link. These systems have been investigated intensively. Moreover, they have initiated the development of the theory of grammar systems. This theory has already resulted in the monograph [4], which contains an exhaustive survey of the state of the art in the area until ca. 1992.

Already, several well-motivated enhancements of these CD grammar systems have been introduced, such as *hybrid* CD grammar systems ([15]), *team* CD grammar systems ([13]) and, most recently, *hybrid team* CD grammar systems ([2]). In hybrid CD grammar systems, a more realistic approach to cooperation is considered, by assuming the grammars to have different capabilities. In team CD grammar systems the

---

[1]This research was supported by a scholarship from the Hungarian Ministry of Culture and Education. Moreover, the facilities provided by the Department of General Computer Science of the Eötvös Loránd University and in particular by the Computer and Automation Research Institute of the Hungarian Academy of Sciences were essential.

198

natural idea of work being done in teams is incorporated in the system by grouping several grammars and use them to rewrite in parallel. The teams are either formed automatically or prescribed and several versions of the maximal competence strategy in CD grammar systems are defined. Hybrid team CD grammar systems combine these two ideas.

In [13] it was shown that there are situations in which the forming of teams enlarges the power of the underlying CD grammar system and that they form an AFL when working in the maximal competence strategy. Moreover, in [6] it was proved that teams of size two suffice. In [19] it was shown that there are situations in which exactly the power of programmed grammars is obtained (recursively enumerable when λ-productions are allowed) and in [11], this result was extended to cover more cases of teams in grammar systems. Another surprising result is that the different maximal competence strategies introduced in each of these papers lead to the same generative power. In [2], finally, it was proved that when hybrid teams are allowed the generative power is not enlarged any further. However, every recursively enumerable language can be generated by a hybrid prescribed team CD grammar system with teams of two members. Moreover, concerning syntactic complexity these systems could well be favoured.

Until now, only team CD grammar systems with context-free productions have been considered. Here, the case of a restriction to regular, linear and metalinear productions is studied. For (hybrid) prescribed team CD grammar systems with teams of constant size and regular productions, the team-forming enlarges their generative power beyond the class of regular languages to the class of regular simple matrix grammars. Hence it extends also beyond the power of regular (hybrid) CD grammar systems. The same holds in the case of a restriction to linear productions. These results lead to several corollaries, one of these being that the class generated by (hybrid) prescribed team CD grammar systems with a restriction to regular or linear productions and teams of constant size is incomparable with the class of context-free languages. On the other hand, (hybrid) (team) CD grammar systems with context-free productions include that class, whereas for the metalinear case, incomparability is only conjectured.

In the case of teams of variable size, no more than the class of regular or linear languages can be generated by (hybrid) prescribed team CD grammar systems with only regular or linear productions, respectively. However, when restricted to metalinear productions, the generative power of (hybrid) prescribed team CD grammar systems extends beyond the class of metalinear languages. Moreover, already the class generated by prescribed team CD grammar systems with this restriction to metalinear productions is equal to the class of programmed grammars with the same restriction and appearance checking in the case of the maximal competence strategies. For the other modes of derivation, the results hold only without appearance checking.

2. Preliminaries

In this section, some prerequisites necessary for understanding the sequel are defined. For details and unexplained notions, the reader is referred to [22] for formal languages, [9] for regulated rewriting, [21] for Lindenmayer systems and [4], [7], [8] and [17] and [2] for (variants of) grammar systems.

The set of all non-empty strings over an *alphabet V* is denoted by V^+. If the *empty* *string*, λ, is included, the notation becomes V^*. The *length* of a string x is denoted by $|x|$.

An *inclusion* is denoted by $\subseteq$, whereas a *proper inclusion* is denoted by $\subset$.

Sometimes, the notation for a family of languages contains a λ between the brackets [and]. This means that the statement holds in the case of allowing λ-productions (indicated by the λ inbetween brackets) as well as in the case of a restriction to λ-free productions (thus neglecting the λ inbetween brackets). Also other symbols between brackets must now be understood.

Without definition, the family of regular (REG), linear (LIN), metalinear ($MLIN$), context-free (CF) and context-sensitive (CS) languages are used in the sequel. Their definitions can be found in, e.g., [9]. The same holds for the family of languages generated by ET0L systems ($ET0L$). Finally, also the family of languages generated by [hybrid] CD grammar systems ($[H]CD$) shall not be defined here. However, their definitions can be found in [4] and will become clear in the sequel.

None of the above families of languages will be used in any construction in the proofs. Those families of languages that are used in (some of) the proofs below, are defined next.

An *unordered scattered context grammar with appearance checking* ([14]) is a construct $G = (N, T, S, P, F)$, where N is the set of nonterminals, T is the set of terminals, $S \in N$ is the axiom, $P = \{p_1, p_2, \ldots, p_n\}$ is a finite set of *rules* (rules are of the form $p_i : (\alpha_1, \alpha_2, \ldots, \alpha_{m_i}) \to (\beta_1, \beta_2, \ldots, \beta_{m_i})$, where $\alpha_j \to \beta_j$ are productions over $N \cup T$) and F is a set of occurrences of productions in P, $1 \le i \le n$. For $w, w' \in (N \cup T)^*$ and $1 \le i \le n$ it is said that w directly derives w', written as

$$
\begin{aligned}
w \Longrightarrow w' \quad \text{iff} \quad &w = w_1 \alpha_{i_1} w_2 \alpha_{i_2} \ldots w_m \alpha_{i_m} w_{m+1}, \ w' = w_1 \beta_{i_1} w_2 \beta_{i_2} \ldots w_m \beta_{i_m} w_{m+1}, \\
&p_i : (\alpha_1, \alpha_2, \ldots, \alpha_p) \to (\beta_1, \beta_2, \ldots, \beta_p) \in P, \ (\alpha_{i_1}, \alpha_{i_2}, \ldots, \alpha_{i_m}) \text{ is a} \\
&\text{permutation of a subsequence of } (\alpha_1, \alpha_2, \ldots, \alpha_p), \ w_l \in (N \cup T)^* \\
&\text{and } 1 \le l \le m + 1 \\
&\text{and} \quad \alpha_j \text{ in } \{\alpha_1, \alpha_2, \ldots, \alpha_p\} \text{ and not in } \{\alpha_{i_1}, \alpha_{i_2}, \ldots, \alpha_{i_m}\} \text{ implies that} \\
&\qquad \alpha_j \text{ is not contained in } w \text{ and } \alpha_j \to \beta_j \in F.
\end{aligned}
$$

If $F = \emptyset$, the unordered scattered context grammar is called an *unordered scattered context grammar without appearance checking* and F is omitted from the construct. Moreover, if F contains all occurrences of productions in P, the unordered scattered context grammar is called *with unconditional transfer*. The language generated by G is $L(G) = \{w \in T^* \mid S \Longrightarrow^* w\}$, where $\Longrightarrow^*$ denotes the reflexive and transitive closure of $\Longrightarrow$.

The family of languages generated by unordered scattered context grammars with λ-free context-free productions in P is denoted by USC_{ac} in the case of grammars with appearance checking; when grammars without appearance checking are considered the subscript ac is omitted and when grammars with unconditional transfer are considered the subscript ac is replaced by ut.

A *programmed grammar* ([20]) is a construct $G = (N, T, S, P)$, where N is the set of nonterminals, T is the set of terminals, $S \in N$ is the axiom and P is a finite set of productions of the form $(r : \alpha \to \beta, \sigma(r), \varphi(r))$, where $r : \alpha \to \beta$ is a production over $N \cup T$, labelled by r. Denote by $Lab(P) = \{r \mid (r : \alpha \to \beta, \sigma(r), \varphi(r)) \in P\}$ the set of labels of productions of G. Then $\sigma(r) \subseteq Lab(P)$ is called the *success field* of production r and $\varphi(r) \subseteq Lab(P)$ the *failure field*. For $(r_1 : \alpha \to \beta, \sigma(r_1), \varphi(r_1)) \in P$ and $w, w' \in (N \cup T)^*$ it is said that w directly derives w', written as

$$(w, r_1) \Longrightarrow (w', r_2) \quad \text{iff} \quad w = w_1 \alpha w_2, \; w' = w_1 \beta w_2 \text{ and } r_2 \in \sigma(r_1)$$
$$\text{or} \quad w = w', \; \alpha \to \beta \text{ cannot be applied to } w \text{ and } r_2 \in \varphi(r_1).$$

If the failure fields are empty for every production, the programmed grammar is called *without appearance checking*; otherwise it is called *with appearance checking*. Moreover, if the success field and the failure field coincide for every labeled production, the programmed grammar is called *with unconditional transfer*. The language generated by G is $L(G) = \{w \in T^* \mid (S, r_0) \Longrightarrow^* (w, r_1), \; r_0, r_1 \in Lab(P)\}$, where $\Longrightarrow^*$ denotes the reflexive and transitive closure of $\Longrightarrow$.

The family of languages generated by programmed grammars with λ-free context-free productions in P is denoted by PR_{ac} in the case of grammars with appearance checking; when grammars without appearance checking are considered the subscript ac is omitted and when grammars with unconditional transfer are considered the subscript ac is replaced by ut.

A *matrix grammar with appearance checking* is a construct $G = (N, T, S, M, F)$, where N is the set of nonterminals, T is the set of terminals, $S \in N$ is the axiom, M is a finite set of *matrices* of the form $m : (r_1, r_2, \ldots, r_n)$, where $r_i : \alpha_i \to \beta_i$ are productions over $N \cup T$ and $|\alpha|_N \geq 1, 1 \leq i \leq n$ and F, finally, is a set of occurrences of productions in M. For $w, w' \in (N \cup T)^*$ and $m : (\alpha_1 \to \beta_1, \alpha_2 \to \beta_2, \ldots, \alpha_n \to \beta_n) \in M$ it is said that w directly derives w', written as

$$w \Longrightarrow w' \quad \text{iff} \quad \text{there exist } w_0, w_1, \ldots, w_n \in (N \cup T)^* \text{ such that}$$
$$w_0 = w \text{ and } w_n = w' \text{ and for all } 0 \leq i \leq n - 1$$
$$\text{either} \quad w_{i-1} = w'_{i-1} \alpha_i w''_{i-1} \text{ and } w_i = w'_{i-1} \beta_i w''_{i-1}$$
$$\text{for some } w'_{i-1}, w''_{i-1} \in (N \cup T)^*$$
$$\text{or} \quad \text{the production } \alpha_i \to \beta_i \text{ cannot be applied to } w_{i-1},$$
$$\alpha_i \to \beta_i \in F \text{ and } w_i = w_{i-1}.$$

If $F = \emptyset$, the matrix grammar is called a *matrix grammar without appearance checking* and F is omitted from the construct. Moreover, if F contains all occurrences of productions in M, the matrix grammar is called *with unconditional transfer*. The language generated by G is $L(G) = \{w \in T^* \mid S \Longrightarrow^* w\}$, where $\Longrightarrow^*$ denotes the reflexive and transitive closure of $\Longrightarrow$.

The family of languages generated by matrix grammars with λ-free context-free productions in M is denoted by MAT_{ac} in the case of grammars with appearance checking; when grammars without appearance checking are considered the subscript ac is omitted and when grammars with unconditional transfer are considered the subscript ac is replaced by ut.

A *simple matrix grammar* ([12]) of *degree* n, $n \geq 1$, is a construct $G = (N_1, N_2, \ldots, N_n, T, S, M)$, where $N_1, N_2, \ldots, N_n$ (sets of nonterminals) and T (the set of terminals) are pairwise disjoint alphabets, $S \notin (\bigcup_{i=1}^{n} N_i \cup T)$ is the start symbol and M is a finite set of matrices, each of one of the following forms.

(a) $(S \to x)$, for $x \in T^*$,

(b) $(S \to A_1 A_2 \ldots A_n)$, for $A_i \in N_i$ and $1 \le i \le n$ or

(c) $(A_1 \to x_1, A_2 \to x_2, \ldots, A_n \to x_n)$, for $A_i \in N_i$, $x_i \in (N_i \cup T)^*$ and $|x_i|_{N_i} = |x_j|_{N_j}$ for all $1 \le i, j \le n$.

For $w, w' \in (\bigcup_{i=1}^{n} N_i \cup T \cup \{S\})^*$ it is said that w directly derives w', written as

$$
\begin{aligned}
w \Longrightarrow w' \quad &\text{iff} \quad w = S \text{ and } (S \to w') \in M \\
&\text{or} \quad w = v_1 A_1 w_1 v_2 A_2 w_2 \ldots v_n A_n w_n, \ w' = v_1 x_1 w_1 v_2 x_2 w_2 \ldots v_n x_n w_n, \\
&\qquad A_i \in N_i, \ v_i \in T^*, \ w_i, x_i \in (N_i \cup T)^*, \ 1 \le i \le n \text{ and} \\
&\qquad (A_1 \to x_1, A_2 \to x_2, \ldots, A_n \to x_n) \in M.
\end{aligned}
$$

The language generated by G is $L(G) = \{w \in T^* \mid S \Longrightarrow^* w\}$, where $\Longrightarrow^*$ denotes the reflexive and transitive closure of $\Longrightarrow$.

A simple matrix grammar is called regular, linear, context-free or λ-free iff the productions appearing in matrices of type (c) in M are all regular, linear, context-free or λ-free, respectively. The family of languages generated by λ-free context-free simple matrix grammars of degree n, $n \ge 1$, is denoted by $SM(n)$. Furthermore, denote $SM = \bigcup_{n \ge 1} SM(n)$ and likewise for the other cases.

For all generative devices mentioned above, only the notation in the case of λ-free context-free productions was given. However, when the productions are of type X, for $X \in \{REG, LIN, MLIN\}$, a subscript X is added to the notation. Moreover, when there is no restriction to λ-free productions a superscript λ is added to the notation.

3. Hybrid Prescribed Teams of Grammars

Definition 1. Let N and T be two disjoint alphabets. A *production* over (N, T) is a pair $(A, x) \in N \times (N \cup T)^*$. Usually, $A \to x$ shall be written instead of (A, x). If $x \ne \lambda$, then $A \to x$ is called a λ-free production. A *team* over (N, T) is a multiset of sets of productions over (N, T). The sets of productions occurring in a team shall be referred to as *components*.

A team rewrites a string in the following manner.

Definition 2. Let N and T be two disjoint alphabets. Let Q be a team over (N, T) and $x, y \in (N \cup T)^*$. Then x is rewritten by Q into y, written as

$$
\begin{aligned}
x \Longrightarrow_Q y \quad &\text{iff} \quad x = x_1 A_1 x_2 A_2 \ldots x_n A_n x_{n+1}, \ y = x_1 y_1 x_2 y_2 \ldots x_n y_n x_{n+1}, \\
&\qquad x_i \in (N \cup T)^*, \ 1 \le i \le n+1, \ A_j \to y_j \in P_j, \ 1 \le j \le n \text{ and} \\
&\qquad Q = \{P_1, P_2, \ldots, P_n\}.
\end{aligned}
$$

A derivation step of a team thus consists of choosing a production from each component of this team and apply these in parallel on the string to be rewritten. If Q is a singleton team, i.e. $Q = \{P\}$ for some set of productions P, then $x \Longrightarrow_P y$ shall be written instead of $x \Longrightarrow_{\{P\}} y$. It is clear that in that case only one symbol in x is rewritten, using a production from P.

So-called modes of derivation are used to prescribe halting requirements on the use of a team. These modes can be divided into three groups. Firstly, mode $*$ has *no restrictions* whatsoever. Any number of derivation steps is allowed. Secondly, modes $\le k$, $= k$ and $\ge k$ restrict the number of derivation steps to *at most, exactly* and *at least k* derivation steps, respectively. Thirdly, modes t_0, t_1 f derivation steps. All three prescribe a slightly different condition which needs to be fulfilled before a team is considered to have successfully worked in that mode. In the case of mode t_0 the work of a team ends successfully when *no further derivation step can be done as a team*, in the case of mode t_1 the work ends when *no component of the team can apply one of its productions any longer* and in mode t_2, finally, the work of a team ends when *there is at least one component that can no longer apply one of its productions.*

Definition 3. Let $Q = \{P_1, P_2, \ldots, P_n\}$ be a team over (N, T) and let $f \in \{\leq k, = k, \geq k \mid k \geq 1\} \cup \{*, t_0, t_1, t_2\}$ be a *mode (of derivation)*. Furthermore, let $x, y, z \in (N \cup T)^*$ and $k \in \mathbf{N}$. Then x is rewritten by Q, working in mode f, into y, written as

$$x \Longrightarrow_Q^{\leq k} y \quad \text{iff} \quad x \Longrightarrow_Q^{k'} y \text{ for some } k' \leq k,$$

$$x \Longrightarrow_Q^{=k} y \quad \text{iff} \quad x \Longrightarrow_Q^{k} y,$$

$$x \Longrightarrow_Q^{\geq k} y \quad \text{iff} \quad x \Longrightarrow_Q^{k'} y \text{ for some } k' \geq k,$$

$$x \Longrightarrow_Q^{*} y \quad \text{iff} \quad x \Longrightarrow_Q^{k} y \text{ for some } k,$$

$$x \Longrightarrow_Q^{t_0} y \quad \text{iff} \quad x \Longrightarrow_Q^{*} y \text{ and there is no } z \text{ such that } y \Longrightarrow_Q z,$$

$$x \Longrightarrow_Q^{t_1} y \quad \text{iff} \quad x \Longrightarrow_Q^{*} y \text{ and for no component } P_i \in Q \text{ and no } z$$
$$\text{there is a derivation } y \Longrightarrow_{P_i} z \text{ and}$$

$$x \Longrightarrow_Q^{t_2} y \quad \text{iff} \quad x \Longrightarrow_Q^{*} y \text{ and there is a component } P_i \in Q$$
$$\text{for which there is no derivation } y \Longrightarrow_{P_i} z.$$

The three variants of the t-mode of derivation first appeared in [11] (t_0), [13] (t_1) and [19] (t_2); the other modes of derivation are the natural extension of the modes in CD grammar systems (see [4]) to teams of grammars.

Now the definition of hybrid prescribed teams in the theory of grammar systems from [2] can be introduced.

Definition 4. A *hybrid prescribed team CD grammar system* is a construct

$$\Gamma = (N, T, S, P_1, P_2, \ldots, P_n, (Q_1, f_1), (Q_2, f_2), \ldots, (Q_m, f_m)),$$

where N is the set of nonterminals, T is the set of terminals, with $N \cap T = \emptyset$, $S \in N$ is the axiom, $P_1, P_2, \ldots, P_n$ are sets of productions over (N, T), $Q_1, Q_2, \ldots, Q_m$ are teams with components from $P_1, P_2, \ldots, P_n$ and $f_1, f_2, \ldots, f_m$ are modes of derivation.

This definition is more general than those from [13] and [19]. If, in this construct, $f_i = f_j$ for all $1 \leq i, j \leq m$, the definition of a prescribed team CD grammar system as in [19] is obtained.

Note that in this definition, there is no restriction on the size of a team. In the original definition of teams in [13], however, they are of constant size. A natural number $s \geq 1$ is given and the teams are formed such that the number of components of every team is exactly s; these teams are called of constant size s. Moreover, in that definition the teams are not prescribed, but each set of components can be a team (so-called *free* teams) as long as the size restriction is fulfilled.

It is now clear that one can differentiate between the following four variants of teams in the theory of grammar systems. For all four, hybridity is another possibility.

Free teams of constant size: this is the original definition of [13], as explained above.

Free teams of variable size: each subset of components can be a team.

Prescribed teams of constant size: all prescribed teams consist of the same number of components.

Prescribed teams of variable size: these are defined in Definition 4.

In the case of teams of constant size, whether prescribed or free, a finite set of axioms $W \subseteq (N \cup T)^*$, with only one string in it containing nonterminals, is allowed. This is done since otherwise in the case of λ-free productions no string shorter than s could be generated. In the case of free teams with teams of constant size, the construct thus becomes $\Gamma = (N, T, W, P_1, P_2, \ldots, P_n)$. The modifications in the other cases are obvious.

Definition 5. Consider a hybrid prescribed team CD grammar system Γ as in Definition 4. Then the language generated by Γ is

$$L(\Gamma) = \{z \in T^* \mid S \Longrightarrow_{Q_{i_1}}^{f_{i_1}} w_{i_1} \Longrightarrow_{Q_{i_2}}^{f_{i_2}} \cdots \Longrightarrow_{Q_{i_p}}^{f_{i_p}} w_{i_p} = z, \ 1 \le i_j \le m, \ 1 \le j \le p\}.$$

When dealing with a language generated by teams of constant size, the notation of Definition 5 is modified to $L(\Gamma, s)$. When the teams are not hybrid, the mode of derivation is added as a subscript to this notation.

The family of languages generated by CD grammar systems with hybrid prescribed teams of variable size and λ-free productions of type X is denoted by HPT_*CD_X. When teams are of constant size s, the $*$ in the notation is replaced by s and when there is no restriction to λ-free productions, λ is added to the notation as a superscript. When dealing with context-free productions this need not be specified and the subscript is thus omitted. Finally, when the teams are not hybrid (prescribed) the H (P) in the notation is omitted.

Some relations concerning the generative power of several of these grammar systems discussed above are given next. A more complete overview can be found in [1]. In the first paper on teams in grammar systems, [13], it was proved that, for $f \in \{=1, \ge 1, *\} \cup \{\le k \mid k \ge 1\}$,

$$CF = T_1CD(f) \subset T_2CD(f) \text{ and}$$
$$ET0L = T_1CD(t) \subset T_2CD(t_1).$$

These relations prove that there are modes of derivation for which the forming of teams strictly increases the power of CD grammar systems, since $CD(t) = ET0L$ and $CF = CD(=1) = CD(\ge 1) = CD(*) = CD(\le k)$ for a $k \ge 1$ were already known to hold (see, e.g., [4]). In [6] it was proved that teams of size two suffice, i.e. for $s \ge 2$

$$T_sCD(t_1) \subseteq T_2CD(t_1).$$

The main results of [19] are, for $s \geq 2$, $f \in \{*\} \cup \{\leq k, = k, \geq k \mid k \geq 1\}$ and $g \in \{t_1, t_2\}$,

$$PR^{[\lambda]} = PT_sCD^{[\lambda]}(f) = PT_*CD^{[\lambda]}(f) \text{ and}$$
$$PR_{ac}^{[\lambda]} = T_sCD^{[\lambda]}(g) = PT_sCD^{[\lambda]}(g) = PT_*CD^{[\lambda]}(g)$$

and the main result of [11] is, for $s \geq 2$ and $h \in \{t_0, t_1\}$,

$$MAT_{ac}^{[\lambda]} = T_sCD^{[\lambda]}(h) = PT_sCD^{[\lambda]}(h) = PT_*CD^{[\lambda]}(h) = T_*CD^{[\lambda]}(h).$$

In [2] it was proved that $HPT_*CD \subseteq MAT_{ac}$ which, together with the results stated above, leads to the following relations for hybrid teams. For $s \geq 2$

$$PR_{ac}^{[\lambda]} = HPT_sCD^{[\lambda]} = HPT_*CD^{[\lambda]}.$$

4. The Sub-Context-Free Cases

In the previous section, results concerning (hybrid) (prescribed) team CD grammar systems with context-free productions were presented. In this section some results concerning a restriction to regular, linear or metalinear types of productions will be presented.

Recall the fact that, whether free or prescribed, teams with constant size are allowed to have a string axiom, whereas teams of variable size always have a single start symbol.

4.1. The Regular and the Linear Cases

First, a result for the regular case of prescribed team CD grammar systems with constant team-size 1 is presented.

Lemma 1. *For $f \in \{*, t\} \cup \{\leq k, = k, \geq k \mid k \geq 1\}$ and $g \in \{= k, \geq k \mid k \geq 2\} \cup \{t_0, t_1, t_2\}$*

$$REG = CD_{REG}(f) \subset PT_1CD_{REG}(g).$$

Proof. The equality is proved in [4] and it is obvious that $CD_{REG}(f) \subseteq PT_1CD_{REG}(g)$ for $f \in \{*, t\} \cup \{\leq k, = k, \geq k \mid k \geq 1\}$ and $g \in \{*, t_0, t_1, t_2\} \cup \{\leq k, = k, \geq k \mid k \geq 1\}$. Furthermore, the prescribed team CD grammar system, with teams of constant size 1,

$$\Gamma_1 = (\{A_0, A_0', A_1, A_1', \ldots, A_{k-2}', B, B'\}, \{a, b\}, AB, P_1, P_2, P_3, \{P_1\}, \{P_2\}, \{P_3\}),$$

where

$$\begin{aligned} P_1 &= \{A_0 \to A_1, A_1 \to A_2, \ldots, A_{k-2} \to aA_0', B \to bB'\}, \\ P_2 &= \{A_0' \to A_1', A_1' \to A_2', \ldots, A_{k-2}' \to A_0, B' \to B\} \text{ and} \\ P_3 &= \{A \to A_1, A_1 \to A_2, \ldots, A_{k-2} \to a, B \to b\}. \end{aligned}$$

contains only regular productions and it generates $L_f(\Gamma_1, 1) = \{a^n b^n \mid n \geq 1\} \in PT_1CD_{REG}(f) \setminus REG$ for $f \in \{= k, \geq k \mid k \geq 2\} \cup \{t_0, t_1, t_2\}$. □

Hence already a prescribed team CD grammar system with only regular productions and teams of size 1 can generate more than the class of regular languages and more than a CD grammar system with only regular productions. The next lemma states that also in the linear case the prescribed team CD grammar systems with teams of any constant size can generate more than the class of linear languages as well as more than CD grammar systems with only linear productions.

Lemma 2. *For* $f \in \{*, t\} \cup \{\leq k, = k, \geq k \mid k \geq 1\}$, $g \in \{= k, \geq k \mid k \geq 2\} \cup \{t_0, t_1, t_2\}$ *and* $g' \in \{*, t_0, t_1, t_2\} \cup \{\leq k, = k, \geq k \mid k \geq 1\}$

$$LIN = CD_{LIN}(f) \subset PT_1 CD_{LIN}(g) \subseteq PT_1 CD(g') = CD(f).$$

Proof. The first equality can be proved with a similar proof as for the regular case (see Lemma 1) and $CD_{LIN}(f) \subseteq PT_1 CD_{LIN}(g)$ is obvious, for $f \in \{*, t\} \cup \{\leq k, = k, \geq k \mid k \geq 1\}$ and $g \in \{*, t_0, t_1, t_2\} \cup \{\leq k, = k, \geq k \mid k \geq 1\}$. Furthermore, the prescribed team CD grammar system, with teams of constant size 1,

$$\Gamma_2 = (\{A_0, A_0', A_1, A_1', \dots, A_{k-2}', B, B'\}, \{a, b, c\}, AB, P_1, P_2, P_3, \{P_1\}, \{P_2\}, \{P_3\}),$$

where

$$\begin{aligned}
P_1 &= \{A_0 \to A_1, A_1 \to A_2, \dots, A_{k-2} \to aA_0'b, B \to cB'\}, \\
P_2 &= \{A_0' \to A_1', A_1' \to A_2', \dots, A_{k-2}' \to A_0, B' \to B\} \text{ and} \\
P_3 &= \{A \to A_1, A_1 \to A_2, \dots, A_{k-2} \to ab, B \to c\}.
\end{aligned}$$

contains only linear productions and it generates $L_f(\Gamma_2, 1) = \{a^n b^n c^n \mid n \geq 1\} \in PT_1 CD_{LIN}(f) \setminus LIN$ for $f \in \{= k, \geq k \mid k \geq 2\} \cup \{t_0, t_1, t_2\}$. The last inclusion in the statement of the lemma is obvious and to prove the last equality, only the inclusion $PT_1 CD(g') \subseteq CD(f)$ is not obvious. To prove this inclusion, all teams of size 1 become a component of the CD grammar system and a component $\{S \to S, S \to w \mid w \in W\}$, S being the axiom of the CD grammar system and W being the finite set of string axioms of the prescribed team CD grammar system with teams of constant size, is added. The mode of derivation remains the same, except that for t_0, t_1 and t_2 it becomes t. $\square$

These two results lead to the following corollary for hybrid prescribed team CD grammar systems with teams of constant size 1 and only regular or linear productions.

Corollary 1.

$$REG = HCD_{REG} \subset HPT_1 CD_{REG} \subseteq HPT_1 CD_{LIN} \text{ and}$$
$$LIN = HCD_{LIN} \subset HPT_1 CD_{LIN} \subseteq HPT_1 CD = HCD.$$

Proof. The equality $REG = HCD_{REG}$ is proved in [15], a similar proof can prove this equality for the linear case. The inclusions of hybrid CD grammar systems with only regular or linear productions in hybrid prescribed team CD grammar systems with teams of constant size 1 and only regular or linear productions, respectively, are obvious. Moreover, Lemma 1 and 2 prove their properness. The remaining two inclusions are also obvious and the last equality can be proved with a similar construction as for the proof of $PT_1 CD(g') = CD(f)$ in Lemma 2. $\square$

Hence also hybrid prescribed team CD grammar systems with only regular (linear) productions and teams of size 1 can generate more than the class of regular (linear) languages as well as more than hybrid CD grammar systems with only regular (linear) productions can.

In fairness, it must be noted that all proper inclusions proved in this section so far are due to the existence of a "non-linear" axiom, not to the very use of teams.

In fact, the following holds. To be more precise, denote $[H]P_nT_1CD_X(f)$ for the class of [hybrid] prescribed team CD grammar systems with at most n occurrences of nonterminals in the string axiom, teams of size 1, only components of type X and working in mode f (omitted in the hybrid case).

Theorem 1. *For $n \geq 1$, $X \in \{REG, LIN\}$ and $f \in \{t_0, t_1, t_2\} \cup \{= k, \geq k \mid k \geq 2\}$*

$$HP_nT_1CD_X = P_nT_1CD_X(f) = SM_X(n) =$$
$$SM_X^\lambda(n) = P_nT_1CD_X^\lambda(f) = HP_nT_1CD_X^\lambda.$$

Proof. In [4], so-called extended CD' grammar systems are defined. In the terminology of this paper, these systems are CD grammar systems with a string axiom. In [10] these extended CD' grammar systems with only regular productions, at most n nonterminals in the string axiom and working in mode $f \in \{t\} \cup \{= k, \geq k \mid k \geq 2\}$ $(E_nCD'_{REG}(f))$ are proved to be equal to the regular simple matrix grammars of degree n.

Clearly, $E_nCD'_{REG}(f) = P_nT_1CD_{REG}(f)$ for $f \in \{*\} \cup \{\leq k, = k, \geq k \mid k \geq 1\}$ and $E_nCD'_{REG}(t) = P_nT_1CD_{REG}(g)$ for $g \in \{t_0, t_1, t_2\}$. When observing the proof, it can be seen that it holds for the linear case as well. Moreover, the construction can easily be modified to hold for the hybrid case as well. (One just has to code all nonterminals, thus indicating which mode is currently being simulated.) Finally, $SM_X^\lambda(n) = SM_X(n)$ for $X \in \{REG, LIN\}$ was proved in [16] and the proof thus holds for both the case of forbidding and the case of allowing λ-productions. $\square$

This theorem has some interesting corollaries, since the families of regular and linear simple matrix grammars are well-investigated. A survey of simple matrix grammars can be found in [9], where the proofs of the results corresponding to the coming corollaries can be found.

Corollary 2. *For $n \geq 1$ and $f \in \{= k, \geq k \mid k \geq 2\} \cup \{t_0, t_1, t_2\}$*

$$P_nT_1CD_{REG}(f) = HP_nT_1CD_{REG} \subset P_nT_1CD_{LIN}(f) = HP_nT_1CD_{LIN}.$$

Corollary 3. *The number of nonterminal occurrences in the axioms of prescribed team CD grammar systems, with teams of size 1 and only regular or only linear productions, defines an infinite hierarchy of languages generated in all modes $f \in \{= k, \geq k \mid k \geq 2\} \cup \{t_0, t_1, t_2\}$. The same holds for the hybrid versions of these families of languages.*

Corollary 4. *For $s \geq 1$ and $f \in \{= k, \geq k \mid k \geq 2\} \cup \{t_0, t_1, t_2\}$*

$$[H]PT_sCD_{REG}(f) \text{ is incomparable with } LIN \text{ and}$$
$$[H]PT_sCD_{LIN}(f) \text{ is incomparable with } CF.$$

The question is now what can be said about the generative power of (hybrid) prescribed team CD grammar systems with only regular or linear productions and teams of constant size s, for $s \geq 2$. From the results presented in Section 3, a comparison with the programmed (or matrix) grammars with only regular or linear productions seems natural. These, however, are equal to the classes of regular and linear languages, respectively, even when appearance checking is used. The proofs for these equalities in the regular case can be found in [9] and the proofs for the linear case can be proved similarly. Hence the inclusions $PR_{REG} = PR_{REG,ac} \subset PT_1CD_{REG}(f)$ and $PR_{LIN} = PR_{LIN,ac} \subset PT_1CD_{REG}(f)$, for $f \in \{=k, \geq k \mid k \geq 2\} \cup \{t_0, t_1, t_2\}$, are obvious.

Moreover, the equalities between the programmed grammars and matrix grammars hold in the regular and linear case as well, even with appearance checking. Again, proofs of these equalities can be found in [9]. Note that these proper inclusions hold already for teams of constant size 1. Thus to find a good comparison for the generative power of (hybrid) prescribed team CD grammar systems with only regular or linear productions and teams of constant size s, $s \geq 2$, remains an open problem.

After these results for (hybrid) prescribed team CD grammar systems with teams of constant size, some results for the case of teams of variable size are presented next. The difference is the use of a single nonterminal as axiom in the case of teams of variable size, whereas in the case of teams with constant size a finite set of string axioms, with only one of them containing nonterminals, is used.

Lemma 3. *For $f \in \{*, t_0, t_1, t_2\} \cup \{\leq k, = k, \geq k \mid k \geq 1\}$*

$$HPT_*CD_{REG} = PT_*CD_{REG}(f) = REG \text{ and}$$
$$HPT_*CD_{LIN} = PT_*CD_{LIN}(f) = LIN.$$

Proof. For teams with more than one component at least two nonterminals must be present in a sentential form, in order to use that team to rewrite that sentential form. This is in contradiction with the facts that every $\Gamma \in \{HPT_*CD_{REG}, PT_*CD_{REG}(f), HPT_*CD_{LIN}, PT_*CD_{LIN}(f) \mid f \in \{*, t_0, t_1, t_2\} \cup \{\leq k, = k, \geq k \mid k \geq 1\}\}$ has a single nonterminal as axiom and regular or linear productions, respectively. For teams of size one, the equality with (hybrid) CD grammar systems is obvious for the regular case as well as for the linear case, keeping in mind the use of a single nonterminal as axiom. From [4] ([15]) it is known that (hybrid) CD grammar systems with only regular productions do not generate more than the class of regular languages and similar proofs can be used to prove these results for the linear case as well. □

4.2. The Metalinear Case

It is obvious that the (hybrid) prescribed team CD grammar systems with teams of variable size and metalinear productions are able to generate languages beyond the class of regular or linear languages. What's more, the following lemma holds.

Lemma 4. *For $f \in \{*, t\} \cup \{\leq k, = k, \geq k \mid k \geq 1\}$ and $g \in \{=1, \geq 1, *, t_0, t_1, t_2\} \cup \{\leq k \mid k \geq 1\}\}$*

$$MLIN = CD_{MLIN}(f) = HCD_{MLIN} \subset PT_*CD_{MLIN}(g).$$

Proof. The first two equalities can be proved by the proofs of $REG = CD_{REG}(f)$ ([4]) and $REG = HCD_{REG}$ ([15]), with the obvious modifications. Furthermore, it is clear that $MLIN \subseteq PT_*CD_{MLIN}(f)$, for $f \in \{*, t_0, t_1, t_2\} \cup \{\leq k, = k, \geq k \mid k \geq 1\}\}$. Moreover, the prescribed team CD grammar system

$$\Gamma_3 = (\{S, A, B, C\}, \{a, b, c\}, S, P_1, P_2, \dots, P_7, \{P_1\}, \{P_2, P_3, P_4\}, \{P_5, P_6, P_7\}),$$

with teams of variable size and the metalinear productions

$$P_1 = \{S \rightarrow ABC\}, \qquad P_2 = \{A \rightarrow aA\}, \qquad P_5 = \{A \rightarrow a\},$$
$$P_3 = \{B \rightarrow bB\}, \qquad P_6 = \{B \rightarrow b\},$$
$$P_4 = \{C \rightarrow cC\} \text{ and } \quad P_7 = \{C \rightarrow c\},$$

generates $L(\Gamma_3) = \{a^n b^n c^n \mid n \geq 1\} \in PT_*CD_{MLIN}(g) \setminus CF$, for $g \in \{= 1, \geq 1, *, t_0, t_1, t_2\} \cup \{\leq k \mid k \geq 1\}\}$. Since it is known that $\{a^n b^n c^n \mid n \geq 1\} \in CS \setminus CF$ and from the Chomsky hierarchy that $MLIN \subset CF \subset CS$, the inclusion is proper indeed. $\qquad\square$

Hence even languages beyond the class of metalinear languages can be generated already by a prescribed team CD grammar system with teams of variable size and metalinear productions for some modes of derivation. For prescribed team CD grammar systems with teams of constant size, no version containing only metalinear productions is defined due to the string axiom they already possess. Note, however, that the lemma above does not cover all modes of derivation, which Lemma 7 below will.

The following theorem is obtained by combining the results of the previous section and the results obtained so far in this section.

Theorem 2. *For* $f \in \{*, t_0, t_1, t_2\} \cup \{\leq k, = k, \geq k \mid k \geq 1\}$ *and* $g \in \{= 1, \geq 1, *, t_0, t_1, t_2\} \cup \{\leq k \mid k \geq 1\}$

$$PT_*CD_{REG}(f) = HPT_*CD_{REG} \subset PT_*CD_{LIN}(f) = HPT_*CD_{LIN} \subset$$
$$MLIN \subset PT_*CD_{MLIN}(g) \subseteq HPT_*CD_{MLIN}.$$

The question is now how far these (hybrid) prescribed team CD grammar systems with teams of variable size and metalinear productions extend beyond the class of metalinear languages. Before presenting a theorem that answers this question, two lemmas are needed.

The proofs of these lemmas are given because the metalinear case is not covered in [9]. Moreover, since the proofs are based on the proofs for the context-free case in [9], they explain the techniques that are used to prove those frequently used results of the next lemmas in the context-free case.

Lemma 5.

$$USC^{[\lambda]}_{MLIN} \subseteq PR^{[\lambda]}_{MLIN} \text{ and } USC^{[\lambda]}_{MLIN,ac} \subseteq PR^{[\lambda]}_{MLIN,ac}.$$

Proof. Only the second statement is proved here (for the λ-free case), the others can be proved in a similar way. Consider an unordered scattered context grammar

$$G = (N, T, S, P, F)$$

with appearance checking and only metalinear productions. Define the homomorphism h from $(N \cup T)^*$ into $(\{A' \mid A \in N\} \cup T)^*$ by

$$h(a) = a \text{ for } a \in T \text{ and } h(A) = A' \text{ for } A \in N.$$

Next, for a rule $r : (\alpha_1, \alpha_2, \ldots, \alpha_n) \rightarrow (\beta_1, \beta_2, \ldots, \beta_n) \in P$, denote $h(\beta_1 \beta_2 \ldots \beta_n) = w_1 B_1' w_2 B_2' \ldots w_m B_m' w_{m+1}$ with $w_i \in T^*$ for $1 \leq i \leq m+1$. To simulate this unordered scattered context grammar with appearance checking, construct the programmed grammar with appearance checking

$$G' = (N', T, S', P'),$$

where

N' = $N \cup \{A' \mid A \in N\} \cup \{S'\}$ and

P' contains   for S' the starting productions $(s : S' \to S, \{[r, 1, 0] \mid r \in P\}, \emptyset)$
and for every production $r : (\alpha_1, \alpha_2, \ldots, \alpha_n) \to (\beta_1, \beta_2, \ldots, \beta_n)$
in P the productions

$$([r, i, 0] : \alpha_i \to h(\beta_i), \{[r, i+1, 0]\}, \{\emptyset \mid \alpha_i \to \beta_i \notin F\} \cup$$
$$\{[r, i+1, 0] \mid \alpha_i \to \beta_i \in F\}),$$

$$([r, n, 0] : \alpha_n \to h(\beta_n), \{[r, 1, 1]\}, \{\emptyset \mid \alpha_n \to \beta_n \notin F\} \cup$$
$$\{[r, 1, 1] \mid \alpha_n \to \beta_n \in F\}),$$

$$([r, j, 1] : B'_j \to B_j), \{[r, j+1, 1]\}, \{[r, j+1, 1]\}) \text{ and}$$

$$([r, m, 1] : B'_m \to B_m), \{[p, 1, 0] \mid p \in P\}, \{[p, 1, 0] \mid p \in P\})$$

for $1 \leq i \leq n$ and $1 \leq j \leq m$.

Since the scattered context grammar contains only metalinear productions, it is clear that also the productions in this programmed grammar are all metalinear. Moreover, the productions in the programmed grammar simulating the productions in a scattered context rule are applied in a fixed order, possibly passing over a production in case it is contained in F. The use of primes guarantees that the simulating productions are applied only to nonterminals already appearing in the sentential form to be rewritten and not to the ones introduced by a former production of the scattered context rule that is being simulated.

This allows the parallel fashion of a scattered context rule to be simulated by the sequential order of programmed grammar productions. Note that the proof requires the unordered characteristic of the scattered context grammar, for a production $\alpha \to \beta$ can rewrite any occurrence of α in the current sentential form. Obviously, $L(G) = L(G')$ and thus $USC_{MLIN,ac} \subseteq PR_{MLIN,ac}$ holds. $\qquad\square$

Lemma 6.

$$MAT^{[\lambda]}_{MLIN} \subseteq USC^{[\lambda]}_{MLIN} \text{ and } MAT^{[\lambda]}_{MLIN,ac} \subseteq USC^{[\lambda]}_{MLIN,ac}.$$

Proof. Again, only the second statement is proved (for the λ-free case), the others can be proved in a similar way. Consider a matrix grammar

$$G = (N, T, S, M, F)$$

with appearance checking and only metalinear productions. Denote

$$Lab(M) = \{m_{i,j} \mid m_i : (\alpha_1 \to \beta_1, \alpha_2 \to \beta_2, \ldots, \alpha_n \to \beta_n) \in M,$$
$$M = \{m_1, m_2, \ldots, m_m\}, 1 \leq i \leq m, 1 \leq j \leq n\}.$$

To simulate this matrix grammar with appearance checking, construct the unordered scattered context grammar with appearance checking

$$G' = (N', T, S', P', F),$$

where

$$N' \quad = \quad N \cup \{[\alpha, \beta] \mid \alpha \in (N \cup T), \beta \in Lab(M)\} \cup \{S'\} \text{ and}$$

P' contains for S' the starting rules $(S') \to ([S, m_{i,1}])$ for $1 \leq i \leq n$ and

for every matrix (with only metalinear productions)

$m_i : (\alpha_1 \to \beta_1 \gamma_1, \alpha_2 \to \beta_2 \gamma_2, \ldots, \alpha_n \to \beta_n \gamma_n) \in M$,

$\beta_j \in (N \cup T)$, $\gamma_j \in (N \cup T)^*$ and $1 \leq j \leq n$

the scattered context rules

$([\alpha_j, m_{i,j}]) \to ([\beta_j, m_{i,j+1}] \gamma_j)$,

$([\alpha_n, m_{i,n}]) \to ([\beta_n, m_{k,1}] \gamma_n)$,

$([\delta, m_{i,j}], \alpha_j) \to ([\delta, m_{i,j+1}], \beta_j \gamma_j)$,

$([\delta, m_{i,n}], \alpha_n) \to ([\delta, m_{k,1}], \beta_n \gamma_n)$ and

$([\tau, m_{i,1}]) \to (\tau)$

for $1 \leq i, k \leq m$, $\delta \in (N \cup T)$ and $\tau \in T^*$.

The matrices can be simulated by unordered scattered context rules by adding a label to every symbol of the alphabet. The matrices are split and for every production of it some scattered context rules are created. The labels define an ordering on the use of the various scattered context rules, thus simulating the strict order of matrices by unordered scattered context rules.

At any moment in time, the number of symbols with a label in the sentential form is zero or one. This can be seen from the definitions. If the number is zero, either the sentential form is a terminal one and the derivation is terminated or the sentential form contains a nonterminal and the derivation is blocked since every rule requires a labeled symbol (except the initial rules). If the number is one, it can be replaced by another labeled symbol (the label being the one of the next production in the matrix or the one of the first production of a new matrix if it was the last production of the matrix) while rewriting the symbol according to the production of a matrix being simulated.

Naturally, a production of a scattered context rule can be "passed over" if the same production could be passed over in the matrix grammar, in which case the other production of the scattered context rule replaces the label by the label from the next production in the matrix or the one from the first production of a new matrix if this was the last production of the matrix. Naturally, terminating rules eliminating the labels are present, to be used only when a matrix has been completely simulated. It can now be seen that $L(G) = L(G')$ and $MAT_{MLIN,ac} \subseteq USC_{MLIN,ac}$ holds. $\square$

Theorem 3. For $f \in \{*\} \cup \{\leq k, = k, \geq k \mid k \geq 1\}$ and $g \in \{t_0, t_1, t_2\}$

$$USC_{MLIN}^{[\lambda]} = PR_{MLIN}^{[\lambda]} = MAT_{MLIN}^{[\lambda]} = PT_* CD_{MLIN}^{[\lambda]}(f) \subseteq HPT_* CD_{MLIN}^{[\lambda]} \text{ and}$$

$$USC_{MLIN,ac}^{[\lambda]} = PR_{MLIN,ac}^{[\lambda]} = MAT_{MLIN,ac}^{[\lambda]} = PT_* CD_{MLIN}^{[\lambda]}(g) = HPT_* CD_{MLIN}^{[\lambda]}.$$

Proof. It can be seen from the proofs of $PR_{ac}^{[\lambda]} \subseteq T_s CD^{[\lambda]}(t_1)$ and $PR_{ac}^{[\lambda]} \subseteq T_s CD^{[\lambda]}(t_2)$ in [19] that these results continue to hold in the metalinear case. The same holds for the proofs, in [19] as well, of $PR^{[\lambda]} \subseteq PT_* CD^{[\lambda]}(f)$ and $PT_* CD^{[\lambda]}(f) \subseteq$

$MAT^{[\lambda]}$, for $f \in \{*\} \cup \{\leq k, = k, \geq k \mid k \geq 1\}$. Finally, also the proof of $HPT_*CD^{[\lambda]} \subseteq MAT_{ac}^{[\lambda]}$ in [2] can be seen to hold in the case of a restriction to metalinear productions as well. The theorem is hence a simple combination of these results and some obvious inclusions with Lemma 5 and 6. □

Note that this theorem strengthens Theorem 2 to an equality for modes t_0, t_1 and t_2 instead of the last inclusion there. An open problem remains, however, for the other modes of derivation. The next lemma strengthens Lemma 4 and thereby Theorem 2, even more.

Lemma 7. *For $f \in \{*\} \cup \{\leq k, = k, \geq k \mid k \geq 1\}$ and $g \in \{t_0, t_1, t_2\}$*

$$MLIN \subset USC_{MLIN} = PR_{MLIN} = MAT_{MLIN} = PT_*CD_{MLIN}(f) \subseteq$$
$$PT_*CD_{MLIN}(g) = HPT_*CD_{MLIN}.$$

Proof. The first three equalities are proved in Theorem 3. Moreover, the unordered scattered context grammar

$$G_1 = (\{S, A, B, C\}, \{a, b, c\}, S, \{p_1, p_2, p_3\}),$$

with the rules (consisting of only metalinear productions)

$$
\begin{aligned}
p_1 &: (S) \to (ABC), \\
p_2 &: (A, B, C) \to (aA, bB, cC) \text{ and} \\
p_3 &: (A, B, C) \to (a, b, c)
\end{aligned}
$$

generates $L(G_1) = \{a^n b^n c^n \mid n \geq 1\} \in USC_{MLIN} \setminus CF$. Since it is known that $\{a^n b^n c^n \mid n \geq 1\} \in CS \setminus CF$ and from the Chomsky hierarchy that $MLIN \subset CF \subset CS$, the first inclusion is proper indeed. The last inclusion is obvious, since clearly $USC_{MLIN} \subseteq USC_{MLIN,ac}$ and, according to Theorem 3, $USC_{MLIN,ac} = PT_*CD_{MLIN}(f)$ for $f \in \{t_0, t_1, t_2\}$. Finally, the last equality was proved in Theorem 3. □

Hence already an unordered scattered context, programmed or matrix grammar without appearance checking and with λ-free productions and only metalinear productions can generate languages beyond the class of metalinear languages. Moreover, also a prescribed team CD grammar system (for all modes of derivation) and a hybrid prescribed team CD grammar system, both with teams of variable size and only metalinear productions, can already generate languages beyond this class of metalinear languages.

For matrix and programmed grammars (with appearance checking) and regular, linear, context-sensitive or recursively enumerable productions only, it is known (see, e.g., [9]) that these cannot generate more than the class of regular, linear, context-sensitive or recursively enumerable languages, respectively. Hence, no interesting results may be expected for unordered scattered context grammars in these cases either.

The next lemma says something about the relation between prescribed team CD grammar systems with teams of bounded size and exactly 1 metalinear production per component and linear simple matrix grammars of degree n. Because of Theorem 1 and its corollaries, this establishes a relation, presented in Corollary 5 right after the coming proof, with the (hybrid) prescribed team CD grammar systems with teams of size 1 and linear or regular productions only.

To be more precise, denote $PT_{(1,n)}CD_{MLIN,1}(f)$ for the class of prescribed team CD grammar systems with teams of size 1 for the teams containing a production with the axiom as its left-hand side, teams of size n for the teams containing other productions, only 1 production per component (the second 1 in the notation), working in mode f and containing only metalinear productions.

Lemma 8. *For $n \geq 1$ and $f \in \{=1, \geq 1, *, t_0, t_1, t_2\} \cup \{\leq k \mid k \geq 1\}$*

$$SM_{LIN}(n) \subseteq PT_{(1,n)}CD_{MLIN,1}(f).$$

Proof. Consider the linear simple matrix grammar

$$G = (N_1, N_2, \ldots, N_k, T, S, M)$$

of degree k, $k \geq 1$. To simulate this linear simple matrix grammar, construct the prescribed team CD grammar system

$$\Gamma = (N, T, S, P_1, P_2, \ldots, P_n, Q_1, Q_2, \ldots, Q_m),$$

where

$$N = \bigcup_{i=1}^{n} N_i,$$

$P_1, P_2, \ldots, P_n$ are the components $\{\alpha \to \beta\}$ for every $\alpha \to \beta$ in matrices of M, $\alpha \in \{S\} \cup \bigcup_{i=1}^{n} N_i$ and $\beta \in (\bigcup_{i=1}^{n} N_i \cup T)^*$ and

$Q_1, Q_2, \ldots, Q_m$ are the teams $\{\{S \to \beta\}\}$ for every matrix $(S \to \beta) \in M$ and $\beta \in \bigcup_{i=1}^{n} N_i \cup T^*$ and

the teams $\{\{A_j \to x_j\}\}$ for every matrix of the form $(A_1 \to x_1, A_2 \to x_2, \ldots, A_k \to x_k) \in M, A_i \in N_i$ $x_i \in (N_i \cup T)^*$ and $1 \leq i, j \leq k$.

Note that due to the pairwise disjoint alphabets of simple matrix languages a production $A_j \to x_j$, $1 \leq j \leq k$, does not rewrite a nonterminal introduced by a production $A_i \to x_j$, $1 \leq i < j \leq k$, of the same matrix, but a nonterminal already present in the sentential form before applying this particular matrix to it. It is this property of simple matrix grammars that allows the strict sequential order of rewriting of them to be simulated by one parallel rewriting step of a team of a prescribed team CD grammar system.

Do note also that a characteristic of linear simple matrix grammars is that there can never be two of the same nonterminals in any sentential form. Hence leftmost rewriting is equal to free rewriting in linear simple matrix grammars, thus free rewriting in the simulating prescribed team CD grammar system suffices. These notes imply the restriction to the modes of derivation as stated in the lemma. Moreover, the metalinear productions of the prescribed team CD grammar system allow exactly the axiom to be the left-hand side of non-linear productions, which are precisely the only non-linear productions in a linear simple matrix grammar.

It is clear that $L(G) = L(\Gamma)$. Furthermore, it is easy to see that teams with one component are constructed for productions with the axiom as left-hand side and teams of k components, k being the degree of the simple matrix grammar, are constructed for the other productions. Moreover, all these components of the prescribed team CD grammar system contain only one production. □

Compare the following relations with Theorem 2.

Corollary 5. For $f \in \{t_0, t_1, t_2\} \cup \{= k, \geq k \mid k \geq 2\}$, $g \in \{*\} \cup \{\leq k, = k, \geq k \mid k \geq 1\}$ and $g' \in \{t_0, t_1, t_2\}$

$$PT_1CD_{REG}(f) = HPT_1CD_{REG} \subset PT_1CD_{LIN}(f) = HPT_1CD_{LIN} \subseteq$$
$$PT_*CD_{MLIN}(g) \subseteq PT_*CD_{MLIN}(g') = HPT_*CD_{MLIN}.$$

Remark 1. According to Corollary 4, there is a language that can be generated by a (hybrid) prescribed team CD grammar system with teams of size 1 and only linear productions, but which cannot be generated by a context-free grammar. Hence the inclusion $PT_1CD_{LIN}(f) \subseteq PT_*CD_{MLIN}(g)$ in the above corollary is either proper and $CF \subseteq PT_*CD_{MLIN}(g)$ holds or the family of languages generated by prescribed team CD grammar systems with teams of variable size and only metalinear productions is incomparable with the class of context-free languages.

My conjecture is an incomparability result. An intuition supporting a possible proof is the following. It is clear that the context-free grammar $G_2 = (\{S, A\}, \{a, b\}, S, \{S \rightarrow aAbS, S \rightarrow aAb, S \rightarrow ab, A \rightarrow aAb, A \rightarrow ab\})$ generates $L(G_2) = \{a^n b^n \mid n \geq 1\}^+ \in CF$. A characteristic of this language is its unknown width and depth, i.e. the number of $a^n b^n \mid n \geq 1$'s next to each other and for each the amount of n are unknown. Obviously, metalinear productions can simulate the depth with productions similar to the last four productions in G_2. The width, however, has to be known in advance in the case of metalinear productions since the axiom is the only production which can have more than one nonterminal on its right-hand side and should thus introduce a sufficient amount of them. This amount has to be known in advance and the set of productions is finite, hence it seems that $\{a^n b^n \mid n \geq 1\}^+ \notin (PT_*CD_{MLIN}(f) \cup PT_*CD_{MLIN}^\lambda(f))$ for $f \in \{*, t_0, t_1, t_2\} \cup \{\leq k, = k, \geq k \mid k \geq 1\}$.

Finally, note that if this conjecture holds, then also the classes of unordered scattered context, matrix and programmed grammars (even with appearance checking) with only metalinear productions are incomparable with the class of context-free languages. For a proof of this, consider for example Theorem 3 and the proof of Lemma 7.

Hence for linear (and regular) simple matrix grammars, a prescribed team CD grammar system with only metalinear productions can be constructed generating the same language. Whether this also holds the other way around and for other modes of derivation, is an open problem.

Another open problem is the relation between simple matrix grammars with only context-free productions and prescribed team CD grammar systems and hence also matrix grammars with only context-free productions (and appearance checking). The leftmost rewriting of simple matrix grammars makes it unlikely to have a similar relation between them and prescribed team CD grammar systems, though. For matrix grammars with only metalinear productions, however, the following corollary does present an interesting relation with regular and linear simple matrix grammars.

Corollary 6. *For* $n \geq 1$

$$SM_{REG}(n) = SM_{REG}^{\lambda}(n) \subset SM_{LIN}(n) = SM_{LIN}^{\lambda}(n) \subseteq MAT_{MLIN} \subseteq MAT_{MLIN}^{\lambda}.$$

Proof. For $n \geq 1$, $SM_{REG}(n) = SM_{REG}^{\lambda}(n) \subset SM_{LIN}(n) = SM_{LIN}^{\lambda}(n)$ (see, e.g., [9]) From Lemma 8 follows that $SM_{LIN}(n) \subseteq PT_{(1,n)}CD_{MLIN,1}(f)$ for $n \geq 1$ and $f \in \{=1, \geq 1, *, t_0, t_1, t_2\} \cup \{\leq k \mid k \geq 1\}$. Moreover, it is clear that $PT_{(1,n)}CD_{MLIN,1}(f) \subseteq PT_*CD_{MLIN}(f)$ for all modes of derivation and thus $SM_{LIN}(n) \subseteq PT_*CD_{MLIN}(f)$ is obtained for $n \geq 1$ and $f \in \{=1, \geq 1, *\} \cup \{\leq k \mid k \geq 1\}$. Finally, Theorem 3 finishes the proof of the corollary. $\quad\square$

$$CF = CD(*) = CD(=1) = CD(\geq 1) = CD(\leq k) \text{ (for a } k \geq 1)$$

$$\boldsymbol{PT_*CD_{MLIN}(h_2)} = \boldsymbol{HPT_*CD_{MLIN}} = \boldsymbol{USC_{MLIN,ac}} = \boldsymbol{PR_{MLIN,ac}} = \boldsymbol{MAT_{MLIN,ac}}$$

$$h_2 \in \{t_0, t_1, t_2\}$$

$$MLIN = [H]CD_{MLIN}(f)$$

$$f \in \{*, t\} \cup \{\leq k, = k, \geq k \mid k \geq 1\}$$

$$h_1 \in \{=1, \geq 1, *\}$$

$$\boldsymbol{PT_*CD_{MLIN}(h_1)} = \boldsymbol{USC_{MLIN}} = \boldsymbol{PR_{MLIN}} = \boldsymbol{MAT_{MLIN}}$$

$$LIN = [H]CD_{LIN}(f) = [H]PT_*CD_{LIN}(f) \; [H]PT_*CD_{LIN}^{[\lambda]}(g) = SM_{LIN}^{[\lambda]}$$

$$f \in \{*, t\} \cup \{\leq k, = k, \geq k \mid k \geq 1\} \qquad g \in \{t_0, t_1, t_2\} \cup \{= k, \geq k \mid k \geq 2\}$$

$$REG = [H]CD_{REG}(f) = [H]PT_*CD_{REG}(f) [H]PT_*CD_{REG}^{[\lambda]}(g) = SM_{REG}^{[\lambda]}$$

A very interesting corollary indeed, knowing that $SM_{LIN}(n) \subseteq SM(n)$ for $n \geq 1$ (see, e.g., [9]) and keeping in mind the unknown relation between simple matrix grammars and matrix grammars, in the case of context-free productions only, already mentioned above.

5. Summary

A summary of the results presented here will be given in the form of a diagram. A hierarchy along the lines of (the sub-context-free part of) the Chomsky hierarchy (see, e.g., [9]), is chosen. In this way, readers will obtain a clear insight into the power of teams in grammar systems in the sub-context-free cases.

In this diagram, a dashed arrow indicates an inclusion which is not known to be proper, whereas a straight arrow indicates a proper inclusion; in both cases the class the arrow leaves is included in the class the arrow points at. Families which are not connected are not necessarily incomparable. Moreover, all relations of which a proof is included in here are printed in boldface.

Observing this diagram, it is clear that some open problems remain, even though a good insight into the power of (hybrid) prescribed teams in CD grammar systems is offered. One such an open problem concerns a possible hierarchy that can be found in this diagram and it is formulated next.

What is the generative power of prescribed (hybrid) team CD grammar systems with only regular or linear productions and teams of constant size s, for $s \geq 2$?

Acknowledgements. This work has benefited from discussions with and comments and suggestions from E. Csuhaj-Varjú, H.C.M. Kleijn and Gh. Păun. This paper is an excerpt from Part III: *Teams in CD grammar systems* of my master's thesis ([1]).

References

1. M. H. ter Beek, Teams in grammar systems, *IR-96-32 (master's thesis)*, Leiden University, 1996.

2. M. H. ter Beek, Teams in grammar systems: hybridity and weak rewriting. To appear in *Proceedings Workshop Grammar Systems: Recent Results and Perspectives, Budapest, 26-27 July 1996*.

3. E. Csuhaj-Varjú and J. Dassow, On cooperating distributed grammar systems. *J. Inf. Process. Cybern. EIK* 26 (1990), 49 - 63.

4. E. Csuhaj-Varjú, J. Dassow, J. Kelemen and Gh. Păun, *Grammar Systems. A Grammatical Approach to Distribution and Cooperation*, Gordon and Breach, London, 1994.

5. E. Csuhaj-Varjú and J. Kelemen, Cooperating grammar systems: a syntactical framework for the blackboard model of problem solving. In *Proc. AI and information-control systems of robots '89* (I. Plander, ed.), North-Holland Publ. Co., 1989, 121 - 127.

6. E. Csuhaj-Varjú and Gh. Păun, Limiting the size of teams in cooperating grammar systems. *Bulletin EATCS* 51 (1993), 198 - 202.

7. E. Csuhaj-Varjú, Eco-grammar systems: recent results and perspectives. In [18] (1995), 79 - 103.

8. J. Dassow, Cooperating grammar systems (definitions, basic results, open problems). In [18] (1995), 40 - 52.

9. J. Dassow and Gh. Păun, *Regulated Rewriting in Formal Language Theory*, Springer-Verlag, 1989.

10. J. Dassow and Gh. Păun, Cooperating distributed grammar systems with regular components. *Computers and AI* (1992).

11. R. Freund and Gh. Păun, A variant of team cooperation in grammar systems. *J. UCS* 1, 2 (1995), 105 - 130.

12. O. H. Ibarra, Simple matrix languages. *Inform. Control* 17 (1970), 359 - 394.

13. L. Kari, A. Mateescu, Gh. Păun and A. Salomaa, Teams in cooperating grammar systems, *J. Exper. Th. AI* 7 (1995), 347 - 359.

14. O. Mayer, Some restricted devices for context-free languages. *Inform. Control* 20 (1972), 69 - 92.

15. V. Mitrana, Hybrid cooperating distributed grammar systems. *Computers and AI* 2 (1993), 83 - 88.

16. Gh. Păun, On eliminating the λ-rules from simple matrix grammars. *Fundamenta Informaticae* 4 (1981), 185 - 195.

17. Gh. Păun, Grammar systems: a grammatical approach to distribution and cooperation. In *Automata, Languages and Programming; 22nd International Colloquium, ICALP'95, Szeged, Hungary, Lecture Notes in Computer Science* 944 (1995), 429 - 443.

18. Gh. Păun, ed., *Artificial Life: Grammatical Models*, Black Sea Univ. Press, Bucharest, Romania, 1995.

19. Gh. Păun and G. Rozenberg, Prescribed teams of grammars. *Acta Informatica* 31 (1994), 525 - 537.

20. D. J. Rosenkrantz, Programmed grammars and classes of formal languages. *J. ACM* 16, 1 (1969), 107 - 131.

21. G. Rozenberg and A. Salomaa, *The Mathematical Theory of L Systems*, Academic Press, New York, 1980.

22. A. Salomaa, *Formal Languages*, Academic Press, New York, 1973.

A Note on the Incomparability of the E0L Family with Certain Families of Languages Generated by Cooperating Grammar Systems

Mohamed AMIN[1]

Institute of Mathematics, Gdańsk University
Wita Stwosza 57, 80-952 Gdańsk, Poland
and
Department of Mathematics and Computer Science, Faculty of Science
Menoufia University, Shebin Elkom, Egypt
E-mail :Amin@ksinet.univ.gda.pl

Abstract. We show that the family of languages generated by cooperating distributed (CD) grammar systems with context-free components in the derivation modes $= k, \geq k$, for $k \geq 2$, and the family of E0L languages are incomparable.

1. Notions and Results

For formal definitions we refer the reader to the monograph [1]. We only specify some notations. A CD grammar system of degree n is a construct

$$G = (T, G_1, G_2, \ldots, G_n, S)$$

where $G_i = (N_{G_i}, T_{G_i}, P_i), 1 \leq i \leq n$, are Chomsky grammars without an axiom, T is the terminal alphabet such that $T \subseteq \cup_{i=1}^{i=n} T_{G_i}$ and $S \in \cup_{i=1}^{i=n} N_{G_i}$.

A k step derivation with respect to a component grammar G_i is denoted $\Longrightarrow_{G_i}^{=k}$ and $\Longrightarrow_{G_i}^{\leq k}, \Longrightarrow_{G_i}^{\geq k}, \Longrightarrow_{G_i}^{*}$, denote a derivation consisting of at most k steps, at least k steps, an arbitrary number of steps, respectively. If $x \Longrightarrow_{G_i}^{*} y$ and there is no $z \in (\cup_{i=1}^{i=n}(T_{G_i} \cup N_{G_i}))^{*}$, such that $y \Longrightarrow_{G_i}^{*} z$ then we write $x \Longrightarrow_{G_i}^{t} y$.

The language generated by G according to the mode of derivation f, for $f \in \{*, t\} \cup \{\leq k, = k, \geq k \mid k \geq 1\}$ is defined as

$$L_f(G) = \{x \in T^* \mid S = x_0 \Longrightarrow_{G_{i_1}}^{f} x_1 \Longrightarrow_{G_{i_2}}^{f} x_2 \ldots \Longrightarrow_{G_{i_m}}^{f} x_m = x,$$
$$m \geq 1, 1 \leq i_j \leq n, 1 \leq j \leq m\}.$$

We denote by $\mathcal{L}_f(CDCF)$ the family of languages generated by CD grammar systems with context-free components working in the mode f, for $f \in \{*, t\} \cup \{\leq k, = k, \geq k \mid k \geq 1\}$. We also denote by $\mathcal{L}(CF), \mathcal{L}(E0L), \mathcal{L}(ET0L), \mathcal{L}(MAT)$ the families of context-free, E0L, ET0L and matrix languages, respectively.

Recall that the length set of an arbitrary language L is the collection of lengths of its words, that is $lg(L) = \{|x| \mid x \in L\}$.
We have

---
[1]Research partially supported by Gdańsk University, Grant Nr. BW 5100-5-0069-6.

Theorem 1. [2] *If* $L \in \mathcal{L}_f(CDCF)$, $f \in \{= k, \geq k \mid k \geq 2\}$, *is an infinite language, then* $lg(L)$ *includes an infinite arithmetical progression.*

Theorem 2. *The family* $\mathcal{L}(E0L)$ *is incomparable with each of the families* $\mathcal{L}_f(CDCF)$, $f \in \{= k, \geq k \mid k \geq 2\}$.

Proof. Consider the languages

$$L_1 = \{a^{2^n} \mid n \geq 1\},$$
$$L_2 = \{a^n b^m a^n \mid m \geq n \geq 1\}.$$

The first language is in $\mathcal{L}(E0L)$ [4] and not in $\mathcal{L}_f(CDCF)$, $f \in \{= k, \geq k \mid k \geq 2\}$ (as a consequence of Theorem 1). In Corollary 4.7 in [4] it is proved that the second language $L_2 \notin \mathcal{L}(E0L)$. On the other hand, for the CD grammar system

$$\Gamma_2 = (\{a, b\}, G_1, G_2, G_3, G_4, G_5, S)$$

with

$$
\begin{aligned}
G_1 &= (\{A, B\}, \{a\}, \{A \to a, B \to a\}),\\
G_2 &= (\{A, B\}, \{a, b, X, A', B'\}, \{A \to aA'X, B \to aB'\}),\\
G_3 &= (\{A', B'\}, \{A, B\}, \{A' \to A, B' \to B\}),\\
G_4 &= (\{S, S',\}, \{A, B, X\}, \{S \to S', S' \to AXB\}),\\
G_5 &= (\{X, X'\}, \{b\}, \{X \to X', X' \to bX', X' \to X', X' \to b\}).
\end{aligned}
$$

we have

$$L_{=2}(\Gamma_2) = L_{\geq 2}(\Gamma_2) = \{a^n b^m a^n \mid m \geq n \geq 1\}.$$

In the above grammar system, we note that

- every symbol X is eventually replaced by one b or several $b's$,

- the derivations start by using G_4, thus generating the string AXB,

- all sentential forms contain at most one occurrence of the nonterminal pair (A, B) or (A', B').

The component grammar G_2 transforms a string $a^i AX^{i-q+1}(b^{m_q})^q a^i B$, $i, q \geq 0$, $q \leq i$, $m_q > 0$ to $a^{i+1} A' X^{i-q+2}(b^{m_q})^q a^{i+1} B'$ (at the beginning, after using G_4, we have $i = 0$ and either G_1, G_5, or G_2 can be applied). After using G_2 we have to apply G_3 and we get the string $a^{i+1} AX^{i-q+2}(b^{m_q})^q a^{i+1} B$ which is of the form we have started with, hence G_2, G_3 can be iterated. This iterative process ends by applying G_1 and finally (or possibly between two uses of G_2, G_3) we use G_5 to rewrite X by b or generating arbitrary many number of $b's$. In conclusion we obtain $a^n b^m a^n, m \geq n \geq 1$, hence the derivation is terminated. (Clearly, the ≥ 2 derivations in Γ_2 are in fact $= 2$ derivations.)

For $k \geq 3$ we replace the first rule, let us denote it by $Z \to w$, of each set P_i, $1 \leq i \leq 5$, by the following $k - 1$ rules (all $Z_j, 1 \leq j \leq k - 2$, are new symbols)

$$Z \to Z_1, Z_1 \to Z_2, \ldots, Z_{k-3} \to Z_{k-2}, Z_{k-2} \to w.$$

Denote by Γ_k the obtained CD grammar system. As in the case of Γ_2, it is easy to see that $L_{=k}(\Gamma_k) = L_{\geq k}(\Gamma_k) = L_2$, which completes the proof. $\square$

In Corollary 1 in [2] it is shown that $\mathcal{L}(E0L)$ is incomparable with each of the families $\mathcal{L}_f(CDCF), f \in \{= k, \geq k \mid k \geq 2\}$. To this aim, one uses the languages

$$L_1 = \{a^{2^n} \mid n \geq 1\},$$
$$L_2 = \{a^n b^n c^n \mid n \geq 1\}.$$

The language $L_2 = \{a^n b^n c^n \mid n \geq 1\}$ is supposed not to be in $\mathcal{L}(E0L)$, which however is not true: see Example 1.13 in [4].

The above theorem shows that the result in [2] is still true, there are languages $L \in \mathcal{L}_f(CDCF) - \mathcal{L}(E0L)$, $f \in \{= k, \geq k \mid k \geq 2\}$ (hence the involved families are incomparable, indeed).

At the end of [2] it is asked whether or not the one-letter languages in families $\mathcal{L}_f(CDCF), f \in \{= k, \geq k \mid k \geq 2\}$, are regular. Because the similar conjecture for $\mathcal{L}(MAT)$ has been recently confirmed, [3], in view of the inclusion $\mathcal{L}_f(CDCF) \subseteq \mathcal{L}(MAT), f \in \{= k, \geq k \mid k \geq 2\}$ [1], the property holds also for the families $\mathcal{L}_f(CDCF)$, f as above. On the other hand, in view of the relations,

$$\mathcal{L}_f(CDCF) = \mathcal{L}(CF), f \in \{*, = 1, \geq 1\} \cup \{\leq k, \mid k \geq 1\},$$
$$\mathcal{L}_t(CDCF) = \mathcal{L}(ET0L),$$

(shown in [1]), the family $\mathcal{L}_t(CDCF)$ contains non-regular one-letter alphabet languages. Thus we have a full characterization of languages over one-letter alphabet generated in the basic derivation modes by CD grammar systems.

References

1. E. Csuhaj-Varju, J. Dassow, J. Kelemen, Gh. Păun, *Grammar Systems. A Grammatical Approach to Distribution and Cooperation*, Gordon and Breach, London, 1994.

2. J. Dassow, Gh. Păun, S. Vicolov, On the generative capacity of certain classes of cooperating grammar systems, *Fundamenta Informaticae*, 22 (1995), 217 – 226.

3. D. Hauschild, M. Jantzen, Petri nets algorithms in the theory of matrix grammars, *Acta Informatica*, 31 (1994), 719 – 728.

4. G. Rozenberg, A. Salomaa, *The Mathematical Theory of L Systems*, Academic Press, New York, 1980.

Colonies as Models of Reactive Systems[1]

Jozef KELEMEN

Department of Applied Informatics, University of Economics
852 35 Bratislava, Slovakia
and
Institute of Mathematics and Computer Science, Silesian University
746 01 Opava, Czech Republic
E-mail: kelemen@{euba.sk, fpf.slu.cz}

1. Introduction

Considering complex systems we typically need – cf. (McClamrock, 1995) – to know *what* a complex system is doing at a higher level in order to find out *how* at the lower level it accomplishes that task. In other words, we often need to know the function of the complex system being analyzed to know what aspects of structure to look at. Understanding the behavior of a complex system requires knowing which aspects of the complex mass of lower-level properties are significant in making a contribution to the overall behavior of the system. In real situations such a distinction may be problematic because the identification of which aspects of the lower-level activity of the system are significant and which are noise – the process of the so called *destillation strategy* (McClamrock, 1995) – is often complicated.

In the following we deal with complex systems which behave without noises. We will concentrate to systems which produce (infinite) sets of strings of symbols, and we will look for as simple as possible structure (architecture) of such systems. Simplicity means in our context, roughly speaking,

– the simplicity of rules which describe the behavior of the components of our complex systems, and

– the simplicity of communication between the components in order to provide the behavior of the complex system.

Another difficult problem is to find the right boundaries of a complex system; cf. (Bechtel, Richardson, 1993). The solution is crucial for identification of the loci of control of the complex systems. There are two extremes here:

– to consider the environment of the system as the locus of control – the case of *external control*, and

– to consider the system itself as the locus of its own control – the case of *internal control*.

The result of emphasizing the external factors is, according to (Bechtel, Richardson, 1993), to reduce the importance of the system, treating it as responding to external factors, or shaped by them, but not itself an important element in accounting for the responses. On the other hand, limited responsivness in the face of wide environmental variation it taken as an indicative of internal control, and the solution is to search for specialized and complex internal mechanisms. The system makes its own contribution and influences what happens to it. We will deal with both of the mentioned cases in the framework of the presented formalisation.

---

[1]Research supported partially by the Grant No. 201/95/0134 of the Grant Agency of the Czech Republic.

Concerning complex systems, our considerations will be motivated mainly by the situation in today artificial intelligence (AI) research. In AI, two main point of views appeared in the past decade – the traditional *deliberative* line of systems designing, and the point of view which stress the idea of *situated action*, or *reactivity* of systems (Maes, 1993), (Kushmerick, 1996).

The *traditional view* of AI emphasizes the role of internal symbolic representation of the outer environment of the systems, and the symbolic computations of plans of systems behavior on the base of these representations, so, this view supposes the internal control of the systems. The *situated action view* stresses the pure reactivity of systems to situations sensed when observing their outer environment. Systems components purely react to the observed situations. Their behavior is controlled externally, by situations sensed in the systems environments.

The situated action and the symbolic deliberative approaches are often considered to be antithetical. However, (Vera, Simon, 1993) argues that there is no such antithesis[2]: situated action systems are in fact symbol systems, and some past and present symbol systems are situated action systems. We will show a possibility to deal with situated action (reactive) systems in the symbolic formal framework, and we will sketch a border-line between the pure reactive symbol systems and those capable to deliberate. We will formulate precisely the possible behavior (generative power) of some classes of reactive symbol systems.

2. Reactive Systems

The *destillation strategy* applied in the following to study complex systems leads us to consider as simple as possible components appearing in the architecture of complex systems organized in as simple as possible ways. We will attempt to describe the possible behaviors of complex systems set up from such simple components with respect to the principles of their communication.

To consider as simple as possible components leads to considering outer control of the complex systems. The control of actions of complex systems lays in this case in the *structure* and *dynamics* of the systems environment. Actions are in such cases in fact *reactions* of systems components to environment structure and changes, only.

In the case of reactivity, the systems macro-goals may be explicit. However, the local details of the (generation of) behaviors are determined by reactions of systems components to the feedback acquired during the activities; cf. (McClamrock, 1995). In this sense the current state of the environment may trigger some macro-goals, too. Benson and Nilsson (1994) write in this context on *teleo-reactivity*: teleo-reactive systems can react appropriately and rapidly to commonly occurring situations that require stereotypical programs of actions. But their functions are influenced by their macro-goals (hence "teleo"). Teleo-reactivity in dynamic, uncertain environments implies a short sense-act cycle of the sort common in feedback control systems.

In order to emphasize the "short sense-act cycles" and the requirement to allocate the control into the environment in the framework of symbol processing systems, a *reactive component* will be formalized as a component capable to execute only a finite number of computations which need no iterations (because of the shortness of the sense-act cycle), and triggered only by appearance of some "start-symbols" in the

---

[2]This view is supported also by some more technical approaches, e.g. by that presented in (Benson, Nilsson, 1994).

structures which will formalize the environment of the systems. So, the simplest type of components – when triggered by start-symbols appearing in their environment – will generate – *without any iterations* – only a finite number of behaviors.

To be reactive only to the states of the outer environment of the systems, the simplest organizational principle of cooperation of reactive components consist in sharing the common symbolic environment in which the components are able to execute changes (rewritings), and which they are able to "sense".

Systems set up from just specified reactive components which communicate only through the shared environment we will call *reactive systems*.

3. Colonies – Models of Reactive Systems in Structured but Static Environments

A colony is a formal model of reactive systems, where the systems reactive components are modelled by *very simple* formal grammars, and the *structured* (but *static*) environment by a string of symbols over which the formal grammars operate either in sequential or in parallel manner. *Very simple* means *regular* grammars which generate *finite languages* only. This capacity of grammars models the intuitively specified capacity of already mentioned reactive components of reactive systems. The environment (the string of symbols) is static in the sense that its changes appear as consequences of components activity (rewritings of symbols appearing in the string by grammars) only.

Colonies represent the simplest architecture reflecting the idea of total decentralization and completely emergent behavior of systems set up from purely reactive components. Particular experiences, e.g. in (Connell, 1990), prove the practical usability of the architecture, e.g. in real-world robotic systems design. The formalized concept of colonies proposed first in (Kelemen, Kelemenová 1992) offers a formal framework for description and study of the behaviors of systems set up according this architecture principles from purely reactive (non-iterating) components. For further technical details and results concerning colonies see e.g. (Dassow et al. 1993), (Csuhaj-Varjú, Păun, 1993-1994), (Kelemenová, Csuhaj-Varjú 1994a,b), (Kelemenová, Kelemen 1994), (Păun, 1995), (Baník 1996), etc.

3.1. The Basic Model

The above described basic model of a colony as well as of some of the closely related notions are formally described as follows.

A *colony* $\mathcal{C}$ is a 3-tuple $\mathcal{C} = (\mathcal{R}, V, T)$, where

(i) $\mathcal{R} = \{R_i \mid 1 \leq i \leq n\}$ is a finite set of regular grammars $R_i = (N_i, T_i, P_i, S_i)$ producing finite languages $L(R_i) = F_i$ for each i. R_i will be referred to as a *component* of $\mathcal{C}$.

(ii) $V = \bigcup_{i=1}^{n} (T_i \cup N_i)$ is an *alphabet* of the colony, and

(iii) $T \subseteq V$ is a *terminal alphabet* of the colony.

We note that a terminal symbol of one grammar can occur as a nonterminal symbol of another grammar.

Elementary changes of strings are determined by a *basic* derivation step of a colony: For $x, y \in V^*$ we define $x \stackrel{b}{\Longrightarrow} y$ iff

$$x = x_1 S_i x_2, \ y = x_1 z x_2, \text{ where } z \in F_i \text{ for some } i, \ 1 \leq i \leq n.$$

The *language* determined by a colony $\mathcal{C}$ starting with the word $w_0 \in V^*$ is given by

$$L(\mathcal{C}, w_0) = \{v \mid w_0 \stackrel{b}{\Longrightarrow}{}^* v, \ v \in T^*\}.$$

A colony $\mathcal{C}$ is *stable* on a set $W \subset (N \cup T)^*$ iff $L(\mathcal{C}, w_i) = L(\mathcal{C}, w_j)$ for arbitrary w_i and w_j from W. The language generated by $\mathcal{C}$ from elements of W will be denoted by $L(\mathcal{C}, W)$.

If it is sufficient for formulation and solution of problems, components are characterized simply by pairs (S_i, F_i).

3.2. Some Variations of the Basic Model

Many natural variants of colonies have been defined which differ in the definition of single derivation step, in the choice of terminal alphabet or other termination mode, in global characterization of derivation process (additional limitations and controls of derivation process can be considered), etc.

Basic differences among the definitions of derivation steps are due to the number of components used in one step as well as to the amount of start symbols (of components), rewritten in one step by each component.

In a colony with *sequential derivation* exactly one component works in a derivation step. The basic derivation step $\stackrel{b}{\Longrightarrow}$ is a sequential derivation step in which one component changes one letter of the string.

In a *sequential* model discussed in (Kelemenová, Csuhaj-Varjú, 1994a), in the derivation step (denoted by $\stackrel{t}{\Longrightarrow}$) one component is used to rewrite all occurrences of its start symbol in string (not necessary by the same word).

In (Păun, 1995), intermediate situations between $x \stackrel{b}{\Longrightarrow} y$ and $x \stackrel{t}{\Longrightarrow} y$ are studied for a given k, where *exactly* (*less than*, *more than*) k occurrences of S_i are rewritten.

In (Dassow et al., 1993) a *parallel* model of derivation is proposed and studied. According to this model of rewriting all components of a colony which *can* work *must* work simultaneously on the tape and each of them rewrites at most one occurrence of its start symbol. The case when more components (S_i, F_i) have the same associated nonterminal S_i requires a special discussion:

If (S, F_i), and (S, F_j) are two components of a colony $\mathcal{C}$ and if (at least) two symbols S appear in a current string, then both these components must be used, each rewriting one occurrence of S.

If only one S appears in a current string, then each component *can* be used, but not both in parallel, hence in such a case we discuss two possibilities:

– the derivation is blocked – *strongly competitive parallel* way of derivation denoted by $\stackrel{sp}{\Longrightarrow}$, and

– the derivation continues and the maximal number of components is used, nondeterministically chosen from all the components which can be used – *weakly competitive parallel* way of derivation denoted by $\stackrel{wp}{\Longrightarrow}$.

If the start symbols of all components in a colony are different, then both $\stackrel{sp}{\Longrightarrow}$ and $\stackrel{wp}{\Longrightarrow}$ define the same relation denoted by $\stackrel{p}{\Longrightarrow}$.

According to different selections of the terminal set of a colony colonies with different *styles of acceptance* are distinguised in (Kelemenová, Csuhaj-Varjú, 1994a,b).

The colony $\mathcal{C} = (\mathcal{R}, V, T)$ with components $R_i = (N_i, T_i, P_i, S_i)$, $(1 \leq i \leq n)$ has – by the definition – an acceptance style

- "arb" iff $T \subseteq \bigcup_{i=1}^{n} T_i$;
- "one" iff $T = T_i$ for some i $(1 \leq i \leq n)$;
- "ex" iff $T = \bigcup_{i=1}^{n} T_i$;
- "all" iff $T = \bigcap_{i=1}^{n} T_i$;
- "dist" iff $T = (\bigcup_{i=1}^{n} T_i) - (\bigcup_{i=1}^{n} N_i)$.

The *language* generated by $\mathcal{C}$ with the derivation step $\overset{x}{\Longrightarrow}$ for $x \in \{b, t, =k, \leq k, \geq k, sp, wp, p\}$ starting with $w_0 \in V^*$ is defined by

$$L_x(\mathcal{C}, w_0) = \{v \mid w_0 \overset{x}{\Longrightarrow}^* u, \ v \in T^*\}.$$

The corresponding families of languages are denoted by COL_x or by COL_x^f in order to stress the style of acceptance $f \in \{one, arb, ex, all, dist\}$. If colonies with exactly n components are considered, $COL_x(n)$ and $COL_x^f(n)$ are used to denote this fact.

Further mechanisms used for regulation of derivation in colonies are *time delays* of components, *hypothesis languages* and *transducer-colony pairs*.

A time delay, associated to each component of a colony, was proposed and studied in (Kelemen, Kelemenová, 1992). It determines a minimal "time" period between two consecutive applications of a component using the so called *delay vector* $d = (d_1, \ldots, d_k)$ of nonnegative integers for a colony $\mathcal{C}_T$.

A derivation step of a colony with delay is defined for pairs $\langle w, t \rangle$, where w is a string and t is a n-tuple of integers (determining possible active components of a colony). So, Let $\mathcal{C}_T = (\mathcal{R}, V, T, d)$ be a colony with delay. Then

$\langle w_1, t \rangle \Longrightarrow_{\mathcal{C}_T} \langle w_2, t' \rangle$ iff $w_1 = x_1 S_j x_2$, $t = (t_1, \ldots, t_n)$ with $t_j = 0$ for some j, $1 \leq j \leq n$ $w_2 = x_1 z x_2$ for some $z \in L(G_j)$, $t' = (t_1', \ldots, t_k')$, where $t_j' = d_j$ and $t_i' = max\{0, m_i - 1\}$ for all i, $i \neq j$.

Note that to put $d = (0, \ldots, 0)$ gives the basic definition of colonies. The derivation step for a colony without delay corresponds to t being the zero vector.

A *language* defined by a colony $\mathcal{C}_T$ with axiom w_0 and with start delay vector t_0 is the set

$$L(\mathcal{C}_T, w_0, t_0) = \{w \in T^* \mid \langle w_0, t_0 \rangle \Longrightarrow_{\mathcal{C}_T}^* \langle w, t \rangle\}.$$

The corresponding family of languages is denoted by $\mathcal{D}COL$.

A colony is a model of a system designed for solving certain problems, hence it is supposed that its actions tend to some expected results. This can be captured in the framework of colonies e.g. by considering a target language for selecting the sentential forms generated by the colony (Păun, 1995).

A *colony with a (regular) hypothesis language* is a quadruple

$$\mathcal{C}_{\mathcal{H}} = (\mathcal{R}, V, T, H),$$

where $(\mathcal{R}, V, T)$ is a colony and H is a regular language in $V^* - T^*$.

For $f \in \{*, t\} \cup \{\leq k, = k, \geq k \mid k \geq 1\}$ and i $(1 \leq i \leq n,)$ the colony accepts a derivation $x \overset{f}{\Longrightarrow} y$ only if $y \in H$ or $y \in T^*$.

The *language* generated by $\mathcal{C_H}$ in the mode f starting with w_0 is the set

$$L_f(\mathcal{C_H}, w_0) = \{x \in T^* \mid w_0 \overset{f}{\Longrightarrow} w_1 \overset{f}{\Longrightarrow} \ldots \overset{f}{\Longrightarrow} w_s = x,$$
$$s \geq 1, 1 \leq i_j \leq n, 1 \leq j \leq s, \text{ and}$$
$$w_j \in H, 1 \leq j \leq s - 1\}.$$

(No hypothesis is made about the last string, the terminal word.)

(Păun, 1995) proposes a model for situation when different components "speak different languages", and a transducer is required to intermediate them:

A *colony-transducer pair* is a couple $(\mathcal{C}, g)$, where $\mathcal{C} = (\mathcal{R}, V, T)$ is a colony, and $g = (V, V, Q, s_0, F, P)$ is a generalized sequential machine (gsm) (Q is the set of states, s_0 is the initial state, F is the set of final states, P is the set of translation rules of the form $sa \to xs'$, $s, s' \in Q$, $a \in V$, $x \in V^+$).

The *language* generated by a colony $(\mathcal{C}, g)$ in the mode f starting with w_0 is

$$L_f(\mathcal{C}, g, w_0) = \{x \in T^* \mid w \Longrightarrow^f_{i_1} w_1 \Longrightarrow g(w_1) \Longrightarrow^f_{i_2} w_2 \Longrightarrow g(w_2) \Longrightarrow \ldots$$
$$\ldots \Longrightarrow^f_{i_s} w_s = x, s \geq 1, 1 \leq i_j \leq n, 1 \leq j \leq s\}.$$

Variants of colonies for modelling "life-like" features as parasitism and symbiosis – the so called *structured colonies* – are proposed and studied in (Csuhaj-Varjú, Păun, 1993-1994):

A *structured colony* is a construct $\sigma = (N, T, w, C_1, \ldots, C_n, \phi)$, where $(N, T, w, C_1, \ldots, C_n)$ is a colony and $\phi : \{C_1, \ldots, C_n\} \to 2^{\{C_1, \ldots, C_n\}}$ is a mapping. (ϕ describes the dependences between the components.)

By different usage of ϕ different modes of derivation can be defined, for instance: For $x, y \in (N \cup T)^*$ we say that x derives y in σ by a direct derivation step under *strong dependence relation*, denoted by $x \Longrightarrow_{sd} y$, iff either

- $x = x_1 S_i S_{j_1} S_{j_2} \ldots S_{j_s} x_2$, $\phi(C_i) = \{C_j\}$, and $y = x_1 z_i z_{j_1} z_{j_2} \ldots z_{j_s} x_2$ or
- $x_1 S_{j_s} \ldots S_{j_2} S_{j_1} S_i x_2$, $\phi(C_i) = \{C_j\}$, and $x_1 z_{j_s} \ldots z_{j_2} z_{j_1} z_i x_2$

for $z_i \in L_i$, $z_j \in L_j$, $z_{k_r} \in L_{k_r}$, $1 \leq s$, $\phi(C_j) \subseteq \{C_i, C_{k_1}\}$, $C_{k_1} \in \phi(C_j)$, $\phi(C_{k_1}) \subseteq \{C_{k_2}, C_j\}$, $C_{k_2} \in \phi(C_{k_1})$, $\phi(C_{k_r}) \subseteq \{C_{k_{r-1}}, C_{k_{r+1}}\}$, $C_{k_{r+1}} \in \phi(C_{k_r})$, $2 \leq r \leq s - 1$, $\phi(C_{k_r}) \subseteq \{C_{k_{s-1}}\}$. or

- $x = x_1 S_{k_s} \ldots S_{k_1} S_j S_i S_l S_{t_1} \ldots S_{t_p} x_2$, $\phi(C_i) = \{C_j, C_l\}$ and $y = x_1 z_{k_s} \ldots z_{k_1} z_j z_i z_l z_{t_1} \ldots z_{t_p} x_2$ or
- $x = x_1 S_{t_p} \ldots S_{t_1} S_l S_i S_j S_{k_1} \ldots S_{k_s} x_2$, $\phi(C_i) = \{C_j, C_l\}$ and $y = x_1 z_{t_p} \ldots z_{t_1} z_l z_i z_j z_{k_1} \ldots z_{k_s} x_2$

for $z_i \in L_i$, $z_j \in L_j$, $z_l \in L_l$, $z_{t_r} \in L_{t_r}$, $1 \leq r \leq p$, $z_{k_r} \in L_{k_r}$, $1 \leq r \leq s$, and for

- $\phi(C_j) \subseteq \{C_i, C_{k_1}\}$, $C_{k_1} \in \phi(C_j)$, $\phi(C_{k_1}) \subseteq \{C_{k_2}, C_j\}$, $C_{k_2} \in \phi(C_{k_1})$, $\phi(C_{k_r}) \subseteq \{C_{k_{r-1}}, C_{k_{r+1}}\}$, $C_{k_{r+1}} \in \phi(C_{k_r})$, $2 \leq r \leq s - 1$, $\phi(C_{k_s}) \subseteq \{C_{k_{s-1}}\}$, and
$\phi(C_l) \subseteq \{C_i, C_{t_1}\}$, $C_{t_1} \in \phi(C_l)$, $\phi(C_{t_1}) \subseteq \{C_{t_2}, C_l\}$, $C_{t_2} \in \phi(C_{t_1})$, $\phi(C_{t_r}) \subseteq \{C_{t_{r-1}}, C_{t_{r+1}}\}$, $C_{t_{r+1}} \in \phi(C_{t_r})$, $2 \leq r \leq p - 1$, $\phi(C_{t_p} \subseteq \{C_{t_{p-1}}\}$.

The language $L_\alpha(\sigma)$ generated by a colony σ (by α-derivations, where α means a particular type of derivation step among those definable for structured colonies) is

$$L_\alpha(\sigma) = \{w \mid S \Longrightarrow^*_\alpha w, w \in T^*\}.$$

The above notion of strong dependence covers both the symbiosis and the parasitism: when $C_j \in \phi(C_i)$ and $C_i \in \phi(C_j)$ we have a symbiotic dependence of C_i and

C_j but when $C_j \in \phi(C_j)$, $C_i \notin \phi(C_j)$ we can say that a parasitic dependence of C_i and C_j is met (C_i is supported by C_j, cannot live alone, whereas C_j is independent of C_i).

The most intensively studied topic of colonies is their *generative power*. The reader can find such type of result in all of the above cited literature. However, in the following we will concentrate on slighly different questions.

4. On the Rationality of Behavior of Reactive Systems

Considering another aspect of colonies behavior, we start with an example of a very simple mechanical device mentioned in (Thorpe, 1989). Ch. Thorpe in his critics of the idea of reactive robotics mentioned that "it is possible to build an extremely simple robot with no models, only reflexes, that does some tasks such as wanders on a table top and turns when it encounters an edge. Such robots don't need models, computers, or even electronics; everything is done mechanically."

The next three figures offer a particular design of the Thorpe's Machine – a fully mechanical child-toy in camouflage of a $\mathcal{LADYBUG}$ – together with the main layers of its subsumed parts $\mathcal{FOR}$ providing the forward motion, and $\mathcal{CURV}$ making curving possible.

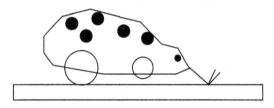

Figure 1. The $\mathcal{LADYBUG}$

The $\mathcal{LADYBUG}$ wanders a table top, and turns when it encounters an edge, so it (almost) *never crashes* off the table. In other words, the behavior of the $\mathcal{LADYBUG}$ is in certain intuitive sense a *rational* because:
– it has perceptual capabilities (to identify the edge of the table by its antennae),
– it has a possibility to execute different actions (through wheels it may roll straightforward and it may change the direction of rolling) – it executes actions having the maximal expected utility for it (it finds the direction of the rolling in order to avoid crashing off the table).

In terms of expectations and beliefs about utilities of performable acts in actual states of environment the systems rationality means that the executed acts are of the *maximal expected utility* for the agent among the actions available at some instant (Doyle 1988). This is the core of the formalization of rationality in the framework of the classical *decision theory*.

The mathematical way of formalization of such concept of rationality is as follows; cf. (Pollock 1992):

Let $\mathcal{A}$ be a system with sensation and action capabilities which connect it with its environment – the so called *agent* – described by a finite set A of *alternative acts* between which it must decide, a finite set O of possible *states of the world*, a function u assigning numerical values – *utilities* – to the possible states of the world, and a set of *beliefs* about the values of the probabilities $p(O/A)$ of each possible state of the world on each act. The *expected utility* of an act a is then defined as

$$e(a) = \sum_{o \in O} u(o)p(o/a)$$

A *decision problem* for the agent $\mathcal{A}$ consists in maximizing the expected utility of its acts. An agent which is able to solve the decision problem is a *rational agent*.

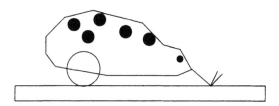

Figure 2. The part $\mathcal{FOR}$ of the $\mathcal{LADYBUG}$

In (Kelemen 1996) a special type of rationality – the so called *low-level rationality* of agents – is defined and studied. The idea behind that level of rationality consists of eliminating probabilities and minimizing the number of considered states of the world.

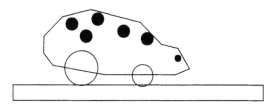

Figure 3. The part $\mathcal{CURV}$ of the $\mathcal{LADYBUG}$

Formally, an agent $\mathcal{A}$ with a finite set $A = \{a_1, a_2, \ldots, a_n\}$ of acts has the property of *low-level rationality* (is an *llr-agent*) if it is able to solve the decision problem under the conditions that:
(i) $\mathcal{A}$ "recognizes" only two states of its world, so $O = \{t, f\}$,
(ii) $\mathcal{A}$ has a binary utility function defined by $u(t) = 1$ and $u(f) = 0$,
(iii) the belief function of $\mathcal{A}$ for given a_i is either

$$p(t/a_i) = 1 \text{ and } p(f/a_i) = 0$$

or

$$p(t/a_i) = 0 \text{ and } p(f/a_i) = 1.$$

Consequently,

$$e(a_i) = \begin{cases} 1 & \text{for } p(t/a_i) = 1 \\ 0 & \text{for } p(t/a_i) = 0 \end{cases}$$

The *behavior* $L_\mathcal{A}$ of an llr-agent $\mathcal{A}$ is the set of all sequences $a_1 \ldots a_k$ $(k \geq 1)$ of acts of $\mathcal{A}$ such that $e(a_1 \ldots a_k) = 1$ where $e(a_1 \ldots a_k) = e(a_1) \ldots e(a_k)$.

An equivalent characterization of the behaviors of llr-agents can be given as follows: *The behavior $L_\mathcal{A}$ of an llr-agent $\mathcal{A}$ is the set of all sequences $a_1 \ldots a_k$ $(k \geq 1)$ of acts of $\mathcal{A}$ such that $p(t/a_i) = 1$ for arbitrary a_i $(1 \leq i \leq k)$ appearing in $a_1 \ldots a_k$.* For the proof see (Kelemen 1996).

5. A Language-Theoretic Treatment of Systems Rationality

To act in an environment means for an agent to perform a sequence of acts. Each such sequence may be labeled by the corresponding sequence of symbols denoting the individual acts performed by the agent. From a *language-theoretic* point of view, the set of symbols denoting acts from A of an agent $\mathcal{A}$ may be understood as a *finite alphabet*, and a behavior of $\mathcal{A}$ (the set of sequences of acts performed by this agent) can be considered as a *language $L_\mathcal{A}$* over that alphabet. Formally, $L_\mathcal{A} \subseteq A^*$, where A^* states for the set of all (finite) sequences (including the empty sequence) defined from the elements of A with respect of the binary operation of concatenation of (strings of) symbols. Thus:

 – A^* states, in fact, for all possible sequences (including the empty one) which may be formed from the acts performable by $\mathcal{A}$,

 – $L_\mathcal{A}$ is the set of all sequences, which can be effectively generated by $\mathcal{A}$,

 – if $\mathcal{A}$ is a *procedurally rational* agent, then there are some mechanisms of $\mathcal{A}$ for selecting (generating) only a subset $L_\mathcal{A}^{rat} \subseteq L_\mathcal{A}$ of rational behaviors of $\mathcal{A}$,

 – if $\mathcal{A}$ is a *substantively rational* [3] agent, then $\mathcal{A}$ is able to produce *only* behaviors from $L_\mathcal{A}^{rat}$, so $L_\mathcal{A}^{rat} = L_\mathcal{A}$.

From the definition of the expected utility function it follows that the behavior $L_\mathcal{A}$ of an arbitrary llr-agent $\mathcal{A}$ has the following property:

For arbitrary i, j $(1 \leq i \leq k; 1 \leq j \leq k)$, if $a_1 \ldots a_i \ldots a_j \ldots a_k \in L_\mathcal{A}$ then $a_1 \ldots a_j \ldots a_i \ldots a_k \in L_\mathcal{A}$. There exists an infinite class of infinite languages which satisfy this property.

The rational behavior of the $\mathcal{LADYBUG}$ can be (approximately) described by the set of all finite sequences of acts f (executable because of the physical limitations of the table maximally k-times) and c (executable because of the same reason maximally l-times), so we have:

$$L_{\mathcal{TM}} = \{(g^m c^n g^r)^+ \mid 1 \leq m \leq k; 1 \leq n \leq l; 1 \leq r \leq k\}.$$

Clearly, this is a regular language.

6. Low-Level Rationality of Colonies

The decision-theoretic model of the $\mathcal{LADYBUG}$ presents it as a system with *internal* and centralized control. It does not reflect the architectural principle applied in construction of the $\mathcal{LADYBUG}$ considered as a totally decentralized set of independent, autonomous, fully reactive components acting in a shared environment.

However, we mentioned already that the $\mathcal{LADYBUG}$ is set up from two functionally separable mechanical parts, $\mathcal{FOR}$ and $\mathcal{CURV}$. Realize now that none of these

---

[3]The notions of *substantive* and *procedural rationality* are taken from (Simon 1982); also cf. (Simon 1978).

parts has any level of rationality – both of them (under suitable conditions, see below) crash off the table. But subsuming them into an agent they generate a rational behavior thanks to their reactivity to situations sensed in their shared environment. So, we can consider the $\mathcal{LADYBUG}$ also as a decentralized system with an external control.

Let the behaviors of the parts are

$$L_{\mathcal{FOR}} = \{f^m s_1 \mid 0 \leq m \leq k\},$$

and

$$L_{\mathcal{CURV}} = \{c^n s_2 \mid 0 \leq n \leq l\}.$$

Both of behaviors are finite because in all cases the strings of actions of the components lead (after executing a number of forward or curving steps) inevitably to the state s_1 and s_2, resp. (by crashing of the $\mathcal{FOR}$ or $\mathcal{CURV}$ off the table; let us suppose a slighly idealized conditions that the table is quite small, so that the "infinite" rotation of $\mathcal{CURV}$ is eliminated, that there are no obstacles on the table, no problems with parts' energy income, etc.).

Trying to describe $\mathcal{FOR}$ and $\mathcal{CURV}$ as llr-agents in the decision-theoretic framework we have serious troubles with defining the beliefs: accepting the previous idealizations we may easily realize, that if the parts $\mathcal{FOR}$ or $\mathcal{CURV}$ roll towards the table's edge, they necessarily crash (so, that $p(crash/g) = p(crash/c) = 1$). Thereupon, the parts $\mathcal{FOR}$ and $\mathcal{CURV}$ are not llr-agents. However, both of the behaviors can be described by corresponding formal grammars in an obvious way.

The languages $L_{\mathcal{FOR}}$ and $L_{\mathcal{CURV}}$ are finite, while the colony formed with their grammars generates an infinite language, $L_{\mathcal{TM}}$.

In (Kelemen 1996) is proved that *the class of llr-agents with behaviors generated by colonies is infinite.*

This proposition shows, that at least the low-level rationality of systems may appear as an *emergent effect* of unsupervised individual behaviors of a finite number of autonomous purely reactive and non-rational components. It is also clear that this rationality is *substantive* in its nature, because of the lack of any internal control mechanisms in colonies.

7. Integrative Societies of Agents

Societies (at least the animal and robotic ones) can be grouped into two basic categories (Parker 1993): In the case of *differentiating societies* the individual members of the societies are formed within the group according to the needs of the society. In this case, the individual exists for the good of the society. On the contrary, *societies that integrate* depend upon the attraction of individual independent components to each other. In the case of integrating behavior, the components of the society are driven by a selfish motivation which leads them to seek group life because it is in their own best interests.

One of the most important problems of inventing any particular architecture for robots intended as individual agents in integrative societies consists of inventing mechanisms of adaptive action selection by an individual agent which selects actions appropriate with respect its individual mission. Actions must be selected on the one hand without any global control strategy, on the other, they must contribute to emergence of a global behavior of the society accomplishing certain global task. This section shows how one mechanism of action selection – the mechanism of *motivation* proposed in (Parker 1993) – may be considered as externally controlled and treated in the formal framework of colonies; for more details see (Kelemen 1993).

According to Parker's proposal, the individual agents are supposed to be designed using the *behavior-based* approach as collections of simple reactive components each receiving sensory input and controlling some aspects of the actuator output. The behavior of each agent emerges from the behaviors of its parts without any central control or global strategy of cooperation of its components.

A robot receives information from its environment through its sensors and through an explicit communication with the other robots. Communication is, however, treated as a behavior. Both sensory data and explicit communication are *inputs*, and make the action selection *adaptive* to tasks performed by other agents *without* introducing any global control.

Unlike typical behavior-based approaches, the architecture delineates several *behavior sets* that are either *active* as a group or are *hibernating*. Each behavior set corresponds to those levels of competence required to perform some task.

Because of the alternative goals that may be pursued by the agents, they must have some means of selecting the appropriate behavior set to become active. For achieving this *action selection* the *motivational behavior* is utilized, which controls the activation of each behavior set.

The *output* of a motivational behavior is the *activation level* of its corresponding behavior set. When this activation level exceeds a given threshold, the behavior set becomes active. Once a behavior set is activated, other behavior sets are suppressed. Then, over the time, the motivation for performing a behavior set increases as long as the corresponding task is not accomplished, as determined from sensory feedback.

Suppose now that a robot belonging to a society is described formally by a colony C each component of which being a description of the reactive behavior of a corresponding component of the robot. Suppose C to be stable on a set W, and the behavior of C to be L. Let W be the set of the samples of data observed by the real agent and communicated by other real agents. Because of the finite scalling capacity of any sensor and the limited exchange of information among the real agents, we suppose W to be finite.

As it was already mentioned, a real agent is able to perform different (but a finite number of) behavior sets. Describing the real agent by a corresponding colony C, these sets can be formally expressed as subsets L_i of the behavior L of a colony C such that $L = \bigcup_{i=1}^{n} L_i$. A motivational behavior for the behavior set L_i is then a set W_i such that C is stable on W_i and $L(C, W_i) = L_i$.

Having in the mind the sensory and communication limitations of real agents it is meaningful to suppose also W_i to be finite. Then to *motivate* an agent to *select a behavior set* L_i means to generate the appropriate *motivational behavior* W_i for it. Because W_i is finite, this task can be done by extending the original architecture of C by a simple specialized component-like agent with behavior W_i which is stable on certain set U_i. Note that the set U_i may contain also elements consisting of sensed/communicated data which are inaccesible to the original C. This extension models certain aspects of action selection and envisions the basic architectural principle which makes the purely distributive cooperative control scheme possible. Since individual agents remain fully autonomous, they have the ability to perform useful actions even amidt the failure of other agents.

The basic theoretical question concerning action selection by motivation can be now posed as follows: Is it possible to find an appropriate motivational behavior W_i for a given behavior set L_i of C, and a colony with the behavior W_i which is stable on a set U_i? The answers proved formally in (Kelemen 1993) may be recapitulated as follows:

For motivation of disjoint behavior sets the corresponding motivational behaviors must be disjoint. If the motivational behaviors are not disjoint, then they cannot motivate different behavior sets.

If the behavior sets are disjoint then motivational behaviors for them must be disjoint, too.

If disjoint finite sets are given then it is possible to construct an agent with such sets as behavior sets motivated by disjoint motivational behaviors.

8. The Role of the Environment

In the previous sections we demonstrated how some "mentalistic" explanations of rationality may be (at least in certain level) replaced by "interactionistic" ones which emphasize the interactions among the (relatively) independent (autonomous) non-rational parts of a rational system. Now, we complete our views by adding some remarks on the role of interactions of rational systems with their *environments*.

It is clear, that an agent is rational only in some "natural" surrounding environment. (All the human rationality disappears if the hunam being is faced with an absolutely unknown environment; in fact, we can't imagine such an environment. Similarly, all the low-level rationality of the $\mathcal{LADYBUG}$ disappears in an environment with vertical obstacles – say, boxes on the table top.) As (Horswill 1995) pointed out, a rational agent should take advantage of the special properties of its environments which may simplify the decision problems which face it. Thus, from the standpoint of the agent and its designer, environments have some important properties. If we try to understand the behavior of an agent in its environment, we must make these properties explicit and draw out their significance for the agent. We will try to do that and expand appropriately our previous grammatical model.

Horswill (1995) considers an environment as a *concrete thing*, a place in which a particular agent acts. The set of environments in which an agent can perform its activities he calls a *habitat*. A *habitat constraint* is a predicate on environments. Its extension is the set of environments which satisfy it. A given environment or habitat can be partially characterized by the set of constraints which it satisfies. Thus the habitat forms a useful descriptive language for environments and habitats.

In our framework we understand a *habitat* of an agent as a formal specification of the states of agent's environment in terms in which the agent's possibilities to act in this environments are expressed.

Formally, let L_C^{rat} be the set of rational behaviors of an agent modelled by the colony C. Then the set $H \subseteq (N_C \cup T_C)^*$ we will call the *habitat* of C if for arbitrary $w \in H$, $w \Longrightarrow^* x$ implies $x \in L_C^{rat}$.

Relating the concept of *habitat* to the concept of the *stability* defined in Section 3, we can – immediatly on the base of definitions – state that *every set in which the colony C is stable forms a habitat for the agent modelled by C.*

With respect of the $\mathcal{LADYBUG}$, in Section 5 we specified its behavior as the language $L_{\mathcal{TM}}$. The parameters k and l appearing in its specification reflect some physical properties of a particular table on which the $\mathcal{LADYBUG}$ rolls, some properties of $\mathcal{LADYBUG}$'s environment. To construct a habitat for the $\mathcal{LADYBUG}$ means to determine the descriptions of $\mathcal{LADYBUG}$'s environments in which it behaves rationally (does not fall the table top). What is very important in this respect is to express the environments regularities (the minitheory of the environment) in concepts which are related to the $\mathcal{LADYBUG}$'s concepts of it environment. In this particular example this means to express the characteristics of the environment in $\mathcal{LADYBUG}$'s possibilities to sense the table tops edge, and to move forward or to change the direction of the motion.

9. Colonies in Dynamic Environments

The agent/environment interactions play a crucial role mainly in situations when the environments in which the agents act have their own dynamics. For the situations when the laws of environment dynamics are known and may be characterized in the symbolic level, in (Csuhaj-Varjú et al. 1994b, 1996) a formal framework – the concept of so called *eco-grammar system* is proposed and studied. Colonies may be considered as a simplfyied variant of such systems based on purely reactive components sharing a common string – their environment – which has its own dynamics governed by some rules. We may imagine these rules in the form of rewritings. The overall dynamics of the whole system set up in this style consists then in two main phases: In the first one the colony executes one step of its modification of the environment. Then, in the second phase, the rules describing environments dynamics are applied – in parallel – and execute environment changes.

More formally, a *colony with dymanic environment* – or an *extended colony*, according (Csuhaj-Varjú, 1996) – may be defined as a structure

$$E = (V, T, H_1, \ldots, H_s, R_1, \ldots, R_n, S)$$

where V and T $(T \subseteq V)$ are the total and the terminal alphabets of E, H_i is a finite set of context-free or regular rewriting rules defined over V, R_i is a component defined as in the basic case of colonies $(V_i \subseteq V)$, S – the starting symbol of E – is an element from V, and T is a subset of the union of all T_is.

The functioning of the structure consists of an action of a component on the environment as in the case of basic colonies, and of a development of the environment acording the rules included in H_is and applied in a parallel way in the sense accepted in the theory of *L-systems* – in the $0L$ manner; cf. (Rozenberg, Salomaa, 1980).

The basic model of derivation in colonies with dynamic environment can be defined as follows:

Let $x, y \in V^+$. Then x directly derives y (in the basic mode of derivation; in the b-mode), if one of the following cases hold:

– there is a start symbol S_i of some of components R_i such that $x = x_1 S_i x_2, x_1, x_2 \in V^*$. Then $y = y_1 w y_2, w \in L(R_i)$, and $x_1 \Longrightarrow_{H_j} y_1, x_2 \Longrightarrow_{H_j} y_2$, for some j, and H_j is applied in the $0L$ style.

– $x \neq x_1 S_i x_2$ for any i for $x_1, x_2 \in V^*$. Then $x \Longrightarrow_{H_j} y$ for some j, and H_j is applied in the $0L$ manner.

The language defined by such a type of colonies can be defined in the usual way. Similarly as in the cases discussed in Section 3, we can define the acceptance styles *arb, one, all* and *ex*.

The generative power of the just defined type of colonies overcomes the generative power of $ET0L$-systems for the basic variant of derivation and the acceptance style *arb*.

10. Conclusions

The previous sections present a conceptual framework for dealing with some properties of systems set up from simple, purely reactive components. The framework is based on the theory of *grammar systems* – a well-founded mathematical approach to distributed or decentralized processing simple symbol structures (Csuhaj-Varjú et al., 1994a). Thus, the presented approach is in many directions limited. No formalization reflects the whole complexity and all of the details of the formalized entities and/or phenomena.

The presented framework is intended mainly to express formally the idea of *pure reactivity*, and *minimal comunication* of the individually simple components – the architectural principle of and the mechanisms of *emergence* of complicated behaviors from the simple ones. It is not intended for dealing with another very important aspect of systems set up from *real* reactive parts – their *situatedness* in real dynamic environments with a lot of uncertainties and sensory noises. Any sensor of a real robotic system realizes only a many-to-one mapping from states of a world to the just sensed data. Moreover, the robot deals with noises when interpreting sensor data. The robotic system decides its actions based on these data, leading to unexpected changes in the environment caused by robots actuators.

In a grammar agent, however, when a symbol is read, the agent is assured that it really *did* read that particular symbol – i.e. it does not have to deal with noises when interpreting the sensed data nor when expecting the changes in the sentential form just under rewriting, when executes a rewriting step. Likewise, when a grammar agent changes some part of a string, it can be assured that the update was what the agent intend – writing a symbol A will result in an A being written. When a robot decides to grasp an object A, the result may or may not the A being grasped. Thus, the abstract description of an environment equals the actual environment for the grammar agents which is not the usual situation in the case of real embodied robots situated in real changing environments. Only having these in mind we can state that the components of a colony of grammars are *situated* in their symbolic environments.

However, the behavior of a colony really *emerges* from interactions of its components acting autonomously in their symbolic environment and can considerably overcome the individual behaviors of the components. Similarly, the analysis of the level of rationality of colonies proves that at least this level of rationality may in principle appear in behaviors of the real purely reactive robots or other kinds of agents. The framework enables also to deal with some aspects of the interactions of environments and agents, and with some phenomena appearing when we see agents as societies of simple autonomous components.

As a generalization, let us repeat the position expressed first in (Kelemen 1993): We recognize four main principles reflected by the grammatical theory of colonies, which appear in behavior-based robotics and in some other branches of research connected with autonomous agents as well. There are:

- The principle of *total decentralization* of complex systems into simple components.

- The *transparent simplicity* of components behaviors in comparison with the behavior performed by the whole system.

- The principle of *liberalism* – components behave without any explicitly defined obligatory strategy of cooperation.

- The principle of *emergence* – the behavior of the system emerges as some kind of side-effect of the behavior of components.

The sketched framework enables us to deal with any of these principles in a symbol-manipulating level. In discussions on the *reactionistic* and *cognitive* approaches to intelligent systems (cf. e.g. (Vera, Simon 1993)) our framework supports the idea that some of the principles are present in both of them, but has been emphasized with different intensity up to now.

References

1. Baník, I.: Colonies with position. *Computers and Artificial Intelligence 15* (1996) 141 – 154

2. Bechtel, W., Richardson, W. C.: *Discovering Complexity.* Princeton University Press, Princeton, NJ, 1993

3. Benson, S., Nilsson, N. J.: Reacting, planning, and learning in an autonomous agent. In: *Machine Intelligence vol. 14* (D. Michie, S. Muggleton, eds.) Oxford University Press, Oxford, 1994, 1 – 33

4. Connell, J. H.: *Minimalist Mobile Robotics.* Academic Press, New York, 1990

5. Csuhaj-Varjú, E.: Colonies - a multi-agent approach to language generation. Text distributed during the *ECAI'96 Workshop on Extended Finite State Models of Language*, Budapest, August 11 and 12, 1996

6. Csuhaj-Varjú, E., Dassow, J., Kelemen, J., Păun, Gh: *Grammar Systems.* Gordon & Breach, London, 1994

7. Csuhaj-Varjú, E., Kelemen, J., Kelemenová, A., Păun, Gh.: Eco-grammar systems - a grammatical framework for life-like interactions. *Artificial Life* (accepted)

8. Csuhaj-Varjú, E., Păun, Gh.: Structured colonies - models of symbiosis and parasitism. *Analele Universtităţii Bucureşti, Matematică-Informatică XLII – XLIII* (1993 – 1994) 15 – 31

9. Dassow, J., Kelemen, J., Păun, Gh.: On parallelism in colonies. *Cybernetics and Systems 24* (1993) 37 – 49

10. Doyle, J. 1988. *Artificial Intelligence and Rational Self-Government.* Computer Science Department, Carnegie Mellon University, Pittsburgh, Penn., Technical Report CMU-CS-88-124

11. Horswill, I.: Analysis of adaptation and environment. *Artificial Intelligence 73* (1995) 1 – 30

12. Kelemen, J.: Multiagent symbol systems and behavior-based robots. *Applied Artificial Intelligence 7* (1993) 419 – 432

13. Kelemen, J.: A note on achieving low-level rationality from pure reactivity. *Journal of Experimental & Theoretical Artificial Intelligence 8* (1996) 121 – 127

14. Kelemen, J., Kelemenov, A.: A grammar-theoretic treatment of multiagent systems. *Cybernetics and Systems 23* (1992) 621 – 633

15. Kelemenová, A., Csuhaj-Varjú, E.: Languages of colonies. *Theoretical Computer Science 134* (1994a) 119 – 130

16. Kelemenová, A., Csuhaj-Varjú, E.: On the power of colonies. In: *Words, Languages and Combinatorics* (M. Ito, H. Jürgensen, eds.) World Scientific, Singapore, 1994b

17. Kelemenová, A., Kelemen, J.: From colonies to eco(grammar)systems - an overview. In: *Results and Trends in Theoretical Computer Science* (J. Karhumäki, H. Maurer, G. Rozenberg, eds.) Springer-Verlag, Berlin, 1994

18. Kushmerick, N.: Cognitivism and situated action - two views on intelligent agency. *Computers and Artificial Intelligence 15* (1996) 393 – 417

19. Maes, P.: Behavior-based artificial intelligence. In: *From Animals to Animates 2* (J.-A. Mayer, H. Roitblat, S. W. Wilson, eds.) The MIT Press, Cambridge, Mass., 1993

20. McClamrock, R.: *Existential Cognition - Computational Minds in the World.* The University of Chicago Press, Chicago, Ill., 1995

21. Păun, Gh.: On the generative power of colonies. *Kybernetika 31* (1995) 83 – 97

22. Parker, L. E.: Adaptive action selection for cooperative agent teams. In: *From Animals to Animates 2* (J.-A. Mayer, H. Roitblat, S. W. Wilson, eds.) The MIT Press, Cambridge, Mass., 1993

23. Pollock, J. L.: New foundations for practical reasoning. *Mind and Machines 2* (1992) 113 – 144

24. Rozenberg, G., Salomaa, A.: *The Mathematical Theory of L Systems.* Academic Press, New York, 1980

25. Simon, H. A.: Rationality as process and as product. *American Economic Review 68* (1978) 1 – 16

26. Simon, H. A.: *The Sciences of the Artificial (2nd Edition).* The MIT Press: Cambridge, Mass. 1982

27. Thorpe, Ch.: Contribution to the Panel on robot navigation. In: *Proc. 11th IJCAI.* Detroit, Mich., 1989

28. Vera, A. H., Simon, H. A.: Situated action - a symbolic interpretation. *Cognitive Science 17* (1993) 7 – 48

Grammatical Inference of Colonies[1]

Petr SOSÍK, Leoš ŠTÝBNAR

Institute of Mathematics and Computer Science
Silesian University, Opava, Czech Republic

Abstract. A concept of accepting colonies is introduced. A hybrid connectionist-symbolic architecture ("neural pushdown automaton") for inference of colonies based on presentation of positive and negative examples of strings is then described, together with an algorithm for extracting a colony from trained neural network. Some examples of the inference of colonies generating/accepting simple context-free languages illustrate the function of the architecture.

1. Introduction

The problem of grammatical inference is generally hard and even for regular languages it is NP in the worst cases. There have been various heuristic methods developed, trying to find a suitable solution with reasonable computational expenses. We shall focus our attention on hybrid architectures coupling principles of neural and symbolic computation.

There have been many such architectures presented, concerning mostly (but not exclusively) the connectionist–symbolic grammatical inference of regular [1], [6], context-free [22] or context-sensitive [2] language acceptors. For a broader description of these results we refer to [21]; a brief overview can be found in [20]. The unifying approach of these results inheres mostly in unfolding input strings into the time-series, so they are presented one symbol at a time and processed *serially*. This seems to be not due to the nature of *artificial neural networks* (ANNs), which is inherently parallel. In fact, this drawback isn't overcome in this paper still, but some attention is devoted to accepting *grammar systems* (GS) – possibly parallel accepting devices.

There are many links between ANNs and GSs: parallelism, independently working elements (agents/neurons), communication of the elements, absence of centralized control. On the other hand, there remain many problems of representing one paradigm by another: fixed communication graph of ANN vs. dynamic communication of GS, virtually *unlimited potential* of GS agents (each agent must be able to act simultaneously on an arbitrary number of symbols of the generated string), and so on [20]. The model of the accepting grammar system presented here doesn't involve some of these problems (balanced by its less accepting power) and can be successfully extracted from a trained ANN.

2. Basic Definitions and Properties

In this section the basic definitions of the constructions necessary to describe our model are given. Often only a special form of a definition is given, simple enough to have the properties necessary for the model; the general forms can be found in the references cited. Also some properties of accepting colonies are derived.

---

[1]Research supported by the Grant Agency of Czech Republic, grant No. 201/95/0134.

We denote the classes of finite languages, regular languages, linear languages, Dyck languages, languages accepted by the deterministic pushdown automata without λ-transitions (DPDA) and context-free (CF) languages by $\mathcal{L}(FIN)$, $\mathcal{L}(REG)$, $\mathcal{L}(LIN)$, $\mathcal{L}(DYCK)$, $\mathcal{L}(DPDA)$ and $\mathcal{L}(CF)$, respectively.

If $x \in V^*$, where V is some alphabet, and if $W \subseteq V$, then $|x|_W$ denotes the number of occurrences of letters from W in x.

2.1. Artificial Neural Networks

Here we only briefly describe the basics of the ANN model used below. For a more detailed tutorial we refer to [9], a broad explanation can be found in [8].

Our ANN is a finite set of interconnected autonomous agents – *neurons*. All the neurons in the network compute the same function

$$y_i = \theta(\sum_{j=1}^{N} a_{ij} x_j),$$

where x_{ij} are the inputs, the y_i is the output of the neuron, θ is the *threshold function*, see figure 1. The constants a_{ij} are called the *weights* of the inputs.

The input of ANN is some n-tuple and the output some m-tuple of real-valued signals. There are *feedforward* and *feedback* connections, which leads to nontrivial dynamics of the network. Such a type of network is called a *recurrent neural network* (RNN).

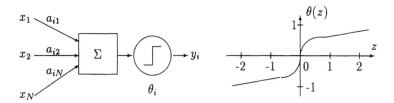

Figure 1. The basic model of neuron and the treshold function.

2.2. Colonies

Colonies and the languages they generate have been described e.g. in [15], [11], [12]. There have been various generating modes and styles of acceptance defined. Here we restrict ourselves to the basic mode and the *dist* style of acceptance used in our model, although the other styles could be modelled as well. In this sense the following definitions are simplified compared to the original ones.

Definition 2.1. A *colony* is an $(n+3)$-tuple $C = (N, T, R_1, \ldots, R_n, S)$, where

(i) N is the set of nonterminals of C;

(ii) T is the set of terminals of C; $N \cap T = \emptyset$;

(iii) $R_i = (S_i, F_i)$, for every $i, 1 \leq i \leq n$, is the component of C; $S_i \in N$ is the start symbol of R_i; $F_i \subseteq (T \cup N - \{S_i\})^*$ is a finite language;

(iv) $S = S_i$ for some $i, 1 \leq i \leq n$; S is the start symbol of C.

238

We denote the total alphabet of C by V, i.e. $V = T \cup N$. We can assume $N = \{S_1, S_2, \ldots, S_n\}$ and $F_i \neq \emptyset$ for every $i, 1 \leq i \leq n$, without loss of generality.

Definition 2.2. Let $C = (N, T, R_1, \ldots, R_n, S)$ be a colony and let $x, y \in V^*$, where V is the total alphabet of C. We write $x \Rightarrow_{\text{gen}} y$, iff there is a component R_i of C for some $i, 1 \leq i \leq n$, such that $x = x_1 S_i x_2$ and $y = x_1 w x_2$ holds, where $x_1, x_2 \in V^*$ and $w \in F_i$.

Definition 2.3. Let $C = (N, T, R_1, \ldots, R_n, S)$ be a colony. The language generated by C is defined by $L_{\text{gen}}(C) = \{w \mid S \Rightarrow^*_{\text{gen}} w, w \in T^*\}$, where $\Rightarrow^*_{\text{gen}}$ denotes the reflexive transitive closure of $\Rightarrow_{\text{gen}}$.

Let us denote $\mathcal{L}_{\text{gen}}(COL)$ the class of languages generated by the colonies defined above. It has been proven in [10], that $\mathcal{L}_{\text{gen}}(COL) = \mathcal{L}(CF)$.

2.3. Accepting Colonies

A concept of accepting grammar systems has been introduced in [3], [4], [5]. We now introduce accepting colonies in a similar way, together with the concept of determinism, since our neural model is deterministic.

Definition 2.4. Let $C = (N, T, R_1, \ldots, R_n, S)$ be a colony and let $x, y \in V^*$, where V is the total alphabet of C. We write $y \Rightarrow_{\text{acc}} x$, iff $x \Rightarrow_{\text{gen}} y$.

Definition 2.5. Let $C = (N, T, R_1, \ldots, R_n, S)$ be a colony. The language accepted by C is defined by $L_{\text{acc}}(C) = \{w | w \Rightarrow^*_{\text{acc}} S, w \in T^*\}$, where $\Rightarrow^*_{\text{acc}}$ denotes the reflexive transitive closure of $\Rightarrow_{\text{acc}}$.

We denote $\mathcal{L}_{\text{acc}}(COL)$ the class of languages accepted by the colonies defined above.

If $y \Rightarrow_{\text{acc}} x_1$ and $y \Rightarrow_{\text{acc}} x_2$ implies $x_1 = x_2$ for every $y \in L_{\text{acc}}(C)$, then we call the system dynamically deterministic; in this case, we add the letter D_d to the notation of the system. This form of determinism guarantees that the accepting colony can at each derivation step perform at most one possible action; if there are more possibilities, the string is rejected.

If $F_i \cap F_j = \emptyset$ for every $i, j, 1 \leq i < j \leq n$, we call the system statically deterministic; in this case, we add the letter D_s to the notation of the system. This guarantees that for every y there is at most one i such that $y \Rightarrow_{\text{acc}} S_i$.

If no set F_i contains the empty word λ, we call the system propagating; in this case, we add the letter P to the notation of the system.

Theorem 2.6.

(i) $\mathcal{L}_{\text{acc}}([P][D_d/D_s]COL) = \mathcal{L}_{\text{gen}}([P][D_d/D_s]COL)$,

(ii) $\mathcal{L}_{\text{acc}}(PD_dCOL) = \mathcal{L}_{\text{acc}}(D_dCOL) \subset \mathcal{L}(LIN)$; $\mathcal{L}_{\text{acc}}(D_dCOL)$ and $\mathcal{L}(REG)$ are incomparable,

(iii) $\mathcal{L}_{\text{gen}}(D_sCOL) = \mathcal{L}_{\text{gen}}(COL)$.

Proof. (i) The statement follows directly from definitions. Note that the concept of both the dynamic and the static determinism is the same for the generating and the accepting case.

(ii) First, note that the existence of the empty word λ in some F_i would destroy the dynamical determinism. Now, let $C = (N, T, R_1, \ldots, R_n, S)$ be a colony in the class $D_d COL$. Without loss of thee geenerality, we can assume that for every $x \in \bigcup_{i=1}^{n} F_i$ there exists a derivation $S \Rightarrow_{gen}^{*} wS_i y \Rightarrow_{gen} wxy \Rightarrow_{gen}^{*} u, u \in T^*$ for some $i, 1 \leq i \leq n$. Then $|x|_N \leq 1$ for every $x \in \bigcup_{i=1}^{n} F_i$. Let us assume for contradiction, that there existed a derivation $S \Rightarrow_{gen}^{*} wS_i y \Rightarrow_{gen} wx_1 S_j x_2 S_k x_3 y \Rightarrow_{gen}^{*} w' x_1' z_1' x_2' z_2' x_3' y' \equiv u, u \in T^*$ such, that $S_j \Rightarrow_{gen}^{*} z_1 \Rightarrow_{gen} z_1'$ and $S_k \Rightarrow_{gen}^{*} z_2 \Rightarrow_{gen} z_2'$ for some i, j, k, $1 \leq i, j, k \leq n$ and some $w', x_1', x_2', x_3', y' \in T^*$, $w, x_1, x_2, x_3, y \in V^*$, $z_1', z_2' \in T^+$ and $z_1, z_2 \in V^+$. Then $u \in L_{acc}(C)$ and $u \Rightarrow_{acc} w' x_1' z_1 x_2' z_2' x_3' y'$ and $u \Rightarrow_{acc} w' x_1' z_1' x_2' z_2 x_3' y'$ would hold.

Now, let $G = (N, T, P, S)$ be a context-free grammar such that $P = \bigcup_{i=1}^{n} (\bigcup_{x \in F_i} S_i \rightarrow x)$. Then $L(G) = L_{acc}(C)$ and G is linear. For the proof of the second statement, note that $\{a^n | n \geq 1\} \notin \mathcal{L}_{acc}(D_d COL)$ and $\{a^n b^n | n \geq 1\} \in \mathcal{L}_{acc}(D_d COL)$.

(iii) We follow the proof of Lemma 2.3 in [4].

Let $C = (N, T, R_1, \ldots, R_n, S)$ be a colony. We define $N' = N \cup \{S_{n+1}\}$, where S_{n+1} is a new symbol. Let $R_{n+1} = (S_{n+1}, \{\lambda\})$ be a new component of the colony.

For each $F_i, 1 \leq i \leq n$, we define

$$\text{conflict}(F_i) = \{x \in F_i | (\exists j \neq i)(x \in F_j)\},$$

$$\text{no} - \text{conflict}(F_i) = F_i - \text{conflict}(F_i).$$

Define

$$\text{DET}(R_i) = (S_i, \text{no} - \text{conflict}(F_i) \cup \{x S_{n+1}^i | x \in \text{conflict}(F_i)\}).$$

Consider the statically deterministic system

$$C' = (N', T, \text{DET}(R_1), \ldots, \text{DET}(R_n), R_{n+1}, S).$$

It is easily seen that $L_{gen}(C) = L_{gen}(C')$. □

We do not know much about the class $\mathcal{L}_{acc}(PD_sCOL)$; we conjecture that it contains $\mathcal{L}(DPDA)$.

3. Hybrid Neural-Symbolic Architecture

The idea of these architectures was introduced first in the classical paper [13]. As it was mentioned in [20], RNN needs some external stimuli during its work, otherwise it tends to reach a stable state soon, which is in contrast with recurrent application of the same rules during the accepting of a string by a grammar system. Moreover, the RNN should be of finite size, but the grammar system should be able to accept a string of an arbitrary length.

The simplest possibility of how to solve these problems is to present the input string serially, which nevertheless leads to a lack of parallelism. The occurrence of the empty string λ in some F_i would cause another problem, so we will restrict ourselves to the propagating systems.

Consider an accepting colony $C = (N, T, R_1, \ldots, R_n, S)$ with the serial access to the accepted string w. We start with the leftmost part of the string w and find a component R_i for some $i, 1 \leq i \leq n$, such that there is $x \in F_i, x = uy$ and $w = uv$ for some $u, v \in T^+$ and some $y \in (\{\lambda\} \cup NV^*)$. Hence the component R_i becomes active. Whenever there occurs the symbol $S_j \in N$ within x for some $j, 1 \leq j \leq n$, the component R_j becomes active, but we must remember that after it finishes its work, the component R_i may has to continue. On the one hand it becomes clear that there has to be a stack for storing calling sequence of the components of the colony.

On the other hand, we must take into the account the fact that in the phase of inference we know neither the number nor the language of components of the colony being inferred; they must be the result of the inference algorithm. As it seems to be much more difficult to change the structure of the RNN in the phase of learning than to change the weights of the neurons only, it follows that we perhaps should not incorporate an expected structure of the colony into the network topology. Moreover, as storing and retrieving information to/from the stack have to be subjected to adaptation, these operations must be continuous in some sense (see the next section).

Again, the simplest solution seems to be the use of a homogeneous RNN, which can store/retrieve to/from the stack some information, no matter what they represent. Then after training we can extract the result from the structure of the internal states of the network and assign an interpretation to it.

3.1. Neural Deterministic Pushdown Automaton

It has become clear during the last years that enhancing the computational power of an RNN over that of finite automata requires an expansion of resources. The disadvantage of many models as in [17], [18] is that they do not involve effective adaptation.

The idea of deterministic *neural pushdown automaton* (NPDA) has been reported first by [17]. We follow the model described in [22], which has the following advantages:

- the stack is considered to be external and not necessarily represented within the RNN; some arguments supporting this approach can be found in [20];

- the model needs only very brief preliminary information about the expected size of the inferred system;

- both the finite neural automaton and the stack operations are subjected to an adaptation process, thanks to the concept of continuous stack memory;

- effective procedures for training such a system have been provided, together with algorithms for extracting the pushdown automaton from the trained network.

There are also some necessary restrictions of the described model; the most important seems to be the request that every rule of the NPDA must be in one of the following forms:

(a) $\delta(q_i, a, b) = (q_j, \lambda)$,

(b) $\delta(q_i, a, b) = (q_j, b)$,

(c) $\delta(q_i, a, b) = (q_j, ab)$.

Moreover, the tape and the stack alphabets are the same, except the starting stack symbol $\perp$. No λ transitions are allowed. If there are no restrictions applied to the strings stored into the stack in the rule forms (b) and (c), the automaton is be equivalent to a CF grammar in the 2-SNF [23] and it is be able to accept any language in $\mathcal{L}(DPDA)$. With these restrictions the class of accepted languages is reduced.

Theorem 3.1. *Let* $M = (Q, \Sigma, \Gamma, \delta, s, F)$ *be a DPDA such, that* $\Gamma = \Sigma \cup \{\perp\}$ *and each rule of* δ *is in one of the forms* (a),(b),(c), *where* $q_i, q_j \in Q$, $a \in \Sigma$, $b \in \Gamma$. *Denote* $\mathcal{L}(M)$ *the class of the languages accepted by the automata of the described type. Then* $\mathcal{L}(DYCK) \subset \mathcal{L}(M) \subset \mathcal{L}(DPDA)$ *and* $\mathcal{L}(M)$ *is incomparable with* $\mathcal{L}(LIN)$.

Proof. As it has been shown in [23], the rule forms (a) and (c) are enough for constructing a DPDA with one state accepting any Dyck language. The form (b) together with more states extends the power of the automaton over the class of DYCK languages. Note, that for instance $\{a^{2n}b^n | n \geq 1\} \in \mathcal{L}(M)$ and $\{a^{2n}b^n \mid n \geq 1\} \notin \mathcal{L}(DYCK)$.

Now, consider the language generated by the linear grammar $G = (\{S\}, \{a, b, u, v, w, x\}, \{S \rightarrow aaSu/abSv/baSw/bbSx/\lambda\}, S)$. It is easily seen that $L(G) \in \mathcal{L}(DPDA)$ and $L(G) \notin \mathcal{L}(M)$. To finish the proof, it remains to note that there are nonlinear Dyck languages. $\square$

The whole NPDA consists of a finite size neural network controller (an extended version of a neural network finite state automata) and an infinite continuous stack memory. The controller is an RNN consisting of third order neurons (also second order would be possible) trained by the real-time recurrent learning (RTRL) algorithm. The infinite continuous stack memory consists of two parallel stacks: the discrete one, which stores the symbols, and the continuous one, which stores the continuous length L of every symbol, $0 \leq L \leq 1$. There are three actions defined upon the stack memory, each of them having the strength A_i, $0 \leq A_i \leq 1$:

- *push*, which stores the input tape symbol onto the top of the stack with the assigned length A_i;

- *pop*, which removes the top symbol(s) so that the total depth of the continuous stack is decreased by A_i;

- *no-op*, which causes no change in the stack memory.

The configuration of the automaton is defined in the usual way. The language accepted by the NPDA consists of the strings which transfer the automaton from the initial configuration $(q_1, \perp, w)$ to the configuration (q_F, λ, λ), so that the final state must be reached and simultaneously the stack must be emptied. Each input string is finished with a special symbol e.

The schematic diagram of the model is presented in figure 2. For more details about the continuous stack, training algorithm, symbol representation and state dynamics we refer to [22], [14].

3.2. Extraction of a Colony from the Trained NPDA

The NPDA is trained using a set of positive and negative samples of strings (that have to be accepted/rejected) of some language in $\mathcal{L}(M)$. During the training the topology of the NPDA is not changing, but the space of the internal states is evolving.

The training is finished, when (almost) every string of the training set is correctly classified. But the final output state consist of analogous values between 0 and 1, so the classification is not strict. There exist analogous errors, which can accumulate as the input string become longer, due to the NPDA nature of a continuous dynamic system.

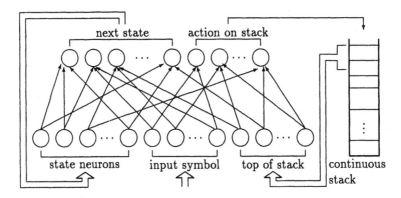

Figure 2. The architecture of the NPDA.

For a correct classification of strings of an arbitrary length, it is necessary to extract a discrete accepting device from the trained NPDA. The result of this process highly depends on the quality of the extracting algorithm, based mostly on clustering in the space of neuron states. Generally, we want to extract as small an accepting device as possible, but still homogeneous with the set of training samples. More detailed descriptions of the clustering algorithms can be found in [1], [6], [22], etc.

We present here an algorithm for extracting a colony from the NPDA $M = (Q, \Sigma, \Gamma, \delta, s, F)$ having already performed hierarchical clustering of states. It employs some special features of the NPDA to obtain as simple a grammar system as possible. Let us denote by $q_1, \ldots, q_F$ the clusters of state neuron output values of NPDA, let us quantize the action neuron states to three levels with assigned labels *push, pop, no-op*. Let us express the state transitions in the form of the oriented graph with the starting node q_1 and the final node q_F. To every edge a triple (a, b, act) is assigned, for $a \in \Sigma$, $b \in \Gamma$, $act \in \{push, pop, no\text{-}op\}$. The nodes from which the final node is inaccessible are ignored.

Algorithm 3.2.

1. Let us denote $C = (N, T, R_1, \ldots, R_n, S)$ the derived colony. Let us assign $T := \Sigma$, $N := \{[q_1, \perp, q_F]\}$, $n := 0$.

2. If there is $[q_i, b, q_j] \in N$ such that $[q_i, b, q_j]$ is not the starting symbol of any component R_k for some $k, 1 \leq k \leq n$, then continue, otherwise go to step 5.

3. Assign $n := n + 1$, add a new component $R_n := ([q_i, b, q_j], \emptyset)$ to the colony. For every edge (a, b, act) from the node q_i to the node q_m for some $q_m \in Q$ do the following:

(a) if $act = pop$ and $q_m = q_j$, add the string a to the F_n;

(b) if $act = no\text{-}op$, add the string $a[q_m, b, q_j]$ to the F_n; add the symbol $[q_m, b, q_j]$ to N;

(c) if $act = push$, add the string $a[q_m, a, q_p][q_p, b, q_j]$ to the F_n for every $q_p \in Q$ such that the node q_p is accessible from the node q_i and q_j is accessible from q_p; add the symbols $[q_m, a, q_p], [q_p, b, q_j]$ to N; *accessible* means the transitive non-reflexive closure of the graph edge transitions.

4. Go to step 2.

5. Apply an algorithm for excluding the nonterminating components of the colony (quite similar as excluding the nonterminating symbols of the CF grammar). Exclude S_i from N for any nonterminating component (S_i, F_i). Exclude the strings containing S_i from F_j for every $j, 1 \leq j \leq n$. Adjust the value of n.

6. For every component (S_i, F_i) for some $i, 1 \leq i \leq n$, such that $F_i \subset T^*$, do the following:

   (a) Replace every string $x_1 S_i x_2$ in F_j for some $j, 1 \leq j \leq n$ and $x_1, x_2 \in V^*$ with the strings $x_1 y x_2$ for every $y \in F_i$.

   (b) Exclude the component (S_i, F_i) from the colony.

7. For every two components $(S_i, F_i), (S_j, F_j)$, for some $i, j, 1 \leq i < j \leq n$, such that $F_i = F_j$, do the following:

   (a) Replace every string $x_1 S_j x_2$ in F_k for some $k, 1 \leq k \leq n$ and $x_1, x_2 \in V^*$ with the string $x_1 S_i x_2$.

   (b) Exclude the component (S_j, F_j) from the colony.

8. For every component (S_i, F_i) for some $i, 1 \leq i \leq n$, such that there is a string $x_1 S_i x_2 \in F_i$ for some $x_1, x_2 \in V$, do the following:

   (a) Assign $n := n + 1$, add a new component $R_n := (S_n, \{S_i\})$ to the colony.

   (b) Replace all occurrences of S_i within the strings in F_i with S_n.

It is easily seen that $L(C) = L(M)$, where C is the colony derived from M by the use of the algorithm described above.

4. Simulation Results

There are three examples given in [22]. Due to the fact that we use the same training process in our model, we can utilize these results at the situation when the RNN has been trained and the hierarchical clustering of the states has been already performed. Then our algorithm for extracting a colony from the trained network will be applied and the results will be presented.

Example 4.1. *The Balanced Parenthesis Language*
The input alphabet consists of symbols [,] (we omit the final transition coupled with an end symbol e). The training set contains fifty strings with an approximately balanced number of the strings to accept and to reject. The trained NPDA is presented

244

in figure 3 (the nodes from which the final node is inaccessible are omitted). The state $(1, .25, .25)$ is final.

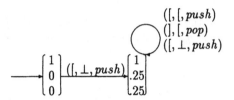

Figure 3. Trained NPDA accepting balanced parenthesis language.

After applying Algorithm 3.2, the resulting colony with five components looks as follows: $C = (\{S, S_1, S_2, S_3, S_4\}, \{[,]\}, e), (S, \{[S_1 S_2]\}), (S_1, \{[S_3 S_3, 0]\}),$ $(S_2, \{1 S_1 S_4, e\}), (S_3, \{S_1\}), (S_4, \{S_2\}), S)$.

Example 4.2. *The language $1^n 0^n$*

The input alphabet is $\{0, 1\}$. The training set consists of 12 legal and 15 illegal strings. In order to have only short strings in the training set, and due to the fact there are relatively few short legal strings in this language, the training set replicates some of the short legal strings. The trained NPDA is presented in figure 4. The state $(1, 1, 1, 1, 1), (1, 0, 1, 1, 1)$ is final. This state (and the second one denoted by two vectors of the neuron outputs) was created by merging of two equivalent clusters.

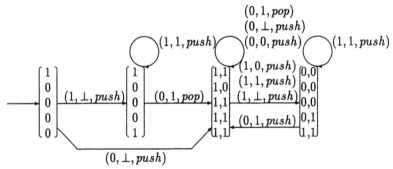

$(0, \perp, push)$

Figure 4. Trained NPDA accepting $0^n 1^n$ language.

The resulting colony with three components is $C = (\{S, S_1, S_2\}, \{0, 1, e\},$ $(S, \{1 S_1 e\}), (S_1, \{1 S_2 0, 0\}), (S_2, \{S_1\}), S)$.

Example 4.3. *The Palindrom Language*

This problem was found to be the most difficult among the presented ones. It has been shown in [14] that the described neural structures are not able to learn this grammar without "hints". The so called *full third-order network structure* has been used in [22] to overcome this problem.

The input alphabet is $\{a, b, c\}$, the palindroms are of the form $wcw^T, w \in \{a, b\}^+$. Two training sets containing 39 and 363 strings were used. The trained NPDA has six states from which the final state is accessible. The resulting colony with five components is $C = (\{S, S_1, S_2, S_3, S_4\}, \{a, b, e\}, (S, \{b S_1 e, a S_2 e\}), (S_1, \{[b S_3 b, a S_4 b, cb]\}),$ $(S_2, \{a S_4 a, b S_3 a, ca\}), (S_3, \{S_1\}), (S_4, \{S_2\}), S)$.

5. Conclusion

The class of accepting colonies has been defined and some of its properties have been derived. It was shown that to present an input string serially (which is needed for the described hybrid connectionist-symbolic architecture), it is necessary to have an infinite memory (stack).

The adaptive neural pushdown automaton together with the algorithm for extracting a colony from the learned neural network was presented and some colonies were successfuly inferred. This documents the possibility of constructing the artificial life models with the ability of adaptation to the surrounding environment.

The drawback of this model is its serial access to the input string. So the direction of the further research is constructing parallel adaptive neural models of parallel working grammar systems, which could couple the abilities of the both paradigms.

References

1. R. Alquézar, A. Sanfeliu: An algebraic framework to represent finite state machines in single-layer recurrent neural networks.*Neural Computation,* No. 7, 931–949 (1995).

2. R. Alquézar, A. Sanfeliu, J. Cueva: Learning of context-sensitive language acceptors through regular inference and constraint induction. In: *Proc. ICGI'96,* L.Miclet and C.de la Higuera (eds.), Springer-Verlag, Lecture Notes in Artificial Intelligence 1147, 134-145, 1996.

3. H. Bordihn, H. Fernau: Accepting grammars and systems. TR 9/94, Universität Karlsruhe, Fakultät für Informatik 1994.

4. H. Fernau, H. Bordihn: Remarks on accepting parallel systems. *Intern. J. Computer Math.,* vol. 56, 51–67.

5. H. Fernau, M. Holzer, H. Bordihn: Accepting multi-agent systems: the case of cooperating distributed grammar systems. *Computers and Artificial Intelligence,* vol. 15 (1996), No. 2–3, 123–139.

6. C. Giles, C. Omlin: Extraction, insertion and refinement of symbolic rules in dynamically-driven recurrent neural networks. In: [21], p.307.

7. M. Goudreau, C. Giles, S. Chakradhar, D. Chen: First-order vs. second-order single layer recurrent neural networks. In: *IEEE Trans. on Neural Networks,* vol. 5, no. 3, p. 511, 1994.

8. J. Hertz et.al.: *Introduction to the Theory of Neural Computation.* Addison-Wesley 1991.

9. J. Hořejš: A view on neural network paradigms development. *Neural Network World,* IDG Prague, 1991,1992.

10. J. Kelemen, A. Kelemenová: A grammar-theoretic treatment of multiagent systems. *Cybernet. Systems* 23 (1992), 621–633.

11. A. Kelemenová, E. Csuhaj-Varjú: Languages of colonies. *Theoretical Computer Science*, 134, Elsevier 1994, 119–130.

12. A. Kelemenová, J. Kelemen: From Colonies to Eco(grammar)systems: An Overview. In: *Results and Trends in Theoretical Computer Science* 812, (eds.) J.Karhumäki, H.Maurer, G.Rozenberg, Springer Verlag, Berlin, 1994, 213–231.

13. S. C. Kleene: Representation of events in nerve nets and finite automata. In: C. E. Shannon, J. McCarthy (eds.): *Automata Studies*, 3–41, Princeton Univ. Press 1956.

14. M. Mozer, S.Das: A connectionist symbol manipulator that discover the structure of context-free languages. *Advances in Neural Information Processing Systems*, vol. 5 (1993), S. Hanson, J. Cowan, C. Gilles (eds.), Morgan Kaufmann, p.863.

15. Gh. Păun (ed.): *Artificial Life: Grammatical Models*. The Black Sea University Press, Bucharest, 1995.

16. Gh. Păun, L. Sântean: Parallel communicating grammar systems: the regular case, *Ann. Univ. Buc., Math.-Informatics Series 38* (1989) 55–63.

17. J. Pollack: Recursive ditribute representation. *Journal of Artificial Intelligence*, vol. 46 (1990), 77–105.

18. H. Siegelmann, E. D. Sontag: On the computational power of neural nets. In: *Proc. Fifth ACM Workshop on Computational Learning Theory*, 440–449, Pittsburgh 1992.

19. P. Sosík: Eco-grammar systems and artificial neural networks. *Computers and Artificial Intelligence*, No. 2–3 (1996), 247–264.

20. P. Sosík: On hybrid connectionist-symbolic models. *Acta Cybernetica*, accepted, 1997.

21. Special issue on architectures for integrating symbolic and neural processes. *Connection Science*, vol. 5, No. 3-4, 1993.

22. G. Sun, C. Giles, H. Chen, Y. Lee: The neural network pushdown automaton: model, stack and learning simulations. Univerzity of Maryland TR Nos. UMIACS-TR-93-77 & CS-TR-3118, 1995.

23. D. Wood: *Theory of Computation*. John Wiley & Sons 1987.

Chapter 3. Parallel Communicating Grammar Systems

A Grammar Characterization of Logarithmic-Space Computation

Karl ABRAHAMSON

Department of Mathematics, East Carolina University
Greenville, NC 27858, USA
E-mail: karl@cs.ecu.edu

Liming CAI

School of Electrical Engineering and Computer Science
Ohio University, Athens, Ohio 45701, USA
E-mail: cai@ace.cs.ohiou.edu

Steve GORDON

Department of Mathematics, East Carolina University
Greenville, NC 27858, USA
E-mail: magordon@ecuvax.cis.ecu.edu

Abstract. It is shown that nondeterministic logarithmic space-bounded Turing machines recognize exactly the closure (under log-space reduction) of the languages generated by a variant of regular parallel communicating grammars systems.

1. Introduction

Establishing correspondences between resource-bounded computational models and classes of generative grammars has long been an important research activity in theoretical computer science. Such correspondences yield valuable insights into the behavior of both computational models and grammars. Typical examples include the equivalence of finite state automata and regular grammars, nondeterministic pushdown automata and context-free grammars, and nondeterministic linear space-bounded Turing machines and context-sensitive grammars [7]. Some resource-bounded computational models do not seem to have equivalent grammars. One approach to characterizing those systems grammatically has been to show that they are equivalent to a closure of the class of languages generated by a given grammar, under an appropriate notion of reduction. For instance, it has been proven that logarithmic space-bounded nondeterministic Turing machines (log-space NTMs) with the help of a stack (e.g., auxiliary push-down automata) recognize exactly the closure (under log-space reduction) of the context-free languages [4], [18]. Although context-free grammars characterize auxiliary push-down automata from the point of view of complexity theory, we know of no grammar that has been shown to characterize logarithmic space-bounded nondeterministic Turing machines (without a stack). This paper demonstrates that the closure (under log-space reduction) of the languages generated by a variant of regular parallel communicating grammars systems characterizes this model of computation.

Recently, parallel communicating grammar (PCG) systems have been introduced to characterize, at the syntactic level, the behavior of complex systems [13]. Characteristics of PCG systems have been studied by several authors [5], [6], [10], [12], [14], [16], [17]. A PCG system consists of a finite number of grammars whose derivations proceed synchronously in parallel. The separate derivations can query one another, and so communicate. The querying mechanism allows any component to copy what another component has produced. To make a query, a derivation generates a query symbol that refers to the grammar whose derivation is to be queried. Several components may copy the same string by generating the same query symbol at the same time.

It has been proven that PCG systems with more than one component grammar of any type in the Chomsky hierarchy is more powerful than a single grammar of the same type. For example, there are regular PCG systems that generate non-context-free languages. The complexity of languages generated by PCG systems have been studied by [2], [3], [8], [9].

The generative power of PCG systems depends on the communicating protocol or the query mechanism for derivations. Under the query mechanism introduced in [13], it has been proven that any language generated by a linear PCG system can be recognized by a log-space NTM [2], [3]. The query mechanism of [13] does not seem powerful enough to generate the computationally hardest languages recognizable in logarithmic space. A small, natural change to the query mechanism, however, increases the power of regular PCG systems sufficiently to generate log-space complete languages. According to the definition in [13], when one component queries another, it gets the string generated by the latter so long as that string does not contain any query symbols. If this string happens to contain a nonterminal symbol that is not in the grammar of the querying component, the entire derivation fails. We propose allowing the querying component to wait until every nonterminal in the string being queried is in its grammar. The motivation for extending the query mechanism in this way is that the information returned from a query would always be coherent with the querying grammar. Moreover, this protocol allows a querying component to wait any number of steps before completing a query, making synchronization among components much easier to achieve. We call this query mechanism *coherent* queries. Grammar systems whose derivations use coherent queries are called coherent PCG systems, or CPGC systems.

We prove that regular CPCG systems can generate one of the computationally hardest languages that can be recognized by log-space NTMs. In particular, we show that the language ORDERED REACHABILITY (a variant of graph reachability) can be generated by a CPCG system of fifteen regular grammar components. On the other hand, we show that log-space NTMs are still powerful enough to recognize any language generated by a regular CPCG system. These two results establish that log-space NTMs recognize exactly the closure (under log-space reduction) of the languages generated by regular CPCG systems.

The paper is organized as follows. Section 2 defines CPCG systems. In Section

3, we define the language ORDERED REACHABILITY and construct a regular CPCG system that generates it. Section 4 presents the main result. We conclude in Section 5.

2. Preliminaries

In this section we define CPCG systems. We are only interested in PCG systems whose components are regular grammars. See [5], [13] for more general definitions of PCG systems, on which our definition will be based.

We assume that the reader is familiar with log-space NTMs and log-space reducibility, as described for example in [7], [1], [11], and with basic concepts of formal language theory as can be found in [15]. We use λ to denote the empty string.

Definition. A *Coherent Parallel Communicating* grammar system (CPCG system) with $k \geq 1$ regular components is a $(k+2)$-tuple $\Gamma = (Q, \Sigma, G_1, \ldots, G_k)$ where Σ is a terminal alphabet, $Q = \{Q_1, Q_2, \ldots, Q_k\}$ is a set of *query symbols*, and each $G_i = (N_i \cup (Q - \{Q_i\}), \Sigma, P_i, S_i)$, for $i = 1, \ldots, k$, is a Chomsky regular grammar with nonterminal set $N_i \cup (Q - Q_i)$, terminal set Σ, productions P_i and start symbol S_i. It is required that sets $N_1 \cup \cdots \cup N_k$, Q and Σ are mutually disjoint. Let $\Longrightarrow_i$ be the single-step derivation relation for grammar G_i.

Informally, a derivation in a CPCG system consists of parallel, synchronized derivations of its component grammars. The separate derivations are independent of one another up to the point where one derivation does a query of one of the others, in which case information can flow from one component to another.

Derivations for system Γ are defined as follows. Consider a k-tuple $(x_1, \ldots, x_k)$ that has been derived so far. For $i = 1, \ldots, k$, if $x_i \notin \Sigma^*$, choose X_i to be the member of $N_i \cup Q$ that occurs at the end of x_i, and let $x_i = z_i X_i$. If $x_i \in \Sigma^*$, then let $X_i = \lambda$. Let $\Longrightarrow_i$ be the single-step derivation relation for grammar G_i. Say that $(x_1, \ldots, x_k) \Longrightarrow (y_1, \ldots, y_k)$ if one of the following cases holds.

1. If $X_i = \lambda$, then one of the following holds.

   (a) If there is no j such that $X_j = Q_i$, then $y_i = x_i$.

   (b) If there is a j such that $X_j = Q_i$, then $y_i = S_i$.

2. If $X_i \in N_i$, then one of the following holds.

   (a) If there is no j such that $X_j = Q_i$ and $X_i \in N_j$, then $x_i \Longrightarrow_i y_i$.

   (b) If there is a j such $X_j = Q_i$ and $X_i \in N_j$, then $y_i = S_i$.

3. If $X_i = Q_j$, then one of the following holds.

   (a) If $X_j = \lambda$ or $X_j \in N_i$, then $y_i = z_i x_j$.

   (b) If $X_j \neq \lambda$ and $X_j \notin N_i$, then $y_i = x_i$.

We would like to explain the difference between our definition of PCG systems and the original definition in [13]. According to [13], when one component queries to another, it waits and gets the word generated by the latter so long as the word does not contain query symbols. However, the word to be queried might contain a nonterminal symbol that never occurs in the querying component. This causes the derivation to cease, and no string of terminals to be derived. When coherence is introduced, this circumstance is avoided by allowing the querying component to wait until all nonterminal symbols in the word to be queried also belong to the grammar of the querying component.

The CPCG systems defined here are called *returning* systems since each derivation component returns to its start symbol once it is queried by another component. A system is *non-returning* if a queried component proceeds with its normal derivation in spite of the query. Only returning PCG systems are discussed in this paper.

By $\Longrightarrow^*$ we denote the reflexive transitive closure of relation $\Longrightarrow$. Say that $(y_1, \ldots, y_k)$ is derivable in t steps from $(x_1, \ldots, x_k)$ if there is a chain of tuples $s_0 \Longrightarrow s_1 \Longrightarrow \cdots \Longrightarrow s_t$ where $s_0 = (x_1, \ldots, x_k)$ and $s_t = (y_1, \ldots, y_k)$.

The language generated by a PCG system Γ is

$$L(\Gamma) = \{x \in \Sigma^* \mid (S_1, S_2, \ldots, S_k) \Longrightarrow^* (x, \alpha_2, \ldots, \alpha_k) \text{ for some } \alpha_2, \ldots, \alpha_m\}$$

3. Generating NL-Complete Languages

In this section, we show that regular CPCG systems are powerful enough to generate *NL*-complete languages.

We will use a variant of the graph reachability problem, which is known to be *NL*-complete. Stated in terms of graphs, the graph reachability problem is "Given a directed graph G and vertices s and t of G, decide whether there is a directed path in G from s to t". For discussing languages, we must encode graphs as strings. Let $\langle G \rangle$ be an encoding of G of the form $(u_1 \$ v_1) \cdots (u_m \$ v_m)$, where $(u_1, v_1), \ldots, (u_m, v_m)$ are the edges of G. Vertices are encoded as strings over alphabet $\{0, 1\}^*$, where the vertices of a graph with n vertices must be encoded as the binary representations of the numbers $0, \ldots, n - 1$. Our encodings of graphs do not explicitly mention vertices; the vertices are those mentioned in edges, and we forbid graphs with isolated vertices. In our encodings of graphs, we permit an edge to occur more than once in the encoding; duplicated edges occur only once in the graph though.

We use the following variant of the graph reachability problem. Given an encoding $\langle G \rangle$ of a directed graph G, an *ordered path* in $\langle G \rangle$ is a directed path p in G whose edges occur in $\langle G \rangle$ in the same order in which they occur in path p. So if a $\langle G \rangle$ has an ordered path from vertices s to t, then $\langle G \rangle$ must be of the form $\cdots (s \$ v_1) \cdots (v_1 \$ v_2) \cdots (v_{h-1} \$ v_h) \cdots (v_h \$ t) \cdots$ for some $h \geq 1$, where $v_i \in \{0, 1\}^*$, for $i = 1, \cdots, h$. Define

ORDERED REACHABILITY =
$$\{s \# t \# \langle G \rangle : \langle G \rangle \text{ has an ordered path from } s \text{ to } t\}$$

Theorem 3.1. *Language* ORDERED REACHABILITY *is NL-complete.*

Proof. First we show ORDERED REACHABILITY to be in the class *NL*. It is easy to see that the syntax of the encoding $s \# t \# \langle G \rangle$ can be checked deterministically in logarithmic space. To check for an ordered path from s to t, copy s and t to a work tape, and copy s to a tape that holds the "current vertex". Scan through the edge list for a nondeterministically chosen distance until an edge of the form (s, v) is found, and copy v to the current vertex tape. Continue scanning ahead, each time searching a nondeterministic distance for an edge that goes from the current vertex to another vertex. At the end of the edge list, check that the current vertex is t.

It is straightforward to reduce graph reachability to ordered graph reachability. Given a graph G of n vertices, simply write n consecutive copies of all of the edges in G, and ask whether there is an ordered path in the resulting encoding. □

In the following, we show that there is a regular PCG system that generates language ORDERED REACHABILITY.

Theorem 3.2. *There are regular PCG systems generating language* ORDERED REACHABILITY.

Proof. We construct a PC grammar system Γ with 15 components that can exactly generate members of ORDERED REACHABILITY. Let $\Gamma = (Q, \Sigma, G_0, G_1, \cdots, G_{14})$ where $Q = \{Q_0, \cdots, Q_{14}\}$ is the set of query symbols, $\Sigma = \{0, 1, (,), \$, \#\}$ is the set of terminal symbols and the components $G_0, \cdots, G_{14}$, categorized in six groups, are described as follows.

Group I consists of three components that generate word s and duplicate it.

G_1:	G_2:	G_3:
$S_1 \to 0S_1 \mid 1S_1 \mid 0S \mid 1S$	$S_2 \to Q_1$	$S_3 \to Q_1$
$S \to S$	$S \to V$	$S \to J$
	$V \to V$	$J \to J$

Group II, similarly to group I, consists of three components that generate the word t and its duplicate.

G_4:	G_5:	G_6:
$S_4 \to 0S_4 \mid 1S_4 \mid 0T \mid 1T$	$S_5 \to Q_4$	$S_6 \to Q_4$
$T \to T$	$T \to L$	$T \to K$
	$L \to L$	$K \to K$

Group III consists of two components that generate a sequence of edges of the form $(u\$v) \cdots (x\$y)$

G_7:	G_8:
$S_7 \to (A$	$S_8 \to Q_7 \mid \lambda$
$A \to 0A \mid 1A \mid 0\$B \mid 1\$B$	$C \to Q_7 \mid D$
$B \to 0B \mid 1B \mid 0)C \mid 1)C$	$D \to D$
$C \to C$	

Group IV consists of three components generating word w_i and its duplicate for each i

G_9:	G_{10}:	G_{11}:
$S_9 \to 0S_9 \mid 1S_9 \mid 0W \mid 1W$	$S_{10} \to Q_{11}$	$S_{11} \to H$
$W \to W$	$H \to I$	$H \to Q_9$
	$I \to Q_9$	$W \to Y$
	$W \to X$	$Y \to Y \mid Z$
	$X \to X$	

Group V consists of two components that can generate the first and last sequences of edges in the graph

G_{12}:	G_{13}:	G_{14}:
$S_{12} \to (A$	$S_{13} \to Q_{12} \mid C$	$S_{14} \to Q_{12} \mid E$
$A \to 0A \mid 1A \mid 0\$B \mid 1\$B$	$C \to Q_{12} \mid C$	$E \to Q_{12} \mid E \mid F$
$B \to 0B \mid 1B \mid 0)C \mid 1)C$		
$C \to C$		

Group VI consists of only one component, the master component

G_0:	
$S_0 \to Q_2$	$D \to (Q_{11}$
$V \to \#Q_5$	$Y \to \$Q_{10}$
$L \to \#Q_{13}$	$Z \to \$Q_6$
$C \to (Q_3$	$K \to)Q_{14}$
$J \to \$Q_{10}$	$F \to \lambda$
$X \to)Q_8$	

We briefly explain how the system Γ works to generate a word of the form
$s\#t\# \cdots (s\$w_1) \cdots (w_1\$w_2) \cdots (w_{h-1}\$w_h) \cdots (w_h\$t) \cdots$

In order to derive the $s\#t\#$, component G_0 first makes a query to component G_2 that derives the word s, a copy of which is derived by component G_3. Then G_0 makes a query to component G_5 that derives word t. A copy of t is derived by G_6 at the same time. G_0 then is ready to derive the encoding of a graph.

G_0 generates an arbitrary sequence of edges by making a query to component G_{13}. Then G_0 derives an edge (s, w_1) by making queries to G_3 that has kept the copy of s and to G_{10} that derives word w_1. At the same time, component G_{11} generates the duplicate of w_1. The subsequent derivation process of Γ can be described in the following loop.

Let $i = 1$. G_0 makes a query to component G_8 that generates an arbitrary sequence edges. Then G_0 derives edge (w_i, w_{i+1}) by making queries to component G_{11} that has kept the copy of w_i and to component G_{10} that has just generated word w_{i+1}. At the same time, component G_{11} generates the duplicate of w_{i+1}. Let $i \leftarrow i + 1$. The system repeats the above process until G_0 derives an edge (w_h, t) by making queries to component G_6 and G_{11} that have kept the copies of t and of w_h respectively. Finally, G_0 makes a query to G_{13} to get the last sequence of edges.

It is instructive to examine the interactions among G_0, G_9, G_{10} and G_{11}. Grammar G_9 is responsible for derive a new word w_i. Grammar G_{10} carries this to G_0, and G_{11} keeps a copy of w_i. It is necessary to make simultaneous copies of queried strings, since the derivation rules are returning. Note that G_{10} will not be able to query G_9 to get a new word w_{i+1} until the copy of w_i maintained by G_{11} is queried by G_0. The production rules in G_{10} force G_{10} to query G_{11} before querying G_9. Since G_{11} holds a word w_iY in which symbol Y does not belong to component G_{10}, G_{10} has to wait until G_{11} being queried by by G_0 and returning to its start. Therefore the synchronization is established for G_{10} and G_{11} to generate the same copy of the new word w_{i+1}, for $i = 1, \cdots, h - 1$.

Whether to terminate the looping process or not can be decided by choosing rules $Y \to Y$ or $Y \to Z$ in component G_{11}. Symbol Y allows the loop process to repeat, and symbol Z forces G_0 to derive (w_h, t) and may lead to terminating the whole process.

Finally, it is easy to see that our construction of the grammar system only generate words that encode $s\#t\#\langle G \rangle$ where G contains an ordered path from s to t. $\qquad\square$

Corollary 3.1. *There are NL-complete languages that can be generated by regular PCG systems.*

4. Simulating Regular PC Grammar Systems in Small Space

Theorem 4.1. *All languages generated by regular CPCG systems can be recognized by log-space NTMs.*

Proof. Given a CPCG system $\Gamma = (Q, \Sigma, G_1, \cdots, G_k)$ with k regular components, we construct a Turing machine M such that, for any input $x \in \Sigma^*$, M simulates the derivation of x by Γ and accepts x if and only if $x \in L(\Gamma)$.

During the process of a derivation by the system Γ, at each step and for each $i = 1, \cdots, k$, component i would like to remember the string $\alpha_i X_i$ derived up to that step, where $\alpha_i \in \Sigma^*$ and $X_i \in N_i \cup Q \cup \{\lambda\}$. Unfortunately, the length of α_i may be larger than logarithm of the input length, so α_i cannot be directly stored in the work-tape of the machine M. We follow the construction in [2] to overcome this difficulty.

The idea for the construction of M is based on the following observation. If component G_i derives word $\alpha_i X_i$ where α_i is *not* a substring of the input x, then α_i will not contribute to recognition of the input x. The reason is that if the master component G_1 makes a query to G_i, then it will not derive x unless it is later queried by some other component and returns to its start symbol.

If component G_i derives word $\alpha_i X_i$ for some α_i that is not a substring of the input x, then G_i is called *void* until it is queried and returns to its start symbol. Note that it suffices to store only the terminal strings derived by components that are not void. Because any such a string is a substring of x, its information can be recorded by two indices that point to the beginning and ending positions of the terminal string x in the input tape. Turing machine M stores the indices instead of the terminal string in the simulation. As a result, M is log-space bounded.

Besides the terminal strings α_i and nonterminal symbols X_i, machine M records the query relationship between each pair of components. At each step, M works according the the information given in the k-tuple $(\alpha_1 X_1, \cdots, \alpha_k X_k)$. Initially, $\alpha_i = \lambda$, $X_i = S_i$ and $void(G_i) = FALSE$ for $i = 1, \cdots, k$. For each $i = 1, \cdots, k$, and each step, M performs one of the following computations

1. If $X_i \in \Sigma^*$ and there is no j such that $X_j = Q_i$ then M does not change α_i or X_i.

2. If $X_i \notin Q$ and if there is no j such that $X_j = Q_i$ or there is a j such that $X_j = Q_i$ but $X_i \notin N_i \cup \{\lambda\}$, then M choose a production $X_i \rightarrow \beta_i Y_i$. If there is no such production, then M rejects x and halts. Otherwise, M updates X_i with Y_i and α_i with $\alpha_i \beta_i$. If the new α_i is not a substring of x, M sets $void(G_i) = TRUE$;

3. If $X_i \notin Q$ and there is a j such that $X_j = Q_i$ and $X_i \in N_j \cup \{\lambda\}$, then M sets X_j to be X_i, α_j to be $\alpha_j \alpha_i$, X_i to be S_i, and α_i to be λ. M sets $void(G_i) = FALSE$. If the new α_j is not a substring of x, M sets $void(G_j) = TRUE$;

M repeats (if it can) the above steps until either G_1 derives the word x or there is a circular query. In the former case, it accepts x. In the latter, it rejects x.

It is easy to verify that the above strategies follow precisely the derivation process defined in Section 2, and that the space is logarithmic in the length of the input. □

Now we are ready for our main result

Theorem 4.2. *Log-space NTMs recognize exactly the closure under log-space reductions of the class of languages generated by regular CPCG systems.*

Proof. Since the composition of two log-space reductions is also a log-space reduction, by Theorem 4.1, the closure under log-space reductions of the class of languages generated by regular PC grammar systems can be recognized by log-space NTMs.

On the other hand, by Theorem 3.2, any language reducible via log-space reduction to language ORDERED REACHABILITY is in that closure. By Theorem 3.1, all languages recognized by log-space NTMs belong to the closure. □

Finally, note the following relationship between regular CPCG systems and a long-standing open problem in computational complexity.

Theorem 4.3. *If regular CPCG systems can generate all context-free languages, then log-space NTMS are equivalent in power to auxiliary pushdown automata.*

Proof. It has been shown [18], [4] that auxiliary pushdown automata recognized exactly the closure of context-free languages under log-space reduction. □

5. Conclusion

We have shown that the class *NL* is exactly the closure under the log-space reduction of the class of languages generated by regular CPCG systems, and have given the first grammatical characterization for logarithmic space-bounded Turing computations.

We would like to point out that the query mechanism adopted for CPCG systems is natural for describing inter-component communications of complex systems. Yet it does not greatly increase the power of regular PCG systems.

References

1. J. Balcázar, J. Díaz and J. Gabarró, *Structural Complexity I and II*, (Springer-Verlag, 1990).

2. L. Cai, The computational complexity of PCGS with regular components. *Proceedings 2nd International Conference on Development in Language Theory*, World Sci. Publ., Singapore, 1996, 209-219.

3. L. Cai, The complexity of linear PCGSs, *Computers and Artificial Intelligence*, 15, 2-3 (1996), pp. 199-210.

4. S. Cook, A Taxonomy of problems with fast parallel algorithms, *Information and Control*, **64** (1985), 2-22.

5. E. Csuhaj-Varjú, J. Dassow, J. Kelemen, and Gh. Păun, *Grammar Systems*, (Gordon and Breach Sci. Publishers Ltd., 1993).

6. R. Freund, Gh. Păun, C. Procopiuc and O. Procopiuc, Parallel Communicating Grammar Systems with Context-sensitive Components, *Artificial Life: Grammatical Models*, Gh. Păun ed. (The Black sea Univ. Press, 1995).

7. J. E. Hopcroft and J. D. Ullman, *Introduction to automata theory, languages and computation* (Addison Wesley, 1979).

8. J. Hromkovič, J. Kari and L. Kari, Some hierarchies for the communication complexity measures of cooperating grammar systems, *Theoretical computer Science*, **127**, 123-147.

9. J. Hromkovič, J. Kari, L. Kari and J. Pardubská, Two lower bounds on distributive generation of languages, *Proc. 19th MFCS'94, Lecture Notes in Computer Science* **841**, 423-432.

10. J. Hromkovič and D. Wierzchula, Note on nondeterministic linear time, real time, and parallel communicating grammar systems, *manuscript*.

11. D. S. Johnson, A catalog for complexity classes, in: J. van Leeuvan, ed., *The handbook of Theoretical Computer Sciences* Vol **A** (Elsevier Science Publishers, 1990), 69-161.

12. Gh. Păun, On the synchronization in parallel communicating grammar systems, *Acta Informatica*, **30** (1993), 351-367.

13. Gh. Păun and L. Santean, Parallel communicating grammar systems: the regular case, *Ann. Univ. Buc., Series Matem.-Inform.*, **38** (1989), 55-63.

14. Gh. Păun and L. Santean, Further remarks on parallel communicating grammar systems, *International Journal on Computing Mathematics*, **34** (1990), 187-203.

15. A. Salomaa, *Formal Languages* (Academic Press, 1973).

16. L. Santean, Parallel communicating systems, *Bulletin EATCS*, **42** (1990), 160-171.

17. L. Santean and J. Kari, The impact of the number of cooperating grammars on the generative power, *Theoretical Computer Science*, **98** (1992), 249-262.

18. I. Sudborough, On the tape complexity of deterministic context-free languages, *Journal of ACM*, **25** (1978), 405-414.

On the Computational Complexity of Context-Free Parallel Communicating Grammar Systems

Ştefan BRUDA

Romanian Academy of Sciences
Centre for Advanced Research in Machine Learning, Natural
Language Processing and Conceptual Modelling
Email: bruda@valhalla.racai.ro

Abstract. In this paper we investigate the computational complexity for Parallel Communicating Grammar Systems (PCGSs) whose components are context-free grammars. We show that languages generated by non-returning context-free PCGSs can be recognized by $O(n)$ space-bounded Turing machines. Also we state a sufficient condition for linear space complexity of returning context-free PCGSs. Based on this complexity characterization we also investigate the generative power of context-free PCGSs with respect to context-sensitive PCGSs and context-sensitive grammars.

1. Introduction

Parallel Communicating Grammar Systems (PCGSs) have been introduced as a language-theoretic treatment of multiagent systems [4]. A PCGS consists of several components (grammars) which work in parallel, in a synchronized manner. This is done according to the communicating protocol in which one grammar (component) may query strings generated by others and several components may make queries at the same time [4]. Formal definitions will be reviewed in the next section. Because of the synchronization and communication facilities, PCGSs whose components are of a certain type are more powerful than a single Chomsky grammar of the same type [1], [4].

The study of computational complexity of PCGS is a stand alone problem. It is also a feasible approach toward the generative power of PCGSs. By proving the upper-bound or lower-bound complexity for PCGSs of a certain type, it is possible to find out the relationship between the generative power of such PCGSs and that of other generative devices.

In this paper, the study of the computational complexity of context-free PCGSs is based on space-bounded Turing machines. We will show that languages generated by non-returning context-free PCGSs can be recognized by nondeterministic Turing machines using $O(|w|)$ tape cells for each input instance w. This result is obtained for both centralized and non-centralized non-returning PCGSs and a sufficient condition for the returning case was stated. Starting from these results, we will analyze the generative power of context-free PCGSs according to the generative power of context-sensitive grammars and context-sensitive PCGSs.

The present paper is organized as follows. The next section reviews some fundamental concepts, the third section presents the computational complexity of context-free PCGSs and the fourth section discusses the generative power of this kind of PCGSs. We present some final remarks and further studies in the last section.

2. Fundamentals

In this section, we will briefly review the notion of PCGS and that of space-bounded Turing computation. More detailed descriptions can be found in [1] and [2] respectively. We also assume that the reader is familiar with basic concepts in formal language and computational complexity theories.

We will use the notations from [1]. For $x \in V^*$, and a set U, $|x|_U$ denotes the number of occurrences of elements of U in x. We also define $\|U\|$ to be the cardinality of set U. The null string is denoted by λ.

The next definitions are also conforming to [1].

Definition 2.1. Let $n \geq 1$ be a natural number. A PCGS with n components is a $(n+3)$-tuple

$$\Gamma = (N, K, T, G_1, \ldots, G_n),$$

where N is the set of nonterminals, T is a terminal alphabet, $K = \{Q_1, Q_2, \ldots, Q_n\}$ (the sets N, K and T are mutually disjoint) and $G_i = (N \cup K, T, P_i, S_i), 1 \leq i \leq n$, are Chomsky grammars. Let $V_\Gamma = N \cup K \cup T$.

The grammars G_i, $1 \leq i \leq n$, are the components of the system and the elements of K are called query symbols; their indices point to $G_1, \ldots, G_n$ respectively.

The derivation in a PCGS is defined as follows.

Definition 2.2. Given a PCGS $\Gamma = (N, K, T, G_1, \ldots, G_n)$ as in the definition above, for the tuples $(x_1, x_2, \ldots, x_n)$, $(y_1, y_2, \ldots, y_n)$, $x_i, y_i \in V_\Gamma^*, 1 \leq i \leq n$, we write $(x_1, x_2, \ldots, x_n) \Rightarrow (y_1, y_2, \ldots, y_n)$ if one of the following cases holds:

1. $|x_i|_K = 0$, $1 \leq i \leq n$, and for all i, $1 \leq i \leq n$, we have $x_i \Rightarrow y_i$ in G_i or $x_i \in T^*$ and $x_i = y_i$;

2. there is i, $1 \leq i \leq n$, such that $|x_i|_K > 0$ and for each such i let $x_i = z_1 Q_{i_1} z_2 Q_{i_2} \dot{s} z_t Q_{i_t} z_{t+1}$, $t \geq 1$; in that case, for $z_j \in V_\Gamma^*$, $|z_j|_K = 0$, $1 \leq j \leq t+1$, if $\left|x_{i_j}\right|_K = 0$, $1 \leq j \leq t$, then $y_i = z_1 x_{i_1} z_2 x_{i_2} \ldots z_t x_{i_t} z_{t+1}$ [and $y_{i_j} = S_{i_j}$, $1 \leq j \leq t$]. If exists j, $1 \leq j \leq t$, and $\left|x_{i_j}\right|_K \neq 0$ then $y_i = x_i$. For all i, $1 \leq i \leq n$, for which y_i was not specified above we have $y_i = x_i$.

The first case is called a componentwise derivation step and the second a communication step. Note that communications have priority over componentwise derivations. The query symbol to which a string has been communicated is called *satisfied*.

A tuple $(x_1, x_2, \ldots, x_n)$ is called a *configuration* of the system. We will call x_i a *component of the configuration*.

Note that rules $Q_j \to \alpha$ are never used, so we can assume that there are no such rules [1].

The derivation in a PCGS is blocked if no rewriting rule can be applied to a nonterminal symbol in any component or circular queries appear (this happens when G_{i_1} introduces Q_{i_2}, G_{i_2} introduces Q_{i_3}, $\ldots$, $G_{i_{k-1}}$ introduces Q_{i_k} and G_{i_k} introduces Q_{i_1}; in this case no rewriting step is applicable, because the communication has priority, but also no communication steps are applicable).

Definition 2.3. The language generated by a PCGS Γ is: $L(\Gamma) = \{x \in T^* \mid (S_1, S_2, \ldots, S_n) \Rightarrow^* (x, \alpha_2, \ldots, \alpha_n), \alpha_i \in V_\Gamma^*, 2 \leq i \leq n\}$.

The derivation starts from the tuple of axioms $(S_1, S_2, \ldots, S_n)$. A number of rewriting and/or communication steps are performed until G_1 produces a terminal string. Note that $L(\Gamma)$ contains only strings generated by the first component, with no care about the strings generated by the others, which may contain query symbols.

Definition 2.4. Let $\Gamma = (N, K, T, G_1, \ldots, G_n)$ be a PCGS. If only G_1 is allowed to introduce query symbols, then Γ is called *centralized*. The unrestricted case is called *non-centralized*.

Definition 2.5. A PCGS is called *returning* (to the axiom) if, after communication, a component which has communicated a string resumes the work from its axiom as described by sentence [and $y_{i_j} = S_{i_j}, 1 \leq j \leq t$] in the second case of Definition 2.2. A PCGS is called *non-returning* if components continue working using the current string after a query (i.e. the sentence above is erased from the definition).

Notations: A centralized, returning PCGS with components of type X is denoted by PC_*X. For the centralized case we add a C and for non-returning case a N (see [1] for details). We obtain the classes PC, CPC, NPC, $NCPC$.

The notion of the *coverability tree* of a non-returning PCGS has been introduced in [5]. We will summarize here this notion and its relevant properties for this paper.

The set of natural numbers $\mathbf{N}$ is extended by a special symbol ω to the set $\mathbf{N}_\omega = \mathbf{N} \cup \{\omega\}$. The operations $+, -, \cdot$ and the relation $\leq$ over $\mathbf{N}$ are extended to $\mathbf{N}_\omega$ by $\omega + \omega = \omega + n = n + \omega = \omega$, $\omega - n = \omega$, $\omega \cdot n = n \cdot \omega = \omega$, $n \leq \omega$ for all $n \in \mathbf{N}$.

The set N (of nonterminals) of a PCGS $\Gamma = (N, K, T, G_1, \ldots, G_n)$ is ordered: $A_1, \ldots, A_{n+m}$, $m \geq 0$, such that $A_1 = S_1, \ldots, A_n = S_n$.

Let $w = (w_1, \ldots, w_n)$ be a configuration of Γ. M_w denotes the vector

$$M_w = ((|w_1|_{X_1}, \ldots, |w_1|_{X_{2n+m}}), \ldots, (|w_n|_{X_1}, \ldots, |w_n|_{X_{2n+m}})),$$

where $X_i = A_i$, $1 \leq i \leq n + m$, $X_{n+m+j} = Q_j$, $1 \leq j \leq n$. $M_w(i, j)$ denotes the element $|w_i|_{X_j}$.

We can assume [5] that for each component of Γ there is a phantom production which does not change the string and which can be applied only to terminal strings in the synchronized case. So, a rewriting step in Γ is an n-tuple $t = (r_1, \ldots, r_n)$, where r_i denotes either a production in G_i or the phantom production, for all $1 \leq i \leq n$. For uniformity, we say that communication steps are produced by a special transition Λ. The set of all $t = (r_1, \ldots, r_n)$ as above is denoted by $TR(\Gamma)$, $\Lambda \in TR(\Gamma)$. A transition t is enabled in a certain configuration if the corresponding rewriting or communication step can be applied in that configuration.

If a transition t is enabled for a configuration w of Γ then we write $M_w[t >_\Gamma$; if, after t is performed, the new configuration is w' then we write $M_w[t >_\Gamma M_{w'}$.

Let A and B be two arbitrary sets. $\mathcal{T}(V, E, l_1, l_2)$ is an (A, B)-labeled tree if (V, E) is a tree and $l_1 : V \to A$ is the node labelling function and $l_2 : E \to B$ is the edge labelling function. We denote by $d_T(v_1, v_2)$ the set of all nodes on the path from v_1 to v_2.

For each PCGS Γ there is a $((\mathbf{N}_\omega^{2n+m})^n, TR(\Gamma))$-labeled tree called *the coverability tree* for Γ defined as follow, [5].

Definition 2.6. Let $\Gamma = (N, K, T, G_1, \ldots, G_n)$ be a PCGS. An $((\mathbf{N}_\omega^{2n+m})^n, TR(\Gamma))$-labeled tree, $\mathcal{T} = (V, E, l_1, l_2)$, is called a *coverability tree* of Γ if the following hold:

1. the root, denoted by v_0, is labeled by M_{x_0}, where $x_0 = (S_1, \ldots, S_n)$ (the initial configuration);

2. for any node $v \in V$ the number of outgoing edges $|v^+|$ is

- 0, if either there is no transition enabled at $l_1(v)$ or there is $v' \in d_T(v_0, v)$ such that $v \neq v'$ and $l_1(v) = l_1(v')$

- the number of transitions enabled at $l_1(v)$ otherwise;

3. for any $v \in V$ with $|v^+| > 0$ and any transition t which is enabled at $l_1(v)$ there is a node v' such that:

(a) $(v, v') \in E$,

(b) $l_2(v, v') = t$,

(c) $l_1(v')$ is given by

- let M be such that $l_1(v)[t >_\Gamma M$;
- if M contains queries then $l_1(v') = M$ else
  if exists $v^* \in d_T(v_0, v)$ such that $l_1(v^*) \leq M$ and $l_1(v^*)(i,j) < M(i,j)$
  then $l_1(v')(i,j) = \omega$ else
  $l_1(v')(i,j) = M(i,j)$,
  for all i, j, $1 \leq i \leq n$ and $1 \leq j \leq 2n + m$.

For non-returning synchronized PCGSs such a tree is always finite and can be effectively constructed (see [5] for demonstrations and details). The coverability tree for a PCGS Γ is denoted by $T(\Gamma)$.

From the construction of the coverability tree it follows that if, for some configuration w, $M_w(i,j) = \omega$, then, in that configuration, the number of occurrences of X_j in the i-th component can be made arbitrarily large [5]. This implies that *if $M_w(i,j) = \omega$ then X_j cannot be totally removed by any successive derivation steps from x_i, i.e. such nonterminals cannot block the derivation.*

Definition 2.7. Given a Turing machine M and an input string $x \in T^*$, the *working space* of M on x is the length of work tapes for M to halt on x. More generally, let S be any function from $\mathbf{N}$ to $\mathbf{N}$; let $L \subseteq T^*$. We say that M decides[1] L in space S provided that M decides L and uses at most $S(n)$ tape cells on any input of length n in T^*. If M is a nondeterministic Turing machine we write $L \in NSPACE(S(n))$. We say also that M is a $S(n)$ space-bounded Turing machine.

For the rate of growth of a function we have the following definition [2]:

Definition 2.8. Let f and g be natural functions. We write $f = O(g)$ iff there is a constant $c > 0$ and an integer n_0 such that $f(n) \leq c \cdot g(n)$ for all $n \geq n_0$.

3. The Complexity of Context-Free PCGS

In this section we will study the computational complexity of PCGSs whose components are context-free grammars. We suppose that there are not λ-productions. A discussion on λ-productions will be done at the end of this section.

---

[1] A Turing machine M decides a language L if, for any input string w, M halts and writes on its tape a specified symbol Y if $w \in L$ or another symbol N if $w \notin L$. If M writes Y we say it *accepts* the string, otherwise it *rejects* the input [2].

Definition 3.1. During a derivation process in a PCGS, a component of the current configuration x_i is called *non-direct-significant* for the recognizing of the string w if

(i) either $i \neq 1$ and x_i is not queried anymore or

(ii) i=1 and the derivation from x_1 to w in G_1 cannot end successfully unless x_1 is reduced to the axiom sometime in the future or

(iii) $i \neq 1$ and x_i is queried by x_j, $j \neq i$, and x_j becomes non-direct-significant.

All the others components are called direct-significant. Any component which is reduced to the axiom becomes direct-significant.

In other words, a non-direct-significant component of a PCGS cannot directly participate at a successful derivation. It can only produce lateral effects (by queries which can modify other components) or block the derivation (by circular queries or by its nonterminals for which there are no applicable rewriting rules).

This definition introduces the class of components for which the structure is irrelevant for the derivation. Therefore, these components can be erased if the information relevant for lateral effects is kept.

Starting from this definition we can consider the following lemmas.

Lemma 3.1. *Let* $\Gamma = (N, K, T, G_1, \ldots, G_n)$ *be a centralized PCGS* ($\Gamma \in CPC_*CF \cup NCPC_*CF$) *and* $w \in T^*$ *a string. Let also* $(x_1, \ldots, x_n)$ *be a configuration of the system. Then, if the length of a component* x_i *becomes greater than* $|w|$, *that component becomes non-direct-significant for the recognizing of* w.

Proof. We will consider two situations:

(i) Let $i = 1$. If $|x_1|_K = 0$, then x_1 will be rewritten using the rules of G_1. But these are context-free rules and there are not λ-productions, so the length of x_1 does not decrease. If $|x_1|_K \neq 0$, a communication step will be performed. But the communication step does not reduce the length of the component because there are not null components to be queried (there are not λ-productions). So, the length of x_1 does not decrease anymore and this leads to the rejection of w because the first component is not queried (we have a centralized PCGS) so it can not be reduced to the axiom. Therefore x_1 is non-direct-significant according to the Definition 3.1.

(ii) For $i \geq 2$, only the first component can introduce query symbols, so if x_i is queried by the first component (if x_i is not queried then it is obviously non-direct-significant), the length of x_1 becomes greater than $|w|$, therefore x_1 becomes non-direct-significant (according to the point (i)). So x_i is non-direct-significant. □

Lemma 3.2. *Let* $\Gamma = (N, K, T, G_1, \ldots, G_n)$ *be a non-centralized non-returning PCGS* ($\Gamma \in NPC_*CF$) *and* $w \in T^*$ *a string. Let also* $(x_1, \ldots, x_n)$ *be a configuration of the system. Then, if the length of a component* x_i *becomes greater than* $|w|$, *that component becomes non-direct-significant for the recognizing of* w.

Proof. The proof is basically similar to the proof of Lemma 3.1. The case $i = 1$ has the same proof as the case (i) in the proof above, because x_1 can not decrease even if it is queried (the system is non-returning).

For $i \geq 2$, either the component x_i is never queried therefore it is non-direct-significant, or it is queried by the first component and we have the same situation as in the case (ii) of the proof above, or it is queried by another component x_j, $j \neq i$, $j \neq 1$, which becomes in this way longer than w and also can not decrease. □

Lemma 3.3. *Let* $\Gamma = (N, K, T, G_1, \ldots, G_n)$ *be a non-centralized returning PCGS* ($\Gamma \in PC_*CF$) *and* $w \in T^*$ *a string. Let also* $(x_1, \ldots, x_n)$ *be a configuration of the system. Then, if the length of a component* x_i *becomes greater than* $|w|$, *that component becomes non-direct-significant for the recognizing of* w.

Proof. We have the same proof as for Lemma 3.2 with the mention that, if a component is queried, it is reduced to the axiom and then it become direct-significant. But this situation is allowed by the definition (a non-direct-significant component can become direct-significant iff it is reduced to the axiom). □

Using the lemmas above, the complexity of context-free PCGS can be studied. We first consider the non-returning case.

Lemma 3.4. *Let* Γ *be a non-returning PCGS with* n *context-free components* ($n \geq 1$). *Then there is a Turing machine* M *that recognizes the language* $L(\Gamma)$ *using at most* $O(|w|)$ *amount of work tape space for each input instance* w.

Proof. Let $\Gamma = (N, K, T, G_1, \ldots, G_n)$ be a non-returning PCGS, where $G_i = (N \cup K, T, P_i, S_i)$, $1 \leq i \leq n$, are context-free grammars. We will construct the nondeterministic Turing machine M which recognizes $L(\Gamma)$.

M will be a standard Turing machine, with a work tape equipped with a read/write-head. The alphabet of the tape of M is $N \cup K \cup T \cup \{@, \omega\}$, $@, \omega \notin N \cup K \cup T$. Given an input string $w \in T^*$, M will simulate step by step the derivation of w by Γ. First, M computes the coverability tree $T(\Gamma)$ of Γ. Note that this computation can be done [5] and its space complexity is not w-dependent, so it does not modify the space complexity of the whole computation if this complexity is a function of w. Then M finds the number $m_{max} = max\{l_1(v)(i, j) \mid 1 \leq i \leq n, 1 \leq j \leq 2n+m, l_1(v)(i, j) \neq \omega\}$. After that, M erases the coverability tree and keeps on its tape the number m_{max} [2].

The simulation of the derivation is done according to Definition 2.2. Therefore, there are two types of derivation steps to simulate: the componentwise rewriting and the communication. M will keep on its tape the current configuration and will work on it as follows:

(i) If $|x_i|_K = 0$ for all i, $1 \leq i \leq n$, M simulates rewriting for each component x_i, $1 \leq i \leq n$. If $|x_i|_N = 0$, then x_i remains unchanged. Otherwise, M nondeterministicaly selects a rule from the rule set P_i and rewrites x_i according to this rule. If there are some i for which such a rule does not exist, then M rejects the input and halts.

If $|x_i| > |w|$ then, according to Lemma 3.1 (if we have a centralized PCGS) or 3.2 (if the system is non-centralized), x_i becomes non-direct-significant. Therefore its structure is irrelevant and it will be replaced by the string

$$@t_1 T_1 \ldots t_j T_j q_1 Q_1 \ldots q_k Q_k \tag{1}$$

where $@$ is a special symbol ($@ \notin N \cup T \cup K$), T_1, $\ldots$, T_j are the distinct nonterminals in x_i and Q_1, $\ldots$, Q_k are the distinct query symbols in x_i; t_h ($1 \leq h \leq j$) is either the number of occurrences of the nonterminal T_h in x_i if the number of these occurrences is smaller than m_{max} or ω otherwise. Also q_h ($1 \leq h \leq k$) is either the number of occurrences of the query symbol Q_h in x_i if these occurrences are fewer than m_{max} or ω otherwise.

---

[2] Or, m_{max} being a property of Γ and not of w, it can be considered a parameter of M. Therefore it should not be computed (and so M does not need to compute $T(\Gamma)$) but it should be on the tape at the beginning of the computation

Note than if the number of occurrences of X in x_i ,$X \in K \cup N$, becomes greater than m_{max}, then $l_1(v)$ must contain ω in the position corresponding to x_i and X (where v is the node in $T(\Gamma)$ corresponding to the current configuration), so the number of occurrences of X cannot decrease (in fact it can grow indefinitely), therefore X cannot be eliminated from x_i, so it is not necessary to count its occurrences in x_i anymore.

We have to explain now how the rewriting works on strings of the form (1). Let the rewriting rule be $A \to \alpha_1 A_1 \alpha_2 A_2 \ldots \alpha_m A_m \alpha_{m+1}$, where $A \in N$, $A_1, \ldots, A_m \in N \cup K$ and $\alpha_1, \ldots, \alpha_m \in T^*$. Then, there is $T_r = A$, $1 \leq r \leq j$ (if not, the rule is not applicable) and M increases the counter for each nonterminals or query symbol A_j (if that counter is ω then it remains unchanged), $1 \leq j \leq m$, in x_i; if that counter becomes greater than m_{max}, then it is replaced by ω and if A_j does not already exists in x_i, then a new pair $1A_j$ is added to x_i. Finally, M decrements the counter of A, excepting when this counter is ω, when it remains unchanged. If that counter becomes zero, both this counter and A are erased from x_i.

The reason for keeping nonterminals in non-direct-significant components is that these nonterminals can introduce query symbols when a rewriting is performed. Also the absence of a nonterminal can block the derivation.

(ii) If there are query symbols in the current configuration, then M simulates communication steps. If there are circular queries, M rejects the input and halts. Otherwise, M nondeterministicaly selects a component x_i for which Q_j, $1 \leq j \leq q$, are all the query symbols and $|x_j|_K = 0$, $1 \leq j \leq q$. M sequentially replaces Q_j by x_j. If either the current x_j is of the form (1) or, after replacement, x_i becomes longer than $|w|$, then x_i becomes non-direct-significant, so it will be replaced by a string of the form (1).

This communication step is repeatedly performed until there are no query symbols in the current configuration.

M repeats steps of type (i) and (ii) until:

1. either x_1 and w are identical or,

2. the first symbol of x_1 is @ or,

3. the number of iterations exceeds a fixed positive number c.

In the first case M accepts the input and halts, in the other two cases M rejects w and halts.

Let us count the amount of work space used by M during the derivation. If the length of a component x_i is smaller than $|w|$ then this component is kept on the tape as it is, so less than $|w|$ tape cells are necessary in order to keep it. If a component has a length greater than $|w|$, it become of the form (1). Because we have a fixed finite number t of nonterminals for a given PCGS and exactly n query symbols, the length of such component on the tape is independent of $|w|$ and is less than $1 + \log m_{max}(t + n)$, where $t = \|N\|$.

A communication step may use temporary an amount of tape space double than the space used by a single component (e.g. a string of length $|w|$ is queried by another string of length $|w|$; before the reduction to form (1) we have to use $2|w|$ tape cells).

Therefore, the number of cells used by a component is smaller than

$$2max(|w|, 1 + \log m_{max}(t + n)).$$

We have n components and we need some extra space on the tape to keep the rules of the system and m_{max}. So, the space used by M is upper-bounded by

$$2n \cdot \max(|w|, 1 + \log m_{max}(t + n)) + pl + \log m_{max}.$$

But t, n and m_{max} are not $|w|$-dependent so, conforming to Definition 2.8 of the rate of growth of the functions, the space used is

$$O(2n|w| + pl + \log m_{max}).$$

Finally we have to show that the fixed integer c we claimed before exists. But this is immediate from the following property of space-bounded Turing machines [2]:

$$NSPACE(S) \subseteq \cup \{NTIME(d^S) \mid d \geq 1\}.$$

If the number of the iterations of M becomes greater than c, M have repeated some configurations, so M should reject the input because, if the input is in $L(\Gamma)$, it would have been accepted before the configuration is repeated at the second time (this happens because of the nondeterminism of M). □

The same result cannot be obtained for returning PCGS unless there is a limit for the number of significant occurrences for each nonterminal (i.e. if the number of occurrences of any nonterminal in any component x_i of the configuration exceeds that limit, then that nonterminal cannot be eliminated from x_i by any further derivation). We will call this limit *a limit of significant occurrences*.

Note that this limit was found for the non-returning case by constructing and inspecting the coverability tree of the system in discussion. This is possible because this tree can be effectively constructed for the non-returning case [5]. The construction of the coverability tree is not necessary effective for returning PCGSs.

Lemma 3.5. *Let Γ be a returning centralized PCGS with n context-free components, $(n \geq 1)$. Then there is a Turing machine M that recognizes the language $L(\Gamma)$ using at most $O(|w|)$ amount of work tape space for each input instance w if there is a finite limit $m_{max} = m(|w|)$ of significant occurrences for any nonterminal, where $m : N \to N$, $m = O(d^n)$, $d > 1$.*

Proof. Let $\Gamma = (N, K, T, G_1, \ldots, G_n)$ be a non-returning PCGS, where $G_i = (N \cup K, T, P_i, S_i)$, $1 \leq i \leq n$, are context-free grammars. We will construct the nondeterministic Turing machine M which recognizes $L(\Gamma)$.

M will be a standard Turing machine, with a work tape equipped with a read/write-head. The alphabet of the tape of M is $N \cup K \cup T \cup \{@, \omega, \}$. Given an input string $w \in T^*$, M will simulate step by step the derivation of w by Γ. The construction of M is basically similar to the one used in the proof of Lemma 3.4 excepting that M does not compute the coverability tree of Γ.

The reference to Lemma 3.2 from the above demonstration should be replaced in the current demonstration by the reference to Lemma 3.3.

Differently from the non-returning case, when a component x_i is queried, M has to simulate the returning of x_i to the axiom. This is done by replacing x_i by the axiom of its grammar (S_i).

Note that this replacement does not depend of the form of x_i so the processing of strings longer than $|w|$ is correct, i.e. the rewriting of such components in the form (1) does not lose any necessary information. Moreover, a number of occurrences (of any terminal X in any component of the configuration x_i) greater than m_{max} implies that X cannot be eliminated from x_i, as in the proof of Lemma 3.4. Therefore, the non-direct-significant components are correctly stored.

M halts if

1. x_1 is identical with w; in this case M accepts the input or

2. no derivation steps are available (there are not rules applicable for some components or there are circular queries) and M rejects the input or

3. the number of iterations exceeds a fixed positive number (similar with the one in Lemma 3.4); also in this case M rejects the input.

Even if the circularity of a PCGS is not a decidable problem for the returning case, M halts in any situation because of the limit c of its possible configurations. M does not decide the circularity of the system at the beginning of the derivation (which can be an undecidable problem) but it halts when any circularity appears.

Finally, the space used by M is, analogous with the proof of Lemma 3.4,

$$O(2n \cdot max(|w|, 1 + \log m_{max}(t + n)) + pl + \log m_{max}) =$$
$$= O(2n \cdot max(|w|, 1 + \log m(|w|)(t + n)) + pl + \log m_{max}) =$$
$$= O(2n \cdot max(|w|, 1 + \log d^{|w|})(t + n)) + pl + \log d^{|w|}) =$$
$$= O(max(|w|, |w|) + |w|) = O(|w|)$$

(because $m_{max} = O(2^{|w|})$), and a limit c for the possible configurations of the tape can be found. $\square$

By Lemmas 3.4 and 3.5 we have

Theorem 3.1. $\mathcal{L}(X_*CF) \subseteq NSPACE(n)$ for $X \in \{NPC, NCPC\}$ and there are no λ-productions.

Theorem 3.2. $\mathcal{L}(X_*CF) \subseteq NSPACE(n)$ for $X \in \{PC, CPC\}$ and there are no λ-productions if a limit in $O(d^{|w|})$, $d > 1$, of significant occurrences exists.

Also we can consider a subclass of context-free PCGS with λ-productions. This subclass is very restrictive but we can consider in this way PCGSs which can generate the null string.

Definition 3.2. We say that $\Gamma \in X_*CF_{\lambda^*}$, $X \in \{PC, NPC, CPC, NCPC\}$, if $\Gamma \in X_*CF$, X as above, and either Γ does not contain λ-productions or

(i) P_i, $i > 1$, do not contain λ-productions and

(ii) P_1 contains only the three productions $S_1 \rightarrow \lambda$, $S_1 \rightarrow S_1$ and $S_1 \rightarrow Q_2$ and

(iii) x_1 is not queried anymore (i.e. Q_1 does not appear in the right side of any production of the system).

Note than the subclasses introduced by this definition are similar with usual context-free grammars in which λ-productions are eliminated [2].

We have the following theorem.

Theorem 3.3. $\mathcal{L}(X_*CF_{\lambda^*}) \subseteq NSPACE(n)$, $X \in \{NPC, NCPC\}$.

Proof. Let $\Gamma = (N, K, T, G_1, \ldots, G_n)$. We will construct Turing machines which simulate the derivation of an input string w. Such a machine M works as follows:

If w is the null string, which belongs to the language in discussion, M accepts it and halts. Otherwise, M continues the derivation for the system $\Gamma' =$

$(N, K, T, G_2, \ldots, G_n)$ as the machine for the appropriate class X_*CF does. Note that, by erasing the first component, the system becomes without λ-productions, so the machine works properly. Also, the first component in Γ only waits for the second component to obtain a terminal string and queries it. $\qquad\square$

Corollary 3.1. $\mathcal{L}(X_*CF_{\lambda^*}) \subseteq NSPACE(n)$, $X \in \{PC, CPC\}$, *if a limit in* $O(d^{|w|})$, $d > 1$, *of significant occurrences exists.*

4. Generative Power of Context-Free PCGS

In this section we will analyze the generative power of context-free PCGS with respect to context-sensitive grammars but also to other types of PCGSs.

Theorrem 4.1. $\mathcal{L}(X_*CF) \subseteq \mathcal{L}(CS)$, $X \in \{NPC, NCPC\}$.

Proof. It has been proved that the class of languages recognized by linear space-bounded Turing machines is identical to the class of context-sensitive languages [2]. This and Theorem 3.1 imply that $\mathcal{L}(CS)$ includes $\mathcal{L}(X_*CF)$. $\qquad\square$

Corollary 4.1. $\mathcal{L}(X_*CF) \subseteq \mathcal{L}(Y_*CS)$, $X \in \{NPC, NCPC\}$, $Y \in \{NPC, NCPC\}$.

We have proved that any language generated by non-returning context-free PCGSs is context-sensitive. An open problem is if there are context-sensitive languages which can not be generated by such PCGS, i.e. if the inclusion in the Theorem 4.1 is proper.

The above results are obtained for the classes X_*CF, $X \in \{NPC, NCPC\}$, but they can be extended for $X \in \{PC, CPC\}$ if a limit of significant occurrences as above exists. Also these results are true for the classes $X_*CF_{\lambda^*}$, X as above.

5. Conclusions

In this paper we have investigated the computational complexity of context-free PCGSs. We have proved the linear space complexity of languages generated by non-returning context-free PCGS, proving so that these languages are context-sensitive. Also, we have found some results concerning returning systems. Finding the limit of significant occurrences we mentioned above is an open problem which we are working on.

Systems which contains λ-productions were not considered and this is a possible extension of this study. We think a feasible approach to this problem consists in finding some transformations which eliminates λ-productions (in the same manner as for context-free grammars [2]) even if there are synchronization problems. Theorem 3.3 is a support for this approach. We believe that these systems have linear space complexity too.

Also a possible extension of this study is the investigation of time-bounded complexity of context-free PCGSs. We intend to pursue further studies on these issues.

References

1. E. Csuhaj-Varjú, J. Dassow, J. Kelemen, Gh. Păun, *Grammar Systems. A Grammatical Approach to Distribution and Cooperation*, Gordon and Breach, London, 1994.

2. H. R. Lewis, C. H. Papadimitriou, *Elements of the Theory of Computation*, Prentice-Hall, 1981.

3. L. Cai, *The Computational Complexity of Linear PCGS*, Computer and AI, 15, 2 - 3 (1996), 199 - 210;

4. Gh. Păun, L. Sântean, *Parallel Communicating Grammar Systems: The Regular Case*, Ann. Univ. Buc., Matem. Inform. Series, 38, 2(1989), 55 - 63.

5. F. L. Ţiplea, O. Procopiuc, C. M. Procopiuc, C. Ene, *On the Power and Complexity of PCGS*, Artificial Life: Grammatical Models (Gh. Păun, ed.), Black Sea University Press, Bucharest, 1995.

Parallel Communicating Grammar Systems with Communication by Signals

Daniel POPESCU

Faculty of Mathematics, University of Bucharest
Str. Academiei 14, 70109 Bucureşti, Romania

Abstract. We consider PC grammar systems with communication by request, but with the communicated strings defined dynamically, according to certain regular languages associated to system components (like in *CCPC* grammar systems). The power of such systems is investigated.

1. Introduction

The orientation of the contemporary operating systems to multitasking, the building of computers with multiprocessor architectures, as well as the last projects in the area of the distributed operating systems (for instance: Plan 9, Spring) show us the great importance of the parallel and distributed architectures.

To investigate them it can be a valuable source to elaborate relevant theoretical models of the parallel and distributed computing. In view of this, we consider, as a start point, the UNIX operating system, a first major system oriented to multitasking, that can be met on all hardware platforms (from microcomputers to supercomputers) and that has decisively influenced the building of most of the contemporary operating systems.

It is often desirable to construct software systems that consist of several cooperating processes rather than a single, monolithic program. There are several possible reasons for this:

- a single program might, for example, to be too large for the machine it is running on (in terms of physical memory or available address space, for instance),

- part of the required functionality may already reside in an existing program,

- it is easier to design small programs, with a well–defined functionality, rather than a big program with several functionalities.

Therefore, the problem might be solved in a better way with a server process that cooperates with an arbitrary number of client processes. Of course, for two or more processes to cooperate in performing a task, they need to have interprocess communication mechanisms and, luckily, UNIX is rich in such mechanisms.

In what follows we shortly describe one of the most used mechanisms in UNIX, the communication by signals (see [4], [5]). In UNIX a signal is a query sent from a process to another process or from a process to a group of processes. Whenever a process receives a signal it performs a special routine to handle this signal (for instance, the routine transmits on a communication channel some information that was processed of it).

Several facts are worth mentioning:

268

- on a UNIX system, there exists a well–defined number of signal types (regardless of the number of processes in the system);

- for each type of signal, a process has at most one routine to handle it, whatever process has sent it;

- if, for a type of signal, a process has not a routine to handle it, then there exists a default routine defined by system, the same for any process;

- the process that receives the signal has no information about the sender process, hence, the responsibility for the correctness of the received dates belongs to the receiver process.

Because, from the point of view of the receiver process, the signal may come asynchronously with the execution of the process (for instance, the receiver process can not communicate the information to the sender process because it has not processed all data), we need a mechanism to synchronize the execution of the processes according to the reception of the signals.

For this, the UNIX systems provides a waiting mechanism by means of which a process turns on an inactivity state. This action will be performed a well–determined period of time or a undetermined period that lasts until a event would occur. Thus a process may turn on a waiting state whenever a signal was not satisfied and waits until it is satisfied.

2. Preliminaries

For an alphabet V, we denote by V^* the free monoid generated by V under the operation of concatenation. The empty string is denoted by λ and $V^+ = V^* - \{\lambda\}$. The length of $x \in V^*$ is denoted by $|x|$. If $x \in V^*$ and $U \subseteq V$ then $|x|_U$ is the number of occurrences in x of symbols in U (the length of the string obtained by erasing from x all symbols in $V - U$). If Va is a set of symbols we denote $V' = \{a' \mid a \in V\}$. A Chomsky grammar is denoted by $G = (N, T, S, P)$, where N is the non terminal alphabet, T is the terminal alphabet, $S \in N$ is the axiom and P is the set of rewriting rules (written in the form $u \to v, u, v \in (N \cup T)^*, |u|_N \geq 1$).

The direct derivation step with respect to G is defined by:

$$x \Rightarrow y \text{ iff } x = x_1 u x_2, y = x_1 v x_2, \text{ for some } u \to v \in P.$$

Denoting by $\overset{*}{\Rightarrow}$ the reflexive and transitive closure of the relation $\Rightarrow$, the language generated by G is define as follows:

$$L(G) = \{x \in T^* \mid S \overset{*}{\Rightarrow} x\}.$$

A *PC grammar system* ([6], [1]) is a construct of the form:

$$\Gamma = (N, T, K, (S_1, P_1), (S_2, P_2), \ldots, (S_n, P_n)),$$

for some $n \geq 1$, where N is the nonterminal alphabet, T is the terminal alphabet, $K = \{Q_1, Q_2, \ldots, Q_n\}$ is the set of query symbols (N, T, K are pairwise disjoint sets), and $(S_i, P_i), 1 \leq i \leq n$, are the components of the system.

S_i is the axiom, and P_i is the set of rewriting rules (over $N \cup T \cup K$) of the i-th component.

The work of the system starts from the initial configuration $(S_1, \ldots, S_n)$ and proceeds by componentwise rewriting steps and communication steps, resulting in new configurations.

In the case of componentwise rewriting steps each component rewrites its current sentential form by applying a rule to it.

In the case of communication steps, when a component G_j introduces some query symbol Q_i, $1 \le i \le n$, then the currently generated string of the i-th component is transmitted to the j-th component in order to replace Q_i in its sentential form.

The communication has priority over rewriting. If a query symbol appears in the sentential form of some component, then a communication must be executed. If circular queries are introduced, then the process is blocked; the system also gets stuck when a derivation must be done and a component is not able to rewrite its sentential form, although it is not a terminal string. After sending its sentential form to another component, a component either resumes working from its axiom (the returning mode), or it continues processing the current string (the non-returning mode).

The set of terminal strings generated in this way by the first component is the language generated by the system.

We denote by REG, LIN, CF, RE the families of regular, linear, context–free, context–sensitive, recursively enumerable languages, respectively.

3. Definitions and Examples

Definition 3.1. Let $n \ge 1$ be a natural number. A *parallel communicating grammar system with communication by signals* (an SPC grammar system, for short) of degree n is a $(n+3)$-tuple:

$$\Gamma = (N, T, K, (S_1, P_1, R_1), (S_2, P_2, R_2), \ldots, (S_n, P_n, R_n)),$$

where N is a nonterminal alphabet, T is a terminal alphabet, $K = \{Q_1, Q_2, \ldots, Q_p\}$ is the set of signals of the system (the sets N, T, K are mutually disjoint), P_i is a finite set of rewriting rules over $N \cup T \cup K$, $S_i \in N$, and R_i is a set of p regular languages over $N \cup T$ associated to symbols $Q_1, \ldots, Q_p$, for all $1 \le i \le n$

We denote $V_\Gamma = N \cup T \cup K$. The sets $P_i, 1 \le i \le n$, are called components of the system.

Here we work only with λ-free SPC grammar systems.

The derivation in an SPC grammar system is defined as follows:

Definition 3.2. Let $\Gamma = (N, T, K, (S_1, P_1, R_1), (S_2, P_2, R_2), \ldots, (S_n, P_n, R_n))$ be a SPC grammar system and two n-tuples $(x_1, x_2, \ldots, x_n), (y_1, y_2, \ldots, y_n)$, $x_i, y_i \in V_\Gamma^*, 1 \le i \le n$ (we call them configurations). We define two types of derivation:

1. (derivation without waiting): $(x_1, x_2, \ldots, x_n) \Rightarrow (y_1, y_2, \ldots, y_n)$, where $x_i \Rightarrow y_i$ by a rule from P_i, $x_i \in (N \cup T)^*, 1 \le i \le n$, or $y_i = x_i$ if $x_i \in T^*, 1 \le i \le n$.

2. (derivation with waiting): $(x_1, x_2, \ldots, x_n) \Rightarrow (y_1, y_2, \ldots, y_n)$, where $x_i \Rightarrow y_i$ by a rule from P_i, $x_i \in (N \cup T \cup K)^*, 1 \le i \le n$ or $y_i = x_i$ if $x_i \in T^*, 1 \le i \le n$, or $x_i \in (N \cup T \cup K)^*$ contains at least a signal $Q_l \in K, 1 \le l \le p$, and we cannot use any rules from P_i to derive x_i. If there exist no components to derive the configuration and $x_1 \notin T^*$, then Γ is blocked.

Definition 3.3. We denote the step of communication by

$$(x_1, x_2, \ldots, x_n) \vdash (y_1, y_2, \ldots, y_n)$$

and we define it as follows:

For $x_i = \alpha_1 Q_{i_1} \alpha_2 Q_{i_2} \ldots Q_{i_j} \alpha_{j+1}$ a word with $Q_{i_l} \in K, 1 \leq l \leq p$, and $\alpha_l \in (T \cup N)^*, 1 \leq l \leq j+1$, we define for each Q_{i_l}:

$$\delta_i(Q_{i_l}, x_k) = \begin{cases} x_k, & \text{if } x_k \in R^i_{Q_{i_l}}, k \neq i, \\ \lambda, & \text{if } x_k \notin R^i_{Q_{i_l}} \text{ or } k = i, \end{cases}$$

for $1 \leq k \leq n$.

We denote $\delta_i(Q_{i_l}) = \delta_i(Q_{i_l}, x_1)\delta_i(Q_{i_l}, x_2)\ldots\delta_i(Q_{i_l}, x_n)$ and

$$\Delta_i(Q_{i_l}) = \begin{cases} \delta_i(Q_{i_l}), & \text{if } \delta_i(Q_{i_l}) \neq \lambda, \\ Q_{i_l}, & \text{if } \delta_i(Q_{i_l}) = \lambda. \end{cases}$$

Finally:

$$y_i = \alpha_1 \Delta_i(Q_{i_1})\alpha_2 \Delta_i(Q_{i_2})\ldots\Delta_i(Q_{i_j})\alpha_{j+1}.$$

Definition 3.4. We define the language generated by Γ as follows :

$$\begin{aligned} L(\Gamma) = \ & \{w \in T^* \mid (S_1, S_2, \ldots S_n) \Rightarrow (x_1^{(1)}, x_2^{(1)}, \ldots, x_n^{(1)}) \vdash (y_1^{(1)}, y_2^{(1)}, \ldots, y_n^{(1)}) \\ & \Rightarrow (x_1^{(2)}, x_2^{(2)}, \ldots, x_n^{(2)}) \vdash (y_1^{(2)}, y_2^{(2)}, \ldots, y_n^{(2)}) \Rightarrow \ldots \models (x_1^{(s)}, x_2^{(s)}, \ldots, x_n^{(s)}), \\ & \text{for some } s \geq 1 \text{ such that } w = x_1^{(s)}, \text{ where } \models \in \{\Rightarrow, \vdash\}\}. \end{aligned}$$

In words, Γ has a set of signal types K and the appearance of a symbol $Q_l \in K$ in the sentential form of the component G_i means sending of the signal Q_l from G_i to all other components of the system Γ (all components of Γ are seen as a group of processes). The routine of any component $G_j, 1 \leq j \leq n$, for handling the signal Q_l consists in the writing of its sentential form on an accessible communication channel to all components of Γ (i.e., the group of processes). From the communication channel the component G_i selects the data sent by G_j only if them are acceptable according to the regular language $R^i_{Q_l}$ (thus G_i verifies that the signal Q_l was properly satisfied by G_j). With respect to the type of derivation of Γ we have:

- in the case of the derivation without waiting, the system is blocked whenever a signal is not satisfied,

- in the case of derivation with waiting, if a signal (of a component G_i) is not satisfied at a step of communication and at the next step (of derivation) we can not perform a rule from P_i, then G_i turns on a waiting state (until the signal will be satisfied).

Definition 3.5. Let $\Gamma = (N, T, K, G_1, G_2, \ldots, G_n)$ be an SPC grammar system. If only G_1 is allowed to introduce signals, then we say that Γ is a centralized SPC grammar system; in the unrestricted case Γ is called non–centralized.

A SPC grammar system is said to be returning (to axiom) if, after a communicating step, each component that has communicated its string to another component returns to axiom. The other systems are called non–returning.

Notations. We denote $SPC_n X$ the class of non–centralized, returning SPC grammar systems of degree at most n of type X with derivation without waiting. When we use only centralized SPC grammar systems we add the letter C, thus obtaining the classes $CSPC_n X$. When non–returning systems are considered, we add the letter N, thus obtaining the classes $NSPC_n X$, $NCSPC_n X$. If we consider the systems with derivation with waiting we denote that by WG where $G \in \{SPC_n X, CSPC_n X, NSPC_n X, NCSPC_n X\}$. We denote all these classes by C_{SPC}. X can be REG, LIN, CF, CS, RE (for REG we consider right–linear grammars) and we suppose that P_i, $1 \le i \le n$, contains only λ–free rules.

If we consider $n = \infty$ in the previously notations, then we say that we have grammar systems with an arbitrary number of components.

The first component of Γ is called the master of the system.

In the following constructions we shall assume that when the regular language associated to a signal $Q_l \in K$ is not specified, then, by default, $R_{Q_l}^i = \emptyset$ (and Q_l does not appear in any right member of the rules from P_i).

Here are two examples:

Example 3.1. Consider the system

$$\Gamma_1 = (N, T, K, (S_1, P_1, R_1), (S_2, P_2, R_2)),$$
$$N = \{S_1, S_1', S_2\}, \ K = \{Q_1\}, \ T = \{a, b\},$$
$$P_1 = \{S_1 \to a^2 S_1', S_1' \to a S_1', S_1' \to a Q_1, S_2 \to b\},$$
$$P_2 = \{S_2 \to b S_2\}, \ R_{Q_1}^1 = b^* S_2.$$

We have:

$$(S_1, S_2) \Rightarrow (a^2 S_1', b S_2) \Rightarrow \ldots \Rightarrow (a^{n-1} S_1', b^{n-2} S_2)$$
$$\Rightarrow (a^n Q_1, b^{n-1} S_1) \vdash (a^n b^{n-1} S_2, S_2) \Rightarrow (a^n b^n, b S_2)$$

Hence, $L(\Gamma_1) = \{a^n b^n \mid n \ge 3\} \in LIN - REG$.

Example 3.2. Consider the system

$$\Gamma_2 = (N, T, K, (S_1, P_1, R_1), (S_2, P_2, R_2)),$$
$$N = \{S_1, S_1', S_2\}, \ K = \{Q_1\}, \ T = \{a, b, c\},$$
$$P_1 = \{S_1 \to a^2 S_1' c^2, S_1' \to a S_1' c, S_1' \to a Q_1 c, S_2 \to b\},$$
$$P_2 = \{S_2 \to b S_2\}, \ R_{Q_1}^1 = b^* S_2.$$

We have:

$$(S_1, S_2) \Rightarrow (a^2 S_1' c^2, b S_2) \Rightarrow \ldots \Rightarrow (a^{n-1} S_1' c^{n-1}, b^{n-2} S_2)$$

$$\Rightarrow (a^n Q_1 c^n, b^{n-1} S_1) \vdash (a^n b^{n-1} S_2 c^n, S_2) \Rightarrow (a^n b^n c^n, b S_2)$$

Hence, $L(\Gamma_1) = \{a^n b^n c^n \mid n \ge 3\} \in CS - CF$.

4. On the Generative Capacity

From definitions, the following results are true:

Lemma 4.1. $X = G_1 X \subseteq G_2 X \subseteq \ldots \subseteq G_\infty X$, for all $X \in \{REG, LIN, CF, CS, RE\}, G \in C_{SPC}$.

Lemma 4.2. $G_n X \subseteq G_n Y$, for all $n \geq 1, X \subseteq Y, X, Y \in \{REG, LIN, CF, CS, RE\}, G \in C_{SPC}.$

From the previous examples, we have:

Lemma 4.3. (1) $REG \subset G_2 REG$, (2) $LIN \subset G_2 LIN$, where $G \in C_{SPC}.$

Lemma 4.4. $WSPC_3 REG$ contains one-letter non context–free languages.

Proof. Let Γ be the system

$$\Gamma = (N, T, K, (S_1, P_1, R_1), (S_2, P_2, R_2), (S_3, P_3, R_3)),$$
$$N = \{S_1, S_2, S_3, A, B\}, \ K = \{Q_1\}, \ T = \{a\},$$
$$P_1 = \{S_1 \rightarrow A, B \rightarrow A, B \rightarrow a, S_1 \rightarrow Q_1\}, \ R^1_{Q_1} = B^+,$$
$$P_2 = \{S_2 \rightarrow Q_1, A \rightarrow B\}, \ R^2_{Q_1} = A^+,$$
$$P_3 = \{S_3 \rightarrow Q_1, A \rightarrow B\}, \ R^3_{Q_1} = A^+.$$

Examine a derivation in Γ. From (S_1, S_2, S_3) we can either perform $(S_1, S_2, S_3) \Rightarrow (Q_1, Q_1, Q_1)$ or $(S_1, S_2, S_3) \Rightarrow (A, Q_1, Q_1) \vdash (S_1, A, A)$. In the first case we are blocked. In the second one we can either continue $(S_1, A, A) \Rightarrow (A, B, B)$ and we are blocked, or $(S_1, A, A) \Rightarrow (Q_1, B, B) \vdash (BB, S_2, S_3) \Rightarrow (AB, Q_1, Q_1) \Rightarrow (AA, Q_1, Q_1) \vdash (S_1, AA, AA)$. We can continue with $(S_1, AA, AA) \Rightarrow (A, BA, BA)$ and we are blocked, or $(S_1, AA, AA) \Rightarrow (Q_1, BA, BA) \Rightarrow (Q_1, BB, BB) \vdash (B^4, S_2, S_3) \overset{*}{\Rightarrow} (A^4, Q_1, Q_1) \vdash (S_1, A^4, A^4) \Rightarrow \ldots \vdash (S_1, A^{2^{n-1}}, A^{2^{n-1}}) \overset{*}{\Rightarrow} (Q_1, B^{2^{n-1}}, B^{2^{n-1}}) \vdash (B^{2^n}, S_2, S_3) \overset{*}{\Rightarrow} (a^{2^n}, Q_1, Q_1).$

It follows that $L(\Gamma) = \{a^{2^n} \mid n \geq 1\}$, which is not a context-free language. $\square$

Theorem 4.1. $LIN \subset WSPC_\infty(REG).$

Proof. Because $WSPC_3(REG) - CF \neq \emptyset$ (Lemma 4.4), we have to prove $LIN \subseteq WSPC_\infty(REG).$

Let $L \in LIN$ and $G = (N, T, S, P)$ such that $L = L(G)$. We can write:

$$L = (L \cap \{\lambda\}) \cup \bigcup_{a \in T} \partial^r_a(L)\{a\},$$

(where ∂^r_a denotes the right derivative with respect to the symbol a). We denote $L_a = \partial^r_a(L)$. We have $L_a \in LIN$ for each $a \in T$.

Let $G_a = (N_a, T_a, S_a, P_a)$ be a grammar such that $L(G_a) = L_a$. We construct $\Gamma_a \in WSPC_\infty(REG)$ such that $L(\Gamma_a) = L_a\{a\}$. We define a relation $\bowtie$ on the set of rules P_a such that, if:

$$r : X_1 \rightarrow uX_2v \in P_a, r' : X'_1 \rightarrow u'X'_2v' \in P_a,$$

with $X_1, X_2, X'_1, X'_2 \in N_a$ and $u, v, u', v' \in T^*$, we say that $r \bowtie r'$ iff $X_2 = X'_2$.

The relation $\bowtie$ divides P_a in a set of classes $\mathcal{M}$ such that each $M \in \mathcal{M}$ is associated to a nonterminal $A \in N_a$ such that

$$M = \{X \rightarrow uYv \in P_a \mid X, Y \in N_a, u, v \in T^*, Y = A\}.$$

If $p = \max\{2, \max\{card(M) \mid M \in \mathcal{M}\}\}$ then we define $K = \{Q, Q_1, Q_2, \ldots, Q_p\}$. Let $m = card(\mathcal{M})$. For each $M_k \in \mathcal{M}$, $1 \leq k \leq m$, we number its rules with $1, 2, \ldots, r_k$. We define Γ_a as

$$\Gamma_a = (\overline{N}, T_a, K, (S_0, P_0, R_0), (S_1, P_1, R_1), (S'_1, P'_1, R'_1), \ldots, (S_m, P_m, R_m), (S'_m, P'_m, R_m)),$$

where:

$$\overline{N} = \{\overline{S}, S_0, S_1, S_1', \ldots, S_m, S_m'\} \cup N_a \cup N_a' \cup \bigcup_{k=1}^{m} \bigcup_{i=1}^{r_k} \{[X, k, i] \mid X \in N_a\}.$$

We define the components of Γ_a as follows:

$$P_0 = \{\overline{S} \to a\} \cup \{S_0 \to Q\} \cup \{A' \to A \mid \forall A \in N_a\} \cup \{S_0 \to xA \mid A \to x \in P_a, x \in T^*\}.$$

Moreover, $R_Q^0 = T^*\overline{S} \cup \{T^*A' \mid A \in N_a\}$. Let $M_k \in \mathcal{M}$ be the class associated to the nonterminal $A \in N_a$. To M_k we associate the components P_k, P_k' of Γ_a defined by

$$P_k = \{S_k \to Q\} \cup \{A \to v[X, k, j] \mid j : X \to uAv\},$$

where j is the number of the rule in M_k. Moreover $R_Q^k = T^*A$.

$$
\begin{aligned}
P_k' &= \{S_k' \to uQ_j \mid j : X \to uAv\} \cup \{[A, k, j] \to A' \mid 1 \le j \le r_k\} \\
&\cup \{[A, k, j] \to \overline{S} \mid 1 \le j \le r_k, \text{ if } A = S_a\}.
\end{aligned}
$$

Moreover, $R_{Q_j}'^k = T^*[X, k, j]$.

From the definition of the languages $R_0, R_j, R_j', 1 \le j \le m$, we observe that P_0 communicates to $P_i, 1 \le i \le m$, P_i communicates to $P_i', 1 \le i \le m$, and P_i' communicates to $P_0, 1 \le i \le m$. If

$$S_0 \Rightarrow u_1 X_1 v_1 \Rightarrow u_1 u_2 X_2 v_2 v_1 \Rightarrow \ldots \Rightarrow u_1 u_2 \ldots u_n X_n v_n v_{n-1} \ldots v_1$$
$$\Rightarrow u_1 u_2 \ldots u_n w v_n v_{n-1} \ldots v_1 = x \in T^*, \qquad (*)$$

is a derivation in G_a then we have in Γ_a a derivation that gets xa, in the reverse way to $(*)$, with the following rules:

i) S_0 starts the derivation by the rule $S_0 \to wX_n$.

ii) If $X_{i-1} \to u_i X_i v_i \in M_{k_i}$ (with the number j in M_{k_i}) is a rule that has to be used in $(*)$, then a communication step between P_0 and P_{k_i} (being in a waiting state after using the rule $S_{k_i} \to Q$) we shall apply the rule $X_i \to v_i[X_{i-1}, k_i, j]$ and, after that, we shall communicate to P_{k_i}' (being in a waiting state after using the rule $S_{k_i}' \to u_iQ_j$). In P_{k_i}' we use the rule $[X_{i-1}, k_i, j] \to X_{i-1}'$ if $i > 1$, otherwise (when $X_{i-1} = S_a$) we can, also, use the rule $[X_{i-1}, k_i, j] \to \overline{S}$ and we communicate to P_0 (being in a waiting state after using the rule $S_0 \to Q$).

iii) The last rule to apply will be in P_0, that is $\overline{S} \to a$, obtaining the string xa.

We can easily observe that any deviation from this scenario leads to blocked derivations in Γ_a. Consequently, we obtain $L(\Gamma_a) = L_a\{a\}$.

We suppose that we constructed Γ_a, for all $a \in T$.

Let Γ_a, Γ_b be two systems as above. We construct Γ_{ab} such that $L(\Gamma_{ab}) = L(\Gamma_a) \cup L(\Gamma_b)$. We assume:

$$
\begin{aligned}
\Gamma_a &= (N', T', K', G_1', G_2', \ldots, G_n'), \\
\Gamma_b &= (N'', T'', K'', G_1'', G_2'', \ldots, G_m'').
\end{aligned}
$$

We define:

$$
\begin{aligned}
\Gamma_{ab} &= (N' \cup N'' \cup \{S_0\}, K' \cup K'' \cup \{Q_0', Q_0''\}, T' \cup T'', G_0, G_1', G_2', \\
&\quad \ldots, G_n', G_1'', G_2'', \ldots, G_m''),
\end{aligned}
$$

with S_0, Q_0', Q_0'' new symbols. The rules of G_0 are $S_0 \rightarrow Q_0'$, $S_0 \rightarrow Q_0''$, and the associated languages are $R_{Q_0'}^0 = T'^*a$, $R_{Q_0''}^0 = T'''^*b$. Obviously, we have $L(\Gamma_{ab}) = L(\Gamma_a) \cup L(\Gamma_b)$.

In the same manner we recursively construct a grammar system such that $L(\Gamma) = \bigcup_{a \in T} L(\Gamma_a)$. □

The following example illustrates the previous algorithm.

Example 4.1. Consider the linear language $L = \{a^n b^n \mid n \geq 1\}$. We have

$$L = \partial_b^r(L)\{b\}, \ \partial_b^r(L) = \{a^n b^{n-1} \mid n \geq 1\}$$

and $\partial_b^r(L)$ is generated by $G_b = (\{X, A\}, \{a, b\}, X, \{X \rightarrow aA, A \rightarrow aAb\})$. We construct Γ_b such that $L(\Gamma_b) = \partial_b^r(L)\{b\}$, with

$$\overline{N} = \{\overline{S}, S_0, S_1, S_1'\} \cup \{X, A', X, A'\} \cup \{[X, 1, 1], [X, 1, 2]\} \cup \{[A, 1, 1], [A, 1, 2]\},$$
$$P_0 = \{S_0 \rightarrow Q, X' \rightarrow X, A' \rightarrow A, \overline{S} \rightarrow b, S_0 \rightarrow abA\}, R_Q^0 = T^*\overline{S} \cup T^*X' \cup T^*A',$$
$$P_1 = \{S_1 \rightarrow Q, A \rightarrow [X, 1, 1], A \rightarrow b[A, 1, 2]\}, R_Q^1 = T^*A,$$
$$P_1' = \{S_1' \rightarrow aQ_1, S_1' \rightarrow aQ_2, [X, 1, 1] \rightarrow X', [A, 1, 2] \rightarrow A', [X, 1, 1] \rightarrow \overline{S}\}.$$

Moreover $R_{Q_1}' = T^*[X, 1, 1], R_{Q_2}' = T^*[A, 1, 2]$.

Here is a derivation in Γ:

$$(S_0, S_1, S_1') \Rightarrow (abA, Q, aQ_2) \vdash (S_0, abA, aQ_2) \Rightarrow (Q, ab^2[A, 1, 2], aQ_2) \vdash$$
$$(Q, S_1, a^2b^2[A, 1, 2]) \Rightarrow (Q, Q, a^2b^2A') \vdash (a^2b^2A', Q, S_1') \Rightarrow (a^2b^2A, Q, aQ_1) \vdash$$
$$(S_0, a^2b^2A, aQ_1) \Rightarrow (Q, a^2b^2[X, 1, 1], aQ_1) \vdash (Q, S_1', a^3b^2[X, 1, 1]) \Rightarrow$$
$$(Q, S_1', a^3b^2\overline{S}) \vdash (a^3b^2\overline{S}, -, -) \Rightarrow (a^3b^3, -, -).$$

Theorem 4.2. $CS \subseteq WSPC_\infty(CF)$.

Proof. Let L be a context–sensitive language and $G = (N, T, S, P)$ such that $L(G) = L$.

We suppose that G is in (weak) Kuroda normal form, hence it has the rules of the form: $A \rightarrow a, A \rightarrow B, A \rightarrow BC, AB \rightarrow CD$, where $A, B, C, D \in N$ and $a \in T$. Without loss of the generality, we may assume that $A \neq B$ in rules of the form $AB \rightarrow CD$ (if $r : AA \rightarrow CD \in P$, then we replace it by $A \rightarrow [A, r], [A, r]A \rightarrow CD$).

We define a relation $\bowtie$ on the set P of the rules. If

$$r_1 : XZ \rightarrow \alpha \in P, r_2 : YZ' \rightarrow \beta \in P,$$

where $Z, Z' \in N \cup \{\lambda\}$, $X, Y \in N$ and $\alpha, \beta \in (N \cup T)^*$, we say that $r_1 \bowtie r_2$ iff $X = Y$. The relation $\bowtie$ divides P in a set of classes $\mathcal{M}$; let $n = \text{card}(\mathcal{M})$. We define Γ a grammar system such that $L(\Gamma) = L$ as:

$$\Gamma = (\overline{N}, T, K, G_0, G_1, G_2, \ldots, G_n),$$

where

$$\overline{N} = N \cup N' \cup \{S_0, S_1, \ldots, S_n\}$$
$$\cup \ \{[A, r] \mid A \in N \text{ and } r : A \rightarrow x \in P \text{ or } r : AB \rightarrow CD \in P$$
$$\text{or } r : BA \rightarrow CD \in P\},$$

$$K = \{Q_0, Q_1, Q_2, \ldots, Q_n\},$$

$$
\begin{aligned}
P_0 &= \{S_0 \to Q_0\} \cup \{A' \to A \mid \forall A \in N\} \\
&\cup \{A \to [A,p] \mid p : A \to a \in P \text{ or } p : A \to B \in P \text{ or } p : A \to BC \in P\} \\
&\cup \{A \to [A,q], B \to [B,q] \mid q : AB \to CD \in P\},
\end{aligned}
$$

$$R_{Q_0}^0 = (T \cup N')^*,$$

$$
\begin{aligned}
P_k &= \{S_k \to Q_k\} \cup \{[A,p] \to a \mid p : A \to a\} \cup \{[A,r] \to B'C' \mid r : A \to BC\} \\
&\cup \{[A,s] \to B' \mid s : A \to B\} \cup \{[A,q] \to C', [B,q] \to D' \mid q : AB \to CD\},
\end{aligned}
$$

$$
\begin{aligned}
R_{Q_k}^k &= \{\alpha[A,p]\beta \mid \alpha, \beta \in (N \cup T)^*, p : A \to a \in P \text{ or } p : A \to B \in P \\
&\quad \text{or } p : A \to BC \in P\} \\
&\cup \{\alpha[A,q][B,q]\beta \mid \alpha, \beta \in (N \cup T)^*, q : AB \to CD \in P\},
\end{aligned}
$$

for $M_k \in \mathcal{M}$ asssociated to $A \in N$.

From the definition of the languages $R_i, 0 \le i \le n$, we observe that the communication is made only between G_0 and a unique component $G_i, 1 \le i \le n$, or between G_i, $1 \le i \le n$, and G_0 (the communication between G_i and $G_j, 1 \le i,j \le n$, is not possible). From this construction, it follows that $L(G) = L(\Gamma)$. □

Definition 4.1. Let Γ be a PC grammar system given by:

$$\Gamma = (N, T, K, G_1, G_2, \ldots, G_n)$$

and a query symbol $Q_i \in K, 1 \le i \le n$.

We say that Q_i has "the property C" if every replacing of it by a communicated string $u_1 X_1 u_2 X_2 \ldots X_p u_{p+1}$ $(X_i \in N, 1 \le i \le p, u_i \in T^*, 1 \le i \le p + 1)$ in a component G_k, $1 \le k \le n$, is followed by the transformation of all non-terminal symbols $X_1, X_2, \ldots, X_n$ (by rules from G_k) before G_k performs a communication step.

A derivation in Γ is called "with the property C" if all query symbols that appear in it, have the property C. We define:

$$L^C(\Gamma) = \{x \in T^* \mid x \in L(\Gamma) \text{ and } x \text{ is obtained by a derivation with propery C}\}.$$

Moreover, we define $PC_n^C(X)$, the set of languages generated by derivation with property C in PC grammar systems of type X and degree n. Analogously we define $CPC_n^C(X), NPC_n^C(X), NCPC_n^C(X)$.

From the definitions we obtain the following result:

Lemma 4.5. $G_n^C(X) = G_n(X)$ where $n \ge 1$, $G \in \{PC, CPC, NPC, NCPC\}$ and $X \in \{REG, LIN\}$.

Theorem 4.3. $G_n^C(X) \subseteq H_n(X)$ where $n \ge 1$, $X \in \{REG, LIN, CF, CS, RE\}$ and $(G, H) \in \{(PC, SPC), (CPC, CSPC), (NPC, NSPC), (NCPC, NCSPC)\}$.

Proof. We suppose $X = CF$ and $(G, H) = (PC, SPC)$ (the other cases are analogous).

Let $\Gamma = (N, T, K, G_1, G_2, \ldots, G_n)$ be a PC grammar system with property C. We construct a SPC system $\Gamma' = (\overline{N}, T, K', G_1', G_2', \ldots, G_n')$ such that $L^C(\Gamma') = L(\Gamma)$, as follows:

$$\overline{N} = \bigcup_{j=1}^{n} \{[A, j] \mid A \in N\} \text{ and } K' = \{Q_1', Q_2' \ldots, Q_n'\}.$$

Let $G_i = (N \cup K, T, S_i, P_i), 1 \leq i \leq n$. We define $G_i' = (\overline{N} \cup K', T, [S_i, i], P_i')$ where P_i' is given by:

$$P_i' = \bigcup_{j=1}^{n} \{[A, j] \rightarrow u_1[X_1, i]u_2[X_2, i] \ldots [X_p, i]u_{p+1} \mid A \rightarrow u_1 X_1 u_2 X_2 \ldots X_p u_{p+1} \in P_i,$$
$$u_1, u_2, \ldots, u_{p+1} \in T^*, X_1, X_2 \ldots, X_p \in N\}.$$

Moreover, we define $R_{Q_j'}^i = (T \cup N_j)^*$, where $N_j = \{[A, j] \mid A \in N\}, 1 \leq j \leq n$.

The theorem follows from the following observation: Γ' works like Γ and the property C of Γ gives us the possibility to communicate atthe same time as in Γ. □

Corollary 4.1. $LIN \subset SPC_\infty(REG)$.

Proof. It is known that $LIN \subset PC_\infty(REG)$ (see [3]). From Lemma 4.5 and Theorem 4.3 we have $LIN \subset PC_\infty(REG) = PC_\infty^C(REG) \subseteq SPC_\infty(REG)$. □

5. A Generalization

As we said in Introduction, in UNIX it is possible to send signals to a group of processes (a case modeled by SPC grammar systems), but also to a process with a defined address.

We model this general case by the concept of *"Parallel communicating grammars systems with communication by signals to addresses"* (ASPC, for short).

Definition 5.1. Let $n \geq 1$ be a natural number. A parallel communicating grammar system of degree n with communication by signals to addresses is an $(n+3)$–tuple:

$$\Gamma = (N, T, K, (S_1, P_1, R_1), (S_2, P_2, R_2), \ldots, (S_n, P_n, R_n)),$$

where N is a nonterminal alphabet, T is a terminal alphabet, $K = \{Q_1, Q_2, \ldots, Q_p\}$ is the set of signals of the system (the sets N, T, K are mutually disjoint). We define: $\overline{K} = \bigcup_{k=1}^{p} Q_k(-1) \cup \bigcup_{k=1}^{p} \bigcup_{i=1}^{n} Q_k(i)$. $Q_k(-1)$ means that the signal Q_k is sent to all components of the systems (like in SPC systems) and $Q_k(i)$ means that the signal Q_k is sent to the component P_i of the system.

P_i is a finite set of rewriting rules over $N \cup T \cup \overline{K}$ and $S_i \in N$, for all $1 \leq i \leq n$

For all $1 \leq i \leq n$, R_i is defined as a set of regular languages $R_i = (R_{Q_j}^i)_{1 \leq j \leq p}$ where $R_{Q_j}^i$ is a regular language associated to the signal Q_j (of the component P_i of Γ).

We assume that the rules of $P_i, 1 \leq i \leq n$, are λ–free and there exist no rules $Q_l(j) \rightarrow \alpha \in P_i, 1 \leq i \leq n, 1 \leq l \leq p, j = -1$ or $1 \leq j \leq n$.

The derivation in an ASPC grammar systems is defined as follows:

Definition 5.2. Let $\Gamma = (N, T, K, (S_1, P_1, R_1), (S_2, P_2, R_2), \ldots, (S_n, P_n, R_n))$ be an ASPC grammar system and two n-tuples $(x_1, x_2, \ldots, x_n), (y_1, y_2, \ldots, y_n), x_i, y_i \in V_\Gamma^*, 1 \leq i \leq n$. We define two types of derivation:

1. (derivation without waiting): $(x_1, x_2, \ldots, x_n) \Rightarrow (y_1, y_2, \ldots, y_n)$, where $x_i \Rightarrow y_i$ by a rule from P_i, $x_i \in (N \cup T)^*, 1 \leq i \leq n$ or $y_i = x_i$ if $x_i \in T^*, 1 \leq i \leq n$.

2. (derivation with waiting): $(x_1, x_2, \ldots, x_n) \Rightarrow (y_1, y_2, \ldots, y_n)$, where $x_i \Rightarrow y_i$ by a rule from P_i, $x_i \in (N \cup T \cup \overline{K})^*, 1 \le i \le n$, or $y_i = x_i$ if $x_i \in T^*, 1 \le i \le n$, or $x_i \in (N \cup T \cup \overline{K})^*$ contains at least a signal $Q_l(j) \in \overline{K}, 1 \le l \le p$, and we can not use any rules from P_i to derive x_i. If there exist no components to derive the configuration and $x_1 \notin T^*$ then Γ is blocked.

Definition 5.3. We denote the step of communication by $(x_1, x_2, \ldots, x_n) \vdash (y_1, y_2, \ldots, y_n)$ and we define it as follows:

If $x_i = \alpha_1 Q_{i_1}(j_1) \alpha_2 Q_{i_2}(j_2) \ldots Q_{i_l}(j_l) \alpha_{l+1}$ a word with $Q_{i_k}(j_k) \in \overline{K}, 1 \le k \le l$, and $\alpha_k \in (T \cup N)^*, 1 \le k \le l+1$, then, for $Q_{i_k}(j_k)$ with $j_k = -1$ communication is done like in the SPC systems, otherwise (when $1 \le j_k \le n$) we replace $Q_{i_k}(j_k)$ by x_{j_k} if $x_{j_k} \in R^i_{Q_{i_k}}$ else it remains unmodified.

The definition of the language generated by an ASPC grammar system is the same as for SPC systems.

From the definitions, we have:

Theorem 5.1. i) *The SPC systems are a particular case of ASPC systems when all addresses are* -1.

ii) *The PC systems are a particular case of ASPC systems with derivation without waiting, with all addresses different from* -1 *and no control on the received information by communication* (i.e, $R^i_{Q_j} = (N \cup T)^*, 1 \le i, j \le n$).

References

1. E. Csuhaj-Varjú, J. Dassow, J. Kellmen, Gh. Păun, *Grammar Systems. A Grammatical Approach to Distribution and Cooperation* , Gordon and Breach, London, 1994.

2. E. Csuhaj-Varjú, J. Kellmen, Gh. Păun, Grammar Systems with WAVE–like Communication, *Computers and Artificial Intelligence*, 15, 5 (1996), 419-436.

3. S. Dumitrescu, Gh. Păun, On the Power of Parallel Communicating Grammar Systems with Right–Linear Components, submitted, 1995.

4. K. Haviland, B. Salama, *Unix System Programming*, Addison–Wesley, 1987.

5. B. W. Kernighan, R. Pike, *The Unix Programming Enviroment*, Prentice Hall, 1984.

6. Gh. Păun, L. Sântean, Parallel Communicating Grammar Systems: The Regular Case, *Ann. Univ. Buc., Ser. Matem.-Inform.*, 38 (1989), 55-63.

7. A. Salomaa, *Formal Languages*, Academic Press, New York, 1973.

PC Grammar Systems Versus Some Non-Context-Free Constructions from Natural and Artificial Languages

Adrian CHIŢU

University of Bucharest, Faculty of Mathematics
Str. Academiei 14, 70109 Bucureşti, Romania

Abstract. We systematically examine the possibility of generating the three basic non-context-free constructions in natural and artificial languages – replication, multiple agreements and crossed agreements – by means of various types of parallel communicating grammar systems. Answering a problem left open in [2], we prove that also the last construction specified above can be covered by centralized (context-free) parallel communicating grammar systems, both in the returning and the non-returning case. Several problems remain open (mainly concerning stronger forms of the results mentioned here).

1. Introduction

The parallel communicating (PC) grammar systems were introduced in [7], as a grammatical model of parallel computing. Roughly speaking, several grammars work together, synchronously, each one on its own sentential form; when certain special symbols are introduced, a *communication* operation is performed: the current sentential form of a component grammar is transmitted to the component which has introduced the query symbol, and the occurrences of the query symbol in the sentential form of the receiving component are replaced by the communicated string. The language generated in this way by a specified component of the system (the *master*) is the language generated by the system.

Two basic classifications of PC grammar systems are the following ones. When only the master is allowed to introduce query symbols, then the system is said to be *centralized*; non-restricted systems are called *non-centralized*. On the other hand, a system is called *returning* if every component resumes working from its axiom after communicating its string to another component; if, after communicating, the components continue the rewriting of the current string, then the system is called *non-returning*. According to the form of the rules, a PC grammar system can be regular, linear, context-free, etc.

We refer to the monograph [1], to [2], etc. for results in this area. We only mention that the cooperation of grammars in the form of a PC grammar system increases the power of regular and of context-free grammars: systems of all forms mentioned above with regular rules are able to generate non-context-free languages. This is useful in view of the fact that one knows that natural languages as well as most of the significant artificial languages are not context-free (see, e.g., [3], [4], [8]).

The three basic non-context-free constructions in natural and artificial languages are the *replication*, the *multiple agreements*, and the *crossed agreements*, modelled by the following languages

$$L_1 = \{xx \mid x \in \{a, b\}^+\},$$
$$L_2 = \{a^n b^n c^n \mid n \geq 1\},$$
$$L_3 = \{a^n b^m c^n d^m \mid n, m \geq 1\}.$$

They are used in many papers as common examples of languages generated by PC grammar systems of various types. However, several problems are still open in this area. For instance, in [6] it is proved that L_3 can be generated by context-free non-centralized PC grammar systems both in the returning and the non-returning modes, but it is formulated the conjecture that centralized systems cannot generate this language. The problem of the place of this language in the hierarchy of families of languages generated by PC grammar systems is formulated as open also in [2].

We solve here this problem, proving that L_3 can be generated by centralized systems both in the returning and the non-returning modes. Still, we do not know whether or not regular PC grammar systems can generate this language (the answer is affirmative in the case of the language L_1, for systems working in the non-returning mode).

2. PC Grammar Systems

As usual, we denote by V^* the free monoid generated by an alphabet V; its identity (the empty string) is denoted by λ and $V^* - \{\lambda\}$ is denoted by V^+. The length of $x \in V^*$ is denoted by $|x|$, whereas $|x|_U$ is the number of occurrences of symbols in $U \subseteq V$ in the string $x \in V^*$. The families of regular, linear, context-free, context-sensitive, and recursively enumerable languages are denoted by *REG, LIN, CF, CS, RE*, respectively. Further elements of formal language theory we shall use here can be found in [9], [10], etc.

A *PC grammar system* (of degree $n, n \geq 1$) is a construct

$$\Gamma = (N, K, T, (S_1, P_1), \ldots, (S_n, P_n)),$$

where N, K, T are mutually disjoint alphabets, with $K = \{Q_1, \ldots, Q_n\}$, $S_i \in N$, and P_i are finite sets of rewriting rules over $N \cup K \cup T$, $1 \leq i \leq n$.

The alphabet N is the nonterminal one, T is the terminal alphabet, the elements of K are called *query symbols*, and the pairs (S_i, P_i) are the *components of the system*. Often, we call P_i a component. Note the one-to-one correspondence between the query symbols and the components. The symbol S_i is the axiom of the component i. An n-tuple $(x_1, \ldots, x_n)$, with $x_i \in (N \cup K \cup T)^*$, is called a *configuration* of Γ.

For two configurations $(x_1, \ldots, x_n)$, $(y_1, \ldots, y_n)$ with $x_1 \notin T^*$, we write $(x_1, \ldots, x_n) \Longrightarrow_{rw} (y_1, \ldots, y_n)$ iff the following conditions hold:

1. $|x_i|_K = 0$, for all $1 \leq i \leq n$;

2. either $x_i \Longrightarrow_{P_i} y_i$, or $x_i = y_i \in T^*$, $1 \leq i \leq n$.

For two configurations as above, we write $(x_1, \ldots, x_n) \Longrightarrow_{com,r} (y_1, \ldots, y_n)$ iff the following conditions hold:

1. there is $i, 1 \leq i \leq n$, such that $|x_i|_K > 0$;

2. if $x_i = z_1 Q_{i_1} z_2 \ldots z_k Q_{i_k} z_{k+1}$, $k \geq 1$, for $z_j \in (N \cup T)^*$, $1 \leq j \leq k+1$, and $|x_{i_j}|_K = 0$ for each j, $1 \leq j \leq k$, then $y_i = z_1 x_{i_1} z_2 \ldots z_k x_{i_k} z_{k+1}$ and $[y_{i_j} = S_{i_j}, 1 \leq j \leq k]$; otherwise, $y_i = x_i$;

3. for all i for which y_i has not been defined at point 2, we have $y_i = x_i$.

The relation $\Longrightarrow_{rw}$ represents a rewriting step (performed in parallel, synchronously, on all components whose current sentential forms are not terminal), the relation $\Longrightarrow_{com,r}$ defines a communication step. The query symbols are replaced by the strings identified by their indices (we say that the query symbols are satisfied), providing that these strings do not contain further query symbols. The communication has priority over rewriting. If some query symbols are not satisfied at a given step, then they might be satisfied at the next ones, providing that the requested strings were modified by the previous communications in such a way that they do not contain query symbols. If circular queries appear, the system is blocked. The system can be also blocked in the rewriting mode, when a component cannot rewrite its sentential form although it is a nonterminal one. Note that neither a rewriting nor a communication is possible when the sentential form of the first component, x_1 above, is terminal. The work of the system stops in that moment.

The above defined communication step is a *returning* one: after communicating, a component resumes working from its axiom. If we remove the brackets, $[y_{i_j} = S_{i_j}, 1 \leq j \leq k]$, then we obtain a *non-returning* communication, denoted by $\Longrightarrow_{com,nr}$: after communicating, a component continues processing the current sentential form.

We write, in general, $\Longrightarrow_r, \Longrightarrow_{nr}$ for denoting both a rewriting and a communicating step (this second one in the returning or non-returning mode, respectively), and $\Longrightarrow_r^*, \Longrightarrow_{nr}^*$ for the reflexive and transitive closure of these relations. The language generated by Γ in the mode $q \in \{r, nr\}$ is

$$L_q(\Gamma) = \{x \in T^* \mid (S_1, \ldots, S_n) \Longrightarrow_q^* (x, y_2, \ldots, y_n),$$
$$y_i \in (N \cup K \cup T)^*, 2 \leq i \leq n\}.$$

The first component of the system is called the *master*; its language is the language of the system. Note that no restriction on the sentential forms of the other components is imposed.

When only the master can introduce query symbols (formally, $|w|_K = 0$ for all $A \to w \in P_i$, $2 \leq i \leq n$), then we say that the system is *centralized*; otherwise, the system is *non-centralized*.

We denote by $PC_n X$ the family of languages $L_r(\Gamma)$ generated (in the returning mode) by non-centralized PC grammar systems with at most n components, $n \geq 1$, of type X. When centralized systems with at most n components, $n \geq 1$, are used, we write $CPC_n X$, when the non-returning mode of working is used we add the letter N, getting $NPC_n X$, $NCPC_n X$. When no bound is imposed on the number of components, we replace the subscript n with $*$. In what concerns the type of the components, we consider here $X \in \{REG, CF\}$, where REG indicates λ-free right-linear rules (that is rules of the form $A \to xB, A \to x$, where A, B are nonterminal symbols and x is a terminal string, different from λ) and CF indicates λ-free context-free rules. When defining the type of rules, the query symbols are considered nonterminals.

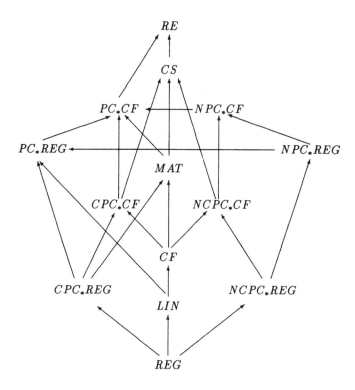

Syntheses of the results about the generative power of PC grammar systems can be found in [1], [5], [6]. The diagram in figure above is borrowed from [2]. An arrow from a family F_1 to a family F_2 indicates the (not necessarily proper) inclusion $F_1 \subseteq F_2$ (MAT is the family of languages generated by λ-free matrix grammars without appearance checking).

3. The Languages L_1, L_2, L_3 in the PC Hierarchy

The following results are known (see the papers mentioned in the previous section):

1. $L_1 \in CPC_2CF \cap NCPC_2CF$,
2. $L_2 \in CPC_3REG \cap NCPC_3REG$,
3. $L_3 \in PC_3CF \cap NPC_{10}CF$.

In [6] and [2] it is asked whether or not L_3 can also be generated by centralized PC grammar systems. We shall affirmatively answer this question, but first we improve the first result above: in the non-returning case, L_1 can be generated also by regular centralized PC grammar systems.

Theorem 1. $L_1 \in NCPC_2REG$.

Proof. Let us consider the following system

$$\Gamma_1 = (N, K, \{a, b\}, (P_1, S_1), (P_2, S_2)),$$

$$N = \{S_1, S_2, A, B, X, Y, [a], (a), [b], (b)\},$$
$$P_1 = \{S_1 \to aa, \ S_1 \to bb, \ S_1 \to A, \ A \to B, \ B \to A, \ B \to Q_2,$$
$$[a] \to aQ_2, \ [b] \to bQ_2, \ (a) \to a, \ (b) \to b\},$$
$$P_2 = \{S_2 \to aX, \ S_2 \to bX, \ X \to S_2,$$
$$S_2 \to [a], \ S_2 \to [b], \ [a] \to (a), \ [b] \to (b), \ (a) \to Y, \ (b) \to Y\}.$$

The derivation in the first component, if it is different from the one step derivations $S_1 \Longrightarrow aa$ and $S_1 \Longrightarrow bb$, starts with $S_1 \Longrightarrow A \Longrightarrow B$ and continues with pairs of steps $B \Longrightarrow A \Longrightarrow B$. Only B can "break" such a cycle, by the rule $B \to Q_2$. Hence Q_2 is introduced after an odd number of derivation steps. If the second component starts by one of the rules $S_2 \to [a], S_2 \to [b]$, then after two more steps we get the symbol Y which cannot be rewritten in P_2 or in P_1, hence the derivation is blocked. After using $S_2 \to aX$ or $S_2 \to bX$, we have to use $X \to S_2$. These cycles can be iterated, hence at even moments we have in the second component a string of the form xS_2. The symbol X cannot be rewritten in P_1, hence when P_1 introduces Q_2 we have to have in the second component a string of the form $x[a]$ or $x[b]$, for some $x \in \{a, b\}^+$. We get the configuration $(x[\alpha], x[\alpha]), \alpha \in \{a, b\}$, hence we continue by

$$(x[\alpha], x[\alpha]) \Longrightarrow_{nr} (x\alpha Q_2, x(\alpha)) \Longrightarrow_{nr} (x\alpha x(\alpha), x(\alpha)) \Longrightarrow_{nr} (x\alpha x\alpha, xY),$$

for $\alpha \in \{a, b\}$. Consequently, $L_{nr}(\Gamma_1) = L_1$. $\qquad\square$

We believe that the result above cannot be extended to regular centralized PC grammar systems working in the returning mode. Clearly, from Figure 1, the previous theorem and the relation $L_1 \in CPC_2CF \cap NCPC_2CF$, this is the only case which remains to be settled for the language L_1.

For the language L_2, the results pointed out at the beginning of this section are the strongest possible (if not considering the question of the number of components of the involved PC grammar systems). We consider now the language L_3.

Theorem 2. $L_3 \in CPC_4CF$.

Proof. Let us consider the system

$$\Gamma_2 = (N, K, \{a, b, c, d\}, (P_1, S_1), (P_2, S_2), (P_3, S_3), (P_4, S_4)),$$

where

$$N = \{S_1, S_2, S_3, S_4, A, A_1, A_2, B, B_1, B_2, B_3, X, X_1, X_2, Y, C, D, \},$$
$$P_1 = \{S_1 \to A_1, \ A_1 \to A_2, \ A_2 \to aAcC, \ A_2 \to a^2Ac^2C,$$
$$S_1 \to aB_1, \ B_1 \to aB_2, \ B_2 \to aB_3, \ B_3 \to aB_1,$$
$$B_2 \to aAQ_4, \ B_2 \to a^2AcQ_4, \ B_2 \to a^3Ac^2Q_4,$$
$$A \to Q_2, \ C \to Q_3, \ B \to b, \ D \to d\},$$
$$P_2 = \{S_2 \to X, \ X \to Y, \ Y \to S_2, \ X \to bA,$$
$$S_2 \to X_1, \ X_1 \to X_2, \ X_2 \to B\},$$
$$P_3 = \{S_3 \to X, \ X \to Y, \ Y \to U, \ U \to X, \ U \to dC,$$
$$S_3 \to U, \ U \to D\},$$
$$P_4 = \{S_4 \to cC, \ C \to cC\}.$$

If the derivation in the first component starts by using the rule $S_1 \rightarrow A_1$, then after two more steps we get here the sentential form $a^i Ac^i C$, $i \in \{1,2\}$; hence the configuration is $(a^i Ac^i C, u, v, c^3 C)$. The symbol Q_4 will be never introduced in P_1.

If the first used rule in P_1 is $S_1 \rightarrow aB_1$, then after one more step we get the string $a^2 B_2$, that is we have a configuration of the form $(a^2 B_2, u_1, v_1, c^2 C)$, for some strings u_1, v_1 which will be specified latter. We have to continue with

$$(a^2 B_2, u_1, v_1, c^2 C) \Longrightarrow_r^* (a^{3l+2} B_2, u_2, v_2, c^{3l+2} C)$$
$$\Longrightarrow_r (a^{3(l+1)+i} Ac^i Q_4, u_3, v_3, c^{3(l+1)} C) \Longrightarrow_r (a^{3(l+1)+i} Ac^{3(l+1)+i} C, u_3, v_3, S_4),$$

where the phase $\Longrightarrow_r^*$ consists of $3l$ derivation steps, $l \geq 0$, and $i \in \{0,1,2\}$.

Therefore, after $3(l+1)$ rewriting steps and a communication step we get a configuration

$$(a^n Ac^n C, u, v, y),$$

where $n = 3(l+1) + i$, for $l \geq 0, i \in \{0,1,2\}$, hence $n \geq 3$. From now on, the symbol Q_4 will be never introduced in P_1.

Let us now examine the work of P_2, P_3 in the first $3(l+1)$ derivation steps. After the first derivation step we get a configuration of the form $(x_1, \alpha, \beta, y_1)$.

If $\alpha = X_1$, then after two more derivation steps one introduces the symbol B which cannot be rewritten in P_2, hence the system is blocked (no query from P_1 can appear at that time). Therefore, we must have $\alpha = X$, which has to continue by using the rule $X \rightarrow Y$ (using $X \rightarrow bA$ blocks the system).

Now, if $\beta = U$, then we obtain

$$(x_1, X, U, y_1) \Longrightarrow_r (x_2, Y, X, y_2) \Longrightarrow_r (x_3, S_2, Y, y_3) \Longrightarrow_r^* (a^n Ac^n C, S_2, Y, y_4),$$

where the phase $\Longrightarrow_r^*$ consists of $3l, l \geq 0$, rewriting steps followed by a communication step. (In P_3 we cannot use one of the rules $U \rightarrow dC, U \rightarrow D$ because they block the system.) If we continue by using the rule $A \rightarrow Q_2$ in P_1, then the symbol X or X_1 is brought from P_2 to the master; if one applies $C \rightarrow Q_3$ in P_1, then one communicates from P_3 to the master the symbol U. In all cases the system is blocked. Consequently, we must have $\beta = X$ and the derivation is

$$(S_1, S_2, S_3, S_4) \Longrightarrow_r (x_1, X, X, y_1) \Longrightarrow_r (x_2, Y, Y, y_2)$$
$$\Longrightarrow_r (x_3, S_2, U, y_3) \Longrightarrow_r^* (a^n Ac^n C, S_2, U, y_4),$$

where the phase $\Longrightarrow_r^*$ consists of $3l, l \geq 0$, rewriting steps followed by a communication step.

Therefore, after $3(l+1)$ derivation steps, the only possible configuration is

$$(a^n Ac^n C, S_2, U, y_4).$$

If we continue by using $A \rightarrow Q_2$ in P_1, then the derivation is blocked. Hence, we have to continue with $C \rightarrow Q_3$, that is we have

$$(a^n Ac^n C, S_2, U, y_4) \Longrightarrow_r (a^n Ac^n Q_3, u_4, v_4, y_5).$$

If $v_4 = X$, then the system is blocked. We distinguish several cases:

1. If $u_4 = X_1$ and $v_4 = dC$, then after the communication step we obtain $(a^n Ac^n dC, X_1, S_3, y_4)$ and the system is blocked after one rewriting step $(A \to Q_2$ or $C \to Q_3$ in $P_1)$ and a communication step (we bring one of X_2, X, U to the first component).

2. If $u_4 = X$ and $v_4 = dC$, then we can continue, leading to the configuration $(a^n Ac^n dC, X, S_3, y_5)$. If we use now $C \to Q_3$ in P_1, then the system is blocked after communicating X or U to the master. We have to continue with $A \to Q_2$ in P_1. If in P_2 we use $X \to Y$, then Y will be communicated to the first component and again the system is blocked. The only remaining possibility is to use $X \to bA$ in P_2. If in P_3 we use $S_3 \to X$, then we have

$$(a^n Ac^n Q_3, X, dC, y_5) \Longrightarrow_r (a^n Ac^n dC, X, S_3, y_5) \Longrightarrow_r (a^n Q_2 c^n dC, bA, X, y_6)$$
$$\Longrightarrow_r (a^n bAc^n dC, S_2, X, y_6)$$

and after a rewriting step $(A \to Q_2$ or $C \to Q_3$ in $P_1)$ and a communication step one of X, X_1, Y is obtained in the first component, blocking the system. Thus, the only possibility is to use $S_3 \to U$ in P_3 at the last step above, hence we get the configuration

$$(a^n bAc^n dC, S_2, U, y_6).$$

We have a configuration with the same nonterminals as those we have started with, hence the operation can be iterated.

3. If $u_4 = X$ and $v_4 = D$, then the derivation can continue by

$$(a^n Ac^n Q_3, u_4, v_4, y_5) \Longrightarrow_r (a^n Ac^n D, X, S_3, y_5).$$

If we apply $D \to d$ in the first component, then the system will be blocked after using in P_2 one of the rules $X \to Y$, $X \to bC$, because Q_2 is introduced in the first component. The system is blocked also when we continue with $A \to Q_2$ in P_1, whichever is the continuation in P_2: the use of $X \to Y$ blocks the system immediately; if we apply $X \to bA$, we get

$$(a^n Q_2 c^n D, bC, v_5, y_6) \Longrightarrow_r (a^n bAc^n D, S_2, v_5, y_6).$$

If we apply the rule $A \to Q_2$, then the system is immediately blocked (one of X, X_1 is introduced on the first component).

If we apply the rule $D \to d$, then the system is blocked in three steps, irrespective which is the continuation; for instance, consider

$$(a^n bAc^n D, S_2, v_5, y_6) \Longrightarrow (a^n bAc^n d, X, v_6, y_7)$$
$$\Longrightarrow (a^n bQ_2 c^n d, bA, v_7, y_8) \Longrightarrow (a^n b^2 Ac^n d, S_2, v_7, y_8),$$

hence at the next communication step we bring X or X_1 in the first component.

4. If $u_4 = X_1$ and $v_4 = D$, then we produce the configuration $(a^n Ac^n D, X_1, S_3, y_4)$. If we use $A \to Q_2$ in P_1, then we bring X_2 to the master and the system is blocked. If we apply $D \to d$, then we continue as follows.

$$(a^n Ac^n d, X_2, v_5, y_5) \Longrightarrow_r (a^n Q_2 c^n d, B, v_6, y_6) \Longrightarrow_r (a^n Bc^n d, S_2, v_6, y_6)$$
$$\Longrightarrow_r (a^n bc^n d, u_5, v_7, y_7).$$

Consequently, after a phase

$$(S_1, S_2, S_3, S_4) \Longrightarrow_r^* (a^n Ac^n C, S_2, U, y),$$

consisting of $3(l+1), l \geq 0$, derivation steps, we have two possibilities to continue without blocking the system:

1. $(a^n Ac^n C, S_2, U, y) \Longrightarrow_r^* (a^n bAc^n Cd, S_2, U, y')$, and
2. $(a^n Ac^n C, S_2, U, y) \Longrightarrow_r^* (a^n bc^n d, u, v, y')$,

where $n \geq 1$.

Using $m-1$ times the first derivation (it can be iterated, because the nonterminals in the obtained configuration are the same as in the starting configuration), and then the second derivation, we get on the first component the string $a^n b^m c^n d^m$. Therefore, $L_3 \subseteq L_r(\Gamma_2)$. From the above discussion, we see that also the converse inclusion is true, that is $L_r(\Gamma_2) = L_3$. □

A similar result holds true also for the non-returning case.

Theorem 3. $L_3 \in NCPC_4CF$.

Proof. Let us consider the PC grammar system

$$\Gamma_3 = (N, K, \{a, b, c, d\}, (P_1, S_1), (P_2, S_2), (P_3, S_3), (P_4, S_4)),$$

where

$$
\begin{aligned}
N &= \{S_1, S_2, S_3, S_4, S_5, A, A', A_1, A_2, B, B_1, B_2, B_3, X, X_1, X_2, \\
&\quad Y, C, C', C_1, C_2, D, \}, \\
P_1 &= \{S_1 \rightarrow A_1, \ A_1 \rightarrow aAcC, \ S_1 \rightarrow abcd, \\
&\quad S_1 \rightarrow aB_1, \ B_1 \rightarrow aB_2, \ B_2 \rightarrow aB_1, \ B_1 \rightarrow aAQ_4, \ B_1 \rightarrow a^2 AcQ_4, \\
&\quad S_1 \rightarrow aC_1, \ C_1 \rightarrow aC_2, \ C_2 \rightarrow aC_1, \ C_1 \rightarrow aA'Q_5, \\
&\quad A \rightarrow Q_2, \ C \rightarrow Q_3, \ B \rightarrow b, \ D \rightarrow d, \ A' \rightarrow b, \ C' \rightarrow d\}, \\
P_2 &= \{S_2 \rightarrow bX, \ X \rightarrow A, \ A \rightarrow Y, \ Y \rightarrow A, \\
&\quad A \rightarrow X_1, \ X_1 \rightarrow X_2, \ X_2 \rightarrow B, \ B \rightarrow X_3\}, \\
P_3 &= \{S_3 \rightarrow dX, \ X \rightarrow Y, \ Y \rightarrow C, \ C \rightarrow Y, \\
&\quad Y \rightarrow D, \ D \rightarrow X_1, \ X_1 \rightarrow X_2, \ X_2 \rightarrow X_3\}, \\
P_4 &= \{S_4 \rightarrow cC, \ C \rightarrow cC\}, \\
P_5 &= \{S_5 \rightarrow cC', \ C' \rightarrow cC'\}.
\end{aligned}
$$

The analysis of the work of this system, in the non-returning mode, is similar to the argument in the previous proof.

For instance, after $2k, k \geq 1$, derivation steps in Γ_3, we can perform a communication from the second or from the third component to the master, and we get

$$(S_1, S_2, S_3, S_4, S_5) \Longrightarrow_{nr}^* (a^n Ac^n C, \alpha, \beta, x, y),$$

where $n \geq 1$.

We have $\alpha \in \{bA, bX_2, bX_3\}$ and $\beta \in \{dY, dX_1, dX_3\}$.

286

If $\alpha = bX_3$ or $\beta \in \{dX_1, dX_2\}$, then the system will be blocked in a few further steps. If $\alpha = bX_2$, $\beta = dY$, then we obtain the derivation

$$(a^n Ac^n C, bX_2, dY, x, y) \Longrightarrow_{nr} (a^n Q_2 c^n C, bB, dZ, x', y')$$
$$\Longrightarrow_{nr} (a^n bBc^n C, bB, dZ, x', y'),$$

where $Z \in \{D, C\}$. If $Z = D$, then in at most two steps we bring to the master a symbol which cannot be rewritten. If $Z = C$, then after one more step the system is blocked, because P_2 cannot continue rewriting its string. The only non-blocking possibility is $\alpha = bA$, $\beta = dY$, that is we have the derivation (consisting of $2k$ steps)

$$(S_1, S_2, S_3, S_4) \Longrightarrow_{nr}^* (a^n Ac^n C, bA, dY, y).$$

In the same way as in the previous proof, one can see that there are only two possible continuations which do not block the system:

1. $(a^n Ac^n C, bA, dY, x, y) \Longrightarrow_{nr}^* (a^n bAc^n dC, bA, dY, x', y')$, and
2. $(a^n Ac^n C, bA, dY, x, y) \Longrightarrow_{nr}^* (a^n b^2 c^n d^2, u, v, x'', y'')$,

where $n \geq 1$.

The first derivation can be iterated. Using it $m - 1$ times, $m \geq 1$, then closing the derivation by a derivation of type 2 above, we can generate every string $a^n b^{m+1} c^n d^{m+1}$ on the first component of the system.

The strings of the form $a^n bc^n d$, $n \geq 2$, can be generated by starting the work of the master with the rule $S_1 \to aC_1$. Then the derivation runs as follows

$$(S_1, S_2, S_3, S_4, S_5) \Longrightarrow_{nr}^* (a^{n-1} C_1, x_1, y_1, z_1, c^{n-1} C')$$
$$\Longrightarrow_{nr} (a^n A' Q_5, x_2, y_2, z_2, c^n C') \Longrightarrow (a^n A' c^n C', x_2, y_2, z_2, c^n C')$$
$$\Longrightarrow_{nr} (a^n bc^n C', x_3, y_3, z_3, c^{n+1} C') \Longrightarrow (a^n bc^n d, x_4, y_4, z_4, c^{n+2} C').$$

The string $abcd$ is directly produced by the rule $S_1 \to abcd$.

Conversely, all the terminal strings obtained by the master component of Γ_3 are of the forms discussed above, hence $L_{nr}(\Gamma_3) = L_3$. □

We do not know whether or not the language L_3 can be generated also by regular PC grammar systems (centralized or not). A related question is whether or not Theorems 2, 3 can be improved by using systems with less than four components.

References

1. E. Csuhaj-Varju, J. Dassow, J. Kelemen, Gh. Păun, *Grammar Systems. A Grammatical Approach to Distribution and Cooperation*, Gordon and Breach, London, 1994.

2. J. Dassow, Gh. Păun, G. Rozenberg, *Grammar systems*, in *Handbook of Formal Languages* (G. Rozenberg, A. Salomaa, eds.), Springer-Verlag, Berlin, Heidelberg, 1997.

3. R. W. Floyd, On the non-existence of a phrase-structure grammar for Algol-60, *Comm. of the ACM*, 5, 9 (1962), 483 – 484.

4. B. H. Partee, A. ter Meulen, R. E. Wahl, *Mathematical Methods in Linguistics*, Kluwer Academic Publ., Dordrecht, Boston, London, 1990.

5. Gh. Păun, Grammar systems: A grammatical approach to distribution and cooperation, *Proc. ICALP 95 Conf., LNCS 944* (1995), 429 – 443.

6. Gh. Păun, Parallel comunicating grammar systems. A survey, *XIth Congress on Natural and Formal Languages*, Tortosa, 1995, 257 – 283.

7. Gh. Păun, L. Sântean, Parallel communicating grammar systems: the regular case, *Ann. Univ. Buc., Ser. Matem.-Inform.*, 38 (1989), 55 – 63.

8. W. C. Rounds, A. Manaster Ramer, J. Friedman, Finding natural languages a home in formal language theory, in *Mathematics of language* (A. Manaster Ramer, ed.), John Benjamins, Amsterdam, Philadelphia, 1987, 349 – 360.

9. G. Rozenberg, A. Salomaa (eds.), *Handbook of Formal Languages*, Springer-Verlag, Berlin, Heidelberg, 1996.

10. A. Salomaa, *Formal Languages*, Academic Press, New York, 1973.

Grammar Systems for the Description
of Certain Natural Language Facts

Maria Dolores JIMÉNEZ-LÓPEZ[1], Carlos MARTÍN-VIDE

Research Group in Mathematical Linguistics and Language Engineering
Rovira i Virgili University
Pl. Imperial Tàrraco, 1
43005 Tarragona, Spain
E-mail: {mdjl,cmv}@astor.urv.es

Abstract. We intend to approach some phenomena of natural languages
by means of grammar systems. Problems as word order, constituents
movements, subcategorization and the working of the linguistic system –
considered as a set of independent modules that work together to produce
natural language– will be tackled taking into account grammar systems
theory.

1. Word Order and Grammar Systems

The way in which the elements of a sentence are arranged from left to right varies
in the different languages. In the research work about word order, three elements
have been identified as relevant in the sentence pattern (subject, verb, and object),
and taking into account their position in the sentence some language classifications
have been proposed. In the same way, we have heard about free word order languages
and fixed word order languages. In spite of such theoretical classification, it seems
that we may not speak in absolute terms neither about fixed word order languages,
nor about languages whose word order does not admit the simplest transformation.

In generative syntax, it has been raised the question of determining whether word
order is or not a phenomenon coming from deep structure. The most preponderant
opinion has been that one in which it has been defended that disarrangements between
underlying word order and surface word order must be solved using transformations.

In Spanish, the basic word order is equivalent to the pattern SVO (subject-verb-
object), though this pattern can be frequently altered. With regard to these word
order alterations, we will pay attention to the following two cases: left-dislocation
and topicalization.

Some linguists have defended the existence of a sentence functional structure organized around two elements: the theme, or subject which a sentence deals with, and
the rheme, or enunciation about that subject.

The known information or theme usually appears at the beginning of the sentence,
being followed by the new information or rheme. However, some movements can occur
in such order. Some people talk about an objective order, where the theme precedes
the rheme, and a subjective order, where the rheme goes before the theme.

Starting from the above-mentioned dichotomy, we can define two procedures by
means of which the selection of the constituent operating as theme or rheme can

---

[1]Research supported by a FI fellowship from Direcció General de Recerca/CIRIT, Generalitat de
Catalunya.

cause important modifications in the syntactical configuration of the sentence: left-dislocation and topicalization.

1.1. Left-Dislocation and PC Grammar Systems with Renaming

First of all, we will talk about left-dislocation. It is defined as a device which makes the theme to have a peripheral position within the sentence, being this position usually an initial one. Some examples of left-dislocation are the following:

(1) *A María* Juan **la** vio ayer. [Spanish]

(2) *A tu hermano*, Juan no **lo** puede ni ver. [Spanish]

(3) *Ese libro* el niño debe leer**lo** cuanto antes. [Spanish]

(4) *A Pedro la carta* hay que escribír**sela** pronto. [Spanish]

(5) *Di questo* non **ne** voglio parlare. [Italian]

(6) *A Roma* io no **ci** vado. [Italian]

(7) *Al jardí* els nens s'**hi** diverteixen molt. [Catalan]

The main syntactical features involved in these examples of left-dislocation are:

a) the constituent occupying a thematic position (italics in the examples above) can belong to different syntactical categories;

b) there is no theoretical boundary as for the number of phrases occupying a left position;

c) within the sentence, the left-dislocated constituent has a correlative pronominal element which must be a clitic (bold in the examples above);

d) a close structural link between the left-dislocated constituent and the clitic one with which it is associated is set up: the left-dislocated element must carry out the same grammatical function and must be given the same thematic role as the pronoun.

The problems arisen in the research about left-dislocation turn on the question whether the left-dislocated element either is the result of a moving process or, on the contrary, is already present in the deep structure in the position of theme. Several reasons, among them the clitic presence, have supported the idea that left-dislocated constituents are already born in the theme position, because, if this would not be the case, i.e. if left-dislocation were a moving process result, the position taken up in the deep structure by the moved phrase should be occupied by a trace, that is to say an empty element.

Putting aside all these questions arisen in generative syntax, the left-dislocation phenomenon might be easily explained using a new type of PC grammar system: the so-called PC grammar system with renaming (introduced by Gh. Păun in May 1996: personal communication).

Definition 1. A *PC grammar system with renaming* is a construct:

$$\Gamma = (N, K, T, (S_1, P_1), \ldots, (S_n, P_n), h_1, \ldots, h_m),$$

where N, K, T are disjoint alphabets, $K = \{Q_1, Q_2, \ldots, Q_n\}, (S_1, P_1), \ldots, (S_n, P_n)$ are the constituents of the system, and $h_1, \ldots, h_m$ are weak codes.

The elements of N are non-terminals, the ones in T are terminal, and $Q_1, Q_2, \ldots, Q_n$ are query symbols associated through a one-to-one correspondence with the system components. $S_i \in N$, is the axiom and P_i are finite sets of rewriting rules over $N \cup T \cup K \cup K'$, where $K' = \{[h_j, Q_i] \mid 1 \leq i \leq n, 1 \leq j \leq m\}$ and each $[h_j, Q_i]$ is considered a symbol. Moreover, $h_j : (N \cup T)^* \to (N \cup T)^*, 1 \leq j \leq m$, are weak codes such that:

$$(i) \quad h_j(A) = A, \text{ for } A \in N,$$
$$(ii) \quad h_j(a) \in T \cup \{\lambda\}, \text{ for } a \in T.$$

These systems work in the same way as usual PC grammar systems, [4], [9], with the only difference than when the symbol $[h_j, Q_i]$ appears in the sentential form, it has to be replaced not by the string x_i, as it is done in a usual PC grammar system, but by $h_j(x_i)$.

This modification, therefore, allows us to rename a string, that is, to get the same string with a different form. This idea fits quite well all the facts previously mentioned about left-dislocation. We have stated that the left-dislocated constituent has a correlative pronominal element in the sentence with which it has a close structural link, due to the fact that both carry out the same grammatical function and are given the same thematic role. So, really they are a unique string with a different form, which is the same string that has been renamed.

For a PC grammar system with renaming to give account of left-dislocation phenomena, it would be enough to consider a grammar system where each constituent generated a particular phrase type (NP, VP, PP) and, at the same time, the master introduced, in a certain moment, two query symbols, Q_i and $[h_j, Q_i]$, placing the first one in an initial position and the second one in an inner position of the sentence. In this way, the left-dislocated phrase x_i would be placed in a peripheral position, and the same phrase translated by a morphism $h(x_i)$ –that is, a pronominal form– in an internal position.

1.2. Topicalization and Grammar Systems

As it has been said previously, with regard to the objective order, the sentence constituents in a final position are understood as new information or rheme. Now, in the subjective order the rheme is placed in initial position. The syntactical processes due to which the rheme appears in a first position within the sentence are called topicalization. The two processes involved in topicalization are emphasis and questions.

Examples of emphasis could be the following:

(8) EN VERANO visitó María Budapest.

(9) DE DOS PARTES consta el examen.

(10) CON ANTONIO se casará María.

(11) UN TRABAJO necesitas tú.

(12) EN PEDRO confía María.

(13) LAS ACELGAS detesta María.

Among the syntactical features attributed to topicalization, we can take into account the following:

a) it can affect to distinct syntactical categories,

b) it involves obligatorily the inversion of subject-verb order,

c) there cannot be a clitic coindexed with the topicalized element,

d) there cannot be more than one emphasized constituent.

Keeping apart all problems generative linguists have had to face when talking about topicalization phenomena, we can here approach these processes using grammar systems.

A PC grammar system might be used in which each one of the components generated a type of phrases, with the master introducing a query symbol in whatever position it wanted. Thus, if we intend to get an objective order (rheme in final position), the master will introduce the query symbol that settles the rheme sending in a final position; on the other hand, if we wish to emphasize a particular information –that is, topicalize a particular constituent–, the master will place the corresponding query symbol in an initial position.

At first sight, the existence of a prominent component –the master– in PC grammar systems [4], [9] seems to offer a lot of possibilities to give account of movements of constituents and word order alterations within the sentence. Given that the language generated by a PC grammar system is the one produced by the master, this one has in its hands the chance to order the strings produced by the other system components in the most suitable manner. So, the movements produced in processes like topicalization could be explained only mentioning the master's freedom to introduce query symbols in any place in the string.

More difficult to be solved would be the subject-verb inversion within the sentences with topicalization. Nevertheless, the easy solution could be chosen again, and it could be pointed out that in cases of topicalization the master of the grammar system places the query symbol referring to the subject after the query symbol referring to the verb.

The matter about interrogative sentences would have the same treatment as emphasis, so that we might distinguish interrogatives like:

(14) ¿A quién enviará Juan una postal?

(15) ¿Cuándo viene María?

(16) ¿Dónde ha ido Pedro?

from interrogatives with the form:

(17) ¿Juan enviará una postal a quién?

(18) ¿María viene cuándo?

(19) ¿Pedro ha ido dónde?

We should talk again about the introduction of query symbols in some place or another in the string: in the first type of interrogative sentences the master would choose the introduction of the query symbols in initial position, with the corresponding inversion subject-verb, while in the second type the query symbol would be placed in final position.

2. X-bar Theory and Grammar Systems

The X-bar theory states that every complex syntactical constituent is the result of the expansion or projection of a nucleus. Due to the structural similarities among the lexical nucleus projections, two schemes that cover all of them under a unique basic type are proposed:

$$X'' \to (\text{Esp})X',$$
$$X' \to X'(\text{Compl}).$$

These schemes allow us the interpretation of the apparent variety of syntactical structures as realizations of a single underlying pattern.

To the different grammatical categories (N, Adj, V, P) can be given some complements and specifiers, as well as they can reject others, that is to say there are several restrictions at the moment of giving a complement to a particular category: not all the categories are given the same type of complement. This idea of restriction might be collected in a PC grammar systems variant: the so-called PC grammar systems with communication by command.

Before establishing the possible relation between this variant and X-bar theory, let's see which are the differences provided by this new type with regard to the standard PC grammar systems.

While in usual PC grammar systems the communication is achieved by means of request –that is, in a particular moment a component of the system introduces a query symbol that determines the communication of a particular string–, in this type of PC grammar systems communication is achieved by means of commands. We have a system made up of differents grammars, like in a usual PC grammar system, which operate separately, have their own sentential forms and also have a regular language or a pattern associated to them. On some particular occasions, rewriting is interrupted because some components send their sentential form to other components, particularly to those ones that have the mentioned sentential form in their selector language. As in a usual PC grammar system, the set of terminal strings generated by the master is the language generated by the system.

Definition 2. A *PC grammar system with communication by command* is a construct

$$\Gamma = (N, T, (S_1, P_1, R_1), \dots, (S_n, P_n, R_n)), n \geq 1,$$

where N,T are disjoint alphabets, and $(S_1, P_1, R_1), \dots, (S_n, P_n, R_n)$ are the components of the system. The elements of N are nonterminals, the ones in T are terminals, $S_i \in N$ is the axiom, P_i are the production rules over $N \cup T$, and $R_i \subseteq (N \cup T)^*$ is the selector language of the $i-th$ component.

In this new type of PC grammar system, a message or string x will be sent to the component i when x will be part of R_i. R_i can be defined either as a regular set or as a pattern. If it is considered as a pattern π, then

$$R_i = L_{N \cup T}(\pi_i), 1 \le i \le n.$$

A pattern can be defined as follows: having an alphabet with constants A and another alphabet with variables V, a pattern is a string over $A \cup V$. The language associated to a pattern π over $A \cup V$ is denoted with $L_A(\pi)$ and consists of the strings obtained from π consistently replacing the variables by non-empty A strings ("consistently" means that all equal variables will be replaced by the same strings).

For instance, having two alphabets $A = \{a, b\}, V = \{X_1, X_2\}$, a pattern $\pi = aaX_1X_1bX_2bb$ defines the set of all strings over A with two occurrences of a, a reduplication of any string over A, one occurrence of b, any string over A, and a double occurrence of b. So that, $x = aa(abb)(abb)b(bab)bb$ has the form specified in π, but $y = aaabbababbabbb$ has not. The language associated to the pattern π will be

$$L_A(\pi) = \{aawwbzbb \mid w, z \in \{a, b\}^+\}.$$

Two kinds of derivations in a PC grammar system with communication by command can be distinguished:

a) rewriting,

b) communication.

Concerning rewriting steps, we can discern two possibilities:

a) each component may use a rule rewriting its sentential form, except those components whose strings are terminal;

b) each component must perform a maximal derivation, that is the rewriting step may finish only when it is not possible to go on rewriting its sentential form.

In both a) and b), when the rewriting step has finished, it is checked whether it is possible or not to execute a communication step. In the second case, if a communication step cannot be fulfilled, we cannot carry out any other step. In the first case, on the contrary, if we cannot communicate the string, we continue rewriting.

Defining a communication step needs tackling the following three problems:

a) definition of the string to be communicated,

b) solution of problems at target components,

c) definition of the next string for the components which have sent messages.

The first problem admits two solutions:

1. Communication without splitting, in which only the completed strings are considered as messages. If $x_i \in R_j$, then x_i as a whole is transmitted to the component j.

2. Communication with splitting, where, for each decomposition:

$$x_i = x_{i,1}x_{i,2}\ldots x_{i,k}, k \geq 1$$

such that $x_{i,j} \in R_{s_j}$ (for some $1 \leq s_j \leq n, 1 \leq j \leq k$), the component i will produce the messages $x_{i,1}, x_{i,2}, \ldots, x_{i,k}$ which will be sent to the components $s_1, s_2, \ldots, s_k$.

With regard to the second problem, we can take into account two possible solutions:

1. the messages received can be enclosed in the string of the component that receives them, or

2. they can replace the string of the component to which messages are sent.

In both 1 and 2, we can either choose a single message among the ones sent or use all messages sent, concatenating them in a specified order.

Finally, the third problem can be solved taking into account a returning or non-returning derivation mode, like in usual PC grammar systems.

Formally, rewriting and communication steps (considering a system with maximal derivation, without splitting, replacing the strings of the target component by a concatenation of the messages received, and in the returning mode) can be defined as follows:

Definition 3. (*rewriting*): $(x_1, \ldots, x_n) \Rightarrow (y_1, \ldots, y_n)$ iff:

$$x_i \Rightarrow^* y_i \text{ in } P_i \text{ and there is no } z_i \in (N \cup T)^*$$
$$\text{such that } y_i \Rightarrow z_i \text{ in } P_i$$
$$(\text{if } x_i \in T^*, \text{ then } y_i = x_i; \text{ otherwise, } x_i \Rightarrow^+ y_i).$$

Definition 4. (*communication*): We denote:

$$\begin{aligned}
\delta_i(x_i, j) &= \lambda, \text{ if } x_i \notin R_j \text{ or } i = j, \\
\delta_i(x_i, j) &= x_i, \text{ if } x_i \in R_j \text{ and } i \neq j, \text{ for } 1 \leq i, j \leq n. \\
\Delta(i) &= \delta(x_1, i)\delta(x_2, i)\ldots\delta(x_n, i), \text{ for } 1 \leq i \leq n. \\
\delta(i) &= \delta(x_i, 1)\delta(x_i, 2)\ldots\delta(x_i, n), \text{ for } 1 \leq i \leq n.
\end{aligned}$$

Under such conditions, $(x_1, \ldots, x_n) \vdash (y_1, \ldots, y_n)$ iff, for $1 \leq i \leq n$:

$$\begin{aligned}
y_i &= \Delta(i), \text{ if } \Delta(i) \neq \lambda, \\
y_i &= x_i, \text{ if } \Delta(i) = \lambda \text{ and } \delta(i) = \lambda, \\
y_i &= S_i, \text{ if } \Delta(i) = \lambda \text{ and } \delta(i) \neq \lambda.
\end{aligned}$$

Definition 5. The *language* generated by a PC grammar system with communication by command is the following:

$$\begin{aligned}
L(\Gamma) = \{w \in T^* \mid (S_1, \ldots, S_n) &\Rightarrow (x_1^{(1)}, \ldots, x_n^{(1)}) \vdash (y_1^{(1)}, \ldots, y_n^{(1)}) \\
&\Rightarrow (x_1^{(2)}, \ldots, x_n^{(2)}) \vdash (y_1^{(2)}, \ldots, y_n^{(2)}) \Rightarrow \ldots \Rightarrow (x_1^{(s)}, \ldots, x_n^{(s)}), \\
&\text{for some } s \geq 1 \text{ such that } w = x_1^{(s)}\}.
\end{aligned}$$

After seeing how a PC grammar system with communication by command works, we can relate this variant with X-bar theory. The restrictions existing at the moment of including a particular complement or specifier in a particular grammatical category can be connected with the idea of a selector language. Thus, we could say, for example, that the fact that in Spanish the items which can function as noun complements are the Adjectival Phrase, the Prepositional Phrase and the Relative Sentence is due to the fact that the component of our grammar system with the task of generating Noun Phrases has a pattern already defined in its language selector, this pattern stating that only strings with the form AP, PP or Relative Sentence can be admitted as Noun Complements. The selector language itself would determine the limited stock of items that can occupy the position of NP specifier.

To sum up, following the idea mentioned above, a syntactical category could only be given those complements or specifiers with a structure equal to the pattern defined by the selector language associated to it. So, the task now for linguists would be to define such patterns for a particular natural language.

3. Subcategorization and Grammar Systems

In generative linguistics theoretical framework, every lexical entry is considered as a matrix of features, and through it phonetic, semantic and syntactical characteristics can be expressed. According to this theory, we can distinguish several types of syntactical information in the lexicon:

a) categorial features, which specify the grammatical category a particular word belongs to;

b) grammatical features, like person, number and gender, which are present in the morphological agreement existing between some elements; and

c) categorial selection features.

The categorial selection features which are the only ones we will be concerned with in this paragraph state the syntactical context in which a particular lexical entry can appear. Thus, for example, the verb 'introduce' would be defined as follows:

$$\text{introduce } [+\_NP\ PP],$$

that is to say, such verb selects two complements realized as a Nominal Phrase and a Prepositional Phrase; thus, the verb 'introduce' is subcategorized to take a NP and a PP.

The idea that each lexical entry is subcategorized to take a particular type of complements might also be covered by the concept of a PC grammar system with communication by command. This variant of PC grammar systems seems to be near the subcategorizations claimed by generative linguists. So that we could say that each entry has a selector language Ri associated to it which specifies the class of complements it can be given. We would say, for example, that the selector language of the verb 'introduce' specifies that this verb will only admit strings with the form NP and PP, that is this component will only be allowed to receive strings with the pattern the selector language has associated to it. Again, the work is now for descriptive linguists.

4. Human Language Device: a Grammar System with Grammar Systems as Components?

Grammar systems can have different types of generative devices as components. Besides Chomsky grammars, also Lindenmayer systems, pure grammars or contextual grammars, among others, can appear as components. If we think a bit about the linguistic system working, we will find a system in which distinct independent modules operate (syntax, semantics, phonology, lexicon) interplaying. Such modules are in their turn divided into submodules, being also independent and interrelated. If we approach closely this functioning, it seems reasonable to think that each one of the linguistic system modules might be seen as a grammar system made up of different grammars working independently and interplaying in particular moments. It seems coherent too to think that the linguistic system as a whole is a grammar system, composed by different generative devices that work independetly and interchange information, contributing to the common task to produce a (complex) language. Therefore, should we talk about a grammar system with grammar systems as components?

If, instead of considering the linguistic system as a grammar system with grammar systems as components, we considered that it is just a system in which the components are usual Chomsky grammars or any other generative device, we would lose many of the advantages that grammar systems theory offers. For instance, one aspect of the theory which makes it to be felt attractive for a linguist is the easy generation of non-context-free structures present in natural languages; structures like:

$$\{a^n b^n c^n \mid n \geq 1\},$$
$$\{xx \mid x \in \{a, b\}^*\},$$
$$\{a^n b^m c^n d^m \mid n, m \geq 1\}$$

are generated without any difficulty (even with rules less powerful than context-free) using a grammar system (see [1], [8]). But, if we thought that the linguistic system is a grammar system whose components are Chomsky context-free grammars, for example, then we would have to claim that syntax -one of the system modules- is just represented by a Chomsky context-free grammar, clearly losing in this way the possibility of generating, among others, non-context-free structures as the ones mentioned previously. This problem would be solved if we support the possibility of a grammar system whose components were grammar systems.

If we support the possibility of a grammar system with grammar systems as components, we have to wonder which kind of grammar systems should be used. We propose that the linguistic system is a PC grammar (macro)system, with each one of its components working in an independent way and intercommunicating on some occasions. The components of such (macro)system might be either CD grammar (micro)systems or PC grammar (micro)systems: the problem remains open.

We could also go even further with this intuition and regard the linguistic system as a PC grammar system with renaming. In fact, generative linguists have claimed that the semantical features of lexical items determine to a great extent the syntactical structure of a sentence. There has been talked about structural canonical realizations, a device to define the categorial nature of an argument depending on the thematic properties of the predicate selector. According to this hypothesis, each argument is carried out in a particular categorial form: the structural canonical realization.

For example, the structural canonical realization of a Theme or of an Agent will be a NP, whenever this syntactical category can satisfy the requirements imposed by such thematical roles; on the contrary, the structural canonical realization of a Locative will be a PP. Thus, we can see how to a particular semantic information a particular syntactical structure corresponds. Therefore, we could hold up that the syntactical component (which is a grammar system) receives the information from the semantic component (which is also a grammar system), translating it by means of the weak codes existing in the linguistic system (which is a PC grammar system with renaming). When the syntactical component introduces a query symbol referring to the semantic component string, it does not introduce a simple symbol Q, but a complex symbol $[hQ]$; if the syntactical component string was, in a particular moment, [Agent- Theme-Locative], it would not introduce the query symbol Q, which would have as a consequence the sending of the mentioned string to the syntax module, but it would use the symbol $[hQ]$, which would translate the semantic information into syntactical information ([NP-NP-PP]), through the codes the grammar system has:

$$h(\text{Agent}) = NP,$$
$$h(\text{Theme}) = NP,$$
$$h(\text{Locative}) = PP.$$

We would have to set out something similar in the case of interrelations between the other components of language.

Thus, stating that the linguistic system is a PC grammar system with renaming, we will have the possibility to translate or rename the information of any component of the system. So, when a component receives the information from any other component, it receives it in its own language, not in the component's one it has interplayed with. Going on with the previous example, we will say that the syntactical component would not receive strings like [Agent-Theme-Locative], but, before introducing them in its sentential form, it would translate them using codes of the linguistic system to obtain strings like [NP-NP-PP], that is, strings written in a language it knows. Such new strings written in syntactical language would respect the whole set of features of the semantic strings from which they come: they would say the same but in a different manner.

5. Final Remarks

In this paper we have attempted to tentatively apply some notions of grammar systems theory to some aspects of natural languages. We have seen the potential utility provided by grammar systems for a rigorous description of phenomena such as word order, subcategorization and the functioning of the linguistic system itself. What has been presented in this paper has been just a series of intuitive ideas about possible applications in the field of natural language description. The whole set of applications of these new generative devices are not known thoroughly yet. However, it seems beyond any doubt that they can be quite useful in the study of natural languages, due to the fact that they show clear advantages with respect to classical models, and they also perfectly agree with the idea of modularity that has a system like the linguistic one, in which different components work separately and cooperate to reach the common aim to build a language.

References

1. Chiţu, A. (1997), "Parallel comunicating grammar systems versus some non-context-free constructions from natural and artificial languages", in this volume.

2. Csuhaj-Varjú, E. (1994), "Grammar systems: a multi-agent framework for natural language generation" , in Gh. Păun, ed., *Mathematical aspects of natural and formal languages*: 63-78. World Scientific, Singapore.

3. Csuhaj-Varjú, E. & R. Abo Alez (1995), "Multiagent systems in natural language processing", unpublished ms.

4. Csuhaj-Varjú, E., J. Dassow, J. Kelemen & Gh. Păun (1994), *Grammar systems: a grammatical approach to distribution and cooperation.* Gordon and Breach, London.

5. Csuhaj-Varjú, E., J. Kelemen & Gh. Păun (1996), "Grammar systems with WAVE-like communication", *Computers and AI*, 15, 5, 419-436.

6. Păun, Gh. (1995), "Generating languages in a distributed way: grammar systems", in C. Martín Vide, ed., *Lenguajes naturales y lenguajes formales*: 45-71. PPU, Barcelona.

7. Păun, Gh. (1995), "Grammar systems: a grammatical approach to distribution and cooperation", *Proceedings of ICALP Conference*, Szeged.

8. Păun, Gh. (1995), "Parallel communicating grammar systems. A survey", in C. Martín Vide, ed., *Lenguajes naturales y lenguajes formales*: 257-283. PPU, Barcelona.

9. Gh. Păun, L. Sântean, Parallel Communicating Grammar Systems: The Regular Case, *Ann. Univ. Buc., Ser. Matem.–Inform.*, 38 (1989), 55-63.

Networks of Parallel Language Processors

Erzsébet CSUHAJ-VARJÚ[1]

Computer and Automation Research Institute
Hungarian Academy of Sciences
H-1528 Budapest, Hungary

Arto SALOMAA

Academy of Finland and Mathematics Department
University of Turku
SF-20014 Turku, Finland

Abstract. A network of language processors (an NLP system) consists of several language identifying devices (language processors) associated with nodes of a network (in particular case with nodes of a virtual complete graph). The processors rewrite strings (representing the current state of the nodes) according to some prescribed rewriting mode and communicate them along the network via input and output filter languages. In this paper we study properties of NLP systems with L systems in the nodes.

1. Introduction

Parallel and distributed symbolic processing has been in the phocus of interest in present day computer science. One of the recent paradigms for data flow in parallel and distributed environment is the Logic Flow paradigm ([13], [4], [5]) in which data is organized by a virtual graph and the processing is performed by moving agents (processes) that navigate in this graph. This concept can serve as a basic architecture for parallel symbolic processing, with simplifications as in the Connection Machine design ([7]). Namely, a symbolic process develops in the virtual (complete) graph which has nodes being processors that are able to handle data. The process starts by injecting some data in the nodes, or in some node(s). Then each node processor starts with local data processing (there are strict conditions which prescribe the way and the time of these actions), and, then the data is communicated to some target nodes, where the local data processing continues. Only such data can be communicated that match some (previously fixed) patterns, that is, successfully pass a filtering process. The target nodes handle the simultaneously arriving messages according to some strategies; for example, the Boltzmann machine ([6]) and the Connection machine ([7], [14]) combines from the multiple messages a single output in various ways.

Since data can be given in the form of strings, it is reasonable to investigate how the above idea can be interpreted in terms of formal grammars and languages. There have been several models introduced and examined in formal language theory, each of them having the following properties: the system consists of several language identifying devices (language processors) associated with nodes of a network (in particular cases with nodes of a virtual complete graph) that rewrite strings (representing the current state of the nodes) according to some prescribed rewriting mode and communicate

---
[1]Research supported by the Academy of Finland, Project 11281

the obtained strings along the network using input and output filter languages. A string of some node can be successfully communicated to another one if it is able to pass the output filter of the node (it is a member of the corresponding language) and it can pass the input filter of the target node. The system is functioning by alternating rewriting and communication steps. The communicated string can be data (a sentential form) or it can be program (a production, for example), thus, we distinguish data and/or program communicating system. Since all the models have the above common characteristics, we can introduce a general framework for them, called networks of language processors (NLP systems). Networks of language processors are both computational and language identifying devices, but the concept can be extended to a framework for modelling parallel and distributed computation of multisets of strings (string collections with several occurrences of the same string), too. In this this case we speak about networks of multiset string processors (NMP systems, for short). Both NLP systems and NMP systems provide new aspects in the description of string collections.

Particular cases of NLP systems exhibit nice properties: a recent model, the parallel communicating grammar system with communication by command, the CCPC grammar system, for short (introduced in [2]), with regular grammars and regular filter languages in the nodes and with concatenating the arriving messages, exhibit the universal computational power, that is, they are able to identify any recursively enumerable language (for details see [2], [8], [9]).

Another example, with a local string processing mechanism essentially different from a grammar, is the test tube distributed system based on splicing, a concept from DNA computing ([1]). In this case the components (the test tubes) are splicing schemes (in the sense of T. Head) which communicate with each other by redistributing their available sets of strings (the contents of the test tubes, in a similar way to the separate operation of Lipton-Adleman) according to filter languages. Such systems with finite initial contents of the tubes and finite sets of splicing rules associated to every component are not only computationally complete (that is they are able to compute any recursively enumerable language), but the existence of universal test tube distributed systems can be proven on this basis, that is, such systems provide the possibility of designing universal programmable computers based on their structure.

In this paper we deal with networks of parallel language processors, that is, we study properties of NLP systems with 0L systems (T0L systems) and finite sets of axioms in the nodes. We show that if we design a master node for selecting the words of the language determined by the system and we describe filter languages by context conditions, then these networks of language processors are as powerful as ET0L systems with the same kind of context conditions. The results imply that such networks of parallel language processors with regular (or some special regular) filter languages are of the universal computational power. We provide a result about the string population of NMP systems (networks of multiset string processors): we show that the growth of the string population in a network with D0L systems, finite multisets of axiom strings, and random context exit and entrance filters in the nodes can be characterized by a growth function of a D0L system. Finally, we give some examples of the rich possibilities that become available when the nodes are represented by DT0L systems and the choice of the developmental tables depends on the work of the other agents in the network.

2. Formal Language Theoretic Prerequisites

Throughout the paper we assume that the reader is familiar with the basics of formal language theory. We list here only some notions, notations and properties which are necessary to follow the paper; for more details we refer to [12], [11] and [3].

For an alphabet V, V^+ denotes the set of all nonempty strings (words) over V. The empty string is denoted by λ, V^* stands for $V^+ \cup \{\lambda\}$. A language L is a subset of V^*. The cardinality of L is denoted by $card(L)$. The length of a string $w \in V^*$ is the number of symbols in w, denoted by $|w|$. For a word w, we use notation $alph(w)$ for the set of symbols that have an appearance in w (we say w is with alphabet $alph(w)$.)

Throughout we use the following convention: if V is an alphabet, then $V^{(i)}$, $1 \leq i \leq n$, denotes $\{A^{(i)} \mid A \in V\}$. For a word $w \in V^*$, where $w = x_1 x_2 \ldots x_n$, $x_j \in V$, $1 \leq j \leq n$, we denote by $w^{(i)}$ the string $x_1^{(i)} x_2^{(i)} \ldots x_n^{(i)}$.

A collection of strings that is allowed to have multiple occurrences of the same string is said to be a multiset of strings. A multiset of strings over an alphabet V with elements, say, $a, a, b, c, c, c \in V$, is denoted by $\{\{a, a, b, c, c, c\}\}$. The elementary operations: union, intersection, etc. are defined for multisets of strings in the same way as in the case of languages. A multiset M of strings is finite if it consists of a finite number of elements.

We denote the family of context-free, context-sensitive and recursively enumerable languages by CF, CS and RE, respectively. If no confusion arises, then we use the same notation, CF and CS, for the corresponding grammar class, too.

A *0L system* (an interactionless L-system) is a triple $H = (V, P, w)$, where V is an alphabet, $w \in V^*$, the axiom, and P is a set of productions (rules) of the form $a \to v$, where $a \in V$ and $v \in V^*$. Moreover, production set P is complete: for every $a \in V$ there is a rule of the form $a \to v$, $v \in V^*$ in P. If for each $a \in V$ there is exactly one production of the form $a \to v$ in P, then we speak of a *deterministic 0L system* or a D0L system. If the axiom is replaced by a finite language, then we have an F0L system, an 0L system with a finite number of axioms.

The direct derivation relation in an 0L system $H = (V, P, w)$ is defined as follows: for $x, y \in V^*$ we write $x \Longrightarrow_P y$ if $x = a_1 \ldots a_n$, $y = z_1 z_2 \ldots z_n$, $a_i \in V$, $z_i \in V^*$, $1 \leq i \leq n$, and $a_i \to z_i \in P$.

We denote by $\Longrightarrow_P^*$ the reflexive and transitive closure of $\Longrightarrow_P$.

The language generated by H is $L(H) = \{v \in V^* \mid w \Longrightarrow_P^* v\}$.

Since production set P in the case of a D0L system $H = (V, P, w)$ defines a homomorphism $h : V \to V^*$, therefore we often write $H = (V, h, w)$ instead of the first notation.

By a word sequence of a D0L system $H = (V, h, w)$ we mean the following sequence of words : $h^0(w) = w$, $h(w)$, $h^2(w)$, $h^3(w), \ldots$. The function $f : \mathbb{N} \to \mathbb{N}$ defined by $f(t) = |h^t(w)|$, $t \geq 0$, is called the growth function of H, and the sequence $|h^t(w)|$, for $t = 0, 1, 2, \ldots$, is said to be its length sequence.

L systems with several sets of productions (tables) are called tabled L systems.

A *T0L system* (a tabled 0L system) with n tables, $n \geq 1$, is a construct $H = (V, P_1, \ldots, P_n, w)$, where each triple (V, P_i, w) is an 0L system. A string x directly derives a string y in H, $x, y \in V^*$, iff y is directly generated from x by applying some of the tables of H, say, P_i.

A T0L system, whose alphabet is divided into two disjoint sets (the nonterminal alphabet, N, and the terminal alphabet, T), written as $H = (N, T, P_1, \ldots, P_n, w)$, is called an *ETOL system* (an extended TOL system) and its language is defined by $L(H) = \{v \in T^* \mid w \Longrightarrow^* v\}$.

The class of languages generated by DOL, OL, FOL, TOL, FTOL and ETOL systems is denoted by *DOL, OL, FOL, TOL, FTOL* and *ETOL*, respectively. If λ-rules (rules of the form $a \to \lambda$) are not allowed to use, then we speak about propagating L systems and use notations *PDOL, POL, PFOL, PTOL, PFTOL* and *EPTOL*, respectively, to denote the corresponding families of languages.

Some basic relations concerning the above language classes are the following:

- $CF \subset CS \subset RE$,

- $DOL \subset OL \subset FOL \subset ETOL$,

- $OL \subset TOL \subset TFOL \subset ETOL$,

- $CF \subset ETOL \subset CS$,

- CF is incomparable with both OL and TOL.

Further regulations in the application of the productions can lead to the enhancement of the generative power of the grammar class. One of the variants is where the production (or the table) can be applied only to that string which satisfies some context condition associated with the production (with the table).

By a context condition ρ over V^*, where V is an alphabet, we mean a mapping $\rho : V^* \to \{\underline{true}, \underline{false}\}$.

We say that ρ is of type

- *reg*, or it is a regular context condition over V^*, given by a regular language $L \subseteq V^*$, if $\rho(w) = \underline{true}$ for any $w \in V^*$ where $w \in L$ otherwise $\rho(w) = \underline{false}$.

- *sc*, or it is a semi-conditional context condition over V^*, given by a pair of strings (u, v), with $u, v \in V^+$, if $\rho(w) = \underline{true}$ for any $w \in V^*$ which has as a subword u but not v and $\rho(w) = \underline{false}$ otherwise. String u is called the permitting context condition and v is the forbidding context condition. If either u or v or both are not given, then no corresponding context check is required. In this case we speak of a corresponding empty context condition and we indicate the empty set in the notation.

- *rc*, or it is of random context condition over V^*, given by a pair (Q, R), where $Q, R \subseteq V$, if $\rho(w) = \underline{true}$ for any $w \in V^*$ which contains each element of Q but no element of R and $\rho(w) = \underline{false}$ otherwise. By definition, Q and R can be empty sets, in this case we omit the corresponding context check. As above, Q forms the permitting context condition and R is the forbidding context condition.

Context conditions can be introduced for any kind of rewriting mechanisms, for further information we refer to [3], here we restrict ourselves only to the case of *ETOL* systems.

By an (X)-type conditional ETOL system (an E(X)TOL system, for short), where $X \in \{reg, sc, rc\}$ we mean a construct $H = (N, T, \rho_1 : P_1, \ldots, \rho_n : P_n, w)$, where

$(N, T, P_1, \ldots, P_n, w)$ is a usual ET0L system and ρ_i is a context condition over $V^* = (N \cup T)^*$, $1 \leq i \leq n$.

The direct derivation step in H is defined in the following manner: for $x, y \in V^*$ we write $x \Longrightarrow_H y$ iff there is a table P_i, $1 \leq i \leq n$, such that x satisfies context condition ρ_i and y is obtained from x by applying table P_i.

The language class generated by ET0L systems of (X)-type context conditions is denoted by $E(X)T0L$, in the propagating case we write $E(X)PT0L$.

The following important relations will be used in the sequel:

- $ET0L \subset E(rc)T0L$,

- $E(rc)PT0L \subseteq E(sc)PT0L = E(reg)PT0L = CS$,

- $E(rc)T0L \subseteq E(sc)T0L = E(reg)T0L = RE$.

3. NLP Systems: the Basic Definitions

In this section we introduce a basic variant of NLP systems and define its functioning. We discuss some possible definitions of the languages associated to such systems, and illustrate the notions by an example.

Networks of parallel language processors are NLP systems with L systems as components. We start with the simple case where the nodes are represented by F0L systems, that is, by 0L systems with a finite set of axioms.

Definition 3.1. An *NLP_F0L system* (of degree n, $n \geq 1$) is a construct

$$\Gamma = (V, (P_1, F_1, \rho_1, \sigma_1), \ldots, (P_n, F_n, \rho_n, \sigma_n)),$$

where

- V is an alphabet (the alphabet of the system),

- $(P_i, F_i, \rho_i, \sigma_i)$, $1 \leq i \leq n$, is called a component (a node) of the system (the i-th component or the i-th node), where

- P_i is a set of 0L rules over V, the production set of the component;

- $F_i \subset V^*$ is a finite set, the set of axioms of the component;

- ρ_i and σ_i are context conditions over V^*

  (mappings from V^* to $\{\underline{true}, \underline{false}\}$), called the exit filter and the entrance filter of the component, respectively.

(Notice that the axiom set of a component can be empty set.)

According to the type of context conditions, ρ_i and σ_i, $1 \leq i \leq n$, we distinguish regular, or semi-conditional or random context exit and/or entrance filters. We say that an NLP_F0L system is with exit and entrance filters of type (X) iff its each component is associated by an (X)-type exit filter and entrance filter, where $X \in \{reg, sc, rc\}$.

If each P_i (the production set of the i-th component) is chosen to be a set of D0L rules or is replaced by tables of a T0L system, then we speak of an NLP_FD0L system or an NLP_FT0L system, respectively. If each axiom set consists of a single word, then we omit letter F from the notation.

The NLP system is functioning via changing its configurations (states).

Definition 3.2. By a configuration (a state) of an NLP_F0L system $\Gamma = (V, (P_1, F_1, \rho_1, \sigma_1), \ldots, (P_n, F_n, \rho_n, \sigma_n))$, $n \geq 1$, we mean an n-tuple $C = (L_1, \ldots, L_n)$, where $L_i \subseteq V^*$, $1 \leq i \leq n$.

L_i is called the state of the i-th component (node) and it represents the set of strings which are present at component (at node) i at that moment.

$C_0 = (F_1, \ldots, F_n)$ is said to be the initial configuration (initial state) of the system.

A configuration can change either by a rewriting step or by a communication step. When a rewriting step happens, then every node derives from its each available string a new one, by applying its productions in the 0L manner. At a communication step, each node j receives a copy of all of such strings that are present at some other node, say, node i, and are able to pass the exit filter of node i and the entrance filter of node j. (These strings satisfy context conditions ρ_i and σ_j). Each rewriting step is followed by a communication step, and reversely, resulting in a pulsating way of functioning.

Definition 3.3. Let $\Gamma = (V, (P_1, F_1, \rho_1, \sigma_1), \ldots, (P_n, F_n, \rho_n, \sigma_n))$, $n \geq 1$, be an NLP_F0L system and let $C_1 = (L_1, \ldots, L_n)$, and $C_2 = (L'_1, \ldots, L'_n)$, be two configurations of Γ.

We say that C_1 directly changes for C_2 by a rewriting step, written as

$$(L_1, \ldots, L_n) \Longrightarrow (L'_1, \ldots, L'_n),$$

if L'_i is the set of words obtained by performing a derivation step on each element of L_i by production set P_i in the 0L manner.

By definition, if L_i is the emptyset, then $L'_i = \emptyset$.

Notice a significant point in the definition: by a rewriting step we obtain from any available string exactly one new string, L'_i is not necessarily the same as the set of words that can be derived from the elements of L_i by one derivation step.

In the case of NLP_FT0L systems the rewriting step is defined by the obvious modification: for producing words of L'_i from L_i the same nondeterministically chosen table (production set) of node i is used.

The communication step is defined as follows:

Definition 3.4. Let $C_1 = (L_1, \ldots, L_n)$ and $C_2 = (L'_1, \ldots, L'_n)$ be two configurations of an NLP_F0L system $\Gamma = (V, (P_1, F_1, \rho_1, \sigma_1), \ldots, (P_n, F_n, \rho_n, \sigma_n))$, $n \geq 1$. We say that C_1 directly changes for C_2 by a communication step in Γ, written as

$$(L_1, \ldots, L_n) \vdash (L'_1, \ldots, L_n),$$

if for every i, $1 \leq i \leq n$,

$$L'_i = L_i \bigcup_{j=1, j \neq i}^{n} A_{i,j},$$

where $A_{i,j} = \{v \mid v \in L_j, \rho_j(v) = \underline{true} \text{ and } \sigma_i(v) = \underline{true}\}$.

The output filters, formally, provide broadcast of the strings along the network, but together with the input filters they implicitly determine a dynamically changing virtual digraph describing the actual successful communication actions in the system: at any moment in time there is an edge leading from node i to node j in the digraph if the i-th component of the NLP system successfully communicates at least one string to the j-th component.

During the functioning of the NLP_F0L system configurations follow each other, each of them arising either from a rewriting step or a communication step. Such sequence of configurations determines a computation in Γ.

Definition 3.5. Let $\Gamma = (V, (P_1, F_1, \rho_1, \sigma_1), \ldots, (P_n, F_n, \rho_n, \sigma_n))$, $n \geq 1$, be an NLP_F0L system. By a computation C in Γ we mean a sequence of configurations $C_0, C_1, \ldots$, where

- $C_i \Longrightarrow C_{i+1}$ if $i = 2j$, $j \geq 0$, and

- $C_i \vdash C_{i+1}$ if $i = 2j + 1$, $j \geq 0$.

Thus, a computation is an alternating sequence of rewriting steps and communication steps in Γ.

We speak about a finite computation in Γ if the sequence of configurations is finite.

The result of a computation C at node i at step t, for i, $1 \leq i \leq n$, and $t \geq 0$, supposing that the corresponding configuration is $(L_1^{(t)}, \ldots, L_n^{(t)})$, is $L_i^{(t)}$.

Thus, the result of a finite computation at node i is the result of this computation at this node at the last step.

NLP_F0L systems are both computational and language identifying devices; the latter property arises from the fact that the nodes, at any moment in time during the functioning of the system, are associated with sets of strings. The first aspect provides information on the dynamism of the behaviour of the system, while the second one refers to the set of all possible behavioural stages of the network.

Languages can be associated to networks of F0L systems in various manners. One possibility is, if we distinguish a master node (a selector node) and collect all strings into a language which are results of a rewriting step at this node during some finite computation. Another reasonable variant is, if all such strings that appear at any of the nodes identify the language of the NLP system.

The first notion resembles to the notion of the language generated by an extended L system (any extended L language can be generated by an NLP system with two nodes, where the first node produces sentential forms of the corresponding L system and the second node selects the terminal words), while the second variant is analogous to the definition of the language of a non-extended L system, namely, every string that is produced by some derivation (computation) in the system belongs to the language.

The behaviour of the NLP system can also be characterized by languages describing communication happened during the functioning of the system: the collection of strings that are succesfully communicated from one node to another one at some computation step form the language of communication of the network of language processors. It provides information both on the filters and the inner rewriting mechanisms of the components. Also, those strings that cannot be communicated from some node to another one, form a language that gives an insight into the intricate inner behaviour of the components. Notice that this case differs from the definition of the language of the master node, among the words of that language there are allowed to be ones that can be successfully communicated.

We choose the first variant, namely, we define the language of the master node.

Definition 3.6. Let $\Gamma = (V, (P_1, F_1, \rho_1, \sigma_1), \ldots, (P_n, F_n, \rho_n, \sigma_n))$, be an NLP_F0L system.

The language $L(\Gamma)$ identified by Γ is

$$L(\Gamma) = \{w \in L_1^{(s)} \mid (F_1, \ldots, F_n) = (L_1^{(0)}, \ldots, L_n^{(0)}) \Longrightarrow (L_1^{(1)}, \ldots, L_n^{(1)})$$
$$\vdash (L_1^{(2)}, \ldots, L_n^{(2)}) \Longrightarrow \cdots \Longrightarrow (L_1^{(s)}, \ldots, L_n^{(s)}), s \geq 1\}.$$

Thus, the language $L(\Gamma)$ identified by Γ is the result of any finite computation in the system that ends by a rewriting step at node 1. This definition supposes at least one rewriting step performed in the system, thus, the elements of the axiom set of strings at the master node belong to the language only in that case if they can be obtained as a result of some rewriting step.

Let us have a very simple example for NLP_F0L systems.

Example 3.1. Let $L = \{a^{2^n}, a^{3^n} \mid n \geq 0\}$. It is easy to see that $L \notin T0L$, moreover, $L \notin (rc)T0L$.

However, $L \in E(rc)T0L$, since it can be generated by the E(rc)T0L system
$H = (\{a, b, c, d\}, \{a\}, (\{b\}, \emptyset) : \{c \to c, b \to b^2, a \to a, d \to d\}, (\{d\}, \emptyset) : \{c \to c, d \to d^3, a \to a, b \to b\}, \{b \to a, d \to a, a \to a, c \to c\}, \{c \to b, c \to d, c \to a, d \to d, b \to b, a \to a\}, c)$.

This language can be generated by a very simple NLP_F0L system Γ with three components. Moreover, there is only one symbol, a, in the system. Let Γ have the following components:
$P_1 = \{a \to a\}$,
$F_1 = \{a\}$,
$\rho_1(u) = false$ for $u \in \{a\}^*$, otherwise $\rho_1(u) = true$,
$\sigma_1(u) = true$ for $u \in \{a\}^*$, otherwise $\sigma_1(u) = false$.
(The component collects the strings of the form a^{2^n}, a^{3^n} and does not issue any string.);
$P_2 = \{a \to a^2\}$,
$F_2 = \{a\}$,
$\rho_2(u) = true$ for $u \in \{a\}^*$, otherwise $\rho_2(u) = false$,
and $\sigma_2(u) = false$ for $u \in \{a\}^*$, otherwise $\sigma_2(u) = true$.
(The node produces the strings of the form a^{2^n} and does not accept any string.);
$P_3 = \{a \to a^3\}$,
$F_3 = \{a\}$,
$\rho_3(u) = true$ for $u \in \{a\}^*$, otherwise $\rho_3(u) = false$, and
$\sigma_3(u) = false$ for $u \in \{a\}^*$, otherwise $\sigma_3(u) = true$.
(It provides strings of the form a^{3^n} and does not accept any string from the other nodes.).
By the above explanations we can easily see that $L(\Gamma) = L$.

We can observe that the set of all strings that appear at the nodes at some computation step is the same language, $L = \{a^{2^n}, a^{3^n} \mid n \geq 0\}$, and if we take those strings that never leave the first node, we obtain again the same set of words. Moreover, the language of the successfully communicated strings is $L - \{a\}$.

Already the above example suggests that NLP_FOL systems are able to compute complicated languages. Before starting with the examination of the language classes they determine, we introduce some notations.

We denote by $(X)NLP_n\_Y$, where $X \in \{reg, sc, rc\}$, $Y \in \{D0L, PD0L, 0L,$ $P0L, F0L, FP0L, T0L, PT0L, FT0L, etc.\}$, $n \geq 1$, the class of languages generated by NLP_Y systems with n components and X-type filters.

If the number of the components is not significant, then we omit n from the notation.

4. Language Classes of NLP Systems

In this section we study language classes of networks of language processors with FOL and FTOL systems as components. We prove that in both cases the determined language class (of the master node) equals to the corresponding class of context conditional ETOL systems (if the NLP system is with X-type filters, then the same kind of context conditions are associated to the tables of the corresponding ETOL system, and reversely), and thus, NLP_FOL systems and NLP_FTOL systems are equally powerful devices. In the case of regular or semi-conditional filters and without erasing rules (λ-rules), the above networks of parallel language processors reach the power of the context-sensitive language class, and having erasing rules they exhibit the universal computational power, that is, they are able to identify any recursively enumerable language.

We first show that X-conditional ETOL languages (random context, semi-conditional or regular context conditional ETOL languages) are languages of NLP_FOL systems with the same kind of filters.

Theorem 4.1. *Let L be a language generated by an $E(X)T0L$ system with n components, where $X \in \{rc, reg\}$ and $n \geq 1$. Then L is a language that can be identified by an $(X)NLP\_F0L$ systems with $n + 2$ components.*

Proof. We give the proof only for the case $x = reg$, the case $x = rc$ can be proven by using the same construction with the appropriate modification in the filters. Let $H = (N, T, K_1 : H_1, \ldots, K_n : H_n, w)$ be an ETOL system with regular context conditions ($K_1, \ldots, K_n$ are the corresponding regular languages). We construct a (reg)NLP_FOL system Γ such that $L(\Gamma) = L(H)$ holds.

Let $V = N \cup T$, and let $V^{(i)}, N^{(i)}, T^{(i)}$ denote superscripted variants of the alphabets V, N, and T, respectively, where $i = 1, \ldots, n$. Let Y be a symbol not in any of the above alphabets. Let us denote $\bar{V} = V \cup_{i=1}^n V^{(i)} \cup \{Y\}$.

Let us define components of $\Gamma = (\bar{V}, (P_0, F_0, \rho_0, \sigma_0), \ldots, (P_{n+1}, F_{n+1}, \rho_{n+1},$ $\sigma_{n+1}))$ as follows: (For the simplicity of reading the construction, we denote the master component by $(P_0, F_0, \rho_0, \sigma_0)$.)

Let
$P_0 = \{A \rightarrow A \mid A \in V\} \cup_{i=1}^n \{A^{(i)} \rightarrow A^{(i)} \mid A^{(i)} \in V^{(i)}\} \cup \{Y \rightarrow Y\}$,
$F_0 = \emptyset$,
$\rho_0(u) = \underline{false}$ for any $u \in \bar{V}^*$ and
$\rho_0(u) = \underline{true}$ otherwise,

$\sigma_0(u) = \underline{true}$ for $u \in T^*$ and $\sigma_0(u) = \underline{false}$ otherwise
(The component selects the terminal strings.);
for $i = 1, \ldots, n$
$P_i = \{A \to \alpha^{(i)} \mid A \to \alpha \in H_i\} \cup \{A^{(i)} \to Y \mid A^{(i)} \in V^{(i)}\} \cup \{Y \to Y\},$
$F_i = \emptyset,$
$\rho_i(u) = \underline{true}$ for any $u \in (V^{(i)})^*$ and $\rho_i(u) = \underline{false}$ otherwise, and
$\sigma_i(u) = \underline{true}$ for $u \in K_i$ and $\sigma_i(u) = \underline{false}$ otherwise.
(The node accepts the strings satisfying K_i, starts with the simulation of the application of table H_i and sends the rewritten string to the $(n+1)$-st node in order to complete the simulation.);
$P_{n+1} = \cup_{i=1}^{n} \{A^{(i)} \to A \mid A \in V\} \cup \{A \to A \mid A \in V\} \cup \{Y \to Y\},$
$F_{n+1} = \{w\},$
$\rho_{n+1}(u) = \underline{true}$ for any $u \in V^*$ and $\rho_{n+1}(u) = \underline{false}$ otherwise,
and $\sigma_{n+1}(u) = \underline{true}$ for $u \in (\cup_{i=1}^{n}(V^{(i)})^*$ and $\sigma_{n+1}(u) = \underline{false}$ otherwise.
(The component completes the simulation of the application of the corresponding table and, then, sends the strings to the other components either to continue the rewriting or to be selected as a terminal string.)

By the above explanations it can be seen that Γ produces all words of $L(H)$. We show that only words of $L(H)$ can be obtained by Γ. We prove that only such strings are able to reach the master node that correspond in any state of their computation to an appropriate sentential form in a terminating derivation in H. This holds for the following reasons: At any moment in time, only such strings are present at nodes $1, \ldots, n$ that are either sentential forms of H, or appropriate coded versions of sentential forms of H, or they are strings consisting of letter Y. Since only the coded versions of the sentential forms of H are communicated to another nodes (by sending a copy of them), and only these strings take part in the further computation steps, therefore nodes $1, \ldots, n$ do not issue any string which does not satisfy the above criteria. We examine strings appearing at node $n + 1$. After arriving at node $n + 1$ from some other nodes, say, from node i, and being rewritten to the corresponding string over V, the new string will be never changed during the further computation steps, but only communicated. Thus, node $n + 1$ has only such strings available at any moment in time that correspond to some sentential form generated in H. Moreover, because each communication step follows a rewriting step, and reversely, any computation in Γ corresponds to a derivation in H.

Hence, Γ does not produce any word which does not belong to $L(H)$. Thus, $L(\Gamma) = L(H)$. $\qquad \square$

Since any ET0L language can be generated by an ET0L system with two tables we obtain

Corollary 4.1. $ET0L \subseteq (reg)NLP_4\_0L.$

Next we turn to the case when the context condition is semi-conditional. Remember that in this case the presence and/or the absence of a subword in a word has to be decided, so, whether or not a string is in T^* cannot be checked in one step.

Theorem 4.2. *Let L be a language generated by an $E(sc)T0L$ system $H = (N, T, \rho_1 : H_1, \ldots, \rho_n : H_n, w)$. Then L can be identified by an $(sc)NLP\_F0L$ system with $n + m + 2$ components, where $m = card(N)$.*

Proof. The proof is based on similar ideas to that of the proof of Theorem 4.1, therefore we give only the necessary details. We first note that instead of contructing an (sc)NLP_FOL system for $L(H)$ we shall construct a system Γ such that $L(\Gamma) = cL(H)$, where c is a symbol not in $V = N \cup T$.

Because $E(sc)T0L = CS$ and the context-sensitive language class is closed under operation left derivative, therefore we can make this modification without losing the generality. Moreover, we explicit context condition ρ_i in the form (u_i, v_i), $1 \leq i \leq n$. (Remember, ρ_i holds true for $x \in V^*$ iff u_i is a subword of u but v_i is not. If no context check is required, then the empty set is given as context condition.)

We construct Γ with the following components:

Let, first, $N = \{B_1, \ldots, B_m\}$ and let us denote by $V^{(i)}$, $1 \leq i \leq n$, $\underline{V}^{(j)}$, $1 \leq j \leq m = card(N)$, superscripted variants of V.

Let $Z, Z_0, Z_1, \ldots, Z_m, Y$ and c be symbols not in any of the above alphabets. Let us denote by $\bar{V} = V \cup_{i=1}^n V^{(i)} \cup_{j=1}^m \underline{V}^{(j)} \cup \{Z, Z_0, \ldots, Z_m, Y, c\}$. (We note that for simplicity of reading, we list only that productions at the components which are necessary to understand the construction: for any letter $D \in \bar{V}$ for which there is no production with D on the left-hand side indicated, production $D \to D$ has to be added to the production set. Moreover, we slightly differ from the customary notation, we denote the master node by $(P_0, F_0, \rho_0, \sigma_0)$: P_0 is the set of productions, F_0 is the set of axioms, ρ_0 is the exit filter and σ_0 is the entrance filter of the component).

Let for $i = 1, \ldots, n$
$$P_i = \{A \to \alpha^{(i)} \mid A \to \alpha \in H_i\} \cup \{A^{(i)} \to Y \mid A^{(i)} \in V^{(i)}\} \cup \{Y \to Y\} \cup \{Z_0 \to Z, Z \to Y\},$$ let
$F_i = \emptyset$, and let the exit filter be defined by $(\emptyset, \emptyset)$ (no context check is necessary, copies of the strings can leave freely the node), and let the entrance filter be given by (u_i, v_i).

Let us define
$$P_{n+1} = \cup_{i=1}^n \{A^{(i)} \to A\} \cup \{A \to Y \mid A \in V\} \cup \{Z \to Z_0, Z_0 \to Y\},$$
$F_{n+1} = \{Z_0 w\}$ and let the component be with exit filter $(\emptyset, \emptyset)$ and with entrance filter $(Z, \emptyset)$.

These components simulate the application of the tables of H, in the same manner as we have shown it in the previous proof, therefore we omit the detailed explanations. The further components are for selecting the terminal words.

Let
$$P_{t,1} = \{Z_0 \to Z_1, Z_1 \to Y\} \cup \{A \to \underline{A}^{(1)} \mid A \in V\} \cup \{\underline{A}^{(1)} \to Y\} \cup \{Y \to Y\},$$
$F_{t,1} = \emptyset$, and let the entrance filter be given by (Z_0, B_1) and the exit filter defined by $(\emptyset, \emptyset)$. (In the latter case no context check is necessary.)

Let us define for j, $2 \leq j \leq m$,
$$P_{t,j} = \{Z_{j-1} \to Z_j, Z_j \to Y\} \cup \{\underline{A}^{(j-1)} \to \underline{A}^{(j)} \mid A \in V\} \cup \{\underline{A}^{(j)} \to Y\} \cup \{Y \to Y\},$$
$F_{t,j} = \emptyset$, and let the entrance filter be given by $(Z_{j-1}, \underline{B}_j^{(j-1)})$ and the exit filter by $(\emptyset, \emptyset)$. ($\underline{B}_j^{(j-1)}$ denotes the $j-1$-th coded version of nonterminal B_j.)

Finally, let
$$P_0 = \{Z_m \to c, c \to c\} \cup \{\underline{A}^{(m)} \to A, A \to A \mid A \in V\},$$
$F_0 = \emptyset$, where the entrance filter is given by $(Z_m, \emptyset)$ and the exit filter is defined by $(Y, \emptyset)$.

We explain the work of the components $(t, 1), \ldots, (t, m)$ given above. Suppose that we have stopped with the simulation of the application of the tables of H (at some derivation in H) at node $n+1$ and we would like to decide whether the obtained string is of the form $Z_0 v$ or not, where v is a terminal word in H. This is simulated in Γ in the following manner: From component $n + 1$ string $Z_0 v$ is communicated to node $(t, 1)$. The arrival is successful, if nonterminal B_1 does not appear in v. Then the string, after the appropriate coding, continues its way along components $(t, 2), \ldots, (t, m)$. Every component (t, j), $2 \le j \le m - 1$, checks whether v contains the corresponding coded variant of nonterminal B_j, and, if the answer is negative, after coding the string is communicated to the next node, $(t, j + 1)$. The communication is successful only in that case if the coded variant of nonterminal B_{j+1} is not present in the string. At the end of this procedure, if the original string, v, does not contain any nonterminal, then the corresponding coded word $Z_m v^{(t,m)}$ is communicated to node 0 and there it is rewritten onto cv. If v is not a terminal word in H, then the above procedure stops before the last coded variant of the string reaches node (t, m), because at some state during the computation the coded string cannot be communicated from the node, say, (t, k), $1 \le k < t$ anymore.

Thus, $cL(H) \subseteq L(\Gamma)$. We show that the reverse inclusion also holds. During any computation in Γ each component communicates only such string that is either a sentential form or it is some coded variant of a sentential form from a terminating derivation in H. Moreover, because after one rewriting step the string is communicated, but it is never communicated successfully after being rewritten more than once at the node, the rewriting steps and the communication steps, together, in Γ correspond to derivation steps in H. Thus, $L(\Gamma)$ has no element which is not in $L(H)$, hence $L(\Gamma) = L(H)$. $\qquad\square$

Next we show that conditional $ETOL$ systems simulate networks of parallel language processors with TOL components.

Theorem 4.3. *For* $X \in \{rc, sc, reg\}$, $(X)NLP\_FTOL \subseteq E(X)TOL$.

Proof. Let $\Gamma = (V, (P_{1,1}, \ldots, P_{1,m_1}, F_1, \rho_1, \sigma_1), \ldots, (P_{n,1}, \ldots, P_{n,m_n}, F_n, \rho_n, \sigma_n))$, $n \ge 1$, $m_i \ge 1$, $1 \le i \le n$, be an (X)NLP_FTOL system for $X \in \{rc, sc, reg\}$. We construct an E(X)TOL system H such that $L(\Gamma) = L(H)$ holds. Here we take $x = rc$, the other cases can be handled analogously.

The idea of the proof is that the constructed tables of the E(X)TOL system simulate the way of the strings around the nodes of Γ and indicate the status of the string, that is, whether it is a copy of a string just going to be communicated, it has just been communicated, or it is going to be rewritten at the node.

First, instead of notations ρ_i and σ_i, $1 \le i \le n$, we use notations (Q_i, R_i) and (Q_i', R_i'), respectively, that is, to satisfy ρ_i (respectively, σ_i) the string has to contain each letter of Q_i and no letter of R_i (respectively, Q_i' and R_i'). (If some of the above sets is empty, then we omit the corresponding context check.)

Let us denote by $V^{(i)}$, $\bar{V}^{(i)}$, $V^{(i,j)}$, $1 \le i \le n$, $1 \le j \le m_i$, superscripted variants of alphabet V, and let S be a symbol not in any of the above alphabets. Moreover, let $\bar{V} = V \cup_{i=1}^{n} V^{(i)} \cup \bar{V}^{(i)} \cup_{i=1}^{n} \cup_{j=1}^{m_i} V^{(i,j)}$.

Tables of H are constructed as follows:

(We note that, as in the previous case, we indicate only those productions which are necessary to understand the construction: for any letter D from $\bar{V}$ for which there is no production with D on the left-hand side, we consider production $D \to D$ to be included in the table.)

Let
$$H_s = \{S \to \bar{w}^{(i)} \mid w \in F_i, 1 \le i \le n\}$$
(It simulates the starting configuration).
Let for each i, $1 \le i \le n$, and for each l, $1 \le l \le m_i$,
$$H_b^{(i,l)} = \{A^{(i)} \to \tilde{A}^{(i)}, \tilde{A}^{(i)} \to \bar{A}^{(i,l)} \mid A \in V\},$$
(The string at node i is going to be rewritten by table $P_{i,l}$.), and let
$$H_a^{(i,l)} = \{\bar{A}^{(i,l)} \to \alpha^{(i,l)} \mid A \to \alpha \in P_{i,l}\} \cup \{A^{(i,l)} \to A^{(i,l)} \mid A \in V\},$$
(The string, present at node i, is rewritten by table $P_{i,l}$.).
Let
$$H_t^{(i,l)} = \{A^{(i,l)} \to A^{(i)}, A^{(i)} \to A^{(i)} \mid A \in V\},$$
(The string is prepared for rewriting and communication.).
Let for $1 \le i, k \le n$, $i \ne k$,
$$(Q_{ik}, R_{ik}) : P^{(i,k)} = \{A^{(i)} \to \bar{A}^{(k)}, A^{(k)} \to \bar{A}^{(k)}, \mid A \in V\},$$
where $Q_{ik} = Q_i^{(i)} \cup Q'^{(i)}_k$ and $R_{ik} = R_i^{(i)} \cup R'^{(i)}_k$.
(A copy of the string leaves node i and arrives at node k passing successfully the
exit filter of node i and the entrance filter of node k.)
And, finally, let
$$H_t = \{A^{(1)} \to A, A \to A \mid A \in V\}.$$
(It selects the terminal strings.)
The terminal set of E(rc)T0L system H is V, any other symbol appearing in any of
the tables is a nonterminal letter for it. The startsymbol of H is S. By the explanations
added to the tables, it comes easily that any string which appears at the first node just
after performing a rewriting step during a finite computation of Γ can be generated
by the E(rc)T0L system H. Moreover, H generates only the words of the language
identified by Γ, because the tables of H can be applied after each other only in such
sequence that simulates the way of a string in a terminating computation in Γ.   □

Summarizing Theorems 1, 2 and 3, we obtain:

Theorem 4.4. *For* $x \in \{rc, sc, reg\}$, *we have* $E(x)T0L = (x)NLP\_F0L = (x)NLP\_FT0L$.

Corollary 4.2.

(i) $CS = E(sc)PT0L = (sc)NLP\_PF0L = (sc)NLP\_PF0L = (reg)NLP\_PF0L$
$= (reg)NLP\_PFT0L$

(ii) $RE = E(sc)T0L = (sc)NLP\_F0L = (sc)NLP\_FT0L = (reg)NLP\_F0L = (reg)NLP\_FT0L$.

Remark 4.1. The proof of Theorem 4.3 gives a direct method for constructing an
equivalent NLP_F0L system for any NLP_FT0L system: each table of the E(X)T0L
system corresponds to a production set of some node and the asssociated context
condition to the entrance filter of the node. The exit filters in the system are empty,
the string copies can freely leave the nodes. The axiom sets are empty sets except of
one node that has strings $\{\bar{w}^{(k)} \mid w \in F_k, 1 \le k \le n\}$ as axioms.

5. Size of String Populations

In the previous sections we considered networks of language processors as language identifying devices, but the concept is a convenient tool for describing such communicating symbol processing mechanisms where the processors compute multisets of strings, that is, the collections of strings are allowed to have multiple occurrences of the same word. In this section we deal with the size properties of such string populations. We prove that the growth of the number of strings being present during the computation in a system which has random context filters and deterministic F0L systems as components can be described by a growth function of a D0L system. The number of the communicated strings and the size of the string population at a fixed node can be calculated from the length sequence of this D0L system.

Networks of multiset string processors (NMP systems, for short) operate in the same way as networks of language processors, therefore we settle only the necessary formalism.

Definition 5.1. An *NMP_F0L system* (of degree n, $n \geq 1$,) is a construct

$$\Gamma = (V, (P_1, F_1, \rho_1, \sigma_1), \ldots, (P_n, F_n, \rho_n, \sigma_n)),$$

$n \geq 1$, where components $V, P_i, \rho_i, \sigma_i, 1 \leq i \leq n$, are defined in the same manner as in Definition 3.1 (the alphabet of the system, the components: the production set, the exit filter and the entrance filter of the component, respectively) and $F_i, 1 \leq i \leq n$, is a finite multiset of strings over V^*.

By a configuration (a state) of an NMP_F0L system $\Gamma = (V, (P_1, F_1, \rho_1, \sigma_1), \ldots, (P_n, F_n, \rho_n, \sigma_n)), n \geq 1$, we mean an n-tuple $C = (M_1, \ldots, M_n)$, where $M_i, 1 \leq i \leq n$, the current state of the i-th component, is a multiset of strings over V^*.

According to the type of the filters and the type of the productions sets we distinguish different classes among NMP systems. We denote by (X)NMP_Y the class of NMP systems with (X)-type filters and Y components, where $X \in \{reg, sc, rc\}$ and $Y \in \{D0L, PD0L, 0L, P0L, T0L, PT0L, etc.\}$.

NMP systems are functioning in the same manner as NLP systems, by modifying collections of strings representing the current state. Since the notions are isomorphic, therefore we omit the definitions.

In the following we examine the size of the changing string populations. If the processors are represented by deterministic $F0L$ systems, we can describe the changes by functions.

Definition 5.2. Let $\Gamma = (V, (P_1, F_1, \rho_1, \sigma_1), \ldots, (P_n, F_n, \rho_n, \sigma_n)), n \geq 1$, be an (X)NMP_FD0L system, where $x \in \{rc, sc, reg\}$ and let $(M_1^{(t)}, \ldots, M_n^{(t)})$ be the state of Γ at step t during the computation in Γ, where $t \geq 0$.

- The function $m(t) : \mathbb{N} \to \mathbb{N}$ defined by $m(t) = \sum_{i=1}^{n} |M_i^{(t)}|$ for $t \geq 0$ is called the population growth function of Γ.

- The function $m_i(t) : \mathbb{N} \to \mathbb{N}$ defined by $m_i(t) = |M_i^{(t)}|$ for $t \geq 0$ is called the population growth function of Γ at node i, $1 \leq i \leq n$.

- The function $f_{i,j}(t) : \mathbb{N} \to \mathbb{N}$ defined by $f_{i,j}(t) = |\{\{v \in M_i^{(t)} \mid \rho_i(v) = \underline{true} \text{ and } \sigma_j(v) = \underline{true}\}\}|$ for $t \geq 0$ is called the communication function of Γ from node i to node j, $1 \leq i,j \leq n$, $i \neq j$.

(Remember that a multiset with elements say, a, b, a, c is denoted by $\{\{a, b, a, c\}\}$.)

Theorem 5.1. *Let* $\Gamma = (V, (P_1, F_1, \rho_1, \sigma_1), \ldots, (P_n, F_n, \rho_n, \sigma_n))$, $n \geq 1$, *be an* $(rc)NMP\_FD0L$ *system. Then there is a D0L system* $H = (\Sigma, h, w)$ *such that*

(i) $m(t) = f(t)$, *where* $m(t)$ *is the population growth function of* Γ *and* $f(t)$ *is the growth function of* H,

(ii) $m_i(t) = |\bar{h}_i(h^t(w))|$ *for some erasing homomorphism* $\bar{h}_i : \Sigma \to \Sigma$, *for* $1 \leq i \leq n$, *where* $m_i(t)$ *is the population growth function of* Γ *at node* i,

(iii) $f_{i,j}(t) = |\bar{h}_{i,j}(h^t(w))|$ *for some erasing homomorphism* $\bar{h}_{i,j} : \Sigma \to \Sigma$, *for* $1 \leq i, j \leq n$, $i \neq j$, *where* $f_{i,j}(t)$ *is the communication function of* Γ *from node* i *to node* j, $1 \leq i,j \leq n$, $i \neq j$.

Proof. (i) The proof is based on the following simple considerations: Since D0L systems define homomorphims, therefore, if we know how many strings with a fixed alphabet are present at some node, then we are able to give the number of strings with the same alphabet obtained after performing a rewriting step at the node. Moreover, because by applying the context conditions we check the presence and/or the absence of some symbols in the string, therefore, if we know the alphabet of the string then we are able to decide whether the string satisfies the context condition or not. Thus, in this case we can represent any multiset of strings which are present at some stage of some computation in Γ by the multiset of their alphabets. We show that at any computation step in Γ the multiset of the alphabets of the words computed by the system is equal to the multiset of the letters of some word of a D0L system H. Moreover, H generates only such words which represent, in the above described manner, states (string collections) of Γ.

Let us construct components of D0L system $H = (\Sigma, h, w)$ as follows:

First, let production sets $P_1, \ldots, P_n$, of components of Γ define homomorphisms $h_1, \ldots, h_n$, respectively, and let us explicit context conditions ρ_i, σ_i, $1 \leq i \leq n$, by using notations (Q_i, R_i) and (Q_i', R_i'), where Q_i, Q_i' are the corresponding sets of permitting symbols and R_i, R_i' are the corresponding sets of forbidding symbols.

Let $\{V_1, \ldots, V_{2^m}\}$ be the set of subsets of V, where $m = card(V)$, and let $\Sigma = \{r_{i_j}, c_{i_j} \mid 1 \leq i \leq n, 1 \leq j \leq 2^m\}$.

For the simplicity of reading, instead of defining homomorphism h of H we present the corresponding production set, P.

Let P consist of the following rules:

For every i, j $1 \leq i \leq n$, $1 \leq j \leq 2^m$, let

(i) $r_{i_j} \to c_{i_l} \in P$ if $alph(h_i(V_j)) = V_l$, where $1 \leq l \leq 2^m$.

Let P have, furthermore, for $1 \leq i \leq n$, $1 \leq j \leq 2^m$, productions

(ii) $c_{i_j} \to r_{i_j} r_{k1_j} r_{k2_j} \ldots r_{ks_j}$, where $k1, \ldots, ks$ are pairwise different numbers, and $\{k1, \ldots, ks\}$ is the maximal subset of $\{1, \ldots, n\} - \{i\}$ such that for every kl it holds that $Q_j \subseteq V_j$, $R_i \cap V_j = \emptyset$ and $Q_{k_l}' \subseteq V_j$ and $R_{k_l}' \cap V_j = \emptyset$, for $1 \leq l \leq s$. If there is no $k1, \ldots, ks$ with the above properties, then P has production $c_{i_j} \to r_{i_j}$.

Let $F_i = \{\{v_{i_1}, \ldots, v_{i_{m_i}}\}\}$, where $m_i = card(F_i)$. Let $g(F_i) = g(v_{i_1}) \ldots g(v_{i_{m_i}})$, where $g(v_{i_j}) = r_{i_j}$, where $alph(v_{i_j}) = V_l$, $1 \leq l \leq 2^m$. Let, moreover, $g(F_i) = \lambda$ if $F_i = \emptyset$. Let $w = g(F_1) \ldots g(F_n)$.

We show that the growth function of H is equal to the population growth function of Γ. It is clear that any symbol, say r_{i_k}, in w corresponds to a word in F_i with alphabet V_k, and reversely, thus, the length of w is equal to the number of axioms of Γ. Productions given by (i) describe a rewriting step in Γ : P_i derives from a word with alphabet V_j a word with alphabet V_l. Since the productions are applied in a parallel manner, therefore the whole new string population at node i, $1 \leq i \leq n$, is represented after a rewriting step. Productions of (ii) describe the communication step: if a word consisting of letters of V_j at node i can be communicated to nodes $k1, \ldots, ks$, then a new word, that is, the copy of the string, over V_j will appear at those nodes. If the string cannot be communicated, then it remains at the node and no other string population will be added by its copy. The above explanations imply that if w_t is the t-th member of the D0L sequence of H, then the length of w_t is equal to the total number of strings being present at the nodes at step t during the computation in Γ. Thus, $m(t) = f(t)$ holds.

(ii) By choosing $\bar{h}_i : \Sigma \to \Sigma$ with $\bar{h}_i(r_{i_j}) = r_{i_j}$, $\bar{h}_i(c_{i_j}) = c_{i_j}$, $1 \leq j \leq 2^m$, and $\bar{h}_i(r_{k_j}) = \lambda$, $1 \leq k \leq n$, $k \neq i$, $1 \leq j \leq 2^m$, we immediately obtain the result.

(iii) The statement follows by choosing $\bar{h}_{i_j} : \Sigma \to \Sigma$ as follows:

For $1 \leq k \leq n$, $1 \leq l \leq 2^m$ let $\bar{h}_{i_j}(r_{k_l}) = \lambda$, $\bar{h}_{i_j}(c_{i_k}) = r_{j_k}$, if $c_{i_k} = r_{i_k}\alpha r_{j_k}\beta$, $\alpha, \beta \in \Sigma^*$, and $c_{i_k} = \lambda$ otherwise.

Thus, Theorem 5.1 shows that we are dealing here with D0L and HD0L growth functions. Consequently, their decidability theory is readily available, see ([11]). We mention here only the following two results.

Corollary 5.1. *The population growth function of an* $(rc)NLP\_MD0L$ *system is either exponential or polynomially bounded.*

Corollary 5.2. *For* $(rc)NLP\_MD0L$ *systems it is decidable whether the population growth function is exponential or polynomially bounded.*

Population growth functions are also interesting in the case of DT0L systems as components, in particular when the selection of the tables to be applied for rewriting is done according to some constraints. Communication functions are of worth to study, too, because they provide information about the information flow in the system.

6. Remarks on Functioning Modes

Networks of parallel language processors are models of communities of developing and communicating agents. The local development at the nodes and the communication protocol of the components together determine the functioning of the system that determines the system's descriptive power. T0L systems in the nodes provide the possibility of sophisticated functioning modes. One of the variants is, if we drop the nondeterministic selection of the tables (which is given by the basic mode of functioning) and we formulate some conditions for the choice of the table to be used in the next rewriting step.

In the following we illustrate these variants by some examples.

Let us have an NLP system with two components, one represented by a D0L system and the other by a DT0L system with two tables. We specify only the $DT0L$ component in full details.

Let $\Gamma_1 = (V \cup \{a, b, c\}, (P_1, F_1, \rho_1, \sigma_1), (P_{2,1}, P_{2,2}, F_2, \rho_2, \sigma_2))$, where $V \cap \{a, b, c\} = \emptyset$,

- P_1 is a D0L set of rules;

- $F_1 = \{w\}$ for some $w \in V^+$;

- $\rho_1(u) = \underline{true}$ iff $u \in V^*$.

- $\sigma_1(u) = \underline{false}$ iff $u \in V^*$.

(This component, from time to time, sends a copy of its generated word to the other component. This node does not accept any string.)

Let

- $P_{2,1} = \{a \rightarrow ab, b \rightarrow b\} \cup \{d \rightarrow \lambda \mid d \in V\}$,

- $P_{2,2} = \{a \rightarrow ac, c \rightarrow c\} \cup \{d \rightarrow \lambda \mid d \in V\}$,

- $F_2 = \{a\}$;

- $\rho_2(u) = \underline{false}$ iff $u \in V^*$;

- $\sigma_2(u) = \underline{true}$ for any $u \in V^*$ which contains any letter from a fixed alphabet $V' \subseteq V$ but no letter from $V - V'$. (u is with alphabet V'.)

(If the word generated by the D0L system is with alphabet V' then it is successfully communicated to this node.)

Moreover, suppose that there is at least one word u generated by H for which $alph(u) = V'$ holds.

Let us define the second component of Γ as the master node. Clearly, if there is no restriction on the usage of the tables, then $L(\Gamma) = \{a\alpha \mid \alpha \in \{b, c\}^+\} \cup \{\lambda\}$. This language is a regular language.

Let us introduce now some control for the selection of tables to be applied. Suppose that Γ is functioning in the following manner: whenever at least one string is successfully communicated to the node (at least one message arrives), then the node chooses such table for rewriting which is different from that was used in the preceding rewriting step (supposing that there are at least two tables at the node; if the node has only one production set, then, obviously that table is applied). If no string is communicated to the node, then the T0L system selects a table in nondeterministic manner. (Thus, the successful communication means an impulse for changing the developmental process.)

It can be easily seen that the above way of impulse controlled functioning, from the point of view of the generative power, is at least as powerful as the original working mode.

Suppose that $\Gamma = (V, (P_{1,1}, \ldots, P_{1,m_1}, F_1, \rho_1, \sigma_1), \ldots, (P_{n,1}, \ldots, P_{n,m_n}, F_n, \rho_n, \sigma_n))$, $n \geq 1$, $m_i \geq 1$, $1 \leq i \leq n$, is an arbitrary NLP_FT0L system working in the basic mode of functioning.

Let X, Y be symbols not in V and let us have $\Gamma' = (V \cup \{X, Y\}, (P'_{1,1}, P"_{1,1}, \ldots, P'_{1,m_1}, P"_{1,m_1}, F_1, \rho_1, \sigma_1), \ldots, (P'_{n,1}, P"_{n,1}, \ldots, P'_{n,m_n}, P"_{n,m_n}, F_n, \rho_n, \sigma_n))$, $n \geq 1$, where $P'_{i,j} = P_{i_j} \cup \{X \to X, Y \to Y\}$, $P"_{i,j} = P_{i_j} \cup \{X \to Y, Y \to X\}$, $1 \leq i \leq n$, $1 \leq j \leq m_i$.

Then, it is easy to see that Γ' in the above impulse controlled manner generates the same language as Γ in the basic mode, because independently from the number of arriving strings, it can choose a table that simulates the table chosen by Γ.

Let us compute the language identified by the NLP_FT0L system Γ_1 of the above example.

It is known (see [11]) that if $w_0, w_1, w_2, \ldots$ is a word sequence generated by a $D0L$ system $H = (\Sigma, h, w)$, then the sets $\Sigma_i = alph(w_i)$, $i \geq 0$, form an almost periodic sequence, i.e., there are numbers $p > 0$ and $q \geq 0$ such that $\Sigma_i = \Sigma_{i+p}$ holds for every $i \geq q$.

We shall use this statement in the sequel. Suppose that $V' = alph(w_i)$ for some word w_i, $i \geq 0$, from the word sequence of the first component and let i be the first number for which this property holds. Then, for appropriate p, a successful string communication takes place at any step of number $i + rp$, where $r \geq 1$, which means that Γ will change the table at any step of number $(i + rp)$.

Then, the computed language contains λ and it contains all prefices of words of the form $a\alpha v_1 v_2 \ldots v_n$, $n \geq 1$, where α is a fixed word, $\alpha \in \{b, c\}^+$, $|\alpha| = i$, $|v_j| = p$, for $1 \leq j \leq n$, and if $v_k = u_k \beta$ and $v_{k+1} = \gamma z_k$, $1 \leq k \leq n-1$, then $\beta \neq \gamma$, $\beta, \gamma \in \{b, c\}$, $u_k, z_k \in \{b, c\}^*$.

This language is a regular language, that is, the controlled table selection did not add power.

The same happens if we modify the above model as follows: when a string successfully arrives at a node, then the node changes the developmental table (chooses such table that differs from the preceding one) and keeps this table for rewriting till such an event again takes place.

In this case, using the above statement concerning D0L systems, we can easily see that Γ_1 computes λ and all prefices of the words of $a\alpha(b^p c^p)^*$, where α is a fixed word of length i, numbers i, p are defined as above, and $\alpha \in \{b, c\}^*$. This language is a regular language, too, due to the periodic behaviour of D0L sytems with respect to symbol occurrence in their words. However, the natural expectation is that controlled functioning adds power to the mechanism, there are cases when the further regulations decrease the generative capacity.

Let us have now an example for such functioning mode when Γ_1 determines a non-context-free context-sensitive language.

In this model, the D0L component sends a message to the DT0L component whenever the new word obtained by a rewriting step is shorter than the old one and this is the only case when a message from the first component to the second is communicated.

The DT0L component has the following strategy for table selection: if the message comes, then the second table of the $DT0L$ component will be applied. If no string arrives at the node, then at the next rewriting step table 1 will be applied. In this way, the changes in the development of the first component control the way of the development at the second component.

By [10] it is known that there exists a D0L length sequence $x_0, x_1, \ldots$, such that there are infinitely many $n \in N$ with $x_{n_0} > x_{n_0+1}$ and for any k there is an i_0 such that $x_{i_0} < x_{i_0+1} < \ldots < x_{i_0+k}$ holds.

Roughly speaking, there are infinitely many points in the development of the D0L system where its growing or stagnating tendency changes but there are arbitrarily long periods without change.

Then, supposing that the D0L component of Γ_1 is a D0L system that has the above property, we obtain that Γ_1 identifies a non-context-free subset of $a(b^*c)^*$.

This Section 6. has a preliminary character. We have only tried to give some examples of the rich possibilities that become available when the hoice of the tables depends on the work of other agents in the network.

References

1. E. Csuhaj-Varjú, L. Kari, Gh Păun, Test Tube Distributed System based on Splicing, *Computers and AI*, **15, 2-3**(1996), 211 – 232.

2. E. Csuhaj-Varjú, J. Kelemen, Gh. Păun, Grammar systems with WAVE-like communication, *Computers and AI*, 1996, **15, 5**(1996), 419 – 436.

3. J. Dassow, Gh. Păun, "Regulated Rewriting in Formal Language Theory", Springer Verlag, Berlin, 1989.

4. L. Errico, "WAVE: An Overview of the Model and the Language", CSRG, Dept. Electronic and Electr. Eng., Univ. of Surrey, UK, 1993.

5. L. Errico, C. Jesshope, Towards a new architecture for symbolic processing, *in* "Artificial Intelligence and Information-Control Systems of Robots '94" (I. Plander, ed.), World Sci. Publ., Singapore, 1994, 31 – 40.

6. S. E. Fahlman, G. E. Hinton, T. J. Seijnowski, Massively parallel architectures for AI: NETL, THISTLE and Boltzmann machines, *in* "Proc. AAAI National Conf. on AI", William Kaufman, Los Altos, 1983, 109 – 113.

7. W. D. Hillis, "The Connection Machine", MIT Press, Cambridge, 1985.

8. L. Ilie, Collapsing hierarchies in parallel communicating grammar systems with communication by command, *Computers and AI*, **15, 2-3**(1996), 173 – 184.

9. L. Ilie, A. Salomaa, On regular characterizations of languages by grammar systems, *Acta Cybernetica*, to appear.

10. J. Karhumäki, Two theorems concerning recognizable N-subsets of σ^*, *Theoretical Computer Science* **1**(1976), 317–323.

11. G. Rozenberg, A. Salomaa, "The Mathematical Theory of L Systems ", Academic Press, New York, 1980.

12. A. Salomaa, "Formal Languages", Academic Press, New York, 1973.

13. P. S. Sapaty, "The WAVE Paradigm", Internal Report 17/92, Dept. Informatics, Univ. of Karlsruhe, Germany, 1992.

14. ***, "Connection Machine, Model CM-2. Tehnical Summary", Thinking Machines T. R. HA 87 – 4, MIT, Cambridge, USA, 1987.

Chapter 4. Splicing Systems

A Reduced Distributed Splicing System for RE Languages

Claudio ZANDRON, Claudio FERRETTI, Giancarlo MAURI[1]

Dipartimento di Scienze dell'Informazione
Università di Milano
via Comelico 39, 20135 Milano, Italy

Abstract. In this paper we prove that each recursively enumerable language can be generated using a distributed splicing system with a fixed number of test tubes. This improves a recent result by Csuhaj-Varjú, Kari, Păun, proving computational completeness only for a system with a number of tubes depending on the cardinality of the used alphabet.

1. Introduction

The family of recursively enumerable languages, RE for short, marks in the usual Chomsky hierarchy for formal languages the computational power equal to that of Turing machines. That's why this family is a benchmark for studying the computational power of new models for formal languages and/or for computation itself.

This is the case with the models of *DNA computation* recently brought to attention [1], [6] as an alternative machinery to the usual silicon based computers. To compare these models to RE we first need to map them to a suitable formal language system, and since they are based on the massively parallel interactions of billions of strings being transformed (DNA sequences), the mind goes to the ideas of grammar systems, [2].

A formal model apt to this domain was already suggested in 1987 by Head [4]. It is called *splicing system* model, and it describes one specific DNA transformation, the one operated by *restriction enzymes*. They cut DNA sequences at the occurrence of specific subsequences, and the thus created halves can successively rejoin with others to create new complete molecules.

The model we consider here has been defined through certain modifications of the original splicing model. As we will see when giving the formal definitions, it considers a set of terminals, as the original model, but also a set of nonterminals. Also, it considers the strings-molecules interacting in groups assigned to different *test tubes*, and to be from time to time redistributed among the different tubes according to filtering rules, as defined in [3]. So we have a system generating strings by interactions at two levels: inside the tubes among strings, and among the tubes in the redistribution of the sets of strings.

The aim of this paper is to improve a result from [3], using the same formalism and some similar ideas, but proving how to reach the power of RE with a *fixed* number of test tubes, instead of a number dependent on the number of symbols contained in the alphabet. We do this by designing a kind of simple encoding/decoding sub-procedure based only on splicing. This result opens way to considerations related to the practical feasibility of this model for DNA computations and, perhaps even more important, to the effectiveness of new general purpose algorithms natively defined for splicing systems. We will diffuse on these issues in the closing section of the paper.

2. Basic Definitions

As usual, V^* is the set of all (finite) strings over a finite alphabet V. The empty string is denoted by λ.

The families of recursively enumerable languages and of finite languages are denoted by RE and FIN, respectively.

We now introduce the definitions of splicing system, and of *distributed* splicing system. This is a kind of PC grammar system where the components are basically splicing systems.

A *Head splicing system* (or H system) is a triple $H = (V, A, R)$, where V is the alphabet of H, $A \subseteq V^*$ is the set of *axioms*, and R is the set of *splicing rules*, with $R \subseteq V^*\#V^*\$V^*\#V^*$ ($\$, \#$ are special symbols not in V).

For $x, y, z, w \in V^*$ and $r = u_1\#u_2\$u_3\#u_4$ in R, we define

$$(x, y) \vdash_r (z, w) \quad \text{if and only if} \quad \begin{aligned} & x = x_1u_1u_2x_2, \ y = y_1u_3u_4y_2, \text{ and} \\ & z = x_1u_1u_4y_2, \ w = y_1u_3u_2x_2, \\ & \text{for some } x_1, x_2, y_1, y_2 \in V^*. \end{aligned}$$

For an H system $H = (V, A, R)$ and a language $L \subseteq V^*$, we write

$$\sigma(L) = \{z \in V^* \mid (x, y) \vdash_r (z, w) \text{ or } (x, y) \vdash_r (w, z), \text{ for some } x, y \in L, r \in R\},$$

and define

$$\sigma^*(L) = \bigcup_{i \geq 0} \sigma^i(L)$$

where

$$\sigma^0(L) = L$$
$$\sigma^{i+1}(L) = \sigma^i(L) \cup \sigma(\sigma^i(L)) \quad \text{for } i \geq 0.$$

An H system is meant to operate starting from the set of strings A, and then generate new strings iterating the splicing step $\vdash_r$ on them and on the strings generated during this process. The language generated in this way is $\sigma^*(A)$.

A *test tube system*, TT for short, is a construct

$$\Gamma = (V, (A_1, R_1, V_1), \ldots, (A_n, R_n, V_n))$$

where $A_i \subseteq V^*, R_i \subseteq V^*\#V^*\$V^*\#V^*$, and $V_i \subseteq V$, for $1 \leq i \leq n$. V_i is called the *selector* of tube i.

Each triple (A_i, R_i, V_i), also called a *tube*, operates individually in the same way as an H system (V, A_i, R_i). According to the definition of H systems, they would generate the language denoted by $\sigma_i^*(A_i)$, but we will see that in a TT they interact among them, accepting from the others the strings belonging to V_i^*. The set B of strings outside any language V_i^* is defined as follows

$$B = V^* - \bigcup_{i=1}^{n} V_i^*$$

Each tube i in the system starts containing only the strings of A_i. One processing step ('$\Rightarrow$') of the system, moves it from the configuration $(L_1, \ldots, L_n)$, where each tube i contains the strings of L_i, to a configuration $(L_1', \ldots, L_n')$, according to the following definition

$$(L_1, \ldots, L_n) \;\Rightarrow\; (L_1', \ldots, L_n') \text{ iff}$$
$$L_i' = \bigcup_{j=1}^{n} \left(\sigma_j^*(L_j) \cap V_i^*\right) \bigcup \left(\sigma_i^*(L_i) \cap B\right))$$
$$\text{for each } i, 1 \leq i \leq n.$$

Finally, we state that the language generated by a TT Γ is the set of words appearing in the tube 1 at any processing step, when starting from the configuration $(A_1, \ldots, A_n)$: ($\Rightarrow^*$ is the reflexive and transitive closure of the relation $\Rightarrow$)

$$L(\Gamma) = \{w \in V^* \mid w \in L_1 \text{ for some } (A_1, \ldots, A_n) \Rightarrow^* (L_1, \ldots, L_n)\}$$

We denote by $TT_n(F_1, F_2)$ the family of languages $L(\Gamma)$ such that Γ is a splicing system with at most n tubes, each with set of axioms from F_1 and set of rules from F_2. The set of languages generated using any number of tubes is defined by

$$TT_*(F_1, F_2) = \bigcup_{n \geq 1} TT_n(F_1, F_2)$$

3. Test Tube Systems and RE Languages

In this section we prove in details our main result.

Theorem 1. $TT_{10}(FIN, FIN) = TT_*(FIN, FIN) = TT_*(F_1, F_2) = RE$ for all families F_1, F_2 such that $REG \subseteq F_i \subseteq RE, i = 1, 2$.

Proof. The inclusions $TT_{10}(FIN, FIN) \subseteq TT_*(FIN, FIN) \subseteq TT_*(F_1, F_2)$ are obvious. The inclusion $TT_{10}(FIN, FIN) \subseteq RE$ is obvious from the Turing/Church thesis. Hence, it is sufficient to prove that $RE \subseteq TT_{10}(FIN, FIN)$.

Take a type-0 Chomsky grammar $G = (N, T, S, P)$. Denote $U = N \cup T$ and construct the system

$$\Gamma = (V, (A_1, R_1, V_1), (A_2, R_2, V_2), (A_3, R_3, V_3), (A_4, R_4, V_4), (A_5, R_5, V_5),$$
$$(A_6, R_6, V_6), (A_7, R_7, V_7), (A_8, R_8, V_8), (A_9, R_9, V_9), (A_{10}, R_{10}, V_{10}))$$

with
$$V = N \cup T \cup \{X, X', Y, Y', Z, Z', H, H', R, K, B, @, Y_@\}.$$

Denote with $U_1, \ldots, U_n$ the symbols of the alphabet U (i.e. non terminal and terminal symbols of G) and with U_{n+1} the special symbol B.

Define

$$A_1 = \emptyset,$$
$$R_1 = \emptyset,$$
$$V_1 = T,$$

$$A_2 = \{XBSY, Z'Z\} \cup \{ZvY \mid u \to v \in P\} \cup \{Z@^iY' \mid 1 \le i \le n+1\},$$
$$R_2 = \{\#uY\$Z\#vY \mid u \to v \in P\} \cup \{\#U_iY\$Z\#@^iY' \mid U_i \in U \cup \{B\}\}$$
$$\cup \{Z'\#Z\$XB\#\},$$
$$V_2 = U \cup \{B, X, Y\},$$

$$A_3 = \{ZY_@, HH'\}$$
$$R_3 = \{\#@Y'\$Z\#Y_@\} \cup \{\alpha\#Y'\$H\#H' \mid \alpha \in U \cup \{B\}\},$$
$$V_3 = U \cup \{X, B, @, Y'\},$$

$$A_4 = \{X'@Z\},$$
$$R_4 = \{X\#\$X'@\#Z\},$$
$$V_4 = U \cup \{X, B, @, Y_@\},$$

$$A_5 = \{ZY'\},$$
$$R_5 = \{\#Y_@\$Z\#Y'\},$$
$$V_5 = U \cup \{X', B, @, Y_@\},$$

$$A_6 = \{XZ\},$$
$$R_6 = \{X'\#\$X\#Z'\},$$
$$V_6 = U \cup \{X', B, Y', @\},$$

$$A_7 = \{XU_iK \mid 1 \le i \le n+1\},$$
$$R_7 = \{X@^i\#\alpha\$XU_i\#K \mid \alpha \in U \cup \{B\}\},$$
$$V_7 = U \cup \{X, B, @, H'\},$$

$$A_8 = \{RY\},$$
$$R_8 = \{\alpha\#H'\$R\#Y \mid \alpha \in U \cup \{B\}\},$$
$$V_8 = U \cup \{X, B, H'\},$$

$$A_9 = \{ZZ\},$$
$$R_9 = \{\#Y\$ZZ\#\},$$
$$V_9 = T \cup \{Y, Z'\},$$

$$A_{10} = \{ZZ\},$$

$$R_{10} = \{\#ZZ\$Z'\#\},$$
$$V_{10} = T \cup \{Z'\}.$$

Let us examine the work of Γ.

The first component only selects the string produced by the others components that are terminal according to G. No such terminal string can enter a splicing, because all rules involves at least one special symbol that we add to the set of terminal and non terminal symbols.

In tube 2 applications of productions of the form $u \to v \in P$ to sentential forms Xw_1Bw_2uY are simulated, where w_2uw_1 is a sentential form of G, and X, Y, B are special symbols, indicating respectively the left end and the right end of the sentential form in Γ and the beginning of the rotating string representing the corresponding sentential form in G.

Tubes 3, 4, 5, 6, 7 and 8 are used to rotate the symbols, so we can simulate the productions of G in the correct place.

Tubes 9 and 10 are used to eliminate special symbols X and Y, so we obtain a terminal string.

The construction works as follows:

In the initial configuration $(A_1, \ldots, A_{10})$, only the second component can execute a splicing. There are three possibilities. We can either use a rule of the form $\#uY\$Z\#vY$, for $u \to v \in P$ (we call this a splicing of type 1), or a rule of the form $\#U_iY\$Z\#@^iY'$ where U_i is the i-th symbol of the alphabet U or, if $i = n + 1$, the symbol B (splicing of type 2), or the rule $Z'\#Z\$XB\#$ (splicing of type 3). In the following, while describing these three cases, we will denote by $\vdash_i$ any splicing of type i, for $i = 1, 2, 3$.

Consider the general case of having in tube 2 a string XwY, with $w \in U^*BU^*$; initially, $w = BS$. We have three possibilities for splicing :

1. $(Xw_1|uY, Z|vY) \vdash_1 (Xw_1vY, ZuY)$, for $u \to v \in P$ and $w = w_1u$

2. $(Xw_1|U_iY, Z|@^iY') \vdash_2 (Xw_1@^iY', ZU_iY)$, for $U_i \in U \cup \{B\}$ and $w = w_1U_i$

3. $(Z'|Z, XB|w_1Y) \vdash_3 (Z'w_1Y, XBZ)$, for $w = Bw_1$

Let us examine the strings we have just created.

The string Xw_1vY is of the same form as Xw_1uY so it will remain in tube 2, entering new splicing of one of the three types. Clearly, the passage from Xw_1uY to Xw_1vY corresponds to using the rule $u \to v \in P$ on a suffix on the string bracketed by X, Y. The string ZuY will remain in tube 2, too. Such a string ZuY can enter a splicing in three cases:

1. ZuY is an axiom, then nothing new appears.

2. ZuY is used as the first term of a splicing of the form $(Zu_1|u'Y, Zv'Y) \vdash_1 (Zu_1v'Y, Zu'Y)$, for $u = u_1u'$ and $u' \to v' \in P$; we obtain two strings of the same form, ZxY, which will remain in tube 2.

3. ZuY is used as the first term in a splicing of the form $(Zu_1|U_iY, Z|@^iY') \vdash_2 (Zu_1@^iY', ZU_iY)$, for $u = u_1U_i, U_i \in U \cup \{B\}$; the string $Zu_1@^iY'$ cannot enter new splicings and cannot be transmitted to another tube.

After any sequence of such splicings, the obtained strings will still be of the form ZxY, hence they will remain in tube 2 and will enter other "legal" splicing, when they are axioms, or they will enter splicings producing "useless" strings ZyY. Therefore, after a series of splicings of type 1, eventually in tube 2 a splicing of type 2 will be performed, producing strings of the form $Xw_1@^iY'$ and ZU_iY. The second string behaves exactly as we discussed above for the string ZuY. If a string $Xw_1@^iY'$ enters a new splicing in tube 2 this can only be splicing of type 3,

$$(Z'|Z, XB|w_2@^iY') \vdash_3 (Z'w_2@^iY', XBZ)$$

for $w_1 = Bw_2$. The string $Z'w_2@^iY'$ cannot enter new splicings in tube 2 and cannot be transmitted to another tube. If the string XBZ enters a new splicing, this can only be of type 3

$$(Z'|Z, XB|Z) \vdash_3 (Z'Z, XBZ)$$

so nothing new can be created.

Any string $Xw_1@^iY'$ is moved from tube 2 to tube 3 where we have to perform

$$(Xw_1@^{i-1}|@Y', Z|Y_@) \vdash (Xw_1@^{i-1}Y_@, Z@Y').$$

The second type of rule of tube 3 will be examined below.

The string $Z@Y'$ cannot be transmitted to another tube and can enter only a splicing of the form

$$(Z|@Y', Z|Y_@) \vdash (Z@Y', ZY_@),$$

hence creating nothing new.

The string $Xw_1@^{i-1}Y_@$ cannot enter new splicing in tube 3, it will be transmitted to tube 4 where we have to perform

$$(X|w_1@^{i-1}Y_@, X'@|Z) \vdash (X'@w_1@^{i-1}Y_@, XZ)$$

The string XZ cannot be transmitted to another tube and can enter only a splicing of the form

$$(X|Z, X'@|Z) \vdash (XZ, X'@Z)$$

hence creating nothing new.

The string $X'@w_1@^{i-1}Y_@$ cannot enter new splicing in this tube; it will be transmitted to tube 5, where the only possible splicing is

$$(X'@w_1@^{i-1}|Y_@, Z|Y') \vdash (X'@w_1@^{i-1}Y', ZY_@)$$

The string $ZY_@$ cannot be transmitted to another tube and can enter only a splicing of the form

$$(Z|Y_@, Z|Y') \vdash (ZY_@, ZY'),$$

so it can creates nothing new.

The string $X'@w_1@^{i-1}Y'$ cannot enter new splicing in this tube; it will be transmitted to tube 6. In tube 6 we can only execute

$$(X'|@w_1@^{i-1}Y', X|Z') \vdash (X@w_1@^{i-1}Y', X'Z')$$

The string $X'Z'$ cannot be transmitted to another tube and can only enter splicing of the form

$$(X'|Z', X|Z') \vdash (X'Z', XZ')$$

hence producing nothing new.

The string $X@w_1@^{i-1}Y'$ cannot enter new splicing in this tube; it will be moved to tube 3.

We started from tube 3 with the string $Xw_1@^iY'$ and now we returned to tube 3 with the string $X@w_1@^{i-1}Y'$. A symbol @ from the right end of the string bracketed by X, Y' has been moved to the left end. The string $X@w_1@^{i-1}Y'$ cannot enter a splicing of the second type in tube 3, but can enter a splicing of the first type in tube 3. By repeating the operations just described, we will return to tube 3 with the string $X@@w_1@^{i-2}Y'$ (i.e. we will rotate another symbol @). This sequence will be repeated until all symbols @ will be moved from the right end to the left end of the string bracketed by X, Y'. It will take i steps.

Then, in tube 3 we obtain a string of the form $X@^iw_1Y'$. This string cannot enter a splicing of first type in tube 3, but it can enter a splicing of second type in this tube, so we can perform

$$(X@^iw_2\alpha|Y', H|H') \vdash (X@^iw_2\alpha H', HY'), \text{ for } w_1 = w_2\alpha, \alpha \in U \cup \{B\}.$$

The string HY' cannot be transmitted to other tubes, and can only enter splicing of the form

$$(H|Y', H|H') \vdash (HY', HH')$$

hence creating nothing new.

The string $X@^iw_1H'$ cannot enter a new splicing in this tube; it will be transmitted to tube 6. In tube 6 we have to perform :

$$(X@^i|\beta w_3H', XU_i|K) \vdash (XU_i\beta w_3H', X@^iK), \text{ for } w_1 = \beta w_3, \beta \in U \cup \{B\}.$$

With this operation we decode the symbol U_i from $@^i$ (we coded U_i in $@^i$ with the splicing of type 2 in tube 2).

The string $X@^iK$ cannot be transmitted to another tube, neither enter new splicings in this tube; hence, it can not create nothing new.

The string XU_iw_1H' cannot enter new splicings in this tube; it will be transmitted to tube 7, where we have to perform

$$(XU_iw_4\chi|H', R|Y) \vdash (XU_iw_4\chi Y, RH'), \text{ for } w_1 = w_4\chi, \chi \in U \cup \{B\}.$$

The string RH' cannot be transmitted to another tube, neither enter new splicings in this tube, so it can't create nothing new.

The string XU_iw_1Y cannot enter new splicing in this tube. It will be moved to tube 2.

After this sequence of operations, we can note that having started with the string Xw_1U_iY in tube 2 we have returned to tube 2 with the string XU_iw_1Y. A symbol from the right end of the string bracketed by X, Y has been moved to the left end. In this way, the string bracketed by X, Y can enter circular permutations as long as we want them to do that. This allows us to pass from a string Xw_1Bw_2Y to any string $Xw_1'Bw_2'Y$ such that $w_2w_1 = w_2'w_1'$. In this way we can "rewind" the string until its suffix is the left-hand member of any rule in P that we want to simulate by a rule in R_2 of the form $\#uY\$\#vY$. As the symbol B is always present (and exactly one copy of it is present as long as we do not use the rule $Z'\#Z\$XB\#$ in R_2), in every moment we know where the "actual beginning" of the string is placed. Consequently, using splicings of type 1 and 2 in tube 2 and splicings in tubes 3, 4, 5, 6, 7 and 8 as described above, we can simulate every derivation in G. Conversely, exactly strings of the form Xw_1Bw_2Y can be obtained in this way, they correspond to strings w_2w_1 that are sentential forms of the grammar G.

We have now to consider the splicing of type 3 in tube 2 and the tubes 9 and 10.

We consider first of all the splicings of type 3 in tube 2. We have already seen what happens for the strings XBZ and $Xw@^iY'$, so we have now to consider the strings of the form $XBqY$ for $q \in U^*$. Using a splicing of type 3 we have

$$(Z'|Z, XB|qY) \vdash_3 (XBZ, Z'qY).$$

If a string $Z'qY$ enter a splicing in tube 2 this can be of type 1 and 2:

$$(Z'q_1|uY, Z|vY) \vdash_1 (Z'q_1vY, ZuY), \text{ for } u \to v \in P, q = q_1u$$
$$(Z'q1|U_iY, Z|@^iY') \vdash_2 (Z'q_1@^iY', ZU_iY), \text{ for } U_i \in U \cup \{B\}, q = q_1U_i$$

We have already discussed the case of ZuY, ZU_iY and $Z'q_1@^iY'$. The string $Z'q_1vY$ can be obtained by performing first

$$(XBq_1|uY, Z|vY) \vdash_1 (XBq_1vY, ZuY)$$

and then

$$(Z'|Z, XB|q_1vY) \vdash_3 (Z'q_1vY, XBZ),$$

so it is a "legal" string.

If the string $Z'qY$, obtained with a splicing of type 3 in the tube 2, have the property that $q \in T^*$ (i.e. q is a terminal string) it can be moved to tube 9. Here the only possible splicing is

$$(Z'q|Y, ZZ|) \vdash (Z'q, ZZY).$$

If ZZY will enter new splicing, these are of the forms

$$(Z'x|Y, ZZ|Y) \vdash (Z'xY, ZZY)$$
$$(ZZ|Y, ZZ|Y) \vdash (ZZY, ZZY)$$

hence no new string is obtained.

The string $Z'q$ cannot enter new splicing in tube 9. It will be moved to tube 10, where we have to perform

$$(|ZZ, Z'|q) \vdash (q, Z'ZZ).$$

If the string $Z'ZZ$ enters new splicings, these are of the forms

$$(Z'|ZZ, Z'|x) \vdash (Z'x, Z'ZZ)$$
$$(Z'|ZZ, Z'|ZZ) \vdash (Z'ZZ, Z'ZZ)$$

hence nothing new can be created.

The string q is terminal. It will be transmitted to all tubes, including the first one. No splicing can be done on a terminal string. As we seen above, such a terminal string q is a string in $L(G)$.

No parasitic string can reach the first tube, consequently $L(\Gamma) = L(G)$.   □

The basic ideas of the construction we have presented here are those already used in [5] and [3]: We simulate the productions of the grammar using splicing operations in tube 2. Unfortunately, using the splicing operation, we can simulate a production (in one step) only if the sub-string we are going to substitute is placed at one end of the string. The splicing operation is not able to do such a substitution (using a finite number of rules) if the sub-string is placed in the internal part of the string.

To deal with this problem, we use the rotation of the symbols. Look at Example 1 below: to simulate the production $u \to v$ we rotate the symbols x_3, x_4 and x_5 so that we can move the sub-string u to the right end of the string. This position is optimal to simulate the production using a splicing operation. After that, we rotate the string v (one symbol at time), and then the symbol x_1 and x_2. Starting with $x_1x_2ux_3x_4x_5$ we obtain $x_1x_2vx_3x_4x_5$, so we have simulate properly the production $u \to v$ of the grammar.

Example 1:

$$x_1x_2ux_3x_4x_5 \;\rightsquigarrow\; x_5x_1x_2ux_3x_4 \;\rightsquigarrow\; x_4x_5x_1x_2ux_3 \;\rightsquigarrow\; x_3x_4x_5x_1x_2u$$
$$\rightsquigarrow\; x_3x_4x_5x_1x_2u \;\rightsquigarrow\; x_3x_4x_5x_1x_2v \;\rightsquigarrow\;$$
$$x_3x_4x_5x_1x_2v \;\rightsquigarrow\; Vx_3x_4x_5x_1x_2 \;\rightsquigarrow\; x_2vx_3x_4x_5x_1 \;\rightsquigarrow\; x_1x_2vx_3x_4x_5$$

The rotation solves the problem we have just mentioned, but it introduces a new problem. When we rotate a symbol, we move it from one end to the other. Using splicing rules, this operation requires more than one step, so the problem we have to deal with, is how to delete the symbol from the right end of the string and to put *the same symbol* in the left end of the string. Due to the multi-step process, we could delete a symbol from the right end and put in the left end a different symbol, generating a word which the grammar was not able to create, even if we do not want to do so.

In [3] the solution to this problem was to substitute the symbol to rotate with a symbol that contains the information on the symbol substituted and then to send the string obtained to a "special" tube that rotates *that specific symbol*. In Example 2 we show how this can be done.

Example 2: We consider the string $x_1x_2x_3x_4x_5w$; the symbol w is replaced with Y_w.

$$x_1x_2x_3x_4x_5w \;\rightsquigarrow\; x_1x_2x_3x_4x_5Y_w$$

Then, the string $x_1x_2x_3x_4x_5Y_w$ is sent to the "special" tube, the only tube able to receive this string. This special tube is the only one that contain the symbol Y_w in the filter, and its function is to rotate *the specific symbol* w. We are sure, in this case, to put in the left end of the string the same symbol we have deleted from the right end of the string.

The problem in this solution is that we need one of these "special" tubes for every symbol of the language we are going to generate (because we need one tube for every type of symbol to rotate). Thus, the number of test tubes needed to generate a language depends on the number of different symbols used in the language we have to generate.

In the model presented here, we introduce some differences. First of all, we number the symbols of the grammar. Before rotating a symbol, we encode it to a number of special symbols @, not present in the alphabet of the grammar. The i-th symbol in the order we give, is substituted with i copies of this symbols. This operation is done by the splicing of type 2 in the second component test tube.

Then the symbol is moved to the left end by rotating, one at a time, the special symbols @. These rotations are executed by the component tubes 2, 3, 4, 5 and 6.

When all the special symbols have been rotated, we decode i special symbols with the correspondent symbol U_i. This is done with the component 7.

In the example below we illustrate these three main phases.

Example 3: We show here the three main phases of the rotation of the symbol x_5 of the string $x_1 x_2 x_3 x_4 x_5$:

$$
\begin{aligned}
\textit{Encoding}: \quad & x_1 x_2 x_3 x_4 x_5 & \rightsquigarrow \quad & x_1 x_2 x_3 x_4 @@@@@ \\
\textit{Rotation}: \quad & @x_1 x_2 x_3 x_4 @@@@ & \rightsquigarrow \quad & @@x_1 x_2 x_3 x_4 @@@ \quad \rightsquigarrow \\
& @@@x_1 x_2 x_3 x_4 @@ & \rightsquigarrow \quad & @@@@x_1 x_2 x_3 x_4 @ \quad \rightsquigarrow \\
& @@@@@x_1 x_2 x_3 x_4 \\
\textit{Decoding}: \quad & @@@@@x_1 x_2 x_3 x_4 & \rightsquigarrow \quad & x_5 x_1 x_2 x_3 x_4
\end{aligned}
$$

This solution offer three advantages:

- A symbol is encoded when it is placed in the right end of the string, thus in a suitable place for the application of splicing rules.

- The only symbol that actually rotates is the special symbol @, so we need just one of the "special" tubes used in [3], about which we have discussed before.

- A symbol is decoded when it is placed in the left end of the string, thus in a suitable place for the application of splicing rules.

These advantages permit us to limit the number of tubes with respect to the construction presented in [3]. Using the construction we have explained, the number of tubes does not depend on the number of the symbols of the language we have to generate: ten test tubes are enough to generate any RE language.

We conclude just saying that the components 8, 9 and 10 are used to control the communication of the strings through the tubes and the component 1, as said in the proof, is used to select the strings which contain terminal symbols only.

4. Conclusions and Perspectives

We proved how to build a distributed splicing system powerful enough to generate any language in RE, and using a fixed number of 10 test tubes.

This is still different from designing in detail a *universal* splicing system, similar to the current programmable computers, but it takes us closer to a practical implementation of a DNA computer: for each computation (language) we want, we just change the starting molecules and the restriction enzymes introduced in the test tubes, we do not change the layout on our workbench for each alphabet we need. Of course it is still a practical problem to have enough real restriction enzymes.

From the grammar systems point of view, this work has been insightful to study a case where a simple algorithm has been designed directly in terms of splicing: an algorithm not simply reproducing an usual grammatical production rule, but doing some different basic operation (encoding/decoding). This, of course, is not the first case in literature, but we feel that the interest in this *molecular algorithm engineering* can eventually lead us to build a kind of universal grammar systems based on molecular-like operations, avoiding the uneffective translations of universal Turing machines seen so far.

Many interesting open problems suggested in [3] still are open, concerning the power of different numbers of test tubes and comparisons to different levels of Chomsky hierarchy. We can only add now that it is interesting to check whether it is possible to use less than 10 tubes for RE, since it is not proved that $TT_9(FIN, FIN)$ is properly contained in RE^2.

References

1. L. M. Adleman, Molecular computation of solutions of combinatorial problems, *Science*, 226 (1994), 1021–1024.

2. E. Csuhaj-Varju, J. Dassow, J. Kelemen, Gh. Păun, *Grammar Systems. A Grammatical Approach to Distribution and Cooperation*, Gordon and Breach, London, 1994.

3. E. Csuhaj-Varjú, L. Kari, Gh. Păun, Test tube distributed system based on splicing, *Computer and AI*, 15, 2-3 (1996), 211–232.

4. T. Head, Formal language theory and DNA: an analysis of the generative capacity of specific recombinant behaviours, *Bull. Math. Biology*, 49 (1987), 737–759.

5. Gh. Păun, Regular extended H systems are computationally universal, *J. Automata, Languages, Combinatorics*, 1, 2 (1996), 27–36.

6. * * *, Proceedings of *Second DIMACS workshop on DNA computing*, Princeton, 1996, to be published by ACM Press.

---

[2]Recently, Gh. Păun has proved that systems as above with *seven* tubes can characterize RE, but still one does not know whether seven is the best result

On the Generative Capacity of Splicing Grammar Systems[1]

Gianina GEORGESCU

Faculty of Mathematics, University of Bucharest
Academiei 14, 70109 Bucureşti, Romania
E-mail: `gianina@math.math.unibuc.ro`

Abstract. The generative capacity of splicing grammar systems is investigated in this paper. It is proved that: 1) any linear language can be generated by a splicing grammar system with two regular components; 2) any context–free language can be generated by a splicing grammar system with three regular components; 3) any recursively enumerable language can be generated by a splicing grammar system with four right linear components. The first two results answer a problem left open in [18], the last result improves results in the same paper.

1. Introduction

In the last years a series of researches were initiated in the field of DNA recombination and computing ([9], [11], [14], [21]). This area is very rich both in theoretical and practical problems, motivated by the possibility of using DNA as a support for computing, [1].

A specific model of DNA recombination is the splicing operation which consists of cutting DNA sequences and then pasting the fragments again, under the influence of restriction enzymes and ligases.

Some generalizations were recently considered in the field. One was to consider arbitrarily large sets of splicing rules, codified in a natural way as strings, hence giving *languages* of splicing rules ([15]). Several ideas about how to handle a regular set of splicing rules were explored in [3], [4], [7], [17], [19], [26]. Another idea was to count the number of copies of the used strings: [6], [7], [16].

A different approach was started in [4], [5]: to use distributed architectures as in grammar system theory [2]. Here we investigate the idea introduced in [5]: to consider a parallel communicating grammar system, as in [23], with the communication replaced by a splicing operation. Thus, a splicing grammar system can be viewed as a set of grammars working in parallel on their own sentential forms and, from time to time, splicing the current strings of two components.

In [5] it is proved that context-free splicing grammar systems with three components can generate all recursively enumerable languages and it is formulated as an open problem the question whether or not two components are enough.

The problem is solved in [18] where the following results are proved:

1) Every recursively enumerable language can be generated by a splicing grammar system with two context–free components.

---

[1]Research supported by the Academy of Finland, project 11281.

2) The family of languages generated by splicing grammar systems with two regular components contains non–context–free languages.

1) Every recursively enumerable language $L \subseteq T^*$ can be written as the intersection of a language generated by a splicing grammar system with three regular components and T^*.

In the above paper are left open the problems whether or not the families of linear and context–free languages are included in the family of languages generated by splicing grammar systems with regular components. We shall prove that every linear language can be generated by a splicing grammar system with two regular components and every context–free language can be generated by a splicing grammar system with three regular components. Also, we shall prove that each recursively enumerable language can be generated by a splicing grammar system with four right linear components.

2. Preliminaries

We assume the reader to be familiar with some basic notions in formal language theory [25]. For grammar system theory, we refer to [2].

For an alphabet V, we denote by V^* the free monoid generated by V under the operation of concatenation; the empty string is denoted by λ and $V^* - \{\lambda\}$ is denoted by V^+. The families of finite, regular, linear, context-free, context-sensitive, recursively enumerable languages are denoted by *FIN, REG, LIN, CF, CS, RE*, respectively.

Convention: Two languages are considered equal if they differ by at most the empty string ($L_1 = L_2$ iff $L_1 - \{\lambda\} = L_2 - \{\lambda\}$).

A *splicing grammar system* (*SGS* for short) is a construct

$$\Gamma = (N, T, (S_1, P_1), (S_2, P_2), \ldots, (S_n, P_n), M),$$

where

(i) N, T are disjoint alphabets and $P_i, 1 \leq i \leq n$, are finite sets of production rules over $N \cup T$,

(ii) M is a finite subset of $(N \cup T)^* \# (N \cup T)^* \$ (N \cup T)^* \# (N \cup T)^*$, with $\#, \$$ two distinct symbols which are not in $N \cup T$.

The sets P_i are called the *components* of Γ.

For two n-tuples (we call them *configurations*) $x = (x_1, x_2, \ldots, x_n)$ and $y = (y_1, y_2, \ldots, y_n)$, $x_i, y_i \in (N \cup T)^*, 1 \leq i \leq n$, we write $x \Longrightarrow y$ if and only if one of the following two conditions holds:

(i) for each $1 \leq i \leq n, x_i \Longrightarrow_{P_i} y_i$,

(ii) there exist $1 \leq i, j \leq n$ such that $x_i = x_i' u_1 u_2 x_i''$, $x_j = x_j' u_3 u_4 x_j''$, and $y_i = x_i' u_1 u_4 x_j''$, $y_j = x_j' u_3 u_2 x_i''$, for $u_1 \# u_2 \$ u_3 \# u_4 \in M$; for $k \neq i, j$, we have $y_k = x_k$.

In the above definition, point (i) defines a rewriting step, whereas point (ii) defines a splicing step, corresponding to a communication step in parallel communicating grammar systems. Note that no priority of any of these operations over the other one is assumed. In case (ii) we usually denote the passing from (x_i, x_j) to (y_i, y_j) by $(x_i, x_j) \vdash (y_i, y_j)$.

The language generated by the ith component of Γ is

$$L_i(\Gamma) = \{x_i \in T^* \mid (S_1, \ldots, S_n) \Longrightarrow^* (x_1, \ldots, x_n), \ x_j \in (N \cup T)^*, j \neq i\},$$

where $\Longrightarrow^*$ is the reflexive and transitive closure of the relation $\Longrightarrow$.

The *total* language associated to Γ is

$$L_t(\Gamma) = \bigcup_{i=1}^{n} L_i(\Gamma).$$

We denote by $ISGS_n(X), TSGS_n(X)$ the families of languages $L_1(\Gamma), L_t(\Gamma)$, respectively, generated by splicing grammar systems of degree at most $n, n \geq 1$, with components of type X, where $X \in \{REG, LIN, RL, CF\}$ when the components are regular, linear, right–linear or context–free, respectively. When no restriction is imposed on the number of components, then we replace the subscript n with $*$.

3. Results

Theorem 1. $LIN \subseteq YSGS_2(REG)$, $Y \in \{I, T\}$.

Proof. Let L be the language generated by a linear grammar $G = (N, T, S, P)$. We can suppose that S does not appear in the right–hand side of any rule from P. For $u, v \in T^*, m(u, v)$ denotes $\max\{|u|, |v|\}$. For p, q two positive integer numbers we denote $\theta(p, q) = \begin{cases} 0, & \text{if } p \leq q \\ p - q, & \text{if } p > q \end{cases}$.

We construct a SGS with two regular components as follows:

$$\Gamma = (N', T', (S_1, P_1), (S_2, P_2), M),$$

where

$$
\begin{aligned}
N' = \ & \{S_1, S_2, S_1', S_2', Y\} \cup N_Z \cup \{(uA, i) \mid B \to uA \in P, \ 1 \leq i \leq |u|\} \cup \\
& \{[uAv, i], [uAv, i]' \mid B \to uAv \in P, \ 1 \leq i \leq m(u, v)\} \cup \\
& \{[uAv], [uAv]' \mid B \to uAv \in P\},
\end{aligned}
$$

$$T' = T \cup \{c_1, c_2\}, c_1, c_2 \notin T,$$

$$
\begin{aligned}
P_1 = \ & \{S_1' \to c_1 S_2'\} \cup && (1) \\
& \{S_1' \to a_1 Z_1, \cdots, Z_{k-1} \to a_k \mid S \to a_1 \cdots a_k \in P, k \geq 0, \\
& \quad a_1 \in T \cup \{\lambda\}, a_2 \cdots a_k \in T, Z_1, \cdots Z_{k-1} \in N_Z\} \cup && (2) \\
& \{S_1' \to a_1(uA, 1) \mid S \to uA \in P, u = a_1 u', a_1 \in T\} \cup && (3) \\
& \{(uA, i) \to a_{i+1}(uA, i+1) \mid u = a_1 \cdots a_{|u|}, 1 \leq i < |u|\} \cup && (4) \\
& \{(uA, |u|) \to a_1(vB, 1) \mid A \to vB \in P, v = a_1 v'\} \cup && (5) \\
& \{(uA, |u|) \to a_1 Z_1, \cdots, Z_{k-1} \to a_k \mid A \to a_1 \cdots a_k \in P, \\
& \quad Z_1, \cdots Z_{k-1} \in N_Z\} \cup && (6) \\
& \{(uA, |u|) \to \alpha[u'Bv', 1) \mid A \to u'Bv' \in P, v' \neq \lambda, \\
& \quad \alpha = \begin{cases} c_1, & \text{if } u' = \lambda \\ a_1, & \text{if } u' = a_1 u'' \end{cases} \} \cup && (7) \\
& \{S_1' \to \alpha[uAv, 1) \mid S \to uAv \in P, v \neq \lambda, \ \alpha = \begin{cases} c_1, & \text{if } u = \lambda \\ a_1, & \text{if } u = a_1 u' \end{cases} \} \cup && (8)
\end{aligned}
$$

$$\{[uAv,i] \rightarrow \alpha[uAv,i+1) \mid 1 \le i < m(u,v), u = a_1 \cdots a_{|u|},$$
$$\alpha = \begin{cases} c_1, & \text{if } |u| < |v|, i \ge |u| \\ a_{i+1}, & \text{otherwise} \end{cases}\}\cup \tag{9}$$
$$\{[uAv,m(u,v)]' \rightarrow c_1[uAv]' \mid B \rightarrow uAv \in P\}\cup \tag{10}$$
$$\{[uAv] \rightarrow \alpha[u'Bv',1] \mid A \rightarrow u'Bv' \in P, \ \alpha = \begin{cases} c_1, & \text{if } u' = \lambda \\ a_1, & \text{if } u' = a_1u'' \end{cases}\}\cup \tag{11}$$
$$\{[uAv] \rightarrow a_1Z_1, \cdots, Z_{k-1} \rightarrow a_k \mid A \rightarrow a_1 \cdots a_k \in P,$$
$$Z_1, \cdots Z_{k-1} \in N_Z\}, \tag{12}$$
$$P_2 = \{S_2 \rightarrow c_2S_1'\}\cup \tag{13}$$
$$\{S_2' \rightarrow c_2(uA,1)'\}\cup \tag{14}$$
$$\{(uA,i)' \rightarrow c_2(uA,i+1)' \mid 1 \le i < |u|\}\cup \tag{15}$$
$$\{(uA,|u|)' \rightarrow c_2(uA,|u|)'\}\cup \tag{16}$$
$$\{(uA,|u|)' \rightarrow b[u'Bv',1]' \mid A \in N, v' \ne \lambda, v' = bv'', \ b \in T\}\cup \tag{17}$$
$$\{S_2' \rightarrow b[uAv,1]' \mid S \rightarrow uAv \in P, \ v \ne \lambda, v = bv', b \in T\}\cup \tag{18}$$
$$\{[uAv,i]' \rightarrow \beta[uAv,i+1]' \mid 1 \le i < m(u,v), v = b_1 \cdots b_{|v|},$$
$$\beta = \begin{cases} c_2, & \text{if } |v| < |u|, i \ge |v| \\ b_{i+1}, & \text{otherwise} \end{cases}\}\cup \tag{19}$$
$$\{[uAv,m(u,v)] \rightarrow c_2[uAv] \mid B \rightarrow uAv \in P\}\cup \tag{20}$$
$$\{[uAv]' \rightarrow \beta[u'Bv',1]' \mid A \rightarrow u'Bv' \in P,$$
$$\beta = \begin{cases} b_1, & \text{if } v' \ne \lambda, v' = b_1v'' \\ c_2, & \text{otherwise} \end{cases}\}\cup \tag{21}$$
$$\{[uAv]' \rightarrow c_2Y, Y \rightarrow c_2Y \mid B \rightarrow uAv \in P\}, \tag{22}$$
$$M = \{\lambda\#c_1S_2'\$c_2\#S_1'\}\cup \tag{23}$$
$$\{u[uAv,m(u,v)]\#\lambda\$c_1\#vc_2^k[uAv,m(u,v)]' \mid B \rightarrow uAv \in P,$$
$$k = \theta(|u|,|v|)\}\cup \tag{24}$$
$$\{[uAv,m(u,v)]v\#c_2^k[uAv,m(u,v)]'\$z\#a \mid B \rightarrow uAv \in P,$$
$$z \in \{c_1,c_2\}, a \in T, \ k = \theta(|u|,|v|), \}\cup \tag{25}$$
$$\{u\#c_1^k[uAv,m(u,v)]\$z\#[uAv,m(u,v)]' \mid$$
$$B \rightarrow uAv \in P, z \in \{c_1,c_2\}, \ k = \theta(|v|,|u|)\}\cup \tag{26}$$
$$\{\lambda\#c_1[uAv]'\$zc_2\#[uAv] \mid B \rightarrow uAv \in P, z \in \{c_1,c_2\}\}. \tag{27}$$

In order to simplify the proof, we denote $G_i = (N_i', T_i', S_i, P_i), i = 1,2$.

The idea of the construction is the following one. For every linear rule $A \rightarrow uBv \in P$, we introduce the nonterminal symbols $[uBv], [uBv]', [uBv,i], [uBv,i]', 1 \le i \le m(u,v)$. Then we try to generate u in P_1 and v in P_2 in a regular manner. When $|u| < |v|$, then $uc_1^{|v|-|u|}$ is generated in P_1, and when $|v| < |u|$, then $vc_2^{|u|-|v|}$ is generated in P_2, where c_1, c_2 are two terminal symbols different from the symbols from T. Then, by using some splicing rules we remove c_1^k from G_1 (if $k > 0$), and we put together substrings u and v such that we will obtain in G_1 the substring $u[uAv,m(u,v)]v$. Then we continue until a terminal string is obtained.

Observation 1. We notice that, in order to apply the splicing rules and thus to obtain a terminal string, it is necessary that the nonterminals which appear in the two components of the grammar are paired, i.e. at every step of a derivation, the two nonterminals are of the form

$$([uAv,i], [uAv,i]'), \text{ or } ([uAv], [uAv]'),$$

where $1 \le i \le m(u,v)$ and there is $B \rightarrow uAv$ a rule in P.

There is only one exception from such a derivation, namely when we apply rules of the form (3), (4), (5) in G_1 (which means rules of the form $S \to u_1 A_1, A_1 \to u_2 A_2$, $\cdots$, $A_{k-1} \to u_k A_k$ in G), followed by terminal rules of the form (6) (i.e. a rule of the form $A_k \to u_{k+1}, u_{k+1} \in T$ in G). Then the string $u_1 \cdots u_{k+1} \in L(G)$ is obtained in $L_1(\Gamma)$.

Let us examine a derivation in Γ. The derivation must start with:

$$(S_1, S_2) \overset{(1)+(13)}{\Longrightarrow} (c_1 S_2', c_2 S_1') \overset{(23)}{\vdash} (S_1', c_2 c_1 S_2').$$

Then it will continue with

a) $(S_1', S_2') \overset{(8)+(18)}{\Longrightarrow^*} (\alpha[uAv, 1], c_2 c_1 b_1[u'A'v', 1])$, where $v' \neq \lambda, v' = b_1 v''$, $b_1 \in T$.

   According to Observation 1, we must have $u = u', A = A', v = v'$. Then the derivation will continue with

$$(\alpha[uAv, 1], c_2 c_1 b_1[uAv, 1]) \overset{(9)+(19)}{\Longrightarrow^*} uc_1^k[uAv, m(u, v)], c_2 c_1 v c_2^p[uAv, m(u, v)]',$$

$$k = \delta(|v|, |u|), p = \delta(|u|, |v|).$$

b) We apply k times, $k \geq 1$, rules of the form (3), (4) and (5) in G_1 and rules of the similar form in G_2, i.e. (14), (15) and (16). Because the nonterminals of the form (uA, i) do not appear in the strings of M, no splicing rule can be applied. Then, if we apply rules of the forms (6) and (16) in G_1 and G_2 respectively, then we obtain a terminal string in G_1 which is also in $L(G)$. If we apply rules of the form (7) and (17), then we obtain

$$(\gamma \alpha[uAv, 1], c_2 c_1 b_1[uAv, 1]')\alpha \in T \cup \{c_1\}, v \neq \lambda, v = b_1 v', \gamma \in T^*.$$

In the general case, we distinguish the following cases:

(i) $(S_1, S_2) \overset{*}{\Longrightarrow} (\gamma u[uAv, m(u, v)]\delta, \mu c_1 v[uAv, m(u, v)]')$, where $\gamma, \delta \in T^*, \delta \neq \lambda, \mu c_1 \in \{c_1, c_2\}^+, |u| = |v|$. Then the derivation will continue with

$$(\gamma u[uAv, m(u, v)]\delta, \mu c_1 v[uAv, m(u, v)]')$$

$$\overset{(24)}{\vdash} (\gamma u[uAv, m(u, v)]v[uAv, m(u, v)]', \mu c_1 \delta)$$

$$\overset{(25)}{\vdash} (\gamma u[uAv, m(u, v)]v\delta, \mu c_1[uAv, m(u, v)]')$$

$$\overset{(26)}{\vdash} (\gamma u[uAv, m(u, v)]', \mu c_1[uAv, m(u, v)]v\delta)$$

$$\overset{(10)+(20)}{\Longrightarrow} (\gamma u c_1[uAv]', \mu c_1 c_2[uAv]v\delta)$$

$$\overset{(27)}{\vdash} (\gamma u[uAv]v\delta, \mu c_1 c_2 c_1[uAv]').$$

(ii) $(S_1, S_2) \overset{*}{\Longrightarrow} (\gamma u c_1^k[uAv, m(u, v)]\delta, \mu c_1 v[uAv, m(u, v)]')$, where $\gamma, \delta \in T^*, \delta \neq \lambda, \mu c_1 \in \{c_1, c_2\}^+, |u| < |v|, k = |v| - |u|$. In this case the derivation will continue with

$$\overset{(24)}{\vdash} (\gamma u c_1^k[uAv, m(u, v)]v[uAv, m(u, v)]', \mu c_1 \delta)$$

$$\overset{(25)}{\vdash} (\gamma u c_1^k[uAv, m(u, v)]v\delta, \mu c_1[uAv, m(u, v)]')$$

$$\overset{(26)}{\vdash} \quad (\gamma u[uAv, m(u,v)]', \mu c_1 c_1^k[uAv, m(u,v)]v\delta)$$

$$\overset{(10)+(20)}{\Longrightarrow} \quad (\gamma u c_1[uAv]', \mu c_1 c_1^k c_2[uAv]v\delta)$$

$$\overset{(27)}{\vdash} \quad (\gamma u[uAv]v\delta, \mu c_1 c_1^k c_2 c_1[uAv]').$$

(iii) $(S_1, S_2) \overset{*}{\Longrightarrow} (\gamma u[uAv, m(u,v)]\delta, \mu c_1 v c_2^k[uAv, m(u,v)]')$, where $\gamma\delta \in T^*, \delta \neq \lambda, \mu c_1 \in \{c_1, c_2\}^+, |u| > |v|, k = |u| - |v|$. Then we obtain

(iii') $v \neq \lambda$;

$$(\gamma u[uAv, m(u,v)]\delta, \mu c_1 v c_2^k[uAv, m(u,v)]')$$

$$\overset{(24)}{\vdash} \quad (\gamma u[uAv, m(u,v)]v c_2^k[uAv, m(u,v)]', \mu c_1 \delta)$$

$$\overset{(25)}{\vdash} \quad (\gamma u[uAv, m(u,v)]v\delta, \mu c_1 c_2^k[uAv, m(u,v)]')$$

$$\overset{(26)}{\vdash} \quad (\gamma u[uAv, m(u,v)]', \mu c_1 c_2^k[uAv, m(u,v)]v\delta)$$

$$\overset{(10)+(20)}{\Longrightarrow} \quad (\gamma u c_1[uAv]', \mu c_1 c_2^k c_2[uAv]v\delta)$$

$$\overset{(27)}{\vdash} \quad (\gamma u[uAv]v\delta, \mu c_1 c_2^{k+1} c_1[uAv]').$$

(iii'') $v = \lambda$;

$$(\gamma u[uA, |u|]\delta, \mu c_1 c_2^{|u|}[uA, |u|]')$$

$$\overset{(26)}{\vdash} \quad (\gamma u[uA, |u|]', \mu c_1 c_2^{|u|}[uA, |u|]\delta)$$

$$\overset{(10)+(20)}{\Longrightarrow} \quad (\gamma u c_1[uA]', \mu c_1 c_2^{|u|} c_2[uA]\delta)$$

$$\overset{(27)}{\vdash} \quad (\gamma u[uA]\delta, \mu c_1 c_2^{|u|+1} c_1[uA]').$$

At the end of the derivation in cases (i), (ii), (iii'), (iii'') we can apply rules of forms (11) and (21) in G_1 and G_2 respectively. Namely, for $\mu' c_1 \in \{c_1, c_2\}^+$, we have

$$(\gamma u[uAv]v\delta, \mu' c_1[uAv]') \overset{(11)+(21)}{\Longrightarrow} (\gamma u a[u'B'v', 1]v\delta, \ \mu' c_1 b[u''B''v'', 1]).$$

According to Observation 1, it is necessary that $u' = u'', B' = B'', v' = v''$. Then the derivation continues until we obtain

$$(\gamma u u' c_1^k[u'B'v', m(u', v')]v\delta, \mu' c_1 v' c_2^p[u'B'v', m(u', v')]'),$$

for $k = \delta(|v|, |u|), p = \delta(|u|, |v|)$, and the process will be repeated in one of cases (i), (ii), (iii'), (iii'').

If at the end of the derivation in cases (i), (ii), (iii'), (iii'') we apply the rules (12) and (21), then we obtain a terminal string.

From these explanations we obtain that $L_1(\Gamma) = L_t(\Gamma) \subseteq L$. On the other hand, it is easy to deduce from the construction that $L \subseteq L_1(\Gamma) = L_t(\Gamma)$. Thus, $L = L_1(\Gamma) = L_t(\Gamma)$ and the theorem is proved. $\qquad\square$

Theorem 2. $CF \subseteq YSGS_3(REG), Y \in \{I, T\}$.

Proof. Let $L \subseteq T^*$ be a language generated by the context–free grammar $G = (N, T, S, P)$ in Greibach normal form. This means that all the rules from P are of the form $A \to ax$ or of the form $A \to a, a \in T, x \in (N \cup T)^*$.

We construct a SGS with three regular components as follows:

$$\Gamma = (N', T', (S_1, P_1), (S_2, P_2), (S_3, P_3), M),$$

where

$$
\begin{aligned}
N' = \ & \{S_1, S_2, S_3, N_2, N_3\} \cup \\
& \{[AaX_1 \cdots X_m, X_1 \cdots X_i] \mid A \to aX_1 \cdots X_m \in P, 1 \le i \le m, \\
& \quad m \ge 0, a \in T, X_1, \cdots, X_m \in N \cup T\} \cup \\
& \{[X], [X]' \mid X \in N \cup T\} \cup \\
& \{(AaX_1 \cdots X_m, X_1 \cdots X_i) \mid A \to aX_1 \cdots X_m \in P, \ m \ge 0, a \in T, \\
& \quad X_1, \cdots, X_m \in N \cup T\} \cup \\
& \{[AaX_1 \cdots X_m, X_1 \cdots X_i]' \mid A \to aX_1 \cdots X_m \in P, \ m \ge 0, a \in T, \\
& \quad X_1, \cdots, X_m \in N \cup T\},
\end{aligned}
$$

$$T' = T \cup N \cup \{z_0, d, e\}, z_0, d, e \notin N \cup T,$$

$$
\begin{aligned}
P_1 = \ & \{S_1 \to a \mid S \to a \in P, a \in T\} \cup & (1) \\
& \{S_1 \to a[SaX_1 \cdots X_m, X_1 \cdots X_m] \mid S \to aX_1 \cdots X_m \in P, \ m \ge 1, \\
& \quad a \in T, X_1, \cdots, X_m \in N \cup T\} \cup & (2) \\
& \{[AaX_1 \cdots X_m, X_1 \cdots X_i] \to X_i[AaX_1 \cdots X_m, X_1 \cdots X_{i-1}] \mid \\
& \quad 2 \le i \le m\} \cup & (3) \\
& \{[AaX_1 \cdots X_m, X_1] \to X_1(AaX_1 \cdots X_m, X_1 \cdots X_m) \mid \\
& \quad A \to aX_1 \cdots X_m \in P, m \ge 1, a \in T, X_1, \cdots, X_m \in N \cup T\} \cup & (4) \\
& \{[X] \to b[XbY_1 \cdots Y_t, Y_1 \cdots Y_t] \mid X \to bY_1 \cdots Y_t \in P, \ t \ge 0, b \in T, \\
& \quad Y_1, \cdots, Y_t \in N \cup T\} \cup & (5) \\
& \{[X] \to X[YbY_1 \cdots Y_t, Y_1 \cdots Y_t]' \mid Y \to bY_1 \cdots Y_t \in P, \ t \ge 0, \\
& \quad b, X \in T, Y_1, \cdots, Y_t \in N \cup T\} \cup & (6) \\
& \{[X] \to X[Y]' \mid X, Y \in T\} \cup & (7) \\
& \{N_2 \to dN_2\} \cup & (8) \\
& \{N_3 \to dN_3\} \cup & (9) \\
& \{[Xb, \lambda] \to d[YcZ_1 \cdots Z_l, Z_1 \cdots Z_l]' \mid Y \to cZ_1 \cdots Z_l \in P, \\
& \quad l \ge 0, c \in T, Z_1, \cdots, Z_l \in N \cup T\} \cup & (10) \\
& \{[Xb, \lambda] \to d[Y]' \mid X \to b \in P, Y \in T\}, & (11) \\
P_2 = \ & \{S_2 \to z_0 N_2\} \cup & (12) \\
& \{N_2 \to dN_2\} \cup & (13) \\
& \{(AaX_1 \cdots X_m, X_1 \cdots X_m) \to d[X_1]' \mid A \to aX_1 \cdots X_m \in P, \\
& \quad m \ge 1, a \in T, X_1, \cdots, X_m \in N \cup T, m \ge 1\} \cup & (14) \\
& \{[Ab, \lambda] \to [Y] \mid A \to b \in P, Y \in N \cup T\} \cup & (15) \\
& \{N_3 \to dN_3\}, & (16) \\
P_3 = \ & \{S_3 \to eN_3\} \cup & (17) \\
& \{N_2 \to dN_2\} \cup & (18) \\
& \{N_3 \to dN_3\} \cup & (19) \\
& \{[AaX_1 \cdots X_m, X_1 \cdots X_m]' \to a[AaX_1 \cdots X_m, X_1 \cdots X_m] \mid \\
& \quad A \to aX_1 \cdots X_m \in P, m \ge 0, a \in T, X_1, \cdots, X_m \in N \cup T\} \cup & (20) \\
& \{[Y]' \to e[Y] \mid Y \in T\}, & (21)
\end{aligned}
$$

$$M = \{a\#d^k[AbX_1\cdots X_m, X_1\cdots X_m]'\$\lambda\#N_2 \mid A \to bX_1\cdots X_m \in P,$$
$$m \geq 0, a, b \in T, k = 0,1\}\cup \tag{22}$$
$$\{\lambda\#dN_2\$a\#[AaX_1\cdots X_m, X_1\cdots X_m] \mid A \to aX_1\cdots X_m \in P,$$
$$m \geq 0, a \in T\}\cup \tag{23}$$
$$\{\alpha\#d^k N_2\$e\#N_3 \mid \alpha \in \{z_0\}\cup N \cup T,$$
$$2 \leq k \leq \max\{|\alpha| - 1 \mid A \to \alpha \in P\} + 2\}\cup \tag{24}$$
$$\{a\#X_m\cdots X_1(AaX_1\cdots X_m, X_1\cdots X_m)\$\beta\#N_2 \mid A \to aX_1\cdots X_m$$
$$\in P, m \geq 1, \beta \in \{z_0\}\cup N \cup T\}\cup \tag{25}$$
$$\{\lambda\#Xd^k[X]'\$\lambda\#N_3 \mid X \in N \cup T, k = 1,2\}\cup \tag{26}$$
$$\{a\#d^2 N_2\$e\#[X] \mid X \in N \cup T, a \in T\}\cup \tag{27}$$
$$\{\lambda\#Xd^k[XbY_1\cdots Y_t, Y_1\cdots Y_t]'\$e\#N_3 \mid X \to bY_1\cdots Y_t \in P,$$
$$t \geq 0, b \in T, k = 1,2\}\cup \tag{28}$$
$$\{a\#dN_3\$e\#[XbY_1\cdots Y_t, Y_1\cdots Y_t] \mid X \to bY_1\cdots Y_t \in P,$$
$$t \geq 0, b \in T\}\cup \tag{29}$$
$$\{a\#[Y]'\$\lambda\#N_2 \mid a, Y \in T\}\cup \tag{30}$$
$$\{\beta\#d^k N_3\$e\alpha\#N_2 \mid \beta \in \{z_0\}\cup N \cup T, k \geq 0, \alpha = d^m,$$
$$0 \leq m \leq \max\{|\alpha| \mid A \to a\alpha \in P, a \in T\} + 4\}\cup \tag{31}$$
$$\{a\#dN_3\$\lambda\#[Y] \mid a, Y \in T\}\cup \tag{32}$$
$$\{z_0\#[SaX_1\cdots X_m, X_1\cdots X_m]'\$\lambda\#N_3 \mid S \to aX_1\cdots X_m \in P\}\cup \tag{33}$$
$$\{a\#[AbY_1\cdots Y_t, Y_1\cdots Y_t]'\$z_0 dN_2\#\lambda \mid A \to bY_1\cdots Y_t \in P, t \geq 0,$$
$$a, b \in T\}\cup \tag{34}$$
$$\{a\#[Y]'\$z_0 dN_2\#\lambda \mid a, Y \in T\}\cup \tag{35}$$
$$\{z_0\#d^m N_2\$e\#N_3 \mid 1 \leq m \leq \max\{|\alpha| - 1 \mid A \to \alpha \in P\}\}. \tag{36}$$

Let us examine a derivation in Γ. We have the following cases:

(i) $(S_1, S_2, S_3) \Longrightarrow (a, z_0 N_2, eN_3)$ and the derivation is stopped, $a \in L_\alpha(\Gamma), \alpha \in \{1, t\}$.

(ii)

$$(S_1, S_2, S_3) \Longrightarrow ([SaX_1\cdots X_m, X_1\cdots X_m], z_0 N_2, eN_3)(*)$$
$$\overset{m}{\Longrightarrow} (aX_m\cdots X_1(SaX_1\cdots X_m, X_1\cdots X_m), z_0 d^m N_2, e^{m+1}N_3)$$
$$\overset{(36)}{\vdash} (aX_m\cdots X_1(SaX_1\cdots X_m, X_1\cdots X_m), z_0 N_3, e^{m+1}d^m N_2)$$
$$\overset{(25)}{\vdash} (aN_2, z_0 N_3, e^{m+1}d^m X_m\cdots X_1(SaX_1\cdots X_m, X_1\cdots X_m))$$

and now the derivation is blocked. If, instead of rule (25) we apply the splicing rule (31) we obtain

$$\overset{(31)}{\vdash} (aX_m\cdots X_1(SaX_1\cdots X_m, X_1\cdots X_m), z_0 N_2, e^{m+1}d^m N_3)$$
$$\overset{(25)}{\vdash} (aN_2, X_m\cdots X_1 (SaX_1\cdots X_m, X_1\cdots X_m), e^{m+1}d^m N_3)$$
$$\Longrightarrow (adN_2, z_0 X_m\cdots X_1 d[X_1]', \cdots eN_3) \quad (**)$$
$$\overset{(26)}{\vdash} (adN_2, z_0 X_m\cdots X_2 N_3, \cdots eX_1 d[X_1]')$$
$$\Longrightarrow (ad^2 N_2, z_0 X_m\cdots X_2 dN_3, \cdots eX_1 de[X_1])$$
$$\overset{(27)}{\vdash} (a[X_1], z_0 X_m\cdots X_2 dN_3, \cdots eX_1 ded^2 N_2])$$

$$\overset{(31)}{\vdash} \quad (a[X_1], z_0X_m \cdots X_2N_2, \cdots d^3N_3]). \qquad (***)$$

In order to simplify the proof, we denote $G_i = (N', T', S_i, P_i), i = 1, 2, 3$.

The point (**) of the above derivation is characterized by the following fact. We started to simulate the rule $S \to aX_1 \cdots X_m \in P, m \geq 1$. The symbol a, followed by some nonterminal, is generated in G_1. In G_2 we keep the string $X_1 \cdots X_m$ in inverse order. G_2 works like a stack. Then, the symbol of the top of the stack, i.e. X_1, is processed. If $X_1 \in N$, then we have the case (iii). Otherwise, we have the other two cases. We notice that, after the application the splicing rule (26) in point (**), X_1 was removed from the stack, i.e. X_1 does not appear in G_2 from now on.

We begin in this way in Γ a simulation of a leftmost derivation in G.

(iii) We continue the derivation in point (***) in the following way:

$$\overset{(5)+(13)+(19)}{\Longrightarrow} (ab[X_1bY_1 \cdots Y_t, Y_1 \cdots Y_t], z_0X_m \cdots X_2dN_2, \cdots eN_3),$$

and, if $t \geq 1$, the derivation will continue as in the point (*). If $t = 0$, then we will continue by:

$$\overset{(5)+(13)+(19)}{\Longrightarrow} \quad (ab[X_1b, \lambda], z_0X_m \cdots X_2dN_2, \cdots eN_3) \qquad (a)$$

$$\overset{(10)+(13)+(19)}{\Longrightarrow} \quad (abd[YcZ_1 \cdots Z_l, Z_1 \cdots Z_l]', \ z_0X_m \cdots X_2dN_2, \cdots eN_3) \quad (b)$$

$$\overset{(22)}{\vdash} \quad (abN_2, z_0X_m \cdots X_2d^2 \ [YcZ_1 \cdots Z_l, Z_1 \cdots Z_l]', \cdots eN_3). \quad (****)$$

Now, the derivation can continue if and only if $X_2 = Y$. Thus:

$$\overset{(28)}{\vdash} \quad (abN_2, z_0X_m \cdots X_3N_3, \ \cdots ed^2[YcZ_1 \cdots Z_l, Z_1 \cdots Z_l]')$$

$$\overset{(8)+(16)+(20)}{\Longrightarrow} \quad (abdN_2, z_0X_m \cdots X_3dN_3, \ \cdots ed^2c[YcZ_1 \cdots Z_l, Z_1 \cdots Z_l])$$

$$\overset{(23)}{\vdash} \quad (abc[YcZ_1 \cdots Z_l, Z_1 \cdots Z_l], \ z_0X_m \cdots X_3dN_3, \cdots ed^3N_2)$$

$$\overset{(31)}{\vdash} \quad (abc[YcZ_1 \cdots Z_l, Z_1 \cdots Z_l], \ z_0X_m \cdots X_3N_2, \cdots ed^4N_3).$$

The derivation will continue as in point (*).

(iv) Another way to continue the derivation in point (***) is, for $X_1 \in T$:

$$\overset{(6)+(13)+(19)}{\Longrightarrow} (aX_1[YbY_1 \cdots Y_t, Y_1 \cdots Y_t]', \ z_0X_m \cdots X_2dN_2, \cdots eN_3) \quad (b')$$

$$\overset{(22)}{\vdash} \quad (aX_1N_2, z_0X_m \cdots X_2d \ [YbY_1 \cdots Y_t, Y_1 \cdots Y_t]', \cdots eN_3)$$

and now we have a case similar to the one in (****).

(v) For $X_1 \in T$, we apply in G_1, in point (***), the rule $[X_1] \to [Y]', Y \in T$. We obtain:

$$\overset{(7)+(13)+(19)}{\Longrightarrow} (aX_1[Y]', z_0X_m \cdots X_2dN_2, \cdots eN_3) \quad (c)$$

$$\overset{(30)}{\vdash} \quad (aXN_2, z_0X_m \cdots X_2d[Y]', \cdots eN_3).$$

The derivation can continue if and only if $X_2 = Y$. This is the case when both X_1, X_2 are terminal symbols and they must appear in G_1 and must be removed from G_2 (the stack). Thus, we have:

$$
\begin{aligned}
&\overset{(26)}{\vdash} && (aX_1N_2, z_0X_m \cdots X_3N_3, \cdots X_2d[X_2]') \\
&\overset{(8)+(16)+(21)}{\Longrightarrow} && (aX_1dN_2, z_0X_m \cdots X_3dN_3, \cdots X_2de[X_2]) \\
&\overset{(32)}{\vdash} && (aX_1[X_2], z_0X_m \cdots X_3dN_3, \cdots \cdots eX_2dedN_2]) \\
&\overset{(31)}{\vdash} && (aX_1[X_2], z_0X_m \cdots X_3N_2, \cdots ed^2N_3]),
\end{aligned}
$$

and now the derivation continues as in case (***).

The examined derivation can be successfully stopped in the points (a), (b), (b') or (c), when the splicing rules (33) (for the first case), (34) (for the follwing two cases) and (35) (for the last case) are applied, respectively. The rules (33), (34), (35) can be applied only when in G_2 there is the string z_0dN_2. This means that 'the stack is empty'. Then, the nonterminal which appears on the right end of the string in G_1 is removed. The terminal string from G_1 is now in $L_1(\Gamma)$ and also in $L_t(\Gamma)$.

Now, if we follow the examined derivation in Γ, $(S_1, S_2, S_3) \overset{*}{\Longrightarrow} (w, \alpha, \beta), w \in T^*$, we can observe that we have simulated in Γ a leftmost derivation for w in G. Hence, $w \in L(G)$ and thus $L_1(\Gamma) = L_t(\Gamma) \subseteq L(G)$. On the other hand, from the construction of Γ it follows that $L(G) \subseteq L_1(\Gamma) = L_t(\Gamma)$. The theorem is proved. □

Theorem 3. $RE = YSGS_4(RL), Y \in \{I, T\}$.

Proof. Let $L \subseteq T^*$ be a recursively enumerable language generated by a phrase–structure grammar $G = (\{S, A, B, C\}, T, S, P)$ in Geffert normal form. This means that P contains rules of the from $S \to x$ and a single extra rule $ABC \to \lambda$.

We construct a SGS with four right linear components as follows:

$$\Gamma = (N', T', (S_1, P_1), (S_2, P_2), (S_3, P_3), (S_4, P_4), M),$$

where

$$
\begin{aligned}
N' = \;& \{S_1, S_2, S_3, S_4, N_2, N_3\} \cup \\
& \{[S \to [Y_1 \cdots Y_t, \alpha], [S \to Y_1 \cdots Y_t, \alpha]', \mid S \to Y_1 \cdots Y_t \in P, t \geq 1, \\
& \alpha \in \{\mu_1, \mu_2, \nu, \tau, \epsilon\} \cup \\
& \{[Y, \alpha], [Y, \alpha]' \mid Y \in T \cup \{A, B, C\}, \alpha \in \{\mu_1, \mu_2, \nu, \tau, \epsilon\}, \\[4pt]
T' = \;& T \cup \{A, B, C\} \cup \{z_0, z_1, e, f\}, z_0, z_1, e, f \notin N \cup T,
\end{aligned}
$$

$$
\begin{aligned}
P_1 = \;& \{S_1 \to z_1N_2, N_2 \to N_2, N_3 \to N_3, S_4 \to S_4\} \cup && (1) \\
& \{[Y, \alpha]' \to [Y, \alpha] \mid Y \in T, \alpha \in \{\nu, \tau\}\} \cup && (2) \\
& \{[Y, \mu_1]' \to [Y, \mu_1] \mid Y \in \{A, B, C\}\}, && (3) \\
P_2 = \;& \{S_2 \to z_0X_m \cdots X_1[S \to Y_1 \cdots Y_t, \mu_1]' \mid S \to X_1 \cdots X_m, \\
& \quad S \to Y_1 \cdots Y_t \in P\} \cup && (4) \\
& \{S_2 \to z_0X_m \cdots X_1[A, \mu_1]' \mid S \to X_1 \cdots X_m \in P\} \cup && (5) \\
& \{S_2 \to z_0X_m \cdots X_1[Y, \mu_2]' \mid S \to X_1 \cdots X_m \in P, Y \in T\} \cup && (6) \\
& \{N_2 \to N_2, N_3 \to N_3\} \cup && (7) \\
& \{[S \to Y_1 \cdots Y_t, \alpha] \to Y_t \cdots Y_1[S \to Z_1 \cdots Z_l, \alpha]' \mid S \to Y_1 \cdots Y_t,
\end{aligned}
$$

$$S \to Z_1 \cdots Z_l \in P, \ \alpha \in \{\nu, \tau, \mu_1\}\} \cup \tag{8}$$

$$\{[S \to Y_1 \cdots Y_t, \alpha] \to Y_t \cdots Y_1[Y, \beta]' \mid S \to Y_1 \cdots Y_t \in P, Y \in T \cup$$

$$\{A, B, C\}, \alpha \in \{\nu, \tau, \mu_1\}, \ \beta = \begin{cases} \mu_1, & \text{if } \alpha = \mu_1, Y \in \{A, B, C\} \\ \tau, & \text{if } \alpha = \tau, Y \in T \\ \nu, & \text{if } \alpha = \tau, Y = A \\ \nu, & \text{if } \alpha = \nu, Y \in \{A, B, C\} \\ \epsilon, & \text{otherwise} \end{cases} \} \cup \tag{9}$$

$$\{[Y, \alpha] \to [S \to X_1 \cdots X_m, \alpha]' \mid Y \in T \cup \{A, B, C\},$$
$$S \to X_1 \cdots X_m \in P, \alpha \in \{\mu_1, \nu, \tau\}\} \cup \tag{10}$$

$$\{[Y, \alpha] \to [Z, \beta]' \mid Y, Z \in T \cup \{A, B, C\}, \ \alpha \in \{\mu_1, \mu_2, \nu, \tau\},$$

$$\beta = \begin{cases} \mu_1, & \text{if } \alpha = \mu_1, Z \in \{A, B, C\} \\ \mu_2, & \text{if } \alpha = \mu_1, Z \in T \\ \tau, & \text{if } \alpha = \tau, Z \in T \\ \nu, & \text{if } \alpha = \tau, Z = A \\ \nu, & \text{if } \alpha = \nu, Z \in \{A, B, C\} \\ \epsilon, & \text{otherwise} \end{cases} \}, \tag{11}$$

$$P_3 = \{S_3 \to eN_3, N_3 \to eN_3\} \cup \tag{12}$$
$$\{[S \to Y_1 \cdots Y_t, \alpha]' \to e[S \to Y_1 \cdots Y_t, \alpha] \mid S \to Y_1 \cdots Y_t \in P,$$
$$\alpha \in \{\nu, \tau, \mu_1\}\} \cup \tag{13}$$
$$\{[C, \nu]' \to e[C, \tau]\}, \tag{14}$$

$$P_4 = \{S_4 \to fS_4\} \cup \tag{15}$$
$$\{[C, \mu_1]' \to f[C, \mu_1]\} \cup \tag{16}$$
$$\{[a, \mu_2]' \to [a, \tau] \mid a \in T\} \cup \tag{17}$$
$$\{[C, \nu]' \to f[C, \nu]\}, \tag{18}$$

$$M = \{\lambda \# S[S \to Y_1 \cdots Y_t, \alpha]' \$e \# N_3 \mid S \to Y_1 \cdots Y_t \in P,$$
$$\alpha \in \{\tau, \nu, \mu_1\}\} \cup \tag{19}$$
$$\{\lambda \# N_3 \$e \# [S \to Y_1 \cdots Y_t, \alpha] \mid S \to Y_1 \cdots Y_t \in P, \alpha \in \{\tau, \nu, \mu_1\}\} \cup \tag{20}$$
$$\{\lambda \# N_2 \$\lambda \# Y[Y, \alpha]' \mid Y \in T \cup \{A, B, C\}, \ \alpha \in \{\tau, \nu, \mu_1, \mu_2\}\} \cup \tag{21}$$
$$\{Y\#[Y, \alpha] \$\lambda \# N_2 \mid \text{either } Y \in T, \alpha \in \{\tau, \nu\},$$
$$\text{or } Y \in \{A, B\}, \alpha = \mu_1\} \cup \tag{22}$$
$$\{a\#ABC[C, \nu]'\$e\#N_3 \mid a \in T\} \cup \tag{23}$$
$$\{Z\#ABC[C, \nu]'\$f\#S_4 \mid Z \in \{A, B, C\}\} \cup \tag{24}$$
$$\{\lambda \# N_2 \$fABC\#[C, \nu]\} \cup \tag{25}$$
$$\{\lambda \# S_4 \$fABC\#N_2\} \cup \tag{26}$$
$$\{\lambda \# N_2 \$e\#[C, \tau]\} \cup \tag{27}$$
$$\{\lambda \# N_3 \$e\#N_2\} \cup \tag{28}$$
$$\{\lambda \# N_2 \$z_0[S \to Y_1 \cdots Y_t, \tau]'\#\lambda \mid S \to Y_1 \cdots Y_t \in P\} \cup \tag{29}$$
$$\{\lambda \# N_2 \$z_0[Y, \tau]'\#\lambda \mid Y \in T\} \cup \tag{30}$$
$$\{Z\#ABC[C, \mu_1]'\$f\#S_4 \mid Z \in \{A, B, C, z_1\}\} \cup \tag{31}$$
$$\{\lambda \# N_2 \$fABC\#[C, \mu_1]\} \cup \tag{32}$$
$$\{\lambda \# z_1 a[a, \mu_2]'\$f\#S_4 \mid a \in T\}\} \cup \tag{33}$$
$$\{\lambda \# N_2 \$fz_1 a\#[a, \tau] \mid a \in T\} \cup \tag{34}$$
$$\{\lambda \# S_4 \$fz_1\#aN_2 \mid a \in T\}. \tag{35}$$

Let us denote $G_i = (N', T', S_i, P_i), i = 1, 2, 3, 4$.

The idea of this construction is the following. First, we notice that for every $w \in L(G)$ there is a derivation which has two parts. In the first part we use only rules of the form $S \to x$. In the last part we use only the rule $ABC \to \lambda$, as long as it is necessary. Moreover, we can consider the first part of this derivation as a leftmost derivation, because we use only context-free rules. Let

$$S \Longrightarrow^* \gamma \Longrightarrow^* w, \gamma \in (T \cup \{A, B, C\})^*, w \in T^*,$$

be a derivation in G such that the derivation $S \Longrightarrow^* \gamma$ is a leftmost derivation, where only rules $S \rightarrow x$ were applied, and in the derivation $\gamma \Longrightarrow^* w$ only rule $ABC \rightarrow \lambda$ is applied.

Now, we try to simulate in Γ the mentioned leftmost derivation with the help of a stack. In the first component of Γ we obtain the terminal strings (which are prefixes of the terminal strings from $L(G)$ when the derivation is succesful), followed by a string over $\{A, B, C\}$. G_2 plays the role of the stack, G_3 and G_4 are used for removing some parasitic strings. Whenever a symbol $X \in T \cup \{A, B, C\}$ is obtained in the top of the stack (i.e. in G_2), it is transferred to the first component of the system, by using a splicing rule. In order to distinguish whether or not $X \in T$ or $X \in \{A, B, C\}$, all nonterminals from Γ are of the form $[S \rightarrow Y_1 \cdots Y_t, \alpha], [S \rightarrow Y_1 \cdots Y_t, \alpha]', [Y, \alpha], [Y, \alpha]'$, where $S \rightarrow Y_1 \cdots Y_t \in P, \alpha \in \{\mu_1, \mu_2, \nu, \tau, \epsilon\}, Y \in T \cup \{A, B, C\}$. ($\nu$ stands for a nonterminal symbol, τ indicates for a terminal symbol, and ϵ indicates for error; the significance of μ_1, μ_2 will be explained later.) If $\alpha = \tau$ (ν), this means that the last transferred symbol in G_1 was a terminal (nonterminal, respectively) symbol. When $\alpha = \nu$ and the last four symbols from G_1 are $ZABC, Z \in \{A, B, C\}$, the substring ABC is transferred from G_1 to G_4 with the help of a splicing rule, and α remains unchanged. When the last symbols from G_1 are of the form $aABC, a \in T$, then ABC is transferred to G_3 and α becomes τ. There is a problem when $\gamma = \gamma_1 \gamma_2$, where $\gamma_1 \in \{A, B, C\}^+$. Then no terminal symbol is in G_1 before γ_1, and we cannot distinguish between the two cases mentioned above.

Then, in order to solve this problem, at the first step of any derivation, the symbol $z_1 \notin T$ is introduced in G_1 and, moreover, initially $\alpha = \mu_1$. As long as a symbol from $\{A, B, C\}$ is transferred from G_2 to G_1, α remains unchanged. When a terminal symbol is obtained in the top of the stack (i.e. in G_2), α becomes μ_2. In this situation, we verify that no symbol A, B or C is now in G_1, with the help of the splicing rule (33): $\lambda \# z_1 a[a, \mu_2]' \$ f \# S_4, a \in T$. Then α becomes τ.

In the other cases, unmentioned above, α becomes ϵ, showing an error case. For example, if α is ν (which means that the last generated symbol in G_1 is A, B or C) and then a terminal string (from T) is in the top of the stack, this string should be transferred to G_1 and thus a parasitic string, over $\{A, B, C\}$, cannot be removed from the string generated in G_1 until this moment. Then the derivation is blocked.

Let us examine in some detail a derivation in Γ.

The first step of any derivation can be:

a)

$$(S_1, S_2, S_3, S_4) \Longrightarrow (z_1 N_2, z_0 X_m \cdots X_1[Y, \mu_2]', eN_3, fS_4)$$

$$\overset{(21)}{\vdash} \quad (z_1 Y[Y, \mu_2]', z_0 X_m \cdots X_2 N_2, \ eN_3, fS_4)$$

$$\overset{(33)}{\vdash} \quad (S_4, z_0 X_m \cdots X_2 N_2, eN_3, fz_1 Y[Y, \mu_2]')$$

$$\Longrightarrow (S_4, z_0 X_m \cdots X_2 N_2, eeN_3, fz_1 Y[Y, \tau])$$

$$\overset{(34)}{\vdash} \quad (S_4, z_0 X_m \cdots X_2[Y, \tau], eeN_3, \ fz_1 Y N_2)$$

$$\overset{(35)}{\vdash} \ (YN_2, z_0X_m \cdots X_2[Y,\tau], eeN_3, \ fz_1S_4).$$

b)

$$(S_1, S_2, S_3, S_4) \Longrightarrow (z_1N_2, z_0X_m \cdots X_1[S \to Y_1 \ \cdots Y_t, \mu_1]', eN_3, fS_4)$$

$$\overset{(19)}{\vdash} \ (z_1N_2, z_0X_m \cdots X_2N_3, \ eS[S \to Y_1 \cdots Y_t, \mu_1]', fS_4)$$

$$\Longrightarrow (z_1N_2, z_0X_m \cdots X_2N_3, eSe[S \to Y_1 \cdots Y_t, \mu_1], f^2S_4)$$

$$\overset{(20)}{\vdash} \ (z_1N_2, z_0X_m \cdots X_2[S \to Y_1 \ \cdots Y_t, \mu_1], eSeN_3, f^2S_4).$$

If rule (8) is applied in G_2, then we can continue in the same way, but if rule (9) is applied in G_2, we continue as at the end of the next case.

c)

$$(S_1, S_2, S_3, S_4) \Longrightarrow (z_1N_2, z_0X_m \cdots X_1[A, \mu_1]', eN_3, fS_4)$$

$$\overset{(21)}{\vdash} \ (z_1A[A, \mu_1]', z_0X_m \cdots X_2N_2, \ eN_3, fS_4)$$

$$\Longrightarrow (z_1A[A, \mu_1], z_0X_m \cdots X_2N_2, e^2N_3, f^2S_4)$$

$$\overset{(22)}{\vdash} \ (z_1AN_2, z_0X_m \cdots X_2[A, \mu_1], e^2N_3, f^2S_4).$$

As long as the symbols A, B, C are generated in G_2, they are transferred to G_1 with rule (21). When $ZABC, Z \in \{A, B, C, z_1\}$, are the last symbols from G_1, then the splicing rule (31) is applied and ABC is removed from G_1. Now, if rule (34) cannot be applied, this means that a string $\gamma \in \{A, B, C\}$ was generated in G_1 from now in such a way that $ABC \to \lambda$ cannot be applied in G. Otherwise, after the application of the rule (33), we apply in G_2 the rule (11) for $\alpha = \mu_1$, and α becomes μ_2. Moreover, the rightmost symbol of the string from G_1 is a terminal one.

After an arbitrary number of steps, assume that we have obtained the configuration

$$(S_1, S_2, S_3, S_4) \overset{*}{\Longrightarrow} (a_1 \ldots a_kN_2, z_0Z_1 \cdots Z_pV, \ldots eN_3, \cdots S_4), \quad (**),$$

where $a_1, \ldots, a_k \in T, k \geq 1, Z_1, \ldots, Z_p \in N \cup T, p \geq 0, \ V = [S \to Y_1 \cdots Y_t, \alpha]$ or $V = [Y, \alpha], \ S \to Y_1 \cdots Y_t \in P, \alpha \in \{\tau, \nu\}, Y \in T \cup \{A, B, C\}$.

Suppose that $V = [S \to Y_1 \cdots Y_t, \alpha]$. We have the following cases:

(i) $p \geq 1$, in G_2 we apply the rule (8):

$$\Longrightarrow (a_1 \ldots a_kN_2, z_0Z_1 \cdots Z_pY_t \ldots Y_1[S \to Z_1 \cdots Z_l, \alpha]', \ldots eN_3, \cdots S_4)).$$

Then, for $Y_1 \neq S$, the derivation is blocked. But, if $Y_1 = S$, we obtain

$$\overset{(19)}{\vdash} \ (a_1 \ldots a_kN_2, z_0Z_1 \cdots Z_pY_t \ldots Y_1N_3, \ldots S[S \to Z_1 \cdots Z_l, \alpha]', \cdots S_4))$$

$$\Longrightarrow (a_1 \ldots a_kN_2, z_0Z_1 \cdots Z_pY_t \ldots Y_1N_3, \ldots S[S \to Z_1 \cdots Z_l, \alpha], \cdots fS_4)$$

$$\overset{(20)}{\vdash} \ (a_1 \ldots a_kN_2, z_0Z_1 \cdots Z_pY_t \ldots Y_2[S \to Z_1 \cdots Z_l, \alpha], \ldots eN_3, \cdots fS_4).$$

Now, we have a similar case as in point (**).

(ii) $p \geq 1$, in G_2 we apply the rule (9):

$$\implies (a_1 \ldots a_k N_2, z_0 Z_1 \cdots Z_p Y_t \ldots Y_1[Y, \beta]', \ldots e N_3, \cdots S_4), Y \in T.$$

If $Y_1 \neq Y$, then the derivation is blocked. Otherwise, the splicing rule (21) is applied:

$$\overset{(21)}{\vdash} (a_1 \ldots a_k Y[Y, \beta]', z_0 Z_1 \cdots Z_p Y_t \ldots Y_2 N_2, \ldots e N_3, \cdots S_4). \qquad (***)$$

For $\beta \neq ABC$, we apply the rule (2) in G_1:

$$\implies (a_1 \ldots a_k Y[Y, \beta], z_0 Z_1 \cdots Z_p Y_t \ldots Y_2 N_2, \ldots e N_3, \cdots f S_4)$$
$$\overset{(22)}{\vdash} (a_1 \ldots a_k Y N_2, z_0 Z_1 \cdots Z_p Y_t \ldots Y_2[Y, \beta], \ldots e N_3, \cdots f S_4),$$

and now the derivation is in a similar case as in (**) (we will continue by applying one of the rules (10) or (11) in G_2).

(iii) In point (***) we have $Y = C, \beta = \nu, a_{k-1} = A, a_k = B, a_{k-2} \in T$. Then we will continue by

$$(a_1 \ldots a_{k-2} ABC[C, \nu]', z_0 Z_1 \cdots Z_p Y_t \ldots Y_2 N_2, \ldots e N_3, \cdots S_4)$$
$$\overset{(23)}{\vdash} (a_1 \ldots a_{k-2} N_3, z_0 Z_1 \cdots Z_p Y_t \ldots Y_2 N_2, \ldots e ABC[C, \nu]', \cdots S_4)$$
$$\implies (a_1 \ldots a_{k-2} N_3, z_0 Z_1 \cdots Z_p Y_t \ldots Y_2 N_2, \ldots e ABCe[C, \tau], \cdots f S_4)$$
$$\overset{(27)}{\vdash} (a_1 \ldots a_{k-2} N_3, z_0 Z_1 \cdots Z_p Y_t \ldots Y_2[C, \tau], \ldots e N_2, \cdots f S_4)$$
$$\overset{(28)}{\vdash} (a_1 \ldots a_{k-2} N_2, z_0 Z_1 \cdots Z_p Y_t \ldots Y_2[C, \tau], \ldots e N_3, \cdots f S_4)$$

and again we are in a similar situation as in (**).

(iv) In point (***) we have $Y = C, \beta = \nu, a_{k-1} = A, a_k = B, a_{k-2} \in \{A, B, C\}$. Then we will continue by

$$(a_1 \ldots a_{k-2} ABC[C, \nu]', z_0 Z_1 \cdots Z_p Y_t \ldots Y_2 N_2, \ldots e N_3, \cdots S_4)$$
$$\overset{(24)}{\vdash} (a_1 \ldots a_{k-2} S_4, z_0 Z_1 \cdots Z_p Y_t \ldots Y_2 N_2, \ldots e N_3, \cdots ABC[C, \nu]')$$
$$\implies (a_1 \ldots a_{k-2} S_4, z_0 Z_1 \cdots Z_p Y_t \ldots Y_2 N_2, \ldots e N_3, \cdots ABC[C, \nu])$$
$$\overset{(25)}{\vdash} (a_1 \ldots a_{k-2} S_4, z_0 Z_1 \cdots Z_p Y_t \ldots Y_2[C, \nu], \ldots e N_3, \cdots f ABC N_2)$$
$$\overset{(26)}{\vdash} (a_1 \ldots a_{k-2} N_2, z_0 Z_1 \cdots Z_p Y_t \ldots Y_2[C, \nu], \ldots e N_3, \cdots f ABC S_4)$$

and again we are in a similar situation as in (**).

(v) In point (**) we have $p = 0$ ('the stack is empty'). Then we can apply only the splicing rule (29), and now the string $a_1 \cdots a_k$ is obtained in G_1. If we follow the 'inputs' and the 'outputs' into and from the stack, we notice that $S \overset{*}{\Longrightarrow}_G a_1 \ldots a_k$. On the other hand, from the construction of Γ it follows that $L(G_1) \subseteq L_1(\Gamma) = L_t(\Gamma)$.

With these explanations we have that $L = L_1(\Gamma) = L_t(\Gamma)$ and $L_2(\Gamma) = L_3(\Gamma) = L_3(\Gamma) = \emptyset$. $\qquad \square$

344

4. Concluding Remarks

Some problems still remain *open* in this area: Is every context-free language an element of $YSGS_2(REG), Y \in \{I, T\}$? Can every recursively enumerable language be generated by a splicing grammar system with regular components? Is the inclusion $YSGS_2(REG) \subseteq YSGS_3(REG)$ proper?

References

1. L. M. Adleman, Molecular computation of solutions to combinatorial problems, *Science*, 226 (Nov. 1994), 1021 – 1024.

2. E. Csuhaj-Varju, J. Dassow, J. Kelemen, Gh. Păun, *Grammar Systems. A Grammatical Approach to Distribution and Cooperation*, Gordon and Breach, London, 1994.

3. E. Csuhaj-Varju, R. Freund, L. Kari, Gh. Păun, DNA computing based on splicing: universality results, *First Annual Pacific Symp. on Biocomputing*, Hawaii, Jan. 1996.

4. E. Csuhaj-Varju, L. Kari, Gh. Păun, Test tube distributed systems based on splicing, *Computers and AI*, 15, 2 – 3 (1996), 211–232.

5. J. Dassow, V. Mitrana, Splicing grammar systems, *Computers and AI*, 15, 2 – 3 (1996), 109–122.

6. C. Ferretti, S. Kobayashi, T. Yokomori, DNA splicing systems and Post systems, *First Annual Pacific Symp. on Biocomputing*, Hawaii, Jan. 1996.

7. R. Freund, L. Kari, Gh. Păun, DNA computing based on splicing: The existence of universal computers, *Technical Report 185-2/FR-2/95*, TU Wien, 1995.

8. V. Geffert, Normal forms for phrase-structure grammars, *RAIRO, Th. Inform. and Appl.*, 25 (1991), 473 – 496.

9. T. Head, Formal language theory and DNA: an analysis of the generative capacity of specific recombinant behaviors, *Bull. Math. Biology*, 49 (1987), 737 – 759.

10. T. Head, Splicing schemes and DNA, in *Lindenmayer Systems: Impacts on Theoretical Computer Science and Developmental Biology* (G. Rozenberg, A. Salomaa, eds.), Springer-Verlag, Berlin, 1992, 371 – 383.

11. T. Head, Gh. Păun, D. Pixton, Language theory and molecular genetics. Generative mechanisms suggested by DNA recombination, in *Handbook of Formal Languages* (G. Rozenberg, A. Salomaa, eds.), Springer–Verlag, 1997.

12. L. Ilie, A. Salomaa, 2-Testability and relabelings produce everything, submitted, 1995.

13. V. Mihalache, Parallel communicating grammar systems with query words, *Ann. Univ. Buc., Matem.-Inform. Series*, 45, 1 (1996), 81 – 92.

14. Gh. Păun, Splicing. A challenge to formal language theorists, *Bulletin EATCS*, 57 (1995), 183 – 194.

15. Gh. Păun, On the splicing operation, *Discrete Appl. Math.*, 70 (1996), 57 – 79.

16. Gh. Păun, On the power of the splicing operation, *Intern. J. Computer Math.*, 59 (1995), 27 – 35.

17. Gh. Păun, Regular extended H systems are computationally universal, *J. Aut. Lang. and Combinatorics*, 1, 1 (1996), 27 – 36.

18. Gh. Păun, On the power of splicing grammar systems, *Ann. Univ. Bucharest. Matem.-Inform. Series*, 55, 1 (1996), 93 – 106.

19. Gh. Păun, Computationally universal distributed systems based on the splicing operation, submitted, 1995.

20. Gh. Păun, G. Rozenberg, A. Salomaa, Computing by splicing, *Theor. Comp. Science*, 168, 2 (1996), 321 – 336.

21. Gh. Păun, A. Salomaa, DNA computing based on the splicing operation, *Acta Mathematica Japonica*, 43, 3 (1996), 607 – 632.

22. D. Pixton, Regularity of splicing languages, *Discrete Appl. Math.*, 69 (1996), 101 – 124.

23. Gh. Păun, L. Santean, Parallel communicating grammar systems: the regular case, *Ann. Univ. Buc., Matem. Inform. Series*, 38 (1989), 55 – 63.

24. D. Pixton, Linear and circular splicing systems, *Proc. 1st Intern. Symp. on Intell. in Neural and Biological Systems*, IEEE, Herndon, 1995, 38 – 45.

25. A. Salomaa, *Formal Languages*, Academic Press, New York, London, 1973.

26. T. Yokomori, S. Kobayashi, C. Ferretti, On the power of circular splicing systems and DNA computability, *Report CSIM 95-01*, Univ. of Electro-Comm., Chofu, Tokyo, 1995.

Array Splicing Systems

Kamala KRITHIVASAN, Venkatesan T. CHAKARAVARTHY

Department of Computer Science and Engineering
Indian Institute of Technology, Madras
Chennai 600 036, India
E-mail: kamala@iitm.ernet.in

Raghavan RAMA

Department of Mathematics
Indian Institute of Technology, Madras
Chennai 600 036, India

Abstract. In this paper the concept of splicing is extended to arrays and array or 2D splicing systems are defined. Various subclasses of 2D splicing systems are defined and a restricted class viz. finite simple splicing systems is studied. The hierarchy among the various subclasses of finite simple splicing systems and their relationship to the strictly locally testable languages are established.

1. Introduction

In formal language theory, lot of work has been done on string languages [9], [4]. It was also found that using restrictions on the manner of applying the rules increased the power of a grammar. [2] gives a detailed discussion on regulated rewriting. The concept of grammar was then extended to arrays and graphs [8]. In these cases shearing and embedding produced some difficulties. Array and Matrix grammars were defined in [10], [11] and [5]. To keep the arrays rectangular, restrictions have to be put on the derivations. In Graph grammars, the embedding restrictions have to be defined properly so that, the grammar generates sensible graphs. Thus we see that, the regulated rewriting is inherent in array and graph grammars.

In [3], Tom Head defined a new type of operation called splicing, motivated by the simulation of recombinant behaviour of DNA sequences. He defined Splicing Systems and the languages generated by them. Several subclasses were defined and studied. In [1], K. Culik and T. Harju defined the Splicing semigroups of dominoes. The systems defined in [3] and [1] are basically equivalent. Păun extended the definition of Head and defined Extended H-Systems. This system has been shown to be computationally universal [7].

In this paper, we give a definition of array splicing systems. The motivation is more from formal language theory, rather than biology, though such systems may find applications for describing splicing of several DNA sequences. We define an array or 2D splicing system and also several restricted classes. As in the case of array grammars, shearing imposes some restrictions on splicing between arrays. Mainly because of this factor, there is a basic difference in the hierarchy in 1D and 2D splicing systems. We define null-context, equal and uniform splicing systems and show that in a restricted class of splicing languages called Finite-Simple splicing languages, the following hierarchy exists among these three classes of languages.

$$uniform \subset equal \subset null - context$$

Such classes in 1D or string splicing have been shown to be equivalent in 1D by Tom Head [3]. They have also been proved to be equivalent to the set of strictly locally testable languages. On extending the definition of strictly locally testability to 2D, we find that, they form a different class altogether.

In section 2, we present the definition of 1D splicing systems and the subclasses, and the main results about them are also given. In section 3 some important notations regarding 2D or array languages are presented. Section 4 defines the 2D or array splicing systems and the main classes of such systems. Section 5 establishes the relationships among these classes and the class of strictly locally testable languages. Section 6 concludes the paper and lists a few directions for future work.

2. 1D Splicing Systems or H-Systems

One dimensional splicing system was introduced by Tom Head[3] and it has its roots in genetic engineering. An attempt to formalize the recombinant behaviour of the DNA has led to the H-systems. In this section we omit the biological perspectives of H-systems and present it from the point of view of formal language theory. The biological background is discussed in [3] and [12].

Definition 2.1. A splicing system S is a 4 tuple, $S = < A, I, B, C >$. 'A' is a finite alphabet, over which S is defined. I, referred as the 'initial set' is the set of initial strings in A^*. B and C are sets of triples $< a, x, b >$, a,b,x $\in A^*$. Each triple $< a, x, b >$ is called a pattern and the string axb is called a site. The string x is called a crossing. Patterns in B are called left patterns and those in C are called right patterns. The language L=L(S) generated by the splicing system S consists of the strings in S and all strings that can be obtained by adjoining to L ucxfq and pexdv whenever ucxdv and pexfq are in L and $< c, x, d >$ and $< e, x, f >$ are patterns of the same hand. A language L is a splicing language(SL) if there exists a splicing system S for which L=L(S).

Definition 2.2. Let $S = < A, I, B, C >$ be a splicing system. Then S is persistent if for each pair of strings ucxdv and pexfq in A^* with $< c, x, d >$ and $< e, x, f >$ being the patterns of the same hand: if y is a subsegment of ucx (respectively xfq) that is the crossing of a site in ucxdv (respectively pexfq) then this same subsegment y of ucxfq contains an occurrence of the crossing of a site in ucxfq.

Definition 2.3. Let $S = < A, I, B, C >$ be a splicing system. It is said to be null context if the patterns are of the form $< 1, x, 1 >$. $x \in A^*$ and 1 is the empty string.

Definition 2.4. A splicing system $S = < A, I, B, C >$ is said to be uniform, if $B = C = \{< 1, x, 1 > | x \in A^k$, where, k is a positive integer.$\}$

Definition 2.5. With respect to a language over the alphabet A, a string c in A^* is a constant if, whenever ucv and pcq are in the language, ucq and pcv are also in the language.

Definition 2.6. A language L over an alphabet A is said to be k-strictly locally testable if there exists sets U,V and W $\subseteq A^k$, such that,
$$L \cap A^k A^* = (UA^* \cap A^*V) \setminus A^*WA^*$$

Example 2.1. An example of a 1D splicing system is presented below.
    S=<A,I,B,C>. A=c,x. I=cxcxc. B=<c,x,c>. C=$\emptyset$.

The language generated L(S) is $(cx)^+c$. Examples for the various types of splicing systems can be found in [3].

Some results in 1D splicing are presented in the theorem below. The proofs and detailed discussions can be found in [3] and [6].

Theorem 2.1.1. *The following conditions on a language L over an alphabet A are equivalent:*

1. *L is a persistent splicing language.*
2. *L is a strictly locally testable language.*
3. *The set of constants for L contains A^p for some positive integer p.*
4. *L is an uniform splicing language.*

This can be expressed by the following relationship.

$pers.SL \Leftrightarrow nullcontext\ SL \Leftrightarrow uniform\ SL \Leftrightarrow SLT\ language.$

In other words, these four classes are equivalent. Later, we shall see that this equivalence is not valid in 2D splicing splicing systems.

3. 2D languages and Array Grammars

String languages have been widely studied in the past [9]. Grammars which generate arrays are called array grammars. One type of array grammar can be found in [11]. We omit the formal definitions regarding arrays and array languages and refer the reader to [10], [11] and [5]. A few definitions and notations widely used throughout the paper are presented here.

Definition 3.1.1. If I is an image, R(I) represents the number of rows of I and C(I) represents the number of columns. $R(\Lambda) = C(\Lambda) = 0$, where Λ is the empty image. Size(I) is a 2 tuple, Size(I) = $< R(I), C(I) >$. The relationships between sizes of images are defined as follows. Let I_1 and I_2 be two images. Let Size(I_1) = $< m, n >$ and Size(I_2) = $< m', n' >$. Then,

Size(I_1) > Size(I_2), if (m $\geq$ m' and n > n') or (n $\geq$ n' and m > m').

Size(I_1) = Size(I_2) if m=m' and n = n'.

if (m > m' and n<n') or (n > n' and m < m') then their sizes cannot be compared.

Definition 3.1.2. Let I be an image. Let Size(I) = $< r, c >$. Then, I[i,j] represents the element in the ith row and jth column. I[i,j] is defined if and only if, $1 \leq i \leq r$ and $1 \leq j \leq c$. The top-left element is represented by I[1,1].

Notation. 'Φ' represents column concatenation of two arrays. 'Θ' represents the row concatenation. The word 'image' refers to rectangular arrays.

Definition 3.1.3. The column concatenation Φ of two images I_1 and I_2 is said to be 'defined' or 'legal' if and only if,

1. $I_1 = \Lambda$ or $I_2 = \Lambda$, where, Λ is the empty image.

or 2. $I_1 \neq \Lambda$ and $I_2 \neq \Lambda$ and R(I_1) = R(I_2).

$I_1 \Phi I_2$ is the image obtained by putting I_2 to the right side of I_1. Similarly, the row concatenation Θ of two images I_1 and I_2 is said to be 'defined' or 'legal' if and only if,

1. $I_1 = \Lambda$ or $I_2 = \Lambda$, where, Λ is the empty image.

or 2. $I_1 \neq \Lambda$ and $I_2 \neq \Lambda$ and C(I_1) = C(I_2). $I_1 \Theta I_2$ is the image obtained by putting I_2 below I_1.

Definition 3.1.4. Let I be a non-empty set of symbols. The set of all arrays over I(including Λ) is denoted by I^{**} and $I^{++} = I^{**} - \Lambda$, where, Λ is the empty image. $I^{m,n}$ denotes the set of all arrays with m rows and n columns defined over I. If 'a' is a sysmbol $a^{m,n}$ denotes an array of a's with m rows and n columns.

Notation. Let I be an alphabet. I^* denotes the horizontal sequences of letters from I and $I^+ = I^* - \{\Lambda\}$. I_* denotes the vertical sequences of letters from I and $I_+ = I_* - \{\Lambda\}$. For example a^n denotes a horizontal sequence of n a's. And a_n denotes a vertical sequence of n a's.

Definition 3.1.5. Let I be an image defined over the alpahbet A and x be its subimage. Then, x is said to be

a 'top-left' subimage of I if, $I \in (x \Phi A^{**}) \Theta A^{**}$.

a 'top-right' subimage of I if, $I \in (A^{**} \Phi x) \Theta A^{**}$.

a 'bottom-left' subimage of I if, $I \in A^{**} \Theta (x \Phi A^{**})$.

a 'bottom-right' subimage of I if, $I \in A^{**} \Theta (A^{**} \Phi x)$.

Definition 3.1.6. A language L defined over an alphabet A is said to be p,q-strictly locally testable (SLT), if 5 sets U, V, Y, Z, W $\subseteq A^{p,q}$ can be constructed such that,

$$L' = (L_U \cap L_V \cap L_Y \cap L_Z) \setminus L_W$$

where,

$$L' = L \cap ((A^{p,q} \Phi A^{**}) \Theta A^{**})$$
$$L_U = ((U \Phi A^{**}) \Theta A^{**})$$
$$L_V = ((A^{**} \Phi V) \Theta A^{**})$$
$$L_Y = (A^{**} \Theta (Y \Phi A^{**}))$$
$$L_Z = (A^{**} \Theta (A^{**} \Phi Z))$$
$$L_W = (A^{**} \Phi (A^{**} \Theta W \Theta A^{**}) \Phi A^{**})$$

It can be easily seen that L' is the set of images in L with size greater than or equal to $< p, q >$, L_U is the set of images over A, with an image in U as 'top-left' subimage; L_V is the set of images over A, with an image in V as 'top-right' subimage; L_Y is the set of images over A, with an image in Y as 'bottom-left' subimage; L_Z is the set of images over A, with an image in Z as 'bottom-right' subimage. L_W is the set of images with an image in W as their subimage.

Algorithm 3.1.1.

An algorithm to test whether an arbitrary image I belongs to a p,q-SLT language L or not, is presented.

Input : The sets U,V,Y,Z and W of the language L, and an input image I, size(I) $\geq < p, q >$

Output: Answers whether I$\in$L or not

Algorithm :

    1. Find the top-left, top-right, bottom-left and bottom-right subimages of I, say u,v,y,z respectively.

    2. If u$\in$U, v$\in$V, y$\in$Y and z$\in$Z

        then

            if there exist a subimage w of I of size $< p, q >$, such that, w$\in$W,

            then

                output "I$\notin$L"

        else

output "I∈L"

    else

        output "I∉L"

This algorithm can be used to prove whether a language L is SLT or not. If there is an image I, size(I) $\geq < p, q >$, such that, $I \notin L$, but the alogorithm outputs "I $\in$ L", then L is not p,q-SLT.

4. Array or 2D Splicing Systems

Definition 4.1. Let S=< $x_{1,1}, x_{1,2}, \ldots, x_{1,n}, x_{2,1}, x_{2,2}, \ldots, x_{2,n}, \ldots, x_{m,1}, x_{m,2}, \ldots, x_{m,n}$ > be a sequence of mn images defined over the alphabet Σ. Let,

$$I_1 = (x_{1,1}\Phi x_{1,2}\Phi x_{1,3}\Phi \ldots \Phi x_{1,n})\Theta$$
$$(x_{2,1}\Phi x_{2,2}\Phi x_{2,3}\Phi \ldots \Phi x_{2,n})\Theta$$
$$\ldots$$
$$(x_{m,1}\Phi x_{m,2}\Phi x_{m,3}\Phi \ldots \Phi x_{m,n})$$
$$I_2 = (x_{1,1}\Theta x_{2,1}\Theta x_{3,1}\Theta \ldots \Theta x_{m,1})\Phi$$
$$(x_{1,2}\Theta x_{2,2}\Theta x_{3,2}\Theta \ldots \Theta x_{m,2})\Phi$$
$$\ldots$$
$$(x_{1,m}\Theta x_{2,m}\Theta x_{3,m}\Theta \ldots \Theta x_{m,n})$$

If I_1 and I_2 are legal (i.e the concatenation operations in the above two expressions are defined as per Definition 3.1.3) and $I_1 = I_2$ then the sequence S is said to be a proper sequence of cardinality $< m, n >$.

Note. The proper sequences can be easily understood by the following two properties. Let S be a proper sequence of cardinality $< m, n >$. Then,

    1. If $x_{i,j} \neq \Lambda$, $1 \leq i \leq m, 1 \leq j \leq n$, then, $R(x_{i,k})=R(x_{i,l})$, for $1 \leq i \leq m$, $1 \leq k, l \leq n$. and $C(x_{k,j})=C(x_{l,j})$, for $1 \leq k, l \leq m, 1 \leq j \leq n$.

    2. If some $x_{i,j}=\Lambda$, then $x_{i,q}=\Lambda$, $1 \leq q \leq n$ or $x_{p,j}=\Lambda$, $1 \leq p \leq m$.

Definition 4.2. Let S=< $x_{1,1}, x_{1,2}, \ldots, x_{1,n}, x_{2,1}, x_{2,2}, \ldots, x_{2,n}, \ldots, x_{m,1}, x_{m,2}, \ldots, x_{m,n}$ > be a proper sequence of cardinality $< m, n >$. Let,

$$I = (x_{1,1}\Phi x_{1,2}\Phi x_{1,3}\Phi \ldots \Phi x_{1,n})\Theta$$
$$(x_{2,1}\Phi x_{2,2}\Phi x_{2,3}\Phi \ldots \Phi x_{2,n})\Theta$$
$$\ldots$$
$$(x_{m,1}\Phi x_{m,2}\Phi x_{m,3}\Phi \ldots \Phi x_{m,n})$$

Then, I is called the matrix-image of S and is represented by MI(S,$< m, n >$).

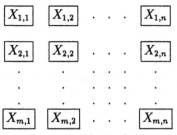

Figure 1. Matrix Split

Definition 4.3. A sequence S of cardinality $< m, n >$ is said to be a matrix split of an image I, if and only if, S is a proper sequence and I is the matrix-image of S.

Figure 1 shows a matrix split of $< m, n >$. Note that, though the figure may misguide by showing $x_{1,1}$ and $x_{1,2}$ to have same number of colums, it need not be the case. Note that for an image more than one matrix-split exists.

Definition 4.4. Let I be an image and M=$< x_{1,1}, x_{1,2}, \ldots, x_{1,5}, x_{2,1}, x_{2,2}, \ldots, x_{2,5}, \ldots, x_{5,1}, x_{5,2}, \ldots, x_{5,5} >$ be a matrix split of I of cardinality $< 5, 5 >$. We define a few prefixes and suffixes of I with respect to M, grouped under four types as follows.

TYPE 1 :

      Prefix : MI($< x_{1,1}, x_{1,2}, x_{1,3}, x_{2,1}, x_{2,2}, x_{2,3}, x_{3,1}, x_{3,2}, x_{3,3} >, < 3, 3 >$).

      LRSuffix: MI($< x_{1,4}, x_{1,5}, x_{2,4}, x_{2,5}, x_{3,4}, x_{3,5} >, < 3, 2 >$).

      BUSuffix: MI($< x_{4,1}, x_{4,2}, x_{4,3}, x_{5,1}, x_{5,2}, x_{5,3} >, < 2, 3 >$).

      CSuffix: MI($< x_{4,4}, x_{4,5}, x_{5,4}, x_{5,5} >, < 2, 2 >$).

TYPE 2 :

      Prefix : MI($< x_{1,3}, x_{1,4}, x_{1,5}, x_{2,3}, x_{2,4}, x_{2,5}, x_{3,3}, x_{3,4}, x_{3,5} >, < 3, 3 >$).

      LRSuffix: MI($< x_{1,1}, x_{1,2}, x_{2,1}, x_{2,2}, x_{3,1}, x_{3,2} >, < 3, 2 >$).

      BUSuffix: MI($< x_{4,3}, x_{4,4}, x_{4,5}, x_{5,3}, x_{5,4}, x_{5,5} >, < 2, 3 >$).

      CSuffix: MI($< x_{4,1}, x_{4,2}, x_{5,1}, x_{5,2} >, < 2, 2 >$).

TYPE 3 :

      Prefix : MI($< x_{3,1}, x_{3,2}, x_{3,3}, x_{4,1}, x_{4,2}, x_{4,3}, x_{5,1}, x_{5,2}, x_{5,3} >, < 3, 3 >$).

      LRSuffix: MI($< x_{3,4}, x_{3,5}, x_{4,4}, x_{4,5}, x_{5,4}, x_{5,5} >, < 3, 2 >$).

      BUSuffix: MI($< x_{1,1}, x_{1,2}, x_{1,3}, x_{2,1}, x_{2,2}, x_{2,3} >, < 2, 3 >$).

      CSuffix: MI($< x_{1,4}, x_{1,5}, x_{2,4}, x_{2,5} >, < 2, 2 >$).

TYPE 4 :

      Prefix : MI($< x_{3,3}, x_{3,4}, x_{3,5}, x_{4,3}, x_{4,4}, x_{4,5}, x_{5,3}, x_{5,4}, x_{5,5} >, < 3, 3 >$).

      LRSuffix: MI($< x_{3,1}, x_{3,2}, x_{4,1}, x_{4,2}, x_{5,1}, x_{5,2} >, < 3, 2 >$).

      BUSuffix: MI($< x_{1,3}, x_{1,4}, x_{1,5}, x_{2,3}, x_{2,4}, x_{2,5} >, < 2, 3 >$).

      CSuffix: MI($< x_{1,1}, x_{1,2}, x_{2,1}, x_{2,2} >, < 2, 2 >$).

In the above definition LR stands for left-or-right;BU stands for bottom-or-up;C stands for corner. It can be easily seen that the image I can be expressed in terms of these prefixes and suffixes. If P,L,B and C represent Prefix, LRsuffix, BUsuffix and CSuffix respectively, then I is

    TYPE 1: I $= (P\Phi L)\Theta(B\Phi C) = (P\Theta B) \ \Phi(L\Theta C)$

    TYPE 2: I $= (L\Phi P)\Theta(C\Phi B) = (L\Theta C) \ \Phi(P\Theta B)$

    TYPE 3: I $= (B\Phi C)\Theta(P\Phi L) = (B\Theta P) \ \Phi(C\Theta L)$

    TYPE 4: I $= (C\Phi B)\Theta(L\Phi P) = (C\Theta L) \ \Phi(B\Theta P)$

These are represented by prefixing with their type. For example, 2-BUSuffix represents a Type-2 BUSuffix. Figure 2 shows Type-1 prefixes and suffixes.

Definition 4.5. A 2D splicing system S is a 4 tuple S=$< \Sigma, I, B, f >$. Σ is the set of symbols used by S. $\Sigma = A \cup A'$, $A \cap A' = \emptyset$. A is the alphabet of the language generated by the splicing system, L(S). A' is called the set of special symbols. f is a mapping f : $A' \rightarrow A$, and is described in detail later. I is the set of initial images. B is a 4 tuple, B $= < B_1, B_2, B_3, B_4 >$. B_i is the set of Type-i patterns. A pattern 'p' is a 9 tuple $< x_1, x_2, x_3, x_4, x_5, x_6, x_7, x_8, x_9 >$, $x_1, x_2, x_3, x_4, x_6, x_7, x_8, x_9 \in \Sigma^{**}$, $x_5 \in \Sigma^{++}$, subjected to the condition that p is a proper sequence of cardinality $< 3, 3 >$. The middle term x_5 is called the crossing of p. The matrix image of p is is called the site of the pattern p.

Splicing products: Four types of splicing operations are defined on any two images and a splicing operation between the two images is uniquely specified by giving the two images, the type of splicing (1,2,3 or 4) and two matrix splits of cardinality $< 5,5 >$, one for each of the two images. And the result of the splicing operation is two reusulatnts or splicing products. But, for the splicing to take place, certain conditions have to be satisfied.

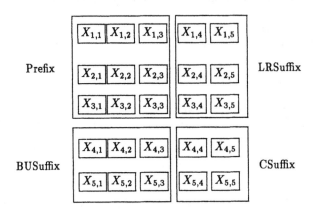

Figure 2. Type-1 prefixes and suffixes

Let X and Y be the two images. Let $MX = < x_{1,1}, x_{1,2}, \ldots x_{1,5}, x_{2,1}, x_{2,2}, \ldots, x_{2,5}, \ldots, x_{5,1}, x_{5,2}, \ldots, x_{5,5} >$ and $MY = < y_{1,1}, y_{1,2}, \ldots, y_{1,5}, y_{2,1}, y_{2,2}, \ldots, y_{2,5}, \ldots, y_{5,1}, y_{5,2}, \ldots, y_{5,5} >$ be the two matrix splits of cardinality $< 5,5 >$ of X and Y respectively. Type-i splicing between X and Y with respect to these matrix splits MX and MY can take place if and only if, the following conditions hold good.

1. $< x_{2,2}, x_{2,3}, x_{2,4}, x_{3,3}, x_{3,4}, x_{3,5}, x_{4,3}, x_{4,4}, x_{4,5} >$ and $< y_{2,2}, y_{2,3}, y_{2,4}, y_{3,3}, y_{3,4}, y_{3,5}, y_{4,3}, y_{4,4}, y_{4,5} >$ are Type-i patterns.

2. $x_{3,3} = y_{3,3}$. That is. the crossings are the same.

3. For the four types of splicing operations, define R_1 and R_2 to be the following. X-P and Y-P represent the Type-i prefixes of X and Y with respect to MX and MY respectively. Similarly for suffixes.

TYPE 1: $R_1 = (\text{X-P}\Phi\text{Y-L})\Theta(\text{Y-B}\Phi\text{Y-C}) = (\text{X-P}\Theta\text{Y-B})\ \Phi(\text{Y-L}\Theta\text{Y-C})$
$R_2 = (\text{Y-P}\Phi\text{X-L})\Theta(\text{X-B}\Phi\text{X-C}) = (\text{Y-P}\Theta\text{X-B})\ \Phi(\text{X-L}\Theta\text{X-C})$

TYPE 2: $R_1 = (\text{Y-L}\Phi\text{X-P})\Theta(\text{Y-C}\Phi\text{Y-B}) = (\text{Y-L}\Theta\text{Y-C})\ \Phi(\text{X-P}\Theta\text{Y-B})$
$R_2 = (\text{X-L}\Phi\text{Y-P})\Theta(\text{X-C}\Phi\text{X-B}) = (\text{X-L}\Theta\text{X-C})\ \Phi(\text{Y-P}\Theta\text{X-B})$

TYPE 3: $R_1 = (\text{Y-B}\Phi\text{Y-C})\Theta(\text{X-P}\Phi\text{Y-L}) = (\text{Y-B}\Theta\text{X-P})\ \Phi(\text{Y-C}\Theta\text{Y-L})$
$R_2 = (\text{X-B}\Phi\text{X-C})\Theta(\text{Y-P}\Phi\text{X-L}) = (\text{X-B}\Theta\text{Y-P})\ \Phi(\text{X-C}\Theta\text{X-L})$

TYPE 4: $R_1 = (\text{Y-C}\Phi\text{Y-B})\Theta(\text{Y-L}\Phi\text{X-P}) = (\text{Y-C}\Theta\text{Y-L})\ \Phi(\text{Y-B}\Theta\text{X-P})$
$R_2 = (\text{X-C}\Phi\text{X-B})\Theta(\text{X-L}\Phi\text{Y-P}) = (\text{X-C}\Theta\text{X-L})\ \Phi(\text{X-B}\Theta\text{Y-P})$

Type-i splicing between X and Y with respect to these matrix splits is said to be defined/legal if the corresponding R_1 and R_2 are legal. i.e. The concatenation operations performed in the above expressions are all legal with respect to Definition 3.1.3. The two images X and Y are i-compatible with respect to these matrix splits if and only if, the Type-i splicing is defined as per the above rules. We can see that, if none of the prefixes and suffixes are Λ, then, the images will be i-compatible if and only if, the i-prefixes of the images are of same size. The four types of splicing and the corresponding resultants are shown in the Figures 3, 4, 5, and 6. In these figures, 'c' represents the crossing.

Note. Now, let us put the above definitions informally to explain the procedure to obtain the Type-i splicing products of two images X and Y. First, we have to locate two subimages in X and Y which are Type-i sites. The two sites are then matrix-split to get the corresponding Type-i patterns. The two patterns should have the same crossing. Let the pattern corresponding to X be $< a_1, a_2, \ldots a_9 >$ and that of Y be $< b_1, b_2 \ldots b_9 >$. The crossings a_5 and b_5 should be the same. X is split into subimages to obtain a matrix-split of $< 5, 5 >$, $x_{1,1}, x_{1,2} \ldots x_{1,5}, \ldots \ldots x_{5,1}, x_{5,1} \ldots x_{5,5}$, such that, $x_{2,2} = a_1; x_{2,3} = a_2; x_{2,4} = a_3; x_{3,2} = a_4; x_{3,3} = a_5, the crossing; x_{3,4} = a_6; x_{4,2} = a_7; x_{4,3} = a_8; x_{4,4} = a_9$. Similarly, Y is split. Then, the Type-i prefixes and suffixes of X and Y with respect to these matrix splits is found. Now, the Type-i splicing prodcuts or resultants of X and Y w.r.t these matrix splits is obtained by exchanging the Type-i prefixes of X and Y. This splicing of X and Y w.r.t to these matrix-splits is said to be 'defined' or 'legal' if BOTH the products obtained are rectangular arrays. And X and Y are said to Type-i comaptible w.r.t these matrix splits. The compatibility condition ensures that the language of the splicing system S, viz. L(S) consists only of rectangular arrays. Note that, if none of the images in the matrix splits of X and Y are Λ, then the Type-i compatibility means that the prefixes of matrix-splits of X and Y are of the same size. Figure 7 shows the matrix split corresponding to the image X with the above mentioned notations. In the figure the subimages are shown with one possible sizes.

		I_1					I_2		
$X_{1,1}$	$X_{1,2}$	$X_{1,3}$	$X_{1,4}$	$X_{1,5}$	$Y_{1,1}$	$Y_{1,2}$	$Y_{1,3}$	$Y_{1,4}$	$Y_{1,5}$
$X_{2,1}$	$X_{2,2}$	$X_{2,3}$	$X_{2,4}$	$X_{2,5}$	$Y_{2,1}$	$Y_{2,2}$	$Y_{2,3}$	$Y_{2,4}$	$Y_{2,5}$
$X_{3,1}$	$X_{3,2}$	c	$X_{3,4}$	$X_{3,5}$	$Y_{3,1}$	$Y_{3,2}$	c	$Y_{3,4}$	$Y_{3,5}$
$X_{4,1}$	$X_{4,2}$	$X_{4,3}$	$X_{4,4}$	$X_{4,5}$	$Y_{4,1}$	$Y_{4,2}$	$Y_{4,3}$	$Y_{4,4}$	$Y_{4,5}$
$X_{5,1}$	$X_{5,2}$	$X_{5,3}$	$X_{5,4}$	$X_{5,5}$	$Y_{5,1}$	$Y_{5,2}$	$Y_{5,3}$	$Y_{5,4}$	$Y_{5,5}$

		R_1					R_2		
$X_{1,1}$	$X_{1,2}$	$X_{1,3}$	$Y_{1,4}$	$Y_{1,5}$	$Y_{1,1}$	$Y_{1,2}$	$Y_{1,3}$	$X_{1,4}$	$X_{1,5}$
$X_{2,1}$	$X_{2,2}$	$X_{2,3}$	$Y_{2,4}$	$Y_{2,5}$	$Y_{2,1}$	$Y_{2,2}$	$Y_{2,3}$	$X_{2,4}$	$X_{2,5}$
$X_{3,1}$	$X_{3,2}$	c	$Y_{3,4}$	$Y_{3,5}$	$Y_{3,1}$	$Y_{3,2}$	c	$X_{3,4}$	$X_{3,5}$
$Y_{4,1}$	$Y_{4,2}$	$Y_{4,3}$	$Y_{4,4}$	$Y_{4,5}$	$X_{4,1}$	$X_{4,2}$	$X_{4,3}$	$X_{4,4}$	$X_{4,5}$
$Y_{5,1}$	$Y_{5,2}$	$Y_{5,3}$	$Y_{5,4}$	$Y_{5,5}$	$X_{5,1}$	$X_{5,2}$	$X_{5,3}$	$X_{5,4}$	$X_{5,5}$

Figure 3. Type-1 splicing

354

Figure 4. Type-2 splicing

I_1

$$\begin{matrix}
X_{1,1} & X_{1,2} & X_{1,3} & X_{1,4} & X_{1,5} \\
X_{2,1} & X_{2,2} & X_{2,3} & X_{2,4} & X_{2,5} \\
X_{3,1} & X_{3,2} & c & X_{3,4} & X_{3,5} \\
X_{4,1} & X_{4,2} & X_{4,3} & X_{4,4} & X_{4,5} \\
X_{5,1} & X_{5,2} & X_{5,3} & X_{5,4} & X_{5,5}
\end{matrix}$$

I_2

$$\begin{matrix}
Y_{1,1} & Y_{1,2} & Y_{1,3} & Y_{1,4} & Y_{1,5} \\
Y_{2,1} & Y_{2,2} & Y_{2,3} & Y_{2,4} & Y_{2,5} \\
Y_{3,1} & Y_{3,2} & c & Y_{3,4} & Y_{3,5} \\
Y_{4,1} & Y_{4,2} & Y_{4,3} & Y_{4,4} & Y_{4,5} \\
Y_{5,1} & Y_{5,2} & Y_{5,3} & Y_{5,4} & Y_{5,5}
\end{matrix}$$

R_1

$$\begin{matrix}
Y_{1,1} & Y_{1,2} & X_{1,3} & X_{1,4} & X_{1,5} \\
Y_{2,1} & Y_{2,2} & X_{2,3} & X_{2,4} & X_{2,5} \\
Y_{3,1} & Y_{3,2} & c & X_{3,4} & X_{3,5} \\
Y_{4,1} & Y_{4,2} & Y_{4,3} & Y_{4,4} & Y_{4,5} \\
Y_{5,1} & Y_{5,2} & Y_{5,3} & Y_{5,4} & Y_{5,5}
\end{matrix}$$

R_2

$$\begin{matrix}
X_{1,1} & X_{1,2} & Y_{1,3} & Y_{1,4} & Y_{1,5} \\
X_{2,1} & X_{2,2} & Y_{2,3} & Y_{2,4} & Y_{2,5} \\
X_{3,1} & X_{3,2} & c & Y_{3,4} & Y_{3,5} \\
X_{4,1} & X_{4,2} & X_{4,3} & X_{4,4} & X_{4,5} \\
X_{5,1} & X_{5,2} & X_{5,3} & X_{5,4} & X_{5,5}
\end{matrix}$$

Figure 4. Type-2 splicing

Figure 5. Type-3 splicing

I_1

$$\begin{matrix}
X_{1,1} & X_{1,2} & X_{1,3} & X_{1,4} & X_{1,5} \\
X_{2,1} & X_{2,2} & X_{2,3} & X_{2,4} & X_{2,5} \\
X_{3,1} & X_{3,2} & c & X_{3,4} & X_{3,5} \\
X_{4,1} & X_{4,2} & X_{4,3} & X_{4,4} & X_{4,5} \\
X_{5,1} & X_{5,2} & X_{5,3} & X_{5,4} & X_{5,5}
\end{matrix}$$

I_2

$$\begin{matrix}
Y_{1,1} & Y_{1,2} & Y_{1,3} & Y_{1,4} & Y_{1,5} \\
Y_{2,1} & Y_{2,2} & Y_{2,3} & Y_{2,4} & Y_{2,5} \\
Y_{3,1} & Y_{3,2} & c & Y_{3,4} & Y_{3,5} \\
Y_{4,1} & Y_{4,2} & Y_{4,3} & Y_{4,4} & Y_{4,5} \\
Y_{5,1} & Y_{5,2} & Y_{5,3} & Y_{5,4} & Y_{5,5}
\end{matrix}$$

R_1

$$\begin{matrix}
Y_{1,1} & Y_{1,2} & Y_{1,3} & Y_{1,4} & Y_{1,5} \\
Y_{2,1} & Y_{2,2} & Y_{2,3} & Y_{2,4} & Y_{2,5} \\
X_{3,1} & X_{3,2} & c & Y_{3,4} & Y_{3,5} \\
X_{4,1} & X_{4,2} & X_{4,3} & Y_{4,4} & Y_{4,5} \\
X_{5,1} & X_{5,2} & X_{5,3} & Y_{5,4} & Y_{5,5}
\end{matrix}$$

R_2

$$\begin{matrix}
X_{1,1} & X_{1,2} & X_{1,3} & X_{1,4} & X_{1,5} \\
X_{2,1} & X_{2,2} & X_{2,3} & X_{2,4} & X_{2,5} \\
Y_{3,1} & Y_{3,2} & c & X_{3,4} & X_{3,5} \\
Y_{4,1} & Y_{4,2} & Y_{4,3} & X_{4,4} & X_{4,5} \\
Y_{5,1} & Y_{5,2} & Y_{5,3} & X_{5,4} & X_{5,5}
\end{matrix}$$

Figure 5. Type-3 splicing

Figure 6. Type-4 splicing

I_1

$$\begin{matrix}
X_{1,1} & X_{1,2} & X_{1,3} & X_{1,4} & X_{1,5} \\
X_{2,1} & X_{2,2} & X_{2,3} & X_{2,4} & X_{2,5} \\
X_{3,1} & X_{3,2} & c & X_{3,4} & X_{3,5} \\
X_{4,1} & X_{4,2} & X_{4,3} & X_{4,4} & X_{4,5} \\
X_{5,1} & X_{5,2} & X_{5,3} & X_{5,4} & X_{5,5}
\end{matrix}$$

I_2

$$\begin{matrix}
Y_{1,1} & Y_{1,2} & Y_{1,3} & Y_{1,4} & Y_{1,5} \\
Y_{2,1} & Y_{2,2} & Y_{2,3} & Y_{2,4} & Y_{2,5} \\
Y_{3,1} & Y_{3,2} & c & Y_{3,4} & Y_{3,5} \\
Y_{4,1} & Y_{4,2} & Y_{4,3} & Y_{4,4} & Y_{4,5} \\
Y_{5,1} & Y_{5,2} & Y_{5,3} & Y_{5,4} & Y_{5,5}
\end{matrix}$$

R_1

$$\begin{matrix}
Y_{1,1} & Y_{1,2} & Y_{1,3} & Y_{1,4} & Y_{1,5} \\
Y_{2,1} & Y_{2,2} & Y_{2,3} & Y_{2,4} & Y_{2,5} \\
Y_{3,1} & Y_{3,2} & c & X_{3,4} & X_{3,5} \\
Y_{4,1} & Y_{4,2} & X_{4,3} & X_{4,4} & X_{4,5} \\
Y_{5,1} & Y_{5,2} & X_{5,3} & X_{5,4} & X_{5,5}
\end{matrix}$$

R_2

$$\begin{matrix}
X_{1,1} & X_{1,2} & X_{1,3} & X_{1,4} & X_{1,5} \\
X_{2,1} & X_{2,2} & X_{2,3} & X_{2,4} & X_{2,5} \\
X_{3,1} & X_{3,2} & c & Y_{3,4} & Y_{3,5} \\
X_{4,1} & X_{4,2} & Y_{4,3} & Y_{4,4} & Y_{4,5} \\
X_{5,1} & X_{5,2} & Y_{5,3} & Y_{5,4} & Y_{5,5}
\end{matrix}$$

Figure 6. Type-4 splicing

We have to note that there could be more than one site in an image and hence, the two images can splice in more than one way even for the same type of splicing. Hence, it is important to specify the $< 5, 5 >$ matrix splits to uniquely specify a splicing operation between the two images. And specifying two $< 5, 5 >$ matrix splits of the two images and the type of splicing , uniquely specifies the splicing operation desired and the resultants.

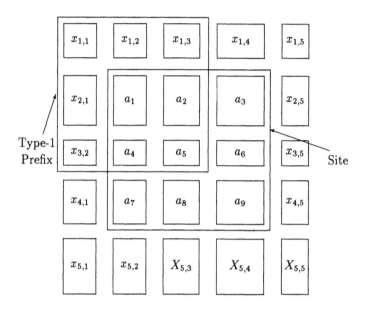

Figure 7. Splitting an image to get splicing products

Auxiliary language L' : The language of the splicing system S, L(S), is obtained as follows. An auxillary language L' is formed by the following procedure.
  1. L' <- ∅.
  2. Add images in I to L'.
  3. Select any two images I_1 and I_2 from L'.
     Splice them in all the possible four types, using all matrix splits.
     If the resultants are rectangular and are not in L' add them to L'.
  4. If no new images are added in step 3 exit else goto step 3.

Language L(S) : For an image X, define F(X), X ∈ L', to be an image obtained by replacing evey special symbol s in X by f(s). Thus, $F : \Sigma^{++} \rightarrow A^{++}$. $L(S) = \{F(X) \mid X \in L'\}$.

4.1. Classes of 2D Splicing Systems

Definition 4.1.1. Let S=$< \Sigma, I, B, f >$ be a splicing system. $\Sigma = A \cup A'$. S is said to be a simple splicing system if A' = ∅. That is there are no special symbols used. Consequently, f is not defined for a simple splicing system. Hence, a simple splicing is represented as S=$< A, I, B >$ and A is the alphabet of L(S).

Definition 4.1.2. A splicing system S=$< \Sigma, I, < B_1, B_2, B_3, B_4 >, f >$, is said to be a finite splicing system if I, B_1, B_2, B_3 and B_4 are all finite.

Definition 4.1.3. A splicing system S is said to be null-context if all the patterns of S are of the form, $< \Lambda, \Lambda, \Lambda, \Lambda, c, \Lambda, \Lambda, \Lambda, \Lambda >$. And $c \in \Sigma^{++}$. Note that in such a system, the crossing itself is a site. The patterns of this form are called null-context patterns. In a null-context pattern of the 9 images, only the crossing 'c' is nonempty image. The null-context patterns are represented by $<< c >>$, where, c is the crossing.

Definition 4.1.4. A null-context splicing system S is said to an equal splicing system, if the four sets of patterns B_1, B_2, B_3 and B_4 are equal to each other. i.e $B_1 = B_2 = B_3 = B_4$. Such a splicing system can be expressed by a 4 tuple $< \Sigma, I, B_1, f >$. B_1 is the set of patterns, and the patterns can be used for any type of splicing.

Definition 4.1.5. A null-context splicing system S is said to be uniform, if the set of patterns are such that,
$$B_1 = B_2 = B_3 = B_4 = \{<< a >> | \ a \in \Sigma^{m,n}, \text{ for some m,n} \geq 0\}.$$
That is every image in $\Sigma^{m,n}$ is a site of all the four types and these are the only sites. An uniform splicing system is represented as $S=< A, I, m, n >$. Note that every uniform splicing system is also null-context.

Definition 4.1.6. An array language L is said to be a finite splicing language, if it can be generated by a finite splicing system. And L is said to be a simple splicing language if it can be generated by a simple splicing system. Similarly, null-context, equal and uniform splicing languages are defined.

4.2. The Pumping Technique

In this section we introduce a technique called the pumping technique, which is used to generate infinite set of images from a finite set of images by splicing. It is very general in nature and hence, an example is provided next to exhibit it, instead of a formal discussion.

Example 4.2.1. The example given next is useful in two ways. It exhibits the concept of pumping infinite set of images from a finite set by splicing; gives a set of images called GRIDS used in a later section.

Let Grid$< X, Y, m, n >$ represent an image G of size $< m, n >$, where, m and n are odd positive numbers; m,n$\geq$3. G is defined by,

$$G[i,j] = \begin{cases} X & \text{if i is odd or j is odd} \\ Y & \text{otherwise} \end{cases}$$

where, $1 \leq i \leq m, 1 \leq j \leq n$

G is said to be a Grid defined over $< X, Y >$ of size $< m, n >$. An example Grid is shown in Figure 8 GRIDS$< X, Y >$ represents the set of all Grids over $< X, Y >$.

GRIDS$< X, Y > = \{$Grid$< X, Y, m, n >$, m and are odd, m,n$\geq$ 3$\}$

Now let us exhibit the pumping technique by generating the infinite set of Grids from a single grid Grid$< X, ., 9, 9 >$. Consider an initial set of images consisting only of Grid$< X, ., 9, 9 >$ and let Grid$< X, ., 5, 5 >$ be a null-context Type-1 site. i.e $<<$ Grid $< X, ., 5, 5 >>$ be a Type-1 pattern. Figures 9, 10 show the Type-1 splicing between two images of the form Grid $< X, ., 9, 9 >$ (Figure 9) giving two resultants R_1=Grid$< X, ., 9, 11 >$ and R_2=Grid$< X, ., 9, 7 >$ (Figure 10). The site used is Grid $< X, ., 5, 5 >$.

```
X X X X X X X
X . X . X . X
X X X X X X X
X . X . X . X
X X X X X X X
X . X . X . X
X X X X X X X
X . X . X . X
X X X X X X X
```

Figure 8. Grid< $X, ., 9, 7$ >

Note. In Figures 9, 10, for I_1 the prefix is I_1 itself and the suffixes are Λ. For I_2, the prefix is Grid< $X, ., 9, 7$ > and BUSuffix=CSuffix=Λ.

$I_1 = Grid < X, ., 9, 9 >$

```
X X X X X X X X X X
X . X . X . X . X
X X X X X X X X X
X . X . X . X . X
X X X X X X X X X
X . X . X . X . X
X X X X X X X X X
X . X . X . X . X
X X X X X X X X X
```

$I_2 = Grid < X, ., 9, 9 >$

```
X X X X X X X X | X X
X . X . X . X . X
X X X X X X X X | X X
X . X . X . X . X
X X X X X X X X | X X
X . X . X . X . X
X X X X X X X X | X X
X . X . X . X . X
X X X X X X X X | X X
```

Figure 9. Splicing between Grids (I)

A similar splicing between R_1 and I_1 produces Grid< $X, ., 9, 13$ >. Thus all possible Grids over < $X, .$ > with number of rows as 9 and any number of columns can be generated. Now, let us consider the splicing between two images $I_1 = I_2 =$ Grid< $X, ., 9, 13$ >. The reader can draw the desired Type-1 splicing. From the definitions it is clear that Grid< $X, ., 11, 13$ > can be generated. Thus by repeatedly applying these two types of splicings we can generate all possible Grids over < $X, ..$ with size greater than < $3, 3$ >.

Property 4.2.1. Whenever in a null-context splicing system, two Grids I_1 and I_2 defined over < X, Y > splice, with a site s(which is also the crossing), size(s) $\geq$< $3, 3$ >, the resultants are also Grids defined over < X, Y >.

5. Finite Simple Splicing Systems

A splicing system S is said to be a finite-simple splicing system (hereafter referred as FS splicing system), if it is both simple and finite. As we have already seen, it can be expressed as, $S = < A, I, B >$, where, I and the four sets of patterns are finite.

The FS splicing system is a direct extension of Tom Head's original -unextended-splicing system [3] to the array languages or to the second dimension. It is interesting to study the properties of these FS splicing systems. The special classes of splicing systems, viz. null-context, uniform and equal are studied under the domain of FS splicing and an hierarchy is established. In the case of H-systems, the null-context splicing languages were shown to be equivalent to uniform splicing languages and strictly locally testable languages. This does not hold good in the case of 2D. In this section, the hierarchy of FS splicing languages is established and their relationship to the strictly locally testable languages is also discussed.

5.1. Hierarchy of FS Splicing Languages

Let $\mathcal{L}_\mathcal{U}$ represent the set of all FS uniform splicing languages, $\mathcal{L}_\mathcal{E}$ the set of all FS equal splicing languages and $\mathcal{L}_\mathcal{NC}$ the set of all FS null-context splicing languages.

$$R_1 = Grid < X, ., 9, 11 > \qquad R_2 = Grid < X, ., 9, 7 >$$

```
X X X X X X X X X X X        X X X X X X X
X . X . X . X . X . X        X . X . X . X
X X X X X X X X X X X        X X X X X X X
X . X . X . X . X . X        X . X . X . X
X X X X X X X X X X X        X X X X X X X
X . X . X . X . X . X        X . X . X . X
X X X X X X X X X X X        X X X X X X X
X . X . X . X . X . X        X . X . X . X
X X X X X X X X X X X        X X X X X X X
```

Figure 10. Splicing between Grids (II)

Theorem 5.1.1. $\mathcal{L}_\mathcal{U} \subset \mathcal{L}_\mathcal{E}$.

Proof. It is directly evident from the definition of uniform and equal splicing systems, that every FS uniform splicing system is an FS equal splicing system. Hence, $\mathcal{L}_\mathcal{U} \subseteq \mathcal{L}_\mathcal{E}$. Now, let us give an example of a language which is FS equal, but not FS uniform. □

Example 5.1.1. Consider the following FS equal splicing system. S=$< A, I, B >$, A=$\{1,0\}$. I=$\{00, b\}$, where b= $\begin{smallmatrix} 1 & 1 \\ 1 & 1 \end{smallmatrix}$. And B=$< B_1, B_1, B_1, B_1 >$.

$B_1 = \left\{ << \begin{smallmatrix} 1 \\ 1 \end{smallmatrix} , >>, \ << 0 >> \right\}$. The language generated is L(S) = $L_1 \cup L_2$, where,

$$L_1 = 0^+, \quad L_2 = \begin{pmatrix} 1 \\ 1 \end{pmatrix}^+.$$

Now let us prove that this language cannot be produced by any FS uniform splicing system. By contradiction, let there be an FS uniform splicing system S'= $< A, I', m, n >$ producing this language. That is L(S') = L(S). I should be such that, I = $I_1 \cup I_2$, where $I_1 \subset L_1$ and $I_2 \subset L_2$. As S' is finite, I_1 and I_2 are also finite. From I_1 the images have to splice and produce L_1. But $I_1 \subset 0^+$ and is finite. So the sites for I_1 should be of the form $0^{1,k}$,k>0. Then only splicing can take place among the images of I_1. Thus, m=1. Now, we can rewrite S' as S'= $< A, I, 1, n >$. This means that, $(0+1)^n$ are all sites and hence, 1^n is also a site. As $(1_2)^n$ belong to L(S'), consider the splicing shown in Figure 11.

Images:

$$
\left.
\begin{array}{cccccc}
1 & 1 & 1 & \ldots & 1 \\
1 & 1 & 1 & \ldots & 1
\end{array}
\right|
\qquad
\left.
\begin{array}{cccccc}
1 & 1 & 1 & \ldots & 1 \\
1 & 1 & 1 & \ldots & 1
\end{array}
\right|
$$

Resultants:

$$
\begin{array}{cccccc}
1 & 1 & 1 & \ldots & 1 \\
1 & 1 & 1 & \ldots & 1 & \qquad 1 \quad 1 \quad 1 \quad \ldots \quad 1 \\
1 & 1 & 1 & \ldots & 1
\end{array}
$$

Figure 11. Splicing for Example 5.1.1

By this, $\begin{pmatrix} 1 \\ 1 \\ 1 \end{pmatrix}^n = (1_3)^n \in L(S')$, which is not in L(S). So, L(S') $\neq$ L(S). Hence the proof.

Theorem 5.1.2. $\mathcal{L}_\mathcal{E} \subset \mathcal{L}_{\mathcal{NC}}$

Proof. It is directly evident from the definitions that, $\mathcal{L}_\mathcal{E} \subseteq \mathcal{L}_{\mathcal{NC}}$ An example of a language is discussed, which is FS null-context but not FS -equal. □

Example 5.1.2. Consider the following FS-null-context splicing system. S=$< A, I, B >$. A = $\{X,+,-,1,2,a,b\}$. I = $\{i_0, i_1, i_2\}$. B=$< B_1, \emptyset, \emptyset, \emptyset >$. $B_1 = \{<< X >>, << c_1 >>\}$. The crossing c_1 and the initial images i_0, i_1 and i_2 are as shown below.

$$
i_0 = XX, \quad i_1 = \begin{pmatrix} 2 & + & + & 1 \\ 2 & X & X & 1 \\ 2 & - & - & 1 \end{pmatrix}, \quad i_2 = \begin{pmatrix} b & + & + & a \\ b & X & X & a \\ b & - & - & a \end{pmatrix}, \quad c_1 = \begin{pmatrix} X \\ - \end{pmatrix}
$$

Let,

$$
L_0 = X^+, \quad L_1 = \begin{matrix} 2 \\ 2 \\ 2 \end{matrix} \begin{pmatrix} + \\ X \\ - \end{pmatrix}^+ \begin{matrix} 1 \\ 1 \\ 1 \end{matrix}, \quad L_2 = \begin{matrix} b \\ b \\ b \end{matrix} \begin{pmatrix} + \\ X \\ - \end{pmatrix}^+ \begin{matrix} a \\ a \\ a \end{matrix},
$$

$$
L_3 = \begin{matrix} 2 \\ 2 \\ 2 \end{matrix} \begin{pmatrix} + \\ X \\ - \end{pmatrix}^+ \begin{matrix} a \\ a \\ a \end{matrix}, \quad L_4 = \begin{matrix} b \\ b \\ b \end{matrix} \begin{pmatrix} + \\ X \\ - \end{pmatrix}^+ \begin{matrix} 1 \\ 1 \\ 1 \end{matrix}, \quad L_5 = \begin{matrix} 2 \\ 2 \\ b \end{matrix} \begin{pmatrix} + \\ X \\ - \end{pmatrix}^+ \begin{matrix} a \\ a \\ a \end{matrix},
$$

$$
L_6 = \begin{matrix} a \\ a \\ 2 \end{matrix} \begin{pmatrix} + \\ X \\ - \end{pmatrix}^+ \begin{matrix} 1 \\ 1 \\ 1 \end{matrix}, \quad L_7 = \begin{matrix} 2 \\ 2 \\ b \end{matrix} \begin{pmatrix} + \\ X \\ - \end{pmatrix}^+ \begin{matrix} 1 \\ 1 \\ 1 \end{matrix}, \quad L_8 = \begin{matrix} b \\ b \\ 2 \end{matrix} \begin{pmatrix} + \\ X \\ - \end{pmatrix}^+ \begin{matrix} a \\ a \\ a \end{matrix}
$$

They are generated as follows.

i_0 by 'pumping' generates L_0.

i_1 by 'pumping' generates L_1.

i_2 by 'pumping' generates L_2.

Images in L_1 and L_2 splice using $<< c_1 >>$ to generate L_3 and L_4

Images in L_1 and L_2 splice using $<< X >>$ to generate L_5 and L_6

Images in L_1 and L_4 splice using $<< X >>$ to generate L_7.

Images in L_2 and L_3 splice using $<< X >>$ to generate L_8.

The languge L=L(S)=$\bigcup L_i$, $0 \leq i \leq 8$. Let $L_\Delta = L - L_0$. Now, we claim that there is no FS equal splicing system generating L. By contradiction, let there exist an FS equal splicing system S'=$< A, I', B' >$, such that L(S') = L(S) = L.

Lemma 5.1.1. *B' should include at least one pattern p of the form $<< X^k >>$, for some k>0.*

Proof. According to our assumption, L(S)=L(S'). I' can be expressed as, $I' = I_0 \cup I_\Delta$, $I_0 \subset L_0$ and $I_\Delta \subset L_\Delta$. If no pattern p of the form, $<< X^k >>$, for some $k> 0$ exists in B', then the initial images in I_0 cannot splice. Let l=Max$\{i/X^i \in I_0\}$. As images in I_0 cannot splice, the image $X^{l+1} \in L$ has to be generated by repeated splicing of images in I_Δ. Note that none of the images in I_Δ have any image of the form X^j, j>0 as their prefix for any type of splicing. A simple induction on the number of splicing steps will prove that, neither the images in I_Δ nor the images generated by repeated splicing of images in I_Δ in the splicing system S' have any prefixes of that form. If we include patterns in B' to generate such images L(S'), then some erroneous images not in L(S) will be produced in L(S'). But, to produce an image of the form X^a, a>0, by splicing, we need an image with an image of the form X^i, i>0, as its prefix. Thus, I_Δ, even on repeated splicing cannot produce the image X^{l+1}. This proves that, to generate all the images in L_0, the images in I_0 have to splice. To satisfy this requirement, B' should include at least one pattern of the form, $<< X^k >>$, k>0. □

In view of this lemma there is k such that, a pattern p = $<< X^k >>\in B'$. Note that S' is an equal splicing system. So,X^k is also a Type-2 site. Consider the Type-2 splicing shown in Figure 12 between I_1 ,$I_2 \in$ L(S') and the resultants R_1 and R_2. R_1 and $R_2 \in$ L(S'), by the rules of splicing.

I_1 $\qquad\qquad$ I_2

```
2  +  +  .  .  +  1      b  +  +  .  .  +  a
2  X  X  .  .  X  1      b  X  X  .  .  X  a
2  -  -  .  .  -  1      b  -  -  .  .  -  a
```

R_1 $\qquad\qquad$ R_2

```
b  +  +  .  .  +  1      2  +  +  .  .  +  a
b  X  X  .  .  X  1      2  X  X  .  .  X  a
b  -  -  .  .  -  a      2  -  -  .  .  -  1
```

Figure 12. Splicing for Example 5.1.2

As, $r_1, r_2 \notin$ L(S), L(S) $\neq$ L(S'). Hence, the proof.

Theorem 5.1.3. $\mathcal{L}_\mathcal{U} \subset \mathcal{L}_\mathcal{E} \subset \mathcal{L}_{\mathcal{NC}}$.

Proof. Straightforward from Theorems 5.1.1 and 5.1.2. □

5.2. Strictly Locally Testability And FS Splicing Languages

In the case of H-systems, the class of null-context H-system languages was shown to be equivalent to the class of strictly locally testable languges. But, that is not the case with 2D FS languages. In fact, the hierarchy established in the previous section is unrelated to the class of SLT languages.

Example 5.2.1. In this example, we present a language which is strictly locally testable, but cannot be generated by any FS null-context splicing system.

Let L be a language over the alphabet A= {1,0} defined as follows. L consists of all images of 1's and 0's which do not have $0^{3,3}$ as subimage. That is the images do not contain the subimage $\begin{pmatrix} 0 & 0 & 0 \\ 0 & 0 & 0 \\ 0 & 0 & 0 \end{pmatrix}$. This language is obviously 3,3 - strictly locally testable with

$$W = \{0^{3,3}\} \text{ and } U = V = Y = Z = A^{3,3} \text{ - W.}$$

Now let us show that this language L cannot be produced by any null-context splicing system. By contradiction, let there be a null-context splicing system S =< $A, I, B >$ with L(S) = L. As I is finite, the language L has to be produced by splicing only. So there should be atleast one pattern in S. Let it be a Type-1 pattern << X >>. Note that X cannot contain $0^{3,3}$ as its subimage. Let Size(X) = < r, c >. Consider two images I_1 and I_2. They are images of same size full of 1's with $0^{2,3}$ and X embedded in them as shown in Figure 13. I_1 and I_2 do not contain $0^{3,3}$ as subimage. Hence, both belong to L. A splicing as shown in the Figure 13 results in a resultant image with $0^{3,3}$ as its subimgae. This image by the rule of splicing should belong to L(S) but does not belong to L. Thus, L(S) $\neq$ L.

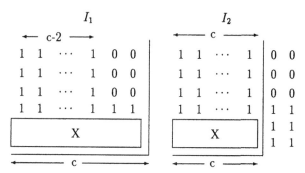

Figure 13. Splicing for Example 5.2.1

Pads. Let I be an image defined over an alphabet Σ of size < m, n >. Let P be an alphabet. Let us define Pad(I,P,a,b,c,d), where a,b,c and d are positive integers, to be the set S as

$$S = \text{Pad(I,P,a,b,c,d)} = P^{(m+a+c),d} \Phi(P^{a,n} \Theta I \Theta P^{c,n}) \Phi P^{(m+a+c),b}$$

If P is a has just one symbol then the Pad(I,P,a,b,c,d) defined above will have only one image. In such a case Pad(I,P,a,b,c,d) is used to represent that single image itself, rather than a set consisting of that single image. The images in set S are said to be padded images of I over the alphabet P of size < a, b, c, d >. Figure 14 shows an example. For this example, I=Grid$< 1,0,5,5 >$. P=$\{c\}$. We give the the single image in the set Pad(I,P,1,2,3,4).

```
c  c  c  c  c  c  c  c  c  c  c
c  c  c  c  1  1  1  1  1  c  c
c  c  c  c  1  0  1  0  1  c  c
c  c  c  c  1  1  1  1  1  c  c
c  c  c  c  1  0  1  0  1  c  c
c  c  c  c  1  1  1  1  1  c  c
c  c  c  c  c  c  c  c  c  c  c
c  c  c  c  c  c  c  c  c  c  c
c  c  c  c  c  c  c  c  c  c  c
```

Figure 14. An example for padding

Property 5.2.1. Let I_1 and I_2 be two images defined over an alphabet Σ. Let $I_1' \in$ Pad(I_1,P,a,b,c,d) and $I_2' \in$ Pad(I_2,P,a,b,c,d). P$\cap\Sigma = \emptyset$. Let m=Max$\{$a,b,c,d$\}$. Then any two resultants R_1' and R_2' obtained by splicing I_1' and I_2' with any nullcontext site s, size(s) $>< m, m >$, are always such that,
$$R_1' \in \text{Pad}(r_1,\text{P,a,b,c,d}) \text{ and } R_2' \in \text{Pad}(r_2,\text{P,a,b,c,d})$$
for some $r_1, r_2 \in \Sigma^{++}$.

In simple terms, whenever padded images with a pad of size $< a, b, c, d >$ splice with a nullcontext site s, then the resultants are also padded images with a pad of size $< a, b, c, d >$, provided s is not a subimage of the padding of the two images.

For brevity, we omit the proof for the above property, but it can be easily proved formally.

Example 5.2.2. In this section we present an example of a language, which is an FS uniform splicing language, but not strictly locally testable.

Let S=$< A, I, 5, 5 >$ be an uniform splicing system with A=$\{$0,1,a,b,c$\}$, I=$\{I_1, I_2, I_3\}$.
$$I_1 = \text{Pad(Grid}< 1,0,9,9 >,\{a\},1,0,1,1)$$
$$I_2 = \text{Pad(Grid}< 1,0,9,9 >,\{b\},1,1,1,0)$$
$$I_3 = \text{Pad}(a^{11}\Phi(a^5b^4\Theta Grid < 1,0,9,9 > \Theta a^5 b^4)\Phi b^{11}), \{c\}, 1,1,1,1)$$

Now let us consider the language of the splicing system, L=L(S). Let L_1, L_2 and L_3 represent the languges produceable from I_1, I_2 and I_3 alone respectively. Formally,
$$L_1 = \text{L}(S_1); S_1 = < A, \{I_1\}, 5, 5 >$$
$$L_2 = \text{L}(S_2); S_2 = < A, \{I_2\}, 5, 5 >$$
$$L_3 = \text{L}(S_3); S_3 = < A, \{I_3\}, 5, 5 >$$
Let
$$L_1' = \{x \mid \text{x=Pad(Grid}< 1,0,i,j >, \{a\}, 1, 0, 1, 1), \text{i,j} \geq 5, \text{i and j are odd}\}$$
$$L_2' = \{x \mid \text{x=Pad(Grid}< 1,0,i,j >, \{b\}, 1, 1, 1, 0), \text{i,j} \geq 5, \text{i and j are odd}\}$$
$$L_3' = \text{Pad}(L_3^\Delta, \{c\}, 1, 1, 1, 1), \text{where}$$
$$L_3^\Delta = (a^{(i+2)}\Phi((a^{(j+1)/2}b^{(j-1)/2})\Theta Grid < 1,0,i,j > \Theta(a^{(j+1)/2}b^{(j-1)/2}))\Phi b^{i+2}),$$
i,j$\geq$5 and i and j odd.

L_1' consists of images of the same form as that of I_1, but of all sizes. Similarly L_2' consists of images of the same as that of I_2 but of all sizes. L_3^Δ consists of Grids with a string $a^k b^{k-1}$, where, k=$\lceil 1/2*(\text{length of the grid})\rceil$, padded on the top and bottom and one pad of a column of 'a' on the left and one pad of a column of 'b' on the right. And L'_3 consists of images of L^A_3 with a padding of 'c' of size $< 1, 1, 1, 1 >$. L'_3 consists of images of the form of I_3, but of all sizes.

By pumping technique, it is clear that, L'_1 can be produced from I_1. i.e $L'_1 \subseteq L_1$. Similarly, $L'_2 \subseteq L_2$ and $L'_3 \subseteq L_3$. But the property of grids, Property 4.2.1 and the property of Pads Property 5.2.1 infer that, $L'_1 = L_1$ and $L'_2 = L_2$. But L'_3 is not equal to L_3. Let $L_3 = L'_3 \bigcup L''_3$. But again, as per Property 4.2.1 and Property 5.2.1,

$L''_3 \subseteq$ Pad(Pad(Grid$< 1, 0, i, j >$, {a,b}, 1, 1, 1, 1), {c}, 1, 1, 1, 1), i and j are odd, i,j$\geq$3

Though L'_3 can be defined formally, the above subset property is enough for our purpose. Now, L(S) may contain images obtained by splicing two images, one from L_1 and other from L_2, L_2 & L_3 and L_1 & L_3. We shall prove that such kind of splicing cannot take place due to the lack of compatability. Only splicing among the images of the same language L_1, L_2 and L_3 can take place. Note that the splicing system S, is an uniform splicing system and all the images of size $< 5, 5 >$ can act as null-context site. Let us consider the case where, g=Grid$< 1, 0, 5, 5 >$ is used as a site for a Type-1 splicing between $I_1 \in L_1$ and $I_2 \in L_2$. It can easily be noted that for any $I_1 \in L_1$, the Type-1 prefix p_1 with respect to the null-context site g, is always such that, size(p_1)=$< i, j >$, with i and j being even numbers. But the corresponding prefix p_2 of any $I_2 \in L_2$ is always such that, size(p_2) = $< i, j >$, with i being even and j being odd. Thus, the prefixes are not of the same size and splicing is illegal and can not take place. The Table 5.2.1 shows the nature of the size of the four different types of splicing prefixes of the images belonging to the three languages L_1, L_2 and L_3 with respect to the site g. For example, the cell corresponding to L_2 and Type-2 reads, $< even, even >$. This means that, if an image s$\in L_2$ is spliced in Type-2, with the image 'g' as a null-context site, then the Type-2 prefix of s, will have even number of rows and even number of columns.

Table 5.2.1 : The table for the Example 5.2.2

	Type-1	Type-2	Type-3	Type-4
L_1	$< even, even >$	$< even, odd >$	$< even, even >$	$< even, odd >$
L_2	$< even, odd >$	$< even, even >$	$< even, odd >$	$< even, even >$
L_3	$< odd, odd >$	$< odd, odd >$	$< odd, odd >$	$< odd, odd >$

From the table it is clear that incompatibilities exist for splicing between 2 images belonging to two different languages of L_1, L_2 and L_3, with respect to the site g. A similar argument can be given for other sites of size $< 5, 5 >$. Thus, L = $L_1 \bigcup L_2 \bigcup L_3$.

We shall show that L is not strictly locallay testable. By contradiction, let L be p,q-strictly locally testable. Let us consider the case where, p and q are even. For the other cases, the proof is similar. As L is p,q-strictly locally testable, there exist sets U,V,Y,Z and W consisting of images of size $< p, q >$ satisfying the equality 3.1.6. Let,

l_1 = Pad(Grid$< 1, 0, p - 1, q - 1 >$, {a},1,0,1,1).
l_2 = Pad(Grid$< 1, 0, p - 1, q - 1 >$, {b},1,1,1,0).

i.e l_1 represents the image in L_1 of size $< p + 1, q >$, l_2 represents the image in L_2 of

364

size $< p+1, q >$. Let,

$u = \text{Pad}(\text{Grid}< 1,0, p-1, q-1 >, \{a\}, 1,0,0,1)$
$v = \text{Pad}(\text{Grid}< 1,0, p-1, q-1 >, \{b\}, 1,1,0,0)$
$y = \text{Pad}(\text{Grid}< 1,0, p-1, q-1 >, \{a\}, 0,0,1,1)$
$z = \text{Pad}(\text{Grid}< 1,0, p-1, q-1 >, \{b\}, 0,1,1,0)$

Note that, u and y are the top-left and bottom-left subimages of l_1 of size $< p, q >$. v and z are top-right and bottom-right subimages of l_2 of size $< p, q >$. As, $l_1, l_2 \in$ L, $u \in$ U; $v \in$ V; $y \in$ Y; $z \in$ Z; Consider the image,

$$X = a_{2p+3}\Phi((a^{q+1}b^q)\ominus X_g(a^{q+1}b^q))\Phi b_{2p+3}$$

where, $X_g = \text{Grid}< 1, 0, 2(p-1)+3, 2(q-1)+3 >$. Let the top-left, top-right, bottom-left and bottom-right images of X be u_x, v_x, y_x and z_x respectively. Note that, u_x=u; v_x=v; y_x=y; z_x=z. And hence, $u_x \in$ U; $v_x \in$ V. $y_x \in$ Y; $z_x \in$ Z. Consider the image X_c=Pad(X,\{c\},1,1,1,1). X is a subimage of X_c. Thus, every subimage of X of size $< p, q >$, is also a subimage of X_c. As, $X_c \in$ L, none of the subimages of X_c of size $< p, q >$ belongs to W. This proves that, X belongs to the language in the right hand side of the equality in Definition 3.1.6. But, $X \notin$ L'. Hence, the equality does not hold good for the language L. Thus, L is not strictly locally testable.

Figure 15 clearly depicts the hierarchy of FS splicing languages and SLT languages.

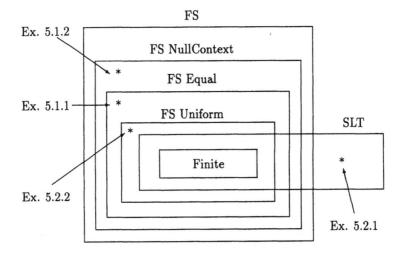

Figure 15. Hierarchy of FS splicing languages and SLT languages

6. Conclusion

In this paper, we have defined 2D splicing systems and several restrictions of it. The hierarchy among these classes is studied. These classes have been compared to the class of strictly locally testable languages. There are several directions for future work. This paper mainly concentrates on hierarchy. Other features like closure properties can be studied. It has also been found that with this definition, by using the mapping function (i.e by using non-simple splicing systems) we are able to generate diffrent interesting languages of pictures more easily than by those given in [11].

In this paper, only finite-simple splicing systems have been considered. It would be interesting to study the systems with infinite set of initial images and patterns. A broader definition as given in [7] can be extended to 2D. It has to be found whether the 2D splicing systems will be universally computational in this case. Another direction of research could be to extend the definition of splicing to graphs. This might have more biological significance. We are working on these lines.

References

1. K. Culik II, T. Harju, Splicing semigroups of dominoes and DNA, *Discrete Applied Mathematics*, 31 (1991), 262 – 277.

2. J. Dassow, Gh. Păun, *Regulated Rewriting in Formal Language Theory*, EATCS Monographs in Computer Science Vol. 18, Springer-Verlag, 1989.

3. T. Head, Formal language theory and DNA – an analysis of the generative capacity of specific recombinant behaviours, *Bulletin of Mathematical Biology*, 49 (1987), 737 – 759.

4. J. E. Hopcroft, J. D. Ullman, *Introduction to Automata Theory, Languages and Computation*, Addison-Wesley Publishing Inc., 1979.

5. K. Krithivasan, R. Siromoney, Array automata and operations on array languages, *International Journal of Computer Mathematics*, 4 (1974), Section A, 3 – 30.

6. A. De Luca, A. Restivo, A characterization of strictly locally testable languages and its application to subsemigroups of a free semigroup, *Information and Control*, 44 (1980), 300 – 319.

7. Gh. Păun, Regular extended H-systems are computationally universal, *Journal of Automata, Languages and Combinatorics*, 1 (1996), 27 – 36.

8. A. Rosenfeld, *Picture Languages*, Academic Press, New York, 1979.

9. A. Salomaa, *Formal Languages*, Academic Press, New York, 1973.

10. G. Siromoney, R. Siromoney, K. Krithivasan, Abstract families of matrices and picture languages, *Computer Graphics and Image Processing*, 1 (1972).

11. G. Siromoney, R. Siromoney, K. Krithivasan, Picture languages with array rewriting rules, *Information and Control*, 22, 5 (1973).

12. M. S. Waterman, *Introduction to Computational Biology: Maps, Sequences and Genomes*, Chapman & Hall, London, 1995.

Chapter 5. Infinite Words

Two Lower Bounds on Computational Complexity of Infinite Words

Juraj HROMKOVIČ[1]

Institute of Informatics, University of Kiel
D-24098 Kiel, Germany

Juhani KARHUMÄKI

Department of Mathematics, University of Turku
20014 Turku, Finland

Abstract. The most of the previous work on the complexity of infinite words has measured the complexity as descriptional one, i. e. an infinite word w had a "small" complexity if it was generated by a morphism or another simple machinery, and w has been considered to be "complex" if one needs to use more complex devices (gsm's) to generate it. In [5] the study of the computational complexity of infinite word generation and of its relation to the descriptional characterizations mentioned above was started. The complexity classes GSPACE(f) = { infinite words generated in space $f(n)$} are defined there, and some fundamental mechanisms for infinite word generation are related to them. It is also proved there, that there is no hierarchy between GSPACE($O(1)$) and GSPACE($\log_2 n$). Here, GSPACE(f) $\subset$ GSPACE(g) for $g(n) \geq f(n) \geq \log_2 n$, $f(n) = o(g(n))$ is proved. The main result of this paper is a new lower bound on the computational complexity of infinite word generation: real-time, binary working alphabet, and $o(n/(\log n)^2$ space is insufficient to generate a concrete infinite word over two-letter alphabet.

1. Introduction

The most of the previous work on infinite word generation has measured the complexity of infinite words as a descriptional complexity. This means an infinite word y was of a "small" complexity if y was generated by a simple machinery (for instance, iterated morphisms [14]), and y has been considered to be "complex" if one needs to use more complex devices (for instance, double DOL TAG - system [2]) to generate y. Hromkovič, Karhumäki and Lepistö [5] proposed to investigate the computational complexity (difficulty) of infinite words as well as its relation to the above mentioned descriptional characterizations. They have defined the time and space complexity of generating infinite word as well as the corresponding complexity

---

[1]This author was partially supported by the Slovak Scientific Grant Agency Grant No. 95/5305/277.

classes GSPACE(s) = {infinite words generated in space $s(n)$}, and GTIME(t) = {infinite words generated in time $t(n)$} for some functions $s, t : \mathbf{N} \to \mathbf{N}$.

The main results of [5] are the following ones:

1. GSPACE($O(1)$) = GSPACE(f) = {ultimately periodic infinite words} for every $f(n) = o(\log_2 n)$, i.e., there is no hierarchy of space complexity classes below $\log_2 n$,

2. the infinite words generated by morphisms are in the smallest nontrivial space complexity class GSPACE($\log_2 n$),

3. Kolakowski sequence [2] is in GSPACE($\log_2 n$), and

4. the infinite words generated by an exponential double DOL TAG - system are in GSPACE($(\log_2 n)^2$).

We recall that Kolakowski sequence was considered as a nontrivial sequence in [2], and that DOUBLE DOL TAG - system introduced in [2] as a unified model to generate infinite words has a very high generating power.

This paper continues the investigation of the computational complexity of infinite word generation. The main attention here is devoted to the development of some lower bound methods on the complexity of infinite word generation. Our first result is the strong, infinite hierarchy GSPACE(f) $\subset$ GSPACE(g) for any $g(n) \geq f(n) \geq \log_2 n$ and $f(n) = o(g(n))$. The main effort of this paper is devoted to the development of a lower bound method on the computational sources needed to generate a specific infinite word. Such a lower bound was already established by Fischer et. al. [4] who show that real-time multicounter machines (i.e. Turing machines working over one-letter alphabet) cannot generate a specific word. Here, we show that real-time 1-tape Turing machines working in space $o(n/(\log_2 n)^2)$ over two-letter alphabet cannot generate a very natural word.

This paper is organized as follows. Section 2 fixes the notation used. Section 3 contains the hierarchy of the space complexity classes, and Section 4 involves our lower bound for our specific infinite word.

2. Definitions and Notations

In this section we fix our computational model - multitape Turing machine - used to define the time and space complexity of generating infinite words.

Our model of computation is *multitape* (or *k-tape*) *Turing machine*, MTM (or k-TM) for short, which consists of

- a finite state control,

- k infinite one way working tapes each of which contains one two-way read/write head,

- one infinite output tape containing one one-way write-only head.

Depending on the current state and the k symbols read by heads on the working tapes the machine makes the following actions (corresponding to one step in a computation):

1. it changes the current state to a new one;

2. it writes a symbol on the output tape and moves the head on the output tape one unit to the right, or it does not do anything on the output tape;

3. each head on a working tape writes a symbol from the finite working alphabet on the currently scanned square and possibly moves to the neighboring square in the right or left.

A *configuration* of a k-TM is $Q = (w, p, x_1, \ldots, x_k)$ where w is a content of the output tape, p is a state, and x_i is the content of the i-th working tape including the position of the head. For a configuration Q, $\overline{Q} = (p, x_1, \ldots, x_2)$ is referred to as its *internal configuration*. The *initial configuration* is the one where all tapes are empty, i. e. containing only blank symbols. As usual a *computation* is a sequence of (consecutive) configurations $Q_0, Q_1, \ldots, Q_n, \ldots$ where Q_0 is the initial one and the machine moves from Q_i to Q_{i+1} in one step. We call the sequence $\overline{Q_0}, \overline{Q_1}, \ldots, \overline{Q_n}, \ldots$ the corresponding *internal computation*.

Next we define central notions how an MTM operates on infinite words.

An *infinite word* $w \in \sum^\omega$ *is generated by an* MTM M if the computation $D = Q_0, Q_1, \ldots$ of M has the following properties:

(i) D is infinite;

(ii) Q_0 is the initial configuration of M, i. e. all the tapes are empty;

(iii) In each configuration Q_i the content of the output tape is a prefix of w;

(iv) For each i there exists an index j such that $j > i$ and the content of the output tape in Q_i is a proper prefix of that in Q_j.

Let M be an MTM generating a word w. The *time* and *space complexities* of M are functions $T_M : \mathbf{N} \to \mathbf{N}$ and $S_M : \mathbf{N} \to \mathbf{N}$ defined as follows:

$T_M(n) = i_n$, where Q_{i_n} is the first configuration of the computation of M having the prefix of w of length n on the output tape.

$S_M(n) = \max\{S(Q_i) \mid i = 0, \ldots, T_M(n)\}$, where $S(Q_i)$ is the space complexity of the configuration Q_i measured as the maximum of the lengths of words on working tapes.

Finally, we define the complexity classes dealt with in this paper in a standard way: For any $t, s : \mathbf{N} \to \mathbf{N}$

GTIME$(t) = \{w \in \sum^\omega \mid \exists$ an MTM M generating w and $T_M(n) \leq t(n)\}$,

GSPACE$(s) = \{w \in \sum^\omega \mid \exists$ an MTM M generating w and $S_M(n) \leq s(n)\}$,

GTIME $-$ SPACE$(t, s) = \{w \in \sum^\omega \mid \exists$ an MTM M generating w and $T_M(n) \leq t(n), S_M(n) \leq s(n)\}$.

3. Space Hierarchy

In [5] it is shown that GSPACE$(f(n)) =$ GSPACE$(g(n))$ for any $f(n) = O(1)$ and $g(n) = o(\log_2 n)$. The natural questions appear: Does there exist an infinite hierarchy for space classes? If yes, how strong is such a hierarchy?

In this section we show that there is a strong space hierarchy for the generation of infinite words, namely, $\mathrm{GSPACE}(f(n)) \subset \mathrm{GSPACE}(g(n))$ for g growing quicker than f.

Theorem 3.1. *Let* f, g *be two nondecreasing functions from* **N** *to* **N** *with the following properties:*

1. $f(n) \leq g(n)$ *for any* $n \in$ **N**,

2. $\sup_{n \to \infty} f(n)/g(n) = 0$,

3. g *is space-constructible*,

4. $g(n) \geq \log_2 n$ *for any* $n \in$ **N**.

Then $\mathrm{GSPACE}(f) \subset \mathrm{GSPACE}(g)$.

Proof. We see two possibilities how to realize the proof. One is to show a one to one correspondence between the generation of infinite words over two-letter alphabet and the recognition of languages over one-letter alphabet. Then, the hierarchy result for $\mathrm{GSPACE}(f)$ is a consequence of the hierarchy results for space-bounded classes of one-letter languages. Here, we prefer to give a direct short proof showing the modification of the well-known diagonalization.

Let $Co(T_1), Co(T_2), \ldots, \ldots,$ be the infinite sequence of binary encoding of 1-TMs in the lexicographical order. We note that we do not need to consider multitape TMs because each MTM can be simulated by a 1-TM with the same space complexity. As usual, there is a Turing machine which, for any given natural number n, constructs $Co(T_n)$.

Let, for any 1-TM $T_i, C_{i1}C_{i2}C_{i3}\ldots$ be the infinite word generated by T_i. Now, we describe a $g(n)$-space bounded 4-TM M which generates an infinite word $\omega_M = d_1 d_2 \ldots$ which differs from $C_{i1}C_{i2}C_{i3}\ldots$ for any i such that T_i is $f(n)$-space bounded. We describe the work of M by giving the procedure of M to generate the n-th bit of ω_M.

Current configuration of M. The output tape contains the first $(n-1)$ symbols of ω_M, and the first working tape contains the binary code of n.

Step 1. M computes the value $g(n)$ and it marks the $g(n)$-th positions on all four working tapes.

Step 2. M writes $1^{g(n)}$ on the second tape.

Step 3. M computes $Co(T_k)$ on the third tape, for a k such that $n = 1 + 2 + 3 + \ldots + (j-1) + j + k$ and $1 \leq k \leq j + 1$. This can be done in $|Co(T_k)|$ space. If Step 3 requires more than $g(n)$ cells of the third tape, then M halts and sets $d_n = 0$. Otherwise M continues with Step 4. Note, that the way in which k is chosen ensures that every Turing machine T_k is infinitely many times asked for computing an element of the infinite word ω_M.

Step 4. M simulates the work of T_k from the initial configuration on the fourth tape except that the produced symbols $C_{k1}C_{k2}\ldots C_{k(n-1)}$ are not written anywhere. M uses binary alphabet to encode the working alphabet of T_k in this simulation. If $g(n)$ cells are not enough to complete the simulation then M halts and sets $d_n = 0$. Besides this M computes the number of simulated steps of T_k on the second tape. If this number is equal to $2^{g(n)}$ then M halts and sets $d_n = 0$. If M succeeds to simulate T_k and T_k computes the symbol C_{kn}, then M sets $d_n = |1 - C_{kn}|$.

Step 5. M writes d_n on the output tape and adds 1 to the binary number coded on the first tape. The contents of all other working tapes is made empty.

Now, we show that $\omega_M = d_1 d_2 \ldots$ is different from $C_{i1} C_{i2} \ldots$ for any i such that T_i is $f(n)$-space bounded. We prove it by contradiction.

Assume that there exists a j such that:

(a) T_j is $f(n)$-space bounded, and

(b) $d_n = C_{jn}$ for all $n \in \mathbf{N}$.

Let Γ be the working alphabet of T_j and let T_j have s states. Since $\sup_{n \to \infty} f(n)/g(n) = 0$ there exists a positive integer m such that

(i) $m = 1 + 2 + 3 \ldots + (r-1) + r + j$ with $0 \le j \le r + 1$,

(ii) $g(m) > |Co(T_j)|$,

(iii) $g(m) > \log_2(|\Gamma| + 1) \cdot f(m)$, and

(iv) $2^{g(m)} > s \cdot (|\Gamma| + 1)^{f(m)}$ which is the number of all different configurations of T_j.

Because of (ii) M is able to perform Step 2. Because of (iii) and (iv) M is able to simulate the generation of of $C_{j1} \ldots C_{jm}$ by T_j. Thus, $d_m = 1 - C_{jm} \neq C_{jm}$, which contradicts to (b). $\qquad \square$

4. A Constructive Lower Bound

One of the hardest tasks in the complexity theory is to prove lower bounds, i. e., the nonexistence of complexity-bounded algorithms (TMs) for given computing problems. Since nobody has been able to prove for a specific language L in NP that L $\notin$ SPACE($\log_2 n$) = DLOG it is very unprobably that somebody will be able to prove for a specific infinite word w that $w \notin$ GSPACE($\log_2 n$). It is also nontrivial to find candidates for this property.

To give a more concrete reason why it is so hard to prove that some infinite word does not belong to GSPACE($\log_2 n$), we note that each prefix of length n of any infinite word algorithmically generated has Kolmogorov complexity at most $\log_2 n$ (see [8] or the original sources [3], [7], [13] for an overview on Kolmogorov complexity). This means that one can always store an encoded content of the output tape on a working tape of the length $\log_2 n$, and use the code of the prefix to generate further output bits. From this point of view the first nontrivial space class GSPACE($\log_2 n$) seems to be very powerful. Thus, the proof of $w \notin$ GSPACE($\log_2 n$) for some w generated by an iterative mechanism cannot be based on the idea that it is impossible to store enough information on the working tape about the already generated prefix on the output tape - the oposite is clearly true. This means that to prove $w \notin$ GSPACE($\log_2 n$) requires to prove the following facts about w:

(i) there is a large prefix y of w whose main part must be stored in order to be able to generate further bits of w, and

(ii) if the information about y is stored in some word x of the length $O(\log_2 n)$, then each algorithm decoding x in order to get the information about y, which is necessary for further generation, has the space complexity greater than $\log_2 n$.

Recently, there has been developed methods to prove (i) [8], [6], but we do not know any method which would allow to go even a little bit in the direction of (ii).

To be able to prove at least a nontrivial lower bound useful for further investigation we restrict the complexity of generation in a very strong way. A 1-TM M is called *strongly real-time* if its working alphabet is identical with its output alphabet (i. e. M cannot use a larger working alphabet than the output alphabet to speed-up the computation), and M writes an output symbol on the output tape in each step.

We consider the following infinite word

$$\omega_{bin} = bin(0)bin(1)bin(2)\ldots bin(i)\ldots,$$

where $bin(i)$ is the binary encoding of i. We shall use Kolmogorov complexity to show that ω_{bin} cannot be generated simultaneously in strongly real-time and in logarithmic space.

Theorem 4.1. ω_{bin} *cannot be generated by any strongly real-time 1-TM working in space* $f(m) = o(m/(\log m)^2)$.

Proof. In order to explain carefully the lower bound proof method developed here, we first prove the following result which is weaker than the assertion of Theorem 4.1.

Theorem A.1. ω_{bin} *cannot be generated by a strongly real-time 1-TM working in logarithmic space.*

Proof. (By contradiction.) Let M be a strongly real-time 1-TM working in space $\log_2 m$, and generating ω_{bin}. Let $Co(M)$ be the binary representation of the code of M and let M have s states. Let, for any word $w \in \{0,1\}^*$, $K(w)$ be the Kolmogorov complexity of w, i.e., the minimum over the lengths of the binary encodings of all Turing machines generating w.

In what follows, if one has a procedure (algorithm) A with input I to generate a finite word w then we consider the Kolmogorov complexity of A, $\mathbf{K}(A)$, as the sum of the Kolmogorov complexity of the binary code of A ($K(Co(A))$) and the Kolmogorov complexity of the binary code of the input ($K(Co(I))$). Obviously, $K(A)$ is an upper bound on $K(w)$ in this case.

Now, we prove a helpful technical fact.

Fact A.1.1. Let M be a strongly real-time 1-TM writing a word $w \in \{0,1\}^*$ on the output tape in a computation part D of the length $|w|$. Then M visits at least
$$K(w) - K(Co(M)) - \lceil \log_2 s \rceil - \log_2 |w| - z$$
different cells of the working tape during the computation part D, where z is a constant independent of w.

Proof of Fact A.1.1. Let M visit $r(w)$ cells of the working tape during the computation part D in which w is generated. Then the following algorithm A can be used to generate w.

Algorithm A

Input: $Co(M)$, the number of the state of M in which M starts to generate w, the contents $X \in \{0,1\}^*$ of the $r(m)$ visited cells of the working tape, and the position of the working head on X in the configuration C from which M starts to generate w.

Output: w.

Procedure: A simulates the work of M from the given configurations C and generates w.

The Kolmogorov complexity of the algorithm A generating w is
$$K(Co(A)) + K(Co(M)) + \lceil \log_2 s \rceil + K(X) + \lceil \log_2 |X| \rceil.$$
Thus, $K(w) \leq K(Co(A)) + K(Co(M)) + \lceil \log_2 s \rceil + r(w) + \lceil \log_2(r(w)) \rceil + z'$ for some constant z' independent of w. Since clearly $r(w) \leq |w|$ we have:
$$
\begin{aligned}
r(w) &\geq K(w) - K(Co(A)) - K(Co(M)) - \lceil \log_2 s \rceil - \lceil \log_2 |w| \rceil - z' \\
&\geq K(w) - K(Co(M)) - \lceil \log_2 s \rceil - \log_2 |w| - z
\end{aligned}
$$
for some constant z independent of w. $\qquad\square$

Using Fact A.1.1 we conclude, that for any subword w generated by M:

$$r(w) \geq K(w) - \lceil \log_2 |w| \rceil - const,$$

where $const$ is a constant independent of w. It is well-known that for any $n \in \mathbf{N}$ there is a word $x_n \in \{0,1\}^n$ with the property $K(x_n) \geq n$. So, for any $n \in \mathbf{N}$ there is a positive integer j_n such that

(i) $bin(j_n) \in 1 \cdot \{0,1\}^{n-2} \cdot 0,$

(ii) $K(bin(j_n)) \geq n - 2.$

Let, for any j_n, D_n be the part of the computation of M in which $bin(j_n)$ is generated. Since $r(bin(j_n)) \geq n - \log_2 n - const$ for any $n \in \mathbf{N}$, M must do at least $n - \log_2 n - const$ steps in one direction (to the left or to the right) on the working tape in the computation part D_n. Without loss of generality assume that M moves the working head at least $n - \log_2 n - const$ times to the right. Obviously, M moves the working head no more than $\log_2 n + const$ times to the left in D_n. Thus, in the first configuration of D_n the working head has the distance at most $3(\log_2 n + const)$ from the left endmarker of the working tape[2], and in the last configuration of D_n the working head is positioned on the d-th cells for some $d \geq n - 3(\log_2 n + const)$. Note that the length of the working tape is bounded by $n + \log_2 n + 1$ when generating $bin(1)bin(2)...bin(j_n)$.

Let, for any $n \in \mathbf{N}, bin(j_n) = bin_1(j_n)bin_2(j_n)$ where $|bin_1(j_n)| = \lceil n/3 \rceil$, and let, for $i = 1, 2, D_n^i$ be the part of D_n in which $bin_i(j_n)$ is generated. Let $z(n)$ be the leftmost cell of the working tape visited in D_n^2. Since $K(bin_1(j_n)) \geq K(bin(j_n))/3 - \log_2 n$ and $K(bin_2(j_n)) \geq 2 \cdot K(bin(j_n))/3 - \log_2 n$ for large enough n. So
$$
\begin{aligned}
z(n) &\geq r(bin_1(j_n)) - 2(\log_2 n + const) \geq \\
&\geq K(bin_1(j_n)) - 3(\log_2 n + const) \geq \\
&\geq (n-2)/3 - 3(\log_2 n + const). \qquad\qquad (*)
\end{aligned}
$$
Here we needed the following basic properties of Kolmogorov complexity: for all words w, x, and y $K(w) \leq |w| + d$ for some d independent of w, and $K(xy) \leq K(x) + K(y) + d'$ for some d' independent of x and y.

Let $X_n^2 = x_{z(n)}x_{z(n)+1}...x_{n+\log_2 n}$ be the suffix of the content $x_1...x_{n+\log_2 n}$ of the working tape in the first configuration of D_n^2. Now, we give an algorithm B generating, for sufficiently large n, $bin(j_n)$ having the Kolmogorov complexity smaller than $n-2$, which will be a contradiction. Before giving the algorithm we note that after the generation of $bin(j_n)$ M generates $bin(j_n + 1)$ which differs from $bin(j_n)$ only in the last bit. Obviously, for any n, $K(bin(j_n+1)) \geq n-b$ where b is a constant independent on n. Fact A.1.1 and the fact that the working head of M is "almost" on the right

---

[2] If not then M cannot realize $n - log_2 n - const$ steps to the right on the working tape of length n in n steps of D_n.

end of the working tape in the last configuration of M imply that when generating $bin(j_n + 1)$ M moves its working head mostly to the left.

Algorithm B

Input: X_n^2, $Co(M)$, n, the state in the first configuration of D_n^2, and the position of the working head on X_n^2 in the first configuration of D_n^2.

Output: $bin(j_n)$

Procedure: **Step 1:** Simulate $n - \lfloor n/3 \rfloor$ steps of M (i. e. D_n^2) to compute $bin_2(j_n)$

Step 2: Simulate further $\lfloor n/3 \rfloor$ steps of M to generate the first $\lfloor n/3 \rfloor$ bits of $bin(j_n + 1)$ which forms exactly $bin_1(j_n)$. (Note that M cannot leave the positions $z(n), \ldots, n + \log_2 n$ in $\lfloor n/3 \rfloor$ steps.)

Step 3: Write $bin_1(j_n)bin_2(j_n)$

Now, we compute the Kolmogorov complexity of this procedure: For any $n \in \mathbf{N}$:
$$K(B) \leq K(Co(B)) + K(Co(M)) + K(X_n^2) + \lceil \log_2 n \rceil + \lceil \log_2 s \rceil + \log_2(|X_n^2|)$$
$$\leq |X_n^2| + \lceil \log_2 n \rceil + \log_2(|X_n^2|) + const'$$
where $const'$ is a constant independent of n.

Following $(*)$ we obtain
$$K(B) \leq n + \log_2 n - z(n) + 2\log_2 n + const' \leq n - (n-2)/3 + 6\log_2 n + 3const + const'$$
Thus, we have for large enough n:

$$K(bin(j_n)) \leq K(B) \leq 3n/4$$

which contradicts the assumption that for any $n \in \mathbf{N}$, $K(bin(j_n)) \geq n - 2$. $\qquad \square$

Now, we shall extend the above proof ideas to prove that ω_{bin} cannot be generated by any strongly real-time 1-TM working in space $f(m) = o(m/(\log_2 m)^2)$. Observe, that each strongly real-time 1-TM works in space m because it cannot write more on the working tape than on the output tape. The idea of the proof is to take a generated subword $bin(j_n)bin(j_n + 1)\ldots bin(j_n + 2^{n/2\log n})$ and to show, for any $k \in \{0, \ldots, 2^{n/2\log n}\}$, that the working head must move much more to the right (or to the left) than to the left (to the right) when generating the word $bin(j_n + k)$. Thus 1-TM will use at least $\Omega(n) \cdot 2^{n/2\log n}$ space to generate $bin(1)bin(2)\ldots bin(j_n + 2^{n/2\log n})$.

Before starting the own proof, we give two helpful technical lemmas ensuring that $bin(j_n + k)$ has still large Kolmogorov complexity for $k \in \{1, \ldots 2^{n/2\log n}\}$ and that $bin(j_n)$ and $bin(j_n + k)$ do not differ in the prefix of the length $\lfloor n/3 \rfloor$.

Lemma A.1. *Let i, j be two positive integers. Then*

$$K(bin(i + j)) \geq K(bin(i)) - \lceil \log_2 j \rceil - k',$$

where k' is a constant independent of i and j.

Proof. The following algorithm C can reconstruct $bin(i)$ from $bin(i + j)$ and j.

Algorithm C

Input: $bin(i + j), j$.

Output: $bin(i)$.

Procedure: Subtract j times 1 from $bin(i + j)$ and write the result $bin(i)$.

Obviously,
$$K(bin(i)) \leq K(C) \leq K(Co(C)) + K(bin(i+j)) + \lceil \log_2 j \rceil$$
$$\leq K(bin(i+j)) + \lceil \log_2 j \rceil + k'$$
for some constant k' independent of i and j.

Lemma A.2. *There exists $n_0 \in \mathbf{N}$ that for all $n \geq n_0$ and all $k \in \{1, \ldots, 2^{n/2 \log n}\}$, $bin(j_n)$ and $bin(j_n + k)$ do not differ in the first $\lceil n/3 \rceil$ bits.*

Proof. To prove Lemma A.2 it is sufficient to show that $bin_2(j_n)$ contains at least $n/2 \log_2 n$ zeros. Let $bin_2(j_n)$ contain fewer than $n/2 \log_2 n$ zeros. Then $bin_2(j_n)$ can be generated by giving the $d < n/2 \log_2 n$ positions of zeros in $bin_2(j_n)$. Thus $K(bin_2(j_n)) < (n/2 \log_2 n) \cdot \lceil \log_2 n \rceil + c$, where c is a constant independent on n.

But, this contradicts to the fact

$$K(bin_2(j_n)) \geq 2(n-2)/3 - \log_2 n$$

for large enough n proved in the proof of Theorem A.1. $\square$

Now, we are ready for the proof.

Proof of Theorem 4.1. Let M be a strongly real-time 1-TM generating ω_{bin}. We again consider the words $bin(j_n)$ with properties (i) and (ii) for any $n \in \mathbf{N}$, and the subwords $bin(j_n)bin(j_n+1)...bin(j_n+2^{n/2\log n})$ for any $n \in \mathbf{N}$. Let b_n^{r+1} be the position of the working head of M on the working tape after the generation of $bin(j_n + r)$. Using Fact A.1.1 we see that for any $r \in \{1, ..., 2^{n/2\log n}\}$

$$|b_n^{r+1} - b_n^r| \geq K(bin(j_n + r)) - 2\lceil \log_2 n \rceil - k',$$

where k' is a constant independent of n and r. Thus, we have from Lemma A.1

$$(1) \quad m|b_n^{r+1} - b_n^r| \geq K(bin(j_n)) - n/2 \log n - 2\lceil \log_2 n \rceil - k' - k \geq n - n/\log_2 n$$

for all sufficiently large n.

We may assume that $b_n^1 - b_n^0 > 0$. Now, we show that this assumption implies that $b_n^{r+1} - b_n^r > 0$ for any $r \in \{1, \ldots, 2^{n/2\log n}\}$. Obviously, this will complete the proof of Theorem 4.1 because it implies

$$b_n^{2^{n/2\log_2 n}} - b_n^0 = \sum_{r=0}^{2^{n/2\log_2 n}} b_n^{r+1} - b_n^r > 2^{n/2\log_2 n} \cdot (n - n/\log_2 n).$$

Since the length m of $bin(1)bin(2)\ldots bin(j_n + 2^{n/\log n})$ is in $O(n \cdot 2^n)$ and M uses at least space $f(m) \geq 2^{n/2\log_2 n} \cdot (n - n/\log_2 n)$ we obtain $f(m) \in \Omega(m/(\log_2 m)^2)$.

Now, we show that $b_n^{r+1} - b_n^r > 0$ for any $r \in \{1, \ldots, 2^{n/2\log n}\}$ by contradiction.

Let $d \geq 1$ be the smallest positive integer with the property $b_n^{d+1} - b_n^d \leq 0$. Then the relation $b_n^{d+1} - b_n^d \leq -n + n/\log_2 n$ follows from (1). We know from Lemma A.2 that $bin(j_n + (d-1)) = bin_1(j_n)x$ and $bin(j_n + d) = bin_1(j_n)y$ for some $x, y \in \{0,1\}^{n - \lceil n/3 \rceil}$. Thus similarly as in Algorithm B in the proof of Theorem A.1, $bin(j_n + (d-1))$ can be generated by simulating first the generation of x by M and then the generation of the first $\lceil n/3 \rceil$ bits of $bin(j_n + d)$ $[bin_1(j_n)]$ by M. Since $b_n^d - b_n^{d-1} \geq n - n/\log_2 n$, $b_n^{d+1} - b_n^d \leq -n + n/\log_2 n$, and $K(x) \geq 2K(bin(j_n + d + 1))/3 - \log n - const$, the number of visited cells of the working tape in this generation procedure can be bounded by $2n/3 + n/\log_2 n$. This and Fact A.1.1 imply that $K(bin(j_n + (d-1))) \leq 2n/3 + n/\log_2 n + \log n + const$ which is the contradiction with the result of Lemma A.1 $K(bin(j_n + (d-1))) \geq (n-2) - n/2 \log n - k$. □

Note, that the lower bound of Theorem 4.1 is for computationally powerful devices. The similar results in [4] are for much weaker machines, namely for real-time MTM's over one letter working alphabet.

5. Conclusion

This paper presents a lower bound result of infinite word generation. Several problems remain open for further investigation. Now, we formulate two of them.

Problem 5.1. Are the words generated by double DOL TAG-systems [2] in the class GSPACE($\log_2 n$)?

Problem 5.2. Prove for some specific infinite word that logarithmic space and linear time do not suffice to generate it. Obviously, the most interesting problem is to prove $x \notin$ GSPACE($\log_2 n$) for some specific infinite word x. But this problem is at least as hard as to prove $L \notin$ DLOG for some $L \in$ NP.

References

1. J. M. Autebert, J. Gabarró: Iterated GSM's and Co-CFL. *Acta Informatica* 26(1989), 749-769.

2. K. Culik II, and J. Karhumäki: Iterative devices generating infinite words. In: *Lecture Notes in Computer Science 577*, Springer-Verlag 1992. (also *Int. J. Found. Comput. Sci.* 5 (1994), 69-97).

3. G. J. Chaitin: On the length of programs for computing finite binary sequences: statistical considerations. *J. Assoc. Comp. Mach. 16* (1969), 145-159.

4. P. C. Fischer, A. Meyer, and A. Rosenberg: Time restricted sequence generation. *J. Comp. Syst. Sci.* 4 (1970), 50 - 73.

5. J. Hromkovič, J. Karkumäki, A. Lepistö: Computational complexity of infinite word generation. In: "Results and Trends in Theoretical Computer Science" (H. Maurer, ed.), *Lecture Notes in Computer Science 812*, Springer Verlag 1994, 169-182.

6. J. E. Hopcroft, J. D. Ullman: *Introduction to Automata Theory, Languages and Computation.* Addison-Wesley Publishing Company, Inc. 1979.

7. A. N. Kolmogorov: Three approaches to the quantitative definition of information. *Problems Inform. Transmission* 1(1968), 662-664.

8. M. Li, P. M. B. Vitányi: Kolmogorov complexity and its applications. In: *Handbook of Theoretical Computer Science A - Algorithms and Complexity* (Jan van Leeuwen, ed.), Elsevier, Amsterdam, New York-Oxford-Tokyo & The MIT Press, Cambridge 1990, 187-254.

9. M. Li, P. M. B. Vitányi: *An Introduction to Kolmogorov Complexity and its Applications*. Springer-Verlag, Berlin, 1993.

10. A. Lepistö: On the computational complexity of infinite words. In: *Developments in Language Theory II* (J. Dassow, G. Rozenberg, and A. Salomaa, eds.), World-Scientific, Singapore, 1996, 35o-359.

11. M. Lothaire: *Combinatorics on Words*. Addison-Wesley, Reading, Massachusetts 1981.

12. A. Salomaa: *Jewels of Formal Language Theory*. Computer Science Press, Rockville, Maryland 1981.

13. R. J. Solomonoff: A formal theory of inductive inference. Part 1 and Part 2. *Inform. and Control* 7(1964), 1-22 and 224-254.

14. A. Thue: Über unendliche Zeichenreihen. *Norske Vid. Selsk. Skr., I Mat. Nat. Kl., Kristiania* 7 (1906), 1-22.

On ω-power Languages

Ludwig STAIGER

Martin-Luther-Universität Halle-Wittenberg
Institut für Informatik
Kurt-Mothes-Str. 1
D–06099Halle (Saale), Germany
E-mail: staiger@informatik.uni-halle.de

0. Introduction

The infinite or ω-power is one of the basic operations to associate with a language of finite words (a finitary language) an ω-language.

It plays a crucial role in the characterization of regular and of context-free ω-languages, that is, ω-languages accepted by (nondeterministic) finite or pushdown automata, respectively (cf. the surveys [St87a, Th90]). But in connection with the determinization of finite ω-automata it turned out that the properties of the ω-power are remarkable elusive; resulting in the well-known complicated proof of MacNaughton's theorem [MN66]. Later work [TB70, Ei74, Ch74] showed a connection between the ω-power of regular ω-languages and a limit operation (called here δ-limit) transferring languages to ω-languages. It was, therefore, asked in [Ch74] for more transparent relationships between the ω-power and the δ-limit of languages. It turned out that this δ-limit is a useful tool in translating the finite to the infinite behaviour of deterministic accepting devices (cf. [Li76, CG78, St87a, Th90, EH93]).

As it was mentioned above ω-power languages play a crucial role in the characterization of ω-languages accepted by nondeterministic finite or push-down automata. In fact, they are useful in general for the characterization of ω-languages accepted by empty storage (cf. [St77]).

Therefore, a general relationship between ω-power and δ-limit could hint for instances where ω-languages accepted nondeterministically via empty-storage-acceptance could be likewise accepted deterministically.

In contrast to the ω-power the δ-limit yields, similar to the adherence of languages, a transparent description of the ω-language derived from the language. Particularly remarkable are the facts that in terms of the natural CANTOR-topology of the space of ω-words it describes exactly G_δ-sets (This being also the reason for calling it δ-limit.) and, moreover, it allows for a specification of the topological (BOREL-) subclasses of G_δ in terms of the underlying (preimage-)languages (cf. [St87b]).

No such properties, however, are known in general for ω-power languages. Except for the representation as an infinite product, the ω-power of a language W, W^ω, is known to be the maximum solution of a linear homogenuous equation in one variable (see Eq. (H) below). The disadvantage of those equations is, in contrast to the language case, that they are not uniquely solvable in ω-languages. This is, however, no obstacle to obtain an axiom system for ω-regular expressions similar to the one for regular expressions given by A. SALOMAA in [Sa66]. K. WAGNER [Wa76] showed that the maximum solution principle of [Re72, St72] is sufficient for this purpose.[1]

Therefore, we start our investigations with the consideration of linear equations for ω-languages. After introducing some necessary notation in the first section we

---

[1] Other axiom systems for ω-regular expressions were given in [DK84, II84]

derive the above mentioned maximum solution principle and some conditions under which equations are equivalent, that is, have the same set of solutions.

In the second section we consider the structure of the set of solutions of a linear equation. To this end we introduce the notion of atomic solutions, that is, nonempty solutions which are in some sense indivisible. Section 3 is devoted to the case when a linear equation has a finite-state or even regular solution. This concludes our investigations on solutions of linear equations, and we turn to the consideration of ω-power languages.

In the fourt part we deal with relationships between the operations of ω-power and δ-limit. Thereby it is natural to consider also toplogical properties of ω-power languages. It turns out that already for topological reasons the δ-limit is not able to describe all ω-power languages.

Moreover, we show which ω-power languages can be found in several low level BOREL-classes (below the class $\mathbf{G}_\delta$). Here the behaviour of ω-power languages is in contrast to the class of so-called strongly-connected ω-languages (cf. [St80a, 83]). Strongly-connected ω-languages are already closed if they are in the BOREL-class $\mathbf{F}_\sigma \cap \mathbf{G}_\delta$, whereas we derive as well examples of open nonclosed as examples of nonopen and nonclosed ω-power languages in $\mathbf{F}_\sigma \cap \mathbf{G}_\delta$.

The final section of this paper deals with another topological property of ω-power languages. It was observed in [St76, 80b] that finite-state (or regular) ω-languages which are nowhere dense in CANTOR-space lack some subword (finite pattern). Here we generalize this result to finite-state ω-languages nowhere dense in an ω-power language.

1. Linear Equations

In this section we introduce some notation used throughout the paper. Further we give some basic results from the theory of ω-languages which are necessary for our investigations. Additional information on the theory of ω-languages can be obtained from the quoted above papers.

After these preparations we introduce linear equations for ω-languages and show how to solve them. An especially interesting way of solving is the maximum solution principle which will be illustrated at the end of this section by two examples. Moreover, we derive a condition under which equations have the same set of solutions.

By $\mathbf{N} = \{0, 1, 2, \ldots\}$ we denote the set of natural numbers. We consider the space X^ω of infinite strings (sequences) on a finite alphabet of cardinality $card\ X \geq 2$. By X^* we denote the set (monoid) of finite strings (words) on X, including the *empty* word e. For $w \in X^*$ and $b \in X^* \cup X^\omega$ let $w \cdot b$ be their *concatenation*. This concatenation product extends in an obvious way to subsets $W \subseteq X^*$ and $B \subseteq X^* \cup X^\omega$. As usual we denote subsets of X^* as *languages* and subsets of X^ω as ω-*languages*. For a language $W \subseteq X^*$ let $W^0 := \{e\}$ and $W^{i+1} := W^i \cdot W$. Then $W^* := \bigcup_{i \in \mathbf{N}} W^i$ is the *submonoid* of X^* generated by W, and by W^ω we denote the set of infinite strings formed by concatenating in W. Furthermore $|w|$ is the *length* of the word $w \in X^*$.

$\mathbf{A}(B) := \{w : w \in X^* \wedge \exists b (b \in X^* \cup X^\omega \wedge w \cdot b \in B)\}$ is the set of all *initial words* (*prefixes*) of the set $B \subseteq X^* \cup X^\omega$. For the sake of brevity we shall write $w \cdot B, W \cdot b$ and $\mathbf{A}(b)$ instead of $\{w\} \cdot B, W \cdot \{b\}$ and $\mathbf{A}(\{b\})$ respectively, and we shall abbreviate the fact that w is an initial word of b, that is $w \in \mathbf{A}(b)$, by $w \sqsubseteq b$. Moreover, we call

$B \subseteq X^* \cup X^\omega$ *prefix-free* iff $w \sqsubseteq b$ and $w, b \in B$ imply $w = b$, a prefix-free subset $C \subseteq X^* \setminus \{e\}$ is also called a *prefix code*.

We consider X^ω as a topological space with the basis $(w \cdot X^\omega)_{w \in X^*}$. Since X is finite, this topological space is homeomorphic to the CANTOR discontinuum, hence compact. In the asequel we shall refer to the space X^ω also as CANTOR-*space*. Open sets in X^ω are of the form $W \cdot X^\omega$ where $W \subseteq X^*$. From this follows that a subset $F \in X^\omega$ is *closed* iff $\mathbf{A}(\beta) \subseteq \mathbf{A}(F)$ implies $\beta \in F$.

The *topological closure* of subset $F \subseteq X^\omega$, that is, the smallest closed subset of (X^ω, ρ) containing F is denoted by $\mathcal{C}(F)$. It holds $\mathcal{C}(F) = \{\xi : \mathbf{A}(\xi) \subseteq \mathbf{A}(F)\}$.

Having defined open and closed sets in X^ω, we proceed to the next classes of the Borel hierarchy (cf. [Ku66]):

$\mathbf{F}_\sigma$ is the set of countable unions of closed subsets of X^ω, and

$\mathbf{G}_\delta$ is the set of countable intersections of open subsets of X^ω.

For $W \subseteq X^* \setminus \{e\}$ and $E \subseteq X^\omega$ we consider the equations

$$T = W \cdot T \qquad (H)$$
$$T = W \cdot T \cup E \qquad (I)$$

which will be referred to as the *homogenuous* and *inhomogenuous* equations, respectively.

It was already observed by TRAKHTENBROT [Tr62] that the simple equation $T = X \cdot T$ has uncountably many ω-languages as solutions (cf. also [St83]). Therefore, in this section and the subsequent ones we address the problem which subsets of X^ω are solutions of the given equations.

From [St72] and [Re72] the following simple properties are known. Let $W \subseteq X^* \setminus \{e\}$ and $E \subseteq X^\omega$. Then

$$F \subseteq W \cdot W^* \cdot F \quad \text{implies} \quad F \subseteq W^\omega \qquad (1)$$
$$W \cdot F \cup E \subseteq F \quad \text{implies} \quad W^* \cdot E \subseteq W^* \cdot F \subseteq F \qquad (2)$$
$$W \cdot F \cup E = F \quad \text{implies} \quad W^* \cdot E \subseteq F \subseteq W^\omega \cup W^* \cdot E, \text{ and} \qquad (3)$$
$$\text{If } F = W \cdot F \quad \text{then} \quad F \cup W^* \cdot E \text{ is a solution of Eq. (I).} \qquad (4)$$

Moreover, it was observed that $W^* \cdot E$ as well as $W^\omega \cup W^* \cdot E$ are solutions of Eq. (I), according to Eq. (3) they are the *minimum* and *maximum* solution, respectively. As a corollary to the above properties we get the maximum solution principle which has been proved useful in establishing identities involving ω-power languages W^ω (e.g. in [Lt88, 91a, 91b, St80a, Wa76]).

Corollary 1. (Maximum solution principle) *Let $F \subseteq X^\omega$ satisfy Eq. (I), and let $W^\omega \subseteq F$. Then*
$$F = W^\omega \cup W^* \cdot E .$$

As a further corollary to Eq. (1) we get

Corollary 2. *If $F \subseteq W \cdot F$ then $W^* \cdot F$ is the minimum solution of the homogenuous equation Eq. (H) containing F.*

This yields the following relation between the solutions of the inhomogenuous and homogenuous converse to Eq. (4):

Lemma 3. *If* $F = W \cdot F \cup E$ *then* $F' := W^* \cdot (F \backslash W^* \cdot E)$ *is the minimum solution of the homogenuous equation Eq. (H) such that* $F = F' \cup W^* \cdot E$.

Proof. We have $F \backslash W^* \cdot E = (W \cdot F \cup E) \backslash W^* \cdot E = W \cdot F \backslash W^* \cdot E \subseteq W \cdot (F \backslash W^* \cdot E)$, and the assertion is immediate with Corollary 2. □

Next we consider pairs of coefficients (W, E) and (V, E') to be *equivalent* if the inhomogenuous equations $T = W \cdot T \cup E$ and $T = V \cdot T \cup E'$ have the same set of solutions.

We obtain the following.

Lemma 4. *Let* $W \cup V \subseteq X^* \backslash \{e\}$, $W^* = V^*$, *and* $W^* \cdot E = V^* \cdot E'$. *Then* (W, E) *and* (V, E') *are equivalent.*

Proof. If F is a solution of Eq. (I), then $W^* \cdot F = F$. This together with the inclusion $W^* \cdot E \subseteq F$ and the identity $W^* = (W \cdot W^*)^*$ yields $F = W \cdot W^* \cdot F \cup W^* \cdot E$.

Conversely, if $F = W \cdot W^* \cdot F \cup W^* \cdot E = W \cdot (W^* \cdot F \cup W^* \cdot E) \cup E$ in virtue of $W^* = (W \cdot W^*)^*$ we have $F = W^* \cdot F$ and $W^* \cdot E \subseteq F$. Thus $F = W \cdot (W^* \cdot F \cup W^* \cdot E) \cup E = W \cdot F \cup E$, and (W, E) is equivalent to $(W \cdot W^*, W^* \cdot E)$. In the same way (V, E') is equivalent to $(V \cdot V^*, V^* \cdot E')$, and the assertion follows. □

Corollary 5. *Let* $e \notin W$ *and* $W^n \subseteq V \subseteq W \cdot W^*$. *Then* $F = W \cdot F \cup E$ *implies* $F = V \cdot F \cup W^* \cdot E$.

Proof. From $F = W \cdot F \cup E$ we have the identity $F = W \cdot F \cup W^* \cdot E$. Inserting the right hand side of this identity n times into itself yields $F = W^n \cdot F \cup W^* \cdot E$. On the other hand $F = W \cdot W^* \cdot F \cup W^* \cdot E$, and the assertion follows. □

The converse statement, however, is not valid. Consider e.g. $W := \{a, b\}$, $V := \{a, b\}^2$, $F := V^* \cdot \{aa, ba\}^\omega$. Then $F = V \cdot F$ but $F \neq \{a, b\} \cdot F$ because $(ab)^\omega \notin F$.

As it was announced above we conclude this section with two instances whose proofs show the usefulness of the simple properties derived in Eqs. (1) ... (4) and Corollary 1 when solving equations like Eq. (H) or Eq. (I).

To every instance we need some preparatory definitions.

As in [Lt88] or [St80] we define the *stabilizer* of an ω-language $E \subseteq X^\omega$,

$$Stab(E) := \{w : w \in \mathbf{A}(E) \backslash \{e\} \wedge w \cdot E \subseteq E\}. \tag{5}$$

Since $\mathcal{C}(w \cdot E) = w \cdot \mathcal{C}(E)$, we have $Stab(E) \subseteq Stab(\mathcal{C}(E))$. Moreover, the stabilizer of an ω-language $E \subseteq X^\omega$, $Stab(E)$, is closed under concatenation, that is, is a subsemigroup of X^*.

Obviously, the stabilizer of an ω-power language W^ω satisfies $W^* \backslash \{e\} \subseteq Stab(W^\omega) \subseteq Stab(\mathcal{C}(W^\omega)) \subseteq \mathbf{A}(W^\omega)$ and $Stab(W^\omega) \cdot W^\omega = W^\omega$.

We obtain a result which is similar to the construction of a minimal generator of the semigroup W^*, $(W \backslash \{e\}) \backslash ((W \backslash \{e\}) \cdot (W^* \backslash \{e\}))$.

Theorem 6. ([Lt88, Proposition IV.3])[2] *Let* $W \subseteq X^* \backslash \{e\}$ *and let* $V := W \backslash (W \cdot Stab(W^\omega))$. *Then* $V^\omega = W^\omega$.

Proof. The inclusion $V^\omega \subseteq W^\omega$ follows from $V \subseteq W$.

On the other hand, we have $V \cdot Stab(W^\omega) \supseteq W^* \backslash \{e\}$. Thus $V \cdot W^\omega = V \cdot Stab(W^\omega) \cdot W^\omega \supseteq W^* \cdot W^\omega = W^\omega$, and Eq. (1) implies $W^\omega \subseteq V^\omega$. □

---

[2]cf. also [Lt91a, Lemma 2] or [Lt91b, Lemma 2.1].

It should be noted that, in contrast to the minimal generator of W^* the language $V := W \setminus (W \cdot Stab(W^\omega))$ defined in Theorem 6 need not be a minimal ω-generator of W^ω contained in $W \subseteq X^* \setminus \{e\}$. In [Lt88, Example IV.4] and [Lt91a, Example 1] it is shown that $W = a \cdot b^* \cup ba \cdot b^*$ satisfies $W = W \setminus (W \cdot Stab(W^\omega))$, but $W^\omega = (W \setminus \{ab\})^\omega$.

Next we derive an instance where the maximum solution principle is used. We give an explicit formula for the closure of W^ω, $\mathcal{C}(W^\omega)$.

To this end let $\mathrm{ls}\, W := \{\xi : \xi \in X^\omega \wedge \mathbf{A}(\xi) \subseteq \mathbf{A}(W)\}$ be the *adherence* of the language $W \subseteq X^*$. Then it is known that $\mathcal{C}(W \cdot E) = W \cdot \mathcal{C}(E) \cup \mathrm{ls}\, W$ when $W \subseteq X^*$, $E \subseteq X^\omega$ and $E \neq \emptyset$. We obtain the formula

$$\mathcal{C}(W^\omega) = W^\omega \cup W^* \cdot \mathrm{ls}\, W \qquad (6)$$

Proof. Since $\mathcal{C}(W^\omega)$ is the closure of W^ω, we have $\mathcal{C}(W^\omega) \supseteq W^\omega$. Now $W^\omega = W \cdot W^\omega$, and from the formula mentioned above we get $\mathcal{C}(W^\omega) = \mathcal{C}(W \cdot W^\omega) = W \cdot \mathcal{C}(W^\omega) \cup \mathrm{ls}\, W$. Our assertion follows from Corollary 1. $\qquad\square$

2. Atomic Solutions of the Homogenuous Equation

In view of Eq. (4) and Lemma 3 every solution of the inhomogenuous equation can be obtained by adding $W^* \cdot E$ to a solution of the homogenuous equation. In this section we, therefore, analyze the structure of the set of solutions of Eq. (H).

To this end we consider nonempty solutions of which are in some sense minimal. We call a nonempty solution S of the homogenuous equation *atomic* if it does not contain two nonempty disjoint solutions of Eq. (H). It is obvious that a nonempty and minimal (with respect to set inclusion) solution of Eq. (H) is atomic, but as we shall see below the converse is not true.

In order to construct atomic solutions we consider so-called W-factorizations of ω-words $\xi \in W^\omega$. A W-*factorization* is a factorization $\xi = w_0 \cdot w_1 \cdots w_i \cdots$ where $w_i \in W \setminus \{e\}$.

Theorem 7. *For every $\beta \in W^\omega$ there is an atomic solution of Eq. (H) containing β.*

Proof. Let $\beta = w_0 \cdot w_1 \cdots w_i \cdots$ be a W-factorization of β and define $\beta_j := w_j \cdot w_{j+1} \cdots w_i \cdots$, that is, $\beta_0 := \beta$ and $\beta_j = w_j \cdot \beta_{j+1}$.

It is easy to verify that $S := W^* \cdot \{\beta_j : j \in \mathbf{N}\}$ is a solution of Eq. (H). It remains to show that S is atomic. Assume $S_1, S_2 \subseteq S$, $S_1 \cap S_2 = \emptyset$ and $W \cdot S_m = S_m$ $(m = 1, 2)$.

If $\{\beta_j : j \in \mathbf{N}\} \subseteq S_1$ then $S_2 = \emptyset$. So let $\beta_{j_m} \in S_m$ and $j_2 < j_1$ (say). Since $W^* \cdot S_1 = S_1$, it follows $\beta_{j_2} \in S_1$, a contradiction to $S_1 \cap S_2 = \emptyset$. $\qquad\square$

The proof of Theorem 7 provides us with a method for constructing atomic solutions of the homogenuous equation.

Corollary 8. *Let $\beta = w_0 \cdot w_1 \cdots w_i \cdots$ be a W-factorization of β. Then for every infinite subset $M \subseteq \mathbf{N}$ the set $S_M := W^* \cdot \{\beta_j : j \in M\}$ is a solution of Eq. (H).*

From the above described construction of atomic solutions the following description of arbitrary solutions is obvious.

Lemma 9. *If $F = W \cdot F$ then F is the union of all atomic solutions of Eq. (H) contained in F.*

382

Though it is not easy, in general, to obtain a concise description of atomic solutions containing $\beta \in W^\omega$, for ultimately periodic ω-words we have the following.

Property 10. *Let $\beta \in X^\omega$ be ultimately periodic. Then every atomic solution of Eq. (H) containing β has the form $W^* \cdot v^\omega$ for an appropriate $v \in W^* \setminus \{e\}$. Conversely, every ω-language $W^* \cdot v^\omega$ where $v \in W^* \setminus \{e\}$ is an atomic solution of Eq. (H).*

Proof. Let $\beta = w \cdot u^\omega$, and let $\beta = w_0 \cdot w_1 \cdots w_i \cdots$ be a W-factorization of β. Then there are infinitely many $j \in \mathbf{N}$ such that $\beta_j = \hat{v}^\omega$ for some $\hat{v} \neq e$. Following Corollary 8 the set $W^* \cdot \hat{v}^\omega$ is an atomic solution of Eq. (H).

We have still to show that $\hat{v}^\omega = v^\omega$ for some $v \in W^* \setminus \{e\}$. To this end observe that if $\beta_j = \beta_k = \hat{v}^\omega$ and $j < k$ then $\beta_j = v \cdot \beta_k$ for an appropriate $v \in W^* \setminus \{e\}$, whence $\beta_j = v^\omega$.

The second assertion is obvious. $\qquad\qquad\qquad\qquad\qquad\qquad\qquad\qquad\square$

Atomic solutions containing a given β, however, may be neither minimal nor unique. Lemma 9 and the proof of Theorem 7 yield only the following sufficient conditions.

Property 11. *If S is a unique atomic solution containing an ω-word β then S is the unique minimal solution containing β.*

Property 12. *If $\beta \in W^\omega$ has a unique W-factorization $\beta = w_0 \cdot w_1 \cdot \ldots \cdot w_i \cdot \ldots$ ($w_i \in W$) then the atomic solution of Eq. (H) containing β is unique.*

Remark. The latter condition is not necessary. Consider e.g. the suffix code $C := \{b, ba, aa\}$. Here ba^ω has two C-factorizations $ba^\omega = b \cdot aa \cdot aa \cdot \ldots = ba \cdot aa \cdot \ldots$ but $C^* \cdot a^\omega$ is the unique atomic solution of the equation $T = C \cdot T$ containing ba^ω.

The following example shows that atomic solutions containing a particular ω-word β may not be unique, even if W is a code[3] and β is ultimately periodic. In addition this example verifies that, though β has more than one W-factorizations all atomic solutions containing β are minimal.

Example 1. Consider the suffix code $W_1 = \{ab, ba, baa\}$, and let $\beta_1 := baa(ba)^\omega = ba(ab)^\omega$. By Property 10, $W_1^* \cdot (ba)^\omega$ and $W_1^* \cdot (ab)^\omega$ are the only atomic solutions containing β_1. Obviously they are incomparable, thus minimal.

Their intersection $W_1^* \cdot (ba)^\omega \cap W_1^* \cdot (ab)^\omega = W_1^* \cdot \beta_1$ does not contain a solution of Eq. (H), because neither $(ab)^\omega \in W_1^* \cdot \beta_1$ nor $(ba)^\omega \in W_1^* \cdot \beta_1$.

We add an example that atomic solutions need not be minimal.

Example 2. Let $W_2 := \{aba, ba, baa\}$ (which is not a code). Then $\beta_2 := (baa)^\omega = ba \cdot (aba)^\omega$ yields the following two atomic solutions $W_2^* \cdot (baa)^\omega$ and $W_2^* \cdot (aba)^\omega$. One easily verifies that $(aba)^\omega \notin W_2^* \cdot (baa)^\omega$ whereas $(baa)^\omega \in W_2^* \cdot (aba)^\omega$. Hence $W_2^* \cdot (baa)^\omega \subset W_2^* \cdot (aba)^\omega$, and the latter atomic solution is not a minimal one.

Atomic solutions are countable subsets of X^ω, hence, as countable unions of closed sets, $\mathbf{F}_\sigma$-sets. Thus Eq. (H) has (if ever) among its nonempty solutions always $\mathbf{F}_\sigma$-sets. Topologically simpler sets than $\mathbf{F}_\sigma$-sets are closed sets. But for Eq. (I) and Eq. (H) it turns out that they have at most one nonempty closed set as solution.

---

[3]That is, for all words $v_1, \ldots, v_l, w_1, \ldots, w_m \in W$ the identity $v_1 \cdots v_l = w_1 \cdots w_m$ implies $l = m$ and $v_i = w_i$ ($i = 1, \ldots, l$).

Lemma 13. *Let $W \neq \emptyset$. Then Eq. (I) has a nonempty closed solution iff* $\mathrm{ls}\, W \cup \mathcal{C}(E) \subseteq W^\omega \cup W^* \cdot E$, *and moreover this solution is the maximum solution.*

Proof. First observe that similar to Eq. (6) the closure of the maximum solution $W^\omega \cup W^* \cdot E$ is calculated as $\mathcal{C}(W^\omega \cup W^* \cdot E) = W^\omega \cup W^* \cdot \mathrm{ls}\, W \cup W^* \cdot \mathcal{C}(E)$, and it satisfies $\mathcal{C}(W^\omega \cup W^* \cdot E) \subseteq W^\omega \cup W^* \cdot E$ if $\mathrm{ls}\, W \cup \mathcal{C}(E) \subseteq W^\omega \cup W^* \cdot E$.

On the other hand if $W^\omega \cup W^* \cdot E = \mathcal{C}(W^\omega \cup W^* \cdot E) = W^\omega \cup W^* \cdot \mathrm{ls}\, W \cup W^* \cdot \mathcal{C}(E)$ the condition is trivially satisfied.

The second assertion is obvious from $W^\omega \subseteq \mathcal{C}(W^* \cdot F)$ whenever $W^* \cdot F$ is nonempty. $\qquad\square$

As a corollary we obtain a necessary and sufficient condition for an ω-power language W^ω to be closed.

Corollary 14. *An ω-power language $W^\omega \subseteq X^\omega$ is closed if and only if* $\mathrm{ls}\, W \subseteq W^\omega$.

We conclude this section with a lower estimate for the possible number of solutions of the inhomogenuous equation Eq. (I). To this end we derive an intersection property.

Lemma 15. *Let $F = V \cdot F$ and $E = W \cdot E$ where $V \subseteq W^* \setminus \{e\}$. If every ω-word $\xi \in E \cap F$ has at most one W-factorization then $F \cap E = V \cdot (F \cap E)$.*

Proof. Since $V \subseteq W^*$, the inclusion $V \cdot (F \cap E) \subseteq F \cap E$ is immediate. To prove the converse we use that every $\beta \in F \cap E$ has a unique W-factorization. First $F = V \cdot F$ implies that $\beta = v \cdot \xi$ for some $v \in V \subseteq W^*$ and $\xi \in F \subseteq W^\omega$.

Let $v = v_1 \cdots v_n$ and $\xi = w_0 \cdot w_1 \cdots w_i \cdots$ where $v_j, w_i \in W \setminus \{e\}$. Thus $\beta = v_1 \cdots v_n \cdot w_0 \cdot w_1 \cdots w_i \cdots$ is the unique W-factorization of β. As $v \in W^n$ and $E = W^n \cdot E$, it follows that $\xi \in E$. Hence $\beta = v \cdot \xi \in V \cdot (E \cap F)$. $\qquad\square$

As a second preparation we derive TRAKHTENBROT's [Tr62] description of all atomic solutions of the equation $T = X \cdot T$.

Example 3. (Atomic solutions of $T = X \cdot T$) Utilizing the technique of the proof of Theorem 7 we observe that for the equation $T = X \cdot T$ and $\beta \in X^\omega$ it holds $\{\beta_i : i \in \mathbf{N}\} = \mathbf{E}(\beta)$ where $\mathbf{E}(\beta)$ is the set of all tails of β. Hence $F_\beta := X^* \cdot \mathbf{E}(\beta)$ is the (unique, according to Property 12) atomic solution of $T = X \cdot T$ containing β.

Consequently, either $F_\beta = F_\xi$ or $F_\beta \cap F_\xi = \emptyset$.

Theorem 16. *If the cardinality of the set $W^\omega \setminus W^* \cdot E$ satisfies* $\operatorname{card} W^\omega \setminus W^* \cdot E = 2^{\aleph_0}$ *then Eq. (I) has $2^{2^{\aleph_0}}$ solutions.*

Proof. Clearly, Eq. (I) can have no more than $2^{2^{\aleph_0}}$ solutions.

According to Lemma 3 the set $F' := W^* \cdot (W^\omega \setminus W^* \cdot E)$ is the minimum solution of Eq. (H) such that $W^\omega = F' \cup W^* \cdot E$. Now applying Lemma 15 and the fact that each one of the sets F_β defined in Example 3 is countable we obtain that the set $\{F' \cap F_\beta : \beta \in W^\omega \setminus W^* \cdot E\}$ is an uncountable family of pairwise disjoint solutions of Eq. (H). Hence, Eq. (H) has all unions $\bigcup_{\beta \in M}(F' \cap F_\beta)$ where $M \subseteq W^\omega \setminus W^* \cdot E$ as solutions, that is, it has at least $2^{2^{\aleph_0}}$ solutions. These solutions differ already on $W^\omega \setminus W^* \cdot E$ which proves that the family of all unions $\bigcup_{\beta \in M}(F' \cap F_\beta) \cup W^* \cdot E$ provides $2^{2^{\aleph_0}}$ solutions of Eq. (I). $\qquad\square$

3. Regular and Finite-State Solutions

In this section we consider solutions of our equation which are closely related to the well-known class of regular ω-languages. To this end we introduce the following.

For a set $B \subseteq X^* \cup X^\omega$ we define the *state* B/w of B generated by the word $w \in X^*$ as $B/w := \{b : w \cdot b \in B\}$, and we call a set B *finite-state* if the number of different states B/w ($w \in X^*$) is finite. Finite-state languages $W \subseteq X^*$ are also known as *regular* languages. Already TRACHTENBROT [Tr62] (cf. also [St83]) observed that the class of finite-state ω-languages is much larger than the class of ω-languages accepted by finite automata (so-called regular ω-languages). An ω-language $F \subseteq X^\omega$ is referred to as *regular* provided there are regular languages $W_i, V_i \subseteq X^*$ ($i = 1, \ldots, n$) such that $F = \bigcup_{i=1}^{n} W_i \cdot V_i^\omega$.

LITOVSKY and TIMMERMAN [LT87] have shown that a regular ω-power language W^ω is already generated by a regular language L. In this section we consider the related case when the coefficients W and E of the inhomogenuous equation Eq. (I) are finite-state or even regular. Our general result follows.

Theorem 17. *If W and E are finite-state, then every solution of Eq. (I) is also finite-state.*

Proof. First we mention that $W^* \cdot E$ is also finite-state if W and E are finite-state.

Let $W^{(n)} := \{w : w \in W^* \wedge |w| \geq n\}$. In view of Corollary 5 $F = W \cdot F \cup E$ implies $F = W^{(n)} \cdot F \cup W^* \cdot E$ for arbitrary $n \in \mathbf{N}$.

Next, we use the property that $W^{(|w|)}/w = W^*/w$. Then $F/w = (W^{(|w|)} \cdot F)/w \cup (W^* \cdot E)/w = (W^*/w) \cdot F \cup (W^* \cdot E)/w$. Thus the number of states of F is not larger than the product of the number of states of W^* and $W^* \cdot E$. □

In the rest of this section we verify that Theorem 17 does not hold in the case of regular sets, and that in order to have only finite-state solutions it is not sufficient to have one finite-state solution.

The first fact is easily verified by the equation $F = X \cdot F$ which has $2^{2^{\aleph_0}}$ solutions. Consequently, most of them cannot be regular.

Next we give an equation which has a regular minimum solution but its maximum solution is not finite-state.

Example 4. Let $W_4 := \{a^{n!} \cdot b : n \in \mathbf{N}\}$ and $E_4 := \{a, b\}^* \cdot a^\omega$. Then Eq. (I) has the minimum solution $W_4^* \cdot E_4 = E_4$ which is regular, but its maximum solution $W_4^\omega \cup W_4^* \cdot E_4$ is not finite-state, because $(W_4^\omega \cup W_4^* \cdot E_4) \cap (a^* \cdot b)^\omega = W_4^\omega$ is not finite-state.

Before proceeding to the next example we need the following lemma.

Lemma 18. *An ω-language of the form $V \cdot \beta$ is finite-state iff there are a regular language V' and a word u such that $V \cdot \beta = V' \cdot u^\omega$.*

Proof. Clearly, the condition is sufficient. Conversely, if $V \cdot \beta$ is finite-state then there are words w and w' such that $w' \neq e$, $w \cdot w' \sqsubset \beta$ and $(V \cdot \beta)/w \cdot w' \subseteq (V \cdot \beta)/w$. Let $\xi := \beta/(w \cdot w')$. Since $\xi \in V \cdot \beta/w$, we have $w \cdot \xi = v \cdot \beta$ for some $v \in V$. On the other hand, $w \cdot w' \cdot \xi = \beta$. Consequently, $w \cdot \xi = v \cdot w \cdot w' \cdot \xi$, that is, $\xi = u^\omega$ where $w \cdot u = v \cdot w \cdot w'$. Then β is also ultimately periodic. Now define $V' := \{w : \xi \in (V \cdot \beta)/w\}$. □

Example 5. The equation $T = X \cdot T \cup \{\xi\}$ has always the finite-state (even regular) maximum solution $F_5 = X^\omega$, but according to our lemma its minimum solution $X^* \cdot \xi$ is finite-state if and only if ξ is ultimately periodic.

4. ω-Power and δ-Limit

In the preceding sections we have seen that, in contrast to the case of languages, the linear equations Eq. (H) and Eq. (I) may have many solutions in the range of ω-languages. One of the solutions of Eq. (H) and a particularly interesting one (its maximum solution) is the ω-power W^ω.

In this section we investigate properties of the ω-power operation and its relation to a limit operation mapping also languages to ω-languages—the so-called δ-limit[4] of a language $W \subseteq X^*$,

$$W^\delta := \{\zeta : \zeta \in X^\omega \wedge \mathbf{A}(\zeta) \cap W \text{ is infinite}\}. \tag{7}$$

We also consider topological properties of ω-power languages. In this section we investigate their relationships to BOREL-classes, and in the subsequent one we focus on (relative) density.

In connection with acceptance results for ω-languages, like those ones as MAC-NAUGHTON's theorem, properties of ω-power languages are remarkably elusive. In this respect the δ-limit has more transparent properties. Therefore it would be desirable to derive some relationships between the operations of ω-power and δ-limit. To this end we first calculate the δ-limit of the concatenation product and the KLEENE-star of languages (cf. [St80a], [Lt88]).

$$W \cdot V^\delta \subseteq (W \cdot V)^\delta \subseteq W \cdot V^\delta \cup W^\delta \tag{8}$$

Particular cases of Eq. (8) are obtained for $W^\delta = \emptyset$ or $e \in V$, respectively.

$$
\begin{array}{lll}
(W \cdot V)^\delta = W \cdot V^\delta & \text{if } W^\delta = \emptyset, \text{ and} & (9) \\
(W \cdot V)^\delta = W \cdot V^\delta \cup W^\delta & \text{if } e \in V & (10)
\end{array}
$$

In virtue of the obvious inclusion $W^\omega \subseteq (W^*)^\delta$ we obtain via the maximum solution principle Corollary 1 the following.

$$(W^*)^\delta = W^\omega \cup W^* \cdot W^\delta \tag{11}$$

We can improve Eq. (8).

Property 19. Let $C \subseteq X^*$ be a prefix code and $W, V \subseteq C^*$. Then

$$W \cdot V^\delta \subseteq (W \cdot V)^\delta \subseteq W \cdot V^\delta \cup (W^\delta \cap (C^* \cdot V)^\omega).$$

Proof. If $\beta \in (W \cdot V)^\delta \setminus W \cdot V^\delta$ then $\beta \in W^\delta$, that is, there are infinitely many prefixes w_i of β in W. To each w_i belongs a $v_i \in V$ such that $w_i \cdot v_i$ is a prefix of β.

Choose the family $(w_i)_{i \in \mathbb{N}}$ in such a way that $|w_{j+1}| > |w_j \cdot v_j|$. Since C is a prefix code and $w_{j+1}, w_j, v_j \in C^*$ there is a $u_{j+1} \in C^*$ such that $w_j \cdot v_j \cdot u_{j+1} = w_{j+1}$. Hence, $\beta = w_1 \cdot v_1 \cdot u_2 \cdot v_2 \cdot \ldots \cdot u_j \cdot v_j \cdot \ldots \in (C^* \cdot V)^\omega$. □

---

[4] The name δ-limit is due to the fact that an ω-language $F \subseteq X^\omega$ is a $\mathbf{G}_\delta$-set in CANTOR-space if and only if there is a language $W \subseteq X^*$ such that $F = W^\delta$.

Remark. In Property 19 it is important that C is indeed a prefix code. Consider e.g. the suffix code[5] $C := \{b, ba\}$. We obtain for $W := C^*$ and $V := \{b\}$ the proper inclusion $C^\omega = (C^* \cdot b)^\delta \supset C^\omega \cap (C^* \cdot b)^\omega$.

As a consequence of Property 19 we obtain that for a prefix code $C \subseteq X^*$ and $V \subseteq C^*$ it holds

$$(C^* \cdot V)^\delta = (C^* \cdot V)^\omega \cup C^* \cdot V^\delta. \qquad (12)$$

We derive two further identities linking the operations of ω-power and δ-limit for languages of a special shape $C^* \cdot V$ or $W \cdot C^*$ where $C \subseteq X^*$ is a prefix code and $W, V \subseteq C^*$.

To this end let $\mathrm{Min}W := W \setminus W \cdot (X^* \setminus \{e\})$ be the set of minimal words with respect to "$\sqsubseteq$" in a language W.

$$(C^* \cdot V)^\omega = (\mathrm{Min}C^* \cdot V^*)^\delta \qquad (13)$$

$$(W \cdot C^*)^\omega = \left(W \cdot C^* \cdot \mathrm{Min}W\right)^\delta \qquad (14)$$

The proof can be easily transferred from the proof in the special case $C = X$ which can be found e.g. in [Pe85, Lt88].

In studying the relations between the ω-power and the δ-limit it is interesting to investigate as an intermediate operation the infinite intersection

$$\mathcal{D}(W) := \bigcap_{i \in \mathbf{N}} (W \setminus \{e\})^i \cdot X^\omega .$$

Though the assumption $W^\omega = \bigcap_{i \in \mathbf{N}} (W \setminus \{e\})^i \cdot X^\omega$ is tempting, it is well-known that in general W^ω and $\mathcal{D}(W)$ do not coincide. It holds only the obvious inclusion

$$W^\omega \subseteq \mathcal{D}(W) \subseteq (W^*)^\delta. \qquad (15)$$

Next we give some examples which show that for both inclusions equality as well as proper inclusion in Eq. (15) may hold, independently of each other.

First we observe that Eq. (8) implies $W^\omega = \mathcal{D}(W) = (W^*)^\delta$ whenever $W^\delta \subseteq W^\omega$. Thus, in particular, the equality $W^\omega = \mathcal{D}(W) = (W^*)^\delta$ holds if W is finite or W is a prefix code (in these cases $W^\delta = \emptyset$).

In connection with the equality $W^\omega = \mathcal{D}(W) = (W^*)^\delta$ we mention the following connection to BOREL-classes.

Property 20. *If W^ω is closed then $W^\omega = \mathcal{D}(W) = (W^*)^\delta$, and if $W^\omega = \mathcal{D}(W)$ then W^ω is a $\mathbf{G}_\delta$-set.*

Proof. In virtue of Corollary 14 W^ω is closed iff $\mathrm{ls}\, W \subseteq W^\omega$. Since $W^\delta \subseteq \mathrm{ls}\, W$ the first assertion follows from Eq. (8). The second assertion follows from the definition of $\mathcal{D}(W)$. $\qquad \square$

Our next example shows that proper inclusion in both cases is possible. Moreover it gives examples of regular languages of special form (one being a suffix code, the othe being prefix-closed) whose ω-power is not a $\mathbf{G}_\delta$-set.

---

[5]This code has, in addition, a delay of decipherability of 1, that is, whenever $w_1 \cdot w_2 \sqsubseteq w_1' \cdot w_2'$ for $w_1, w_2, w_1', w_2' \in C$ then $w_1 = w_1'$.

Example 6. ([Pa81]) Consider the suffix code $C_6 := \{a\} \cup c \cdot \{a, b\}^* \cdot b$.
Then $cbaba^2ba^3 \ldots \in \mathcal{D}(C_6) \setminus C_6^\omega$ and $cb^\omega \in (C_6^*)^\delta \setminus \mathcal{D}(C_6)$, that is, $C_6^\omega \subset \mathcal{D}(C_6) \subset (C_6^*)^\delta$.

Moreover the intersection of C_6^ω with the closed set $c \cdot \{a, b\}^\omega \subseteq \{a, b, c\}^\omega$ satisfies $C_6^\omega \cap c \cdot \{a, b\}^\omega = c \cdot \{a, b\}^* \cdot b \cdot a^\omega \in \mathbf{F}_\sigma \setminus \mathbf{G}_\delta$. Hence $C_6^\omega \notin \mathbf{G}_\delta$.

We continue this example with the prefix-closure of C_6, $W_6 := \mathbf{A}(C_6) = \{e, a\} \cup c \cdot \{a, b\}^*$. Here we have similarly $W_6^\omega \cap c \cdot \{a, b\}^\omega = c \cdot \{a, b\}^* \cdot a^\omega \in \mathbf{F}_\sigma \setminus \mathbf{G}_\delta$, and $W_6^\omega \notin \mathbf{G}_\delta$.

Observe that as for C_6 it holds $cbaba^2ba^3 \ldots \in \mathcal{D}(W_6) \setminus W_6^\omega$, and $cb^\omega \in (W_6^*)^\delta \setminus \mathcal{D}(W_6)$.

The purpose of the next example (due to WAGNER and WECHSUNG, cf. [St86, Example 3]) is twofold. First it shows that $\mathcal{D}(W) = (W^*)^\delta$ while $W^\omega \subset \mathcal{D}(W)$, and second the proper inclusion holds although C_7^ω is a $\mathbf{G}_\delta$-set.

Example 7. Let $w_1 := a$ and $w_{i+1} := w_i^i \cdot b^i \cdot a$ for $i \geq 1$. Then $w_i \sqsubseteq w_i^i \sqsubset w_{i+1}$. Put $C_7 := \{w_i : i \geq 1\}$. It holds $C_7^\delta = \{\eta\}$ where $w_i^i \sqsubset \eta$ for all $i \geq 1$. Thus $\eta \in \mathcal{D}(C_7)$, but $\eta \notin C_7^\omega$. Moreover in [St86, Theorem 7 and Example 3] it is shown that C_7^ω is a $\mathbf{G}_\delta$-set.

In view of the general identities $\mathcal{D}(W) = W^* \cdot \mathcal{D}(W)$ and $(W^*)^\delta = \mathcal{D}(W) \cup W^* \cdot W^\delta$, we have $C_7^* \cdot \eta \subseteq \mathcal{D}(C_7)$ whence the final conclusion $C_7^\omega \subset \mathcal{D}(C_7) = (C_7^*)^\delta$.

It should be noted that in view of Corollary 23 below the language in Example 7 cannot be chosen regular.

The fourth possibility can be verified again by regular languages.

Example 8. Consider $C_8 := b \cdot a^*$ which is a (suffix) code having a delay of decipherability of 1.

Hence, $C_8^\omega = \mathcal{D}(C_8)$ by Theorem 8 of [St86]. Since $b \cdot a^\omega \in C_8^\delta \setminus C_8^\omega$ we have $C_8^\omega = \mathcal{D}(C_8) \subset (C_8^*)^\delta$.

In Theorem 8 of [St86] it is shown that for codes $C \subseteq X^*$ having a bounded delay of decipherability[6] the identity $C^\omega = \mathcal{D}(C)$ holds. We present another class of languages for which this identity is true. Since $C_8^\omega = (b \cdot \{a, b\}^*)^\omega$ the subsequent lemma will also prove that $C_8^\omega = \mathcal{D}(C_8)$.

Lemma 21. Let $W \subseteq X^*$ and $W = W \cdot X^*$. Then $W^\omega = \bigcap_{i \in \mathbf{N}} W^i \cdot X^\omega$.

Proof. If $e \in W$ the assertion is clear.

Let $e \notin W$ and $\eta \in \bigcap_{i \in \mathbf{N}} W^i \cdot X^\omega$. We construct inductively a factorization $\eta = w_1 \cdot v_1 \cdots v_{i-1} \cdot w_i \cdot v_i \cdots$ where $w_i \in W$ and $v_i \in X^*$.
We start with an arbitrary $w_1 \in W$ for which $w_1 \sqsubset \eta$. Having defined $w_1 \cdot v_1 \cdots v_{i-1} \cdot w_i \sqsubset \eta$ let $l_i := |w_1 \cdot v_1 \cdots v_{i-1} \cdot w_i| + 1$. Since $\eta \in W^{l_i} \cdot X^\omega$, we have $w_1^{(l_i)} \cdots w_{l_i}^{(l_i)} \sqsubset \eta$ for words $w_1^{(l_i)}, \ldots, w_{l_i}^{(l_i)} \in W$. By the choice of l_i it follows $w_1 \cdot v_1 \cdots v_{i-1} \cdot w_i \sqsubseteq w_1^{(l_i)} \cdots w_{l_i-1}^{(l_i)}$. Define $v_i \in X^*$ such that $w_1 \cdot v_1 \cdots v_{i-1} \cdot w_i \cdot v_i = w_1^{(l_i)} \cdots w_{l_i-1}^{(l_i)}$ and $w_{i+1} := w_{l_i}^{(l_i)}$. $\square$

A tight relation between W^ω and $\mathcal{D}(W)$ is given by the following lemma.

Lemma 22. Let $v \cdot w^\omega \in \mathcal{D}(W)$ be an ultimately periodic sequence. Then $v \cdot w^\omega \in W^\omega$.

---

[6]For codes having a bounded delay of decipherability see also [BP85] or [Sa81].

Proof. Let $v \cdot w^\omega \in \mathcal{D}(W)$. Then for every $i \in \mathbf{N}$ there is a prefix $u_1 \cdots u_i$ of $v \cdot w^\omega$ such that $u_j \in W^* \setminus \{e\}$. Let u_1 be longer than v and let $i > |w|$. Then there are $j, k \leq i$ with $j < k$ such that $|u_1 \cdots u_k| - |u_1 \cdots u_j|$ is divisible by $|w|$. Hence $v \cdot w^\omega = u_1 \cdots u_j \cdot (u_{j+1} \cdots u_k)^\omega$. $\qquad\square$

Since regular ω-languages are characterized by their ultimately periodic ω-words, $\mathcal{D}(W)$ is not regular if W^ω is regular and $\mathcal{D}(W) \neq W^\omega$. Moreover, we have the following.

Corollary 23. *If W is regular and $\mathcal{D}(W) = (W^*)^\delta$ then $W^\omega = (W^*)^\delta$.*

Next we characterize ω-power languages in several BOREL-classes. A first result for closed sets has been obtained in Corollary 14. We start with the BOREL-class $\mathbf{G}_\delta$. To this end we need the following operation. As in [St87b] we call

$$W \rhd V := \{v : v \in V \wedge \exists W(w \in W \wedge w \sqsubseteq v \wedge \forall u(w \sqsubset u \sqsubset v \rightarrow u \notin V))\}$$

the *continuation* of the language W to the language V. In other words $W \rhd V$ consists of all those words in V which are minimal (w.r.t. "$\sqsubseteq$") prolongations of words in W. The following properties of the operation " $\rhd$ " are shown in [St87b].

$$(W \rhd V)^\delta = W^\delta \cap V^\delta \qquad (16)$$

Property 24. *$W \rhd V$ is a regular language if W and V are regular.*

Lemma 25. *An ω-power language W^ω is a $\mathbf{G}_\delta$-set if and only if there is a $V \subseteq W^*$ such that $W^\omega = (V^*)^\delta$. If, moreover, W is regular then V can be chosen to be also regular.*

Proof. The "if"-part is evident from the above remark on δ-limits.

If $W^\omega \subseteq X^\omega$ is a $\mathbf{G}_\delta$-set then there is a language $U \subseteq X^*$ such that $W^\omega = U^\delta$. Now set $V := U \rhd W^*$. We obtain from Eq. (16) that $V^\delta = U^\delta \cap (W^*)^\delta = W^\omega$. Then in virtue of $V \subseteq W^*$ the assertion $(V^*)^\delta = V^\omega \cup V^* \cdot V^\delta = W^\omega$ follows.

The additional part on the regularity of V follows from Property 24 and the fact that U can be chosen also as a regular language provided W^ω is a regular ω-language. $\qquad\square$

Now we turn to the ω-power languages which are open ω-languages.

Lemma 26. *An ω-power language $V^\omega \subseteq X^\omega$ is open if and only if there is a language $W \subseteq V^*$ such that $V^\omega = W^\omega = (W \cdot X^*)^\omega = W \cdot X^\omega$.*

Proof. Clearly, our condition is sufficient.

If $V^\omega \subseteq X^\omega$ is open there is a language $V' \subseteq X^*$ with $V^\omega = V' \cdot X^\omega$. Define

$$W := V' \cdot X^* \cap (V^* \setminus \{e\}) \,.$$

Obviously, $V^\omega = V' \cdot X^\omega \subseteq W \cdot X^\omega$. As the inclusions $W^\omega \subseteq (W \cdot X^*)^\omega \subseteq W \cdot X^\omega$ are evident, it remains to show that $V^\omega \subseteq W^\omega$.

Let $\xi = v_1 \cdots v_i \cdots$ where $v_i \in V$, $v_i \neq e$. Because of $V^\omega = V' \cdot X^\omega$ it holds $\xi \in v' \cdot X^\omega$ for some $v' \in V'$. Then $v' \sqsubseteq v_1 \cdots v_{|v'|}$ and, by construction, $v_1 \cdots v_{|v'|} \in W$ and $v_{|v'|+1} \cdots v_i \cdots \in V^\omega$. Thus $V^\omega \subseteq W \cdot V^\omega$, and the assertion follows from Eq. (1). $\qquad\square$

For ω-power languages of the form $(W \cdot X^*)^\omega$ we have the following necessary and sufficient conditions to be open.

Lemma 27. *Let* $W \subseteq X^* \setminus \{e\}$ *be a nonempty language. Then the following conditions are equivalent:*

1. $(W \cdot X^*)^\omega$ *contains a nonempty open subset.*

2. $X^* \cdot W$ *contains a finite maximal prefix code.*

3. $(W \cdot X^*)^\omega = W \cdot X^\omega$.

Proof. 3. $\Rightarrow$ 1. is obvious.
2. $\Rightarrow$ 3. Let $X^* \cdot W$ contain a finite maximal prefix code C. Then $X^\omega = C^\omega \subseteq (X^* \cdot W)^\omega$, whence $(W \cdot X^*)^\omega = W \cdot (X^* \cdot W)^\omega = W \cdot X^\omega$.
1. $\Rightarrow$ 2. First we observe that $\xi \in (W \cdot X^*)^\omega$ iff it has some $w_0 \in W$ as prefix and contains infinitely many nonoverlapping subwords $w_i \in W$, that is, ξ has the form $\xi = w_0 \cdot v_0 \cdot w_1 \cdot v_1 \cdots w_i \cdot v_i \cdots$ where $v_i \in X^*$.

Let now $u \cdot X^\omega \subseteq (W \cdot X^*)^\omega$ for some $u \in X^*$. Then every $\zeta \in X^\omega$ has the form $\zeta = v_0 \cdot w_1 \cdot v_1 \cdots w_i \cdot v_i \cdots$ where $w_i \in W$ and $v_i \in X^*$. Consequently, every $\zeta \in X^\omega$ has a prefix in $X^* \cdot W$. Thus $X^* \cdot W \cdot X^\omega = X^\omega$, which is equivalent to Condition 2. $\qquad\square$

This lemma allows us to present examples of ω-power languages which are open but not closed and which are neither open nor closed but a union of an open and a closed set, respectively.

Property 28. *Let* $\eta \in X^\omega \setminus \{x^\omega : x \in X\}$. *Then* $X^\omega \setminus \{\eta\}$ *is an open nonclosed ω-power language.*

Proof. It is evident that $X^\omega \setminus \{\eta\}$ is an open nonclosed subset in CANTOR-space. Moreover, $X^\omega \setminus \{\eta\} = (X^* \setminus \mathbf{A}(\eta)) \cdot X^\omega$.

Since $\eta \notin \{x^\omega : x \in X\}$, it has a prefix $a^n \cdot b$ (say) where $a, b \in X$, $a \neq b$ and $n > 0$. Consequently, $(X \setminus \{a\}) \cup \{a^{n+1}\} \subseteq X^* \setminus \mathbf{A}(\eta)$. Thus X^{n+1} is a finite maximal prefix code contained in $X^* \cdot (X^* \setminus \mathbf{A}(\eta))$, and $X^\omega \setminus \{\eta\} = ((X^* \setminus \mathbf{A}(\eta)) \cdot X^*)^\omega$ follows from Lemma 27. $\qquad\square$

We conclude with an example of an ω-power language which is neither open nor closed, but as a union of an open and a closed ω-language a set in a low level BOREL-class.

Example 9. Let $C := \{a\} \cup \{bab\}^* \cdot bbb$. Then for $X := \{a, b\}$ the language $X^* \cdot C$ contains $\{a, ba, bba, bbb\}$ – a maximal prefix code. Hence $(C \cdot X^*)^\omega = C \cdot X^\omega$ is open and, since C is an infinite prefix code, $C \cdot X^\omega$ is not closed.

Take the prefix code C and consider $F := (C \cdot X^* \cup \{baa\})^\omega$. Due to the identity $(V \cup W)^\omega = (W^* \cdot V)^\omega \cup (W^* \cdot V)^* \cdot W^\omega$ we obtain $F = (\{baa\}^* \cdot C \cdot X^*)^\omega \cup (\{baa\}^* \cdot C \cdot X^*)^* \cdot (baa)^\omega$.

Now we calculate $(\{baa\}^* \cdot C \cdot X^*)^\omega = \{baa\}^* \cdot (C \cdot X^* \cdot \{baa\}^*)^\omega = \{baa\}^* \cdot (C \cdot X^*)^\omega = \{baa\}^* \cdot C \cdot X^\omega$, and $(\{baa\}^* \cdot C \cdot X^*)^* = \{e\} \cup \{baa\}^* \cdot C \cdot X^*$.

Thus $F = \{baa\}^* \cdot C \cdot X^\omega \cup (\{baa\}^* \cdot C \cdot X^*) \cdot (baa)^\omega \cup \{(baa)^\omega\} = \{baa\}^* \cdot C \cdot X^\omega \cup \{(baa)^\omega\}$ is a union of the open set $\{baa\}^* \cdot C \cdot X^\omega$ with the closed set $\{(baa)^\omega\}$. It remains to show that F is neither open nor closed.

To this end observe that $(baa)^\omega \notin \{baa\}^* \cdot C \cdot X^\omega$, thus F is not open, and that $(bab)^\omega \in C(F) \setminus F$.

5. Topological Density

In this section we study the density of regular and finite-state ω-languages in ω-power languages. It turns out that in this case density and subwords are closely related.

Topological density is based on the following notion. A set F is *nowhere dense* in $E \subseteq X^\omega$ provided $C(E \setminus C(F)) = C(E)$, that is, if $C(F)$ does not contain a nonempty subset of the form $E \cap w \cdot X^\omega$. This condition can be formulated as follows.

Lemma 29. *A set $F \subseteq X^\omega$ is nowhere dense in E iff for every $v \in \mathbf{A}(E)$ there is a $w \in X^*$ such that $v \cdot w \in \mathbf{A}(E)$ and $v \cdot w \cdot X^\omega \cap F = \emptyset$.*

Cast in the language of prefixes, our Lemma 29 asserts, that F is not nowhere dense in $E \neq \emptyset$ if and only if there is a $w \in \mathbf{A}(E)$ such that $E/w \subseteq C(F)/w$. From the following equation

$$C(E \setminus C(F)) = C(E \setminus (C(F) \cap E)) = C(C(E) \setminus C(F)) \qquad (17)$$

we see that F is nowhere dense in E iff F is nowhere dense in $C(E)$ and iff $(C(F) \cap E)$ is nowhere dense in E.

A subset $F \subseteq X^\omega$ is called nowhere dense if it is nowhere dense in X^ω. For finite-state nowhere dense ω-languages we have the following.

Lemma 30. *([St76,80b])A finite-state set $F \in X^\omega$ is nowhere dense iff there is a pattern $w \in X^*$ such that $F \subseteq X^\omega \setminus X^* \cdot w \cdot X^\omega$.*

The aim of this section is to generalize the result of Lemma 30 to finite-state ω-languages nowhere dense in an ω-power language W^ω.

We obtain the following version of Lemma 29.

Corollary 31. *Let $W \subseteq X^*$. Then $F \subseteq X^\omega$ is nowhere dense in W^ω if and only if for every $v \in W^*$ there is a $w \in W^*$ such that $v \cdot w \cdot X^\omega \cap F = \emptyset$.*

Cast again in the language of prefixes, we have that F is not nowhere dense in an ω-power language W^ω if and only if there is a $w \in W^*$ such that $W^\omega/w \subseteq C(F)/w$. We obtain the following necessary and sufficient conditions for a finite-state ω-language to be nowhere dense in an ω-power language.

Lemma 32. *Let $W \subseteq X^*$, and let $F \subseteq X^\omega$ be a finite-state ω-language. Then the following conditions are equivalent.*

1. *F is nowhere dense in W^ω.*

2. *$\forall u(u \in W^* \Rightarrow F/u$ is nowhere dense in $W^\omega)$*

3. *$\forall w(w \in Stab(C(W^\omega)) \cup \{e\} \Rightarrow F/w$ is nowhere dense in $W^\omega)$*

4. *$\forall v(v \in X^* \Rightarrow (C(F) \cap W^\omega)/v$ is nowhere dense in $W^\omega)$*

5. *$\forall v(v \in X^* \Rightarrow (C(F) \cap C(W^\omega))/v$ is nowhere dense in $W^\omega)$*

Remark. Observe that, in general, the stabilizer of $\mathcal{C}(W^\omega)$, $Stab(\mathcal{C}(W^\omega))$ contains $Stab(W^\omega) \supseteq W^* \setminus \{e\}$. Thus Condition 3 shows more states F/w of F to be nowhere dense in W^ω than Condition 2.

Proof. The implications 5. $\Rightarrow$ 4., 4. $\Rightarrow$ 1., 3. $\Rightarrow$ 2., and 2. $\Rightarrow$ 1. are obvious.

To conclude the proof, it suffices to show 1. $\Rightarrow$ 3. and 3. $\Rightarrow$ 5. To this end assume first that Condition 5 does not hold, that is, there is a $v \in X^*$ such that $(\mathcal{C}(F) \cap \mathcal{C}(W^\omega))/v$ is not nowhere dense in W^ω. Then according to Corollary 31 there is a $w \in W^*$ satisfying $(\mathcal{C}(F) \cap \mathcal{C}(W^\omega))/v \cdot w \supseteq \mathcal{C}(W^\omega)/w$. Since $w \in W^* \subseteq Stab(\mathcal{C}(W^\omega)) \cup \{e\}$, we have $\mathcal{C}(W^\omega)/w \supseteq \mathcal{C}(W^\omega)$. Consequently, $u := v \cdot w \in Stab(\mathcal{C}(W^\omega)) \cup \{e\}$, and $\mathcal{C}(F)/u \supseteq W^\omega$ which shows that F/u is not nowhere dense in W^ω.

Now assume Condition 3 to be violated, that is, let F/w be not nowhere dense in W^ω for some $w \in Stab(\mathcal{C}(W^\omega)) \cup \{e\}$. According to Corollary 31 there is a $v \in W^* \subseteq Stab(\mathcal{C}(W^\omega)) \cup \{e\}$ such that $\mathcal{C}(F)/w \cdot v \supseteq \mathcal{C}(W^\omega)/v$. Consequently, $u := w \cdot v \in Stab(\mathcal{C}(W^\omega))$.

Since F is finite-state, there are $n, k \geq 1$ such that $F/u^n = F/u^{n+k}$. Hence $\mathcal{C}(W^\omega) \subseteq \mathcal{C}(F)/u$ implies $\mathcal{C}(W^\omega)/u^{n+k-1} \subseteq \mathcal{C}(F)/u^{n+k} = \mathcal{C}(F)/u^n$.

Now observe that $\mathcal{C}(W^\omega)/u^n \subseteq \mathcal{C}(W^\omega)/u^{n+k-1} \subseteq \mathcal{C}(F)/u^n$, because $u \in Stab(\mathcal{C}(W^\omega)) \cup \{e\}$, what proves our assertion. $\quad\square$

As a consequence of Lemma 32 we show the announced generalization of Lemma 30 that for finite-state ω-languages nowhere dense in ω-power languages W^ω there are patterns, that is subwords appearing in the ω-power language W^ω which do not appear in the finite-state ω-language F. Those patterns can be shown to belong to W^*. Due to the possiblity that $F \not\subseteq \mathcal{C}(W^\omega)$ we have to distinguish two cases.

Theorem 33. *Let $F \subseteq X^\omega$ be finite-state, and let $W^* \subseteq X^*$.*

1. *F is nowhere dense in W^ω iff there is a $w \in W^*$ such that $\mathcal{C}(F) \cap \mathcal{C}(W^\omega) \subseteq \mathcal{C}(W^\omega) \setminus W^* \cdot w \cdot X^\omega$.*

2. *If $F \subseteq \mathcal{C}(W^\omega)$ then F is nowhere dense in W^ω iff there is a $u \in W^*$ such that $F \subseteq \mathcal{C}(W^\omega) \setminus X^* \cdot u \cdot X^\omega$.*

Proof. 1. If F is finite-state and nowhere dense in W^ω then according to Lemma 32.2 the set $F' := \bigcup_{u \in W^*} F/u$ as a finite union of sets nowhere dense in W^ω is again nowhere dense in W^ω. Hence, there is a $w \in W^*$ such that $F' \cap w \cdot X^\omega = \emptyset$. Assume that $F \cap W^* \cdot w \cdot X^\omega \neq \emptyset$. Then there is some $v \in W^*$ such that $F \cap v \cdot w \cdot X^\omega = v \cdot (F/v) \cap v \cdot w \cdot X^\omega \neq \emptyset$, which contradicts the fact that $F' \supseteq F/v$ and $w \cdot X^\omega$ are disjoint.

To prove the converse direction, suppose F to be not nowhere dense in W^ω, that is, according to Lemma 32.2 and Corollary 31 there is some $u \in W^*$ such that $\mathcal{C}(F)/u \cdot w \supseteq \mathcal{C}(W^\omega)/w \supseteq \mathcal{C}(W^\omega)$ for some $w \in W^*$. Hence, $\mathbf{A}(F) \supseteq w \cdot u \cdot W^*$ and there is no $v \in W^*$ with $F \cap u \cdot w \cdot v \cdot X^\omega = \emptyset$.

2. In view of Lemma 32.5 from $\mathcal{C}(F) \subseteq \mathcal{C}(W^\omega)$ we obtain that the finite union $F'' := \bigcup_{u \in X^*} F/u$ is also nowhere dense in W^ω provided F is nowhere dense in W^ω. Now the proof proceeds as in 1. The converse direction of the second part is an immediate consequence of the first part. $\quad\square$

For ω-powers of codes we obtain the following corollary to Theorem 33.1.

Corollary 34. *Let $F \subseteq X^\omega$ be finite-state, and let $C \subseteq X^*$ be a code. If F is nowhere dense in C^ω then there are a $k > 0$ and a word $u \in C^k$ such that $F \cap \mathcal{C}(C^\omega) \subseteq \mathcal{C}((C^k \setminus \{u\})^\omega)$*

The converse statement is, however, not true in general. Consider e.g. the suffix code $C := \bigcup_{n \in \mathbf{N}} \{a, b\}^n \cdot b \cdot a^n$. Here $\mathcal{C}((C^k \setminus \{u\})^\omega) = \mathcal{C}(C^\omega) = \{a, b\}^\omega$ for every pair $k > 0$ and $u \in C^k$, but $F := \{a, b\}^\omega$ is dense in C^ω.

References

[BP85] J. Berstel and D. Perrin, Theory of Codes, Academic Press, Orlando 1985.

[Ch74] Y. Choueka, Theories of automata on ω-tapes: A simplified approach, J. Comput. System Sci. 8 (1974), 117–141.

[CG78] R. S. Cohen and A. Y. Gold, ω-computations on deterministic push down machines, J. Comput. System Sci. (1978) 3, 257–300.

[DK84] Ph. Darondeau and L. Kott, Towards a formal proof system for ω-rational expressions, Inform. Process. Letters 19 (1984), 173–177.

[Ei74] S. Eilenberg, Automata, Languages and Machines. Vol. A, Academic Press, New York 1974.

[EH93] J.Engelfriet, H.J. Hoogeboom: X-automata on ω-words. Theoret. Comput. Sci. 110 (1993) 1, 1–51.

[II84] H. Izumi, Y. Inagaki and N. Honda, A complete axiomsystem of the algebra of closed rational expressions, in: *Automata, Languages and Programming* (ed. J. Paradaens), Lect. Notes Comput. Sci 172, Springer-Verlag, Berlin 1984, 260–269.

[Li76] M. Linna, On ω-sets associated with context-free languages, Inform. Control 31 (1976) 3, 272–293.

[Li77] M. Linna, A decidability result for deterministic ω-context-free languages, Theoret. Comput. Sci. 4 (1977), 83–98.

[Lt88] I. Litovsky, Generateurs des langages rationelles de mots infinis. Thèse, Univ. de Lille Flandres Artois 1988.

[Lt91a] I. Litovsky, Prefix-free languages as ω-generators, Inform. Process. Letters 37 (1991) 1, 61–65.

[Lt91b] I. Litovsky, Free submonoids and minimal ω-generators of R^ω, Acta Cybernetica 10 (1991) 1-2, 35–43.

[LT87] I. Litovsky and E. Timmerman, On generators of rational ω-power languages. Theoret. Comput. Sci. 53 (1987) 2/3, 187–200.

[MN66] R. McNaughton, Testing and generating infinite sequences by a finite automaton, Inform. Control 9 (1966), 521–530.

[Pa81] D. Park, Concurrency and automata on infinite sequences, in: *Theoret. Comput. Sci.* (P. Deussen ed.), Lect. Notes Comput. Sci. 104, Springer-Verlag, Berlin 1981, 167–183.

[Pe85] D. Perrin, An introduction to finite automata on infinite words, in: *Automata on Infinite Words* (eds. M. Nivat and D. Perrin), Lect. Notes Comput. Sci. 192, Springer-Verlag, Berlin 1985, 1–17.

[Re72] R.R. Redziejowski, The theory of general events and its application to parallel programming, Tech. paper TP 18.220, IBM Nordic Lab. Lidingö, Sweden, 1972.

[Sa66] A. Salomaa, Two complete axion systems for the algebra of regular events. J.ACM 13 (1966) 1, 158–169.

[Sa81] A. Salomaa, Jewels of Formal Language Theory, Computer Sci. Press, Rockville 1981.

[St76] L. Staiger, Reguläre Nullmengen. Elektron. Informationsverarb. Kybernetik EIK 12 (1976) 6, 307–311.

[St77] L. Staiger, Empty-storage-acceptance of ω-languages. in: *Fundamentals of Computation Theory* '77 (ed. M. Karpiński), Lect. Notes Comput. Sci. 56, Springer-Verlag, Berlin 1977, 516–521.

[St80a] L. Staiger, A note on connected ω-languages. Elektron. Informationsverarb. Kybernetik EIK 16 (1980) 5/6, 245–251.

[St80b] L. Staiger, Measure and category in X^ω. in: *Topology and Measure* II (eds. J. Flachsmeyer, Z. Frolik and F. Terpe) Part 2, Wiss. Beitr. Ernst-Moritz-Arndt-Universität Greifswald, 1980, 129–136.

[St83] L. Staiger, Finite-state ω-languages. J. Comput. System Sci. 27 (1983) 3, 434–448.

[St86] L. Staiger, On infinitary finite length codes. RAIRO Infor. théor. et Appl. 20 (1986) 4, 483–494.

[St87a] L. Staiger, Sequential mappings of ω-languages. RAIRO Infor. théor. et Appl. 21 (1987) 2, 147–173.

[St87b] L. Staiger, Research in the theory of ω-languages. J. Inform. Process. Cybernetics EIK 23 (1987) 8/9, 415–439.

[Th90] W. Thomas, Automata on infinite objects, in: *Handbook of Theoretical Computer Science* (ed. J. Van Leeuwen), Vol. B, Elsevier, Amsterdam 1990, 133–191.

[Tr62] B.A. Trakhtenbrot, Finite automata and monadic second order logic. Siberian Math. J. 3 (1962), 103–131. (Russian; English translation in: AMS Transl. 59 (1966), 23–55.)

Shuffle-Like Operations on ω-words[1]

Alexandru MATEESCU

Academy of Finland and Department of Mathematics
University of Turku, 20014 Turku, Finland

George Daniel MATEESCU

Department of Mathematics, University of Bucharest
Str. Academiei 14, 70109 Bucharest, Romania

Grzegorz ROZENBERG

Leiden University, Department of Computer Science
P.O. Box 9512, NL-2300 RA Leiden, The Netherlands

Arto SALOMAA

Academy of Finland and Department of Mathematics
University of Turku, 20014 Turku, Finland

Abstract. We introduce and investigate some shuffle-like operations on
ω-words and ω-languages. The approach is applicable to concurrency,
providing a method to define the parallel composition of processes. It is
also applicable to parallel computation. The operations are introduced
using a uniform method based on the notion of an *ω-trajectory*. As a
consequence, we obtain a very intuitive geometrical interpretation of the
parallel composition operation. Our main results concern associativity.
A rather surprising interconnection between associativity and periodicity
will be exhibited.

1. Introduction

Parallel composition of words and languages appears as a fundamental operation
in parallel computation and in the theory of concurrency. Usually, this operation
is modelled by the shuffle operation or restrictions of this operation, such as literal
shuffle, insertion, left-merge, infiltration product, etc.

The shuffle-like operations considered below are based on syntactic constraints on
the ω-shuffle operation. The constraints are referred to as syntactic since they do not
concern properties of the ω-words shuffled, or properties of the letters that occur in
these ω-words.

Instead, the constraints describe the general strategy to switch from one ω-word
to another ω-word. Once such a strategy is defined, the structure of the ω-words that
are shuffled does not play any role.

The syntactic constraints that we consider here are based on the notion of an *ω-trajectory*. Roughly speaking, an ω-trajectory is a line in plane, starting in the origin

---
[1]The work reported here has been partially supported by the Project 11281 of the Academy
of Finland and the ESPRIT Basic Research Working Group ASMICS II. All correspondence to
Alexandru Mateescu.

and continuing parallel with the axis Ox or Oy. The line can change its direction only in points with nonnegative integer coordinates.

An ω-trajectory defines how to move from an ω-word to another ω-word when carrying out the shuffle operation.

2. Basic Definitions

The set of nonnegative integers is denoted by ω. If A is a set, then the set of all subsets of A is denoted by $\mathcal{P}(A)$.

A *closure operator* on A, see [2], is a function $\varphi : \mathcal{P}(A) \longrightarrow \mathcal{P}(A)$ such that, (i) for all $B \subseteq A$, $B \subseteq \varphi(B)$, (ii) if $B_1 \subseteq B_2$, then $\varphi(B_1) \subseteq \varphi(B_2)$, where $B_1, B_2 \subseteq A$, and (iii) for all $B \subseteq A$, $\varphi(\varphi(B)) = \varphi(B)$.

Let Σ be an alphabet, i.e., a finite nonempty set of elements called *letters*. The free monoid generated by Σ is denoted by Σ^*. Elements in Σ^* are referred to as *words*. The empty word is denoted by λ.

If $w \in \Sigma^*$, then $|w|$ is the length of w. Note that $|\lambda| = 0$. If $a \in \Sigma$ and $w \in \Sigma^*$, then $|w|_a$ denotes the number of occurrences of the symbol a in the word w. The *mirror* of a word $w = a_1 a_2 \dots a_n$, where a_i are letters, $1 \leq i \leq n$, is $mi(w) = a_n \dots a_2 a_1$ and $mi(\lambda) = \lambda$. A word w is a *palindrome* iff $mi(w) = w$. A *weak coding* is a morphism that maps each letter into a letter or into λ.

For all other notions and results concerning formal languages that are used in this paper we refer the reader to [10].

Let Σ be an alphabet. An ω-*word* over Σ is a function $f : \omega \longrightarrow \Sigma$. Usually, the ω-word defined by f is denoted as the infinite sequence

$$f(0)f(1)f(2)f(3)f(4) \dots$$

An ω-word w is *ultimately periodic* iff $w = \alpha vvvvv\dots$, where α is a (finite) word, possibly empty, and v is a nonempty word. In this case w is denoted as αv^ω. An ω-word w is referred to as *periodic* iff $w = vvv\dots$ for some nonempty word $v \in \Sigma^*$. In this case w is denoted as v^ω. The set of all ω-words over Σ is denoted by Σ^ω. An ω-*language* is a subset L of Σ^ω, i.e., $L \subseteq \Sigma^\omega$. The set of all words and ω-words over an alphabet Σ is denoted by Σ^∞, that is $\Sigma^\infty = \Sigma^* \cup \Sigma^\omega$.

The notation "$\exists^\omega n$" stands for "there exist infinitely many n", whereas the notation "$\exists^{<\omega} n$" stands for "there are only finitely many n".

Let Σ be an alphabet and let $\alpha = a_0 a_1 a_2 a_3 \dots$ be an ω-word over Σ, where $a_i \in \Sigma$ for all $i \in \omega$. The following notations will be used: $\alpha(i, j) = a_i a_{i+1} \dots a_j$, where $i \leq j$, and $\alpha(i, \omega) = a_i a_{i+1} a_{i+2} \dots$, where $i \geq 0$. Moreover, $In(\alpha)$ denotes the set of those letters from Σ that occur infinitely many times in α, i.e.,

$$In(\alpha) = \{\sigma \in \Sigma \mid \exists^\omega n \text{ such that } a_n = \sigma\}.$$

If $L \subseteq \Sigma^*$ is a language, then L^ω denotes the the following ω-language:

$$L^\omega = \{\alpha \in \Sigma^\omega \mid \alpha = w_0 w_1 w_2 \dots, \text{where } w_i \in L, i \geq 0\}.$$

Assume that Σ and Δ are two alphabets. Let $\varphi : \Sigma \longrightarrow \Delta^*$ be a morphism and let $\alpha = a_0 a_1 a_2 \dots$ be an ω-word over Σ, where $a_i \in \Sigma$, for all $i \geq 0$. The image by φ of α is the ω-word over Δ defined as:

$$\varphi(\alpha) = \beta_0 \beta_1 \beta_2 \dots,$$

where $\beta_i = \varphi(a_i)$ for all $i \geq 0$.

Analogously, if $\Sigma : \Sigma \longrightarrow \mathcal{P}(\Delta^*)$ is a substitution, then

$$\Sigma(\alpha) = \{\gamma_0\gamma_1\gamma_2\ldots \mid \gamma_i \in \Sigma(a_i) \text{ for all } i \geq 0\}.$$

A *Büchi automaton* is a quintuple $A = (Q, \Sigma, q_0, \delta, F)$, where Q is a finite set of states, Σ is the *input alphabet*, $q_0 \in Q$ is the *initial state*, δ is the *transition relation*, $\delta \subseteq Q \times \Sigma \times Q$, and $F \subseteq Q$ is the set of *final states*.

Let α be an ω-word over Σ, $\alpha = a_0a_1a_2\ldots$, where $a_i \in \Sigma$, for all $i \geq 0$. A *run* of A on α is a sequence of states $s = s_0s_1s_2\ldots$, such that $s_0 = q_0$ and $(s_i, a_i, s_{i+1}) \in \delta$, for all $i \geq 0$. The run is *successful* iff $In(s) \cap F \neq \emptyset$. α is *accepted* by A iff there exists a successful run of A on α.

The ω-language *recognized* by A is:

$$L(A) = \{\alpha \in \Sigma^\omega \mid \alpha \text{ is accepted by } A\}.$$

An ω-language L is referred to as ω-*regular* or *Büchi recognizable* iff there exists a Büchi automata A such that $L(A) = L$. The reader is reffered to [11] or [9] for a survey on ω-languages and automata.

We now recall some operations for formal languages that simulate the parallel composition of words.

For general results concerning the theory of concurrency the reader may consult [8], [1] or [4].

The *shuffle* operation, denoted by $\amalg$, is defined recursively by:

$$(au \amalg bv) = a(u \amalg bv) \cup b(au \amalg v),$$

and

$$(u \amalg \lambda) = (\lambda \amalg u) = \{u\},$$

where $u, v \in \Sigma^*$ and $a, b \in \Sigma$.

The shuffle operation is extended in a natural way to languages: the *shuffle* of two languages L_1 and L_2 is:

$$L_1 \amalg L_2 = \bigcup_{u \in L_1, v \in L_2} u \amalg v.$$

Example 2.1. $ab \amalg bc = \{abbc, abcb, babc, bacb, bcab\}$.

The *literal shuffle*, denoted by $\amalg_l$, is defined as:

$$a_1a_2\ldots a_n \amalg_l b_1b_2\ldots b_m = \begin{cases} a_1b_1a_2b_2\ldots a_nb_nb_{n+1}\ldots b_m, & \text{if } n \leq m, \\ a_1b_1a_2b_2\ldots a_mb_ma_{m+1}\ldots a_n, & \text{if } m < n, \end{cases}$$

where $a_i, b_j \in \Sigma$.

$$(u \amalg_l \lambda) = (\lambda \amalg_l u) = \{u\},$$

where $u \in \Sigma^*$.

Example 2.2. $aba \amalg_l bc = \{abbca\}$.

398

3. ω-Trajectories

In this section we introduce the notions of the ω-trajectory and shuffle on ω-trajectories. The shuffle of two ω-words has a natural geometrical interpretation related to lattice points in the plane (points with nonnegative integer coordinates) and with a certain "walk" in the plane defined by each ω-trajectory.

Let $V = \{r, u\}$ be the set of *versors* in the plane: r stands for the *right* direction, whereas, u stands for the *up* direction.

Definition 3.1. An ω-*trajectory* is an element t, $t \in V^\omega$. A set T, $T \subseteq V^\omega$, is called a set of ω-*trajectories*.

Let Σ be an alphabet and let t be an ω-trajectory, $t = t_0 t_1 t_2 \ldots$, where $t_i \in V, i \geq 0$. Let α, β be two ω-words over Σ, $\alpha = a_0 a_1 a_2 \ldots, \beta = b_0 b_1 b_2 \ldots$, where $a_i, b_j \in Sigma, i, j \geq 0$.

Definition 3.2. The *shuffle of α with β on the ω-trajectory t*, denoted $\alpha \text{⧢}_t \beta$, is defined as follows:

$\alpha \text{⧢}_t \beta = c_0 c_1 c_2 \ldots$, where, if $|t_0 t_1 t_2 \ldots t_i|_r = k_1$ and $|t_0 t_1 t_2 \ldots t_i|_u = k_2$, then

$$c_i = \begin{cases} a_{k_1-1}, & \text{if } t_i = r, \\ b_{k_2-1}, & \text{if } t_i = u. \end{cases}$$

Remark. The shuffle on (finite) trajectories of (finite) words is investigated in [7]. In this case a trajectory is an element t, $t \in V^*$.

Let Σ be an alphabet and let t be a trajectory, $t = t_0 t_1 \ldots t_n$, where $t_i \in V, 1 \leq i \leq n$. Let α, β be two words over $Sigma$, $\alpha = a_0 a_1 \ldots a_p, \beta = b_0 b_1 \ldots b_q$, where $a_i, b_j \in \Sigma, 0 \leq i \leq p$ and $0 \leq j \leq q$.

The shuffle of α with β on the trajectory t, denoted $\alpha \text{⧢}_t \beta$, is defined as follows: if $|\alpha| \neq |t|_r$ or $|\beta| \neq |t|_u$, then $\alpha \text{⧢}_t \beta = \emptyset$, else $\alpha \text{⧢}_t \beta = c_0 c_1 c_2 \ldots c_{p+q+2}$, where, if $|t_0 t_1 \ldots t_i|_r = k_1$ and $|t_0 t_1 \ldots t_i|_u = k_2$, then

$$c_i = \begin{cases} a_{k_1-1}, & \text{if } t_i = r, \\ b_{k_2-1}, & \text{if } t_i = u. \end{cases}$$

Observe that there is an important distinction between the finite case, i.e., the shuffle on trajectories, and the infinite case, i.e., the shuffle on ω-trajectories: sometimes the result of shuffling of two words α and β on a trajectory t can be empty whereas the shuffle of two ω-words over an ω-trajectory is always nonempty and consists of only one ω-word.

Now we give a recursive definition of the operation ⧢_t, where $t \in V^\omega$. It will lead to the same notion of ⧢_t as Definition 3.2.

Definition 3.3. Let Σ be an alphabet and let $a_i, i \geq 0$ be letters from Σ. Consider the functions $first$ and $last_\omega$ defined as:

$$first(a_0 a_1 a_2 \ldots) = a_0 \text{ and } last_\omega(a_0 a_1 a_2 \ldots) = a_1 a_2 \ldots$$

The operation ⧢_t, where $t \in V^\omega$, $d \in V$ is defined as follows:

$$\alpha \text{⧢}_{dt} \beta = \begin{cases} first(\alpha)(last_\omega(\alpha) \text{⧢}_t \beta), & \text{if } d = r, \\ first(\beta)(\alpha \text{⧢}_t last_\omega(\beta)), & \text{if } d = u. \end{cases}$$

If T is a set of ω-trajectories, the *shuffle of α with β on the set T of ω-trajectories*, denoted $\alpha \amalg_T \beta$, is:

$$\alpha \amalg_T \beta = \bigcup_{t \in T} \alpha \amalg_t \beta.$$

The above operation is extended to ω-languages over Σ, if $L_1, L_2 \subseteq \Sigma^\omega$, then:

$$L_1 \amalg_T L_2 = \bigcup_{\alpha \in L_1, \beta \in L_2} \alpha \amalg_T beta.$$

Notation. If T is V^ω then $\amalg_T$ is denoted by $\amalg_\omega$.

Example 3.1. Let α and β be the ω-words $\alpha = a_0a_1a_2a_3a_4a_5a_6a_7\ldots$, $\beta = b_0b_1b_2b_3b_4\ldots$ and assume that $t = r^2u^3r^5uru\ldots$. The shuffle of α with β on the trajectory t is:

$$\alpha \amalg_t \beta = \{a_0a_1b_0b_1b_2a_2a_3a_4a_5a_6b_3a_7b_4\ldots\}.$$

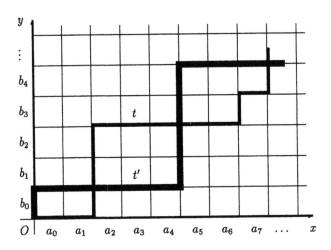

Figure 1

The result has the following geometrical interpretation (see Figure 1): the trajectory t defines a line starting in the origin and continuing one unit right or up, depending of the definition of t. In our case, first there are two units right, then three units up, then five units right, etc. Assign α on the Ox axis and β on the Oy axis of the plane. The result can be read following the line defined by the trajectory t, that is, if being in a lattice point of the trajectory, (the corner of a unit square) and if the trajectory is going right, then one should pick up the corresponding letter from α, otherwise, if the trajectory is going up, then one should add to the result the corresponding letter from β. Hence, the trajectory t defines a line in the plane, on which one has "to walk" starting from the origin O. In each lattice point one has to follow one of the versors r or u, according to the definition of t.

Assume now that t' is another trajectory, say:

$$t' = ur^5u^4r^3\ldots.$$

The trajectory t' is depicted in Figure 1 by a much bolder line than the trajectory t. Observe that:

$$\alpha \amalg_{t'} \beta = \{b_0 a_0 a_1 a_2 a_3 a_4 b_1 b_2 b_3 b_4 a_5 a_6 a_7 \ldots\}.$$

Consider the set of trajectories, $T = \{t, t'\}$. The shuffle of α with β on the set T of trajectories is:

$$\alpha \amalg_T \beta = \{a_0 a_1 b_0 b_1 b_2 a_2 a_3 a_4 a_5 a_6 b_3 a_7 b_4 \ldots, b_0 a_0 a_1 a_2 a_3 a_4 b_1 b_2 b_3 b_4 a_5 a_6 a_7 \ldots\}.$$

The following two theorems are representation results for ω-languages of the form $L_1 \amalg_T L_2$.

Observe that we are using here the obvious associativity of the operation $\amalg_\omega$. We will return to this matter in Section 4.

Theorem 3.1. *For all ω-languages L_1 and L_2, $L_1, L_2 \subseteq \Sigma^\omega$, and for all sets T of ω-trajectories, there exist a gsm M and two letter-to-letter morphisms g and h such that*

$$L_1 \amalg_T L_2 = M(h(L_1) \amalg_\omega g(L_2) \amalg_\omega T).$$

Proof. Let $\Sigma_1 = \{a_1 \mid a \in \Sigma\}$ and $\Sigma_2 = \{a_2 \mid a \in \Sigma\}$ be two copies of Σ such that Σ_1, Σ_2 and V are pairwise disjoint alphabets. Define the morphisms: $g : \Sigma \longrightarrow \Sigma_1^*$, $g(a) = a_1$, $a \in \Sigma$ and $h : \Sigma \longrightarrow \Sigma_2^*$, $h(a) = a_2$, $a \in \Sigma$.

Now consider the gsm $M = (Q, \Sigma', \Delta, q_0, \delta, F)$, where $Q = \{q_0, q_1, q_2\}$, $\Sigma' = \Sigma_1 \cup \Sigma_2 \cup V$, $\Delta = \Sigma$, $F = \{q_0\}$ and

$$\delta(q_0, r) = (q_1, \lambda), \ \delta(q_0, u) = (q_2, \lambda),$$
$$\delta(q_1, a_1) = (q_0, a) \text{ and } \delta(q_2, a_2) = (q_0, a),$$

for all $a_1 \in \Sigma_1$ and $a_2 \in \Sigma_2$.

One can easily verify that $L_1 \amalg_T L_2 = M(h(L_1) \amalg_\omega g(L_2) \amalg_\omega T)$. $\square$

The next theorem shows that the gsm-mapping M of Theorem 3.1 is of a particular type.

Theorem 3.2. *For all ω-languages L_1 and L_2, $L_1, L_2 \subseteq \Sigma^\omega$, and for all sets T of ω-trajectories, there exist a morphism φ and two letter-to-letter morphisms g, h and a regular ω-language R, such that*

$$L_1 \amalg_T L_2 = \varphi((h(L_1) \amalg_\omega g(L_2) \amalg_\omega T) \cap R).$$

Proof. Let Σ_1 and Σ_2 be as before. Define the morphisms: $g : \Sigma \longrightarrow \Sigma_1^*$, $g(a) = a_1$, $a \in \Sigma$ and $h : \Sigma \longrightarrow \Sigma_2^*$, $h(a) = a_2$, $a \in \Sigma$. Let R be the regular ω-language, $R = (r\Sigma_1 \cup u\Sigma_2)^\omega$.

Now consider the morphism:

$$\varphi : (\Sigma_1 \cup \Sigma_2 \cup V) \longrightarrow \Sigma^*,$$

defined as: $\varphi(a_1) = a$, $\varphi(a_2) = a$ and $\varphi(r) = \varphi(u) = \lambda$.

It is easy to see that: $L_1 \amalg_T L_2 = \varphi((h(L_1) \amalg_\omega g(L_2) \amalg_\omega T) \cap R)$. $\square$

Theorem 3.3. *If L_1 and L_2 are regular ω-languages, then $L_1 \amalg_\omega L_2$ is a regular ω-language.*

Proof. Without loss of generality we can assume that L_1 and L_2 are over the same alphabet Σ. Let $A_i = (Q_i, \Sigma, q_0^i, \delta_i, F_i)$ be Büchi automata such that $L(A_i) = L_i$, $i = 1, 2$. We define a Büchi automaton $A = (Q, \Sigma, q_0, \delta, F)$ such that $L(A) = L_1 \, \mathrm{III}_w L_2$ as follows. $Q = Q_1 \times Q_2 \times \{0, 1, 2\}$. Elements in Q are denoted as $[q_1, q_2, k]$, where $q_i \in Q_i, i = 1, 2$ and $0 \leq k \leq 2$. The initial state is $q_0 = [q_0^1, q_0^2, 0]$, the final states are $F = Q_1 \times Q_2 \times \{2\}$. The transition function δ is defined in such a way that it simulates nondeterministically on the first component the automaton A_1 or on the second component the automaton A_2. The third component of the states is used to record an occurrence of a final state from F_1 (by storing the value 1). The value 2 is stored if at some stage later a final state from F_2 does occur. The value 0 is stored in the third component whenever the first two components are not final states.

Formally, the definition of δ is:

$$\delta([q_1, q_2, 0], a) = \{[\delta_1(q_1, a), q_2, 0], [q_1, \delta_2(q_2, a), q_2, 0]\} \text{ if } \delta_1(q_1, a) \notin F_1,$$

$$\delta([q_1, q_2, 0], a) = \{[\delta_1(q_1, a), q_2, 1], [q_1, \delta_2(q_2, a), 0]\} \text{ if } \delta_1(q_1, a) \in F_1,$$

$$\delta([q_1, q_2, 1], a) = \{[\delta_1(q_1, a), q_2, 1], [q_1, \delta_2(q_2, a), 1]\} \text{ if } \delta_2(q_2, a) \notin F_2,$$

$$\delta([q_1, q_2, 1], a) = \{[\delta_1(q_1, a), q_2, 1], [q_1, \delta_2(q_2, a), 2]\} \text{ if } \delta_2(q_2, a) \in F_2,$$

$$\delta([q_1, q_2, 2], a) = \{[\delta_1(q_1, a), q_2, 0], [q_1, \delta_2(q_2, a), q_2, 0]\} \text{ if } \delta_1(q_1, a) \notin F_1,$$

$$\delta([q_1, q_2, 2], a) = \{[\delta_1(q_1, a), q_2, 1], [q_1, \delta_2(q_2, a), q_2, 0]\} \text{ if } \delta_1(q_1, a) \in F_1.$$

Clearly, $L(A) = L_1 \, \mathrm{III}_w L_2$. □

The following theorem provides a characterization of those sets of ω-trajectories T for which $L_1 \, \mathrm{III}_T L_2$ is a regular ω-language, whenever L_1, L_2 are regular ω-languages.

Theorem 3.4. *Let T be a set of ω-trajectories, $T \subseteq \{r, u\}^\omega$. The following assertions are equivalent:*

(i) *for all regular ω-languages L_1, L_2, the ω-language $L_1 \, \mathrm{III}_T L_2$ is a regular ω-language.*

(ii) *T is a regular ω-language.*

Proof. (i) $\Rightarrow$ (ii) Assume that $L_1 = r^\omega$ and $L_2 = u^\omega$ and note that $L_1 \, \mathrm{III}_T L_2 = T$. It follows that T is a regular ω-language.

(ii) $\Rightarrow$ (i) It follows from Theorem 3.2, Theorem 3.3 and from the closure properties of regular ω-languages under intersection and morphisms. □

4. Commutativity and Associativity

Definition 4.1. A set T of ω-trajectories is referred to as *commutative* iff the operation III_T is commutative, i.e., $\alpha \, \mathrm{III}_T \beta = \beta \, \mathrm{III}_T \alpha$, for all alphabets Σ and for all $\alpha, \beta \in \Sigma^\omega$.

Example 4.1. Note that ω-shuffle is a commutative set of trajectories, whereas for instance, the literal ω-shuffle, i.e., the shuffle over the set of ω-trajectories consisting of only one ω-trajectory t,

$$t = (ru)^{\omega} = rururu\ldots$$

is noncommutative.

Notation. The morphism $sym : \{r, u\} \longrightarrow \{r, u\}^*$ is defined by $sym(u) = r$ and $sym(r) = u$.

Remark 4.1. A set T of ω-trajectories is commutative iff $T = sym(T)$.

Proposition 4.1. *If T is a regular set of ω-trajectories, then it is decidable whether or not T is commutative.*

Proof. If T is a regular ω-language, then $sym(T)$ is also a regular ω-language. Hence, the equality $T = sym(T)$ is decidable. □

Notation. Let $\mathcal{C}$ be the family of all commutative sets of ω-trajectories.

Proposition 4.2. *If $(T_i)_{i \in I}$ is a family of commutative sets of ω-trajectories, then T',*

$$T' = \bigcap_{i \in I} T_i \ ,$$

is also a commutative set of ω-trajectories.

Proof. Let α and β be ω-words over Σ. Assume that $w \in \alpha \ \text{Ш}_{T'} \beta$. It follows that for all i, $i \in I$, $w \in \alpha \ \text{Ш}_{T_i} \beta$. But, each T_i is commutative, hence $w \in \beta \ \text{Ш}_{T_i} \alpha$, for all i, $i \in I$. Therefore, $w \in \beta \ \text{Ш}_{T'} \alpha$. Thus,

$$\alpha \ \text{Ш}_{T'} \beta = \beta \ \text{Ш}_{T'} \alpha.$$

This implies that T' is a commutative set of ω-trajectories. □

Definition 4.2. Let T be an arbitrary set of ω-trajectories. The *commutative closure* of T, denoted $\check{T}$, is

$$\check{T} = \bigcap_{T \subseteq T', T' \in \mathcal{C}} T'.$$

Observe that for all $T, T \subseteq \{r, u\}^{\omega}$, $\check{T}$ is an commutative set of ω-trajectories and, moreover, $\check{T}$ is the smallest commutative set of ω-trajectories that contains T.

Remark 4.2. The function $\check{\ \ }: \mathcal{P}(V^{\omega}) \longrightarrow \mathcal{P}(V^{\omega})$ defined as above is a closure operator.

Remark 4.3. One can easily verify that:

$$\check{T} = T \cup sym(T).$$

• Associativity

The main results in this paper deal with associativity. After a few general remarks, we restrict the attention to the set V_+^{ω} of ω-trajectories t such that both r and u occur infinitely often in t. (It will become apparent below why this restriction is important.) It turns out that associativity can be viewed as stability under four particular operations, referred to as $\Diamond$-operations. This characterization exhibits a

surprising interconnection between associativity and periodicity, which in our opinion is of direct importance also for the basic theory of ω-words.

Definition 4.3. A set T of ω-trajectories is *associative* iff the operation $\amalg_T$ is associative, i.e.,

$$(\alpha \amalg_T \beta) \amalg_T \gamma = \alpha \amalg_T (\beta \amalg_T \gamma),$$

for all $\alpha, \beta, \gamma \in \Sigma^\omega$.

The following sets of ω-trajectories are associative:

1. $T = \{r, u\}^\omega$.

2. $T = \{t \in V^\omega \mid |t|_r < \infty\}$.

3. $T = \{\alpha_0 \beta_0 \alpha_1 \beta_1 \ldots \mid \alpha_i \in r^*, \beta_i \in u^*$ and, moreover, α_i and β_i are of even length, $i \geq 0\}$.

Nonassociative sets of ω-trajectories are for instance:

1. $T = (ru)^\omega$.

2. $T = \{t \in V^\omega \mid t$ is a Sturmian ω-word $\}$.

3. $T = \{w_0 w_1 w_2 \ldots \mid w_i \in L\}$, where $L = \{r^n u^n \mid n \geq 0\}$.

Definition 4.4. Let D be the set $D = \{x, y, z\}$. Define the substitutions Σ, $\tau : V \longrightarrow \mathcal{P}(D^*)$, as follows:

$$\Sigma(r) = \{x, y\} \ , \ \Sigma(u) = \{z\},$$

$$\tau(r) = \{x\} \ , \ \tau(u) = \{y, z\}.$$

Consider the morphisms φ and ψ, φ , $\psi : V \longrightarrow D^*$, defined as:

$$\varphi(r) = x \ , \ \varphi(u) = y,$$

$$\psi(r) = y \ , \ \psi(u) = z.$$

Proposition 4.3. *Let T be a set of ω-trajectories. The following conditions are equivalent:*

(i) T is an associative set of ω-trajectories.

(ii) $\Sigma(T) \cap (\varphi(T) \amalg z^\omega) = \tau(T) \cap (\psi(T) \amalg x^\omega)$.

Proof. (i) $\Rightarrow$ (ii). Assume that T is an associative set of ω-trajectories. Consider w such that $w \in \Sigma(T) \cap (\varphi(T) \amalg z^\omega)$. It follows that there exists $t_1, t_1 \in T$, such that $w \in \Sigma(t_1)$ and there exists $t, t \in T$, such that $w \in \varphi(t) \amalg z^\omega$. Assume that

$$t_1 = r^{i_0} u^{j_1} r^{i_1} \ldots u^{j_n} r^{i_n} \ldots,$$

for some nonnegative integers i_g, j_h, $0 \leq g, 1 \leq h$. From the definition of Σ we conclude that

$$w \in \{x, y\}^{i_0} z^{j_1} \{x, y\}^{i_1} \ldots z^{j_n} \{x, y\}^{i_n} \ldots.$$

Since $w \in \varphi(t) \amalg z^\omega$, it follows that $t = s_0 s_1 \ldots s_n \ldots$, such that $s_k \in V^*$ and $|s_k| = i_k$ for all k, $0 \leq k$. Therefore,

$$w \in (x^\omega \amalg_t y^\omega) \amalg_{t_1} z^\omega.$$

Because T is associative, there are t' and t'_1 in T such that

$$(x^\omega \amalg_t y^\omega) \amalg_{t_1} z^\omega = x^\omega \amalg_{t'} (y^\omega \amalg_{t'_1} z^\omega).$$

Hence, we obtain that $w \in x^\omega \amalg_{t'} (y^\omega \amalg_{t'_1} z^\omega)$, for some t' and t'_1 in T. Now, it is easy to observe that this implies that $w \in \tau(T) \cap (\psi(T) \amalg x^\omega)$. Thus, $\Sigma(T) \cap (\varphi(T) \amalg z^\omega) \subseteq \tau(T) \cap (\psi(T) \amalg x^\omega)$. The converse inclusion is analogous. Therefore, the equality from (ii) is true.

$(ii) \Rightarrow (i)$. Let Σ be an alphabet and let α, β, γ be ω-words over Σ. Consider an ω-word w, such that $w \in (\alpha \amalg_T \beta) \amalg_T \gamma$. There exist t and t_1 in T such that $w \in (\alpha \amalg_t \beta) \amalg_{t_1} \gamma$. Let v be the ω-word obtained from w by replacing each letter from α by x, each letter from β by y and each letter from γ by z. Observe that v is in $\Sigma(t_1)$ and also in $\varphi(t) \amalg z^\omega$. Therefore, $v \in \Sigma(T) \cap (\varphi(T) \amalg z^\omega)$. By our assumption, it follows that $v \in \tau(T) \cap (\psi(T) \amalg x^\omega)$. Hence, there are t' and t'_1 in T such that $v \in \tau(t') \cap (\psi(t'_1) \amalg x^\omega)$. Note that this means that $v \in x^\omega \amalg_{t'} (y^\omega \amalg_{t'_1} z^\omega)$. Hence, it is easy to see that $w \in \alpha \amalg_{t'} (\beta \amalg_{t''} \gamma)$, i.e., $w \in \alpha \amalg_T (\beta \amalg_T \gamma)$. Thus, $(\alpha \amalg_T \beta) \amalg_T \gamma \subseteq \alpha \amalg_T (\beta \amalg_T \gamma)$. The converse inclusion is analogous. Therefore, for all $\alpha, \beta, \gamma \in \Sigma^\omega$,

$$(\alpha \amalg_T \beta) \amalg_T \gamma = \alpha \amalg_T (\beta \amalg_T \gamma).$$

Thus, T is an associative set of ω-trajectories. $\square$

Proposition 4.4. *If T is a regular set of ω-trajectories, then it is decidable whether or not T is associative.*

Proof. Observe that if T is a regular ω-language, then the languages $\Sigma(T) \cap (\varphi(T) \amalg z^\omega)$ and $\tau(T) \cap (\psi(T) \amalg x^\omega)$ are regular ω-languages. Hence, the equality (ii) from the Proposition 4.3 is decidable. $\square$

Notation. Let $\mathcal{A}$ be the family of all associative sets of ω-trajectories.

Proposition 4.5. *If $(T_i)_{i \in I}$ is a family of associative sets of ω-trajectories, then T',*

$$T' = \bigcap_{i \in I} T_i \ ,$$

is an associative set of ω-trajectories.

Proof. Analogous to Proposition 4.2. $\square$

Definition 4.5. Let T be an arbitrary set of ω-trajectories. The *associative closure* of T, denoted $\overline{T}$, is

$$\overline{T} = \bigcap_{T \subseteq T', T' \in \mathcal{A}} T'.$$

Observe that for all T, $T \subseteq \{r, u\}^*$, $\overline{T}$ is an associative set of ω-trajectories and, moreover, $\overline{T}$ is the smallest associative set of ω-trajectories that contains T.

Remark 4.4. The function $^- : \mathcal{P}(V^\omega) \longrightarrow \mathcal{P}(V^\omega)$ defined as above is a closure operator.

Notation. Let V_+^ω be the set of all ω-trajectories $t \in V^\omega$ such that t contains infinitely many occurrences both of r and of u.

Now we give another characterization of an associative set of ω-trajectories from V_+^ω. This is useful in finding an alternative definition of the associative closure of a set of ω-trajectories and also to prove some other properties related to associativity.

However, this characterization is valid only for sets of ω-trajectories from V_+^ω and not for the general case, i.e., not for sets of ω-trajectories from V^ω.

Definition 4.6. Let W be the alphabet $W = \{x, y, z\}$ and consider the following four morphisms, ρ_i, $1 \leq i \leq 4$, where

$$\rho_i : W \longrightarrow V_+^\omega , \qquad 1 \leq i \leq 4,$$

and

$$\begin{array}{lll}
\rho_1(x) = \lambda , & \rho_1(y) = r , & \rho_1(z) = u, \\
\rho_2(x) = r , & \rho_2(y) = u , & \rho_2(z) = u, \\
\rho_3(x) = r , & \rho_3(y) = u , & \rho_3(z) = \lambda, \\
\rho_4(x) = r , & \rho_4(y) = r , & \rho_4(z) = u.
\end{array}$$

Next, we consider four operations on the set of ω-trajectories, V_+^ω.

Definition 4.7. Let $\Diamond_i$, $1 \leq i \leq 4$ be the following operations on V_+^ω.

$$\Diamond_i : V_+^\omega \times V_+^\omega \longrightarrow V_+^\omega , \qquad 1 \leq i \leq 4,$$

Let t, t' be in V_+^ω

1. $\Diamond_1(t, t') = \rho_1((x^\omega \amalg_t y^\omega) \amalg_{t'} z^\omega)$,

2. $\Diamond_2(t, t') = \rho_2((x^\omega \amalg_t y^\omega) \amalg_{t'} z^\omega)$,

3. $\Diamond_3(t', t) = \rho_3(x^\omega \amalg_{t'} (y^\omega \amalg_t z^\omega))$,

4. $\Diamond_4(t', t) = \rho_4(x^\omega \amalg_{t'} (y^\omega \amalg_t z^\omega))$.

Definition 4.8. A set $T \subseteq V_+^\omega$ is *stable* under $\Diamond$-operations iff for all $t_1, t_2 \in T$, it follows that $\Diamond_i(t_1, t_2) \in T$, $1 \leq i \leq 4$.

Proposition 4.6. *Let T be a set of ω-trajectories, $T \subseteq V_+^\omega$. The following assertions are equivalent:*

(i) T is an associative set of ω-trajectories.

(ii) T is stable under $\Diamond$-operations.

Proof. The idea of the proof is that for two ω-trajectories t, t' and for the ω-words x^ω, y^ω and z^ω, the operation $\Diamond_1$ applied to t and t' computes the (unique) trajectory t_1' that occurs in the equality:

$$(x^\omega \amalg_t y^\omega) \amalg_{t'} z^\omega = x^\omega \amalg_{t_1} (y^\omega \amalg_{t_1'} z^\omega).$$

The operation $\Diamond_2$ computes the (unique) ω-trajectory t_1 that occurrs in the above equality. Analogously, $\Diamond_3$ applied to t_1 and t_1' computes the (unique) trajectory t whereas $\Diamond_4(t_1, t_1') = t'$.

$(i) \implies (ii)$ Assume that T_+^ω is an associative set of ω-trajectories. Since T is associative, there are t_1 and t_1' in T such that

$$(x^\omega ⧢_t y^\omega) ⧢_{t'} z^\omega = x^\omega ⧢_{t_1} (y^\omega ⧢_{t_1'} z^\omega).$$

Hence,

$$\Diamond_1(t, t') = \rho_1((x^\omega ⧢_t y^\omega) ⧢_{t'} z^\omega) = \rho_1(x^\omega ⧢_{t_1} (y^\omega ⧢_{t_1'} z^\omega)) =$$
$$= r^\omega ⧢_{t_1'} u^\omega = t_1' \in T.$$

Thus T is stable for $\Diamond_1$.

Analogously,

$$\Diamond_2(t, t') = \rho_2((x^\omega ⧢_t y^\omega) ⧢_{t'} z^\omega) = \rho_2(x^\omega ⧢_{t_1} (y^\omega ⧢_{t_1'} z^\omega)) =$$
$$= r^\omega ⧢_{t_1} u^\omega = t_1 \in T.$$

Hence T is stable for $\Diamond_2$.

A similar proof shows that T is also stable for $\Diamond_3$ and $\Diamond_4$.

$(ii) \implies (i)$ Now assume that $T \subseteq V_+^\omega$ is a set of ω-trajectories stable under $\Diamond_i$, $1 \leq i \leq 4$.

Let Σ be an alphabet and consider $\alpha, \beta, \gamma \in \Sigma^\omega$ and $t, t' \in T$. Note that $\Diamond_1(t, t') = t_1'$ and $\Diamond_2(t, t') = t_1$, for some $t_1, t_1' \in T$. Now it is easy to see that

$$(\alpha ⧢_t \beta) ⧢_{t'} \gamma = \alpha ⧢_{t_1} (\beta ⧢_{t_1'} \gamma).$$

Thus, we obtain that

$$(\alpha ⧢_T \beta) ⧢_T \gamma \subseteq \alpha ⧢_T (\beta ⧢_T \gamma).$$

For the converse inclusion, the proof is similar, but using this time the fact that T is stable under $\Diamond_3$ and $\Diamond_4$. □

Remark 4.5. Here we like to point out why we restricted our attention to the set V_+^ω and not to the general case V^ω. The operation $\Diamond_1$ is defined to produce the ω-trajectory t_1' (see the above proof). However, if T contains a trajectory t that is not in V_+^ω, then $\Diamond_1(t, t)$ is not necessarily in V^ω. For instance $t = r u r^\omega$, then $\Diamond_1(t, t) = ur \notin V^\omega$. Thus the operation $\Diamond_1$ is not well defined. A similar phenomenon happens with the operation $\Diamond_3$.

Comment. Observe that $\mathcal{D} = (\mathcal{P}(V_+^\omega), (\Diamond_i)_{1 \leq i \leq 4})$ is a universal algebra. If T is a set of ω-trajectories, then denote by $\tilde{T}$ the subalgebra generated by T with respect to the algebra $\mathcal{D}$.

Proposition 4.7. Let $T \subseteq V_+^\omega$ be a set of ω-trajectories.
(i) $\tilde{T}$ is an associative set of ω-trajectories and, moreover,
(ii) $\tilde{T} = \overline{T}$, i.e., the associative closure of T is exactly the subalgebra generated by T in $\mathcal{D}$.

Proof. (i) $\tilde{T}$ is stable under the operations $\Diamond_i$, $1 \leq i \leq 4$ and thus, by Proposition 4.6, $\tilde{T}$ is an associative set of ω-trajectories.

(ii) Observe that $T \subseteq \tilde{T}$ and that $\tilde{T}$ is associative, hence $\overline{T} \subseteq \tilde{T}$. For the converse inclusion, let $T' \subseteq V_+^\omega$ be an associative set of ω-trajectories such that $T \subseteq T'$. Note that by Proposition 4.6, T' is stable under the operations $\Diamond_i$, $1 \le i \le 4$ and thus $\tilde{T} \subseteq T'$. Therefore $\tilde{T} \subseteq \overline{T}$. $\qquad\square$

Proposition 4.8. *Let $T \subseteq V_+^\omega$ be a set of ω-trajectories.*

(i) If each $t \in T$ is a periodic ω-word, then the associative closure of T, $\overline{T}$, has the same property, i.e., each ω-trajectory in $\overline{T}$ is periodic.

(ii) if additionally, each $t \in T$ has a palindrome as its period, then the associative closure of T, $\overline{T}$, has the same property.

(iii) If T is a set of ultimately periodic ω-trajectories, then the associative closure of T, $\overline{T}$, has the same property, i.e., each ω-trajectory in $\overline{T}$ is ultimately periodic.

Proof. (i) Note that the morphisms ρ_i, $1 \le i \le 4$, preserve the periodicity. Now consider the operation $\Diamond_1$. Let $t_1 = s^\omega$ and $t_2 = s'^\omega$. Define p and q by $p = |s|_r$ and $q = |s|_u$. Observe that $x^\omega = (x^p)^\omega$ and $y^\omega = (y^q)^\omega$. Let v be the unique word $x^p \,\text{Ⅲ}_s\, y^q$ (note that this is the shuffle over a finite trajectory, see Remark 3.1). Observe that $x^\omega \,\text{Ⅲ}_{t_1}\, y^\omega = v^\omega$ is a periodic ω-word for some nonempty word v that contains both r and u $(T \subseteq V_+^\omega)$.

Now assume that $i = |s'|_r$, $j = |s'|_u$ and $k = |v|$. Let n be the smallest common multiple of i, j, k. Assume that $n = ii' = jj' = kk'$ for some positive nonzero integers i', j', k'. Note that

$$(x^\omega \,\text{Ⅲ}_{t_1}\, y^\omega) \,\text{Ⅲ}_{t_2}\, z^\omega = v^\omega \,\text{Ⅲ}_{s'^\omega}\, z^\omega = \left(v^{i'}\right)^\omega \,\text{Ⅲ}_{s'_j s'^\omega} \left(z^{k'}\right)^\omega = \alpha^\omega,$$

where α is the unique word $v^{i'} \,\text{Ⅲ}_{s'_j s'}\, z^{k'}$.

Hence $\Diamond_1(t_1, t_2)$ is a periodic ω-word. Similarly, $\Diamond_i(t_1, t_2)$ is a periodic ω-word, $2 \le i \le 4$.

(ii) Observe that the morphisms ρ_i, $1 \le i \le 4$, are weak codings and hence they preserve the palindromes. The proof now proceeds as above. The resulting periods are palindromes.

(iii) The proof is similar with the proof of (i). $\qquad\square$

The above proposition yields:

Corollary 4.1. *The following sets of ω-trajectories are associative:*

(i) the set of all periodic ω-trajectories from V_+^ω.

(ii) the set of all periodic ω-trajectories from V_+^ω that have as their period a palindrome.

(iii) the set of all ultimately periodic ω-trajectories from V_+^ω.

The next theorem provides a characterization of those ω-trajectories that are periodic. As such it is also a direct contribution to the study of ω-words, exhibiting an interconnection between periodicity and associativity. The theorem gives also a concrete example of a calculation of the associative closure of a set of ω-trajectories.

Theorem 4.1. *Let t be an ω-trajectory such that $t \ne r^\omega$ and $t \ne u^\omega$. The following assertions are equivalent:*

(i) t is a periodic ω-word.

(ii) t is in the associative closure of $(ru)^\omega$.

Proof. (ii) $\Longrightarrow$ (i) It follows from Proposition 4.7, (ii) and Proposition 4.8, (i).

$(i) \implies (ii)$ Let A be the associative closure of the ω-trajectory $(ru)^\omega$. Assume that w is a nonempty word from V^*, $w = d_{i_1}^{j_1} d_{i_2}^{j_2} \ldots d_{i_k}^{j_k}$, where $d_{i_p} \in \{r, u\}$, $1 \leq j_p$, for all $1 \leq p \leq k$ and, moreover, $d_{i_q} \neq d_{i_{q+1}}$, for all $1 \leq q < k$. The *degree* of w, denoted $deg(w)$, is by definition k. Note that for each nonempty word w over V, $deg(w)$ is a unique integer greater than 1. Let t be a periodic ω-word over V such that $t \neq r^\omega$ and $t \neq u^\omega$. It follows that $t = w^\omega$ for some nonempy word w. Clearly, $deg(w) \geq 2$.

We prove by induction on $deg(w)$ that $t = w^\omega$ is in A. First we prove two claims:

Claim A. For all $i, j \geq 1$, the ω-trajectories $t = w^\omega$, where $w = r^i u$ or $w = ur^j$, are in A.

Proof of Claim A. Note that $\diamond_1((ru)^\omega, (ru)^\omega) = (uru)^\omega$. Moreover, $\diamond_3((uru)^\omega, (ru)^\omega) = (ur)^\omega$. Hence we obtain that $(ur)^\omega \in A$.

Assume now that $w = r^i u$, $i \geq 1$. We show by induction on i that $t = w^\omega \in A$. For $i = 1$, obviously $t \in A$. Assume the statement true for all $w = r^i u$ with $i \leq k$ and consider $w = r^{k+1} u$. If k is an even number, say $k = 2j$, then let t_1, t_2 be the ω-trajectories $t_1 = (ru)^\omega$ and $t_2 = (r^j u)^\omega$. By the inductive hypothesis t_2 is in A. Now observe that:

$$\diamond_4(t_1, t_2) = \rho_4(x^\omega \amalg_{t_1} (y^j z)^\omega) = \rho_4((xy)^j xz)^\omega) = (r^{2j+1} u)^\omega = (r^{k+1} u)^\omega.$$

Consider now the other case, i.e., k is an odd number, say $k = 2j - 1$. Let t_1, t_2 be the ω-trajectories $t_1 = (r^j u)^\omega$ and $t_2 = (ur)^\omega$. By the inductive hypothesis t_1 is in A. Now observe that:

$$\diamond_3(t_1, t_2) = \rho_3(x^\omega \amalg_{t_1} (zy)^\omega) = \rho_3((x^j zx^j xy)^\omega) = (r^{2j} u)^\omega = (r^{k+1} u)^\omega.$$

Therefore $(r^i u)^\omega \in A$ for all $i \geq 1$.

A similar proof shows that $(u^j r)^\omega, (ur^j)^\omega, (ru^j)^\omega \in A$ for all $j \geq 1$.

Claim B. For all $i, j, p, q \geq 1$, the ω-trajectories $t = w^\omega$, where $w = r^i u^j$ or $w = u^p r^q$, are in A.

Proof of Claim B. First assume that $w = r^i u^j$, $i, j \geq 1$. The proof is by induction on the number $i + j$. Obviously, if $w = ru$, then $t = w^\omega \in A$. The inductive step: let $t_1 = (r^i u^j)^\omega$ be in A. By Claim A it follows that $t_2 = (r^{i+j} u)^\omega \in A$. Observe that:

$$\diamond_2(t_1, t_2) = \rho_2((x^i y^j) \omega \amalg_{t_2} z^\omega) = \rho_2(x^i y^j z)^\omega) = (r^i u^{j+1})^\omega.$$

Hence Claim B is true also for $w = r^i u^{j+1}$.

Note that the ω-trajectory $t_3 = (ru^{i+j})^\omega$ is also in A, see Claim A. Moreover, $\diamond_4(t_1, t_3) = (r^{i+1} u^j)^\omega$. Therefore, for all words of the form $w = r^i u^j$, $i, j \geq 1$, $w^\omega \in A$. A similar proof shows that for all words of the form $w = u^p r^q$, $p, q \geq 1$, $w^\omega \in A$.

We are now ready to prove Theorem 4.1, $(i) \implies (ii)$. Let $t = w^\omega$ be a periodic ω-word such that $t \neq r^\omega$ and $t \neq u^\omega$. The proof is by induction on $k = deg(w)$. The case $k = 2$ follows from Claim B. Assume the implication true for words w with $deg(w) \leq k$. Let w be an word with $deg(w) = k + 1$, say $w = r^{i_1} u^{i_2} r^{i_3} \ldots r^{i_k} u^q$. Denote $w_1 = r^{i_1} u^{i_2} r^{i_3} \ldots r^{i_k}$ and note that by the inductive hypothesis the ω-trajectory $t_1 = (w_1)^\omega$ is in A. Consider also the ω-trajectory $t_2 = (r^s u^q)^\omega$, where $s = |w_1|$ and note that t_2 is also in A. Observe that:

$$\diamond_2(t_1, t_2) = \rho_2((x^{i_1} y^{i_2} \ldots x^{i_k}) \amalg_{t_2} z^\omega) = \rho_2((x^{i_1} y^{i_2} \ldots x^{i_k} z^q)^\omega) = t.$$

If $w = r^{i_1} u^{i_2} r^{i_3} \ldots u^{i_k} r^p$, then denote $w_1 = r^{i_1} u^{i_2} r^{i_3} \ldots u^{i_k}$ and note that again by the inductive hypothesis the ω-trajectory $t_1 = (w_1)^\omega$ is in A. Consider also the ω-trajectory $t_2 = (u^s r^p)^\omega$, where $s = |w_1|$ and note that t_2 is also in A. Moreover, it is easy to see that: $\Diamond_4(t_2, t_1) = t$.

The situation when w begins with u is similar. □

Comment. Theorem 4.1 provides another proof of Corollary 4.1. The theorem can also be used for calculations of the associative closure of other sets of ω-trajectories. For instance let $T = \{t_1, t_2\}$, where $t_1 = (r^2 u)^\omega$ and $t_2 = (r^3 u)^\omega$. In order to compute $\overline{T}$ observe that $\Diamond_1(t_1, t_2) = (ru)^\omega$. Therefore $\overline{T}$ is the set of all periodic ω-trajectories, except r^ω and u^ω.

• Distributivity

Observe that for each set of ω-trajectories, T, the operation Ш_T is distributive over union both on the right and on the left side. Moreover, we adjoin to V^ω a unit element with respect to each Ш_T, denoted 1. Note that 1 is not an ω-word. Hence, we obtain the following mathematically important result:

Proposition 4.9. *If T is an associative set of trajectories, then for any alphabet* Σ,

$$S = (\mathcal{P}(\Sigma^*), \cup, \text{Ш}_T, \emptyset, 1)$$

is a semiring.

Proof. One can easily verify the axioms of a semiring, see [3]. □

5. Fairness

Fairness is a property of the parallel composition of processes that, roughly speaking, means that each action of a process is performed with not too much delay with respect to performing actions from another process. That is, the parallel composition should be "fair" for both processes performed.

Definition 5.1. Let $T \subseteq \{r, u\}^\omega$ be a set of ω-trajectories and let n be an integer, $n \geq 1$. T has the *n-fairness* property iff for all $t \in T$ and for all $t' \in V^*$ such that $t = t' t''$ for some $t'' \in V^\omega$, it follows that:

$$| \, |t'|_r - |t'|_u \, | \leq n.$$

This means that all ω-trajectories from T are contained in the region of the plane bounded by the line $y = x - n$ and the line $y = x + n$, see Figure 2, for $n = 4$.

Example 5.1. The ω-literal shuffle, i.e., $T = (ru)^\omega$ has the n-fairness property for all n, $n \geq 1$.

Definition 5.2. Let n be a fixed number, $n \geq 1$. Define the language F_n as:

$$F_n = \{t \in V^\omega | \, | \, |t'|_r - |t'|_u \, | \leq n, \text{ for all } t' \text{ such that } t = t' t'', t' \in V^*, t'' \in V^\omega\}.$$

Remark 5.1. Note that a set T of trajectories has the n-fairness property if and only if $T \subseteq F_n$.

410

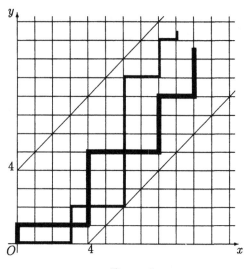

Figure 2

Proposition 5.1. *For every n, $n \geq 1$, the language F_n is a regular ω-language.*

Proof. We omit the straightforward construction of a Büchi automaton for F_n. □

Corollary 5.1. *If T is a regular set of ω-trajectories and n is fixed, $n \geq 1$, then it is decidable whether or not T has the n-fairness property.*

Proof. Note that the inclusion problem for regular ω-languages is decidable. Hence, this corollary follows from Proposition 5.1. □

Proposition 5.2. *The fairness property is preserved by the commutative closure.*

Proof. Assume that T has the n-fairness property for some n, $n \geq 1$. This means that for all $t \in T$ and for all t' such that $t = t't''$ for some $t'' \in V^{\omega}$, it follows that

$$| \, |t'|_r - |t'|_u \, | \leq n.$$

Obviously,

$$| \, |t'|_r - |t'|_u \, | = | \, |sym(t')|_r - |sym(t')|_u \, | \, .$$

□

Proposition 5.3. *The fairness property is not necessarily preserved by the associative closure.*

Proof. Consider the set of trajectories $T = (ru)^{\omega}$. Using Theorem 4.1 we infer that the associative closure of T does not have the fairness property. □

6. Conclusions

Shuffle on trajectories provides a useful tool for the study of a variety of problems in the theory of ω-words as well as in connection with parallel computation and the theory of concurrency. Besides, it opens a new view on the general theory of ω-words, as shown by our exhaustive characterization of the periodicity of ω-words. At the

394

[TB70] B.A. Trakhtenbrot and Ya.M. Barzdin, Finite Automata, Behaviour and Synthesis. Nauka Publishers, Moscow 1970. (Russian; English translation: North Holland, Amsterdam 1973)

[Wa76] K. Wagner, Eine Axiomatisierung der Theorie der regulären Folgenmengen. Elektron. Informationsverarb. Kybernetik EIK 12 (1976) 7, 337–354.

time of this writing, a similar characterization for the ultimate periodicity of ω-words remains an open problem.

Other aspects from the theory of concurrency and parallel computation such as priorities, the existence of critical sections, communication and the use of re-entrant routines are studied using semantic constraints on the shuffle operation. Indeed, these aspects are more related to the inner structure of the words that are shuffled and cannot be investigated using only syntactic constraints. We like to emphasize that perhaps the most useful and realistic types of constraints are mixed, i.e., both syntactic and semantic.

Of a special interest is to extend these operations to more complex objects such as graphs and networks or different types of automata. In this way one can obtain a more general framework to study the phenomena of parallelism and of concurrency.

References

1. J. C. M. Baeten and W. P. Weijland, *Process Algebra*, Cambridge University Press, 1990.

2. P. M. Cohn, *Universal Algebra*, D. Reidel Publishing Company, New York, 1980.

3. J. S. Golan, *The Theory of Semirings with Applications in Mathematics and Theoretical Computer Science*, Longman Scientific and Technical, Harlow, Essex, 1992.

4. M. Hennessy, *Algebraic Theory of Processes*, The MIT Press, Cambridge, Massachusetts, London, 1988.

5. W. Kuich and A. Salomaa, *Semirings, Automata, Languages*, EATCS Monographs on Theoretical Computer Science, Springer-Verlag, Berlin, 1986.

6. A. Mateescu and A. Salomaa, "Formal Languages: an Introduction and a Synopsis", Chapter 1, in *Handbook of Formal Languages*, eds. G. Rozenberg and A. Salomaa, Springer-Verlag, to appear.

7. A. Mateescu, G. Rozenberg and A. Salomaa, "Shuffle on Trajectories: Syntactic Constraints", Technical Report 96-18, University of Leiden, 1996.

8. R. Milner, *Communication and Concurrency*, Prentice Hall International, 1989.

9. D. Perrin and J. E. Pin, *Mots Infinis*, Report LITP 93.40, 1993.

10. A. Salomaa, *Formal Languages*, Academic Press, New York, 1973.

11. W. Thomas, "Automata on Infinite Objects", in *Handbook of Theoretical Computer Science*, Volume B, ed. J. van Leeuwen, Elsevier, 1990, 135-191.

Chapter 6. Algebraic Approaches to Languages

Generalized Lindenmayerian Algebraic Systems

Werner KUICH

Institut für Algebra und Diskrete Mathematik
Abteilung für Theoretische Informatik
Technische Universität Wien
Wiedner Hauptstraße 8–10, A–1040 Wien

Abstract. The Lindenmayerian algebraic systems of Honkala, Kuich [3] are generalized to arbitrary ω-continuous semirings. On the other side, Lindenmayerian algebraic systems for languages with just one symbol are considered. If such a system has a special form then the components of its least solution are rational.

1. Introduction

Formal power series play an important role in generalizing the theory of formal languages and automata theory (see Berstel, Reutenauer [1], Kuich, Salomaa [6] and Salomaa, Soittola [8]). In [3], Honkala and Kuich gave a power series approach to a generalization of ET0L languages (see Rozenberg, Salomaa [7]).

In this paper we generalize this approach to ω-continuous semirings. The background of this research is the following. In Kuich [5], we have shown that many classical theorems of automata theory, of the theory of formal languages and of the theory of formal power series are, in fact, specialized versions of theorems on ω-continuous semirings. For example, the Theorem of Kleene, the equivalence of context-free grammars or algebraic systems and push-down automata, and the Theorem of Parikh can be generalized to ω-continuous semirings.

In [3], Honkala and Kuich considered Lindenmayerian algebraic systems and generalized some results of ET0L languages to Lindenmayerian algebraic power series. In the first part of this paper, we make—in the spirit of Kuich [5]—a further step of generalization. We generalize Lindenmayerian algebraic power series to certain subsemirings of ω-continuous semirings and show some closure properties of these subsemirings.

In the second part of this paper, we consider Lindenmayerian algebraic systems with just one terminal symbol. If such a system has a special form then the components of its least solution are rational.

It is assumed that the reader is familiar with the basics of semiring theory. Notions and notations that are not defined are taken from Kuich [5] and Honkala, Kuich [3].

2. Lindenmayerian Algebraic Systems

In the sequel A is always an ω-continuous semiring, A' is a subset of A containing 0 and 1, and $Y = \{y_1, \ldots, y_n\}$ is an alphabet of variables.

An A'-*Lindenmayerian algebraic system* (with variables in Y) is a system of formal equations

$$y_i = p_i(y_1, \ldots, y_n, h_{11}(y_1), \ldots, h_{1s}(y_1), \ldots, h_{n1}(y_n), \ldots, h_{ns}(y_n)), \quad 1 \le i \le n,$$

where $p_i(y_1, \ldots, y_n, z_{11}, \ldots, z_{1s}, \ldots, z_{n1}, \ldots, z_{ns})$, $1 \le i \le n$, is a semiring-polynomial in $A'(Y \cup Z)$ and $h_{ij} : A \to A$ are complete semiring morphisms such that $h_{ij}(a) \in A'$ for $a \in A'$, $1 \le i \le n$, $1 \le j \le s$. Furthermore, $Z = \{z_{11}, \ldots, z_{1s}, \ldots, z_{n1}, \ldots, z_{ns}\}$ is an alphabet with $Y \cap Z = \emptyset$. We want to emphasize that when we consider the polynomial p_i we do not assume that each z_{ij} actually has an occurrence in p_i, $1 \le i \le n$, $1 \le j \le s$.

If there is no danger of confusion, we use a vectorial notation. We write y for $y_1, \ldots, y_n$, p for $p_1, \ldots, p_n$, h for $h_{11}, \ldots, h_{1s}, \ldots, h_{n1}, \ldots, h_{ns}$ and $h(y)$ for $h_{11}(y_1), \ldots, h_{1s}(y_1), \ldots, h_{n1}(y_n), \ldots, h_{ns}(y_n)$. By this vectorial notation, an A'-Lindenmayerian algebraic system as defined above is now written as

$$y = p(y, h(y)).$$

The development of the theory of A'-Lindenmayerian algebraic systems parallels that of the usual A'-algebraic systems.

A *solution* to the A'-Lindenmayerian algebraic system $y = p(y, h(y))$ is given by $\sigma \in A^n$ such that $\sigma = p(\sigma, h(\sigma))$. It is termed the *least solution* iff $\sigma \sqsubseteq \tau$ holds for all solutions τ of $y = p(y, h(y))$. Hence, a solution (resp. the least solution) of $y = p(y, h(y))$ is nothing else than a fixpoint (resp. the least fixpoint) of the mapping $f : A^n \to A^n$ defined by $f(\sigma) = p(\sigma, h(\sigma))$, $\sigma \in A^n$.

By Theorem 3.2 of Kuich [5] we infer that the mappings h_{ij}, $1 \le i \le n$, $1 \le j \le s$, are ω-continuous. Since ω-continuous mappings are closed under functional composition, the mapping f is ω-continuous. Hence, by the Fixpoint Theorem the least solution of an A'-Lindenmayerian algebraic system $y = p(y, h(y))$ exists and equals the least fixpoint $\text{fix}(f) = \sup\{f^n(0) \mid n \in \mathbf{N}\}$.

To compute this unique least fixpoint, we define the *approximation sequence*

$$\sigma^0, \sigma^1, \sigma^2, \ldots, \sigma^j, \ldots, \qquad \sigma^j \in A^{n \times 1},$$

associated to the A'-Lindenmayerian algebraic system $y = p(y, h(y))$ as follows:

$$\sigma^0 = 0, \qquad \sigma^{j+1} = p(\sigma^j, h(\sigma^j)), \, j \ge 0.$$

Then the least solution is given by $\sup\{\sigma^j \mid j \in \mathbf{N}\}$. This proves our first theorem.

Theorem 2.1. *The least solution of the A'-Lindenmayerian algebraic system $y = p(y, h(y))$ exists and is given by*

$$\sup\{\sigma^j \mid j \in \mathbf{N}\},$$

where $\sigma^0, \sigma^1, \ldots, \sigma^j, \ldots$ is the approximation sequence associated to it.

The collection of all components of the least solutions of A'-Lindenmayerian algebraic systems is denoted by $\mathbf{LAlg}(A')$. Clearly, we have $\mathbf{Alg}(A') \subseteq \mathbf{LAlg}(A')$.

We now connect our definition of an A'-Lindenmayerian algebraic system with the L algebraic systems of Honkala, Kuich [3]. The basic semiring is now $A\langle\langle \Sigma^* \rangle\rangle$, where

A is commutative, Σ is an alphabet, and A' is the semiring of polynomials $A\langle\Sigma^*\rangle$. For each L algebraic system with least solution σ there exists an $A\langle\Sigma^*\rangle$-Lindenmayerian algebraic system with least solution σ.

Theorem 2.2. $A^{\mathrm{Lalg}}\langle\langle\Sigma^*\rangle\rangle \subseteq \mathbf{LAlg}(A\langle\Sigma^*\rangle)$.

Theorem 10 of Kuich [4] and application of the distribution laws prove the next theorem.

Theorem 2.3. *Let A be one of the semirings* $\mathbf{B}$, $\mathbf{N}^\infty$ *or* $\mathbf{R}_+^\infty$. *Then* $A^{\mathrm{Lalg}}\langle\langle\Sigma^*\rangle\rangle = \mathbf{LAlg}(A\langle\Sigma^*\rangle)$.

Our next theorems are similar to Theorems 7.2, 7.4 and 2.7 of Honkala, Kuich [3].

Theorem 2.4. *The components of the least solution of an* $\mathbf{LAlg}(A')$-*algebraic system are in* $\mathbf{LAlg}(A')$.

Proof. Let
$$y_i = p_i(a_1, \ldots, a_m, y_1, \ldots, y_n), \qquad 1 \le i \le n,$$
be an $\mathbf{LAlg}(A')$-algebraic system. The notation indicates that the coefficients of this $\mathbf{LAlg}(A')$-algebraic system are $a_1, \ldots, a_m \in \mathbf{LAlg}(A')$. We now replace the coefficients $a_1, \ldots, a_m$ by new variables $z_1, \ldots, z_m$ and consider the A'-algebraic system
$$y_i = p_i(z_1, \ldots, z_m, y_1, \ldots, y_n), \qquad 1 \le i \le n,$$
and the A'-Lindenmayerian algebraic systems
$$y^j = p^j, \qquad 1 \le j \le m.$$
The variables of the j-th A'-Lindenmayerian algebraic system, i. e. the components of y^j, are $y_1^j, \ldots, y_{n_j}^j$, $1 \le j \le m$. We assume that the least solution of $y^j = p^j$ is given by τ^j with $\tau_1^j = a_j$, $1 \le j \le m$.

We now construct a new A'-Lindenmayerian algebraic system
$$\begin{aligned} y_i &= p_i(y_1^1, \ldots, y_1^m, y_1, \ldots, y_n), & 1 \le i \le n, \\ y^j &= p^j, & 1 \le j \le m, \end{aligned}$$
with variables in $\{y_i \mid 1 \le i \le n\} \cup \{y_i^j \mid 1 \le i \le n_j, \ 1 \le j \le m\}$. We observe that the y^j-subvector of the least solution of this new A'-Lindenmayerian algebraic system equals the least solution of the j-th A'-Lindenmayerian algebraic system $y^j = p^j$, i. e. τ^j, for $j = 1, \ldots, m$, and that the y_i-component of the least solution of the new A'-Lindenmayerian algebraic system equals the y_i-component of the least solution of the original $\mathbf{LAlg}(A')$-Lindenmayerian algebraic system
$$y_i = p_i(a_1, \ldots, a_m, y_1, \ldots, y_n), \qquad 1 \le i \le n.$$
Hence, the components of the least solution of this $\mathbf{LAlg}(A')$-Lindenmayerian algebraic system are elements in $\mathbf{LAlg}(A')$. □

Corollary 2.5. $\mathbf{Alg}(\mathbf{LAlg}(A')) = \mathbf{LAlg}(A')$.

The next corollary means that $\mathbf{LAlg}(A')$ is fully rationally closed.

Corollary 2.6. Rat(LAlg(A')) = LAlg(A').

In the next theorem we consider complete semiring morphisms $g : A \to A$, where $g(b) \in$ **LAlg**(A') for $b \in A'$. The application of these complete semiring morphisms to elements of **Alg**(A') yields elements of **LAlg**(A').

Theorem 2.7. *Let $g : A \to A$ be a complete semiring morphism such that $g(b) \in$ **LAlg**(A') for $b \in A'$. Then $g(a) \in$ **LAlg**(A') for all $a \in$ **Alg**(A').*

Proof. We consider the A'-algebraic system

$$y_i = p_i(a_1, \ldots, a_m, y_1, \ldots, y_n), \qquad 1 \le i \le n.$$

Here $a_1, \ldots, a_m$ are the coefficients of the system and $y_1, \ldots, y_n$ are the variables. Denote the least solution of this A'-algebraic system by σ. Then we show that $g(\sigma_i)$, $1 \le i \le n$, are elements in **LAlg**(A'). The proof is similar to the proof of Theorem 7.4 of Kuich [5].

By Theorem 2.4 we infer that the least solution τ of the **LAlg**(A')-algebraic system

$$y_i = p_i(g(a_1), \ldots, g(a_m), y_1, \ldots, y_n), \qquad 1 \le i \le n,$$

is a vector of elements in **LAlg**(A'). We claim that $\tau_i = g(\sigma_i)$, $1 \le i \le n$.

Let (σ^j) and (τ^j) be the approximation sequences associated to the systems $y_i = p_i(a_1, \ldots, a_m, y_1, \ldots, y_n)$ and $y_i = p_i(g(a_1), \ldots, g(a_m), y_1, \ldots, y_n)$, $1 \le i \le n$, respectively. Then we show by induction on j that $\tau_i^j = g(\sigma_i^j)$, $1 \le i \le n$, $j \ge 0$. Since a complete semiring morphism g is ω-continuous that will show our claim.

We have $\tau_i^0 = 0 = g(0) = g(\sigma_i^0)$, $1 \le i \le n$, and, for $j > 0$ and $1 \le i \le n$,

$$\begin{aligned}
\tau_i^j &= p_i(g(a_1), \ldots, g(a_m), \tau_1^{j-1}, \ldots, \tau_n^{j-1}) \\
&= p_i(g(a_1), \ldots, g(a_m), g(\sigma_1^{j-1}), \ldots, g(\sigma_n^{j-1})) \\
&= g(p_i(a_1, \ldots, a_m, \sigma_1^{j-1}, \ldots, \sigma_n^{j-1})) \\
&= g(\sigma_i^j).
\end{aligned}$$

Hence, $\tau_i = g(\sigma_i)$, $1 \le i \le n$, are in **LAlg**(A'). $\qquad\square$

Theorem 2.8. *Let $g : A \to A$ be a complete semiring morphism such that $g(b) \in A'$ for $b \in A'$. Then $g(a) \in$ **LAlg**(A') for all $a \in$ **LAlg**(A').*

Proof. We consider the A'-Lindenmayerian algebraic system $y = p(y, h(y))$ with the least solution σ. Then the A'-Lindenmayerian algebraic system

$$y_0 = g(y), \qquad y = p(y, h(y))$$

has the least solution $g(\sigma)$. $\qquad\square$

3. Lindenmayerian Algebraic Series with One Terminal Symbol

Througout this section, A denotes a *commutative idempotent ω-continuous* semiring.

We start with an example. This example shows that

$$\mathbf{B}^{\text{alg}}\langle\langle\{x\}^*\rangle\rangle = \mathbf{B}^{\text{rat}}\langle\langle\{x\}^*\rangle\rangle \subset \mathbf{B}^{\text{Lalg}}\langle\langle\{x\}^*\rangle\rangle.$$

Example 3.1. We consider the L algebraic system with just one equation $y = h(y) + x$, where $h(x) = x^2$. The approximation sequence associated to it is given by $\sigma^0 = 0$, $\sigma^j = x^{2^{j-1}} + x^{2^{j-2}} + \cdots + x^2 + x$, $j \geq 0$. Hence, the least solution of $y = h(y) + x$ is given by $\sigma = \sum_{j \geq 0} x^{2^j}$. Since $\{2^j \mid j \geq 0\}$ is not semilinear, σ is not contained in $\mathbf{B}^{\mathrm{alg}}\langle\langle \{x\}^* \rangle\rangle = \mathbf{B}^{\mathrm{rat}}\langle\langle \{x\}^* \rangle\rangle$.

Observe that σ is (by the isomorphism between $\mathbf{B}\langle\langle \{x\}^* \rangle\rangle$ and $\mathbf{P}(\{x\}^*)$) the language generated by the D0L system $G = (\{x\}, h, x)$ (see Rozenberg, Salomaa [7]). $\qquad\square$

We now consider infinite $\mathbf{Rat}(A')$-Lindenmayerian algebraic systems with just one variable y of the form

$$y = \sum_{j \geq 1} a_j(y)y + b, \qquad\qquad (*)$$

where $a_j(y) = c_j h_{j1}(y) \cdots h_{jn_j}(y) y^{m_j - 1}$, $b, c_j \in \mathbf{Rat}(A')$ and $h_{jk} : A \to A$ are complete A'-rational morphisms, $n_j \geq 0$, $m_j \geq 1$, $1 \leq k \leq n_j$, $j \geq 1$. Moreover, we assume that $\mathbf{H} = \{h_{jk} \mid 1 \leq k \leq n_j, \ j \geq 1\}$ is a finite set, $|\mathbf{H}| = m$ for some $m > 0$, and

$$\sum_{j \geq 1} c_j z_{j1} \cdots z_{jn_j} y^{m_j - 1} \in \mathbf{Rat}(A'\langle (Z \cup \{y\})^* \rangle).$$

Here $Z = \{z_1, \ldots, z_m\}$ is a finite alphabet of variables corresponding to the morphisms of $\mathbf{H}$ and $z_{jk} \in Z$, $1 \leq k \leq n_j$, $j \geq 1$.

We call these systems together with all properties described above *infinite* $\mathbf{Rat}(A')$-*Lindenmayerian algebraic* $(*)$-*systems* (with one variable y).

The definitions of solution, least solution and approximation sequence of these $(*)$-systems are analogous to the respective definitions for A'-Lindenmayerian algebraic systems in Section 2 and so is the proof of the next theorem.

Theorem 3.1. *The least solution of an infinite* $\mathbf{Rat}(A')$-*Lindenmayerian algebraic* $(*)$-*system exists and is given by*

$$\sup\{\sigma^j \mid j \in \mathbf{N}\},$$

where $\sigma^0, \sigma^1, \ldots, \sigma^j, \ldots$ *is the approximation sequence associated to it.*

It turns out that certain infinite $\mathbf{Rat}(A')$-Lindenmayerian algebraic $(*)$-systems have a rational least solution. The proof of this result has similarities with Pilling's proof of the Theorem of Parikh (see Section 8 of Kuich [5]).

Theorem 3.2. *Consider an infinite* $\mathbf{Rat}(A')$-*Lindenmayerian algebraic* $(*)$-*system and assume* $h(a^*)a^* = a^*$ *for all* $h \in \mathbf{H}$ *and* $a \in \mathbf{Rat}(A')$. *Then its least solution is given by*

$$\sigma = \Big(\sum_{j \geq 1} a_j(b) \Big)^* b$$

and $\sigma \in \mathbf{Rat}(A')$.

Proof. We first show that $\sigma \in \mathbf{Rat}(A')$. Consider the complete $(A'\langle (Z \cup \{y\})^* \rangle, A')$-rational semiring morphism h defined by $h(z_j) = h_j(b)$, $z_j \in Z$, $h(y) = b$ and

$$h\Big(\sum_{i_1, \ldots, i_m, i \geq 0} a_{i_1, \ldots, i_m, i} z_1^{i_1} \cdots z_m^{i_m} y^i \Big) = \sum_{i_1, \ldots, i_m, i \geq 0} a_{i_1, \ldots, i_m, i} h_1(b)^{i_1} \cdots h_m(b)^{i_m} b^i.$$

Then, by Theorem 7.7 of Kuich [5], the assumption

$$\sum_{j\geq 1} c_j z_{j1} \cdots z_{jn_j} y^{m_j-1} \in \mathbf{Rat}(A'\langle\langle (Z \cup \{y\})^* \rangle\rangle)$$

implies $\sum_{j\geq 1} a_j(b) \in \mathbf{Rat}(A')$. Hence, $\sigma \in \mathbf{Rat}(A')$.

We now show that σ is a solution of our infinite $\mathbf{Rat}(A')$-Lindenmayerian algebraic $(*)$-system. Denote $r(y) = \sum_{j\geq 1} a(y)$. Then $\sigma = r(b)^*b$ and we obtain

$$\begin{aligned}
\sum_{j\geq 1} a_j(\sigma)\sigma + b \; &= \\
&= \sum_{j\geq 1} c_j h_{j1}(r(b)^*)h_{j1}(b)\cdots h_{jn_j}(r(b)^*)h_{jn_j}(b)(r(b)^*)^{m_j}b^{m_j} + b \\
&= \sum_{j\geq 1} c_j h_{j1}(b)\cdots h_{jn_j}(b)r(b)^*b^{m_j} + b \\
&= r(b)r(b)^*b + b = r(b)^*b = \sigma.
\end{aligned}$$

Here the second equality follows by the equality $(r(b)^*)^{m_j} = (r(b)^*)^{n_j+1}$ (see Theorem 8.2(i) of Kuich [5]), by $r(b)^* \in \mathbf{Rat}(A')$ and by the assumption $h(a^*)a^* = a^*$ for all $h \in \mathbf{H}$ and $a \in \mathbf{Rat}(A')$.

Finally, we show that σ is the least solution. Let (σ^j) be the approximation sequence associated to $(*)$. We show by induction that, for $j \geq 0$,

$$\sum_{0\leq k\leq j} r(b)^k b \sqsubseteq \sigma^{j+1}.$$

For $j = 0$ we have $b \sqsubseteq \sigma^1 = b$. For $j > 0$ we obtain

$$\sum_{0\leq k\leq j} r(b)^k b = b + r(b) \sum_{0\leq k\leq j-1} r(b)^k b \sqsubseteq b + r(b)\sigma^j \sqsubseteq b + r(\sigma^j)\sigma^j = \sigma^{j+1}.$$

Here the first inequality follows by the induction hypothesis and the second inequality by $\sigma^j \sqsupseteq \sigma^1 = b$, $j \geq 1$.

Since A is an ω-continuous semiring, the inequality

$$\sum_{0\leq k\leq j} r(b)^k b \sqsubseteq \sigma^{j+1}, \qquad j \geq 0,$$

implies

$$\sum_{k\geq 0} r(b)^k b \sqsubseteq \sup\{\sigma^j \mid j \geq 0\}.$$

Since $\sigma = r(b)^*b$ is a solution we infer that $\sigma = \sup\{\sigma^j \mid j \geq 0\}$, i. e. σ is the least solution. $\square$

We now show that the assumption $h(r^*)r^* = r^*$ in Theorem 3.2 is satisfied by certain morphisms for $r \in \mathbf{B}^{\mathrm{rat}}\langle\langle (\{x\}^*) \rangle\rangle$.

Lemma 3.3. *The following inequalities are valid in* $\mathbf{B}\langle\langle (\{x\}^*) \rangle\rangle$ *for* $p, t \geq 1$:

(i) $(x^{tp})^+ \sqsubseteq (x^p)^+$,

(ii) $(x^{tp})^* \sqsubseteq (x^p)^*$.

Proof. (i) $(x^{tp})^+ = x^{tp} + x^{2tp} + \cdots + x^{ntp} + \cdots \sqsubseteq (x^p)^+$.

(ii) $(x^{tp})^* = 1 + (x^{tp})^+ \sqsubseteq 1 + (x^p)^+ = (x^p)^*$. $\square$

Lemma 3.4. *Let* $h(x) = x^t$ *for some* $t \geq 0$ *and consider a rational power series* $r \in \mathbf{B}^{\mathrm{rat}}\langle\langle\{x\}^*\rangle\rangle$. *Then* $h(r^*)r^* = r^*$.

Proof. By Chapter V of Eilenberg [2], the rational power series r is of the form

$$r = \sum_{1 \leq i \leq s_1} x^{n_i} + \Big(\sum_{1 \leq i \leq s_2} x^{m_i} \Big)(x^p)^*$$

for some $s_1, s_2 \geq 0$, $p \geq 1$. We now compute the rational power series r^*:

$$
\begin{aligned}
r^* &= \Big(\sum_{1 \leq i \leq s_1} x^{n_i} \Big)^* \Big(\Big(\sum_{1 \leq i \leq s_2} x^{m_i} \Big)(x^p)^* \Big)^* \\
&= \Big(\sum_{1 \leq i \leq s_1} x^{n_i} \Big)^* \Big(1 + \Big(\sum_{1 \leq i \leq s_2} x^{m_i} \Big)^+ (x^p)^* \Big) \\
&= \Big(\sum_{1 \leq i \leq s_1} x^{n_i} \Big)^* + \Big(\sum_{1 \leq i \leq s_1} x^{n_i} \Big)^* \Big(\sum_{1 \leq i \leq s_2} x^{m_i} \Big) \Big(\sum_{1 \leq i \leq s_2} x^{m_i} \Big)^* (x^p)^* \\
&= (x^{n_1})^* \cdots (x^{n_{s_1}})^* + \\
&\quad \big((x^{m_1})^+ \cdots (x^{m_{s_2}})^* + \cdots + (x^{m_1})^* \cdots (x^{m_{s_2}})^+ \big)(x^{n_1})^* \cdots (x^{n_{s_1}})^* (x^p)^*.
\end{aligned}
$$

Here the first, second and fourth equality follow by Theorem 8.2 of Kuich [5]. We now compute the power series $h(r^*)$:

$$
\begin{aligned}
h(r^*) &= (x^{tn_1})^* \cdots (x^{tn_{s_1}})^* + \\
&\quad \big((x^{tm_1})^+ \cdots (x^{tm_{s_2}})^* + \cdots + (x^{tm_1})^* \cdots (x^{tm_{s_2}})^+ \big)(x^{tn_1})^* \cdots (x^{tn_{s_1}})^* (x^p)^* \\
&\sqsubseteq r^*
\end{aligned}
$$

Here the inequality follows by Lemma 3.3. Hence, $h(r^*)r^* \sqsubseteq (r^*)^2 = r^*$. Moreover, $h(r^*)r^* = h(r^+)r^* + r^* \sqsupseteq r^*$. These two inequalities imply $h(r^*)r^* = r^*$. $\square$

Theorem 3.5. *The L algebraic system (with one variable y)*

$$y = \sum_{1 \leq j \leq s} x^{i_j} h_{j1}(y) \cdots h_{jn_j}(y) y^{m_j} + b(x),$$

where $b(x) \in \mathbf{B}\langle\{x\}^*\rangle$, $s \geq 0$, $1 \leq j \leq s$, $i_j, n_j \geq 0$, $m_j \geq 1$ *and* $h_{jk} : \mathbf{B}\langle\langle\{x\}^*\rangle\rangle \to \mathbf{B}\langle\langle\{x\}^*\rangle\rangle$ *are morphisms defined by* $h_{jk}(x) = x^{t_{jk}}$, $t_{jk} \geq 0$, $1 \leq k \leq n_j$, *has the least solution*

$$\Big(\sum_{1 \leq j \leq s} x^{i_j} h_{j1}(b(x)) \cdots h_{jn_j}(b(x)) b(x)^{m_j - 1} \Big)^* b(x) \in \mathbf{B}^{\mathrm{rat}}\langle\langle\{x\}^*\rangle\rangle.$$

The question now arises whether we can solve $A\langle \Sigma^\oplus \rangle$-Lindenmayerian algebraic systems over the commutative idempotent ω-continuous semiring $A\langle\langle \Sigma^\oplus \rangle\rangle$ with the methods of Theorem 3.2. Here $\Sigma^\oplus$ is the free commutative monoid generated by an alphabet Σ. The next example shows that this is not possible in general.

Example 3.2. Let $\Sigma = \{x_1, x_2\}$. Our basic semiring is $\mathbf{B}\langle\langle\Sigma^{\oplus}\rangle\rangle$. We consider the $\mathbf{B}\langle\Sigma^{\oplus}\rangle$-Lindenmayerian algebraic system

$$y = h(y)y + x_1 x_2,$$

where $h : \mathbf{B}\langle\langle\Sigma^{\oplus}\rangle\rangle \to \mathbf{B}\langle\langle\Sigma^{\oplus}\rangle\rangle$ is the morphism defined by $h(x_1) = x_1^{t_1}$, $h(x_2) = x_2^{t_2}$, $t_1, t_2 > 0$.

Then σ of Theorem 3.2 is given by

$$\sigma = h((x_1 x_2)^*)x_1 x_2 = (x_1^{t_1} x_2^{t_2})^* x_1 x_2 = \sum_{m \geq 0} x_1^{t_1 m + 1} x_2^{t_2 m + 1}.$$

We now substitute σ into the right side of the above equation and obtain

$$
\begin{aligned}
h(\sigma)\sigma + x_1 x_2 &= h\Big(\sum_{n \geq 0} x_1^{t_1 n + 1} x_2^{t_2 n + 1}\Big)\Big(\sum_{k \geq 0} x_1^{t_1 k + 1} x_2^{t_2 k + 1}\Big) + x_1 x_2 \\
&= \Big(\sum_{n \geq 0} x_1^{t_1^2 n + t_1} x_2^{t_2^2 n + t_2}\Big)\Big(\sum_{k \geq 0} x_1^{t_1 k + 1} x_2^{t_2 k + 1}\Big) + x_1 x_2 \\
&= \sum_{n,k \geq 0} x_1^{t_1(t_1 n + k + 1) + 1} x_2^{t_2(t_2 n + k + 1) + 1} + x_1 x_2.
\end{aligned}
$$

If we assume that σ is a solution, i. e., $h(\sigma)\sigma + x_1 x_2 = \sigma$, then we obtain the following equations: For each choice of n, k t here exists an m such that

$$
\begin{aligned}
t_1(t_1 n + k + 1) + 1 &= t_1 m + 1, \\
t_2(t_2 n + k + 1) + 1 &= t_2 m + 1.
\end{aligned}
$$

This implies $t_1 = t_2$. Hence, in case $t_1 = t_2$ we can apply the methods of Theorem 3.2, while in case $t_1 \neq t_2$ the method of Theorem 3.2 does not solve the equation. □

We now extend the method of Theorem 3.2 to systems with more than one variable. We consider infinite $\mathbf{Rat}(A')$-Lindenmayerian algebraic systems (with commuting variables in Y) of the form

$$
\begin{aligned}
y_i = & r_i(y_1, \ldots, y_n, h_{11}(y_1), \ldots, h_{ns}(y_n))y_i \\
& + b_i(y_1, \ldots, y_{i-1}, h_{11}(y_1), \ldots, h_{i-1\,s}(y_{i-1})),
\end{aligned}
\qquad (**)
$$

where $r_i(y_1, \ldots, y_n, z_{11}, \ldots, z_{ns})y_i + b_i(y_1, \ldots, y_{i-1}, z_{11}, \ldots, z_{i-1\,s}) \in \mathbf{Rat}(A'\langle\langle(Z \cup Y)^{\oplus}\rangle\rangle)$, $h_{ij} : A \to A$ are complete A'-rational morphisms, $1 \leq i \leq n$, $1 \leq j \leq s$, and $Z = \{z_{ij} \mid 1 \leq i \leq n, 1 \leq j \leq s\}$.

We call these systems together with all properties described above *infinite* $\mathbf{Rat}(A')$-*Lindenmayerian algebraic* (**)-*systems* (with commuting variables in Y).

In the sequel we will use the following notations for $1 \leq i \leq n$:

$$
\begin{aligned}
\hat{r}_i(y_1, \ldots, y_n) &= r_i(y_1, \ldots, y_n, h_{11}(y_1), \ldots, h_{ns}(y_n)), \\
\hat{b}_i(y_1, \ldots, y_{i-1}) &= b_i(y_1, \ldots, y_{i-1}, h_{11}(y_1), \ldots, h_{i-1\,s}(y_{i-1})).
\end{aligned}
$$

The definitions of solution, least solution and approximation sequence of these (**)-systems are analogous to the respective definitions for A'-Lindenmayerian algebraic systems in Section 2 and so is the proof of the next theorem.

Theorem 3.6. *The least solution of an infinite* $\mathbf{Rat}(A')$*-Lindenmayerian algebraic* (**)*-system exists and is given by*

$$\sup\{\sigma^j \mid j \in \mathbf{N}\},$$

where $\sigma^0, \sigma^1, \ldots, \sigma^j, \ldots$ *is the approximation sequence associated to it.*

Theorem 3.7. *Consider an infinite* $\mathbf{Rat}(A')$*-Lindenmayerian algebraic* (**)*-system and assume* $h_{ij}(a^*)a^* = a^*$ *for* $1 \le i \le n$, $1 \le j \le s$, *and* $a \in \mathbf{Rat}(A')$. *Then its least solution is in* $\mathbf{Rat}(A')$.

Proof. Observe that, by our assumptions, $r_i(y_1, \ldots, y_n, z_{11}, \ldots, z_{ns}) \in \mathbf{Rat}(A'\langle (Z \cup Y)^\oplus \rangle)$ and $b_i(y_1, \ldots, y_{i-1}, z_{11}, \ldots, z_{i-1\,s}) \in \mathbf{Rat}(A'\langle (Z \cup \{y_1, \ldots, y_{i-1}\})^\oplus \rangle)$, $1 \le i \le n$. This is easily seen by the construction of $A'\langle (Z \cup Y)^\oplus \rangle$-rational transducers (resp. $(A'\langle (Z \cup Y)^\oplus \rangle, A'\langle (Z \cup \{y_1, \ldots, y_{i-1}\})^\oplus \rangle)$-rational transducers, $1 \le i \le n$) that map $r_i y_i + b_i$ into r_i (resp. b_i), $1 \le i \le n$.

The proof now proceeds by induction on n. For $n = 1$ the least solution σ is given by Theorem 3.2: $\sigma = \hat{r}_1(b_1)^* b_1 \in \mathbf{Rat}(A')$. Assume now $n > 1$ and consider the infinite $\mathbf{Rat}(A'\langle \{y_1, \ldots, y_{n-1}, z_{11}, \ldots, z_{n-1\,s}\}^\oplus \rangle)$-Lindenmayerian algebraic (*)-system (with variable y_n)

$$y_n = r_n(y_1, \ldots, y_{n-1}, y_n, z_{11}, \ldots, z_{n-1\,s}, h_{n1}(y_n), \ldots, h_{ns}(y_n))y_n$$
$$+ b_n(y_1, \ldots, y_{n-1}, z_{11}, \ldots, z_{n-1\,s}).$$

By Theorem 3.2, the least solution $t_n(y_1, \ldots, y_{n-1}, z_{11}, \ldots, z_{n-1\,s})$ of this system is in $\mathbf{Rat}(A'\langle \{y_1, \ldots, y_{n-1}, z_{11}, \ldots, z_{n-1\,s}\}^\oplus \rangle)$. Denote $\hat{t}_n(y_1, \ldots, y_{n-1}) = t_n(y_1, \ldots, y_{n-1}, h_{11}(y_1), \ldots, h_{n-1\,s}(y_{n-1}))$. Consider now the infinite $\mathbf{Rat}(A')$-Lindenmayerian algebraic (**)-system (with variables $y_1, \ldots, y_{n-1}$)

$$y_i = \hat{r}_i(y_1, \ldots, y_{n-1}, \hat{t}_n(y_1, \ldots, y_{n-1}))y_i + \hat{b}_i(y_1, \ldots, y_{i-1}), \qquad 1 \le i \le n-1.$$

By induction hypothesis, there exists a least solution $(s_1, \ldots, s_{n-1})$, where $s_i \in \mathbf{Rat}(A')$, $1 \le i \le n$. This means

$$s_i = \hat{r}_i(s_1, \ldots, s_{n-1}, \hat{t}_n(s_1, \ldots, s_{n-1}))s_i + \hat{b}_n(s_1, \ldots, s_{i-1}), \qquad 1 \le i \le n-1.$$

Moreover, $\hat{t}_n(s_1, \ldots, s_{n-1})$ is the least solution of

$$y_n = \hat{r}_n(s_1, \ldots, s_{n-1}, y_n)y_n + \hat{b}_n(s_1, \ldots, s_{n-1}).$$

Hence, $(s_1, \ldots, s_{n-1}, \hat{t}_n(s_1, \ldots, s_{n-1}))$ is a solution of

$$y_i = \hat{r}_i(y_1, \ldots, y_n)y_i + \hat{b}_i(y_1, \ldots, y_{i-1}), \qquad 1 \le i \le n,$$

and $s_1, \ldots, s_{n-1}, \hat{t}_n(s_1, \ldots, s_{n-1}) \in \mathbf{Rat}(A')$.

We now show that this is the least solution. Let $(\sigma_1, \ldots, \sigma_n)$ be an arbitrary solution of our (**)-system. Since $\hat{t}_n(\sigma_1, \ldots, \sigma_{n-1})$ is the least solution of

$$y_n = \hat{r}_n(\sigma_1, \ldots, \sigma_{n-1}, y_n)y_n + \hat{b}_n(\sigma_1, \ldots, \sigma_{n-1}),$$

we obtain $\hat{t}_n(\sigma_1, \ldots, \sigma_{n-1}) \sqsubseteq \sigma_n$. Define, for $1 \le i \le n-1$,

$$s_i^0 = 0, \qquad s_i^{j+1} = \hat{r}_i(s_1^j, \ldots, s_{n-1}^j, \hat{t}_n(s_1^j, \ldots, s_{n-1}^j))s_i^j + \hat{b}_i(s_1^j, \ldots, s_{i-1}^j).$$

Since $(s_1^j, \ldots, s_{n-1}^j)$, $j \geq 0$, is the approximation sequence associated to

$$y_i = \hat{r}_i(y_1, \ldots, y_{n-1}, \hat{t}_n(y_1, \ldots, y_{n-1}))y_i + \hat{b}_i(y_1, \ldots, y_{n-1}), \qquad 1 \leq i \leq n-1,$$

we obtain $\sup(s_i^j \mid j \geq 0) = s_i$, $1 \leq i \leq n-1$. We claim now $s_i^j \sqsubseteq \sigma_i$, $1 \leq i \leq n-1$, $j \geq 0$, and prove it by induction on j.

For $j = 0$, we have $s_i^0 = 0 \sqsubseteq \sigma_i$, $1 \leq i \leq n-1$. The inductive step is proved by

$$
\begin{aligned}
s_i^{j+1} &\sqsubseteq \hat{r}_i(\sigma_1, \ldots, \sigma_{n-1}, \hat{t}_n(\sigma_1, \ldots, \sigma_{n-1}))\sigma_i + \hat{b}_i(\sigma_1, \ldots, \sigma_{n-1}) \\
&\sqsubseteq \hat{r}_i(\sigma_1, \ldots, \sigma_{n-1}, \sigma_n)\sigma_i + \hat{b}_i(\sigma_1, \ldots, \sigma_{n-1}) = \sigma_i, \qquad 1 \leq i \leq n-1.
\end{aligned}
$$

Hence, $s_i \sqsubseteq \sigma_i$, $1 \leq i \leq n-1$. Moreover,

$$\hat{t}_n(s_1, \ldots, s_{n-1}) \sqsubseteq \hat{t}_n(\sigma_1, \ldots, \sigma_{n-1}) \sqsubseteq \sigma_n.$$

This proves that $(s_1, \ldots, s_{n-1}, \hat{t}_n(s_1, \ldots, s_{n-1}))$ is the least solution of our (∗∗)-system. □

Our last corollary is a generalization of Theorem 3.5 to more than one variable.

Corollary 3.8. *The components of the least solution of an L algebraic system with commuting variables $y_1, \ldots, y_n$ of the form*

$$
\begin{aligned}
y_i = {} & r_i(y_1, \ldots, y_n, h_{11}(y_1), \ldots, h_{ns}(y_n))y_i \\
& + b_i(y_1, \ldots, y_{i-1}, h_{11}(y_1), \ldots, h_{i-1\,s}(y_{i-1})),
\end{aligned}
$$

where $r_i(y_1, \ldots, y_n, z_{11}, \ldots, z_{ns}) \in \mathbf{B}\langle\{x, y_1, \ldots, y_n, z_{11}, \ldots, z_{ns}\}^*\rangle$, $b_i(y_1, \ldots, y_{i-1}, z_{11}, \ldots, z_{i-1\,s}) \in \mathbf{B}\langle\{x, y_1, \ldots, y_{i-1}, z_{11}, \ldots, z_{i-1\,s}\}^*\rangle$ and $h_{ij} : \mathbf{B}\langle\langle\{x\}^*\rangle\rangle \to \mathbf{B}\langle\langle\{x\}^*\rangle\rangle$ are finite substitutions defined by $h_{ij}(x) = x^{t_{ij}}$ for some $t_{ij} \geq 0$, $1 \leq i \leq n$, $1 \leq j \leq s$, are in $\mathbf{B}^{\mathrm{rat}}\langle\langle\{x\}^*\rangle\rangle$.

References

1. Berstel, J., Reutenauer, C.: Rational Series and Their Languages. EATCS Monographs on Theoretical Computer Science, Vol. 12. Springer, 1988.

2. Eilenberg, S.: Automata, Languages and Machines. Vol. A. Academic Press, 1974.

3. Honkala, J., Kuich, W.: On Lindenmayerian algebraic power series. Theor. Comput. Sci., to appear.

4. Kuich, W.: Representations and complete semiring morphisms. Inf. Process. Letters 56(1995)293–298.

5. Kuich, W.: Semirings and formal power series: Their relevance to formal languages and automata. In: G. Rozenberg and A. Salomaa, eds., Handbook on Formal Languages, Springer, to appear.

6. Kuich, W., Salomaa, A.: Semirings, Automata, Languages. EATCS Monographs on Theoretical Computer Science, Vol. 5. Springer, 1986.

7. Rozenberg, G., Salomaa, A.: The Mathematical Theory of L Systems. Academic Press, 1980.

8. Salomaa, A., Soittola, M.: Automata-Theoretic Aspects of Formal Power Series. Springer, 1978.

The Structure of the Basic Morphisms[1]

Virgil Emil CĂZĂNESCU

University of Bucharest, Faculty of Mathematics
Str. Academiei 14, 70109 Bucharest
E-mail: vec@math.math.unibuc.ro

Abstract. In [1] we gave presentations as abstract data types for some classes of finite relations (functions, partial functions, injections, bijections and so on) and we proved that each relation may be written in a unique normal form. The algebraic structures introduced there include some elements which model the finite relations at the abstract level. These elements are called abstract relations. Our paper proves that each abstract relation may be written in a normal form.

1. Preliminaries

In a category we use the diagramatic order for composition, i.e. $fg : a \longrightarrow c$ is the composite of $f : a \longrightarrow b$ and $g : b \longrightarrow c$. The first and the second axioms in table 1 are for categories.

A category C is said to be **strict monoidal** if its set of objects $\mathrm{Ob}(C)$ is a monoid and if it is endowed with a sum

$$+ \; : C(a,b) \times C(c,d) \longrightarrow C(a+c, b+d)$$

which satisfies axioms C3-C6 in table 1, where ε is the neutral element of monoid $\mathrm{Ob}(C)$.

A subcategory of C which has the same objects as C and is closed under sum is called a strict monoidal subcategory of C. If G is a set of morphisms of C, then the least strict monoidal subcategory of C which includes G consists of all the finite composites of morphisms of type $1_a + g + 1_b$ where $g \in G$.

A strict monoidal category B is said to be **symmetric** if it contains a morphism ${}^a\mathsf{x}^b : a + b \longrightarrow b + a$ for each $a, b \in \mathrm{Ob}(B)$ and satisfies axioms C7-C9 in table 1. For short, instead of symmetric strict monoidal category we shall write ssmc.

Let $B_{a\alpha}$ be the least strict monoidal subcategory of C which includes $\{\, {}^a\mathsf{x}^b \mid a, b \in \mathrm{Ob}(B)\}$. A morphism in $B_{a\alpha}$ is called an $a\alpha$-**morfism**.

Besides the symmetric strict monoidal categories(in the sequel they are called $a\alpha$-ssmc, too) which models the intuitive concept of bijection we shall use 15 types of ssmc which models other types of finite relations as function, partial function, injective function, surjective function, partial injective function and so on. These 16 concepts are called in the sequel xy-ssmc, where $x \in \{a, b, c, d\}$ and $y \in \{\alpha, \beta, \gamma, \delta\}$.

These concepts use some distinguished morphisms: $\top, \bot, \vee, \wedge$. The second column in table 3 shows the distinguished morphisms we use in each case. We mention that one uses such a distinguished morphism for each object which is written as a subscript or a superscript. The domains and the codomains of these morphisms are:

$$\top_a : \varepsilon \longrightarrow a \qquad \bot^a : a \longrightarrow \varepsilon$$
$$\vee_a : a + a \longrightarrow a \qquad \wedge^a : a \longrightarrow a + a$$

[1]Research partially supported by the Academy of Finland, Project 11281

These distinguished morphisms must satisfy their axioms in table 2. The axiom list which must be satisfied in each case is given in the last column of table 3. In table 2 the superscript ° shows a categorial duality. Notice that $\top$ and $\bot$ are dual. The same for $\vee$ and $\wedge$.

$(C1)$ $f(gh) = (fg)h$

$(C2)$ $1_a f = f = f 1_b$

$(C3)$ $f + (g + h) = (f + g) + h$

$(C4)$ $1_e + f = f = f + 1_e$

$(C5)$ $1_a + 1_b = 1_{a+b}$

$(C6)$ $(f + g)(u + v) = fu + gv$

$(C7)$ ${}^b\times^a (f + g) {}^c\times^d = g + f$

$(C8)$ ${}^a\times^e = 1_a$

$(C9)$ ${}^a\times^{b+c} = ({}^a\times^b + 1_c)(1_b + {}^a\times^c)$

Table 1. Axioms for csms

An xy-ssmc is a ssmc endowed with the distinguished morphisms mentioned in the second column of table 3 and which satisfies the axioms mentioned in the last column of table 3.

Let B_{xy} be the least strict monoidal subcategory of B which includes $B_{\alpha\alpha}$ and all the distinguished morphisms coresponding to the case xy.

(A) $(\vee_a + 1_a)\vee_a = (1_a + \vee_a)\vee_a$
$(A°)$ $\wedge^a (\wedge^a + 1_a) = \wedge(1_a + \wedge^a)$

(B) ${}^a\times^a \vee_a = \vee_a$
$(B°)$ $\wedge^a \, {}^a\times^a = \wedge^a$

(C) $(\top_a + 1_a)\vee_a = 1_a$
$(C°)$ $\wedge^a (\bot^a + 1_a) = 1_a$

(D) $\vee_a \bot^a = \bot^a + \bot^a$
$(D°)$ $\top_a \wedge^a = \top_a + \top_a$

(E) $\top_a \bot^a = 1_e$

(F) $\vee_a \wedge^a = (\wedge^a + \wedge^a)(1_a + {}^a\times^a + 1_a)(\vee_a + \vee_a)$

(G) $\wedge^a \vee_a = 1_a$

$(SV1)$ $\top_e = 1_e$
$(SV1°)$ $\bot^e = 1_e$

$(SV2)$ $\top_{a+b} = \top_a + \top_b$
$(SV2°)$ $\bot^{a+b} = \bot^a + \bot^b$

$(SV3)$ $\vee_e = 1_e$
$(SV3°)$ $\wedge^e = 1_e$

$(SV4)$ $\vee_{a+b} = (1_a + {}^b\times^a + 1_b)(\vee_a + \vee_b)$
$(SV4°)$ $\wedge^{a+b} = (\wedge^a + \wedge^b)(1_a + {}^a\times^b + 1_b)$

Table 2. Axioms for xy-csms

2. Basic Morphisms

We use the following notation:

$$x' = \begin{cases} a & \text{if } x = b \\ c & \text{if } x = d \end{cases} \quad \text{and} \quad y' = \begin{cases} \alpha & \text{if } y = \beta \\ \gamma & \text{if } y = \delta \end{cases}$$

Theorem 1. *Let B be an xy-ssmc.*

1. *If $x \in \{b, d\}$ then each xy-morphism can be written as $j(1_a + \bot^b)$, where j is a $x'y$-morphism.*

2. If $y \in \{\beta, \delta\}$ then each xy-morphism can be written as $(T_a + 1_b)j$, where j is a xy'-morphism.

3. If $x \in \{b, d\}$ and $y \in \{\beta, \delta\}$ then each xy-morphism can be written as $(T_c + 1_a)j(1_b + \perp^d)$, where j is a $x'y'$-morphism.

Case xy	Existing basic morphisms	Specific identities satisfied
$a\alpha$	–	–
$a\beta$	$\top$	SV1-2
$a\gamma$	$\vee$	A, B, SV3-4
$a\delta$	$\top, \vee$	A-C, SV1-4
$b\alpha$	$\perp$	SV1°-2°
$b\beta$	$\perp, \top$	E, SV1-2, SV1°-2°
$b\gamma$	$\perp, \vee$	A, B, D, SV3-4, SV1°-2°
$b\delta$	$\perp, \top, \vee$	A-E, SV1-4, SV1°-2°
$c\alpha$	$\wedge$	A°, B°, SV3°-4°
$c\beta$	$\wedge, \top$	A°, B°, D°, SV1-2, SV3°-4°
$c\gamma$	$\wedge, \vee$	A, B, F, G, A°, B°, SV3-4, SV3°-4°
$c\delta$	$\wedge, \top, \vee$	A-C, F, G, A°, B°, D°, SV1-4, SV3°-4°
$d\alpha$	$\perp, \wedge$	A°-C°, SV1°-4°
$d\beta$	$\perp, \wedge, \top$	A°-D°, E, SV1°-4°, SV1-2
$d\gamma$	$\perp, \wedge, \vee$	A, B, D, F, G, A°-C°, SV3-4, SV1°-4°
$d\delta$	$\perp, \wedge, \top, \vee$	A-G, A°-D°, SV1-4, SV1°-4°

Table 3. xy-csms

Proof. In each case one shows the set of all the morphisms having the above form is a sub-xy-ssmc.

In the third case, $x \in \{b, d\}$, $y \in \{\beta, \delta\}$, we prove that this set is closed under composition and sum. For composition let $j \in B(c + a, b + d)$, $k \in B(e + b, f + g)$ be two $x'y'$-morphisms. In the composition

$(T_c + 1_a)j(1_b + \perp^d)(T_e + 1_b)k(1_f + \perp^g) =$
$(T_e + 1_a)j(T_e + 1_b + \perp^d)k(1_f + \perp^g) =$
$= (T_c + 1_a)j(T_e + 1_{b+d})(1_{e+b} + \perp^d)k(1_f + \perp^g)$
$= [T_e + (T_c + 1_a)j][k(1_f + \perp^g) + \perp^d]$
$= (T_e + T_c + 1_a)(1_e + j)(k + 1_d)(1_f + \perp^g + \perp^d)$
$= (T_{e+c} + 1_a)[(1_e + j)(k + 1_d)](1_f + \perp^{g+d})$

we remark that $(1_e + j)(k + 1_d)$ is an $x'y'$-morphism.

For sum let $j \in B(c + a, b + d)$, $k \in B(e + h, f + g)$ be two $x'y'$-morphisms. In the sum

$$(\mathsf{T}_c + 1_a)j(1_b + \bot^d) + (\mathsf{T}_e + 1_h)k(1_f + \bot^g) =$$
$$= (\mathsf{T}_c + 1_a + \mathsf{T}_e + 1_h)(j + k)(1_b + \bot^d + 1_f + \bot^g)$$
$$= [\mathsf{T}_c + (\mathsf{T}_e + 1_a)\,^e\!\!\times^a + 1_h]\,(j + k)\,[1_b + \,^{d}\!\!\times^f(1_f + \bot^d) + \bot^g]$$
$$= (\mathsf{T}_c + \mathsf{T}_e + 1_a + 1_h)\,[(1_c + \,^e\!\!\times^a + 1_h)(j+k)(1_b + \,^{d}\!\!\times^f + 1_g)]\,(1_b + 1_f + \bot^d + \bot^g)$$
$$= (\mathsf{T}_{c+e} + 1_{a+h})\,[(1_c + \,^e\!\!\times^a + 1_h)(j + k)(1_b + \,^{d}\!\!\times^f + 1_g)]\,(1_{b+f} + \bot^{d+g})$$

we remark that $(1_c + \,^e\!\!\times^a + 1_h)(j + k)(1_b + \,^{d}\!\!\times^f + 1_g)$ is an $x'y'$-morphism.
    As

$$1_a = (\mathsf{T}_e + 1_a)1_a(1_a + \bot_e)\,, \quad \,^a\!\!\times^b = (\mathsf{T}_e + 1_{a+b})\,^a\!\!\times^b(1_{b+a} + \bot^e)$$

$$\bot^a = (\mathsf{T}_e + 1_a)1_a(1_e + \bot^a) \text{ and } \mathsf{T}_a = (\mathsf{T}_a + 1_e)1_a(1_a + \bot^e)$$

we deduce that all the morphisms of the above given form makes a sub-xy-ssmc, therefore we get the conclusion. □

Proposition 2. *Let B be an xy-ssmc.*

1. If $x \in \{b, d\}$ and $y \in \{\beta, \delta\}$, then

- *each $a\beta$-morphism is a monic which has a right converse,*
- *each $b\alpha$-morphism is an epic which has a left converse.*

2. If $y = \delta$, then

- *each $a\gamma$-morphism is an epic which has a left converse.*

2°. If $x = d$, then

- *each $c\alpha$-morphism is a monic which has a right converse.*

3. If $x \in \{b, d\}$ and $y = \delta$, then

- *each $b\gamma$-morphism is an epic which has a left converse.*

3°. If $x = d$ and $y \in \{\beta, \delta\}$, then

- *each $c\beta$-morphism is a monic which has a right converse.*

Proof. One knows that each xy-morphism may be written as a finite composite of morphisms of one of the following type:

a) $1_a + \,^b\!\!\times^c + 1_d$,

b) $1_a + \bot^b + 1_c$ only if $x \in \{b, d\}$,

c) $1_a + \wedge^b + 1_c$ only if $x \in \{c, d\}$,

d) $1_a + \mathsf{T}_b + 1_c$ only if $y \in \{\beta, \delta\}$,

e) $1_a + \vee_b + 1_c$ only if $y \in \{\gamma, \delta\}$.

The morphisms of type **a)** are isomorphisms.

As

$$(1_a + \top_b + 1_c)(1_a + \perp^b + 1_c) = 1_{a+c}$$

we deduce for $y \in \{\beta, \delta\}$ that the morphisms of type **b)** have a left converse and for $x \in \{b, d\}$ the morphisms of type **d)** have a right converse.

For $x = d$, as

$$(1_a + \wedge^b + 1_c)(1_{a+b} + \perp^b + 1_c) = 1_{a+b+c}$$

we deduce that the morphisms of type **c)** have a right converse.

For $y = \delta$, as

$$(1_{a+b} + \top_b + 1_c)(1_a + \vee_b + 1_c) = 1_{a+b+c}$$

we deduce the morphisms of type **e)** have a left converse.

Finally remark that a composite of morphisms having a left converse is a morphism having a left converse. □

In the sequel we use for each nonnegative integer n the following conventions:

1. n satisfies a or α means $n = 1$,

2. n satisfies b or β means $n \leq 1$,

3. n satisfies c or γ means $n \geq 1$,

4. n satisfies d or δ means no conditions.

Fact 3. Let B be an ay-ssmc and let r be a natural number satisfying the condition y. If $n \geq 1$ and $b_i \in Ob(B)$ for $i \in [n]$ then there exists an $a\alpha$-morphism k such that

$$V^r_{b_1 + b_2 + \dots + b_n} = k(V^r_{b_1} + V^r_{b_2} + \dots + V^r_{b_n}).$$

Proof.

- For $n = 1$ take $k = 1_{rb_1}$.

- For $n = 2$ we use an induction on r to prove $V^r_{a+b} = k(V^r_a + V^r_b)$.

$$V^{r+1}_{a+b} = (V^r_{a+b} + 1_{a+b})V_{a+b} = [k(V^r_a + V^r_b) + 1_{a+b}](1_a + {}^b\!\times^a + 1_b)(V_a + V_b)$$

$$= (k + 1_{a+b})(1_{ra} + {}^{rb}\!\times^a + 1_b)(V^r_a + 1_a + V^r_b + 1_b)(V_a + V_b)$$

$$= [(k + 1_{a+b})(1_{ra} + {}^{rb}\!\times^a + 1_b)](V^{r+1}_a + V^{r+1}_b)$$

- Finally we use an induction on n:

$$V^r_{b_1 + b_2 + \dots + b_{n+1}} = k_1(V^r_{b_1 + b_2 + \dots + b_n} + V^r_{b_{n+1}}) = k_1[k_2(V^r_{b_1} + V^r_{b_2} + \dots + V^r_{b_n}) + V^r_{b_{n+1}}]$$

$$= [k_1(k_2 + 1_{rb_{n+1}})](V^r_{b_1} + V^r_{b_2} + \dots + V^r_{b_{n+1}}). \qquad \square$$

Fact 4. Let B an ay-ssmc where $y \in \{\gamma, \delta\}$ and $n \geq 1$. If for each $i \in [n]$ we suppose $a_i \in Ob(B)$ and the natural numbers r_i, t_i satisfy condition y then there exists an $a\alpha$-morphism k such that

$$\left(\sum_{i=1}^n V^{r_i}_{a_i} + \sum_{i=1}^n V^{t_i}_{a_i}\right)V_{a_1 + \dots + a_n} = k \sum_{i=1}^n V^{r_i + t_i}_{a_i}.$$

Proof. Induction on n.

For $n = 1$ we have a known identity $(\vee_{a_1}^{r_1} + \vee_{a_1}^{t_1})\vee_{a_1} = \vee_{a_1}^{r_1+t_1}$.

We assume the equality is true for $n-1$. Let $t = \sum_{i=1}^{n-1} t_i a_i$, $r = \sum_{i=1}^{n-1} r_i a_i$ and $a = \sum_{i=1}^{n-1} a_i$.

$$\left(\sum_{i=1}^{n} \vee_{a_i}^{r_i} + \sum_{i=1}^{n} \vee_{a_i}^{t_i}\right) \vee_{a_1+a_2+\cdots+a_n} =$$

$$= \left(\sum_{i=1}^{n-1} \vee_{a_i}^{r_i} + \vee_{a_n}^{r_n} + \sum_{i=1}^{n-1} \vee_{a_i}^{t_i} + \vee_{a_n}^{t_n}\right)(1_a + {}^{a_n}\!\times^a + 1_{a_n})(\vee_a + \vee_{a_n})$$

$$= \left[\sum_{i=1}^{n-1} \vee_{a_i}^{r_i} + \left(\vee_{a_n}^{r_n} + \sum_{i=1}^{n-1} \vee_{a_i}^{t_i}\right) {}^{a_n}\!\times^a + \vee_{a_n}^{t_n}\right](\vee_a + \vee_{a_n})$$

$$= \left[\sum_{i=1}^{n-1} \vee_{a_i}^{r_i} + {}^{r_n a_n}\!\times^t\left(\sum_{i=1}^{n-1} \vee_{a_i}^{t_i} + \vee_{a_n}^{r_n}\right) + \vee_{a_n}^{t_n}\right](\vee_a + \vee_{a_n})$$

$$= (1_r + {}^{r_n a_n}\!\times^t + 1_{t_n a_n})\left[\left(\sum_{i=1}^{n-1} \vee_{a_i}^{r_i} + \sum_{i=1}^{n-1} \vee_{a_i}^{t_i}\right)\vee_a + (\vee_{a_n}^{r_n} + \vee_{a_n}^{t_n})\vee_{a_n}\right]$$

$$= (1_r + {}^{r_n a_n}\!\times^t + 1_{t_n a_n})\left[k\left(\sum_{i=1}^{n-1} \vee_{a_i}^{r_i+t_i}\right) + \vee_{a_n}^{r_n+t_n}\right]$$

$$= \left[(1_r + {}^{r_n a_n}\!\times^t + 1_{t_n a_n})\left(k + 1_{(r_n+t_n)a_n}\right)\right]\sum_{i=1}^{n} \vee_{a_i}^{r_i+t_i}. \qquad \square$$

Lemma 5. *Let B an ay-ssmc with $Ob(B)$ equidivisible. Each ay-morphism can be written as $k \sum_{i=1}^{n} \vee_{b_i}^{n_i}$, where k is an $a\alpha$-morphism, $n \geq 1$ and for each $i \in [n]$: $b_i \in Ob(B)$ and n_i satisfies condition y.*

Proof. Notice that the morphisms $1_a + {}^b\!\times^c + 1_d$, $1_a + \top_b + 1_c$ if $y \in \{\beta, \delta\}$ and $1_a + \vee_b + 1_c$ if $y \in \{\gamma, \delta\}$ may be written as above.

We prove that the right composite with $1_a + {}^b\!\times^c + 1_d$, $1_a + \top_b + 1_c$ if $y \in \{\beta, \delta\}$ and with $1_a + \vee_b + 1_c$ if $y \in \{\gamma, \delta\}$ of each morphism of the above type may be written as a morphism of the above type.

When the right composite with $1_a + {}^b\!\times^c + 1_d$ is defined we deduce $b_1 + b_2 + \cdots + b_n = a + b + c + d$. Usind the equidivisibility and fact 3 we deduce

$$k\left(\sum_{i=1}^{n} \vee_{b_i}^{n_i}\right)(1_a + {}^b\!\times^c + 1_d) =$$

$$k'\left(\sum_{i=1}^{m} \vee_{c_i}^{m_i}\right)(1_{c_1+c_2+\cdots+c_s} + {}^{c_{s+1}+\cdots+c_r}\!\times^{c_{r+1}+\cdots+c_t} + 1_{c_{t+1}+\cdots+c_m}),$$

where k' is an $a\alpha$-morphism, $m \geq 1$, $c_i \in Ob(B)$ for each $i \in [m]$ and $1 \leq s < r < t < m$. Notice that the last composition is equal to the composite of

$$k'\left(1_{\sum_{i=1}^{s} m_i c_i} + {}^{\sum_{i=s+1}^{r} m_i c_i}\!\times^{\sum_{i=r+1}^{t} m_i c_i} + 1_{\sum_{i=t+1}^{m} m_i c_i}\right)$$

to

$$\left(\sum_{i=1}^{s} \vee_{c_i}^{m_i} + \sum_{i=r+1}^{t} \vee_{c_i}^{m_i} + \sum_{i=s+1}^{r} \vee_{c_i}^{m_i} + \sum_{i=t+1}^{m} \vee_{c_i}^{m_i}\right).$$

When the right composite with $1_a + T_b + 1_c$ is defined we deduce $b_1 + b_2 + \cdots + b_n = a + c$. Therefore

$$k\left(\sum_{i=1}^{n} \vee_{b_i}^{n_i}\right)(1_a + T_b + 1_c) = k'\left(\sum_{i=1}^{m} \vee_{c_i}^{m_i}\right)(1_{c_1+c_2+\cdots+c_s} + T_b + 1_{c_{s+1}+\cdots+c_m})$$

where k' is an $a\alpha$-morphism, $m \geq 1$, $c_i \in Ob(B)$ for each $i \in [m]$ and $1 \leq s < m$, hence

$$k\left(\sum_{i=1}^{n} \vee_{b_i}^{n_i}\right)(1_a + T_b + 1_c) = k'\left(\sum_{i=1}^{s} \vee_{c_i}^{m_i} + \vee_b^0 + \sum_{i=s+1}^{m} \vee_{c_i}^{m_i}\right).$$

When the right composite with $1_a + V_b + 1_c$ is defined we deduce $b_1 + b_2 + \cdots + b_n = a + b + b + c$. Usind the equidivisibility of the monoid $Ob(B)$ and fact 3 we deduce

$$k\left(\sum_{i=1}^{n} \vee_{b_i}^{n_i}\right)(1_a + V_b + 1_c) = k'\left(\sum_{i=1}^{m} \vee_{c_i}^{m_i}\right)(1_{c_1+\cdots+c_s} + V_{c_{s+1}+\cdots+c_r} + 1_{c_{t+1}+\cdots+c_m})$$

where k' is an $a\alpha$-morphism, $m \geq 1$, $c_i \in Ob(B)$ for each $i \in [m]$, $1 \leq s < r < t < m$ and $b = c_{s+1} + \cdots + c_r = c_{r+1} + \cdots + c_t$. Usind again the equidivisibility we deduce the existence of the objects $d_1, d_2, \ldots, d_h \in Ob(B)$ such that:

$c_{s+p} = d_{i_{p-1}+1} + \cdots + d_{i_p}$ for $1 \leq p \leq r - s$

$c_{r+q} = d_{j_{q-1}+1} + \cdots + d_{j_q}$ for $1 \leq q \leq t - r$

where $0 = i_0 < i_1 < \ldots < i_{r-s} = h$ and $0 = j_0 < j_1 < \ldots < j_{t-r} = h$.

Using fact 3, there exists an $a\alpha$-morphism k'' such that

$$k\left(\sum_{i=1}^{n} \vee_{b_i}^{n_i}\right)(1_a + V_b + 1_c) = k''\left(\sum_{i=1}^{s} \vee_{c_i}^{m_i} + \sum_{v=1}^{r-s}\sum_{w=i_{v-1}+1}^{i_v} \vee_{d_w}^{m_s+v} + \right.$$

$$\left. + \sum_{v=1}^{t-r}\sum_{w=j_{v-1}+1}^{j_v} \vee_{d_w}^{m_r+v} + \sum_{i=t+1}^{m} \vee_{c_i}^{m_i}\right)(1_{c_1+c_2+\cdots+c_s} + V_{d_1+d_2+\cdots+d_h} + 1_{c_{t+1}+\cdots+c_m}).$$

To get the conclusion we apply fact 4.

Therefore all the morphisms which may be written as $k\sum_{i=1}^{n} \vee_{b_i}^{n_i}$ form a sub-xy-ssmc, hence this set includes B_{ay}. $\qquad\square$

Fact 6. In each xy-ssmc B if m satisfies condition x, n satisfies condition y and $a \in Ob(B)$, then there exists an $a\alpha$-morphism k such that

$$\vee_a^n \wedge_m^a = (\sum_{i=1}^{n} \wedge_m^a)k(\sum_{i=1}^{m} \vee_a^n).$$

Theorem 7. *Let B an xy-ssmc with $Ob(B)$ equidivisible. Each xy-morphism can be written as*

$$(\sum_{j=1}^{m} \wedge_{m_j}^{a_j}) k (\sum_{i=1}^{n} \vee_{b_i}^{n_i})$$

where $m, n \geq 1$, k is an $a\alpha$-morphism, for $j \in [m]$ $a_j \in Ob(B)$ and m_j satisfies condition x and for $i \in [n]$ $b_i \in Ob(B)$ and n_i satisfies condition y.

Proof. All the morphisms as above make a sub-xy-ssmc. We prove the most dificult part only, i.e. the fact that the composite of two morphisms as above is a morphism as above, therefore

$$\left(\sum_{j=1}^{m} \wedge_{m_j}^{a_j}\right) k \left(\sum_{i=1}^{n} \vee_{b_i}^{n_i}\right) \left(\sum_{j=1}^{p} \wedge_{r_j}^{c_j}\right) j \left(\sum_{i=1}^{q} \vee_{d_i}^{t_i}\right)$$

where $b_1 + b_2 + \cdots + b_n = c_1 + c_2 + \cdots + c_p$. Using the echidivisibility of $Ob(B)$, fact 3, its dual and then fact 6 we get

$$\left(\sum_{j=1}^{m} \wedge_{m_j}^{a_j}\right) k' \left(\sum_{t=1}^{r} \vee_{e_t}^{n_t} \wedge_{v_t}^{e_t}\right) j' \left(\sum_{i=1}^{q} \vee_{d_i}^{t_i}\right) =$$

$$= \left[\left(\sum_{j=1}^{m} \wedge_{m_j}^{a_j}\right) k' \left(\sum_{t=1}^{r} \sum \wedge_{v_t}^{e_t}\right)\right] k'' \left[\left(\sum_{t=1}^{r} \sum \vee_{e_t}^{n_t}\right) j' \left(\sum_{i=1}^{q} \vee_{d_i}^{t_i}\right)\right]$$

Applying in the two square brackets the dual of lemma 5 and lemma 5 we get the conclusion. □

In a is in a free monoid, $\mid a \mid$ denotes its length and $a_1, a_2, \ldots, a_{|a|}$ its letters.

Corollary 8. *Let B be an xy-ssmc such that $Ob(B)$ is a free monoid. Each xy-morphism $f \in B(a,b)$ can be written as*

$$(\sum_{j=1}^{|a|} \wedge_{m_j}^{a_j}) k (\sum_{i=1}^{|b|} \vee_{b_i}^{n_i}),$$

where k is $a\alpha$-morphism, m_j satisfy condition x for $j \in [\mid a \mid]$ and n_i satisfy condition y for $i \in [\mid b \mid]$.

Proof. We apply theorem 7. The terms as $\wedge_{m_j}^{\varepsilon}$ or $\vee_{\varepsilon}^{n_i}$, where ε is the empty word, may be get out from the sum. For the terms $\wedge_m^a$ or $\vee_a^n$ where a is a word of length at least 2, we apply the dual of fact 3 and fact 3, respectively. □

References

1. V. E. Căzănescu, Gh. Ştefănescu, Classes of finite relations as initial abstract data types I, Discrete mathematics **90** (1991), 233 – 265.

2. V. E. Căzănescu, Gh. Ştefănescu, A general result on abstract flowchart schemes with applications to the study of accesibilty, reduction and minimization Theoretical Computer Science **99** (1992), 1 – 63.

3. V. E. Căzănescu, Gh. Ştefănescu, Towards a new algebraic foundation of flowchart scheme theory, Fundamenta Informaticae **13** (1990), 171 – 210.

On Mix Operation

Manfred KUDLEK

Fachbereich Informatik, Universität Hamburg
Germany

Alexandru MATEESCU

Faculty of Mathematics, University of Bucharest
Str Academiei 14, 70109 Bucureşti, Romania

Abstract. We consider operations between languages, based on splitting the underlying alphabet into two disjoint sets. Such operations are generalizations of the classical catenation or shuffle operation. With such operations rational and algebraic languages can be defined similar to the classical case. The basic properties of the corresponding language families are investigated.

1. Introduction

In [9] the *partial shuffle* has been introduced as a new operation on sets of words, based on the normal operations of catenation and shuffle. In [5], [6], [7] another operation on words, *distributed catenation*, similar to partial shuffle, but based only on normal catenation, was considered. In [2] a general extension is studied. In this paper we present another general extension of such operations. These are based on the division of the alphabet into two disjoint sets, and the composition of the new operation by using three (not necessarily different) associative operations on the two disjoint subsets and the entire alphabet. This new operation will be called (*left*) *mix operation*.

Throughout this paper we will omit *left* and use only *mix operation*.

2. Basic Properties of Mix Operation

We start by introducing the basic definitions of mix operation and considering the basic properties of it.

Let Σ be a finite and nonempty set, an alphabet. The empty word is denoted by λ, the set of all nonempty words over Σ by Σ^+, and the set of all words over Σ by $\Sigma^* = \Sigma^+ \cup \{\lambda\}$.

For general results concerning the theory of formal languages the reader may consult the monograph [12].

If Σ is an alphabet, let $\Delta \subseteq \Sigma$ and $\Gamma \subseteq \Sigma$ such that $\Sigma = \Gamma \cup \Delta$ and $\Gamma \cap \Delta = \emptyset$. Note that Γ or Δ can be empty.

Notations. For $\Delta \subseteq \Sigma$ let

$$M_0 = \Gamma^*,$$
$$M_{k+1} = \Gamma^*(\Delta^+\Gamma^+)^k\Delta^+\Gamma^* \cup \{\lambda\}, k \geq 0.$$

Remark 1. Note that:

(i) $\bigcup_{k\geq 0} M_k = \Sigma^*$,

(ii)   if $i \neq j$, then $M_i \cap M_j = \{\lambda\}$,

(iii)   for any $w \in \Sigma^+$, there exists a unique $k \geq 0$, such that $w \in M_k$.

Definition 2. Let w be in Σ^+. The Δ-*degree* of w is:

$$deg_\Delta(w) = k, \text{ where } w \in M_k.$$

By definition, $deg_\Delta(\lambda) = 0$.

Comment. Note that for any word $w \in \Sigma^*$, $deg_\Delta(w)$ has a unique value (see Remark 1).

Any $w \in \Sigma^*$ can be represented in the following *canonical decomposition with respect to* Δ, or shortly, *canonical decomposition*, if Δ is clear from the context: $w = u_0 v_1 u_1 \cdots v_k u_k$ with $u_i \in \Gamma^*, i = 0, \cdots, k$ and $v_j \in \Delta^+, j = 1, \cdots, k$.

Definition 3. Let $\diamond, \triangleright$, and $\circ$ be binary operations on $\mathcal{P}(\Sigma^*)$, defined by $\{\lambda\} \bullet \{\lambda\} = \{\lambda\}$ $\{\lambda\} \bullet \{x\} = \{x\} \bullet \{\lambda\} = \{x\}$ for $\bullet \in \{\diamond, \triangleright, \circ\}$, with $\{x\} \diamond \{y\} \subseteq \Gamma^+$, $\{x\} \triangleright \{y\} \subseteq \Delta^+$, $\{x\} \circ \{y\} \subseteq \Sigma^+$ for $x, y \in \Gamma, \Delta, \Sigma$, respectively, and

$$\{x\} \bullet (\{y\} \bullet \{z\}) = (\{x\} \bullet \{y\}) \bullet \{z\}, \quad A \bullet B = \bigcup_{x \in A, y \in B}(\{x\} \bullet \{y\})$$

for $\bullet \in \{\diamond, \triangleright, \circ\}$ $x, y, z \in \Sigma$.

Then $\diamond, \triangleright, \circ$ are associative operations on $\mathcal{P}(\Sigma^*)$.

For arbitrary $k \geq 0$ a binary operation on M_k is defined by

Definition 4. If $x \in M_k$, $y \in M_k$, $x = u_0 v_1 u_1 \ldots v_k u_k$, $y = u_0' v_1' u_1' \ldots v_k' u_k'$, with $u_0, u_0', u_k, u_k' \in \Gamma^*, u_i, u_i' \in \Gamma^+, i = 1, \cdots, k-1, v_i, v_i' \in \Delta^+, i = 1, \ldots, k$, then:

$$\{x\}[\diamond, \triangleright, \circ, \Delta, k]\{y\} = (\{u_0\} \diamond \{u_0'\}) \circ (\{v_1\} \triangleright \{v_1'\}) \circ (\{u_1\} \diamond \{u_1'\}) \cdots$$
$$(\{v_k\} \triangleright \{v_k'\}) \circ (\{u_k\} \diamond \{u_k'\}).$$

By definition,

$$\{x\}[\diamond, \triangleright, \circ, \Delta, k]\{\lambda\} = \{\lambda\}[\diamond, \triangleright, \circ, \Delta, k]\{x\} = \{x\}.$$

$[\diamond, \triangleright, \circ, \Delta, k]$ is called the k-Δ-mix operation of $\{x\}$ with $\{y\}$.

Trivially,

Lemma 5. *For any* Σ, $\Delta \subseteq \Sigma$ *and* $k \geq 0$, *the operation* $[\diamond, \triangleright, \circ, \Delta, k]$ *is associative, and the triple* $\mathcal{M}_{[\diamond, \triangleright, \circ, \Delta, k]} = (\mathcal{P}(M_k), [\diamond, \triangleright, \circ, \Delta, k], \{\lambda\})$ *is a monoid.*

Proof. Assume $x, y, z \in M_k$ with canonical decompositions

$$x = u_0 v_1 u_1 \cdots v_k u_k, \quad y = u_0' v_1' u_1' \cdots v_k' u_k', \quad z = u_0'' v_1'' u_1'' \cdots v_k'' u_k'',$$

Then

$$(\{x\}[\diamond, \triangleright, \circ, \Delta, k]\{y\})[\diamond, \triangleright, \circ, \Delta, k]\{z\}$$
$$= (\{u_0\} \diamond \{u_0'\}) \diamond \{u_0''\} \circ (\{v_1\} \triangleright \{v_1'\}) \triangleright \{v_1''\}(\{u_1\} \diamond \{u_1'\}) \diamond \{u_1''\} \cdots$$
$$(\{v_k\} \triangleright \{v_k'\}) \triangleright \{v_k''\} \circ (\{u_k\} \diamond \{u_k'\}) \diamond \{u_k''\}$$
$$= \{u_0\} \diamond (\{u_0'\} \diamond \{u_0''\}) \circ \{v_1\} \triangleright (\{v_1'\} \triangleright \{v_1''\})\{u_1\} \diamond (\{u_1'\} \diamond \{u_1''\}) \cdots$$
$$\{v_k\} \triangleright (\{v_k'\} \triangleright \{v_k''\}) \circ \{u_k\} \diamond (\{u_k'\} \diamond \{u_k''\})$$
$$= \{x\}[\diamond, \triangleright, \circ, \Delta, k](\{y\}[\diamond, \triangleright, \circ, \Delta, k]\{z\})$$

and $\{\lambda\}$ is the unit element.

The binary operation $[\diamond, \triangleright, \circ, \Delta, k]$ is extended to arbitrary subsets A, B of M_k in a natural way by

$$A[\diamond, \triangleright, \circ, \Delta, k]B = \bigcup_{x \in A, y \in B} (\{x\}[\diamond, \triangleright, \circ, \Delta, k]\{y\}).$$

Then $\mathcal{M}_{[\diamond, \triangleright, \circ, \Delta, k]} = (\mathcal{P}(M_k), [\diamond, \triangleright, \circ, \Delta, k], \{\lambda\})$ is a monoid. $\qquad \Box$

Moreover,

Lemma 6. *The operation $[\diamond, \triangleright, \circ, \Delta, k]$ is distributive with the operation $\cup$ and the triple $\mathcal{S}_{[\diamond, \triangleright, \circ, \Delta, k]} = (\mathcal{P}(M_k), \cup, [\diamond, \triangleright, \circ, \Delta, k], \emptyset, \{\lambda\})$ is a (generally noncommutative) ω-complete semiring.*

ω-complete means that any sequence (A_i) with $A_i \in \mathcal{P}(M_k)$ and $A_i \subseteq A_{i+1}$ for $i \geq 0$ has a limit (supremum) in $\mathcal{P}(M_k)$. This limit is

$$A = \bigcup_{i \geq 0} A_i.$$

Furthermore, for $B \in \mathcal{P}(M_k)$,

$$B[\diamond, \triangleright, \circ, \Delta, k]\bigcup_{i \geq 0} A_i = \bigcup_{i \geq 0}(B[\diamond, \triangleright, \circ, \Delta, k]A_i)$$

and

$$(\bigcup_{i \geq 0} A_i)[\diamond, \triangleright, \circ, \Delta, k]B = \bigcup_{i \geq 0}(A_i[\diamond, \triangleright, \circ, \Delta, k]B).$$

For the theory of semirings one may consult the monographs [1] and [3].

Definition 7. If $A \subseteq M_k$, $k \geq 0$, then the Δ-k-*mix operation closure* of A is:

$$A^{[\diamond, \triangleright, \circ, \Delta, k]} = \bigcup_{i \geq 0} A^{[\diamond, \triangleright, \circ, \Delta, k](i)}, \text{ where}$$

$$A^{[\diamond, \triangleright, \circ, \Delta, k](0)} = \{\lambda\} \text{ and } A^{[\diamond, \triangleright, \circ, \Delta, k](i+1)} = A[\diamond, \triangleright, \circ, \Delta, k]A^{[\diamond, \triangleright, \circ, \Delta, k](i)}.$$

Comment. Note that $A^{[\diamond, \triangleright, \circ, \Delta, k]}$ is the submonoid generated by A, with respect to $[\diamond, \triangleright, \circ, \Delta, k]$, in the monoid $\mathcal{M}_{[\diamond, \triangleright, \circ, \Delta, k]}$ and in the semiring $\mathcal{S}_{[\diamond, \triangleright, \circ, \Delta, k]}$.

If $\diamond$ and $\triangleright$ are commutative, then $[\diamond, \triangleright, \circ, \Delta, k]$ is commutative too.

The $k - \Delta$-mix operation will now be extended to arbitrary subsets from Σ^*. The new operation will be denoted by $[\diamond, \triangleright, \circ, \Delta]$.

Definition 8. Let x, y be in Σ^+ such that $deg_\Delta(x) = n$ and $deg_\Delta(y) = m$. Assume that $x = u_0 v_1 u_1 \cdots v_n u_n, y = u'_0 v'_1 u'_1 \cdots v'_m u'_m$, with $u_0, u'_0, u_n, u'_m \in \Gamma^*, u_i \in \Gamma^+, i = 1, \cdots, n-1, v_i \in \Delta^+, i = 1, \cdots, n, u'_i \in \Gamma^+, i = 1, \cdots, m-1, v'_i \in \Delta^+, i = 1, \cdots, m$. Then the $\Delta - k$ *mix operation* of $\{x\}$ with $\{y\}$ is:

Case $n \leq m$

$$\begin{aligned}
\{x\}[\diamond, \triangleright, \circ, \Delta]\{y\} = \ &(\{u_0\} \diamond \{u'_0\}) \circ (\{v_1\} \triangleright \{v'_1\}) \circ (\{u_1\} \diamond \{u'_1\}) \cdots \\
&(\{v_n\} \triangleright \{v'_n\}) \circ (\{u_n\} \diamond \{u'_n\}) \circ \\
&\circ \{v'_{n+1}\} \circ \{u'_{n+1}\} \cdots \{v'_m\} \circ \{u'_m\}
\end{aligned}$$

Case $n \geq m$

$$\{x\}[\diamond, \triangleright, \circ, \Delta]\{y\} = (\{u_0\} \diamond \{u_0'\}) \circ (\{v_1\} \triangleright \{v_1'\}) \circ (\{u_1\} \diamond \{u_1'\}) \cdots$$
$$(\{v_m\} \triangleright \{v_m'\}) \circ (\{u_m\} \diamond \{u_m'\}) \circ$$
$$\circ \{v_{m+1}\} \circ \{u_{m+1}\} \cdots \{v_n\} \circ \{u_n\}$$

By definition:

$$\{x\}[\diamond, \triangleright, \circ, \Delta]\{\lambda\} = \{\lambda\}[\diamond, \triangleright, \circ, \Delta]\{x\} = \{x\}.$$

$[\diamond, \triangleright, \circ, \Delta]$ is extended to $\mathcal{P}(\Sigma^*)$ in the usual way by

$$A[\diamond, \triangleright, \circ, \Delta]B = \bigcup_{x \in A, y \in B} \{x\}[\diamond, \triangleright, \circ, \Delta]\{y\}$$

for $A, B \in \mathcal{P}(\Sigma^*)$.

Remark 9. Note that actually we have defined a *left* mix operation. A *right* one can be defined similarly.

For the special cases $\Delta = \emptyset$ and $\Delta = \Sigma$ we get the operations $\diamond$ and $\triangleright$, respectively.

Again, if $\diamond$ and $\triangleright$ are commutative then $[\diamond, \triangleright, \circ, \Delta]$ is commutative.

Lemma 10. *For any* Σ *and* $\Delta \subseteq \Sigma$ *the operation* $[\diamond, \triangleright, \circ, \Delta]$ *is associative, and the triple* $\mathcal{M}_{[\diamond, \triangleright, \circ, \Delta]} = (\mathcal{P}(\Sigma^*), [\diamond, \triangleright, \circ, \Delta], \{\lambda\})$ *is a (noncommutative) monoid.*

Proof. First, observe that λ is the unit element. It remains to show that $[\diamond, \triangleright, \circ, \Delta]$ is an associative operation on $\mathcal{P}(\Sigma^*)$. Let x, y, z be in Σ^+ with $deg_\Delta(x) = i, deg_\Delta(y) = j$, and $deg_\Delta(z) = k$. Assume that x, y, z have canonical decompositions:

$$x = u_0 v_1 u_1 \cdots v_i u_i, \ y = u_0' v_1' u_1' \cdots v_j' u_j', \ z = u_0'' v_1'' u_1'' \cdots v_k'' u_k''.$$

Observe that:
$$(\{x\}[\diamond, \triangleright, \circ, \Delta]\{y\})[\diamond, \triangleright, \circ, \Delta]\{z\} =$$
$$= (\{u_0\} \diamond \{u_0'\} \diamond \{u_0''\}) \circ (\{v_1\} \triangleright \{v_1'\} \triangleright \{v_1''\}) \circ (\{u_1\} \diamond \{u_1'\} \diamond \{u_1''\}) \cdots$$
$$(\{v_s\} \triangleright \{v_s'\} \triangleright \{v_s''\}) \circ (\{u_s\} \diamond \{u_s'\} \diamond \{u_s''\}) \cdot$$
$$\cdot (\{v_{s+1}^{(1)} v_{s+1}^{(2)}\}(u_{s+1}^{(1)} u_{s+1}^{(2)}) \cdots$$
$$(\{v_r^{(1)}\} \triangleright \{v_r^{(2)}\}) \circ (\{u_r^{(1)}\} \diamond \{u_r^{(2)}\}) \circ \{v_{r+1}^{(2)}\} \triangleright \{u_{r+1}^{(2)}\} \cdots$$
$$\{v_t^{(2)}\} \circ \{u_t^{(2)}\} =$$
$$= \{x\}[\diamond, \triangleright, \circ, \Delta](\{y\}[\diamond, \triangleright, \circ, \Delta]\{z\})$$
where $s = min(i, j, k), r = min(\{i, j, k\} - \{s\}), t = max(i, j, k)$ and, moreover:

if $i \leq j \leq k$, then $v_p^{(1)} = v_p', u_p^{(1)} = u_p', v_q^{(2)} = v_q'', u_q^{(2)} = u_q''$, else

if $i \leq k \leq j$, then $v_p^{(1)} = v_p'', u_p^{(1)} = u_p'', v_q^{(2)} = v_q', u_q^{(2)} = u_q'$, else

if $j \leq i \leq k$, then $v_p^{(1)} = v_p, u_p^{(1)} = u_p, v_q^{(2)} = v_q'', u_q^{(2)} = u_q''$, else

if $j \leq k \leq i$, then $v_p^{(1)} = v_p'', u_p^{(1)} = u_p'', v_q^{(2)} = v_q, u_q^{(2)} = u_q$, else

if $k \leq i \leq j$, then $v_p^{(1)} = v_p, u_p^{(1)} = u_p, v_q^{(2)} = v_q', u_q^{(2)} = u_q'$, else

if $k \leq j \leq i$, then $v_p^{(1)} = v_p', u_p^{(1)} = u_p', v_q^{(2)} = v_q, u_q^{(2)} = u_q$,

where $p = s + 1, \ldots, r$ and $q = s + 1, \ldots, t$.

By the normal extension to arbitrary subsets A, B, C of Σ^*,

$$A \circ_\Delta B = \bigcup_{x \in A, y \in B} x \circ_\Delta y,$$

it follows that $[\diamond, \triangleright, \circ, \Delta]$ is an associative operation. □

Then, trivially

Lemma 11. *For any* $\Delta \subseteq \Sigma$, *the triple* $\mathcal{M}_{[\diamond,\triangleright,\circ,\Delta]} = (\mathcal{P}(\Sigma^*), [\diamond,\triangleright,\circ,\Delta], \{\lambda\})$ *is a (noncommutative) monoid, and the quintuple* $\mathcal{S}_{[\diamond,\triangleright,\circ,\Delta]} = (\mathcal{P}(\Sigma^*), \cup, \emptyset, [\diamond,\triangleright,\circ,\Delta], \{\lambda\})$ *is an ω-complete (noncommutative) semiring.*

Definition 12. *If* $A \subseteq \Sigma^*$ *then the Δ-mix operation closure of A is:*

$$A^{[\diamond,\triangleright,\circ,\Delta]} = \bigcup_{i \geq 0} A^{(i)[\diamond,\triangleright,\circ,\Delta]}, \text{ where}$$

$$A^{[\diamond,\triangleright,\circ,\Delta](0)} = \{\lambda\} \text{ and } A^{[\diamond,\triangleright,\circ,\Delta](i+1)} = A[\diamond,\triangleright,\circ,\Delta]A^{[\diamond,\triangleright,\circ,\Delta](i)}.$$

Comment. Note that $A^{[\diamond,\triangleright,\circ,\Delta]}$ is the submonoid generated by A, with respect to $[\diamond,\triangleright,\circ,\Delta]$, in the monoid $\mathcal{T}_{[\diamond,\triangleright,\circ,\Delta]}$ and in the semiring $\mathcal{S}_{[\diamond,\triangleright,\circ,\Delta]}$.

Notation. For any $k \geq 0$ let

$$H_k = \bigcup_{i \leq k} M_i.$$

Lemma 13. *For any* $\Delta \subseteq \Sigma$ *and for any* $k \geq 0$,

$$\mathcal{H}_{[\diamond,\triangleright,\circ,\Delta,k]} = (\mathcal{P}(H_k), \cup, \emptyset, [\diamond,\triangleright,\circ,\Delta,k], \{\lambda\})$$

is also a (noncommutative) semiring.

Proof. This fact follows from Lemma 11. □

Definition 14. *Let* $A \in \mathcal{S}_{[\diamond,\triangleright,\circ,\Delta]}$, $A \neq \emptyset$. *The Δ-degree of A is:*

$$deg_\Delta(A) = max(\{deg_\Delta(x) \mid x \in A\}),$$

if the maximum exists and $deg_\Delta(A) = \infty$ otherwise.
By definition, $deg_\Delta(\emptyset) = 0$.

Note that the following fact holds:

$$deg_\Delta(A \cup B) = max\{deg_\Delta(A), deg_\Delta(B)\}$$

3. Equations and Systems of Equations

Note that the semirings $\mathcal{S}_{[\diamond,\triangleright,\circ,\Delta,k]}$, $\mathcal{H}_{[\diamond,\triangleright,\circ,\Delta,k]}$ and $\mathcal{S}_{[\diamond,\triangleright,\circ,\Delta]}$ are ω-complete semirings, i.e. any increasing sequence $(A_n)_{n \geq 0}$ of elements has the supremum in the corresponding semiring. The supremum of an increasing sequence $(A_n)_{n \geq 0}$ will be denoted by $\bigvee A_n$. Moreover, any of the above semirings has a first element (infimum), the empty set $\emptyset$.

Lemma 15. *Let* $A, B \in \mathcal{S}_{[\diamond,\triangleright,\circ,\Delta]}$. *The equation* $X = A[\diamond,\triangleright,\circ,\Delta]X \cup B$ *has the (minimal) solution* $X_0 = A^{[\diamond,\triangleright,\circ,\Delta]}[\diamond,\triangleright,\circ,\Delta]B$.

Proof. Consider the function:

$$\varphi : \mathcal{P}(\Sigma^*) \rightarrow \mathcal{P}(\Sigma^*) \quad \varphi(C) = A[\diamond,\triangleright,\circ,\Delta]C \cup B.$$

It is easy to verify that φ is an ω-continuous function, i.e. φ commutes with the supremum of increasing sequences of elements from $S_{[\diamond,\triangleright,\circ,\Delta]}$. Therefore, by Kleene's fixed point theorem φ has a least fixed point, $X_0 = \bigvee \varphi^n(\emptyset)$, where φ^n means *identity* if $n = 0$ and $\varphi^{n+1} = \varphi \circ \varphi^n$ if $n > 0$. In our case, we obtain $X_0 = A^{[\diamond,\triangleright,\circ,\Delta]}[\diamond,\triangleright,\circ,\Delta]B$, which completes the proof. □

Corollary 16. *The result of the above lemma remains true if the semiring $S_{[\diamond,\triangleright,\circ,\Delta]}$ is replaced by any of the semirings $S_{[\diamond,\triangleright,\circ,\Delta,k]}$, $\mathcal{H}_{[\diamond,\triangleright,\circ,\Delta,k]}$, $k \geq 0$.*

Let $X = \{X_1, \ldots, X_n\}$ be a set of variables such that $X \cap \Sigma = \emptyset$.

Definition 17. A *monomial* over $S_{[\diamond,\triangleright,\circ,\Delta]}$ with variables in X is a finite string of the form :

$$A_1[\diamond,\triangleright,\circ,\Delta]A_2[\diamond,\triangleright,\circ,\Delta]\ldots[\diamond,\triangleright,\circ,\Delta]A_k$$

where $A_i \in X$ or $A_i \subseteq \Sigma^*$, $|A_i| < \infty, i = 1, \ldots, k$ (without loss of generality, $A_i = \{\alpha_i\}$ with $\alpha_i \in \Sigma^*$ suffices instead of $A_i \subseteq \Sigma^*$).

A *polynomial* $p(X)$ over $S_{[\diamond,\triangleright,\circ,\Delta]}$ is a finite union of monomials.

A *system of equations* over $S_{[\diamond,\triangleright,\circ,\Delta]}$ is a finite set of equations:

$$E = \{X_i = p_i(X) \mid i = 1, \ldots, n\},$$

where $p_i(X)$ are polynomials.

The *solution* of E is a n-tuple $(L_1, \ldots, L_n)$ of languages over Σ, with the property that $L_i = p_i(L_1, \ldots, L_n)$ and the n-tuple is minimal with this property, i.e. if $(L'_1, \ldots, L'_n)$ is another n-tuple that satisfies E, then $(L_1, \ldots, L_n) \leq (L'_1, \ldots, L'_n)$ (where the order is defined componentwise with respect to inclusion).

As in the case of Lemma 15, see also [8], it can be shown that:

Theorem 18. *Any system of equations over $S_{[\diamond,\triangleright,\circ,\Delta]}$ ($S_{[\diamond,\triangleright,\circ,\Delta,k]}$, $\mathcal{H}_{[\diamond,\triangleright,\circ,\Delta,k]}$, $k \geq 0$) has a unique solution.*

Comment. This solution is also the least fixed point, and it is the limit of an iteration starting with $(X_1, \cdots, X_n) = (\emptyset, \cdots, \emptyset)$.

4. Rational and Algebraic Languages with Mix Operation

In this section we will consider properties of languages defined in a way analogous to the classical rational and algebraic languages, but with the operation $[\diamond,\triangleright,\circ,\Delta]$. If necessary, we will also include the alphabet Σ into our notations.

Definition 19. A language L is *(mix operation) algebraic* over (Σ, Δ) if and only if L is the component of the solution of a system of equations over $S_{[\diamond,\triangleright,\circ,\Delta,\Sigma]}$.

Notation.

$$Alg([\diamond,\triangleright,\circ,\Delta,\Sigma]) = \{L \mid L \text{ is } [\diamond,\triangleright,\circ,\Delta]\text{-algebraic over } (\Sigma, \Delta)\},$$

$$Alg([\diamond,\triangleright,\circ,\Sigma]) = \bigcup_{\Delta \subseteq \Sigma} Alg([\diamond,\triangleright,\circ,\Delta,\Sigma]),$$

$$Alg([\diamond,\triangleright,\circ]) = \{L \mid \exists \Sigma, L \in Alg([\diamond,\triangleright,\circ,\Sigma])\}.$$

Definition 20. The family of *(mix operenation)* *rational* languages over the semiring $S_{[\diamond,\triangleright,\circ,\Delta,\Sigma]}$ is the smallest family of languages, denoted $\underline{Rat}([\diamond,\triangleright,\circ,\Delta,\Sigma])$, such that:

(i) if $F \subseteq \Sigma^*$ finite, then $F \in \underline{Rat}([\diamond,\triangleright,\circ,\Delta,\Sigma])$.
(ii) if $A, B \in \underline{Rat}([\diamond,\triangleright,\circ,\Delta,\Sigma])$, then $A \cup B \in \underline{Rat}([\diamond,\triangleright,\circ,\Delta,\Sigma])$.
(iii) if $A, B \in \underline{Rat}([\diamond,\triangleright,\circ,\Delta,\Sigma])$ then $A[\diamond,\triangleright,\circ,\Delta]B \in \underline{Rat}([\diamond,\triangleright,\circ,\Delta,\Sigma])$.
(iv) if $A \in \underline{Rat}([\diamond,\triangleright,\circ,\Delta,\Sigma])$, then $A^{[\diamond,\triangleright,\circ,\Delta]} \in \underline{Rat}([\diamond,\triangleright,\circ,\Delta,\Sigma])$.

Notation.

$$\underline{Rat}([\diamond,\triangleright,\circ,\Sigma]) = \bigcup_{\Delta \subseteq \Sigma} \underline{Rat}([\diamond,\triangleright,\circ,\Delta,\Sigma]),$$

$$\underline{Rat}([\diamond,\triangleright,\circ]) = \{L \mid \exists\, \Sigma, L \in \underline{Rat}([\diamond,\triangleright,\circ,\Sigma])\}.$$

Definition 21. A monomial is *rational* iff it is of the form $\alpha[\diamond,\triangleright,\circ,\Delta]Y$ or of the form α, where Y is a variable and $\alpha \in \Sigma^*$.

A polynomial is *rational* iff it is a finite union of rational monomials.

A system $E = \{X_i = p_i(X) \mid i = 1,\ldots,n\}$ is *rational* if each polynomial p_i is a rational polynomial, $i = 1,\ldots,n$.

The following theorem recovers a fundamental result:

Theorem 22. *The following assertions are equivalent:*

(i) $L \in \underline{Rat}([\diamond,\triangleright,\circ,\Delta,\Sigma])$.

(ii) L *is a component of the solution of a rational system of equations over the semiring* $S_{[\diamond,\triangleright,\circ,\Delta,\Sigma]}$.

Proof. This follows in a straightforward way from the general theory of semirings, see [8] or [1]. □

Comment. The same holds if in Definition 21 *rational* is defined by using $Y[\diamond,\triangleright,\circ,\Delta]\alpha$ instead of $\alpha[\diamond,\triangleright,\circ,\Delta]Y$.

Comment. From the above theorem, it follows that

$$\underline{Rat}([\diamond,\triangleright,\circ,\Delta,\Sigma]) \subseteq \underline{Alg}([\diamond,\triangleright,\circ,\Delta,\Sigma]),$$
$$\underline{Rat}([\diamond,\triangleright,\circ,\Sigma]) \subseteq \underline{Alg}([\diamond,\triangleright,\circ,\Sigma]),$$
$$\underline{Rat}([\diamond,\triangleright,\circ]) \subseteq \underline{Alg}([\diamond,\triangleright,\circ]).$$

The next theorem states some closure properties.

Theorem 23. *For any* Σ *and for any* Δ, $\Delta \subseteq \Sigma$, *the class* $\underline{Alg}([\diamond,\triangleright,\circ,\Delta,\Sigma])$ *is closed under union* $\cup$, *mix operation* $[\diamond,\triangleright,\circ,\Delta]$, *and* $[\diamond,\triangleright,\circ,\Delta]$-*closure* $^{[\diamond,\triangleright,\circ,\Delta]}$.

Proof. (1) Let $L_1, L_2 \in \underline{Alg}([\diamond,\triangleright,\circ,\Delta,\Sigma])$. There exist algebraic systems of equations E_1 and E_2 such that L_i corresponds to the X_i component of the solution. Without loss of generality, we can assume that E_1 and E_2 have disjoint sets of variables. Let X_3 be a new variable and define the following system of algebraic equations:

$$E_3 = E_1 \cup E_2 \cup \{X_3 = X_1 \cup X_2\}.$$

Obviously, the component of the solution of E_3 corresponding to X_3, is $L_3 = L_1 \cup L_2$.

(2) For proving closure under $[\diamond, \triangleright, \circ, \Delta]$ define E_3 as follows:

$$E_3 = E_1 \cup E_2 \cup \{X_3 = X_1[\diamond, \triangleright, \circ, \Delta]X_2\}.$$

Obviously again, the component of the solution of E_3 corresponding to X_3, is the set $L_3 = L_1[\diamond, \triangleright, \circ, \Delta]L_2$.

(3) Finally, for $[\diamond, \triangleright, \circ, \Delta]$-closure define:

$$E_3 = E_1 \cup \{X_3 = X_1[\diamond, \triangleright, \circ, \Delta]X_3 \cup \{\lambda\}\}.$$

The component of the solution of E_3 corresponding to the variable X_3, is the set $L_3 = L_1^{[\diamond, \triangleright, \circ, \Delta]}$. □

5. Rational and Algebraic Languages with Special Mix Operation

In the remaining part of this paper we will assume the following additional conditions on the underlying operations $\diamond$, $\triangleright$, and $\circ$. The first one is on the lengths.

$$\forall z \in \{x\} \bullet \{y\} : |z| = |x| + |y| .$$

Then all sets $\{x\} \bullet \{y\}$ for $\bullet \in \{\diamond, \triangleright, \circ\}$ are finite, as well as the set $\{x\}[\diamond, \triangleright, \circ, \Delta]\{y\}$.

The second one concerns the Parikh vectors. It implies the first condition.

$$\forall z \in \{x\} \bullet \{y\} : \pi(z) = \pi(x) + \pi(y) .$$

The classical catenation $\cdot$ and shuffle $\sqcup\!\sqcup$ are fulfilling these conditions.

Assuming the first condition the following pumping lemmata can be shown as in the classical case (see also [5]):

Lemma 24. Let $L \in Rat([\diamond, \triangleright, \circ])$ with $L \subseteq \Sigma^*$. Then there exist $\Delta \subseteq \Sigma$ and $n(L) > 0$ such that, for any $w \in L$ with $|w| \geq n(L)$, there exist $x_1, x_2, x_3 \in \Sigma^*$ such that:

(i) $w \in \{x_1\}[\diamond, \triangleright, \circ, \Delta]\{x_2\}[\diamond, \triangleright, \circ, \Delta]\{x_3\}$.

(ii) $0 < |x_2| \leq n(L)$.

(iii) $\{x_1\}[\diamond, \triangleright, \circ, \Delta]\{x_2\}^{[\diamond, \triangleright, \circ, \Delta]}[\diamond, \triangleright, \circ, \Delta]\{x_3\} \subseteq L$.

Lemma 25. Let $L \in Alg([\diamond, \triangleright, \circ])$ with $L \subseteq \Sigma^*$. Then there exist $\Delta \subseteq \Sigma$ and $n(L) > 0$ such that, for any $w \in L$ with $|w| \geq n(L)$, there exist $x_1, x_2, x_3, x_3, x_5 \in \Sigma^*$ such that:

(i) $w \in \{x_1\}[\diamond, \triangleright, \circ, \Delta]\{x_2\}[\diamond, \triangleright, \circ, \Delta]\{x_3\}[\diamond, \triangleright, \circ, \Delta]\{x_4\}[\diamond, \triangleright, \circ, \Delta]\{x_2\}$.

(ii) $|x_2 x_3 x_4| \leq n(L)$.

(iii) $0 < |x_2 x_4|$

(iv) $\forall k \geq 0 :$

$\{x_1\}[\diamond, \triangleright, \circ, \Delta]\{x_2\}^{[\diamond, \triangleright, \circ, \Delta](k)}[\diamond, \triangleright, \circ, \Delta]\{x_3\}[\diamond, \triangleright, \circ, \Delta]\{x_4\}^{[\diamond, \triangleright, \circ, \Delta](k)}[\diamond, \triangleright, \circ, \Delta]\{x_5\} \subseteq L$.

438

As in the classical case, it is also possible to prove a result on the set of Parikh vectors of $L \in Alg([\diamond, \triangleright, \circ])$.

Lemma 26. *Let $L \in Alg([\diamond, \triangleright, \circ])$. Then the set $\pi(L)$ of Parikh vectors of L is a semilinear set.*

Proof. This can be shown as in the classical case. Note that $x[\diamond, \triangleright, \circ, \Delta]y$ and xy yield the same Parikh vectors. □

From this follows immediately

Corollary 27. *Let $L \in Alg([\diamond, \triangleright, \circ])$. Then the set of lengths $\nu(L) = \{|w| \mid w \in L\}$ is a semilinear set.*

Lemma 28. $Alg([\diamond, \triangleright, \circ]) \subset CS$.

Proof. For any $L \in Alg([\diamond, \triangleright, \circ])$, i.e. L component of the minimal solution of an algebraic system of equations, it is easy to construct a LBA, verifying for any input w if $w \in L$. Here we must point out that the system can be considered without coefficients λ and thus, in Kleene's iterations the length of words is strictly increasing. Therefore, $Alg([\diamond, \triangleright, \circ]) \subseteq CS$.

Consider the language:

$$L = \{a^n b^{n^2} \mid n > 0\}.$$

Obviously, $L \in CS$, but note that $\nu(L) = \{|w| \mid w \in L\}$ is not a semilinear set. Thus, by Corollary 27, $L \notin Alg([\diamond, \triangleright, \circ])$, hence the inclusion is strict. □

Defining the language families $Alg(\diamond)$, $Rat(\diamond)$, $Alg(\triangleright)$, $Rat(\triangleright)$ in a similar way, and using Remark 9, the relations between these language families can be stated in the following diagram where all relations, except for that stated in Lemma 28, are also valid in the general case.

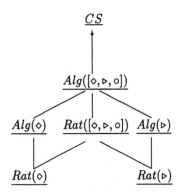

Finally, we show a decidability properties of $Rat([\diamond, \triangleright, \circ])$ which holds only for special mix operation with the first condition.

Theorem 29. *The membership problem, the emptiness problem, and the infinity problem of $Rat([\diamond, \triangleright, \circ])$ are decidable.*

Proof. This can be seen immediately from the finite representation of $L \in Rat([\diamond, \triangleright, \circ])$ by $\cup, [\diamond, \triangleright, \circ, \Delta]$, and $^{[\diamond, \triangleright, \circ, \Delta]}$. □

Conclusion. In [9] the case [·, ⊔⊔, ·] of [◇, ▷, ○] was considered whereas in [5], [6], [7] the case of [·, ·, ·]. In another paper we will investigate the remaining cases with · and ⊔⊔.

References

1. J. S. Golan: The Theory of Semirings with Application in Mathematics and Theoretical Computer Science. Longman Scientific and Technical, 1992.

2. J. S. Golan, A. Mateescu, D. Vaida: Semirings and Parallel Composition of Processes. Journ. of Automata, Languages and Combinatorics, Vol.1 No. 3 199-217, 1996.

3. H. Jürgensen: Syntactic Monoids of Codes. Report 327, Dept.Comp.Sci., The University of Western Ontario, 1992.

4. M. Kudlek: Generalized Iteration Lemmata. PU.M.A., Vol. 6 No. 2, 211-216, 1995.

5. M. Kudlek, A. Mateescu: Distributed Catenation and Chomsky Hierarchy. LNCS 965, Springer, 313-322, 1995.

6. M. Kudlek, A. Mateescu: Rational and Algebraic Languages with Distributed Catenation. 'Developments in Language Theory II', *At the Crossroads of Mathematics, Computer Science and Biology*, ed. J. Dassow, G. Rozenberg, Arto Salomaa, World Scientific, 129-138, 1996.

7. M. Kudlek, A. Mateescu: On Distributed Catenation. Report Fac. Comp. Sci., Univ. Hamburg, FBI-Bericht 182/95, 1995.

8. W. Kuich, A. Salomaa: Semirings, Automata, Languages. EATCS Monographs on Theoretical Computer Science, Springer, 1986.

9. A. Mateescu: On (Left) Partial Shuffle. Proceedings of 'Results and Trends in Theoretical Computer Science', LNCS 812, Springer, 264-278, 1994.

10. C. Reutenauer: Free Lie Algebras. Clarendon Press, 1993.

11. J. Sakarovitch, I. Simon: Subwords, in Combinatorics on Words. M. Lothaire, (ed.), Addison-Wesley, 1983.

12. A. Salomaa; Formal Languages. Academic Press, 1973.

On the Complexity of Iterated Insertions

Markus HOLZER, Klaus-Jörn LANGE

Wilhelm-Schickard-Institut für Informatik
Universität Tübingen
Sand 13, D-72076 Tübingen, Germany
E-mail: {holzer,lange}@informatik.uni-tuebingen.de

Abstract. We investigate complexities of insertion operations on formal languages relatively to complexity classes. In this way, we introduce operations closely related to $LOG(CFL)$ and NP. Our results relativize and give new characterizations of the ways to relativize nondeterministic space.

1. Introduction

There are many close connections between the theory of formal languages and structural complexity theory [14], [17]. While it is obvious to express the complexity of classes of formal languages in terms of completeness results, it is another question to classify the complexity of operations on formal languages [4], [11], [13]. Our approach is to determine relatively to a base complexity class A. In this way, we consider two constructions: on the one hand we analyze the complexity of a single application of an operator op to A. This leads to the class $APPL(A, op)$ of all languages reducible to $op(L)$ for some $L \in A$. The drawback of this class is that it is not necessarily closed under op, even if op is idempotent. Therefore, we consider also the class $HULL(A, op)$ which is the smallest class containing A and closed under op as well as downward under logspace many-one reducibility.

In this notation, for example the relation between the Kleene star $(STAR)$, nonerasing homomorphism (HOM) and the complexity classes $NSpace(\log n)$, NP, and $1DSpace(\log n)$ (the class of languages recognizable by logarithmically space bounded deterministic Turing machines with *one-way* input tape) are:

$$
\begin{aligned}
NSpace(\log n) &= APPL(1DSpace(\log n), STAR) \\
&= HULL(1DSpace(\log n), STAR),
\end{aligned}
$$

whereas for nonerasing homomorphisms we find

$$
\begin{aligned}
NSpace(\log n) &= APPL(1DSpace(\log n), HOM) \quad \text{and} \\
NP &= HULL(1DSpace(\log n), HOM).
\end{aligned}
$$

There are many more relations like this, nearly all pertaining to the classes $NSpace(\log n)$ and NP. We remark that $LOG(CFL)$, the complexity class generated by the context-free languages, has not been characterized in this way.

One of the main results of this paper will be the construction of an operation on formal languages filling this gap. The key observation to do this will be to consider operations which are iterations of simpler operations. As an example, Kleene's star operation may be regarded as the iterated application of the operation of concatenation. We will now replace concatenation by the more complex operation of *(monadic) insertion* of languages. A similar approach was made in [6], [7], [10], [15] in terms of iterated substitution. The difference is that we here are interested in complexity theoretical aspects.

Since insertion is not associative there are several possibilities to iterate the operation of insertion. One is to do it *outside-in (OI)*, i.e., to insert atomic words into composed ones, while *inside-out (IO)* iteration of insertion inserts composed words into atomic ones. It will turn out that outside-in iterated insertion characterizes NP, while inside out iterated insertion characterizes $NSpace(\log n)$. The anticipated operation characterizing $LOG(CFL)$ is now obtained by iterating the operation of *binary insertion*. Again the outside-in iteration of binary insertion characterizes NP, while the inside-out iteration now characterizes $LOG(CFL)$. In particular we obtain the following equations:

1. $NSpace(\log n) = APPL(1DSpace(\log n), IO_{MON})$
   $= HULL(NSpace(\log n), IO_{MON})$,

2. $LOG(CFL) = APPL(1DSpace(\log n), IO_{BIN}) = HULL(LOG(CFL), IO_{BIN})$,

3. $LOG(CFL) = APPL(1DSpace(\log n), OI)$,

4. $NP = APPL(DSpace(\log n), OI) = HULL(NP, OI)$, and

5. $NP = HULL(1DSpace(\log n), OI)$.

In a second part we show that all these relations relativize. It is interesting to see how the different ways to iterate insertions characterize the different ways to equip space bounded complexity classes with oracles: the two most important possibilities to relativize nondeterministic space are that of Ladner and Lynch [12] and that of Ruzzo, Simon, and Tompa [18]. These two notions carry over in a natural way to time and space bounded auxiliary pushdown automata. It turns out that the outside-in iteration of insertion corresponds to LL-relativizations while inside-out iterations pertain to RST-relativizations.

2. Preliminaries

We assume the reader to be familiar with the basics of complexity theory as contained in [1], [9], [20]. In particular, we will deal with the well-known sequence of complexity classes:

$$1DSpace(\log n) \subseteq DSpace(\log n) \subseteq NSpace(\log n) \subseteq P \subseteq NP.$$

Here $1DSpace(\log n)$, $DSpace(\log n)$, $NSpace(\log n)$, P, and NP, respectively, denote the set of all problems recognizable in one-way logarithmic space, logarithmic space, nondeterministic logarithmic space, polynomial time, and nondeterministic polynomial time, respectively.

Completeness and hardness results are always meant with respect to deterministic logspace many-one reducibilities, unless otherwise stated. $L \leq_m^{\log} M$ is used to denote the fact that L is reducible to M. For a class A let $LOG(A) := \{ L \mid \exists_{M \in A} : L \leq_m^{\log} M \}$. In addition, we use λ to denote the empty word, $|w|$ for the length of a word w, and w^R for the mirror image of w.

In the following, we will often make use of the concept of auxiliary pushdown automaton [2], [9]. Let $NAuxPDA\text{-}TimeSpace(t(n), s(n))$ denote the set of all problems accepted by $O(t(n))$ time- and $O(s(n))$ space-bounded nondeterministic pushdown automata. The importance of this automaton model is demonstrated by its ability to represent the classes

$$P = NauxPDA\text{-}TimeSpace(2^{O(n)}, \log n) \quad [2] \text{ and}$$
$$LOG(CFL) = NauxPDA\text{-}TimeSpace(n^{O(1)}, \log n) \quad [19].$$

Throughout this paper, we will consider complexities of operations on formal languages. In this context, we introduce a "measure" for the complexity of an operation relative to a complexity class.

Definition 1. Let op be an operation on formal languages and A some class, then $op(A) := \{ op(L) \mid L \in A \}$.

We define $APPL(A, op)$ to be the logspace many-one closure of $op(A)$, i.e., $APPL(A, op)$ is the set $LOG(op(A))$. For iterating the APPL-operation on a class A of languages we define $APPL^0(A, op) := A$ and $APPL^{i+1}(A, op) := APPL(APPL^i(A, op), op)$.

Finally, let $HULL(A, op)$ be the smallest complexity class closed under op that contains A. In other words $HULL(A, op) := \bigcup_{i \geq 0} APPL^i(A, op)$.

Obviously $APPL(A, op) \subseteq HULL(A, op)$ and sometimes we refer to A in $APPL(A, op)$ or $HULL(A, op)$ as the *base class*.

3. Iterated Insertions

We show that several nondeterministic complexity classes can be characterized in terms of formal language theoretical operations. One of the main results of this section will be the characterization of $LOG(CFL)$. The formal language operations which will be studied in this section are natural generalizations of the concatenation operation, the so called insertion operations. Thus we define:

Definition 2. Let L_1 and L_2 be arbitrary languages. The *monadic insertion* of L_1 into L_2 is defined as $L_1 \rightarrow L_2 := \{ w_1 v w_2 \mid v \in L_1 \text{ and } w_1 w_2 \in L_2 \}$.

In contrast to operations like concatenation or shuffle, the above operation is not associative. Hence, there are several ways to iterate it. The first possibility is to insert composed words into "atomic words," i.e., to make the iteration in an *inside-out* manner. Thus, for monadic insertion we define

Inside-Out monadic insertion

1. Let $IO_{MON}(L, 0) := \{\lambda\}$ and $IO_{MON}(L, (i+1)) := IO_{MON}(L, i) \rightarrow L$.
2. Finally set $IO_{MON}(L) := \bigcup_{i \geq 0} IO_{MON}(L, i)$.

The other possibility to iterate the insertion process is in a so called *outside-in* manner, i.e., to insert "atomic words" into composed ones. Thus, for the monadic insertion we define:

Outside-in monadic insertion

1. Set $OI_{MON}(L, 0) := \{\lambda\}$ and $OI_{MON}(L, (i+1)) := L \rightarrow OI_{MON}(L, i)$.
2. Finally set $OI_{MON}(L) := \bigcup_{i \geq 0} OI_{MON}(L, i)$.

Example 1. Let F be the finite set $\{(,)\}$. Then $IO_{MON}F$ is a linear language generated by the grammar $G = (\{S\}, \{(,)\}, P, S)$ with the productions $P = \{S \to \lambda, S \to (S), S \to S(), S \to ()S, S \to ()\}$. On the other hand one readily verifies that $OI_{MON}(F)$ equals to the Dyck set D_1.

In next subsections, we will see that the complexity of these two iterated monadic insertions lead not to the class $LOG(CFL)$, but again to $NSpace(\log n)$ and NP, only. Thus, in order to find a complete operation for $LOG(CFL)$ we have to define a more "complicated" version of insertion.

Definition 3. Let L_1, L_2, and L_3 be arbitrary languages. The *binary insertion* of L_1 and L_2 into L_3 is defined as

$$(L_1, L_2) \to L_3 := \{ w_1 u w_2 v w_3 \mid u \in L_1, v \in L_2, \text{ and } w_1 w_2 w_3 \in L_3 \}.$$

Again, we have two possibilities to iterate the insertion process:

Inside-Out binary insertion

1. Set $IO_{BIN}(L, 0) := \{\lambda\}$, $IO_{BIN}(L, 1) := L$, and
   $IO_{BIN}(L, (i+1)) := \bigcup_{0 \le j \le i}(IO_{BIN}(L, j), IO_{BIN}(L, (i-j))) \to L$.
2. $IO_{BIN}(L) := \bigcup_{i \ge 0} IO_{BIN}(L, i)$.

Outside-In binary insertion

1. Let $OI_{BIN}(L, 0) := \{\lambda\}$, $IO_{BIN}(L, 1) := L$, and
   $OI_{BIN}(L, (i+1)) :=$
   $$\bigcup_{0 \le j \le 1}(OI_{BIN}(L, j), OI_{BIN}(L, (1-j))) \to OI_{BIN}(L, i).$$
2. $OI_{BIN}(L) := \bigcup_{i \ge 0} OI_{BIN}(L, i)$.

For the outside-in binary insertion $OI_{BIN}(L)$ one shows that this insertion process coincides with the outside-in monadic one. Thus, we have:

Lemma 1. $OI_{MON}(L) = OI_{BIN}(L)$ *for arbitrary language L.*

Because of this lemma, we deal only with *one* outside-in operation in the sequel, and define $OI(L) := OI_{MON}(L)$ for an arbitrary language L. Let us give a further example.

Example 2. Let F be the set of the previous example. By Lemma 1 and the definition of the OI-operation we have $OI(F) = D_1$ and an easy induction on the iteration process shows that $IO_{BIN}(F) = D_1$, too.

3.1. Closure under Iterated Insertion

In this subsection, we show that several complexity classes are closed under iterated insertion. First, we consider inside-out iterated monadic and binary insertion. In both cases, the main idea for an algorithm to check $IO_{MON}(L)$ or $IO_{BIN}(L)$ is the same. The machine that checks $IO_{MON}(L)$ membership works as follows: on input w it guesses a decomposition $w = w_1 u w_2$, checks whether $w_1 w_2 \in L$, and recursively verifies that v belongs to $IO_{MON}(L)$. Then following proposition is easy to see:

Proposition 1. *If $s(n) \geq \log n$, then $IO_{MON}(NSpace(s(n))) \subseteq NSpace(s(n))$.*

In case of binary inside-out iterated insertion we do similarly, but now using an auxiliary pushdown automaton. On input w the machine guesses a decomposition $w_1 u w_2 v w_3$, checks whether $w_1 w_2 w_3 \in L$, and recursively verifies whether both words u and v belong to $IO_{BIN}(L)$. To do so the machine stores the begin and end of the subwords u and v on its pushdown. If the nondeterministic auxiliary pushdown automaton that accepts L is $O(t(n))$-time and $O(s(n))$ space bounded, then the machine that checks $IO_{BIN}(L)$ membership is $O(n \cdot t(n))$-time and $O(s(n))$ space bounded.

Theorem 1. *Let $s(n) \geq \log n$ and $t(n) \geq n^{O(1)}$. If L is a member of the class $NauxPDA\text{-}TimeSpace(t(n), s(n))$, then the language $IO_{BIN}(L)$ belongs to $NauxPDA\text{-}TimeSpace(n \cdot t(n), s(n))$.*

Observe that with a little bit more advanced algorithm we can even check $OI(L)$ membership in $NauxPDA\text{-}TimeSpace(2^{O(s(n))}, s(n))$ if $L \in 1DSpace(s(n))$. The only modification in the construction is, that the automaton which accepts $OI_{MON}(L)$, guesses a decomposition $u_0 w_1 u_1 w_2 u_2 \ldots u_{t-1} w_t u_{t+1}$ while the input head scans the input from left to right, and checks by simulating the one-way nondeterministic $O(s(n))$ space bounded Turing machine whether $w_1 w_2 \ldots w_t$ belongs to L. Then the machine recursively verifies—as described above—whether the words u_i, for $0 \leq i \leq t+1$, belong to $OI_{MON}(L)$.

As an immediate consequence of the characterization of $LOG(CFL)$ and P in terms of nondeterministic auxiliary pushdown automata [2], [19] we get the closure of both classes under inside-out iterated binary insertion.

Corollary 1. $IO_{BIN}(LOG(CFL)) \subseteq LOG(CFL)$ *and* $IO_{BIN}(P) \subseteq P$.

At this point we want to mention two things: (1) The construction presented to check IO_{BIN}-membership can be generalized to IO-membership for insertions where the possible insertion points into a word is constantly bounded. Hence, e.g., $LOG(CFL)$ is also closed under *iterated inside-out ternary insertion*. (2) Moreover, we want to point out that $DSpace(\log^2 n)$ is closed under both types of inside-out iterated insertion.

Finally, we mention the closure of NP under OI-operation. This proof is straightforward and is left to the reader.

Proposition 2. $OI(NP) \subseteq NP$.

3.2. Hardness of Iterated Insertion

For technical reasons we introduce a notation, the so-called insertion tree, which is helpful in analyzing inside-out iterated monadic and binary insertion.

Definition 4. An *insertion tree over a terminal alphabet T* is a construct $I = (V, h, x_0, label, T)$, where

1. (V, h, x_0) is a tree rooted in $x_0 \in V$, i.e., $h : V \to V$ points every node to its father, $h(x_0) = x_0$ and for all $x \in V$ there exists an $n \geq 0$ such that $h^n(x) = x_0$.

2. $label : V \to T^*(VT^*)^*$ is the labelling function.

For an insertion tree I we define the functions

1. $word : V \to T^*$, by $word(x) := w_0 w_1 \ldots w_t$, if $label(x) = w_0 x_1 w_1 \ldots w_{t-1} x_t w_t$,

2. $yield : V \to T*$ inductively by $yield(x) = w_0 yield(x_1) w_1 \ldots w_{t-1} yield(x_t) w_t$, if $label(x) = w_0 x_1 w_1 \ldots w_{t-1} x_t w_t$.

An insertion tree I is called (1) *monadic* if the mapping *label* only takes images in $T^* \cup T^* V T^*$ and (2) *binary* if it only takes images in $T^* \cup T^* V T^* V T^*$.

Obviously, for any language we have:

Lemma 2. *Let $L \subseteq T^*$ and $w \in T^*$. The word w belongs to $IO_{MON}(L)$ ($IO_{BIN}(L)$, $OI(L)$, respectively) if and only if there exists a monadic (binary, arbitrary, respectively) insertion tree $I = (V, h, x_0, label$ such that $yield(x_0) = w$ and for all $x \in V$ we have $word(x) \in L \cup \{\lambda\}$.*

3.2.1. Hardness of the IO_{MON}-Operation

The following theorem shows close relation of IO_{MON} and $NSpace(\log n)$. We state it without proof, since it is very similar to that on showing the analogous results of the Kleene star operation [4], [16].

Theorem 2. *There is a language L_M in $1DSpace(\log n)$ such that $IO_{MON}(L_M)$ is $NSpace(\log n)$-complete.*

Essentially the strings in L_M are of the form $b^n \$(a^* \$ b^* \$)^* \# (\$ a^* \$ b^*)^* \$ a^n$. The Kleene closure of this language is $NSpace(\log n)$-complete. But the power of the IO_{MON}-operation makes it necessary to extend the construction in order to avoid "wrong" insertion. The details are similar to, although less extensive than, those provided in Theorem 3. Using Proposition 1 we get:

Corollary 2. $NSpace(\log n) = APPL(1DSpace(\log n), IO_{MON})$
$= HULL(NSpace(\log n), IO_{MON})$.

This implies the following equalities: $APPL(1DSpace(\log n), IO_{MON}) = APPL(DSpace(\log n), IO_{MON}) = HULL(1DSpace(\log n), IO_{MON})$. Later we will see that the OI-operation is much more sensitive with respect to this difference.

3.2.2. Hardness of the IO_{BIN}-Operation

Before we come to one of the main results of this paper establishing a close link between iterated binary insertion and polynomially time bounded auxiliary pushdown automata we need the following lemma.

Lemma 3. *There exists a $LOG(CFL)$-complete context-free language which is generated by a context-free grammar $G = (N, T, P, S)$, with nonterminals N, terminals T, axiom S, and production set $P \subseteq N \times (T \cup TN^2)$.*

Observe, that context-free grammars which satisfy $P \subseteq N \times (T \cup TN^2)$ can only generate words of odd length. Hence such a normal-form for context-free grammars does not exist in general.

Proof. Without loss of generality one can assume that the $LOG(CFL)$-complete context-free language L is generated by a grammar $G = (N, T, P, S)$ being in 2-standard Greibach normal-form, i.e.,

$$P \subseteq N \times ((T \cup T(N \setminus \{S\})) \cup T(N \setminus \{S\})^2).$$

We will use new symbols $\#$, X with subscripts which are not contained in N and T. We first modify the production set P in the following way:

$$P_1 := \{A \to aa \mid A \to a \in P\} \cup \{A \to aaB \mid A \to aB \in P\} \cup$$
$$\{A \to aaBC \mid A \to aBC \in P\}.$$

Observe that the language $G_1 = (N, T, P_1, S)$ is $LOG(CFL)$-complete, too. Then let us construct a grammar G_2 with $L(G_2) = L(G_1)\{\#\}$. Every word that belongs to $L(G_1)\{\#\}$ has odd length. Set

$$P_2 := \{X_a \to a \mid a \in T\} \cup$$
$$\{X_{Ab} \to aX_aX_b, X_{bA} \to bX_aX_a, X_{bDA} \to bX_{Da}X_a \mid A \to aa \in P_1\} \cup$$
$$\{X_{Ab} \to aX_aX_{Bb}, X_{bA} \to bX_aX_{aB}, X_{bDA} \to bX_{Da}X_{aB} \mid$$
$$A \to aaB \in P_1\} \cup$$
$$\{X_{Ab} \to aX_{aB}X_{Cb}, X_{bA} \to bX_aX_{aBC}, X_{bDA} \to bX_{Da}X_{aBC} \mid$$
$$A \to aaBC \in P_1\}$$

and let

$$G_2 = (N \cup \{X_{S\#}\} \cup \{X_a, X_{aB}, X_{aBC} \mid a \in T \text{ and } B, C \in N\}, T \cup \{\#\}, P_2, X_{S\#}).$$

Then P_2 has the expected normal-form, and obviously $L(G_2)$ is $LOG(CFL)$-complete. $\quad\square$

Theorem 3. *There is a set L_B in $1DSpace(\log n)$ such that both $OI_{MON}(L_B)$ and $IO_{BIN}(L_B)$ are $LOG(CFL)$-complete.*

Proof. We start with a $LOG(CFL)$-complete language L_1 which is generated by a context-free grammar $G = (N, T, P, S)$ satisfying the requirement of the above lemma.

Observe that we do not require L_1 to be a hardest language in the sense of Greibach [6], but only to be $LOG(CFL)$-complete. Our construction closely follows that one of Greibach although we have to be more careful due to the nonsequential nature of iterated insertion (compared to inverse homomorphism).

In the following we will need new symbols \$, $\#$, 0, 2, and F contained in neither N nor T. In addition, let $\bar{N} := \{\bar{A} \mid A \in N \cup \{F\}\}$ be a disjoint copy of $N \cup \{F\}$.

For an arbitrary $a \in T$ consider all productions $p_1, \ldots, p_k$ such that $p_i \in N \times (a \cup aN^2)$ for each $1 \le i \le k$. For each $i \ge 0$ and each $1 \le j \le k$ define

$$f_i^a(j) := \begin{cases} \bar{A}2CB\$^i & \text{if } p_j \text{ equals } A \to aBC^1 \\ \bar{A}0\$^i & \text{if } p_j \text{ equals } A \to a \end{cases}$$

and

$$f_i'^a(j) := \begin{cases} \lambda & \text{if } p_j \text{ equals } A \to aBC \\ \bar{A}2FF\$^i & \text{if } p_j \text{ equals } A \to a. \end{cases}$$

Further on we set

$$g_i^a := \$^i f_i^a(1) f_i^a(2) \ldots f_i^a(k) \quad \text{and} \quad g_i'^a := \$^i f_i'^a(1) f_i'^a(2) \ldots f_i'^a(k).$$

---

[1] Observe the inversion of B and C.

For a word $w = a_1 \ldots a_n \in T^*$ with $a_i \in T$ we define

$$h(a_1 \ldots a_n) := S\#g_1^{a_1}\#g_2^{a_2}\#\ldots\#g_{n-1}^{a_{n-1}}\#g_n'^{a_n}\#\$^{n+1}\bar{F}0\$^{n+1}\#\$^{n+2}\bar{F}0.$$

Obviously, the mapping is computable in deterministic logarithmic space.

Now we define the language L_B. First let

$$R := \{\,\bar{A}0 \mid A \in N \cup \{F\}\,\} \cup \{\,\bar{A}2BC \mid A \in N \text{ and } B,C \in N \cup \{F\}\,\}$$

and for $i \geq 0$ set $R_i := \$^i(R\$^i)^*$. Finally, define

$$L_B := \{\,A\alpha\#\beta\bar{A}c \mid \exists i \geq 1 : \alpha \in R_{i-1}, \beta \in R_i; A \in N \cup \{F\}; c \in \{0,2\}\,\}.$$

Obviously, L_B is a member of $1DSpace(\log n)$.

The idea underlying this construction is to translate a derivation tree of G into an insertion tree as follows: if A is a nonterminal labelling the root of a subderivation tree $\mathcal{D}$ and B and C are the root-labels of the left and right subtrees $\mathcal{D}_L$ and $\mathcal{D}_R$, there will be three elements of L_B, namely $w_A := A\alpha\#\beta\bar{A}2$, $w_B := B\alpha'\#\beta'\bar{B}c'$, and $w_C := C\alpha''\#\beta''\bar{C}c''$. The corresponding part of the insertion tree will consist of w_A on top, w_C inserted at the very right end of w_A, and w_C inserted after the first symbol of w_C, which is the symbol C. That is left brothers become the left sons of the right brothers. This is illustrated in Figure 1.

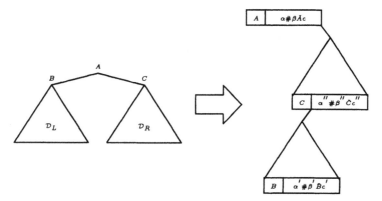

Figure 1. The conversion of a derivation tree into an insertion tree

Now we have to prove $w \in L_1$ if and only if $h(w) \in OI(L_B)$ if and only if $h(w) \in IO_{BIN}(L_B)$. It is easy to show that $w \in L_1$ implies $h(w) \in IO_{BIN}(L_B)$ and hence $h(w) \in OI(L_B)$. The converse makes use of the many additional features which we added to Greibach's construction [6].

Let us assume $h(w) \in OI(L_B)$. Then there exists an insertion tree $I = (V, h, x_0, label)$ with $yield(x_0) = h(w)$ and $word(x) \in L_B$ for all $x \in V$. We proceed in several stages:

Step 1 Let $x \in V$ and $label(x) = w_0x_1w_1 \ldots x_tw_t$. Due to the increasing length of the $\$^i$-blocks it is easy to see that for a typical element $A\alpha\#\beta\bar{A}c \in L_B$ there are only three places to perform insertion: before A, behind A, or after the c. Otherwise the resulting word could no longer be a subword of $h(w)$.

Step 2 We can rearrange I in the following way: First, I no longer has nodes inserting the empty word, and second whenever two nodes in I are directly neighboured, i.e., the concatenation of the yields is a subword of $h(w)$, the right one is inserted as a son at the very right end of the left one. The way to rearrange I is indicated in the Figures 2 and 3.

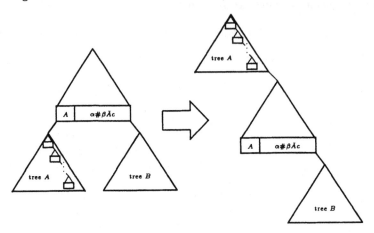

Figure 2. First rearrangement of the insertion tree I.

Step 3 After the rearrangement, each node x of I is either a leaf or has at most two sons, one inserted at the right end of $word(x)$ and one after the first symbol of $word(x)$. Let x be in V and $word(x) = A\alpha\#\beta\bar{A}c \in L_0$. Then we set $nonterminal(x) := A$ and $index(x) := i$ if $\beta \in R_i$ (and $\alpha \in R_{i-1}$). It is not hard to work out that $nonterminal(x_0) = S$.

Step 4 The structure of the mapping h enforces the following claim:

Claim. If $x \in V$ with $word(x) = A\alpha\#\beta\bar{A}c$ possesses a right son y, inserted after the symbol c, then (1) $c = 2$ and (2) y possesses a left son z inserted after the first symbol of $word(y)$.

Proof. If $word(y) = C\alpha''\#\beta''\bar{C}c''$, then $\bar{A}cC$ must be a subword of $h(w)$, since otherwise nothing is inserted left of C. Hence c cannot be 0, but must be 2. But then we need a second nonterminal following the symbol 2. This can be only provided by the insertion of a left son z after symbol c. $\square$

Step 5 Inductively we define the mapping $derive : V \to T^*$ by $derive(x) := a_i$, if x does not possess a right son in I. Here $i := index(x)$. If $i \geq n + 1$, we set $a_i := \lambda$. If x possesses a right son y we know by the previous step that y in turn possesses a left son z. In this case we define $derive(x) := a_i derive(z) derive(y)$. The reader may verify that $derive(x_0) = w$!

Step 6 For each $x \in V$ with $index(x) \leq n$ we have $A \Rightarrow_G^* derive(x)$. In particular $S = nonterminal(x_0) \Rightarrow_G^* w$, i.e., $w \in L_1$.

Proof. If x has no right son, then $word(x) = Aa\#\beta\bar{A}0$ for some $\alpha \in R_{i-1}$, $\beta \in R_i$, and $i := index(x)$. Hence, $\$^i\bar{A}0$ is a subword of $h(w)$ and $g_i^{a_i}$. This implies that $A \to a_i$ is in P. Hence $A \Rightarrow_G^1 a_1 = derive(x)$.

If x possesses a right son y with $nonterminal(y) = C$, then by Step 4 the node y has a left son z with $nonterminal(z) = B$. Then we have that $\$^i\bar{A}2CB$ is a subword of $h(w)$ and hence of $g_i^{a_i}$. This implies $A \to a_iBC$ is in P. Hence, by induction $A \Rightarrow_G^1 a_iBC \Rightarrow_G^* a_i derive(z) derive(y) = derive(x)$. $\qquad\square$

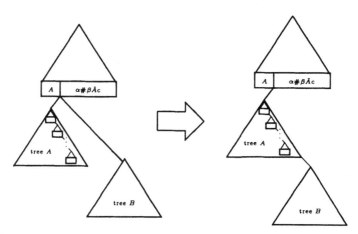

Figure 3. Second rearrangement of the insertion tree I.

Using Corollary 1 we get:

Corollary 3.

1. $LOG(CFL) = APPL(1DSpace(\log n), IO_{BIN})$
   $\qquad\qquad = HULL(LOG(CFL), IO_{BIN}).$

2. $LOG(CFL) = APPL(1DSpace(\log n), OI).$

3.2.3. Hardness of the OI-Operation

In this sub-subsection, we will exhibit some crucial differences in the structural behaviour of OI compared with IO_{MON} and IO_{BIN}.

Theorem 4. $NP = APPL(DSpace(\log n), OI)$
$\qquad\qquad\quad = HULL(1DSpace(\log n), OI) = HULL(NP, OI).$

Proof. We first show the inclusion $NP \subseteq APPL(DSpace(\log n), OI)$. Let L_1 and L_2 bet the sets:

$$L_1 := \{\, \$a_1\$\$a_2\$\$\ldots\$\$a_k\$\#b\# \mid a_1,\ldots,a_k, b \text{ are binary numbers}$$
$$\text{with } \textstyle\sum_{i=1}^k a_i = b \,\} \quad \text{and}$$
$$L_2 := \{\, \$a\$ \mid a \text{ is a binary number} \,\}.$$

Now set $L_{OI} := L_1 \cup L_2$. Obviously, L_{OI} belongs to $DSpace(\log n)$ and language $OI(L_{OI}) \cap ((\${0,1\}^*\$)^*\#\{0,1\}^*\#)$ is the NP-complete subset-sum problem (see, e.g., [20]). Hence, $OI_{MON}(L_{OI})$ is NP-complete, too.

The inclusion $APPL(DSpace(\log n), OI) \subseteq HULL(1DSpace(\log n), OI)$ follows since the former class is included in $APPL^2(1DSpace(\log n), OI)$. Finally, $HULL(1DSpace(\log n), OI) \subseteq HULL(NP, OI)$ is trivial and to close the circle we use Proposition 2 and the fact that NP is closed under deterministic logarithmic space bounded reducibilities, which gives us $HULL(NP, OI) \subseteq NP$. $\qquad\square$

We want to mention that the above given construction even works with an "unbounded" variant of insertion, i.e., the number of insertion points are not bounded any more. Moreover, if one modifies set L_2 to be $\{ \$a_1\$\$a_2\$\$\ldots\$\$a_k\$ \mid a_1, a_2, \ldots, a_k$ are binary numbers $\}$, then one obtains subset-sum with the shuffle operation (SHU). Since NP is closed under shuffle it equals the complexity class $APPL(DSpace(\log n), SHU)$. This strengthens a result in [8].

In the light of construction following Theorem 1 we should not hope to find a language L in $1DSpace(\log n)$ with an NP-complete set $OI(L)$, since this would imply $LOG(CFL) = P = NP$.

This sensitivity of the OI-operation with respect to the used base class leads to surprising phenomena: OI compared to IO_{MON} is idempotent, i.e., $OI(OI(L)) = OI(L)$ while in general $IO_{MON}(L) \subseteq IO_{MON}(IO_{MON}(L))$ for a language L. But on the other hand, we have $APPL(1DSpace(\log n), IO_{MON}) = APPL^2(1DSpace(\log n), IO_{MON})$ while $APPL(1DSpace(\log n), OI) = LOG(CFL)$ seems to be different from the class $APPL^2(1DSpace(\log n), OI) = NP$.

3.3. Relativizations

We show that all the relations found in the previous section relativize. For space bounded complexity classes, there are two main possibilities to relativize them, i.e., to equip space bounded machines with an oracle mechanism. In the approach of Ladner and Lynch [12], further called *LL-relativization*, the machine may use all of its power to generate oracle queries, while in the approach of Ruzzo, Simon, and Tompa [18], further called *RST-relativization*, the queries have to be generated deterministically. As usual, the use of parentheses is reserved for the LL-mechanism, while the use of the RST-relativization is indicated by using angles. Hence, for an arbitrary oracle set A one gets, e.g., in case of nondeterministic logspace bounded Turing machines the LL-relativized class $NSpace(\log n)^{(A)}$ and the RST-relativized version $NSpace(\log n)^{\langle A \rangle}$, respectively. Observe that in case of deterministic logspace bounded machines both relativizations coincide.

In [13] it was shown that the relations

1. $NP = APPL(DSpace(\log n), HOM) = HULL(DSpace(\log n), HOM)$,

2. $NSpace(\log n) = APPL(1DSpace(\log n), HOM)$,

3. $NP = HULL(1DSpace(\log n), HOM)$, and

4. $NSpace(\log n) = APPL(DSpace(\log n), STAR)$
   $\qquad\qquad\quad = HULL(DSpace(\log n), STAR)$

relativize, i.e, for an arbitrary oracle set A we have:

1. $NP^{(A)} = APPL(DSpace(\log n)^{(A)}, HOM) = HULL(DSpace(\log n)^{(A)}, HOM)$,

2. $NSpace(\log n)^{(A)} = APPL(1DSpace(\log n)^{(A)}, HOM)$,

3. $NP^{(A)} = HULL(1DSpace(\log n)^{(A)}, HOM)$, and

4. $NSpace(\log n)^{(A)} = APPL(DSpace(\log n)^{(A)}, STAR)$
   $= HULL(DSpace(\log n)^{(A)}, STAR)$.

Observe that in the fourth relation the RST- and and in the second relation the LL-relativization is used.

We will see this pattern again, when replacing nonerasing homomorphism by outside-in iterated insertion and the Kleene closure by inside-out iterated insertion. Before we can state our theorem, we need the following definition:

Definition 5. A *doubly RST-restricted* nondeterministic polynomially time bounded logspace auxiliary oracle pushdown automaton is a nondeterministic poly-nomially time and logspace bounded pushdown automaton equipped with an oracle mechanism (tape, query- and answer states), which is not allowed to use nondeter-minism or its pushdown store while writing on its oracle tape[2].

The class of languages reducible to an oracle set A via a doubly RST-restricted nondeterministic polynomially time bounded logspace augmented oracle pushdown automaton is denoted by $NauxPDA\text{-}TimeSpace(n^{O(1)}, \log n)^{(A)}$.

Theorem 5. *For an arbitrary oracle set A we have:*

1. $NP^{(A)} = HULL(1DSpace(\log n)^{(A)}, OI)$.

2. $NP^{(A)} = APPL(DSpace(\log n)^{(A)}, OI) = HULL(DSpace(\log n)^{(A)}, OI)$.

3. $NSpace(\log n)^{(A)} = APPL(1DSpace(\log n)^{(A)}, IO_{MON})$
   $= HULL(1DSpace(\log n)^{(A)}, IO_{MON})$.

4. $NauxPDA\text{-}TimeSpace(n^{O(1)}, \log n)^{(A)}$
   $= APPL(1DSpace(\log n)^{(A)}, IO_{BIN})$
   $= HULL(1DSpace(\log n)^{(A)}, IO_{BIN})$.

In the cases 1 till 3 it is possible to put oracle queries in the sets constructed in the Theorem 2 and 4, very similar to the methods used in [13]. The idea to prove 4 is a bit more complicated since one has to deal with pushdown automata instead of grammars. That is, one has to combine the triple-construction with the inside-out iterated binary operation. □

4. Conclusions

We investigated the computational power of operations on formal languages with respect to simple complexity classes. We introduced two new operations which were closely related to $LOG(CFL)$ and NP. We mention in passing that similar results can be obtained when iterating the operation of deletion, defined in correspondence to that of insertion.

There are several questions left open. An interesting aspect is the treatment of abstract storage types. Most results concerning context-free languages and pushdown

---

[2]This is equivalent to a logarithmic bound on the oracle queries, if the oracle has access to the input word.

automata have been shown to remain valid if we replace in the automaton the push-down store by another arbitrary storage device. For languages this led to the notions of abstract families of automata or of automata with abstract storage [3], [5]. Essentially this led to the construction of *permissible sequences of basic instructions* of a storage type. For instance, the Dyck sets are the languages of correct computations of a pushdown store. In our framework this leads to the task to construct to an abstract storage type X a characteristic operation op_X, which would play for X that role which inside-out iterated binary insertion plays for the context-free languages. The advantage of this approach is that all results obtained in this way would relativize.

References

1. J. L. Balcázar, J. Díaz, and J. Gabarró. *Structural Complexity I*, volume 11 of *EATCS Monographs on Theoretical Computer Science*. Springer, 1988.

2. S. A. Cook. Characterizations of pushdown machines in terms of time-bounded computers. *Journal of the ACM*, 18:4–18, 1971.

3. J. Dassow and K.-J. Lange. Complexity of automata with abstract storages. In *Proceedings of the 8th Fundamentals of Computing Theory*, number 529 in LNCS, pages 200–209. Springer, 1991.

4. P. Flajolet and J. Steyaert. Complexity of classes of languages and operators. Rap. de Recherche 92, IRIA Laboria, 1974.

5. S. Ginsburg. *Algebraic and Automata-Theoretic Properties of Formal Languages*. North-Holland, Amsterdam, 1975.

6. S. A. Greibach. The hardest context-free language. *SIAM Journal on Computing*, 2(4):304–310, December 1973.

7. J. Gruska. A characterization of context-free languages. *Journal of Computer and System Sciences*, 5:353–364, 1971.

8. D. Haussler and M. K. Warmuth. On the complexity of iterated shuffle. *Journal of Computer and System Sciences*, 28:345–358, 1984.

9. J. E. Hopcroft and J. D. Ullman. *Introduction to Automata Theory, Languages and Computation*. Addison-Wesley, 1979.

10. L. Kari. Insertion operations: closure properties. *Bulletin of the European Association for Theoretical Computer Science*, 51:181–191, 1993.

11. K.-I. Ko. On some natural complete operations. *Theoretical Computer Science*, 37:1–30, 1985.

12. R. Ladner and N. Lynch. Relativization of questions about log space computability. *Mathematical Systems Theory*, 10:19–32, 1976.

13. K.-J. Lange. Decomposition of nondeterministic reductions. *Theoretical Computer Science*, 58:175–181, 1988.

453

14. K.-J. Lange. Complexity structure in formal language theory. In *Proceedings of the 8th Annual Structure in Complexity Theory*, pages 224–238. IEEE Computer Society Press, May 1993.

15. I. P. McWhirter. Substitution expressions. *Journal of Computer and System Sciences*, 5:629–637, 1971.

16. B. Monien. About the deterministic simulation of nondeterministic ($\log n$)-tape bounded Turing machines. In *2-te GI Fachtagung Automatentheorie und Formale Sprachen*, number 33 in LNCS, pages 118–126. Springer, 1975.

17. B. Monien and I. Sudborough. The interface between language theory and complexity theory. In R. V. Book, editor, *Formal Languages—Perspectives and Open Problems*, pages 287–324, New York, 1980. Academic Press.

18. W. L. Ruzzo, J. Simon, and M. Tompa. Space-bounded hierarchies and probabilistic computations. *Journal of Computer and System Sciences*, 28:216–230, 1984.

19. I. H. Sudborough. On the tape complexity of deterministic context-free languages. *Journal of the ACM*, 25:405–414, 1978.

20. K. Wagner and G. Wechsung. *Computational Complexity*. Mathematics and its applications (East Europeans series). VEB Deutscher Verlag der Wissenschaften, Berlin, 1986.

The Decidability of the Generalized Confluence Problem for Context-Free Languages

Lucian ILIE[1]

Faculty of Mathematics, University of Bucharest
Str. Academiei 14, 70109 Bucureşti, Romania

Abstract. A language $L \subseteq \Sigma^*$ is confluent with respect to a given quasi order $\leq$ on Σ^* if, for any $x, y \in L$, there is $z \in L$ such that $x \leq z$ and $y \leq z$. L is confluent with respect to $\leq$ in generalized sense if it is a finite union of languages confluent with respect to $\leq$. We investigate in this paper the decidability of the generalized confluence problem with respect to the prefix partial order and the factor partial order for context-free languages, thus generalizing previous results concerning the decidability of the ordinary confluence problem.

1. Introduction

Starting from the property of the language of all factors of an infinite word to contain, for any two words of it, one which has the former two as factors, one introduced in [2] the notion of confluence. Generally, for any quasi order on a free monoid, the confluence property is the property of a language to contain, for any two words of it, one which is bigger with respect to the given quasi order than each of the former two. As shown in [2], the decidability of the confluence problem is closely related to the effective regularity of down-sets, where the down-set of a language is the set of all words smaller than the words in the language.

The confluence property was generalized in [6] by considering languages which are finite unions of confluent languages. It was shown there that the generalized confluence property is closely related to the property of a quasi order of being a well quasi order.

We study in this paper the decidability of the generalized confluence problem with respect to the prefix partial order and the factor partial order for context-free languages. Our results generalize the similar ones for the ordinary confluence problem in [2].

The paper is organized as follows. After giving the basic definitions in the next section, we prove in section 3 that the generalized confluence problem with respect to the prefix partial order is decidable for context-free languages. It turns out that this decidability is closely connected with the decidability of the slenderness problem for context-free languages. In section 4 we prove that the same problem is undecidable for the factor partial order.

2. Definitions

For an alphabet Σ, we denote by Σ^* the free monoid generated by Σ and by λ, the empty word, its identity. For a word $w \in \Sigma^*$, $|w|$ denotes the length of w.

---

[1]Research supported by the Academy of Finland, Project 11281

Given a quasi order $\leq$ on Σ^*, we say that a language $L \subseteq \Sigma^*$ is *confluent w.r.t.* $\leq$ if, for any $x, y \in L$, there is $z \in L$ such that $x \leq z$ and $y \leq z$. For a positive integer $k \geq 1$, $L \subseteq \Sigma^*$ is called *k-confluent w.r.t.* $\leq$ if

$$L = \bigcup_{i=1}^{k} L_i,$$

for some $L_i \subseteq \Sigma^*$, L_i confluent w.r.t. $\leq$, for any $1 \leq i \leq k$. L is *confluent w.r.t.* $\leq$ in *generalized sense* if L is k-confluent w.r.t. $\leq$, for some $k \geq 1$.

Notice that this is a generalization of the ordinary confluence since 1-confluent is the same as confluent. Also remark that the empty language is confluent w.r.t. any quasi order and, for any two quasi orders $\leq_1$ and $\leq_2$ on Σ^*, if $\leq_1 \subseteq \leq_2$, then any language confluent w.r.t. $\leq_1$ is confluent also w.r.t. $\leq_2$.

The *down-set of L w.r.t.* $\leq$, denoted $\downarrow_\leq L$, is the set

$$\downarrow_\leq L = \{w \in \Sigma^* \mid w \leq u \text{ for some } u \in L\}.$$

For any quasi order $\leq$ on Σ^*, the down-operator $\downarrow_\leq$ is monotone and idempotent.

The two partial orders we deal with in this paper are as follows, where u, v are finite words over an alphabet Σ:

> prefix: $u \leq_p v$ iff there is $w \in \Sigma^*$ such that $v = uw$,
> factor: $u \leq_f v$ iff there is $w, z \in \Sigma^*$ such that $v = wuz$,

Examples:

1. The language

$$L_1 = \{a^n b \mid n \geq 0\}$$

is obviously confluent w.r.t. $\leq_f$ but it is not confluent w.r.t. $\leq_p$. In fact, L_1 is not confluent w.r.t. $\leq_p$ even in generalized sense. Indeed, if R is a nonempty subset of L_1 such that R is confluent w.r.t. $\leq_p$, then R has exactly one element, since any two elements of L_1 are incomparable w.r.t. $\leq_p$. Thus, as L_1 is infinite, it cannot be written as a finite union of languages confluent w.r.t. $\leq_p$.

2. For any language $L \subseteq \Sigma^*$, the catenation closure of L, L^*, is confluent w.r.t. any quasi order $\leq$ on Σ^* which is an extension of the factor partial order $\leq_f$.

3. For any alphabet Σ such that $card(\Sigma) \geq 2$, the total language Σ^* is not confluent w.r.t. $\leq_p$, even in the generalized sense. To prove this, consider two different letters of Σ, say a and b. For any $k \geq 1$, consider the following $k + 1$ words in Σ^*: $ab^{k+1}, a^2b^k, \ldots, a^{k+1}b$. Since, for any two words x, y of the previous $k + 1$, there is no word $z \in \Sigma^*$ such that $x \leq_p z$ and $y \leq_p z$, it follows that Σ^* is not k-confluent w.r.t. $\leq_p$.

For all formal language theory results we refer to [3] and [9] and for all combinatorics on words results we refer to [1] and [7].

In what concerns the decidability of the generalized confluence problem w.r.t. a given quasi order $\leq$, there are two problems. We formulate them for context-free languages but they can be considered for any family of languages.

1. Given a fixed $k \geq 1$, is it decidable whether or not an arbitrary context-free language is k-confluent w.r.t. $\leq$?

2. Is it decidable whether or not an arbitrary context-free language is confluent w.r.t. $\leq$ in generalized sense, that is, is there some $k \geq 1$ such that the given language is k-confluent w.r.t. $\leq$?

We prove in the next sections that both problems are decidable for the prefix partial order $\leq_p$ and undecidable for the factor partial order $\leq_f$.

3. Prefixes of Words

We prove in this section that both problems, the k-confluence problem w.r.t. $\leq_p$ and the generalized confluence problem w.r.t. $\leq_p$ are decidable for context-free languages.

For an infinite word α, we denote by $Pref(\alpha)$ the set of all finite prefixes of α. The family of languages which are prefixes of infinite words is denoted by $\mathcal{F}_{pref}$, that is,

$$\mathcal{F}_{pref} = \{L \mid L = Pref(\alpha) \text{ for some infinite word } \alpha\}.$$

Our first result is a connection between k-confluence and the family $\mathcal{F}_{pref}$. It generalizes the following result in [2].

Lemma 3.1. *Any language $L \subseteq \Sigma^*$ is in the family $\mathcal{F}_{pref}$ if and only if the following conditions are fulfilled: (i) L is infinite, (ii) $L = \downarrow_{\leq_p} L$, (iii) L is confluent w.r.t. $\leq_p$.*

We need also the next result from [6]. (It was proved first for $k = 1$ in [2].)

Lemma 3.2. *For any quasi order $\leq$ on Σ^* and $k \geq 1$, a language $L \subseteq \Sigma^*$ is k-confluent w.r.t. $\leq$ if and only if $\downarrow_{\leq} L$ is k-confluent w.r.t. $\leq$.*

Lemma 3.3. *Let $k \geq 1$ and $L \subseteq \Sigma^*$ an infinite language such that $L = \downarrow_{\leq_p} L$. Then L is k-confluent w.r.t. $\leq_p$ if and only if*

$$L = \bigcup_{i=1}^{k} L_i$$

such that, for any $1 \leq i \leq k$, $L_i \subseteq \Sigma^*$ and L_i is either finite and confluent w.r.t. $\leq_p$ or infinite and $L_i \in \mathcal{F}_{pref}$.

Proof. Take $k \geq 1$ and $L \subseteq \Sigma^*$, such that L is infinite and $L = \downarrow_{\leq_p} L$. Suppose first that L is k-confluent w.r.t. $\leq_p$ and put

$$L = \bigcup_{i=1}^{k} L_i,$$

for some $L_i \subseteq \Sigma^*$, L_i confluent w.r.t. $\leq_p$, for any $1 \leq i \leq k$. Since

$$\downarrow_{\leq_p} L = \downarrow_{\leq_p} \left(\bigcup_{i=1}^{k} L_i \right) = \bigcup_{i=1}^{k} \downarrow_{\leq_p} L_i,$$

we may suppose that $L_i = \downarrow_{\leq_p} L_i$, for any $1 \leq i \leq k$. Notice that we may indeed make this assumption since L_i is confluent w.r.t. $\leq_p$ and so, by Lemma 3.2, $\downarrow_{\leq_p} L_i$ is also confluent w.r.t. $\leq_p$.

If, for some $1 \leq i \leq k$, L_i is infinite, as $L_i = \downarrow_{\leq_p} L_i$ and L_i is confluent w.r.t. $\leq_p$, it follows by Lemma 3.1 that $L_i \in \mathcal{F}_{pref}$. One implication is proved.

For the converse one, it is enough to observe that any language in the family $\mathcal{F}_{pref}$ is confluent w.r.t. $\leq_p$. The proof is concluded. $\qquad\square$

We need one more definition from [8]. For a language $L \subseteq \Sigma^*$, denote

$$l_n(L) = card\{w \in L \mid |w| = n\},$$

for any $n \geq 0$. For any $k \geq 0$, the language L is called *k-slender* if and only if $l_n(L) \leq k$, for any $n \geq 0$. L is called *slender* if it is k-slender, for some $k \geq 1$.

We remind the following two results from [4] and [5].

Lemma 3.4. ([4]) *A context-free language $L \subseteq \Sigma^*$ is slender if and only if it is a finite union of sets of the form*

$$\{uv^n wx^n y \mid n \geq 0\},$$

where $u, v, w, x, y \in \Sigma^*$.

Lemma 3.5. ([5]) *It is decidable whether or not an arbitrary context-free language $L \subseteq \Sigma^*$ is slender. In the affirmative case, the smallest constant k such that L is k-slender is computable. Also, there are finitely many possibilities of decomposing L into sets of the form in Lemma 3.4 and all of them can be effectively found.*

Lemma 3.6. *Let $k \geq 1$ and $L \subseteq \Sigma^*$ be an infinite context-free language. Then L is k-confluent w.r.t. $\leq_p$ if and only if the following two conditions are fulfilled:*
(i) $\downarrow_{\leq_p} L$ is k-slender,
(ii) $\downarrow_{\leq_p} L$ is a finite union

$$\downarrow_{\leq_p} L = \bigcup_{i=1}^{k} L_i,$$

for some $L_i \subseteq \Sigma^*$, such that for any $1 \leq i \leq k$, L_i is either finite and confluent w.r.t. $\leq_p$ or infinite and of the form

$$L_i = \downarrow_{\leq_p} \{z_{i1} z_{i2}^n \mid n \geq 0\},$$

for some $z_{i1}, z_{i2} \in \Sigma^*, z_{i2} \neq \lambda$.

Proof. Take $k \geq 1$ and $L \subseteq \Sigma^*$, such that L is k-confluent w.r.t. $\leq_p$. By Lemma 3.2, the down-set $\downarrow_{\leq_p} L$ is confluent w.r.t. $\leq_p$ and so, by Lemma 3.3, we have

$$\downarrow_{\leq_p} L = \bigcup_{i=1}^{k} L_i,$$

for some $L_i \subseteq \Sigma^*$, L_i either finite and confluent w.r.t. $\leq_p$ or else infinite and $L_i \in \mathcal{F}_{pref}$.

Clearly, if $L_i \in \mathcal{F}_{pref}$, then $l_n(L_i) = 1$, for any $n \geq 0$. On the other hand, if L_i is finite, then $l_n(L_i) \leq 1$, for any $n \geq 0$. Indeed, if $u, v \in L_i$ such that $|u| = |v|$, then, as L_i is k-confluent w.r.t. $\leq_p$, there is $w \in L_i$ such that $u \leq_p w$ and $v \leq_p w$. Thus, either $u \leq_p v$ or $v \leq_p u$. In any case, it follows that $u = v$.

Therefore, $l_n(\downarrow_{\leq_p} L) \leq k$, for any $n \geq 0$, and (i) is proved.

The following claim will be useful for the proof of (ii).

Claim 1. $\downarrow_{\leq_p} L$ contains no infinite antichain of $\leq_p$.

Proof of Claim 1. Let $A \subseteq \downarrow_{\leq_p} L$ be an antichain of $\leq_p$. We have

$$A = \bigcup_{i=1}^{k}(L_i \cap A).$$

If $u, v \in L_i \cap A$, then, as L_i is confluent w.r.t. $\leq_p$, there is $w \in L_i$ such that $u \leq_p w$ and $v \leq_p w$. Thus either $u \leq_p v$ or $v \leq_p u$. In both cases, since A is an antichain of $\leq_p$, it follows that $u = v$, so $card(L_i \cap A) \leq 1$. Therefore, $card(A) \leq k$ and so A is finite. The claim is proved.

Since $\downarrow_{\leq_p} L$ is slender, it follows by Lemma 3.4 that it is a finite union of the form

$$\downarrow_{\leq_p} L = \bigcup_{i=1}^{m}\{u_i v_i^n w_i x_i^n y_i \mid n \geq 0\},$$

for some $m \geq 1$ and $u_i, v_i, w_i, x_i, y_i \in \Sigma^*, 1 \leq i \leq m$. Thus

$$\downarrow_{\leq_p} L = \bigcup_{i=1}^{m} \downarrow_{\leq_p}\{u_i v_i^n w_i x_i^n y_i \mid n \geq 0\},$$

where we suppose that no set in the union in the right-hand side is redundant, that is, for no $i_0, 1 \leq i_0 \leq m$,

$$\downarrow_{\leq_p} L = \bigcup_{\substack{i=1 \\ i \neq i_0}}^{m} \downarrow_{\leq_p}\{u_i v_i^n w_i x_i^n y_i \mid n \geq 0\},$$

Claim 2. If, for some $1 \leq i \leq m$, $v_i x_i \neq \lambda$, then

$$\downarrow_{\leq_p}\{u_i v_i^n w_i x_i^n y_i \mid n \geq 0\} = \downarrow_{\leq_p}\{z_{i1} z_{i2}^n \mid n \geq 0\},$$

for some $z_{i1}, z_{i2} \in \Sigma^*, z_{i2} \neq \lambda$.

Proof of Claim 2. Because $v_i x_i \neq \lambda$, it follows that the set $\{u_i v_i^n w_i x_i^n y_i \mid n \geq 0\}$ is infinite. As, by Claim 1, there is no infinite antichain of $\leq_p$ in $\downarrow_{\leq_p} L$, we can find a strictly increasing infinite sequence of positive integers $(i_n)_{n\geq 1}$ such that

$$u_i v_i^{i_n} w_i x_i^{i_n} y_i \leq_p u_i v_i^{i_{n+1}} w_i x_i^{i_{n+1}} y_i,$$

for any $n \geq 1$. Thus, for any $n, p \geq 1$,

$$w_i x_i^{i_n} y_i \leq_p v_i^{i_{n+p}-i_n} w_i x_i^{i_{n+p}} y_i.$$

Suppose that $v_i \neq \lambda$ and $x_i \neq \lambda$. Then, as the length of $v_i^{i_{n+p}-i_n}$ tends to infinity with p, for a large enough i_n, $x_i^{i_n}$ and $v_i^{i_{n+p}-i_n}$ will overlap each other on a part longer than $|x_i| + |v_i|$. By Fine and Wilf's theorem, it follows that x_i and v_i are powers of conjugates of the same word. Thus, there are $z', z'' \in \Sigma^*$ such that $x_i = (z'z'')^{r_1}, v_i = (z''z')^{r_2}$, for some $r_1 > 0, r_2 > 0$. Then $w_i = (z''z')^{r_3} z''$, for some

$r_3 \geq 0$ and $y_i = (z'z'')^{r_4}t'$, for some $r_4 \geq 0$ and $t' \in \Sigma^*, t' \leq_p z'z''$. Let us put $z'z'' = t't'', t'' \in \Sigma^*$. Therefore

$$
\begin{aligned}
\{u_i v_i^n w_i x_i^n y_i \mid n \geq 0\} &= \{u_i(z''z')^{nr_2}(z''z')^{r_3}z''(z'z'')^{nr_1}(z'z'')^{r_4}t' \mid n \geq 0\} \\
&= \{u_i z''(z'z'')^{r_3+r_4+n(r_1+r_2)}t' \mid n \geq 0\} \\
&= \{u_i z''(t't'')^{r_3+r_4+n(r_1+r_2)}t' \mid n \geq 0\} \\
&= \{z_{i1} z_{i2}^n \mid n \geq 0\},
\end{aligned}
$$

for

$$
\begin{aligned}
z_{i1} &= u_i z''t'(t''t')^{r_3+r_4}, \\
z_{i2} &= (t''t')^{r_1+r_2}.
\end{aligned}
$$

Notice that $z_{i2} \neq \lambda$.

The cases $v_i \neq \lambda, x_i = \lambda$ and $v_i = \lambda, x_i \neq \lambda$ are treated similarly. The claim is proved.

Claim 3. $m \leq k$.

Proof of Claim 3. By Lemma 3.3, $\downarrow_{\leq_p} L$ is a finite union of k sets of prefixes of some words, finite or infinite, say

$$
L = \bigcup_{i=1}^{k} R_i.
$$

So far, we proved that $\downarrow_{\leq_p} L$ is finite union of m sets of prefixes of some words which are either finite or infinite and ultimately periodic. Since we have supposed that none of the words in the second representation is redundant, it follows that

$$
card\{i \mid R_i \text{ is infinite}\} \geq card\{i \mid z_{i2} \neq \lambda\}.
$$

Indeed, if $\downarrow_{\leq_p} \{z_{i1}z_{i2}^n \mid n \geq 0\} \cap R_j$ is infinite, then $\downarrow_{\leq_p} \{z_{i1}z_{i2}^n \mid n \geq 0\} \subseteq R_j$, since $R_j \in \mathcal{F}_{pref}$. It is also clear that

$$
card\{i \mid R_i \text{ is finite}\} \geq card\{i \mid z_{i2} = \lambda\}.
$$

Therefore $m \leq k$ and the claim is proved.

By Claim 2 and Claim 3, one implication in the statement is proved.

The converse implication is clear since L and $\downarrow_{\leq_p} L$ are k-confluent w.r.t. $\leq_p$ at the same time. The proof is concluded. $\square$

Remark. It is clear that condition (i) in Lemma 3.6 does not imply that L is k-confluent w.r.t. $\leq_p$. We notice that, even with the hypothesis that L is confluent w.r.t. $\leq_p$ in generalized sense, it still does not follow that L is k-confluent w.r.t. $\leq_p$. For instance, the language

$$
L = Pref(ab^\omega) \cup Pref(a^2 b^\omega) \cup \{b\},
$$

where b^ω is the infinite word $bbb\ldots$, is 2-slender but it is not 2-confluent w.r.t. $\leq_p$. L is 3-confluent w.r.t. $\leq_p$.

We can prove now the decidability of the k-confluence problem w.r.t. $\leq_p$ for context-free languages.

Theorem 3.7. *For any $k \geq 1$, it is decidable whether or not an arbitrary context-free language $L \subseteq \Sigma^*$ is k-confluent w.r.t. $\leq_p$.*

Proof. Take $k \geq 1$ and an arbitrary context-free language $L \subseteq \Sigma^*$. We give the following algorithm to decide whether or not L is k-confluent w.r.t. $\leq_p$.

460

Algorithm 3.8.

1. Decide whether or not L is finite [possible for context-free languages]. If yes, then decide directly whether or not L is k-confluent w.r.t. $\leq_p$ [obviously possible], else go to step 2.

2. Construct $\downarrow_{\leq_p} L$ [this is effectively constructable for L context-free].

3. Decide whether or not $\downarrow_{\leq_p} L$ is slender [possible by Lemma 3.5]. If yes, then go to step 4, else answer **no** [correct by Lemma 3.6].

4. Compute the minimal k' such that $\downarrow_{\leq_p} L$ is k'-slender [possible by Lemma 3.5].

5. If $k' \leq k$, then go to step 6, else answer **no** [correct by Lemma 3.6].

6. Find all possibilities of decomposing $\downarrow_{\leq_p} L$ as in Lemma 3.4 [possible by Lemma 3.5].

7. Check whether any of these decompositions [there are finitely many] verifies the conditions in the statement of Lemma 3.6 [this is clearly possible]. If yes, then answer **yes**, else answer **no** [correct by Lemma 3.6].

We move now to the generalized confluence problem w.r.t. $\leq_p$. We intend to prove that also this problem is decidable for context-free languages. We need the following result which is a corollary of Lemma 3.6.

Corollary 3.9. *Let $L \subseteq \Sigma^*$ be a context-free language. Then L is confluent w.r.t. $\leq_p$ in generalized sense if and only if $\downarrow_{\leq_p} L$ is slender and there is a deconposition of L*

$$\downarrow_{\leq_p} L = \bigcup_{i=1}^{k} \downarrow_{\leq_p} \{u_i v_i^n \mid n \geq 0\},$$

for some $k \geq 1$ and $u_i, v_i \in \Sigma^*, 1 \leq i \leq k$.

Proof. Take $L \subseteq \Sigma^*$ a context-free language which is confluent w.r.t. $\leq_p$ in generalized sense. Then, for some $k \geq 1$, L is k-confluent w.r.t. $\leq_p$ and the claim follows by Lemma 3.6.

The converse implication is clear since the set of prefixes of a finite or infinite word is confluent w.r.t. $\leq_p$. $\square$

As a consequence of Corrolary 3.9, we have the next result.

Corollary 3.10. *If $L \subseteq \Sigma^*$ is a context-free language which is confluent w.r.t. $\leq_p$ in generalized sense, then L is regular.*

We can give now the decidability result.

Theorem 3.11. *It is decidable whether or not an arbitrary context-free language is confluent w.r.t. $\leq_p$ in generalized sense.*

Proof. Let $L \subseteq \Sigma^*$ be a an arbitrary context-free language. The algorithm to decide whether or not L is confluent w.r.t. $\leq_p$ in generalized sense is clear now from Corollary 3.9.

Algorithm 3.12.

1. Decide whether or not L is finite [possible for context-free languages]. If yes, then answer **yes** [obviously correct], else go to step 2.

2. Construct $\downarrow_{\leq_p} L$ [this is effectively constructable for L context-free].

3. Decide whether or not $\downarrow_{\leq_p} L$ is slender [possible by Lemma 3.5]. If yes, then go to step 4, else answer **no** [correct by Corollary 3.9].

4. Find all possibilities of decomposing $\downarrow_{\leq_p} L$ as in Lemma 3.4 [possible by Lemma 3.5].

5. Check whether any of these decompositions [there are finitely many] verifies the conditions in the statement of Corollary 3.9 [this is clearly possible]. If yes, then answer **yes**, else answer **no** [correct by Corollary 3.9].

The next corollary is a direct consequence of Theorem 3.7, Theorem 3.11, and Lemma 3.6.

Corollary 3.13. *For a context-free language L which is confluent w.r.t. $\leq_p$ in generalized sense, the minimal k such that L is k-confluent w.r.t. $\leq_p$ is computable. Also*

$$\min\{k' \mid \downarrow_{\leq_p} L \text{ is } k'\text{-slender}\} \leq \min\{k'' \mid L \text{ is } k''\text{-confluent w.r.t. } \leq_p\}.$$

4. Factors of Words

We deal in this section with the factor partial order $\leq_f$ and prove that the k-confluence problem w.r.t. $\leq_f$ and the generalized confluence problem w.r.t. $\leq_f$ are undecidable for context-free languages.

We prove first a general undecidability result concerning the decidability of the k-confluence problem w.r.t. $\leq_f$.

Lemma 4.1. *Let $k \geq 1$ and $\mathcal{L}$ be a family of languages effectively closed under union, catenation with letters, and λ-free catenation closure such that the inclusion problem is undecidable in $\mathcal{L}$. Then also the k-confluence problem is undecidable in $\mathcal{L}$.*

Proof. We argue by contradiction. Suppose that the k-confluence problem w.r.t. $\leq_f$ is decidable in $\mathcal{L}$.

Claim 1. The emptiness problem is decidable in $\mathcal{L}$.

Proof of Claim 1. Take an arbitrary language $L \in \mathcal{L}, L \subseteq \Sigma^*$, and construct the language

$$L_1 = \bigcup_{i=0}^{k} \#L\#_i,$$

where $\#, \#_0, \#_1, \ldots, \#_k \notin \Sigma$ are new letters. It follows by hypothesis that $L_1 \in \mathcal{L}$ and we claim that L is empty if and only if L_1 is k-confluent w.r.t. $\leq_f$.

If $L = \emptyset$, then $L_1 = \emptyset$, so L_1 is k-confluent w.r.t. $\leq_f$.

Conversely, suppose that L_1 is k-confluent w.r.t. $\leq_f$ but $L \neq \emptyset$ and take $w \in L$. We have by definition

$$L_1 = \bigcup_{i=1}^{k} R_i,$$

for some $R_i \subseteq \Sigma^*, R_i$ confluent w.r.t. $\leq_f$. Consider the words $\#w\#_i, 0 \leq i \leq k$. They belong all to L_1. But no R_i can contain two of them. Indeed, if $\#w\#_{i_1}, \#w\#_{i_2} \in R_i$, for some $0 \le i_1, i_2 \le k, i_1 \ne i_2$, then, as R_i is confluent w.r.t. $\le_f$, there is $z \in R_i$ such that $\#w\#_{i_1} \le_f z$ and $\#w\#_{i_2} \le_f z$. Then, from $\#w\#_{i_1} \le_f z$, we get $z = \#w\#_{i_1}$ so $\#w\#_{i_2} \not\le_f z$, a contradiction. Therefore L is empty.

Consequently, to decide whether or not L is empty, we decide whether or not L_1 as constructed above is k-confluent w.r.t. $\le_f$, which is possible by our assumption, since L_1 is effectively in $\mathcal{L}$. The claim is proved.

We show that also the inclusion problem is decidable in $\mathcal{L}$, thus obtaining a contradiction. For, take $L_1, L_2 \in \mathcal{L}, L_1 \subseteq \Sigma^*, L_2 \subseteq \Sigma^*$, and construct the language

$$L = \#L_1\#_0 \cup \bigcup_{i=1}^{k}(\#L_2\#_0\#_i)^+,$$

where $\#, \#_0, \#_1, \ldots, \#_k \notin \Sigma$ are new letters. Then, by hypothesis, $L \in \mathcal{L}$.

Claim 2. L is k-confluent w.r.t. $\le_f$ if and only if either $L_1 \subseteq L_2$ or $1 \le card(L_1) \le k$ and $L_2 = \emptyset$.

Proof of Claim 2. Suppose first that $L_1 \subseteq L_2$. Then

$$\downarrow_{\le_f} L = \downarrow_{\le_f} (\#L_1\#_0) \cup \bigcup_{i=1}^{k} \downarrow_{\le_f} (\#L_2\#_0\#_i)^+ = \bigcup_{i=1}^{k} \downarrow_{\le_f} (\#L_2\#_0\#_i)^+$$

since

$$\downarrow_{\le_f} (\#L_1\#_0) \subseteq \downarrow_{\le_f} (\#L_2\#_0\#_i) \subseteq \downarrow_{\le_f} (\#L_2\#_0\#_i)^+,$$

for any $1 \le i \le k$. As, clearly, $(\#L_2\#_0\#_i)^+$ is confluent w.r.t. $\le_f$, by Lemma 3.2, $\downarrow_{\le_f} (\#L_2\#_0\#_i)^+$ is confluent w.r.t. $\le_f$. Thus $\downarrow_{\le_f} L$ if k-confluent w.r.t. $\le_f$ and so, again by Lemma 3.2, L is k-confluent w.r.t. $\le_f$.

Suppose now that $1 \le card(L_1) \le k$ and $L_2 = \emptyset$. Then, if $L_1 = \{w_1, w_2, \ldots w_p\}$, $1 \le p \le k$, then

$$L = \bigcup_{i=1}^{p}\{\#w_i\#_0\}.$$

As $\{\#w_i\#_0\}$ is confluent w.r.t. $\le_f$, it follows that L is p-confluent w.r.t. $\le_f$ hence also k-confluent w.r.t. $\le_f$.

For the converse part, suppose that L is k-confluent w.r.t. $\le_f$. Suppose also that $L_1 \not\subseteq L_2$ and take $w_1 \in L_1 \backslash L_2$. If $L_2 \ne \emptyset$, then take $w_2 \in L_2$. It follows that

$$\{\#w_1\#_0, \#w_2\#_0\#_1, \#w_2\#_0\#_2, \ldots, \#w_2\#_0\#_k\} \subseteq L$$

and a contradiction with the k-confluence w.r.t. $\le_f$ of L is obtained as in the proof of Claim 1. Thus $L_2 = \emptyset$ and so

$$L = \#L_1\#_0.$$

If $card(L_1) \ge k + 1$, then take $z_1, z_2, \ldots, z_{k+1} \in L_1, z_i \ne z_j$, for any $i \ne j$. We have that

$$\{\#z_1\#_0, \#z_2\#_0, \ldots \#z_{k+1}\#_0\} \subseteq L$$

and again a contradiction with the k-confluence w.r.t. $\le_f$ of L is obtained. Thus $card(L_1) \le k$. As $L_1 \not\subseteq L_2 = \emptyset$, we get also $card(L_1) \ge 1$. The claim is proved.

Claim 3. The inclusion problem is decidable in $\mathcal{L}$.

Proof of Claim 3. Take two arbitrary language $L_1, L_2 \in \mathcal{L}$ and construct the language L as above. We give the following algorithm to decide whether or not $L_1 \subseteq L_2$ and prove the claim.

Algorithm 4.2.
1. Decide whether or not $L_2 = \emptyset$ [the emptiness problem is decidable in $\mathcal{L}$ by Claim 1]. If yes, then go to step 2, else go to step 3.

2. Decide whether or not $L_1 = \emptyset$ [possible by Claim 1]. If yes, then answer **yes** [obviously correct], else answer **no** [again correct].

3. Decide whether or not L is k-confluent w.r.t. $\leq_f$ [the k-confluence problem is decidable in $\mathcal{L}$ by our assumption and L is effectively in $\mathcal{L}$]. If yes, then answer **yes** [correct by Claim 2], else answer **no** [correct also by Claim 2].

Consequently, we have proved that the decidability of the k-confluence problem w.r.t. $\leq_f$ for languages in $\mathcal{L}$ would entail the decidability of the inclusion problem for languages in $\mathcal{L}$. Since the latter is undecidable in $\mathcal{L}$, it follows that also the former is undecidable in $\mathcal{L}$ and the result is proved. $\quad\square$

As a direct corollary of Lemma 4.1, we obtain the undecidability of the k-confluence problem w.r.t. $\leq_f$ for context-free languages.

Theorem 4.3. *For any $k \geq 1$, it is undecidable whether or not an arbitrary context-free language is k-confluent w.r.t. $\leq_f$.*

We consider now the generalized confluence problem w.r.t. $\leq_f$ and give the following general undecidability result.

Lemma 4.4. *Let $\mathcal{L}$ be a family of languages effectively closed under union, catenation, and λ-free catenation closure such that all regular languages are in $\mathcal{L}$. If it is undecidable for an arbitrary language $L \in \mathcal{L}, L \subseteq \Sigma^*$, whether or not $L = \Sigma^*$, then the generalized confluence problem w.r.t. $\leq_f$ is undecidable for languages in $\mathcal{L}$.*

Proof. We argue by contradiction. Suppose that the generalized confluence problem w.r.t. $\leq_f$ is decidable in $\mathcal{L}$. Then we prove that it is decidable for an arbitrary language $L \in \mathcal{L}, L \subseteq \Sigma^*$, whether or not $L = \Sigma^*$. For, take an arbitrary such language L and construct the language

$$L_1 = \#\Sigma^* \#_1 \#_2^* \#_1 \cup (\#L\#_1\#_2^*\#_1)^+,$$

where $\#, \#_1, \#_2 \notin \Sigma$ are new letters. Then, by hypothesis, $L_1 \in \mathcal{L}$.

Claim. L_1 is confluent w.r.t. $\leq_f$ in generalized sense if and only if $L = \Sigma^*$.

Proof of Claim. Suppose first that $L = \Sigma^*$. Then

$$\downarrow_{\leq_f} L_1 = \downarrow_{\leq_f} (\#\Sigma^*\#_1\#_2^*\#_1) \cup \downarrow_{\leq_f} (\#\Sigma^*\#_1\#_2^*\#_1)^+ = \downarrow_{\leq_f} (\#\Sigma^*\#_1\#_2^*\#_1)^+.$$

Then, as $(\#\Sigma^*\#_1\#_2^*\#_1)^+$ is confluent w.r.t. $\leq_f$, it follows, by Lemma 3.2, that $\downarrow_{\leq_f} (\#\Sigma^*\#_1\#_2^*\#_1)^+$ is confluent w.r.t. $\leq_f$, so $\downarrow_{\leq_f} L_1$ is confluent w.r.t. $\leq_f$ and so, again by Lemma 3.2, L_1 is confluent w.r.t. $\leq_f$. It follows also that L_1 is confluent w.r.t. $\leq_f$ in generalized sense.

Conversely, suppose that L_1 is k-confluent w.r.t. $\leq_f$, for some $k \geq 1$, but $L \subset \Sigma^*$ and take $w \in \Sigma^* \backslash L$. Put also

$$L_1 = \bigcup_{i=1}^{k} R_i,$$

for some $R_i \subseteq \Sigma^*$, R_i confluent w.r.t. $\leq_f$. We have then

$$\bigcup_{i=0}^{k} \{\#w\#_1\#_2^i\#_1\} \subseteq L_1.$$

and we can find an $i, 1 \leq i \leq k$, and $i_1 \neq i_2, 0 \leq i_1, i_2 \leq k$, such that $\#w\#_1\#_2^{i_1}\#_1$, $\#w\#_1\#_2^{i_2}\#_1 \in R_i$. As R_i is confluent w.r.t. $\leq_f$, there is $z \in R_i$ such that $\#w\#_1\#_2^{i_1}\#_1 \leq_f z$ and $\#w\#_1\#_2^{i_2}\#_1 \leq_f z$. Because $w \notin L$, it follows that $z \notin (\#L\#_1\#_2^*\#_1)^+$, and so $z = \#x\#_1\#_2^j\#_1$, for some $x \in \Sigma^*, j \geq 0$. From $\#w\#_1\#_2^{i_1}\#_1 \leq_f \#x\#_1\#_2^j\#_1$, we obtain $w = x$ and $i_1 = j$. But, since $i_1 \neq i_2$, $\#w\#_1\#_2^{i_2}\#_1 \not\leq_f z$, a contradiction. It follows that $L = \Sigma^*$. As k above has been chosen arbitrarily, the claim is proved.

Hence, to decide whether or not $L = \Sigma^*$, we can decide whether or not L_1 is confluent w.r.t. $\leq_f$ in generalized sense, which is possible by our assumption, since L_1 is effectively in $\mathcal{L}$. But this contradicts the hypothesis. Therefore the generalized confluence problem w.r.t. $\leq_f$ is undecidable in $\mathcal{L}$ and the result is proved. $\square$

We get imediately the following result.

Theorem 4.5. *It is undecidable whether or not an arbitrary context-free language is confluent w.r.t. $\leq_f$ in generalized sense.*

References

1. C. Choffrut, J. Karhumäki, *Combinatorics of Words*, in *Handbook of Formal Languages*, (G. Rozenberg, A Salomaa, eds.), to appear.

2. T. Harju, L. Ilie, On quasi orders of words and the confluence property, manuscript.

3. J. E. Hopcroft, J. D. Ullman, *Introduction to Automata Theory, Languages, and Computation*, Addison-Wesley, Reading, Mass., 1979.

4. L. Ilie, On a conjecture about slender context-free languages, *Theoretical Computer Science* **132** (1994) 427–434.

5. L. Ilie, On slender context-free languages, manuscript.

6. L. Ilie, A. Salomaa, On well quasi orders of free monoids, manuscript.

7. M. Lothaire, *Combinatorics on Words*, Addison-Wesley, Reading, Mass., 1983.

8. Gh. Păun, A. Salomaa, Thin and slender languages, *Discrete Appl. Math.* **61** (1995) 257–270.

9. A. Salomaa, *Formal Languages*, Academic Press, New York, 1973.

Author Index

Springer
and the
environment

At Springer we firmly believe that an international science publisher has a special obligation to the environment, and our corporate policies consistently reflect this conviction.
We also expect our business partners – paper mills, printers, packaging manufacturers, etc. – to commit themselves to using materials and production processes that do not harm the environment. The paper in this book is made from low- or no-chlorine pulp and is acid free, in conformance with international standards for paper permanency.

 Springer

Lecture Notes in Computer Science

For information about Vols. 1–1141

please contact your bookseller or Springer-Verlag